Bottom Line's HEALTH BREAKTHROUGHS 2010

10 9 8 7 6 5 4 3 2 1

0-88723-581-6

HealthDay

Articles in this book were written by reporters for HealthDay, an award-winning international daily consumer health news service, headquartered in Norwalk, Connecticut.

281 Tresser Boulevard, Stamford, Connecticut 06901

www.bottomlinesecrets.com

Bottom Line Books® is an imprint of Boardroom® Inc., publisher of print periodicals, e-letters and books. We are dedicated to bringing you the best information from the most knowledgeable sources in the world. Our goal is to help you gain greater wealth, better health, more wisdom, extra time and increased happiness.

Printed in the United States of America

Contents

6 • DRUG NEWS

7 • EMOTIONAL WELL-BEING

8 • FAMILY HEALTH

9 • HEART DISEASE

10 • NATURAL REMEDIES

11 • NUTRITION, DIET AND FITNESS

12 • PAIN TREATMENT

13 • SAVVY CONSUMER

14 • STROKE PREVENTION

Preface

We are proud to bring you *Bottom Line's Health Breakthroughs 2010*, a new book filled with the year's latest health discoveries.

When you choose a Bottom Line Book, you are turning to a stellar group of experts in a wide range of specialties—medical doctors, alternative practitioners, nutrition experts, research scientists and consumer-health advocates, to name a few.

We go to great lengths to interview the foremost health experts. Whether it's cancer prevention, breakthrough arthritis treatments or cutting-edge nutritional advice, our editors talk to the true innovators in health care.

How do we find all these top-notch professionals? Over the past 20 years, we have built a network of thousands of leading physicians in both alternative and conventional medicine. They are affiliated with the world's premier medical institutions. We follow the latest research and we regularly talk to our advisors in major teaching hospitals, private practices and government health agencies. We also tap the resources of HealthDay, an award-winning news service devoted to consumer health issues.

Bottom Line's Health Breakthroughs 2010 is a result of our ongoing research and contact with these experts, and is a distillation of their latest findings and advice. We hope that you will enjoy the presentation and glean helpful information about the health topics that concern you and your family.

As a reader of a Bottom Line Book, please be assured that you are receiving reliable and well-researched information from a trusted source. But, please use prudence in health matters. Always speak to your physician before taking vitamins, supplements or over-the-counter medication...changing your diet...or beginning an exercise program. If you experience side effects from any regimen, contact your doctor immediately.

The Editors, Bottom Line Books, Stamford, Connecticut.

1

Aging & Senior Health

Walk Your Way to a Better Memory

Exercise may help treat memory problems in adults, according to research that has emerged from Australia. The study found that a home-based physical activity program led to modest improvements in cognitive function in adults with memory difficulties.

THE STUDY

The participants—138 people age 50 and older who had memory problems but didn't meet criteria for dementia—were randomly assigned to do a 24-week home-based physical activity program or to receive usual care.

Those in the exercise group were encouraged to do at least 150 minutes of moderate-intensity physical activity per week in three 50-minute sessions. Walking was the most frequently recommended type of activity. Participants in the exercise group did an average of 142 minutes more physical activity per week, or 20 minutes more per day, than those in the usual care group.

Over 18 months, participants in the exercise group had better Alzheimer Disease Assessment Scale-Cognitive (ADAS-Cog) scores and delayed recall, and lower Clinical Dementia Rating scores, than those in the usual care group. The ADAS-Cog consists of a number of cognitive tests.

The findings were published in *The Journal of the American Medical Association.*

"To our knowledge, this trial is the first to demonstrate that exercise improves cognitive function in older adults with subjective and objective mild cognitive impairment. The benefits of physical activity were apparent after six months and persisted for at least another 12 months after the intervention had been discontinued," said Nicola T. Lautenschlager, MD, of the University of Melbourne.

American Medical Association news release.

IMPLICATION

"Unlike medication, which was found to have no significant effect on mild cognitive impairment at 36 months, physical activity has the advantage of health benefits that are not confined to cognitive function alone, as suggested by findings on depression, quality of life, falls, cardiovascular function and disability," the researchers added.

They noted that the number of older adults with Alzheimer's disease (AD) could increase from the current 26.6 million to 106.2 million by 2050. If AD onset could be delayed by 12 months, there would be 9.2 million fewer cases of AD worldwide.

EXPERT COMMENTARY

Exercise and other lifestyle factors may benefit older adults at risk for AD, said Eric B. Larson, MD, MPH, of the Group Health Center for Health Studies in Seattle.

"Health advances of the past century have led to more individuals surviving to extreme old age, when their risk of Alzheimer's disease and related dementias increases substantially," Dr. Larson added. "Exercise—and possibly other lifestyle factors—appears to affect vascular risk and late-life brain health."

info For more information on memory loss, visit the National Institute on Aging's Web site, *www.niapublications.org*, and type "forgetfulness" into the search box.

■ ■ ■ ■

Prevent Falls with Push-Ups

Push-ups are excellent exercise for seniors. The ability to do them is more than an indicator of fitness—the exercise increases strength in the upper-body, which helps protect against injury from falls.

Why: When people fall, they instinctively reach out to catch themselves in a manner similar to the push-up motion. Upper-body strength helps break the weight of a fall safely. Those who don't have the strength to do a push-up are at heightened risk of suffering a broken wrist or other injury in a fall—and of not being able to push or lift themselves up, even if not injured.

Fitness guideline: At age 60, men should be able to do 17 push-ups...women should be able to do six of them.

James Ashton-Miller, PhD, director, biomechanics research laboratory, University of Michigan, Ann Arbor.

■ ■ ■ ■

Memory Loss Linked to Low Levels of "Good" Cholesterol

When 3,673 men and women were followed for seven years, researchers found that those with low levels of high-density lipoprotein (HDL) "good" cholesterol (less than 40 mg/dL) at age 60 were 53% more likely to experience memory loss than those with high HDL levels (60 mg/dL or higher).

To increase HDL levels: Exercise regularly ...do not consume trans fats...and replace saturated fats with monounsaturated fats, such as olive oil, whenever possible.

Archana Singh-Manoux, PhD, senior research fellow, French National Institute for Health and Medical Research, Saint-Maurice, France.

Cholesterol Drugs Lower Stroke Risk in People 65 and Older

American Academy of Neurology news release.

Taking a cholesterol-lowering drug after a stroke or mini-stroke reduces an older person's risk of another stroke as much as it does in younger patients, according to a US study.

"Even though the majority of strokes and heart attacks occur in people who are 65 and older, studies have found that cholesterol-lowering drugs are not prescribed as often for older people as they are for younger people. These results show that using these drugs is just as beneficial for people who are 65 as they are for younger people," said study author Seemant Chaturvedi, MD, of Wayne State University in Detroit.

THE STUDY

The researchers looked at 4,731 people who had had a recent stroke or mini-stroke (transient ischemic attack or TIA), including 2,249 people age 65 and older and 2,482 people under age 65. In each group, about half the patients received the cholesterol-lowering drug *atorvastatin* (Lipitor), and about half received a placebo. The participants were then followed for an average of 4.5 years.

Levels of "bad" low-density lipoprotein (LDL) cholesterol were reduced by an average of 61 points in the over-65 group taking atorvastatin and by an average of 59 points in the under-65 group. Stroke risk was reduced by 26% in the younger group and by 10% in the older group.

AGE NOT A FACTOR

"It's estimated that 20% of the US population will be 65 or older by 2010, so it's important to reduce the burden of strokes and other cerebrovascular diseases in this group. This is a step in that direction," Dr. Chaturvedi said.

The study, supported by atorvastatin maker Pfizer Inc., was published in *Neurology.*

info To learn more about the symptoms and treatment of stroke, go to the Know Stroke Web site of the National Institute of Neurological Disorders and Stroke at *http://stroke.nih.gov/.*

Five Ways to Lower Alzheimer's Risk Up to 60%

Marwan Sabbagh, MD, geriatric neurologist, director of clinical research and chief medical scientific officer at Banner Sun Health Research Institute in Sun City, Arizona, and adjunct professor at Arizona State University in Tempe. Dr. Sabbagh is author or coauthor of more than 70 scientific articles on Alzheimer's and author of *The Alzheimer's Answer* (Wiley). *www.thealzheimersanswer.com.*

Last year, the Alzheimer's Association reported that one in six women and one in 10 men age 55 and older in the US will develop Alzheimer's disease. (More women get Alzheimer's, in part, because they tend to live longer.) Many people think that not getting Alzheimer's is more about good genes than good health, but new research suggests that lifestyle factors, such as diet and exercise, play key roles.

Here's what you need to know about the latest scientific advances in the battle against Alzheimer's disease...

PREVENTION

New research shows that the primary feature of Alzheimer's—the accumulation of a protein by-product called *beta-amyloid* that wrecks brain cells—starts decades before symptoms begin, perhaps even in a person's 30s.

How to help prevent or slow that process...

- **Statins.** Researchers from the Netherlands studied nearly 7,000 people age 55 and older. They found that patients who regularly took a cholesterol-lowering statin drug had a 43% lower risk for developing Alzheimer's than those who didn't take the drug.

Theory: Cholesterol may be a "cofactor" in beta-amyloid production.

Bottom line: More studies are needed to show that taking a statin can prevent Alzheimer's, so it's premature for your doctor to prescribe the drug for that purpose. But if you take a statin to control cholesterol, you may experience this very positive "side effect."

- **Weight control.** Researchers at the National Institutes of Health analyzed 23 years of data from more than 2,300 people. Women who were obese at ages 30, 35 or 50, with excess belly fat, had a nearly seven times higher risk for developing Alzheimer's. Men who gained a lot of weight between ages 30 and 50 had a nearly four times higher risk.

Theory: Excess pounds increase chronic low-grade inflammation...increase insulin resistance (prediabetes)...and may increase production of amyloid precursor protein—all factors that may increase the likelihood of Alzheimer's.

Bottom line: Keep your body weight within a healthy range by controlling calories and exercising regularly.

- **Fruits and vegetables.** Oxidative stress —a kind of "internal rust" caused by factors such as a diet loaded with fat and refined carbohydrates...air pollution...and hormones triggered by stress—is believed to play a role in the development of Alzheimer's. In the laboratory, researchers at Cornell University exposed brain cells to oxidative stress and added extracts of apples, bananas and oranges to the mix. The extracts reduced neurotoxicity—damage to brain cells.

Theory: Fruits and vegetables are rich in cell-protecting and strengthening antioxidants that fight the oxidative stress that contributes to Alzheimer's.

Bottom line: Fruits that deliver the most antioxidants include blueberries, blackberries, cherries, red grapes, oranges, plums, raspberries and strawberries. Best vegetables include arugula, bell peppers, broccoli, bok choy, cabbage, collard greens, kale and spinach.

•**Alcohol.** Researchers at Stritch School of Medicine at Loyola University in Chicago reviewed data on alcohol intake and health and found that more than half the studies showed that a moderate intake of alcohol (one drink a day for women, one to two drinks a day for men) was associated with a lower risk for cognitive decline and dementia, including Alzheimer's.

Theory: Alcohol delivers potent antioxidants, and moderate intake reduces inflammation.

Bottom line: One to two drinks a day may slightly decrease Alzheimer's risk. One drink is five ounces of wine, 12 ounces of beer or 1.5 ounces of an 80-proof liquor, such as vodka or gin.

•**Exercise.** Research shows that regular exercise can reduce Alzheimer's risk by up to 60%. A recent study shows that it also may help slow the progression of the disease. Scientists at University of Kansas School of Medicine studied 57 people with early-stage Alzheimer's disease and found that those who were sedentary had four times more brain shrinkage (a sign of Alzheimer's) than those who were physically fit.

Bottom line: Aim for 30 minutes a day of exercise, such as brisk walking outdoors or on a treadmill.

COMBINATION TREATMENT

Medications can slow the development of Alzheimer's symptoms. Research now shows that combining certain drugs maximizes their effectiveness. The FDA has approved two types of drugs to treat Alzheimer's—*cholinesterase inhibitors,* such as *donepezil* (Aricept), which work by slowing the breakdown of *acetylcholine,* a neurotransmitter that helps brain cells communicate...and *memantine* (Namenda), which calms *excitotoxicity,* a type of cellular hyperactivity that harms neurons.

In a 30-month study of nearly 400 people with Alzheimer's, researchers at Harvard Medical School found that taking both drugs together is more effective in reducing Alzheimer's symptoms than taking either a cholinesterase inhibitor alone or a placebo.

Bottom line: Patients who start both drugs at the time of diagnosis may significantly slow the progress of Alzheimer's disease.

WHAT DOESN'T WORK

The following do not seem to be effective against Alzheimer's...

•**NSAIDs.** Some studies have linked regular intake of a nonsteroidal anti-inflammatory drug (NSAID)—such as aspirin, *ibuprofen* (Advil), *naproxen* (Aleve) and *celecoxib* (Celebrex)—with lower rates of Alzheimer's. But in the Alzheimer's Disease Anti-Inflammatory Prevention Trial (ADAPT)—a study conducted by more than 125 researchers, involving more than 2,000 people age 70 and older—celecoxib didn't reduce the risk for developing Alzheimer's. Naproxen had a minor effect that was outweighed by the fact that it increased the rate of heart attacks and strokes.

•**Ginkgo biloba.** A team of dozens of researchers led by scientists at University of Pittsburgh studied more than 3,000 people age 75 and older, dividing them into two groups. One group took a daily dose of 240 milligrams (mg) of ginkgo biloba extract, which is widely touted for invigorating the brain and improving memory. A second group took a placebo. Those taking ginkgo did not have a lower rate of developing Alzheimer's.

•**B vitamins.** Elevated blood levels of the amino acid *homocysteine* have been linked to Alzheimer's. Because B vitamins can lower homocysteine, scientists wondered if B vitamins could slow the development of Alzheimer's.

Researchers in the department of neurosciences at University of California, San Diego, studied 340 people with mild-to-moderate Alzheimer's disease for about four years and found that B vitamins reduced homocysteine levels but didn't slow the progression of Alzheimer's disease.

•**Antipsychotics.** Alzheimer's patients often develop behavioral disturbances, such as wandering, agitation, aggression, paranoia, delusions, anxiety and hallucinations. A standard treatment is an antipsychotic drug, such as *risperidone* (Risperdal), *ziprasidone* (Geodon), *olanzapine* (Zyprexa), *quetiapine* (Seroquel) or *aripiprazole* (Abilify).

New danger: For three years, researchers in England studied 165 Alzheimer's patients who had taken antipsychotics—continuing the drug in half the patients and switching the other half to placebos. After three years, 59% of those on the placebo were alive, compared with 30% on the medication. In other words, those who continued the drug had twice the risk of dying.

New approach: Researchers at Indiana University Center for Aging Research reviewed nine studies on the use of a cholinesterase inhibitor to manage behavioral symptoms and found it to be a "safe and effective alternative" to antipsychotic drugs.

■ ■ ■ ■

New Medicine Prevents Alzheimer's and Even Reduces Symptoms

A recent study found that a type of blood pressure medication—*angiotensin receptor blocker* (ARB)—was associated with a reduced risk for dementia in seniors and slowed its progress in cases where it was already diagnosed.

A study of the medical records of five million people found that patients taking ARBs had a 35% to 40% lower chance of getting Alzheimer's disease or other forms of dementia, while patients taking ARBs who were already suffering from Alzheimer's or other forms of dementia had up to a 45% lower chance of developing delirium, being admitted to nursing homes or dying. How ARBs might produce this benefit is not certain. Consult your doctor.

Benjamin Wolozin, MD, PhD, professor of pharmacology and neurology, Boston University School of Medicine, Boston.

■ ■ ■ ■

Are You at Higher Risk For Alzheimer's?

People whose mothers had Alzheimer's may be at higher risk for the disease than people whose fathers had it.

Recent finding: Adult children of women who had Alzheimer's showed reductions in sugar utilization in the brain—glucose (sugar) was available, but the brain wasn't using it properly. Decreased sugar utilization is common in Alzheimer's patients.

Theory: Maternally inherited genes may alter brain metabolism. Identifying individuals at risk may enable earlier intervention.

Lisa Mosconi, PhD, assistant professor of psychiatry, New York University School of Medicine, New York City, and leader of a study of 49 people, published online in *Proceedings of the National Academy of Sciences.*

Low Vitamin B-12 May Shrink Your Brain

Anna Vogiatzoglou, RD, doctoral candidate, department of physiology, anatomy and genetics, University of Oxford, England.

Jonathan Friedman, MD, associate professor, surgery and neuroscience and experimental therapeutics, Texas A&M Health Science Center College of Medicine, and associate dean, College of Medicine, Bryan-College Station campus, and director, Texas Brain and Spine Institute, College Station, Texas.

Shari Midoneck, MD, associate clinical professor, medicine, Weill Cornell Medical College, and internist, Iris Cantor Women's Health Center, New York City.

Neurology.

Low levels of vitamin B-12 may increase the risk for brain atrophy or shrinkage, recent research suggests. Brain atrophy is associated with Alzheimer's disease and impaired cognitive function.

THE STUDY

The research involved 107 volunteers, ages 61 to 87, who were cognitively normal at the beginning of the five-year study. All participants underwent annual clinical exams, MRI scans and cognitive tests, and had blood samples taken.

Individuals with lower vitamin B-12 levels at the start of the study had a greater decrease in brain volume. Those with the lowest B-12 levels had a sixfold greater rate of brain-volume loss compared with those who had the highest levels of the vitamin.

Interestingly, none of the participants were deficient in vitamin B-12. They just had low levels within a normal range.

"They all had normal B-12 levels, yet there was a difference between the higher levels and the lower levels in terms of brain shrinkage. This is new information which could potentially change what we recommend to people in terms of diet," said Jonathan Friedman, MD, an associate professor of surgery, neuroscience and experimental therapeutics at Texas A&M Health Science Center College of Medicine and associate dean of the College of Medicine, Bryan-College Station campus.

IMPLICATIONS

Although the study, published in *Neurology*, can't confirm that lower levels of B-12 actually cause brain atrophy, they do suggest that "we ought to be more aware of our B-12 status, especially people who are vulnerable to B-12 deficiency [elderly, vegetarians, pregnant and lactating women, infants], and take steps to maintain it by eating a balanced and varied diet," said study coauthor Anna Vogiatzoglou, a registered dietitian and doctoral candidate in the department of physiology, anatomy and genetics at the University of Oxford, in England.

Not only might B-12 levels be a modifiable risk factor for cognitive decline, it might also be a clue to help clinicians assess cognitive problems earlier on.

"It's worth looking at B-12 levels," affirmed Shari Midoneck, MD, an internist at the Iris Cantor Women's Health Center in New York City. "It doesn't hurt to take B-12."

According to the study authors, vitamin B-12 deficiency is a public health problem, especially among older people.

Good sources of the vitamin include meat, fish, milk and fortified cereals.

NEW B-12 CLINICAL TRIAL

It's not clear what the biological mechanisms behind the link might be, nor is it clear whether added B-12 would avert brain atrophy.

"We are doing a clinical trial in Oxford in which we are giving B vitamins [including B-12] to elderly people with memory impairment," Vogiatzoglou said. "In this trial, we are doing MRI scans at the start and the end, and so, we will be able to find out if taking B vitamins really does slow down the shrinking of the brain."

info To learn more, go to the National Institutes of Health Web site, *http://ods.od.nih.gov* and search "vitamin B-12."

"Old Age" Symptoms Could Really Be a Vitamin Deficiency

Sally M. Pacholok, RN, and Jeffrey J. Stuart, DO, coauthors of *Could It Be B-12?* (Linden). Ms. Pacholok has studied vitamin B-12 deficiency for more than 20 years and is an emergency room nurse in Mount Clemens, Michigan. Dr. Stuart is a board-certified emergency medicine physician in Rochester, Michigan.

Millions of Americans suffer tingling, numbness or pain in their hands or feet...dizziness...balance problems... depression...and/or memory loss because they are deficient in vitamin B-12, a nutrient that most of us—including many doctors—rarely think about. Low levels of vitamin B-12 can even raise the risk for heart disease and osteoporosis, according to research.

Good news: You can avoid the potentially serious complications of vitamin B-12 deficiency with simple, inexpensive treatment—if the problem is identified soon enough. Permanent damage can occur if the deficiency is not treated within a year of the development of symptoms.

What you need to know...

A KEY TO PROPER NERVE FUNCTION

Vitamin B-12 is needed to maintain the layers of tissue, called the myelin sheath, that insulate each nerve cell. We need only a very tiny amount of the vitamin each day—2.4 micrograms (mcg).

The vitamin is abundant in meats (such as red meat, poultry and liver), shellfish, eggs and dairy products. Because vitamin B-12 is readily stored by the body (mainly in the liver), doctors have long assumed that deficiency is rare.

But a complex process must occur before vitamin B-12 can do its job. When it is consumed, the vitamin must be split from the proteins to which it is attached, carried into the small intestine and transported throughout the body with the help of other proteins.

If there is a problem—for example, a person takes a drug that interferes with vitamin B-12 absorption—a potentially dangerous deficiency can result. Among adults over age 65, up to 25% have been found in studies to have a clear B-12 deficiency (blood levels of less than 225).

THE TOLL OF B-12 DEFICIENCY

Many so-called symptoms of aging—both physical and mental—actually could be the result of B-12 deficiency. When a lack of this vitamin impairs the nervous system, a variety of problems can result, including weakness, dizziness and tremor—all of which can be mistaken for signs of neurological disorders, such as Parkinson's disease, multiple sclerosis, vertigo or neuropathy (nerve damage that causes pain or numbness).

A B-12 deficiency also can affect how you think, feel and act, resulting in irritability, apathy, confusion, forgetfulness—even serious depression, dementia, paranoia and/or hallucinations. Vitamin B-12 deficiency can lead to symptoms that are sometimes mistaken for Alzheimer's disease.

The cardiovascular system also can be affected. Vitamin B-12—along with vitamin B-6 and folic acid (another B vitamin)—plays a key role in the breakdown of *homocysteine,* a naturally occurring amino acid. Elevated levels of homocysteine damage blood vessels and promote the buildup of fatty deposits in the arteries (atherosclerosis) as well as abnormal blood clotting. Several studies have linked high blood levels of homocysteine to significantly increased risk for heart disease, heart attack, stroke and blood clots in the lungs and/or extremities.

The dangers of elevated homocysteine are widely known, but many doctors—cardiologists among them—simply prescribe high doses of folic acid to lower levels of the amino acid, ignoring the need to test for and possibly correct vitamin B-12 deficiency as well.

Also linked to B-12 deficiency...

- **Breast cancer.** A Johns Hopkins study of 390 women found that those with the lowest levels of B-12 were two to four times more likely to develop breast cancer than those with healthier levels.
- **Infections.** In another study, 30 older adults who had very low levels of B-12 produced fewer antibodies when vaccinated against pneumonia—leaving them with less protection against this potentially fatal infection than adults with adequate levels of B-12.
- **Osteoporosis.** Research shows that B-12 deficiency is linked to osteoporosis—in part, because B-12 is crucial to the function of osteoblasts (bone-forming cells).

ARE YOU AT RISK?

Aging is a primary risk factor for B-12 deficiency. That's because 30% to 40% of people over age 50 suffer from *atrophic gastritis,* which damages the stomach lining, markedly reducing production of the stomach acid needed to absorb vitamin B-12. Many older adults also fail to eat vitamin B-12-rich foods.

Another cause of B-12 deficiency is *pernicious anemia*—an autoimmune disorder in which the body does not produce a substance called *intrinsic factor,* which is necessary for the vitamin's absorption. Pernicious anemia is more common among people who have other autoimmune diseases, such as rheumatoid arthritis, lupus, thyroid disease and type 1 diabetes.

It's now recognized that Crohn's disease (chronic inflammation of the intestinal wall) and celiac disease (intolerance to gluten, a protein found in wheat, barley and rye) can impede absorption of vitamin B-12. So can gastrointestinal surgery—particularly gastric bypass.

In addition, commonly used medications—such as the heartburn drugs known as *proton pump inhibitors,* including *omeprazole* (Prilosec) and *lansoprazole* (Prevacid)...and *H2 blockers,* including *ranitidine* (Zantac) and *famotidine*

(Pepcid)...as well as the oral diabetes drug *metformin* (Glucophage, Glucovance)—can interfere with B-12 absorption.

Because vitamin B-12 is found only in animal products, strict vegetarians are at high risk for a deficiency. Some research shows that 80% of people who do not eat animal products and fail to take a B-12 supplement have a deficiency of the vitamin.

GET THE RIGHT TEST

When doctors order a complete blood count (CBC), among the abnormalities they look for is *macrocytic anemia,* a condition in which red blood cells are abnormally large. This can be a sign of vitamin B-12 deficiency. But in people who take supplements that contain folic acid—as do most multivitamins—blood test results may appear normal even when there is a vitamin B-12 deficiency. (Folic acid can "mask" such a deficiency.) A blood test that specifically measures B-12 levels also is available. However, this test is not always accurate—it has a wide "normal" range and can be inconsistent in its sensitivity.

The most sensitive B-12 test measures the amount of *methylmalonic acid* (MMA) in the urine. Because vitamin B-12 plays a key role in the production of MMA, results of this test can conclusively diagnose or rule out B-12 deficiency. Health insurance will pay for the test if the patient has symptoms of B-12 deficiency or is at high risk for deficiency.

BEST TREATMENT OPTIONS

If you have a B-12 deficiency, injections of 1,000 mcg—daily at first, then weekly, then monthly—are the most dependable solution, especially if neurologic symptoms are present. Sublingual (under-the-tongue) doses may be an alternative for some people. Ask your doctor. The MMA test should be repeated in three months to check the sublingual supplement's effectiveness.

If you have a B-12 deficiency, it's also wise to receive a homocysteine blood test before treatment to determine whether inadequate B-12 has raised your homocysteine levels, thus increasing your risk for vascular disease.

■ ■ ■ ■

Slow Memory Loss with Milk!

Elderly patients with low levels of vitamin B-12 have twice as much brain shrinkage as those with higher levels. Drinking two glasses of milk (even skim) daily is enough to increase vitamin B-12 to normal levels, which could help slow cognitive decline.

Also: Take up to 500 micrograms each day of B-12 supplements.

A. David Smith, FMedSci, professor of pharmacology, Oxford University, Oxford, England.

Aging...What's Normal, What's Not and What Works

Robert N. Butler, MD, president and CEO of the New York City–based International Longevity Center and former medical editor-in-chief of the journal *Geriatrics.* Dr. Butler is author of the Pulitzer Prize–winning *Why Survive? Being Old in America.* His most recent book is *The Longevity Revolution: The Benefits and Challenges of Living a Long Life* (Public Affairs).

Normal aging takes an inevitable toll—for example, joints and tendons don't work as well as they once did, and your circulatory system weakens. As a result, it's often difficult to separate the normal signs of aging from disease and other problems that can be treated to give you a better quality of life.

Conditions you may be able to improve with proper care...

FATIGUE

Fatigue is common among older adults, but the cause often is easy to correct. About 30% of Americans over the age of 60 have a normal age-related decrease in stomach acid, which is needed to absorb vitamin B-12. However, a B-12 deficiency is not normal and can result in *pernicious anemia* (marked by defective production of red blood cells).

What to do: If you feel tired and weak, ask your doctor to test you for pernicious anemia, which is correctable with B-12 shots.

FRAILTY

Frailty—weight loss, weakness, exhaustion and slowed walking speed—increases your risk for a fall, a leading cause of death among adults over age 65. We all lose muscle mass as we age, but frailty is not normal.

What to do: Test the strength of your thighs. Thigh strength is a predictor of frailty.

To test your thighs: Sit down and fold your arms across your chest. While having someone time you, stand up and sit down five times, as rapidly as possible. If five chair-squats take 14 seconds or more, your thighs are weak. Ask your doctor for advice on thigh-strengthening exercises.

HEARING LOSS

One-third of adults over age 65 have *presbycusis* (age-related hearing loss). This is normal but can make conversations hard to hear.

What to do: If hearing loss is interfering with your ability to participate in activities or communicate with others, see an audiologist for an exam. Only one in five adults with hearing loss that leads to communication problems decides to use a hearing aid—usually because of a fear that the device will be conspicuous or work poorly. However, newer models are small and produce high-quality sound.

HIGH BLOOD PRESSURE

Because arteries stiffen with age, a mild increase in blood pressure is to be expected as a person grows older. However, high blood pressure (above 120/80 mmHg) is not a normal part of aging.

What to do: Exercise regularly—for example, walk briskly for 30 minutes at least five times a week. Restrict your salt intake by eating whole foods rather than processed foods, which provide 75% of the typical American's daily salt intake. If these steps fail to lower your blood pressure, talk to your doctor about blood pressure–lowering medication.

MEMORY LOSS

If you forget where you put your car keys, that usually is what doctors call age-related memory loss—and it's a normal part of aging. But if you forget even briefly what your car keys are for, that's a sign of brain damage (due to a head injury, for example) or a form of dementia, such as Alzheimer's.

Depression, which afflicts nearly one out of every five older adults, often causes symptoms (such as apathy and lack of concentration) that mimic those of Alzheimer's.

What to do: If Alzheimer's is suspected in you or a loved one, be sure that the doctor has taken a thorough history to detect symptoms of depression, such as suicidal thoughts, weight loss and sleep disturbances.

SLEEP PROBLEMS

Older adults often suffer sleep problems due to age-related changes in the sleep-wake cycle. However, anyone who is sleeping less than seven hours nightly should attempt to improve his/her sleep.

What to do: Adopt sleep-promoting strategies—for example, reduce the amount of light in the bedroom, get regular exercise and reduce stress. If necessary, sleep medications, such as *zolpidem* (Ambien) and *eszopiclone* (Lunesta), can be valuable for short-term relief. If you snore, experience daytime fatigue or suffer morning headaches, ask your doctor if you should be evaluated for sleep apnea, which causes frequent interruptions in breathing during sleep.

SEXUAL DYSFUNCTION

Older adults have no reason to forgo sexual activity. However, a recent study in *The New England Journal of Medicine* found that older adults rating their overall health as "poor" or "fair" were 60% to 80% less likely to be sexually active than those rating their health as "very good" or "excellent."

What to do: Get regular physical activity and eat a balanced diet that emphasizes whole foods to help prevent or even reverse diabetes and artery-clogging diseases—conditions that can reduce blood flow to the penis, causing erectile dysfunction. For women, such lifestyle habits promote overall physical fitness, which generally leads to good sexual function.

TOOTH LOSS

In 1955, half of Americans over age 65 had lost their teeth due to gum disease. Today, a far greater number of Americans over age 65 retain their teeth as a result of improved dental care. Tooth loss is not a normal part of aging.

What to do: Brush twice a day and floss at least once a day. See your dentist twice a year for a cleaning and a checkup.

URINARY PROBLEMS

If you're a man and suffer increased urgency or frequency, you may have *benign prostatic hyperplasia* (BPH), an age-related enlargement of the prostate.

What to do: See your doctor about medication, such as *finasteride* (Proscar), to help reduce the size of the prostate.

Older women often experience stress urinary incontinence—leaking urine while sneezing, laughing or lifting a heavy object.

What to do: Kegel exercises—squeezing the pelvic floor muscles that stop or slow the stream of urine—can cure or improve up to 90% of cases. Squeeze the muscles 10 to 20 times a day, holding each contraction for 10 seconds.

VISION PROBLEMS

Everyone's eyes change with age. For example, lenses become stiff, leading to *presbyopia* (difficulty reading fine print). But loss of vision is not normal—it is almost always a sign of disease, such as age-related macular degeneration.

What to do: After age 50, get an eye exam at least every two years.

■ **More from Robert N. Butler, MD...**

Get Your Doctor to Detect Diseases Without Costly Tests

No matter what your age, your doctor should take seriously any condition that would be considered abnormal in a younger person. To do otherwise is "ageist." A careful history and physical exam can diagnose 90% of all diseases without costly medical tests. For a person age 65 or over, a good history takes about an hour.

Problem: Doctors rarely spend that much time with a patient because of reimbursement issues—one 60-minute session pays no more than one 30-minute session.

Solution: Ask your doctor to do a thorough history over two sessions rather than one. The second can usually be billed to insurance as a follow-up visit.

Six Great Supplements For Everyone Over 50

Jamison Starbuck, ND, a naturopathic physician in family practice in Missoula, Montana. She is past president of the American Association of Naturopathic Physicians and a contributing editor to *The Alternative Advisor: The Complete Guide to Natural Therapies and Alternative Treatments* (Time-Life).

Of all the changes that occur with aging, one of the most underrecognized is the body's reduced ability to absorb nutrients. As we grow older, our bodies become less efficient at secreting the digestive enzymes that are necessary for the absorption of essential vitamins. Because of this absorption problem, I advise my older patients to follow the nutritious and heart-healthy Mediterranean diet—rich in fresh greens (such as chard, kale and spinach), fresh fruit, whole grains, nuts, seeds, beans, healthful oils (olive, for example) and lean protein, such as turkey and fish. For more on the Mediterranean diet, visit the Web site of the American Heart Association, *www.americanheart.org*.

But it's not always easy to stick to a nutritious eating plan. What's more, many older adults suffer conditions that interfere with appetite—for example, dry mouth, nausea or constipation caused by common medications, such as pain relievers and hypertension drugs. Dentures and waning senses of smell and taste also can interfere with the consumption of healthful meals. In my opinion, all people over age 50 should consider taking certain supplements—in addition to a daily multivitamin—to compensate for nutrients that might be lacking in their diets. *My favorite "healthy aging" supplements (all available at health food stores)...*

- **Vitamin B-12—800 micrograms (mcg) to 1,000 mcg daily,** in sublingual (dissolved under the tongue) form. It helps with poor memory, a lack of energy, depression and neuralgia (nerve pain).
- **Vitamin A—10,000 international units (IU) daily.** It helps promote health of the eyes and skin and general immunity. If you also take a multivitamin containing vitamin A, do not exceed 10,000 IU daily unless recommended by your doctor.
- **Vitamin E—400 IU daily.** It protects nerve and muscle cells, reduces leg cramps and helps prevent heart disease.*
- **Vitamin D—1,000 IU daily.** Recent research shows that many older adults are deficient in vitamin D, a nutrient that is essential for calcium absorption and osteoporosis prevention and may protect against certain malignancies, including cancers of the breast and colon.
- **Essential fatty acids,** in the form of fish oil, containing 1,800 milligrams daily of combined *eicosapentaenoic acid* (EPA) and *docosahexaenoic acid* (DHA). Fish oil acts as a natural antidepressant for patients of all ages and improves brain function.
- **Digestive enzymes.** Typically derived from papaya or pineapple, digestive enzyme supplements promote digestion—and, in turn, the absorption of nutrients from foods and other supplements. Follow the manufacturer's directions for dosages. If you have a gastrointestinal disease, such as an ulcer or diverticulitis, consult your physician before taking plant enzymes, which can irritate an inflamed gastrointestinal tract.

*If you take a blood-thinning drug, such as *warfarin* (Coumadin), check with your doctor before taking vitamin E supplements.

Play Video Games to Boost Your Brainpower

Chandramallika Basak, postdoctoral researcher, University of Illinois.

Paul R. Sanberg, PhD, DSc, professor of neurosurgery and director of the University of South Florida Center of Excellence for Aging and Brain Repair, Tampa.

Psychology and Aging.

Older people who want to stay sharp should consider playing video games, a recent study suggests.

While past studies have shown that playing video games has many positive benefits, ranging from improved problem-solving abilities in young people to improved operating skills in surgeons, the recent study in the journal *Psychology and Aging* went one step further. The research, which was not funded by the gaming industry, is the first to indicate that playing complex video games after receiving training may improve the cognitive functions that typically decline with age.

THE STUDY

The researchers tested the cognitive abilities of 40 people in their 60s and 70s before and after playing the computer game "Rise of Nations," which rewards the complex task of creating a society, including building cities, employing people and expanding territory.

Half of the group received training before playing the game while the other half served as a comparison group and received no training.

Testing showed that people in the trained group performed better, not only on the game, but also on tests of memory, reasoning and the ability to identify rotated objects compared to those who were not trained.

IMPLICATIONS

The results may eventually help older people who are struggling with managing tasks they once found to be simple.

"Juggling multiple tasks such as cooking, answering the door and talking on the phone might be simple for a young person, while an older person might feel overwhelmed and burn their food," said study author Chandramallika

Basak, a postdoctoral researcher at the University of Illinois. "These are the kind of things that older people do in their everyday lives, so if you're not very good at juggling different tasks it does impact your lifestyle."

The study offers welcome news for America's aging baby boomer population. The whole notion that the older brain in aging individuals can improve is of vital interest right now, said Paul R. Sanberg, PhD, DSc, director of the University of South Florida's Center of Excellence for Aging and Brain Repair. "The interesting thing is that less than 24 hours of training not only improved mental and cognitive functions, but also enhanced their ability to function in some other tasks," he said.

BRAIN-IMAGING STUDIES

"This would be a good type of experiment to combine with brain-imaging studies to see the effect of the training on these people, and whether there's increased activity in the brain and new connections," said Dr. Sanberg. "It's also nice to see if there's some correlation with actual brain function."

HOW TO GET THE MOST BRAIN BENEFIT

While a growing number of studies have found that playing video games can be beneficial, experts warn against too much of a good thing, noting that playing video games can be an isolating experience that mitigates other health benefits.

"Clearly mental exercises, whether through a game or another media outlet, aren't bad, but you want to establish societal connections as well," cautioned Dr. Sanberg. "Doing too much of one thing might not be the best idea."

Basak suggested that playing strategy-based games, such as chess or video games with other people, might offer a way to achieve the same benefits without sacrificing social interaction.

"When we look at improvements in cognition, it's not just one thing," said Basak. "There are many factors that go into it."

info To learn more, visit the Web site of the National Institute on Aging, *http://www.nia.nih.gov,* and search "changing brain in healthy aging."

■ ■ ■ ■

Surf the Web—Better Than Reading for Building Your Brain

Middle-aged and senior computer users showed more brain activity in the frontal lobe—an area involved in complex reasoning and decision-making—while searching for information on the internet than while simply reading text. Brain scans also revealed the highest neural activity among experienced Web surfers, though novices, showed a brain-activity boost after searching the internet for one hour per day for five days.

Theory: Even simple computer tasks cultivate neural circuits that may protect the brain against future decline.

Gary Small, PhD, MD, director, University of California, Los Angeles Center on Aging, and leader of a study of 24 people, to be published in *American Journal of Geriatric Psychiatry.*

Stay Healthy to 100+

John Robbins, author of *Healthy at 100: The Scientifically Proven Secrets of the World's Healthiest and Longest-Lived Peoples* (Ballantine), *www.healthyat100.org.* The recipient of the Albert Schweitzer Humanitarian Award, Robbins lives in Northern California. His book *Diet for a New America* (Kramer) was nominated for the Pulitzer Prize and was the basis for a PBS special.

If you were told that it's entirely possible to live in good health to age 100 and beyond, you would probably think that the claim sounds far-fetched.

But health and longevity researcher John Robbins has found people who do just that. The son of the cofounder of Baskin-Robbins (the world's largest chain of ice cream shops), Robbins walked away from the family business in 1968 and has since dedicated himself to studying healthful lifestyle habits, including those of the world's longest-living and healthiest people.

Here's what Robbins had to say in a recent interview...

Where do people live the longest healthy lives? The communities I studied are found in the valley of Vilcabamba in Ecuador...the Hunza region of Pakistan...the Japanese island of Okinawa... and the republic of Abkhazia, which has been in the news due to the recent conflict between Georgia and Russia. I chose to write about centenarians in these regions because they have been exhaustively researched.

What is special about the centenarians in these areas? In these communities, large numbers of people not only live to be 100, but they're also remarkably healthy at this age. In the US, most of us hit our peak of physical fitness, strength and overall health between the ages of 20 and 30 and gradually decline after that. Research shows that by the age of 70, most Americans have lost 30% to 40% of their maximum breathing capacity...40% of their kidney and liver functions...15% to 30% of their bone mass...and 30% of their strength.

In the communities I researched and wrote about, people live extraordinarily long lives and have extremely low rates of heart disease, cancer, arthritis, osteoporosis, asthma, dementia and other degenerative diseases that plague so many older people in the West. Many of the centenarians remain vigorous until weeks or months before their deaths.

What are the eating habits of people living in these regions? They derive their protein primarily from plant sources, including beans, peas, whole grains, seeds and nuts. This style of eating is supported by a recent major international study, which found that a diet based on plant foods—with only a minimal amount of foods derived from animals—results in lower total cholesterol levels.

What else is unique about their diets? The centenarians I studied eat diets that are low in calories. For example, even with their active lifestyles, men in these regions consume an average of about 1,900 calories a day compared with an average daily consumption of 2,650 calories by men in the US, where lifestyles tend to be more sedentary. Also, the fats that the centenarians eat are derived from food sources, including seeds (such as flaxseeds, sesame and sunflower seeds) and many kinds of nuts, and in some cases wild fish, rather than from bottled oils, margarines or saturated animal fats.

Is there any obesity among the centenarians? No. Interestingly, all the longest-lived people eat very slowly. They savor their food and enjoy each other's company, and their evening meal can last for hours. This leisurely pace gives their digestive systems time to register when they have eaten enough—and allows them to stop eating when they feel nearly full. As a result, there is not a single case of obesity among the centenarians in these communities. In contrast, a recent study predicted that nearly 90% of Americans will be overweight or obese by 2030.

Does it help to change one's eating habits later in life? Beginning to eat well can make an extraordinary difference in your health and longevity even if you've eaten poorly for decades. That's because most of your body's cells and tissues are in a constant state of renewal. Almost all the cells of your body—including those lining the stomach—are being continually regenerated, so that what you eat today has a direct impact on your body tomorrow.

What about exercise? In the cultures I studied, daily life involves lots of vigorous walking and, in most cases, mountain climbing. *The Journal of Epidemiology and Community Health* published a study that found mountain dwellers live longer than their lowland counterparts because their hearts get a better daily workout.

Numerous studies have found that physical exercise plays an essential role in preventing a variety of serious illnesses, including Alzheimer's disease. For example, a study published in *Archives of Neurology* found that people who engaged in moderate physical activity (exercise three or more times per week at an intensity equal to walking) had a significant reduction in Alzheimer's risk.

Obviously, few Americans regularly walk up and down mountains, but we still can walk much more than we do, climb stairs instead of taking elevators and, when we do drive, park our cars at the far end of parking lots.

What other habits contribute to the centenarians' longevity? There is a deep sense of human connection in all four of the communities. People continually help one another, believe in one another and enjoy spending time with each other.

For example, when an Abkhazian host invites someone over for dinner, the invitation always says, "Come and be our guest." It never says, "Come for dinner." Of course, dinner is served, but the emphasis is on the pleasure of being together rather than on the meal.

In Vilcabamba, a popular saying addresses social connections: The left leg and the right leg help keep people healthy, since they carry individuals to their friends' homes.

Were any of the lifestyle practices surprising to you? In these societies, people actually look forward to growing old. They expect to be healthy and vital and know that they will be respected, since age is equated with wisdom.

The power of our attitudes toward aging is demonstrated in recent research conducted at the Yale School of Public Health. One landmark study concluded that negative thoughts about aging can undermine a person's health. In fact, one's perceptions about aging proved to be a more accurate indicator of life span than blood pressure, cholesterol level or whether the person smoked or exercised.

How Older Athletes Can Help You Stay Young

Vonda Wright, MD, director of the Performance and Research Initiative for Master Athletes (PRIMA) at the University of Pittsburgh Medical Center. She is author of *Fitness After 40: How to Stay Strong at Any Age* (Amacom). *www.seniorsportsandfitness.com*.

Olympic swimmer Dara Torres won three silver medals in Beijing in 2008 and set an American record in the women's 50-meter freestyle. At 41 years old, she was nearly twice the age of many of her competitors.

Torres is not the first athlete to compete at an elite level after age 40. Baseball Hall of Famer Nolan Ryan threw a no-hitter at age 44...golfer Jack Nicklaus won the Masters Tournament at age 46...quarterback George Blanda remained in the NFL until age 48...tennis star Martina Navratilova won a US Open mixed doubles title at 49...and hockey player Gordie Howe played professional hockey until he was 52.

Here's what older athletes can teach us all about remaining physically active into middle age and beyond...

- **Fight the real enemy.** The enemy isn't age—it's inactivity. The widely held belief that physical decline is inevitable once we pass 30 is a myth. There is no scientific reason why we cannot continue to perform at or near our peaks into our 50s. Serious declines often can be staved off until our late 70s.

Most people over age 40 experience more precipitous physical declines not because their bodies fail them, but because they fail their bodies. The vast majority of Americans get less and less exercise as they age. This inactive lifestyle, not the passage of time, is the single greatest cause of their physical deterioration.

- **Push hard, but not all the time.** Older athletes must make a few concessions to their advancing age, but easing up on the throttle during workouts is not one of them. Don't just go for a walk...go for a jog. Don't just try to repeat the same performance in each exercise session...shoot for faster times and additional reps. (Always check with your doctor before starting an exercise program.)

People over age 40 should not attempt to go all out all the time, however. Older bodies take longer to recover from strenuous workouts than younger bodies. Schedule a rest day without guilt after a physically challenging day.

Example: If you plan a weeklong hiking trip with the grandkids, schedule challenging hikes only every other day, with days off for relaxing at campsites in between.

If you can't see yourself taking a day off from exercise, at least select an activity that challenges a different muscle group.

- **Try to never get out of shape.** Getting back in shape is good, but never getting out of shape is better. Athletes who remain physically competitive after age 40 usually don't have to worry about getting back in shape—most of them have never allowed themselves to get out of shape.

Example: Dara Torres was swimming competitively just three weeks after giving birth.

For those who are in great shape, staying in shape is like taking a well-tuned sports car out for a spin. But for those who are out of shape, exercising is like pushing a broken car up a hill. Their hearts and lungs are inefficient, and their muscles are weak. Exercise is unpleasant, so they avoid it.

The psychological challenge of getting back in shape can be equally daunting. Once middle-aged people let their fitness levels slide, they tend to assume that this decline is natural and inevitable, which makes it easy for them to surrender to the process. Those who never get out of shape continue to think of good health and physical fitness as their natural state and exercise as a natural part of their lives.

As difficult as rebounding from a period of inactivity can be, it will only become more difficult the longer this inactivity lasts. If you are out of shape, the best time to begin your return to fitness is today.

•Ignore advancing age. Successful older athletes don't think of their age as a disadvantage—most don't even think of themselves as old. They feel young, think young and react with surprise when others suggest that competing at their age is unnatural.

Example: NHL hockey player Chris Chelios turned 47 last season. When asked how someone so old managed to stay in the league, he said, "I don't feel old."

When successful older athletes think about their age at all, they tend to focus on its advantages—decades of experience and improved technique. They believe that their younger competitors are at the disadvantage.

•Work on injury-prevention muscles, not cosmetic muscles. Leave the bulging biceps to the younger athletes. The muscles that matter the most to those over 40 are the ones that help us avoid aches and injuries. *Among the most important...*

•Rotator cuff muscles. Injuries of the rotator cuff (the muscles and tendons inside your shoulder) are extremely common among those over 40. These injuries make it painful to swim, swing a golf club or tennis racket, throw a baseball or do virtually anything else that involves the shoulder. To strengthen the rotator cuff, use an exercise band, placing one end under your right foot and the other end in your right hand. Raise the band slowly in front of your body, keeping your elbow straight. Do one set of eight-to-10 reps. Work up to two sets. Repeat on the left side.

•Abdominals and pelvic muscles. The secret to a healthy back is a healthy front. Keep your abs and pelvic muscles toned, and back pain is less likely. A key exercise is the plank. Lie on your stomach, hold in your abs and raise your body on your elbows and toes. Begin by holding for 30 seconds, and work up to two minutes.

•Quads. Knee pain is not always caused by a problem with the joint itself. Strengthening the four large quad muscles on the front of your thighs can make your knees feel as good as new. Quad exercise: Place your back against a wall with your feet about 18 inches in front of the wall. Place two rolled towels between your knees, and squeeze them with your knees. Then lower your back down the wall until your knees are bent about 60 degrees. Hold for 10 to 30 seconds, and work up to doing it 10 times. Keep your stomach pulled in.

•Don't forget flexibility and balance. Successful older athletes almost invariably understand that stretching and "equilibrium training" are just as important as aerobic exercise and strength training.

Our muscles become shorter and stiffer as we age. This shortens our stride when we run and makes full, fluid 360-degree shoulder motion difficult when we swim, golf or play tennis. Daily stretching can allow us to move as we did when we were young.

Stretch the major muscle groups for 30 seconds every day, not just before physical activity. After age 65, double this stretching time to 60 seconds per stretch per muscle group.

Our natural equilibrium begins to decline in our 30s, but most people do not realize that their balance is slowly failing until they start to fall down, typically in their 60s or 70s.

The best way to slow equilibrium loss is to practice balancing every day.

An easy way: Stand on one foot as long as you can while doing the dishes or brushing your teeth, then switch.

It's True—Caregiving Actually Lengthens Your Life

Stephanie Brown, PhD, assistant professor, internal medicine, University of Michigan, Ann Arbor, and researcher, VA Ann Arbor Healthcare System.

Gary Kennedy, MD, director, geriatric psychiatry, Montefiore Medical Center, New York City.

Psychological Science.

Much has been reported about the stress and burden of caregiving, but a recent study suggests there may be a flip side to taking care of someone you love as they age—a decreased risk for death.

"We found that caregivers who spent an average of 14 or more hours a week caregiving lived longer and reduced their risk of dying by about half," said study author Stephanie Brown, PhD, an assistant professor in internal medicine at the University of Michigan in Ann Arbor. She added that even after they controlled the data to account for things such as age or previous illness, "there was about a 36% reduced risk of dying in the seven-year time period."

Results of the study were published in *Psychological Science.*

THE STUDY

The study included 1,688 couples who lived on their own, not in assisted living or a nursing home. All of the study participants were over age 70.

The researchers gathered health and demographic information as well as information on how much each spouse helped the other with normal activities of daily living, such as eating, managing money and taking medications.

Over the seven-year study, 27% of the study volunteers died.

When the researchers analyzed the data and controlled for factors such as age, race, gender, education level and net worth, they found that providing care for your spouse for more than 14 hours a week was associated with a significantly decreased risk of death compared to those who provided no spousal caregiving.

IMPLICATIONS

"Other studies caution against caregiving, but our study suggests that the actual act of caretaking may not be harmful," said Dr. Brown.

"This study shows that the burden of caregiving can sometimes be lightly born," said Gary Kennedy, MD, director of geriatric psychiatry at Montefiore Medical Center in New York City. But he said that the results might be different depending on the type of care a spouse has to provide. Taking care of someone with early-stage Alzheimer's disease, who can still function fairly well and still behaves normally for the most part is much different from taking care of someone in the middle stages of the disease, who may be aggressive or may not sleep well.

THEORIES

Dr. Brown believes that the decreased risk of death comes from physiological benefits from caregiving instead of psychological ones. The authors suggest that stress regulation may play a role in this benefit. Helping others is associated with a release of oxytocin, a hormone that may help buffer the effects of stress, Dr. Brown explained.

Dr. Kennedy said the survival benefit is likely caused by both physiological and psychological factors.

"We know that in rat pups that are prematurely weaned, their heart rate plummets, even before they've lost body temperature, so it's not related to cooling or caloric problems at that point. Simply being separated changes the heart rate. Social interactions have a biological impact," he explained.

Plus, he said, having a partner to care for provides structure and a sense of purpose.

info Learn more about alleviating caregiver stress from the National Women's Health Information Center's Web site, *www.womenshealth.gov/faq/caregiver-stress.cfm.*

■ ■ ■ ■

The Anxiety–Longevity Link

In a recent study, anxiety was linked to longevity. Among seniors, women who scored higher on tests that gauge anxiety lived longer than women with low anxiety levels.

Theory: Anxiety may motivate women to seek prompt medical care.

Jianping Zhang, MD, PhD, researcher, department of psychiatry and psychology, Cleveland Clinic, and leader of a study of 1,000 seniors, presented at a meeting of the American Psychosomatic Society.

The Truth About Testosterone

Abraham Morgentaler, MD, associate clinical professor of urology at Harvard Medical School in Boston. He is the author of *Testosterone for Life* (McGraw-Hill).

When it comes to hormones, testosterone is among the most widely misunderstood. This sex hormone is produced in a man's testes and adrenal glands and, in smaller amounts, in a woman's ovaries and adrenal glands. It affects sex drive in both men and women. In men, it also plays a role in strength, mood, the development of sex organs and secondary male sexual characteristics like hair growth.

Even though a significant number of men over age 50 suffer from a deficiency of the hormone, few receive appropriate treatment. Women also can be affected by symptoms when their bodies do not produce enough testosterone. *What you need to know...*

BEYOND SEXUAL DYSFUNCTION

Until fairly recently, doctors believed that the only casualty of the waning testosterone levels that occur when a man ages was his sex drive (libido).

Now: It's known that low testosterone can cause a variety of other symptoms. *For example...*

- **Fatigue.** Men with low testosterone often tire more easily and take more naps.
- **Low mood.** Irritability and depression can occur.

Low testosterone also can lead to hidden problems, such as...

- **Anemia.** A shortage of red blood cells may be due to such causes as a nutritional deficiency, gastrointestinal bleeding—or low testosterone.
- **Bone loss.** Osteoporosis isn't just a woman's disease—more than 6% of men have developed it by age 65—and testosterone deficiency greatly increases the risk.
- **Loss of muscle mass.** Belly fat also can develop.

ARE YOU DEFICIENT?

Unfortunately, few men who experience these symptoms receive a blood test for testosterone deficiency. The test that measures total testosterone levels is the best known. But free testosterone levels should be measured (also with a blood test) to determine the amount of the hormone that can be used most readily by the body.

Important: There is debate regarding the exact definition of "normal" blood levels of both total and free testosterone. Speak to your physician for an interpretation of your test results.

Low numbers on either test—in addition to the symptoms described earlier—usually warrant a trial of testosterone therapy. It may take up to three months to see benefits.

WHAT ARE THE RISKS?

The long-term effects of testosterone therapy are unknown, but research is beginning to address many of the concerns some men have had regarding the potential risks of testosterone replacement.

Among the most common...

- **Heart disease.** Men are more prone to heart disease than women are, and testosterone was once considered a likely explanation. But there is virtually no evidence that supports this theory.

In fact, one study found that men with higher testosterone levels are less likely to develop atherosclerosis (fatty buildup in the arteries) than those with low testosterone. Low testosterone is associated with diabetes and obesity—major risk factors for heart attack.

Caution: Testosterone boosts red blood cell production. This is good for anemia, but too many red blood cells can raise heart attack risk. Men with high *hematocrit* (a measure of red blood cell concentration) should use testosterone cautiously, if at all. Men with advanced kidney or liver disease should avoid testosterone therapy—it could cause fluid retention, which already is a problem for such men.

•**Prostate cancer.** There has been concern that testosterone may fuel the growth of prostate cancer and that testosterone therapy could stimulate small, unsuspected tumors.

While it is true that lowering testosterone levels to zero does make prostate tumors shrink, there is now strong evidence that raising testosterone levels in men who have testosterone deficiency does not increase prostate cancer risk.

A new and controversial issue is whether men who have been treated for prostate cancer can receive testosterone therapy. Early data suggest that this may be safe in certain men. Discuss it with your doctor.

USING TESTOSTERONE

Testosterone replacement can be administered in a variety of ways...

•**Injections are usually given by a doctor or nurse every two to three weeks.** Some men learn to inject themselves.

Typical cost: About $10 per injection.

•**Gel can be rubbed into the skin** (typically on the chest, shoulders and upper arms) daily. For 80% to 85% of men, the gel works as well as injections.

Typical cost: $200 to $500 per month.

•**Pellets containing testosterone are implanted under the skin** during a five-minute office procedure. Treatment generally lasts for three to six months.

Typical cost: $500 to $600 per treatment.

•**Skin patches** usually are not as effective as the other forms described above.

If you're interested in testosterone therapy, consult your primary care physician, who may refer you to a urologist or an endocrinologist (a doctor who specializes in the treatment of hormone disorders).

Important: Any man who receives testosterone therapy should have his *prostate-specific antigen* (PSA) levels measured at least annually. Elevated PSA levels can indicate prostate cancer or benign enlargement of the prostate. PSA levels often rise within three months of starting testosterone therapy but should stabilize afterward.

HOW WOMEN CAN BE AFFECTED

Like men, women experience a drop in testosterone levels as they age. Low testosterone may be implicated if a woman loses her sex drive—either before or after menopause. None of the testosterone preparations described above are FDA-approved for use in women.

But in a recent study that appeared in *The New England Journal of Medicine* and involved more than 800 postmenopausal women, yearlong use of a testosterone skin patch raised desire and the frequency of satisfying sexual episodes from 0.7 to 2.1 per month, on average.

Women may suffer side effects from testosterone therapy—unwanted hair growth, in particular. The long-term effects of testosterone therapy in women are unknown.

Why Men Get Sick—And How to Keep Them Healthy

Marianne J. Legato, MD, founder of the Partnership for Gender-Specific Medicine at Columbia University, professor of clinical medicine at Columbia University College of Physicians and Surgeons, both in New York City, and adjunct professor of medicine at Johns Hopkins School of Medicine in Baltimore. She is the author of *Why Men Die First: How to Lengthen Your Lifespan* (Macmillan).

Most people know that men tend to develop heart disease at a younger age than women do, but medical researchers now are uncovering other important gender-specific risks that can have a profound effect on men's health.

What you need to know...

COLORECTAL CANCER

Colorectal cancer is slightly more common in men than it is in women. Most of these malignancies begin as small masses of precancerous cells (polyps). By removing these growths before they become cancerous, doctors can prevent most colorectal malignancies.

Interesting fact: Men are most likely to develop polyps in the rectum (the last few inches of the large intestine) and the left side of the colon (the major part of the large intestine, above the rectum), while in women, polyps tend to develop in the right side of the colon.

How men can protect themselves: Starting at age 50, all men should have an annual fecal occult blood test (FOBT). This test can detect hidden blood in the stool, which may signal cancer.

Important: To ensure accurate test results, about three days prior to the FOBT, avoid certain foods, including red meat, radishes, cauliflower and cantaloupe (these foods contain a chemical that can affect test results).

The FOBT should be performed each year in addition to a colonoscopy (the "gold standard" for detecting polyps and early-stage malignancies in the large intestine) every five years. If a polyp is found, a repeat colonoscopy in three years is advisable.

DEMENTIA

Stroke prevention may be especially important for reducing dementia risk in men, according to a recent study published in the *Journal of Neurology, Neurosurgery and Psychiatry.* Researchers found that a history of stroke was a major predictor of dementia in men but not in women, even though stroke rates are similar for both sexes. Researchers theorize that this disparity may be due, in part, to diet.

How men can protect themselves: Pay close attention to blood pressure. High blood pressure (hypertension) is the single most important controllable risk factor for stroke.

In addition, at least every two years, all men over age 40 should have an ultrasound of their carotid (neck) arteries, which deliver blood to the brain. Excessive fatty buildup (plaque) in these arteries may increase stroke risk. If necessary, plaque can be removed with a surgical procedure known as *endarterectomy*—a doctor makes an incision in the affected artery and uses a specially designed tool to remove plaque. In some cases, cholesterol-lowering statin drugs can reduce plaque.

DEPRESSION

Research has shown that a history of depression is an independent risk factor for heart disease in men but not in women. Another study found that men who had suffered depression in their 20s were twice as likely to develop heart disease later in life as those without a history of depression.

Why does depression have such a dramatic effect on men's health?

One theory points to the fact that depression goes undiagnosed and untreated more often in men than in women.

Important: Treatment with prescription antidepressants and/or psychotherapy probably lowers the chance of developing heart disease in people with depression, though this has not been proven in studies.

How men can protect themselves: Any man who suffers symptoms of depression should see his doctor.

Caution: Classic depression symptoms, such as expressing sadness or hopelessness to others, are more likely to occur in women than in men. In men, depression is usually characterized by persistent irritability, increased use of alcohol, disturbed sleep patterns (insomnia or sleeping too much) and an inability to function effectively at work.

Also helpful: Any man who has ever been diagnosed with depression should have a baseline stress echocardiogram (which uses sound waves to produce images of the heart) or a stress thallium test (which involves the use of a radioactive dye to show how well blood flows to the heart).

HIGH BLOOD PRESSURE

One-third of American adults have high blood pressure. *In men, the condition can be affected by such factors as...*

- **Lack of treatment.** Men with high blood pressure are less likely than women to have the problem successfully treated—possibly because of an unwillingness to take medication that has been prescribed for the condition. One study found that only 19% of men with high blood pressure had the condition controlled, compared with 28% of women.

How men can protect themselves: Men over age 40 should have an annual physical that includes a blood pressure check. A reading above 130/80 mmHg requires treatment, including lifestyle measures (such as following a healthful diet, maintaining a normal weight, exercising regularly, not smoking and limiting sodium and alcohol intake) and, in many cases, medication.

Important: Men with high blood pressure should be rechecked after three months if blood pressure medication is prescribed—drug therapy often must be adjusted. Subsequent checks should occur every six months.

• **Obstructive sleep apnea.** This condition, marked by brief interruptions in breathing during sleep, can cause or aggravate high blood pressure. Sleep apnea is more common in men than in women.

How men can protect themselves: If you have symptoms of sleep apnea, such as loud snoring, gasping for air during the night and/or excessive daytime sleepiness, see your doctor. The condition can be treated with lifestyle changes, such as losing weight, and/or the use of a face mask that delivers air pressure to help keep the sufferer's airways open during sleep.

LUNG CANCER

Smoking is the most common culprit in lung cancer, the leading cause of cancer deaths in the US.

Important new study: National Cancer Institute researchers recently compared lung cancer risk in male and female smokers, taking into account not only whether people smoke, but also how much. In men and women who smoked about the same amount, men had a slightly higher risk for lung cancer. Also, male former smokers were more likely to develop lung cancer than female former smokers with similar smoking histories.

Interesting fact: Lung cancer usually produces symptoms at an earlier stage in men than in women—perhaps because men's cancers tend to cluster in the center of the lung, whereas women's are more often located at the periphery of the lung. A centrally located lung malignancy is more likely to cause a cough that produces blood.

How men can protect themselves: In addition to not smoking, any man who has ever smoked—no matter how long ago—should have a chest X-ray to screen for lung cancer even if he has no symptoms of the disease. He should ask to be tested for lung cancer (with a CT scan, for example) if he has symptoms of a lung malignancy, including lung infections more than once a year, hoarseness, shortness of breath, cough or chest pain.

TESTICULAR CANCER

Most people think that testicular cancer is a young man's disease, since most cases occur between ages 15 and 34, but it is also relatively common between ages 50 and 60. The risk is highest in men who have a father or brother who has had testicular cancer and in those with a history of an undescended testicle, in which one of the testes failed to move down from the abdomen into the scrotal sac after birth.

How men can protect themselves: All men should examine their testicles monthly for any hard lumps—the most common warning sign of testicular cancer. Most testicular malignancies are painless, but they may produce a dull ache or a feeling of heaviness in the affected testicle or groin area or cause the affected testicle to enlarge. Breast tenderness or an increase in breast size also can occur with testicular cancer.

Osteoporosis Rates Rising for Men

Mark A. Stengler, ND, naturopathic physician in private practice, La Jolla, California...adjunct associate clinical professor at the National College of Natural Medicine, Portland, Oregon...author of many books and the *Bottom Line/Natural Healing* newsletter.

Osteoporosis in men is substantially underdiagnosed, undertreated and inadequately researched. Rates are expected to increase by nearly 50% in the next 15 years as the population ages. Sufferers are vulnerable to hip fractures, which are projected to double or triple by 2040.

New guidelines: Men over age 50 should be assessed for osteoporosis risk factors, according to the American College of Physicians.

In my view, low body weight, inactivity and weight loss are strong predictors of increased risk for osteoporosis. Most vulnerable are smokers, heavy alcohol drinkers, men with testosterone deficiency and those who have been on steroid therapy. I agree that it is smart for men to join women in being screened for osteoporosis beginning at age 50.

70% of Prostatitis Treatments Don't Work! What Will…

Rodney Anderson, MD, a professor of urology (emeritus) at Stanford University School of Medicine in Stanford, California. Dr. Anderson has authored several scientific studies on chronic prostatitis and is coauthor of *A Headache in the Pelvis: A New Understanding and Treatment for Prostatitis and Chronic Pelvic Pain Syndromes* (National Center for Pelvic Pain Research).

As men age, many begin to suffer problems with the prostate gland. Prostate enlargement is the condition that is most widely recognized, but there can be another culprit.

Often-overlooked condition: At some point in their lives, about one in 10 men will be diagnosed with chronic prostatitis, pain and swelling of the prostate due to inflammation that results from unknown causes or an infection.

Like an enlarged prostate, chronic prostatitis causes urinary difficulties, such as urinary frequency (urinating more than once every two hours)…urinary urgency (urination is hard to delay once the urge occurs)…and reduced stream (slow urinary flow).

Chronic prostatitis also can lead to symptoms that do not typically occur with an enlarged prostate—for example, pain in the perineum (the area between the anus and the scrotum)…the tip of the penis…the testicles…the bladder area…and the rectum. Men with prostatitis may even suffer pain during urination or orgasm.

Symptoms, which last for three months or more, are intermittent or constant. In severe, untreated cases, the condition may interfere with a man's sleep, desire for sex and overall enjoyment of life—indefinitely.

LESSONS LEARNED

When chronic prostatitis is diagnosed, more than 70% of primary care physicians prescribe an antibiotic such as *ciprofloxacin* (Cipro), according to a recent survey. About half of the surveyed doctors prescribe an alpha-blocker drug, such as *alfuzosin* (Uroxatral) or *tamsulosin* (Flomax), which is typically used for prostate enlargement (benign prostatic hyperplasia).

Antibiotics are prescribed because many doctors believe that chronic prostatitis is an infectious disease—but, in fact, bacteria are present in only about 5% of cases. Alpha-blockers are used in the hope they might relax the prostate and the perineum. But recent studies show that these approaches don't work.

New thinking: Because the symptoms are real, but no biochemical or mechanical cause has yet been found, nonbacterial chronic prostatitis is now considered to be a pain "syndrome," called chronic prostatitis/chronic pelvic pain syndrome (CP/CPPS).

DIAGNOSING THE PROBLEM

If you think you have CP/CPPS, see a urologist for a standard urological evaluation. Urinary and prostate fluid cultures should be ordered to look for infection. Urodynamic testing (to measure the functioning of the bladder and prostate) and cystoscopy (an examination of the urethra and bladder) also may be performed. These and other tests will help rule out other diseases, such as prostate cancer or bladder cancer.

TREATMENTS WORTH TRYING

If you are suffering from CP/CPPS, there are several effective therapies to consider…

- **Quercetin.** This antioxidant/anti-inflammatory is found in red wine, onions and green tea. By reducing inflammation, it may help curb the pain and urinary difficulties of CP/CPPS.

Scientific evidence: When researchers at the Harbor-UCLA Medical Center in Los Angeles asked 28 men with CP/CPPS to take either a quercetin supplement or a placebo twice daily for one month, those taking quercetin had a 35% decrease in pain, while the placebo group experienced only a 7.2% reduction.

Resource: Most reputable brands of quercetin should have this effect. In one part of the study described above, men took the quercetin-containing product Prosta-Q, available from the manufacturer Farr Laboratories (877-284-3976, *www.farrlabs.com*).

Caution: Don't take any quercetin product along with a quinolone antibiotic—such as ciprofloxacin...*levofloxacin* (Levaquin)...*norfloxacin* (Noroxin)...or *ofloxacin* (Floxin). The supplement can interfere with the antibiotic's action.

- **Relaxation and trigger point therapy.** Some scientists theorize that CP/CPPS is caused by chronic tension in the pelvis. This, in turn, creates knots (trigger points) in the muscles, reduces blood flow and irritates pelvic nerves. If you consciously learn to relax those muscles, even when you're in pain...and a physical therapist locates and releases the trigger points with pressure and stretching—symptoms can be reduced.

Scientific evidence: When 138 men whose CP/CPPS symptoms did not respond to any treatment underwent a relaxation and trigger point therapy called the Stanford Protocol, 72% said their symptoms were moderately or markedly improved in one month.

Resource: The Stanford Protocol is offered in a six-day program in northern California. To learn more, call 707-874-2225 or consult *www.pelvicpainhelp.com*.

- **Acupuncture.** Researchers believe that pain occurs in CP/CPPS patients when stimulation, such as that caused by sitting or sexual activity, travels up the spinal cord and becomes magnified in the brain. Introducing a different stimulus, such as acupuncture, in the area where the pain originates can interrupt the cycle.

Scientific evidence: When 10 men whose CP/CPPS symptoms did not respond to at least one conventional medical treatment received acupuncture twice a week, their pain and urinary symptom scores dropped by more than 70%.

Resource: To find an acupuncturist near you, consult the National Certification Commission for Acupuncture and Oriental Medicine (904-598-1005, *www.nccaom.org*).

- **Biofeedback.** A biofeedback machine monitors a specific bodily function that we typically are not conscious of, such as muscular tension. When the function is abnormal, the machine gives feedback, such as a beep or flashing light.

Scientific evidence: When 31 men with CP/CPPS underwent a "pelvic floor biofeedback re-education program"—a series of biofeedback treatments that showed them when pelvic muscles were tense and how to relax them—the men had a 52% decrease, on average, in pain and urinary symptom scores.

Resource: To find a biofeedback practitioner near you, consult the Association for Applied Psychophysiology and Biofeedback, Inc., 800-477-8892, *www.aapb.org*.

Best Cures for Common Men's Health Problems

Geovanni Espinosa, ND, MS.Ac, director of clinical trials, clinician and co-investigator at the Center for Holistic Urology at Columbia University Medical Center in New York City (*www.holisticurology.columbia.edu*). Dr. Espinosa is also a certified nutrition specialist and a registered herbalist with the American Herbalists Guild. He is author of the naturopathic section in *1,000 Cures for 200 Ailments* (HarperCollins).

If you've ever had an acute infection of the prostate, you may know that antibiotics often clear up the problem in just a few days.

But as the antibiotics eliminate infection-causing bacteria, these powerful drugs also wipe out "healthy" organisms that aid digestion and help fortify the immune system. You may experience diarrhea, upset stomach or a yeast infection while taking the medication.

What's the answer? Holistic medicine uses alternative therapies, such as dietary supplements, nutritional advice and acupuncture, to complement—or replace—conventional medical treatments, including prescription drugs.

For example, probiotic "good" bacteria supplements help replenish the beneficial intestinal bacteria killed by antibiotics. Ask your doctor about taking 10 billion to 20 billion colony forming units (CFUs) of probiotics, such as lactobacillus or acidophilus, two to three hours after each dose of antibiotics.*

Holistic treatments for other urological problems that affect men...**

ENLARGED PROSTATE

Prescription drugs, such as *finasteride* (Proscar) and *doxazosin* (Cardura), can relieve the urgent need to urinate and other symptoms caused by benign prostatic hyperplasia (BPH). But the drugs' side effects often include reduced libido, fatigue and potentially harmful drops in blood pressure. *Holistic approach...*

• ***Beta-sitosterol* is a plant compound that is found in saw palmetto,** a popular herbal remedy for BPH. Men who do not improve with saw palmetto may want to combine it with beta-sitosterol (125 milligrams, or mg, daily).

• ***Pygeum africanum*,** an herb derived from an African evergreen tree, has anti-inflammatory effects that interfere with the formation of prostaglandins, hormone-like substances that tend to accumulate in the prostate of men with BPH. Take 100 mg two times daily with or without saw palmetto and/or beta-sitosterol.

• **Acupuncture may help ease BPH symptoms.** It can be used in addition to the remedies described above. The typical regimen is one to two treatments weekly for about four weeks.

Whether you're taking medication or herbs, lifestyle changes—such as drinking less coffee (which acts as a diuretic)...avoiding spicy foods and alcohol (which can irritate the bladder)... and cutting down on fluids—are a key part of managing BPH symptoms.

IMPOTENCE

For stronger, more reliable erections, conventional medicine offers several medications, such as *sildenafil* (Viagra) and *vardenafil* (Levitra). But these drugs can have side effects, including painful, prolonged erections and sudden vision loss. *Holistic approach...*

*To find a doctor near you who offers holistic therapies, consult the American Holistic Medical Association, 216-292-6644, *www.holisticmedicine.org*. Holistic doctors can help you choose high-quality supplements—these products may contain impurities.

**Because some supplements can interact with prescription drugs, raise blood sugar and cause other adverse effects, check with your doctor before trying any of the therapies mentioned in this article.

• **Maca is a root vegetable from South America.** In supplement form, it has been shown to increase libido in healthy men.

Recommended dosage: 500 mg to 1,000 mg three times daily.

• **Asian ginseng,** a well-studied herb from China and Korea, can improve erections. Take 900 mg three times daily.

• **Ginkgo biloba,** derived from a tree native to China, may improve erections by boosting circulation. Take 120 mg to 240 mg daily. Maca, Asian ginseng and ginkgo biloba can all be combined.

• **Niacin,** a B vitamin, widens blood vessels when taken in high doses (500 mg to 1,000 mg daily) and may help promote erections in some men who do not improve with the three impotence remedies described above. A doctor should monitor high-dose courses of niacin.

• **Vigorous exercise** (such as weight lifting, jogging or cycling) promotes healthy circulation and boosts testosterone.

Important: Erectile dysfunction may be an early warning of heart problems, so consult a doctor before starting an exercise program. Erectile dysfunction also may be a symptom of diabetes or other systemic illness—or stress and relationship issues. For this reason, men who experience erectile dysfunction should see a doctor for a full evaluation before trying holistic therapies.

CHRONIC PROSTATITIS

Pain and swelling of the prostate (prostatitis) may be caused by inflammation that develops for unknown reasons or by an infection. The prostate enlargement that characterizes BPH, on the other hand, is likely due to hormonal changes that occur as men age. Symptoms of chronic prostatitis, such as pelvic pain and pain when urinating, can linger for months. Conventional medicine has little to offer other than antibiotics.

Holistic approach...

• **Fish oil and quercetin** (a plant-based supplement) are both anti-inflammatories. The fish oil supplements should contain a daily total of about 1,440 mg of *eicosapentaenoic acid* (EPA) and 960 mg of *docosahexaenoic acid* (DHA).

Take 500 mg of quercetin twice daily. Fish oil and quercetin can be combined.

INCONTINENCE

Because incontinence can be caused by various underlying problems, including an infection, a neurological disorder (such as multiple sclerosis) or an enlarged prostate, any man who suffers from incontinence should first be evaluated by a urologist.

Holistic approach...

- **Buchu,** cleavers and cornsilk are herbal remedies that often help when overactive bladder (marked by a sudden, intense need to urinate) causes incontinence. Some products contain all three herbs. For dosages, follow label instructions.
- **Bromelain,** an enzyme derived from pineapple, acts as an anti-inflammatory to help treat incontinence caused by an inflamed prostate. Take 500 mg to 2,000 mg daily in two divided doses.
- **Pumpkin seed oil extract** may ease incontinence in men when overactive bladder is related to an enlarged prostate. *Typical dosage:* 160 mg of pumpkin seed oil extract, taken three times daily with meals. Pumpkin seed oil extract can be combined with saw palmetto. Ask your doctor for advice on combining pumpkin seed oil extract with any of the other incontinence remedies described above.

■ ■ ■ ■

Urinary Problems Make Men 21% More Likely to Fall

In a recent four-year study of 5,872 men (age 65 or older), those who reported moderate lower urinary tract problems, such as urgency to urinate or urinary frequency, were 21% more likely to fall at least twice within a one-year period than those without urinary problems.

Theory: Falls may occur when a man is rushing to the bathroom—during the day or at night. If you have urinary tract symptoms, ask your doctor about treatment.

J. Kellogg Parsons, MD, assistant professor of surgery/urology, Moores Cancer Center, University of California, San Diego.

Seven Hidden Causes of Slips, Trips and Falls

Rosanne M. Leipzig, MD, PhD, vice chair for education and professor in the Brookdale Department of Geriatrics and Adult Development at Mount Sinai School of Medicine in New York City. She is a recipient of the American Geriatrics Society's Dennis W. Jahnigen Award for contributions in geriatric education.

Anyone can trip and be thrown momentarily off balance. But can you regain your balance—or do you go down? Anything that makes an initial misstep more likely or that interferes with a person's ability to self-correct increases the risk for falls. And many such factors become more common with age. *For example...*

- **Muscle weakness.** If you stumble, it requires coordinated actions of your feet, ankles, knees and hips to prevent a fall. Muscle weakness in any of those areas impairs this ability. That's why physical inactivity is a common—though often unrecognized—cause of falls.

Exercise helps slow the loss of muscle mass that occurs with aging. Stair-climbing is an excellent way to strengthen critical thigh muscles.

Also helpful: Leg extensions—while sitting in a chair, raise your lower leg until it is in line with the thigh. Repeat 10 times and switch legs. Perform this exercise three times a day.

- **Impaired nerve function.** The nervous system plays a part in sensing loss of balance early and guiding the self-correction process. Blunted nerve function in the feet often is due to peripheral neuropathy, which can be caused by diabetes, vitamin B-12 deficiency or low thyroid levels (hypothyroidism).
- **Thinning bones.** Bone mass declines with age. If the thinning process goes far enough, osteoporosis can develop—in both women and men—and those dangerously fragile bones are liable to fracture. Osteoporosis can worsen the consequences of a fall, but in some cases, weakened bones are the cause, not the effect.

Here's what happens: As bones lose density, the body's center of gravity shifts forward, causing an older person to lean progressively forward. Balance becomes more precarious, so a slip is more likely to become a fall. Small fractures of the vertebrae caused by osteoporosis accentuate the forward shift.

•**Low vitamin D levels.** A 2005 analysis of five studies published in *The Journal of the American Medical Association* found a more than 20% reduction in falls in healthy older people who took vitamin D supplements, compared with those who didn't.

Researchers theorize that vitamin D may have an effect on muscle that helps reduce falls. Although the Daily Value (the FDA's reference guideline for daily nutrient intake) for vitamin D is 400 international units (IU), most studies have found that daily doses of 700 IU to 800 IU are needed to prevent falls and fractures.

Vitamin D deficiency is more common than previously believed—it's often due to a lack of regular sun exposure and/or a low intake of foods containing or fortified with vitamin D. If either of these factors applies to you, ask your doctor to check your blood level of vitamin D.

VISION AND HEARING LOSS

"Silent" vision problems, such as cataracts and glaucoma that have not yet caused difficulties in reading or other activities, can increase a person's risk for falls. Subtle vision changes, such as a decline in the ability to see contrasts in color or light and dark, can be missed as well. This makes tripping over curbs and on stairs or escalators more of a danger.

Correcting nearsightedness or farsightedness with glasses will help but initially can be risky. It takes time to adjust to new glasses—particularly when they have multifocal (bifocal, trifocal or variable) lenses. An Australian study found that in the period just after patients got new glasses, they were more likely to fall.

Even hearing loss may be linked to increased falls—possibly because some hearing problems reflect damage to the eighth cranial nerve, which also controls the inner-ear system that maintains balance.

DANGEROUS MEDICATIONS

Any drug that causes sedation can impair alertness, slow reaction time and disable the coordinated interplay of nerves and muscles that protects against falls. Some medications lower blood pressure when you stand up—these can cause weakness and light-headedness that can lead to a fall.

Among the most common culprits: Some antidepressants and anti-anxiety drugs...medications taken for enlarged prostate...painkillers, such as *codeine* and *oxycodone* (OxyContin)... and pills for high blood pressure.

Important: The more medications you take, the higher your risk of falling.

Hidden menace: Over-the-counter (OTC) drugs. For example, older OTC antihistamines that can have sedating effects, such as *diphenhydramine* (Benadryl), should not be used by older adults, who may experience confusion when taking such drugs. First try a nonsedating antihistamine, such as *loratadine* (Claritin).

SLEEP PROBLEMS

Lack of sleep can increase fall risk by impairing alertness and slowing reaction time. However, sleeping pills aren't the solution—their effects often linger, dulling the senses and slowing reaction time. Even newer sleep medications, such as *zolpidem* (Ambien), which are designed to be shorter acting, keep working longer in older people, possibly contributing to falls.

Anything that gets you out of bed in the middle of the night—such as an urgent need to urinate—also increases your fall risk. Keep a clear path to the bathroom, use night-lights and keep a cane or walker easily accessible, if necessary.

UNDIAGNOSED ILLNESS

Falls also can be a harbinger of a new health problem, such as pneumonia, a urinary tract infection, heart attack or heart failure. In some cases, weakness that can lead to a fall is more evident than the usual symptoms for these illnesses.

SMALL CHANGES THAT HELP

The exact cause of a fall is often impossible to pin down and may actually be due to several subtle factors working together—such as a slight loss of sensation in the feet, mild sedation due to medication and minor difficulty with balance.

Fortunately, safety is cumulative, too. Slight adjustments can be lifesaving. For example, avoid shoes that don't fit snugly or have slippery soles...instead, wear sneakers or walking shoes. In addition, get rid of any throw rugs...

make sure that lighting is adequate and handrails are available where needed...and don't be vain about using a cane or walker if it helps you move about safely.

■ **More from Rosanne M. Leipzig, MD, PhD...**

How to Prevent Falls

There are several different steps you can take to reduce your risk for falling...

•**Exercise to increase muscle strength and balance.** This reduces the risk of falling and increases the chance of escaping a fall unhurt.

•**Have your vision checked.** Not seeing an obstacle can lead you to trip on it.

•**Remove obstacles that may cause a fall,** such as loose rugs, low tables and clutter. Install railings, handles and lighting where they can improve safety.

•**Design for safety.** Remodel cupboards, shelves, drawers and other home fixtures to eliminate excessive reaching and bending.

•**Check medication side effects.** Your drugs may affect balance or coordination.

New Study Helps Predict Age-Related Eye Disease

American Academy of Ophthalmology news release.

Poor night vision might be a predictor of age-related macular degeneration (AMD), a recent study says.

AMD, the leading cause of vision loss in people ages 60 and older, results in the destruction of the macula in the eye's retina, the area that normally provides detailed, central vision.

THE STUDY

More than 1,000 people with early signs of AMD were given a 10-item questionnaire asking them to rate their difficulties with night driving and low-light activities, such as reading or watching movies, then were followed annually for up to six years. Those with the worst night vision at the start were most likely to develop reduced visual acuity and advanced AMD.

The study was published in *Ophthalmology.*

IMPLICATION

Study leader Gui-shuang Ying, MD, PhD, assistant professor of ophthalmology at the University of Pennsylvania School of Medicine, said the simple questionnaire could prove useful in identifying patients at high risk of vision loss and advanced AMD.

Info For more information about AMD, visit the National Eye Institute Web site, *www.nei.nih.gov,* and type "age-related macular degeneration" into the search box.

Five Signs You May Have Cataracts

David F. Chang, MD, clinical professor of ophthalmology at the University of California, San Francisco. Dr. Chang codiscovered intraoperative floppy iris syndrome (IFIS), an iris problem that can complicate cataract surgery. He serves as chair of the Cataract Clinical Committee of the American Society of Cataract and Refractive Surgery and is coauthor of *Cataracts: A Patient's Guide to Treatment* (Addicus).

Cataracts can develop so slowly in some people that they do not even realize they have an eye problem. In the early stages, just a small portion of the eye's lens may become cloudy. Only when the cloudiness of the eye's lens increases over time—sometimes over a period of years—does the person's vision worsen.

Even though cataracts are quite common—about half of people over age 65 have some signs of the condition—few people are aware that many common vision problems actually can be the result of cataracts.

To learn more about diagnosis and the latest treatment options, we spoke with internationally recognized cataract surgeon and researcher David F. Chang, MD...

SYMPTOMS THAT CAN BE MISSED

If your vision starts to appear cloudy or blurry, you might suspect a cataract—these are among the most widely recognized symptoms. But there are many other symptoms that are not nearly as well-known and that can prevent people from getting proper eye care. Symptoms can vary greatly, depending on the location, severity and type of cataract. Cataracts may be age-related, due to an eye injury, congenital (present at birth) or appearing in childhood. *Questions to ask yourself...*

•**Do colors appear faded or washed out?**

•**Do I have trouble seeing distant objects,** such as highway signs, while wearing eyeglasses?

•**Do I need more light than I used to for close work,** such as reading small print and sewing? Do my eyes tire more easily when I'm engaged in these activities?

•**Does glare make it much harder for me to drive at night** or see well in bright sunlight?

•**Do I ever experience "ghost images,"** such as seeing multiple moons at night?

If you answered "yes" to several of these questions, consult an ophthalmologist (a physician who specializes in medical and surgical eye care) or an optometrist (a nonphysician who can test for common eye problems, such as nearsightedness and cataracts, but who does not perform surgery).

A doctor can identify a cataract by dilating a patient's pupil and examining the eye with a table-mounted microscope called a slit lamp.

Important: Even if you do not experience any of the symptoms described above, get your eyes checked regularly after age 40 to help identify any treatable eye problems, such as glaucoma, a vision-robbing eye disease marked by increased pressure within the eyeball.

ARE YOU AT INCREASED RISK?

Age is a primary risk factor for cataracts. After age 50, cataracts are the most common cause of decreased vision. *Other risk factors...*

•**Family history.** In some families, cataracts tend to occur at an earlier age. If a family member, such as a parent or sibling, developed cataracts before age 60, you also may be at increased risk of developing cataracts at around the same age.

•**Medical conditions.** Diabetes increases the risk for cataracts three- to fourfold. This is because elevated blood sugar levels can cause changes in the lens that, in turn, can lead to cataracts.

Self-defense: Work with your doctor to manage your blood sugar levels.

•**Nearsightedness.** For reasons that are not yet understood, severely nearsighted people often develop cataracts at an earlier age.

•**Steroid use.** Long-term (one year or more) oral steroid use can increase risk for cataracts. Long-term use of inhaled steroids, taken at high doses, also may increase risk.

•**Eye diseases.** Some eye diseases, such as chronic eye inflammation (uveitis), increase risk for cataracts. Prior eye surgery—for retinal problems, for example—also raises risk.

•**Eye injuries.** Cataracts may develop, sometimes years later, as a result of eye injuries, such as those that can occur when being struck by a blunt object (like a ball).

Self-defense: Wear polycarbonate safety goggles (available at sporting-goods stores) when playing sports such as squash and racketball.

•**Sun exposure.** The sun's ultraviolet rays also can increase cataract risk. Wear a broad-brimmed hat and UV-blocking sunglasses.

DO YOU NEED SURGERY?

If cataracts interfere with your ability to read, drive or enjoy a hobby, you may need surgery.

Most ophthalmologists in the US perform "small-incision" surgery, a 20- to 30-minute outpatient procedure in which the surgeon uses an ultrathin blade to make an incision of about one-eighth inch in the cornea. The cataract is removed with ultrasound wave technology, vibrating at 40,000 times per second, to break up the cloudy lens into smaller fragments.

After these pieces of the lens are gently suctioned out, an artificial lens, called an intraocular lens, is permanently implanted in place of the natural lens. Once removed, cataracts will never recur, and the artificial lens will last for the patient's lifetime.

Small-incision surgery can be performed with topical anesthesia (eyedrops) and usually requires no sutures. (A tiny flap is created that closes on its own.) The success rate of cataract surgery in otherwise healthy eyes approaches 98%. Severe complications, such as infection or bleeding in the eye, are rare.

Latest development: New artificial lens implants that can reduce a patient's dependence on eyeglasses are now available. These multifocal lenses may provide focus for both near and far distances, allowing many patients to read without eyeglasses.

Because multifocal lenses are considered a convenience—rather than a medical necessity—patients must pay an additional out-of-pocket cost ($2,000 to $3,000 per lens) under Medicare and private insurance plans.

Important new finding: Recent research has shown that use of drugs called alpha-blockers, such as *tamsulosin* (Flomax) taken for an enlarged prostate, can interfere with the necessary dilation of the pupil during surgery. Known as *intraoperative floppy iris syndrome*, this condition can make cataract surgery more difficult for your surgeon.

If you are planning to have cataract surgery, tell your doctor if you are taking an alpha-blocker, such as tamsulosin. Patients with cataracts or symptoms of poor vision should have an eye exam before starting to take an alpha-blocker drug.

A Healthy Mouth Lowers Risk for Heart Disease, Diabetes and More

Robert J. Genco, DDS, PhD, distinguished professor in the department of oral biology, School of Dental Medicine, and in the department of microbiology, School of Medicine and Biomedical Sciences at the State University of New York at Buffalo. He is also a professor in the department of immunology at the Roswell Park Cancer Institute and a recipient of the American Dental Association's Gold Medal for Excellence in Research.

Until recently, most people who took good care of their teeth and gums did so to ensure appealing smiles and to perhaps avoid dentures. Now, a significant body of research shows that oral health may play a key role in preventing a wide range of serious health conditions, including heart disease, diabetes, some types of cancer and perhaps even dementia.

Healthy teeth and gums also may improve longevity. Swedish scientists recently tracked 3,273 adults for 16 years and found that those with chronic gum infections were significantly more likely to die before age 50, on average, than were people without gum disease.

What's the connection? Periodontal disease (called gingivitis in mild stages...and periodontitis when it becomes more severe) is caused mainly by bacteria that accumulate on the teeth and gums. As the body attempts to battle the bacteria, inflammatory molecules are released (as demonstrated by redness and swelling of the gums). Over time, this complex biological response affects the entire body, causing systemic inflammation that promotes the development of many serious diseases. *Scientific evidence links poor oral health to...*

- **Heart disease.** At least 20 scientific studies have shown links between chronic periodontal disease and an increased risk for heart disease. Most recently, Boston University researchers found that periodontal disease in men younger than age 60 was associated with a twofold increase in angina (chest pain), or nonfatal or fatal heart attack, when compared with men whose teeth and gums are healthy.

- **Diabetes.** State University of New York at Buffalo studies and other research show that people with diabetes have an associated risk for periodontitis that is two to three times greater than that of people without diabetes. Conversely, diabetics with periodontal disease generally have poorer control of their blood sugar than diabetics without periodontal disease—a factor that contributes to their having twice the risk of dying of a heart attack and three times the risk of dying of kidney failure.

- **Cancer.** Chronic gum disease may raise your risk for tongue cancer. State University of New York at Buffalo researchers recently compared men with and without tongue cancer and found that those with cancer had a 65% greater loss of alveolar bone (which supports the teeth)—a common measure of periodontitis. Meanwhile, a Harvard School of Public Health study shows that periodontal disease is associated with a 63% higher risk for pancreatic cancer.

•**Rheumatoid arthritis.** In people with rheumatoid arthritis, the condition is linked to an 82% increased risk for periodontal disease, compared with people who do not have rheumatoid arthritis.

Good news: Treating the periodontitis appears to ease rheumatoid arthritis symptoms. In a recent study, nearly 59% of patients with rheumatoid arthritis and chronic periodontal disease who had their gums treated experienced less severe arthritis symptoms—possibly because eliminating the periodontitis reduced their systemic inflammation.

•**Dementia.** When Swedish researchers recently reviewed dental and cognitive records for 638 women, they found that tooth loss (a sign of severe gum disease) was linked to a 30% to 40% increased risk for dementia over a 32-year period, with the highest dementia rates suffered by women who had the fewest teeth at middle age. More research is needed to confirm and explain this link.

STEPS TO IMPROVE YOUR ORAL HEALTH

Even though the rate of gum disease significantly increases with age, it's not inevitable. To promote oral health, brush (twice daily with a soft-bristled brush, using gentle, short strokes starting at a 45-degree angle to the gums) and floss (once daily, using gentle rubbing motions—do not snap against the gums). *In addition...*

•**See your dentist at least twice yearly.** Ask at every exam, "Do I have gum disease?" This will serve as a gentle reminder to dentists that you want to be carefully screened for the condition. Most mild-to-moderate infections can be treated with a nonsurgical procedure that removes plaque and tartar from tooth pockets and smooths the root surfaces. For more severe periodontal disease, your dentist may refer you to a periodontist (a dentist who specializes in the treatment of gum disease). Note: Patients with gum disease often need to see a dentist three to four times a year to prevent recurrence of gum disease after the initial treatment.

Good news: Modern techniques to regenerate bone and soft tissue can reverse much of the damage and halt progression of periodontitis, particularly in patients who have lost no more than 30% of the bone to which the teeth are attached.

•**Boost your calcium intake.** Research conducted at the State University of New York at Buffalo has shown that postmenopausal women with osteoporosis typically have more alveolar bone loss and weaker attachments between their teeth and bone, putting them at substantially higher risk for periodontal disease. Other studies have linked low dietary calcium with heightened periodontal risk in both men and women.

Self-defense: Postmenopausal women, and men over age 65, should consume 1,000 mg to 1,200 mg of calcium daily to preserve teeth and bones. Aim for two to three daily servings of dairy products (providing a total of 600 mg of calcium), plus a 600-mg calcium supplement with added vitamin D for maximum absorption.

Helpful: Yogurt may offer an edge over other calcium sources. In a recent Japanese study involving 942 adults, ages 40 to 79, those who ate at least 55 grams (about two ounces) of yogurt daily were 40% less likely to suffer from severe periodontal disease—perhaps because the "friendly" bacteria and calcium in yogurt make a powerful combination against the infection-causing bacteria of dental disease.

•**Control your weight.** Obesity is also associated with periodontitis, probably because fat cells release chemicals that may contribute to inflammatory conditions anywhere in the body, including the gums.

•**Don't ignore dry mouth.** Aging and many medications, including some antidepressants, antihistamines, high blood pressure drugs and steroids, can decrease saliva flow, allowing plaque to build up on teeth and gums. If you're taking a drug that leaves your mouth dry, talk to your doctor about possible alternatives. Prescription artificial saliva products—for example, Caphosol or Numoisyn—also can provide some temporary moistening, as can chewing sugarless gum.

•**Relax.** Recent studies reveal a strong link between periodontal disease and stress, depression, anxiety and loneliness. Researchers are focusing on the stress hormone cortisol as a possible culprit—high levels of cortisol may exacerbate the gum and jawbone destruction caused by oral infections.

•**Sleep.** Japanese researchers recently studied 219 factory workers for four years and found that those who slept seven to eight hours nightly suffered significantly less periodontal disease progression than those who slept six hours or less. The scientists speculated that lack of sleep lowers the body's ability to fend off infections. However, more research is needed to confirm the results of this small study.

Best Ways to Treat Unsightly Varicose Veins

John Blebea, MD, a vascular surgeon and professor of vascular surgery and endovascular therapy at Case Western Reserve University School of Medicine in Cleveland.

Varicose veins—enlarged, colored and twisted veins just beneath the skin—affect up to 25% of adults, and as many as half of all adults over age 50.

For many, varicose veins are merely unsightly. For some, aching legs may be a symptom, although these are not really a health risk. The main health risk is that, over the long term, skin ulcers may develop around the site of varicose veins.

The good news: The newest varicose vein treatments are quick, safe and highly effective. Most can be done quickly in your doctor's office.

FINDING A SPECIALIST

Veins are responsible for returning blood to the heart to be reoxygenated. They contain a series of one-way valves that let blood move forward but not backward. But aging, obesity, pregnancy and other factors can make certain valves—especially those in the legs—malfunction, causing blood to pool in these veins, making them enlarged, twisted and purplish.

Varicose veins are unsightly but usually not medically dangerous. However, they may also be the sign of a valve dysfunction either in the deep or superficial veins.

Common mistake: Failing to seek evaluation from a board-certified vascular surgeon, interventional radiologist or other doctor who specializes in treating varicose veins. To find one, go to the Web site for the Society for Vascular Surgery (*www.vascularweb.org*) or the Society of Interventional Radiology (*www.sirweb.org*). These specialists will give you a careful exam to determine if the veins are linked to a more serious problem.

Another benefit: If underlying medical problems are detected, your health insurance is likely to cover the treatment cost. Varicose vein treatments for purely cosmetic reasons are typically *not* covered by insurance.

GETTING EXAMINED

When the doctor examines you, he/she will start with a visual exam and take a full history, including symptoms such as swelling (a possible sign of a more serious problem), itching or painful, aching legs at the end of the day and any history of blood clots.

The most important exam element is a venous duplex ultrasound scan of the veins in both legs, from hip to ankle. The scan takes about 30 minutes. The doctor may have the equipment in his office or refer you to an accredited vascular lab. The scan will detect any blood clots or other blockages in the deep veins of your legs. If there is a blockage in the deep veins, your superficial veins could be providing a pathway for blood going to your heart—and treatment for superficial varicosities without tending to the deep-vein issues could cause serious leg swelling and other complications.

The scan also maps out the network of varicose veins and determines if they're linked to a dysfunction in the major valves of the great saphenous vein—the large superficial vein running the length of each leg. If these valves—principally located in the groin and top of the thigh—are dysfunctional, this vein must be closed from groin to knee before treating any tributary veins. Otherwise, lower varicose veins will persist and new ones develop.

SAPHENOUS VEIN TREATMENT

Treatment for great saphenous veins used to involve inserting a plastic tube through an incision and pulling out the vein ("stripping"). Technology developed during the past five years has now replaced the old method with two new treatments: *Radiofrequency endovenous obliteration* and *endovenous laser therapy.*

In both procedures, a catheter is inserted into the vein—usually from the knee to the groin—heated and gradually withdrawn, causing the vein to collapse. (Following the procedure, the blood previously flowing through the vein becomes naturally redirected into other leg veins.) Results are immediate. The process uses local anesthesia and may be done in the doctor's office, though many physicians prefer a hospital or surgical center. The patient is up and walking after the procedure and wears compression bandages for 24 to 48 hours afterward. The procedure is only minimally painful, and patients are able to resume normal activity after 48 hours.

I prefer to treat smaller varicose veins at the same time as well.

SMALLER VARICOSE VEINS

Once the great saphenous veins have been treated—or if ultrasound reveals that the saphenous valves are fine—the doctor can then treat any smaller varicose veins requiring attention.

Sclerotherapy is the "gold standard" for treating small- to medium-sized varicose veins. A small needle is used to inject a solution that irritates the vein's internal lining, causing it to collapse. The vein is still there, but it visually disappears since it no longer contains any blood.

The doctor typically makes a series of injections along the vein. The procedure is relatively painless, though the injections may sting slightly. The patient is up and walking afterward and then wears compression bandages for several weeks. Depending on the number of varicose veins, more than one session may be needed. Although both legs can be injected during one session (if there are multiple veins to be treated), for patient comfort and to limit session duration to less than one hour, you may need several sessions. I like to schedule sessions four to six weeks apart.

Sclerotherapy, delivered by an experienced doctor, has an excellent success rate and is quite safe. Still, it's not completely without side effects. Some patients may experience temporary bruising, sores, redness or brown pigmentation around the injection site. In rare cases, the patient may have an allergic reaction (itching, swelling) to the sclerosing liquid—this is seldom serious. Doctors sometimes test a small area before the procedure if the patient has a history of allergies. Or some liquid may escape from the vein, causing temporary irritation.

Sodium tetradecyl sulfate (Sotradecol) and concentrated saline solutions are the only FDA-approved sclerosing agents in the US. *Polidocanol* (Aethoxysklerol) is used extensively in Europe and by some US doctors but is not approved by the FDA—so I do not use it for that reason. Several more agents are expected to become available soon—including Varisolve, a foam version of polidocanol used widely in Europe and currently in clinical trials in the US. The foam delivers the sclerosant more efficiently because it is less likely than a liquid to be diluted and deactivated when it mixes with the blood. This makes it more effective than other agents, especially in larger veins.

Ambulatory ("stab") phlebectomy is used for varicose veins too large to be treated with sclerotherapy. Instead, the veins are removed. The doctor makes a series of tiny incisions along the vein, then uses a tiny hooked instrument to pull vein segments out through the incisions. The procedure is typically done in the doctor's office using local anesthesia. The incisions are so small that often no stitches are required. The patient can walk immediately following the procedure and wears compression bandages or compression hosiery for at least two weeks afterward.

TREATING SPIDER VEINS

A common variation of varicose veins are spider veins (networks of tiny purple or red blood vessels just under the skin surface), a purely cosmetic problem. Treating them is generally not covered by insurance. Two treatments are sclerotherapy—an approach made possible by the recent introduction of extra-small sclerotherapy needles—or laser therapy, in which a laser is beamed through the skin to collapse the blood vessels. Both treatments have a success rate of more than 90%.

Estrogen Cream Can't Help Sun-Damaged Skin

Laure Rittié, PhD, research investigator, department of dermatology, University of Michigan Medical School, Ann Arbor.
Doris Day, MD, attending physician, dermatology, Lenox Hill Hospital, New York City.
Archives of Dermatology.

The hormone cream *estradiol* can repair aging skin, but only if the damaging ultraviolet rays of the sun have never touched that skin, new research finds.

Decades of sun damage on the face and arms and other exposed areas seem to undermine the power of the cream, according to a study in the *Archives of Dermatology.*

Unfortunately, these are the exact areas that are most in need of repair.

BACKGROUND

"There was a general belief that estrogen was good for the skin," explained study author Laure Rittié, PhD, a research investigator in the department of dermatology at the University of Michigan Medical School in Ann Arbor. But most, if not all, previous studies that had purported to show this looked at sun-protected areas of the skin, not sun-exposed areas.

"When we look for treatments for aging skin, we usually want to treat the face or hands or neck—in other words, sun-exposed areas," Dr. Rittié explained. "We decided to go ahead and carefully test these questions."

THE STUDY

Researchers applied topical estradiol for two weeks to both sun-exposed areas on the forearm and nonexposed skin near the hip in 40 women and 30 men, average age 75.

A biopsy was taken from each volunteer 24 hours after the last treatment.

The study was partially supported by Pfizer.

THE RESULTS

The cream stimulated collagen production in sun-protected skin areas but not in areas that were damaged by the sun. The collagen-promoting effects were found in both men and women but were more pronounced in women volunteers.

"Despite commonly held beliefs, estrogen was not able to raise collagen when the skin was damaged by sunlight," said Dr. Rittié. "Apparently, chronic exposure to sunlight breaks something in the way estrogen increases collagen, which makes damaged skin even harder to repair."

The authors acknowledge that treating volunteers for more than two weeks might have yielded different results in sun-exposed skin areas; additional studies would be needed to test this.

EXPLANATION

"What makes a hormone a hormone is that it is made in one place but works somewhere else in the body," said Doris Day, MD, an attending physician in dermatology at Lenox Hill Hospital in New York City. "It's like a light switch; it's small but, when you turn it on, the whole room lights up. Estradiol cream is like a little switch, but we're only just beginning to understand the different parts of the body it affects and how it affects them. This is putting the science behind the anecdote."

info For sun-safety tips, visit the Web site of the American Academy of Dermatology, *www.aad.org*, and choose "Sun Safety" under the Public Center tab.

2

Asthma and Allergy

Eating Peanuts May Cure Peanut Allergy

Exposing children with peanut allergies to a carefully administered daily oral dose of peanuts helped them build tolerance to the point where some of them appear to have lost their allergies, a recent study found.

However, the researchers, from Duke University Medical Center and Arkansas Children's Hospital, cautioned that the approach is still experimental and should not be tried by parents on their own.

"This is not something to be done at home," said Wesley Burks, MD, chief of pediatric allergy and immunology at Duke and a coauthor of the research. "It truly is an investigational study."

Dr. Burks and his colleagues presented their findings at a meeting of the American Academy of Asthma, Allergy & Immunology in Washington, DC.

BACKGROUND

About four million Americans have allergies to foods, and nut allergies, including peanut allergies, are among the most common. For the highly allergic, exposure to even a trace amount of peanuts can provoke a life-threatening reaction. Nearly half of the 150 deaths attributed to food allergies each year are caused by peanut allergies, according to background information in the study.

THE STUDY

For the study, which began five years ago, Dr. Burks and his colleagues gave children with a history of peanut allergy gradually larger daily doses of peanut protein, while other allergic

Wesley Burks, MD, chief of the division of pediatric allergy and immunology, Duke University Medical Center, Durham, North Carolina.

Scott H. Sicherer, MD, chair, American Academy of Pediatrics' Section on Allergy and Immunology, associate professor of pediatrics and researcher at Jaffe Food Allergy Institute, Mount Sinai School of Medicine, New York City, and author of *Understanding and Managing Your Child's Food Allergies* (Johns Hopkins University Press).

American Academy of Asthma, Allergy & Immunology meeting, Washington, DC.

children were given a placebo. The starting doses were very small, as little as 1/1,000th of a peanut. The doses increased until the children ate the equivalent of up to 15 peanuts a day about 10 months later. They then stayed on this daily therapy while continuing to be monitored.

Nine of the 33 children participating in the study have been on maintenance therapy for more than 2.5 years, and four of them were able to discontinue the treatment and eat peanuts, the researchers said.

When the researchers tracked immunologic changes—specifically, levels of an antibody called immunoglobulin E, which the body makes in response to allergens—they found the levels had declined to nearly nothing at the end of the trial.

IMPLICATION

"I think what has been shown in this [research] is that the threshold [at which allergic reactions begin] really can change with treatment," Dr. Burks said.

Changing the threshold is valuable, he said, because it could mean that if a child with a peanut allergy accidentally ate something with peanut in it, he may have no reaction. "If you do that alone, you give the family comfort."

Still to be answered is whether doctors can "make the disease go away," Dr. Burks said, adding that his research will continue.

EXPERT REACTION

The concept of exposing an allergic person to small amounts of the allergen isn't new, of course, said Scott H. Sicherer, MD, associate professor of pediatrics at Mount Sinai School of Medicine in New York City. That's the idea behind allergy shots.

Dr. Sicherer, who's also chairman of the American Academy of Pediatrics' Section on Allergy and Immunology, thought the test results were very promising.

info To learn more about food allergies, visit the American Academy of Allergy, Asthma & Immunology Web site, *www.aaaai.org/patients/publicedmat/tips/foodallergy.stm.*

Herbal Remedy Reverses Peanut Allergy

Xiu-Min Li, MD, associate professor, pediatrics, and director, Center for Chinese Herbal Therapy for Allergy and Asthma, Mount Sinai School of Medicine, New York City.
David L. Katz, MD, MPH, director, Prevention Research Center, Yale University School of Medicine, New Haven, Connecticut.
The Journal of Allergy and Clinical Immunology online.

A new herbal formula based in ancient Chinese medicine may be able to control allergic reactions to peanuts and other foods, researchers from New York City's Mount Sinai School of Medicine report.

"We can reverse the peanut allergic reaction," said lead researcher Xiu-Min Li, MD, director of the Center for Chinese Herbal Therapy for Allergy and Asthma at Mount Sinai.

BACKGROUND

Food allergies are potentially life-threatening for children and adults. Food allergies among children have increased 18% since 1997, and in 2007, some 3 million US children had food allergies, according to the National Center for Health Statistics. Currently, there is no treatment for the allergies, so avoidance is the only protection.

Allergic reactions to food can range from mild hives to vomiting to difficulty breathing to anaphylaxis, the most severe reaction. Anaphylaxis causes muscles to contract, blood vessels to dilate and fluid to leak from the bloodstream into the tissues. This can result in narrowing of the upper or lower airways, low blood pressure, shock or a combination of these symptoms, and also can lead to a loss of consciousness and even death.

THE STUDY

For the study, Dr. Li's team tested their new herbal remedy, called Food Allergy Herbal Formula (FAHF-2), on mice allergic to peanuts. They found that the formula protected mice from allergic reactions to peanuts.

In fact, FAHF-2 protected the animals from anaphylaxis for more than 36 weeks after treatment was stopped. This is one-quarter of the mouse life span, Dr. Li noted.

Protection from less severe allergic reactions to peanuts persisted for almost nine months after treatment was stopped, Dr. Li said. "The herbal formula can stop peanut allergy and produce a prolonged protection," she said. "This formula may be effective for human peanut allergy."

The report was published in *The Journal of Allergy and Clinical Immunology.*

Dr. Li's team has also shown the formula protects mice against other food allergies including tree nut, fish and shellfish.

HUMAN TRIAL UNDER WAY

Based on these findings, FAHF-2 has been given investigational new drug approval by the US Food and Drug Administration and a human trial is underway.

The trial is testing the safety and effectiveness of the remedy for a variety of food allergies including peanut, tree nut, fish and shellfish, Dr. Li said. "The results of the trial have shown that FAHF-2 is safe and well-tolerated," she noted.

Dr. Li's team has developed an additional herbal formula to treat asthma. That formula is also being tested in human trials, she said.

EXPERT REACTION

David L. Katz, MD, MPH, director of the Prevention Research Center at Yale University School of Medicine, said that no matter where it comes from, a cure for peanut allergy would be an important breakthrough.

"This paper suggests that traditional Chinese medicine may offer promising therapy for peanut allergy," Dr. Katz said.

info For more information on food allergies, visit the National Library of Medicine's Web site, *www.nlm.nih.gov/medlineplus/foodallergy.html.*

Herb Eases Allergies as Well as Drugs

Mark A. Stengler, ND, naturopathic physician in private practice, La Jolla, California...adjunct associate clinical professor at the National College of Natural Medicine, Portland, Oregon...author of many books and the *Bottom Line/Natural Healing* newsletter.

Butterbur, also called *Petasites hybridus,* is commonly used in Europe for relief of allergic rhinitis—and scientific evidence has shown it to be effective. For instance, several studies have found that butterbur alleviated nasal congestion, sneezing, itchy eyes and other symptoms about as effectively as the drugs *cetirizine* (Zyrtec) and *fexofenadine* (Allegra)—but without the medications' sedating side effects. Butterbur appears to work by decreasing the body's production of histamine, a chemical that triggers allergy symptoms.

Butterbur is commonly sold at health food stores in capsule form. Select a product labeled "standardized extract" that contains 7.5 mg to 16 mg of the active ingredient *petasin* per capsule. Take three or four times daily until allergy season is over. (Ideally, begin this regimen about two weeks before your allergy season typically starts to prevent symptoms). Rare side effects include headache, itchy eyes, drowsiness and nausea. As a general precaution, do not take butterbur if you are pregnant or breast-feeding.

Good brand: Petadolex by Enzymatic Therapy (60 softgels for $49.95, 800-783-2286, *www.enzy.com*). Butterbur is not known to have any drug interactions.

Study Reveals Startling New Cause of Asthma

University of Cincinnati news release.

Traffic pollution may cause genetic changes in the womb that increase a child's risk of developing asthma, say researchers who studied umbilical cord blood from New York City children.

STUDY FINDINGS

The researchers found evidence of a possible new biomarker—an epigenetic alteration in the gene ACSL3—associated with prenatal exposure to polycyclic aromatic hydrocarbons (PAHs), which are created as byproducts of incomplete combustion of carbon-containing fuels such as gasoline.

Epigenetic changes can disrupt the normal functioning of genes by affecting their expression, but don't cause structural changes or mutations in the genes. PAH levels are high in heavy-traffic areas, and exposure to PAHs has been linked to such diseases as cancer and childhood asthma.

IMPLICATIONS

The findings, published in the journal *PLoS One*, offer a potential clue for predicting environmentally-related asthma in children, said the researchers from the University of Cincinnati and Columbia University Mailman School of Public Health in New York City.

"Our data support the concept that environmental exposure can interact with genes during key developmental periods to trigger disease onset later in life, and that tissues are being reprogrammed to become abnormal later," said the study's senior author, Shuk-mei Ho, PhD, professor and chair of University of Cincinnati's Department of Environmental Health.

If the findings are confirmed, changes in the ACSL3 gene could offer a new biomarker for early diagnosis of pollution-related asthma.

"Understanding early predictors of asthma is an important area of investigation because they represent potential clinical targets for intervention," said study coauthor Rachel Miller, MD, director of the Asthma Project of the Columbia Center for Children's Environmental Health at Columbia University Medical Center in New York City.

info To learn more, visit the Web site of the American Lung Association, *www.lungusa.org,* and search "childhood asthma."

The "Country Cure" For Asthma

Giovanni Piedimonte, MD, professor and chairman, Department of Pediatrics, West Virginia University School of Medicine, physician in chief, WVU Children's Hospital, and director, WVU Pediatric Research Institute, Morgantown.

Andrew MacGinnitie, MD, PhD, allergist/immunologist, Children's Hospital of Pittsburgh.

Pediatrics.

After a week away from urban air pollution, children with mild persistent asthma begin to show dramatic changes in their respiratory health.

A study published in *Pediatrics* reports that just seven days after a group of school-age children left the city for a rural area, airway inflammation went down and lung function increased.

BACKGROUND

Previous studies have found that exposure to particulate matter from air pollution increases the use of asthma medicines and leads to more hospitalizations for asthma. Other pollutants have been associated with a predisposition to respiratory infections, wheezing and a stronger reaction to inhaled allergens.

What had not been studied, according to the authors, was whether the negative response to air pollution is reversible.

THE STUDY

To try to answer that question, the researchers took 37 children who lived in an urban area in Italy and brought them to a rural hotel for a week of camp. All of the children had allergies and mild persistent asthma, though none were being treated at the time of the study.

Air pollution, pollen counts and meteorological conditions were monitored at both sites. The children underwent testing at both sites as well. Tests included measuring nasal eosinophils, white blood cells linked to allergies, and lung function.

THE RESULTS

After a week in the rural environment, there was a fourfold decrease in nasal eosinophil levels and an increase in lung function, as measured by peak expiratory flow (the strength at which you can breathe out).

"I was quite surprised by our findings," said the study's senior author, Giovanni Piedimonte, MD, professor and chairman of the pediatrics department at the West Virginia University School of Medicine. "I thought we would see a difference, but I didn't think we'd have such statistically significant changes. What I was particularly surprised by was that the most statistically significant change was in pulmonary function. Virtually every single child more or less increased pulmonary function."

EXPERT COMMENTARY

Andrew MacGinnitie, MD, PhD, an allergist and immunologist at Children's Hospital in Pittsburgh, said the study was "impressive, and it adds to a growing body of evidence that pollution is a big driver of asthma." He added that he would have preferred it if, in addition to testing biomarkers of allergies and testing for lung function, the researchers had assessed the children's symptoms in both the urban and rural environments.

The good news from the study, he noted, is that "it does suggest that changes we see with pollution may be reversible."

IMPLICATIONS

"Clean air is good. The air where you live is probably more important than we generally think," Dr. Piedimonte said. "One of the best things we could accomplish is to clean the air in cities. Our situation in the US has improved, but there's much more to do. If we cut funding to agencies like the EPA [Environmental Protection Agency], the implications for children's health are going to be very dire."

info To learn more about air quality and asthma, visit the Web site of the Nemours Foundation, *www.kidshealth.org/parent* and search "asthma and pollution."

Is Your Nagging Cough a Sign of A Serious Illness?

Peter V. Dicpinigaitis, MD, professor of clinical medicine at Albert Einstein College of Medicine and founder and director of the Montefiore Cough Center at Montefiore Medical Center, both in the Bronx, New York.

Coughing is so prevalent—especially during the winter months—that most people dismiss it as a minor ailment that will go away on its own.

Coughing is actually a vital reflex that helps clear mucus, airborne chemicals and other substances from the airways, which extend from the throat to the lungs. Foreign substances trigger coughing by irritating receptors (nerve endings that line the airways).

Recent development: A highly contagious type of cough that often is accompanied by classic cold symptoms, such as sneezing and a runny nose, is on the rise among American adults. Reported cases of pertussis, commonly known as whooping cough, recently reached a 40-year high in the US—and the disease now strikes up to 600,000 Americans each year.

SHOULD YOU SEE A DOCTOR?

A cough that accompanies a cold usually goes away within a matter of days. But sometimes a cough can linger for weeks or months. If a cough lasts more than two months, it is considered chronic and should be evaluated by a physician. Regardless of how long it has lasted, any cough that seriously disturbs your sleep, work or family or social life should be treated by a doctor. If violent enough, a cough can cause sore muscles—and even break ribs or precipitate bouts of fainting or vomiting.

Important: A cough that occurs with certain other symptoms may signal a potentially serious illness. For example, if you have a high fever and/or cough up dark-colored phlegm or blood, it may indicate pneumonia...chest pain and shortness of breath could mean a collapsed lung...and blood-streaked sputum and wheezing could indicate lung cancer. These conditions require immediate medical care.

To treat a nagging cough that occurs without the additional symptoms described above, the underlying cause must be identified.

MAIN CULPRITS

If you exclude smoking and medication side effects—blood pressure–lowering drugs known as *angiotensin-converting enzyme* (ACE) inhibitors, such as *enalapril* (Vasotec), often trigger coughing—more than 90% of all chronic coughs are caused by three conditions (in order of prevalence)...

- **Upper-airway cough syndrome** is a new term for what used to be called postnasal drip. The syndrome includes coughing due not only to postnasal drip (mucus accumulation in the back of the nose or throat), but also resulting from other effects of nose, sinus or throat irritation or inflammation.

Best treatment options: Older over-the-counter antihistamines, such as *chlorpheniramine* (Chlor-Trimeton), and decongestants, such as *pseudoephedrine* (the active ingredient in Sudafed), are the only medications shown in studies to provide much relief—especially when taken in combination. (Pseudoephedrine is available "behind-the-counter" at drugstores.) Newer antihistamines, such as *loratadine* (Claritin) and *fexofenadine* (Allegra), are easier to take because they don't make you as drowsy but don't seem to work as well against cough.

There's little evidence that expectorant or suppressive cough syrups do much—they don't get at the cause of the cough. But a potent cough suppressant, such as one with codeine or hydrocodone, can offer temporary relief when a severe cough prevents sleep. For allergic rhinitis (due to such conditions as hay fever or an allergy to animal dander), inhaled steroids are the best choice, while antibiotics treat chronic sinusitis.

•**Asthma** is the next most common cause of cough. If accompanied by wheezing and shortness of breath, asthma is easy to diagnose. But much of the time, cough is the only symptom. This condition is known as cough-variant asthma.

Best treatment options: Cough-variant asthma usually responds to the same treatments as traditional asthma—inhaled steroids, plus other drugs, such as bronchodilators, if needed. Some of the newest asthma medications—*leukotriene receptor antagonists,* such as *montelukast* (Singulair)—are particularly effective for asthmatic cough.

Important: Once cough-variant asthma goes away, it is tempting to stop treatment. But experts now agree that this type of asthma may affect the lungs much the way traditional asthma does, causing chronic inflammation and thickening of the airway wall that could lead to irreversible obstruction. For this reason, it's safest to continue treatment as instructed by your physician.

New development: Nonasthmatic eosinophilic bronchitis (NAEB) recently has been recognized as a cause of chronic cough. The prevalence of this condition in the US is unknown, but European studies have found that 13% of people with chronic cough have NAEB. Like asthmatic cough, NAEB responds well to inhaled steroids.

•**Gastroesophageal reflux disease** (GERD) is one of the most common causes of chronic cough in the US. GERD is associated with heartburn but also can cause a cough—with or without heartburn. Coughing results when stomach contents back up into the esophagus, stimulating cough receptors. If acid reaches the voice box (larynx), coughing may occur with other upper respiratory symptoms, such as hoarseness.

Best treatment options: Cough caused by GERD generally improves with standard lifestyle changes (such as avoiding alcohol, caffeine and chocolate...and not eating within two hours of bedtime) and acid-suppressing medication prescribed for ordinary reflux. In some cases, two drugs—a proton pump inhibitor, such as *omeprazole* (Prilosec), and an H2 blocker, such as *ranitidine* (Zantac)—may be needed to eliminate cough-causing GERD.

In some people, bile and other nonacidic contents of the stomach are to blame, and drugs, such as *metoclopramide* (Reglan), are needed to strengthen the sphincter valve at the base of the esophagus and hasten stomach emptying.

A type of laparoscopic surgery (which involves wrapping part of the upper stomach around the sphincter to strengthen it) is helpful if drugs don't work, but may only reduce—not cure—the cough.

•**Pertussis,** which was first identified in the early 1900s, causes a nagging cough that often lingers for weeks or even months. The disease was largely eradicated in the US with widespread use of a childhood vaccine, but pertussis is now reemerging as immunity from the illness has begun to weaken in some people during adulthood.

The Centers for Disease Control and Prevention recommends a booster pertussis vaccine, which has been approved for adults ages 19 to 64. Because the vaccine is acellular (made from bacterial fragments, rather than the whole organism), it is unlikely to cause arm soreness, fever or other adverse reactions.

If treated during the two weeks of acute infection, pertussis responds well to antibiotics, such as *erythromycin* (E-Mycin). But because early symptoms resemble those of the common cold—and there's often nothing distinctive about the cough (adults are unlikely to display the loud and forceful "whoop" from which the disease gets its common name)—pertussis often remains undiagnosed until the cough has become severe. At this point, antibiotics are less effective, because the infection is too advanced. The infection resolves with time.

Caution: Pertussis is extremely contagious—one person can infect most or all of the people in his/her household. If a member of your household has pertussis, you should be seen by a physician as a precaution.

Acetaminophen Triples Risk for Asthma

Mark A. Stengler, ND, naturopathic physician in private practice, La Jolla, California...adjunct associate clinical professor at the National College of Natural Medicine, Portland, Oregon...author of many books and the *Bottom Line/Natural Healing* newsletter.

Researchers from Europe, led by a team from Imperial College in London, asked 1,028 people, about half of whom had asthma, how often they took painkillers containing *paracetamol,* known as *acetaminophen* (Tylenol) in the US. They compared this with use of painkillers that do not contain paracetamol, such as aspirin or ibuprofen.

Result: Participants who took paracetamol-containing painkillers at least once a week were 2.87 times more likely to suffer from asthma than those who took it less often. There was no association between asthma and other painkillers.

In my view, acetaminophen depletes levels of *glutathione,* an antioxidant that protects against airway inflammation. Studies also show that the painkiller reduces the antioxidant capacity in the blood, which could be why people who regularly use this drug are more susceptible to asthma. I recommend avoiding repeated use of acetaminophen whenever possible. Instead, try natural pain relievers, such as *methylsulfonylmethane* (MSM), *glucosamine* and *boswellia,* all available at health-food stores. Acupuncture and homeopathy can treat all types of pain. Chiropractic treatments also can be used for muscles and joints.

Cleaning House Risky for Women With Asthma

American College of Allergy, Asthma & Immunology news release.

Housecleaning products may pose a threat to women with asthma, US researchers say.

THE STUDY

During a 12-week study, researchers compared cleaning-related health effects in women who did and did not have asthma and found more lower respiratory tract symptoms among the asthmatic women.

Jonathan A. Bernstein, MD, of the University of Cincinnati College of Medicine, and colleagues found that "women in both groups exhibited increased upper and lower respiratory tract symptoms in response to cleaning agents rated mild in toxicity, suggesting a subtle but potentially clinically relevant health effect of long-term, low-level chemical exposures."

The study was published in the *Annals of Allergy, Asthma & Immunology.*

IMPLICATIONS

The researchers recommended "that women with asthma should be routinely interviewed as to whether they clean their home and cautioned about the potential respiratory health effects of these activities."

Asthma affects about 22 million people in the United States. Death rates from the disease are higher among women than men. In many homes, women are the primary cleaners.

Authors of the study concluded that "...longer, prospective studies of nonprofessional household cleaners are needed to determine whether there is an association between household cleaning agent exposure and the development of asthma."

info For more information about asthma, visit the Web site of the National Heart, Lung and Blood Institute, *www.nhlbi.nih.gov* and search "What is asthma?"

■ ■ ■ ■

Household Sprays Raise Asthma Risk by 76%

Using a spray furniture or glass cleaner or a spray air freshener just once a week increased the risk of developing asthma by up to 76%.

Best: Use nonspray products.

Jan-Paul Zock, PhD, research fellow, Center for Research in Environmental Epidemiology, Barcelona, Spain, and lead author of a study of 3,503 people, published in *American Journal of Respiratory and Critical Care Medicine.*

■ ■ ■ ■

Thunderstorms Linked to Asthma Attacks

When researchers recently analyzed about 10 million emergency room visits, those due to asthma attacks were 3% higher on days following a thunderstorm versus days when a storm had not occurred.

Theory: During thunderstorms, rain, possibly combined with the electrical fields produced by lightning, breaks up pollen grains that are spread by gusty winds.

If you have asthma: Try to stay indoors during and immediately after thunderstorms.

Andrew Grundstein, PhD, associate professor, climatology research laboratory, University of Georgia, Athens.

Sweat More, Wheeze Less

Warren Lockette, MD, head of clinical research, Naval Medical Center, San Diego, California.

Don't complain about how much you sweat when you work out—it could actually be one of the reasons you *can* work out. A recent study shows that people who sweat more are less likely to have exercise-induced asthma, a type of asthma that typically arises suddenly, five to 10 minutes into a workout, or even after the workout is over. One moment you are playing tennis or basketball or running...the next, you're experiencing symptoms of asthma, such as wheezing, coughing, chest pain and/or a shortage of breath. It can even happen in people with no history of asthma.

WHO GETS EXERCISE-INDUCED ASTHMA?

Exercise-induced asthma (or EIA) is brought on by continuous, strenuous aerobic activity, such as running or cross-country skiing. A research study on EIA has provided some insight into who those particularly susceptible individuals might be. At the US Naval Medical Center in San Diego, Warren Lockette, MD, and his team of researchers analyzed the rate of fluid secretion (in sweat, saliva and tears) in young members of the military suspected of having EIA. To identify those with the condition, researchers gave 56 healthy volunteers a drug that produced similar physiological effects as EIA and then measured their airflow. Those who experienced a 20% or more drop in airflow were confirmed to have EIA. Next he measured their sweating rates, along with fluid secretions from the mouth and eyes.

The results (published in a recent issue of *Chest*) showed that people least likely to have EIA produced more sweat and had more saliva and tears than those who are prone to the condition. Those with low airflow also had the lowest rates of fluid secretion in their mouths or eyes and on their skin from sweat. Dr. Lockette said he was surprised by the magnitude of the correlation between sweating rates and EIA.

SWEAT IS A GOOD THING

How is sweat linked to exercise-induced asthma? Dr. Lockette thinks that external secretions, such as sweat and saliva, reflect how much water is normally secreted within the lung's airways. The drier the airways, the more likely EIA will occur. If this is true, then "giving attention to hydration and nutrition is the next area to study," said Dr. Lockette. He is doing just that. More information about the root causes of EIA may lead to solutions—such as better hydration—that are easier and safer than current options, including prescription medications taken orally or with inhalers, which carry their own risks.

■ ■ ■ ■

Delicious Fruit Reduces Coughing by 76%

Researchers from three research centers gave 42 people with asthma (average age 36) 150 milligrams (mg) of purple passion fruit peel extract or a placebo daily. After four weeks, coughing was reduced by 76% in the passion fruit group, compared with 47% for those taking a placebo. Of patients who experienced wheezing, only 19% still wheezed after taking the extract, compared with 79% of those taking a placebo.

Purple passion fruit, native to South America, traditionally has been used there to treat asthma and bronchitis. In this study, the peels were soaked in water, then concentrated to produce high levels of the antioxidant chemicals *anthocyanins*. Study authors theorize that anthocyanins reduce allergenic and inflammatory reactions in asthmatics. No side effects were reported. These impressive results may have been even better if the study had lasted longer than four weeks. The extract is not yet available in the US, but it should be shortly.

Mark A. Stengler, ND, naturopathic physician in private practice, La Jolla, California...adjunct associate clinical professor at the National College of Natural Medicine, Portland, Oregon...author of many books and the *Bottom Line/Natural Healing* newsletter.

3

Breast Cancer Treatments

Hodgkin's Survivors 40 Times More Likely To Get Cancer

In an ironic testament to the success of childhood cancer treatments, researchers report that women who were treated as children with radiation for Hodgkin's disease, cancer of the lymphatic system, were nearly 40 times more likely to develop breast cancer later in life.

"We can cure most patients now who have Hodgkin's disease. Back in 1950, it was regarded as a universally fatal disease," said study coauthor Nancy Mendenhall, MD, a professor of radiation oncology at the University of Florida College of Medicine in Gainesville. "[But] when you've got a high cure rate, as people age, you begin to identify some of the unanticipated effects that seem to be related to the treatments. If you don't cure the patients, they don't survive to see those effects."

The risk rose with the radiation dose, and there was also a higher risk of developing malignancies in both breasts.

BACKGROUND

Often, treatment for Hodgkin's involves some radiation to the breast, explained study leader Louis S. Constine, MD, a professor of radiation oncology at the James P. Wilmot Cancer Center, University of Rochester Medical Center in New York state.

The amounts of radiation used are much lower now than in the past, Dr. Constine added, as is the proportion of the body irradiated. Chemotherapy is also sometimes substituted for radiation in more modern treatment.

Nancy Mendenhall, MD, professor of radiation oncology, University of Florida College of Medicine, Gainesville.

Louis S. Constine, MD, professor, radiation oncology and pediatrics, and vice chair, department of radiation oncology, James P. Wilmot Cancer Center, University of Rochester Medical Center, New York.

Rajaram Nagarajan, MD, assistant professor, hematology/oncology, Cincinnati Children's Hospital Medical Center.

The International Journal of Radiation Oncology Biology Physics.

THE STUDY

The findings, published in *The International Journal of Radiation Oncology Biology Physics,* are part of a larger study involving 930 children treated for Hodgkin's disease between 1960 and 1990 at five US centers. Overall, survivors of childhood Hodgkin's disease, especially female survivors, were found to be at higher risk for second malignancies.

This analysis followed nearly 400 female survivors of childhood Hodgkin's disease for an average of almost 17 years.

THE RESULTS

Women who had had this childhood cancer were 37 times more likely to develop breast cancer as compared with women who had not had Hodgkin's disease, although the absolute risk was low (29 women overall were diagnosed with breast cancer). Women were diagnosed as early as 9.4 years after radiation and as late as 36.1 years after the initial treatment. More women are likely to be diagnosed with breast cancer as follow-up continues.

Women who were diagnosed at an earlier stage of Hodgkin's disease or were older than 12 were more likely to develop breast cancer, possibly a result of different radiation doses or the developing breast tissue being more susceptible to harm from radiation.

About one-third of women in the group had cancer in both breasts.

Radiation of the pelvic area lowered breast cancer risk, although Dr. Mendenhall speculated that this surprising finding could be due to impact on hormone production in the ovaries.

IMPORTANT SCREENING GUIDELINES

While guidelines recommend that women, in general, start getting mammograms at age 40, women who received radiation that potentially impacted breast tissue are urged to start screening 10 years after radiation or at age 30, whichever comes first.

Research released recently, however, found that almost half of female childhood cancer survivors under the age of 40 who had chest radiation as part of their treatment are not following the recommended advice to get screening mammograms sooner than other women.

BREAST CANCER RISK MAY DECREASE

It's unclear how different treatment paradigms will affect survivors.

"The majority of these patients were treated in an earlier era, and current treatment protocols are certainly much different in terms of the amount of radiation and the field size," said Rajaram Nagarajan, MD, an assistant professor of hematology/oncology at Cincinnati Children's Hospital Medical Center. "But it will still take some time until we are able to assess how current changes are going to change these risks. The assumption is that they are going to reduce the risk."

Regardless, Dr. Nagarajan said, survivors need to receive regular care in centers and clinics specializing in the follow-up of pediatric cancer survivors.

"We have made a lot of changes in the past 10 to 15 years," he said. "The problem is, we are always five or 10 years behind in terms of assessing."

Info For follow-up guidelines for survivors of childhood cancers, visit the Web site of the Children's Oncology Group, *www.survivorshipguidelines.org/.*

High Insulin Raises Risk of Breast Cancer

Journal of the National Cancer Institute news release.

Women with high levels of insulin in their blood appear to be more likely to develop breast cancer than those with lower insulin levels.

And that might be the link between obesity and breast cancer, say researchers from the Albert Einstein College of Medicine in New York City. High insulin levels have already been associated with obesity.

THE STUDY

The researchers compared insulin levels in 835 women who developed breast cancer and 816 women who did not. All women were participating in the Women's Health Initiative study. Those whose fasting insulin levels were the highest had a 1.5 times greater risk of breast cancer than did women with the lowest fasting insulin levels, the study found.

The risk was even greater among women who were not taking hormone therapy. The study found that those women were 2.4 times more likely to have developed breast cancer if their insulin levels were high than if they were low.

The findings were published in the *Journal of the National Cancer Institute.*

IMPLICATIONS

In laboratory studies, insulin has been shown to stimulate the growth of breast cells. And, being overweight or obese has been identified as a risk factor for breast cancer, according to the American Cancer Society.

"These data suggest that *hyperinsulinemia* [excess insulin in the blood] is an independent risk factor for breast cancer and may have a substantial role in explaining the obesity–breast cancer relationship," said the researchers.

info To learn more about breast cancer risk factors, visit the Web site of the American Cancer Society, *www.cancer.org,* and search "What causes breast cancer."

■ ■ ■ ■

Get to Know Your Breasts

Know how your breasts feel. Breast tissue might normally feel like butter...bubble wrap...gravel...even rocks. If you notice any difference between or change in the texture of your breasts, call your doctor—you may need to be screened for cancer.

M. Ellen Mahoney, MD, breast surgeon, Stanford University, and cofounder of the Community Breast Health Project, both in Palo Alto, California, reported at *www.strengthforcaring.com,* an information and support Web site from Johnson & Johnson.

■ ■ ■ ■

Combo Technique Detects 91% of Breast Cancer

When 2,637 women—about half with a personal history of breast cancer—were screened with both mammography and ultrasound, the combined techniques detected 91% of the 40 tumors diagnosed in the women...ultrasound alone found 80%...and mammography alone found 78%.

Theory: Certain types of breast cancer are detected only by mammography, while others are found only via ultrasound.

W. Phil Evans, MD, professor of radiology, University of Texas Southwestern Center for Breast Care, Dallas.

■ ■ ■ ■

Nearly Painless Mammograms

Before undergoing mammograms, 418 women took an oral painkiller or placebo and/or applied a 4% lidocaine anesthetic gel or placebo gel to their breasts, then removed it 30 to 65 minutes before the test.

Result: The lidocaine gel group reported significantly less discomfort during the test than women who did not receive the treatment. Oral painkillers had no significant effect on comfort.

Before your next mammogram appointment: Speak to your pharmacist about a 4% lidocaine gel.

Colleen Lambertz, FNP, family nurse practitioner, breast care services, radiation oncology, St. Luke's Mountain States Tumor Institute, Boise, Idaho.

■ ■ ■ ■

Find Tumors Mammograms Miss

An MRI of the other breast is vital for women diagnosed with cancer in one breast—the sooner, the better. In up to 10% of breast cancer patients, both breasts are affected. Magnetic resonance imaging (MRI) often detects cancer missed by mammography.

Constance D. Lehman, MD, PhD, professor and head of breast imaging, University of Washington, Seattle, and leader of a study of 969 women, published in *The New England Journal of Medicine.*

Eat Up! Walnuts May Reduce Breast Cancer

American Association for Cancer Research news release.

Walnuts contain compounds that may help prevent breast cancer, suggest findings from a study involving mice specially created to develop tumors.

THE STUDY

One group of mice was fed a daily diet that included what would be equivalent to two ounces of walnuts in humans, while another group of mice ate a regular diet. The mice that ate the diet with walnuts had a much lower incidence of breast tumors, fewer glands with a tumor and smaller-sized tumors.

"These laboratory mice typically have 100% tumor incidence at five months; walnut consumption delayed those tumors by at least three weeks," said study author Elaine Hardman, PhD, an associate professor of medicine at Marshall University School of Medicine.

Molecular analysis revealed that increased consumption of omega-3 fatty acids, antioxidants and *phytosterols* found in walnuts contributed to tumor resistance in the mice. The findings were presented at the American Association for Cancer Research's annual meeting in Denver.

"With dietary interventions, you see multiple mechanisms when working with the whole food," Dr. Hardman said. "It is clear that walnuts contribute to a healthy diet that can reduce breast cancer."

RECOMMENDATIONS

Though the study was done with mice, Dr. Hardman suggested that it's still a good idea for people to eat more walnuts.

"Walnuts are better than cookies, french fries or potato chips when you need a snack," Dr. Hardman said. "We know that a healthy diet overall prevents all manner of chronic diseases."

The study was funded with matching grants from the American Institute for Cancer Research and the California Walnut Commission.

info For more information on how to eat healthfully to lower your cancer risk, visit the Web site of the American Institute for Cancer Research, *www.aicr.org,* and click on "Diet and Cancer."

Seven Ways to Fight Breast Cancer After Menopause

JoAnn E. Manson, MD, DrPH, is a professor of medicine and women's health at Harvard Medical School and chair of the division of preventive medicine at Brigham and Women's Hospital, both in Boston. She is a lead investigator for two highly influential studies on women's health—the Harvard Nurses' Health Study and the Women's Health Initiative. Dr. Manson is coauthor of *Hot Flashes, Hormones and Your Health* (McGraw-Hill).

Many postmenopausal women think their primary risk factor for breast cancer is genetics. Yet most breast cancers occur in women with no family history of the disease, and the major breast cancer genes (BRCA1 and BRCA2) account for only 5% to 10% of cases. *The primary risk factors...*

- **Age.** Average age at diagnosis is 61, and rates are highest after age 70.
- **Estrogen.** This hormone stimulates growth of breast tissues—including abnormal cells. Estrogen levels are highest during the childbearing years, so the earlier you started menstruating and the later you reached menopause, the higher your risk.

To help prevent breast cancer...

- **Guard against vitamin-D deficiency.** Vitamin D may fight formation of blood vessels that nourish tumors and inhibit division of cells that line the breast. Many experts now recommend that all adults get 1,000 international units (IU) daily.

Sources: Sunlight (from which skin synthesizes vitamin D)...cod liver oil, fatty fish (mackerel, tuna), fortified milk and cereals...and supplements of vitamin D-3 (cholecalciferol).

• **Get adequate folate,** a B vitamin involved in DNA synthesis and repair. Eat three one-cup servings daily of folate-rich foods—leafy green vegetables, garbanzo beans, peas, citrus fruits.

• **Avoid unnecessary hormone therapy.** Consider taking estrogen (plus progestin to guard against uterine cancer, if you have not had a hysterectomy) only if hot flashes and night sweats significantly disrupt your sleep or quality of life. Use the lowest effective dose...try to limit use to less than four or five years.

• **Watch your weight.** Obesity after menopause may double breast cancer risk, perhaps because fat cells take over the ovaries' job of producing estrogen. Nearly one-quarter of postmenopausal breast cancers in the US are due to excess weight.

• **Exercise 30 minutes or more per day.** Exercise lowers blood levels of insulin and estrogen, both of which are risk factors for breast cancer.

• **Eat less saturated fat.** In a study of 48,835 postmenopausal women, those who were accustomed to a high-fat diet reduced their breast cancer risk by adopting a diet in which less than 25% of daily calories came from fat.

• **Limit alcohol intake.** Even moderate drinking raises breast cancer risk by increasing estrogen and decreasing folate absorption. Also, alcohol can be metabolized into acetaldehyde, a potential carcinogen, so have no more than one drink daily.

If you're at high risk: The drugs tamoxifen and raloxifene can reduce breast cancer risk—but increase the odds of blood clots, hot flashes, uterine cancer and perhaps stroke. Ask your doctor if these drugs are right for you.

■ ■ ■ ■

Wine Helps Block Estrogen from Causing Cancer

Taking the amount of resveratrol found in a glass of red wine (0.1 grams) decreases the ability of estrogen to change into toxins that react with DNA in breast cells, causing cancer. Resveratrol is an antioxidant and can boost the immune system. Speak to your doctor before taking resveratrol supplements.

Eleanor G. Rogan, PhD, professor, University of Nebraska Medical Center, Omaha.

■ ■ ■ ■

Warning! Even Short-Term Hormone Use Is Dangerous

Previous research suggested that taking estrogen and progestin (to relieve menopausal symptoms) for less than five years did not increase breast cancer risk.

New finding: Taking these hormones for three years or more may triple the risk for lobular breast cancer, which accounts for only about 16% of invasive breast cancers in the US but is hard to detect.

Recommended: If you have been taking hormones for three years or more, ask your doctor if it is time to consider discontinuing them.

Christopher I. Li, MD, PhD, associate member, epidemiology program, Fred Hutchinson Cancer Research Center, Seattle, and lead author of a study of 1,513 women, published in *Cancer Epidemiology, Biomarkers & Prevention.*

Strange but True: HRT Users Less Likely to Die From Breast Cancer

Sarah F. Marshall, epidemiologist, University of California, Irvine.
Victor G. Vogel, MD, MHS, national vice president, research, American Cancer Society, and professor, medicine and epidemiology, University of Pittsburgh.
San Antonio Breast Cancer Symposium, Texas.

Taking hormone replacement therapy (HRT) after menopause is known to increase the risk of getting breast cancer, but women who take hormone therapy and then develop breast cancer have a lower risk of dying from the disease, a recent study suggests.

Why?

"Hormone therapy seems to give you a particular type of cancer that is easier to treat," explained study author Sarah F. Marshall, a senior statistician at the University of California, Irvine. She reported her finding at the San Antonio Breast Cancer Symposium, in Texas.

THE STUDY

Marshall and her colleagues evaluated nearly 2,800 postmenopausal women who were diagnosed with a primary invasive breast cancer after joining the study in 1995 and 1996. The researchers then tracked outcomes through the end of 2005, or until the women's death.

"We looked at self-reported use of hormone therapy before their diagnosis," Marshall said. "We compared three groups—those without [current or previous hormone use], those on estrogen alone, and those on estrogen-progestin."

Those taking estrogen-progestin had a 47% reduced risk of death from breast cancer during the follow-up compared with those with breast cancer who did not take hormone therapy. Those on estrogen alone had an 18% reduced risk of breast cancer death, but that was not statistically significant, she said.

"We found that women who took hormone therapy before their diagnosis were more likely to be diagnosed with estrogen receptor-positive cancer, as well as having breast cancers that were more favorable in other ways, [such as being] smaller and detected at an earlier stage," Marshall said.

Estrogen receptor–positive breast cancers depend on estrogen to grow. Giving anti-estrogen therapy (such as *tamoxifen*) treats the cancer.

IMPLICATIONS

The study results may be somewhat reassuring for women who took hormone replacement therapy, Marshall said.

"The results of this study tell us that if you are taking HRT, your risk of getting breast cancer is higher, but your risk of dying from breast cancer is less [than women with breast cancer who did not take hormones]," said Victor G. Vogel, MD, MPH, national vice president of research for the American Cancer Society and a professor of medicine and epidemiology at the University of Pittsburgh.

info To learn more about breast cancer, visit the National Cancer Institute Web site, *www.cancer.gov.* Select "Breast Cancer" under "Types of Cancer."

■ ■ ■ ■

Osteoporosis Drug Reduces Breast Cancer Risk

Estrogen protects bones but makes breasts more vulnerable to cancer. In a landmark study, women who took the osteoporosis drug *raloxifene* (Evista) were about half as likely to develop invasive, estrogen receptor (ER)–positive breast cancer—the most common postmenopausal breast cancer—as women who did not take it. Raloxifene provides the protective effects of estrogen to bones while having antiestrogenic effects on breast tissue.

Downside: Like estrogen, the drug increases risk for blood clots and perhaps stroke.

Best: If you are considering medication for osteoporosis, ask your doctor if raloxifene is appropriate for you.

Elizabeth Barrett-Connor, MD, chief, division of epidemiology, University of California, San Diego School of Medicine, and leader of a study of 10,101 women, published in *The New England Journal of Medicine.*

■ ■ ■ ■

Drug that Blocks Tumor Growth

Trastuzumab (Herceptin) blocks a protein that promotes tumor growth. It is currently given primarily to early-stage patients whose tumors have a lot of the protein.

But: Two federally run studies suggest that some women who test negative for the protein actually may have enough of it to benefit from Herceptin.

JoAnne Zujewski, Md, Senior Disciplinary Scientist, Clinical Investigations Branch, National Cancer Institute, Bethesda, Maryland.

Beautiful Breasts After Cancer Surgery

Jeffrey A. Ascherman, MD, chief of the division of plastic surgery and associate professor of clinical surgery, Columbia University Medical Center, New York City. He has published studies in various medical journals on breast surgery and has presented his research findings both nationally and internationally. Dr. Ascherman has performed more than 1,500 breast procedures.

Despite the victory of surviving cancer, losing a breast (or two) can be devastating. That's why many cancer patients choose to have breast reconstruction after mastectomy (total removal of a breast) or even after lumpectomy (removal of a breast tumor) if a large amount of tissue was removed.

Having reconstruction at the time of mastectomy makes cancer recovery emotionally easier...and does not significantly delay chemotherapy or increase the risk for complications. It is also possible to have reconstruction months or years after a mastectomy or lumpectomy.

There are two main surgical options—implants and tissue flaps (in which the patient's own tissue is used to create a new breast mound). Each has its advantages and can provide good cosmetic results.

TISSUE FLAP PROCEDURE

This involves rebuilding a breast using skin, fat and blood vessels from elsewhere on the body. The procedure takes about six hours. The new breast is in place when the woman awakens from her mastectomy, but it may require follow-up surgery to adjust shape and size. It generally feels and looks more natural than an implant. Results last forever, and you may get a tummy tuck in the bargain, because the tissue is often taken from the abdomen.

In my research, I have found less than a 1% incidence of abdominal hernia (when part of an organ or other tissue protrudes through the abdominal wall, which may have been weakened by the tissue flap procedure), a complication that requires additional surgery.

New finding: Patients who opt for the tissue flap procedure may be less prone to postsurgical infections than breast implant patients.

Best for: Women who have had no prior abdominal surgery that required a vertical midline incision...have sufficient fat on the abdomen, back, thighs or buttocks...and have no other major medical problems.

Recovery: The hospital stay is about four days. A patient must avoid strenuous activity and heavy lifting for six to eight weeks.

Interesting: Since the reconstruction uses living tissue, breast size changes if a woman loses or gains weight, just as a natural breast does.

IMPLANT SURGERY

All implants are encased in a silicone shell. The inside is filled with silicone gel or saline solution.

- **Silicone implants tend to be softer and feel more natural than saline.** Despite fears raised by past studies, recent clinical trials have shown no link between silicone implants and autoimmune disease.

- **Saline implants are filled with salt water that is easily reabsorbed into the body if the implant leaks or ruptures.** With saline implants, the breasts tend to feel slightly firmer and therefore less natural than with silicone-filled implants, and the skin may be more prone to rippling.

Recent studies show no proven health risks from leaking implants. A saline leak is easy to detect—the skin around the implant contracts, and the breast looks smaller. A silicone leak is harder to detect—scar tissue keeps the implant in place, and the breast maintains its shape—but it can be found with a physical exam or MRI.

With both types of implants, manufacturers report a 1% to 5% rate of leaking—though in my practice, I have found it to be lower. Although no implant is guaranteed to last a lifetime, an implant can be left in place for the rest of a woman's life if no problem develops.

The procedure: Implant surgery is usually done in two steps. Part one can be done at the time of mastectomy or lumpectomy and takes an additional one to two hours. After the original breast tissue is removed, a tissue expander is placed beneath the chest muscle. Through a tiny valve buried beneath the skin, the expander is filled periodically with saline to gradually stretch the skin. A few months later, when the skin has stretched, an implant of the appropriate size is inserted during an outpatient procedure that takes 60 to 90 minutes.

Recovery: Hospitalization for the first surgery is one to two days...recovery takes one to two weeks. The second surgery generally causes only temporary mild discomfort. After each step, the patient should avoid strenuous activity for two weeks. After that, any activity is okay unless it involves direct pressure on your chest, such as deep-sea diving or going off a high diving board.

Best for: Women who need reconstruction on both breasts...or who are very thin. Implants can be more challenging in patients who have received radiation to the breast area—loss of tissue elasticity makes it difficult to create a breast that looks real.

FINISHING TOUCHES

A replacement nipple and areola can be constructed in the doctor's office under local anesthesia several months after completion of either type of reconstruction.

To create a nipple, skin flaps lifted from the reconstructed breast are wrapped around one another. In the past, the areola was grafted from skin elsewhere and sometimes a tattoo was applied to enhance the color. Like many surgeons today, I prefer to avoid additional surgical sites by creating an areola from a tattoo alone. Healing takes a few weeks.

Insurance: Policies that cover mastectomy also must cover reconstruction plus surgery on the other breast (a lift, reduction or enhancement) if necessary to achieve symmetry.

If you're dissatisfied: Breast surgery can be revised or corrected. I've personally redone prior surgeries performed at our institution or elsewhere, with excellent results.

Follow-up: Different surgeons have different protocols. Once all is healed, I see my patients yearly to ensure that breasts are intact. Additional testing of the reconstructed breast usually is not necessary.

▪ **More from Dr. Ascherman...**

Finding a Great Breast Surgeon

Interview at least two surgeons before making a decision.

Referrals: American Society of Plastic Surgeons (888-475-2784, *www.plasticsurgery.org*). *Key questions...*

- **Are you board certified as a plastic surgeon?**

Only acceptable answer: Yes.

- **What is the ideal result?**

Best answer: To make the two breasts look as similar and natural as possible.

- **How many of this type of breast surgery have you done?**

Best answer: At least 10 to 20 surgeries per year.

- **Can I speak to some other patients of yours?**

Best answer: Contact information for at least two references.

▪ ▪ ▪ ▪

Don't Worry—Many Breast Implants Require Repeat Surgery

About 30% of postmastectomy reconstruction patients develop wound infections, implant asymmetry or displacement, capsular contracture (contraction of the tissue surrounding the implant) or other localized problems, usually within the first year after the surgery. About 20% require follow-up surgery. Before undergoing a mastectomy, women should discuss the pros and cons of implants and what kind of reconstruction—if any—is best for their individual situations.

Joseph K. McLaughlin, PhD, president of the International Epidemiology Institute, Rockville, Maryland, and professor of medicine at Vanderbilt University Medical Center and Vanderbilt-Ingram Cancer Center, Nashville. His study of 574 women was published in *Archives of Surgery*.

■ ■ ■ ■

Relax! Yoga Helps Breast Cancer Patients

In a recent study of breast cancer survivors, it was found that engaging in the Iyengar method—one of the more active forms of yoga—during treatment for breast cancer promotes psychological well-being...benefits the immune system...and generally improves patients' quality of life.

Sally E. Blank, PhD, associate professor, program in health sciences, Washington State University, Spokane, and researcher of a study of breast cancer survivors, presented at a meeting of the American Physiological Society.

■ ■ ■ ■

Weight Loss May Ease Lymphedema

Overweight women are at higher risk for chronic arm swelling (*lymphedema*), a side effect that can persist for decades after breast cancer surgery. Lymphedema is abnormal swelling due to accumulation of lymph fluid in a limb. It can develop some time after the original surgery.

Recent finding: Weight loss may alleviate lymphedema.

Clare Shaw, PhD, RD, consultant dietitian in oncology, Royal Marsden NHS Foundation Trust, London, England, and leader of a study of 64 women, published in *Cancer.*

■ ■ ■ ■

Calcium May Protect Bones From Cancer

About 70% of patients with advanced breast cancer also get bone tumors.

Study finding: Calcium deficiency makes it easier for cancer cells to penetrate bones...perhaps by causing bone breakdown. Increasing dietary calcium—from foods (such as milk) or supplements—may reduce bone breakdown.

Colin R. Dunstan, PhD, ANZAC Research Institute, Sydney, Australia, and senior author of a study of tumor growth in mice, published in *Cancer Research.*

■ ■ ■ ■

Beware! Popular Supplement May Cause Cancer to Spread

Black cohosh does not increase a woman's breast cancer risk, but in women who already have breast tumors, it may make the cancer more likely to spread to the lungs and other organs. Products with black cohosh, including Remifemin, often are used to ease symptoms of menopause, but they are not FDA regulated. To be safe, women with breast cancer or at high risk for it should avoid any products containing black cohosh.

Vicki L. Davis, PhD, assistant professor of pharmacology, Duquesne University, Pittsburgh, and leader of a study of the effects of black cohosh on female mice, published in *Cancer Research.*

4

Cancer Breakthroughs

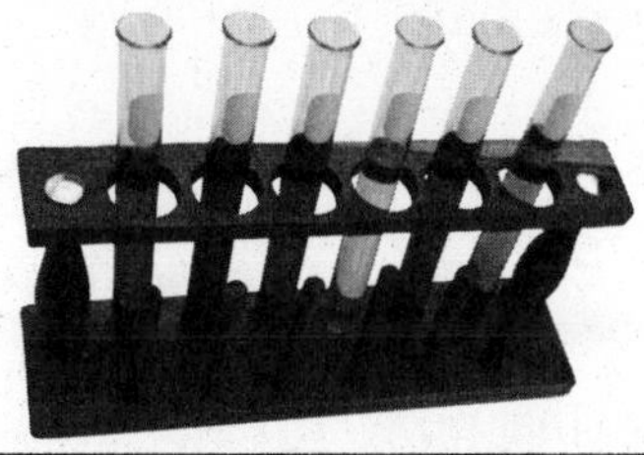

Beta-Blockers May Slow Melanoma

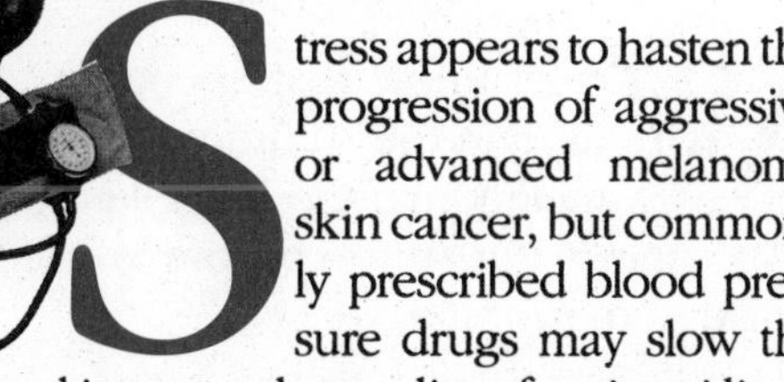

Stress appears to hasten the progression of aggressive or advanced melanoma skin cancer, but commonly prescribed blood pressure drugs may slow the disease and improve the quality of patients' lives, according to an Ohio State University study.

BACKGROUND

Each year in the United States almost 50,000 cases of melanoma—the most serious type of skin cancer—are diagnosed and nearly 8,000 people die of the disease, according to the American Cancer Society.

THE STUDY

In laboratory tests, the researchers exposed samples of three melanoma cell lines to the stress hormone norepinephrine and looked for changes in the levels of certain proteins released by the cells. The three proteins studied were *vascular endothelial growth factor* (VEGF), which stimulates the growth of new blood vessels to feed a growing tumor, and *interleukin-6* (IL-6) and *interleukin-8* (IL-8), which play a role in tumor growth.

THE FINDINGS

When exposed to norepinephrine, all three melanoma cell lines increased production of the three proteins. In C8161 cells—the most aggressive and advanced form of melanoma—there was "a 2,000 percent increase in IL-6. In untreated samples from this cell line, you normally can't detect any IL-6 at all," said Eric V. Yang, PhD, a research scientist at the Institute for Behavioral Medicine Research at Ohio State University.

"What this tells us is that stress might have a worse effect on melanoma that is in a very aggressive or advanced stage, and that one marker for that might be increased levels of IL-6," Dr. Yang said.

The researchers found that norepinephrine molecules bind to receptors on the surface of

Ohio State University news release.

cancer cells, which stimulates the release of the pro-cancer proteins.

Further tests showed that common beta-blocker blood pressure drugs significantly reduced melanoma cells' production of IL-6 and the other two proteins. The drugs did this by blocking the receptors on the surface of the cancer cells.

CONCLUSION

The findings, published in the journal *Brain, Behavior and Immunity*, suggest that beta-blockers may help slow the progression of melanoma, Dr. Yang and colleagues said.

info For more information on melanoma, visit the American Academy of Dermatology Web site, *www.aad.org*, and search "melanoma."

■ ■ ■ ■

Skin Cancer Patients at Risk For Other Cancers

In a 16-year study, researchers found that people previously diagnosed with nonmelanoma skin cancer (basal cell or squamous cell skin cancer) were twice as likely to develop other types of malignancies—such as breast, colon or lung cancer—as those without a history of skin cancer.

Theory: People who develop skin cancer may have an inherited tendency to develop other cancers.

If you have a history of nonmelanoma skin cancer: Be sure that your doctors know about it.

Anthony Alberg, PhD, associate director for cancer prevention and control, Hollings Cancer Center, Medical University of South Carolina College of Medicine, Charleston.

■ ■ ■ ■

Curable Cancers Doctors Don't Look For

Researchers from the University of Miami and the University of North Carolina at Chapel Hill analyzed data on 38,124 adults and found that only 15% reported ever having a skin cancer screening. Screening rates were lowest among those who work outside, such as farmers and construction workers.

Skin cancer is the most common cancer in the US, with more than one million cases and 10,000 deaths annually. Ask your dermatologist to examine your skin (from head to toe) yearly for signs of cancer. And if you have any suspicious lesions—including a mole that has changed shape or color—see a doctor. When caught early, cancerous skin lesions are 100% curable.

Mark A. Stengler, ND, naturopathic physician in private practice, La Jolla, California...adjunct associate clinical professor at the National College of Natural Medicine, Portland, Oregon...author of many books and the *Bottom Line/Natural Healing* newsletter.

New Ways to Protect Against Melanoma

Albert M. Lefkovits, MD, an associate clinical professor of dermatology at Mount Sinai School of Medicine and codirector of the Mount Sinai Dermatological Cosmetic Surgery Program, both in New York City. He is a member of the Medical Advisory Council of the Skin Cancer Foundation (SCF), *www.skincancer.org*, and recently presented "New Strategies for Melanoma Prevention" at an international gathering of the SCF.

We all know that spending too much time in the sun increases the risk for melanoma, the most serious form of skin cancer. But sun exposure is not the only cause of melanoma.

What you may not know: Genetic factors may play a significant role in the development of skin cancer. Melanoma can develop on parts of the body that get little or no sun (for example, on the palms of your hands or soles of your feet ...between the fingers, toes and buttocks...and on the genitals). Melanoma also can develop under a fingernail or toenail...in the eye...and, in rare cases, in the nose and mouth.

People with a family (or personal) history of melanoma or pancreatic cancer must be especially vigilant about checking their skin for changes even if they spend little time in the sun. (Pancreatic cancer has been linked to melanoma via a mutation in a particular gene.)

Even though we cannot change our genes, we can control our sun exposure and be vigilant about skin exams. *My advice...*

UV DANGERS

Ultraviolet (UV) radiation, produced by the sun and tanning beds and lamps, is a carcinogen (cancer-causing agent) that increases risk for all types of skin cancer. Specifically, sunshine contains UVB radiation, which causes tanning and sunburn, and UVA radiation, which damages deeper skin layers. Tanning beds produce primarily UVA radiation and should be avoided.

Important: UVA skin damage can occur even if your skin does not appear red.

BETTER SUNSCREENS

The most effective sunscreens are "broad-spectrum"—they protect the skin against both UVA and UVB radiation. Within the next few years, virtually all sunscreens will be broad-spectrum. Until then, you must read the label.

Avobenzone (Parsol 1789) or *oxybenzone*, both of which absorb UV radiation, are compounds that are commonly found in broad-spectrum sunscreens of high quality.

Titanium dioxide and zinc oxide are broad-spectrum sunscreen ingredients that prevent all of the sun's rays from reaching the skin by reflecting the rays back. Products that contain at least 5% of titanium dioxide or zinc oxide are recommended for people who burn easily or work outdoors, those with a history of skin cancer or those who take certain medications that increase sun sensitivity, such as certain antihistamines, diuretics and tetracycline and sulfa antibiotics.

What you may not know: The FDA has proposed a new one- to four-star rating system to alert consumers to a sunscreen's protective effect. The FDA is finalizing this rule and plans to implement it within the next few years.

Other advice...

- **Don't spend more for ultra-high SPF sunscreens.** I recommend using a sunscreen with a sun protection factor (SPF) of 30.

Exception: A sunscreen with an SPF higher than 30 should be used by people with extremely sun-sensitive skin, a history of skin cancer and/or a photosensitivity disease, such as lupus.

- **Apply a sufficient amount of sunscreen.** Most people apply only a thin layer. It takes about one ounce of sunscreen—approximately two tablespoons—to protect the average-sized person's face and all exposed areas of the body (including the hands and feet).

Also important: Apply sunscreen at least every two hours and reapply immediately after getting out of the water and drying off. Also, apply it 30 to 60 minutes before going outside to allow the active ingredients to penetrate into deeper layers of skin.

- **Protect your scalp and eyes.** Wear a hat with at least a three-inch brim and UV-blocking sunglasses.

TEA EXTRACTS

Many skin-care products, including some sunscreens, now contain tea extracts. Reliable studies have shown that both green and black tea (applied topically) reduce inflammation caused by sun exposure. Tea contains antioxidants that reduce free radicals, harmful molecules released in the skin during excessive sun exposure. Controlling free radicals protects skin DNA and can help reduce the risk for skin cancer.

A SUNSCREEN YOU SWALLOW

The dietary supplement Heliocare (available online or by special order at your pharmacy) contains an extract of *Polypodium leucotomos*, a tropical plant, which improves the skin's resistance to UV radiation. Studies published in the *Journal of the American Academy of Dermatology* found that the extract significantly reduced sunburn as well as cell damage—both can increase cancer risk.

How to use: Take one 240-milligram (mg) capsule in the morning on a day when you're planning to spend time in the sun. Take a second capsule at noon if you will be exposed to intense sunlight (such as that in a tropical climate). The extract has no known side effects.

Caution: Heliocare should be used in conjunction with—not as a substitute for—sunscreen.

IMPROVED EXAMS

A monthly self-exam of the skin is one of the best ways to identify signs of melanoma anywhere on the body. Most skin cancers, including melanoma, can be cured when they are confined to the outermost layer of skin.

Use a mirror to look at hard-to-see areas—and don't forget to part the hair and examine the scalp. If necessary, ask another person, such as your hair stylist or barber, to examine your scalp. A thorough self-exam also should include the back of the neck and behind the ears—like the scalp, these areas sometimes are missed, allowing a melanoma lesion to reach an advanced stage before being detected.

Everyone should see a dermatologist for a full-body exam each year—especially people who burn easily or have a personal or family history of skin cancer.

What you may not know: A relatively new technology known as *epiluminescence microscopy* (ELM) allows a doctor to detect cancers or precancerous changes that would get missed during a routine skin examination. With digital ELM, the doctor uses a handheld device to examine and photograph large areas of the skin. The images are magnified and stored electronically.

The equipment is expensive, so only certain dermatologists in private practice—for example, those who specialize in the treatment of melanoma—use ELM. However, many large hospitals and academic medical centers now utilize the technology.

NEW RULE FOR DETECTION

Melanoma deaths could be curbed by 60% if everyone performed monthly self-exams. Patients have traditionally been advised to see a doctor if a mole or other growth can be described by the "A, B, C, D" guidelines—that is, it is **Asymmetric**, in which the two halves are different...has an irregular **Border**...has variations in **Color**...and/or has a **Diameter** greater than the size of a pencil eraser.

What you may not know: "E" for **Evolving** has been added to the guidelines. If a mole or other growth changes in appearance, sensation (itching and tenderness) or size, see a dermatologist. Lesions that change, particularly over a period of a few months, are far more likely to be melanoma than areas that stay the same over a period of years.

Warning: It's unusual for patients to develop new moles after age 40. To be safe, if you develop a new mole after age 40, see a doctor right away, particularly if you have melanoma risk factors—a personal or family history of melanoma, a large number of moles (more than 20) or fair skin that burns easily.

Could Your Thyroid Stop Cancer?

Rebecca Shannonhouse, editor, *Bottom Line/Health* newsletter, 281 Tresser Blvd., Stamford, Connecticut 06901.

Cancer patients with underactive thyroid hormone (hypothyroidism) sometimes live longer than those with normal thyroid function—but, until recently, oncologists didn't know why.

What has been discovered?

In a study where a hypo (low) thyroid state was induced in patients with recurrent gliomas (aggressive brain tumors), their survival rates were about three times longer than those patients with the same cancer who had normal thyroid function, says Aleck Hercbergs, MD, a radiation oncologist at the Cleveland Clinic. It appears that thyroxine, the body's main thyroid hormone, may stimulate cancer cell growth.

Interestingly, when the charts of nearly 2,000 lung cancer patients were reviewed, those with a history of hypothyroidism were diagnosed at an average age that was 4.3 years older than those with normal thyroid function—suggesting that these cancers took longer to grow to a diagnosable stage. Similar patterns have been noted in patients with breast and kidney cancers.

Even though the link between thyroid hormone and cancer growth is still speculative, some doctors now advise hypothyroid patients with an active cancer (or a history of cancer) to use the lowest possible dose of thyroid hormone replacement—or forgo it altogether. Cancer patients may want to ask their oncologists if thyroid manipulation—using available drugs to artificially create a low-thyroid status—though experimental, might improve their outcomes.

On the horizon: A hormonally inactive chemical byproduct of thyroxine may help prevent cancer cells from proliferating—perhaps leading to new anticancer drugs.

■ ■ ■ ■

Amazing! Dogs that Sniff Out Cancer

In the lab, trained dogs can detect samples of ovarian malignancies, including those at an early stage, by scent. These tumors apparently have a different odor than other gynecological malignancies.

Integrative Cancer Therapies.

Six Ways Statins Fight Prostate Cancer

Lionel L. Bañez, MD, Division of Urologic Surgery and Duke Prostate Center, Duke University Medical Center, Durham, North Carolina.

Robert J. Hamilton, MD, MPH, urology resident, University of Toronto Medical Center, Ontario, Canada.

Stacy Loeb, MD, department of urology, Johns Hopkins University.

Rodney H. Breau, MD, oncology fellow, department of urology, Mayo Clinic, Rochester, Minnesota.

Jennifer L. St. Sauver, PhD, epidemiologist, Mayo Clinic, Rochester, Minnesota.

Ajay Nehra, MD, professor of urology, Mayo Clinic, Rochester, Minnesota.

American Urological Association annual meeting, Chicago.

Several recent studies suggest statins help prevent prostate cancer and reduce the risk for erectile dysfunction.

"At this point in time, there seems to be mounting evidence that there may be a future role for statins in prostate cancer treatment or prostate cancer prevention," said Lionel L. Bañez, MD, from the Division of Urologic Surgery and Duke Prostate Center at Duke University Medical Center and lead author of one study. "There will definitely be more men taking statins for cardiovascular reasons, and this is a great opportunity for us to see how many of these men develop prostate cancer and whether these prostate cancers are aggressive."

All the reports were presented at a meeting of the American Urological Association.

STUDY #1: RECURRENCE

One study found that men who were taking statins before undergoing surgical removal of their prostate had a lower risk of having the cancer return. "The use of statins at the time of surgery was associated with a 30% reduction in the risk of recurrence of prostate cancer," said lead researcher Robert J. Hamilton, MD, MPH, a urology resident at the University of Toronto Medical Center in Ontario, Canada.

Dr. Hamilton thinks that the anti-inflammatory properties of statins may explain the finding. However, it might also be the ability of these drugs to lower cholesterol that has an effect on cancer cells, he said.

Although these results are promising, Dr. Hamilton is cautious about recommending statins to reduce the risk of recurrent prostate cancer. "At this point, we cannot with confidence say that that's true," he stressed.

There are also several unanswered questions, including the optimal dose, the length of time one needs to be taking statins to achieve a benefit, and whether starting statin therapy after surgery would have the same effect.

"Although the results of these studies are exciting, they need to be confirmed," he said.

STUDY #2: TUMOR INFLAMMATION

Another study focused on inflammation inside prostate cancer tumors. "We looked at the association between statin use and prostate tumor inflammation," Dr. Bañez said.

"We found that men who were using statins prior to surgery had a significantly lower risk for inflammation within their prostate tumor," Dr. Bañez said.

In fact, men taking statins had a 72% reduction in the risk for inflammation of the prostate tumor. The researchers also found that obesity appears to be associated with increased inflammation and more aggressive prostate cancer.

STUDY #3:
AGGRESSIVENESS OF CANCER

In a third report, researchers led by Stacy Loeb, MD, from Johns Hopkins University, found statins may help in reducing the aggressiveness of prostate cancer. Our examination of prostate cancer that was surgically removed suggests that the use of statins may result in a less aggressive cancer, the researchers said.

STUDY #4:
PREVENTION

In a fourth report, researchers led by Rodney H. Breau, MD, from the Mayo Clinic, found that statins were associated with a lower risk of developing prostate cancer.

"In recent years, it has been suggested that statin medications may prevent development of cancer. However, until now, there has been limited evidence to support this theory," Dr. Breau said. "Our research provides evidence that statin use is associated with a threefold reduced risk of being diagnosed with prostate cancer."

There may come a time when people will be taking statins to treat or prevent prostate cancer, Dr. Hamilton noted. "If these studies keep rolling in suggesting that there is something there with prostate cancer, then the use of statins could go up," he said.

STUDY #5:
URINARY TRACT SYMPTOMS
AND ENLARGED PROSTATE

In a fifth study, Mayo Clinic researchers found that statin users had fewer lower urinary tract symptoms related to an enlarged prostate.

The researchers found that statin users were 63% less likely to develop lower urinary tract problems and 57% less likely to develop an enlarged prostate.

"Statin drugs have been shown to have anti-inflammatory effects, and previous research suggests inflammation may be associated with benign prostate disease," said lead researcher Jennifer L. St. Sauver, PhD. "This study suggests that men's urinary health could be improved by taking statin medications."

STUDY #6:
ERECTILE DYSFUNCTION

In another report from Mayo Clinic researchers, older men taking statins over an extended period had a lower risk of developing erectile dysfunction (ED).

Statins were associated with a decreased risk of ED among men older than 60. And the longer men took statins, the lower their risk. For example, men taking statins for nine years or more were 64% less likely to develop ED. Men who took statins for less than three years had about the same risk of developing ED as men who did not take statins, the researchers found.

Protection of vascular health is important in preserving erectile health. "Our data suggest that longer use of statins may result in the lowest risk of erectile dysfunction," said study author Ajay Nehra, MD.

info For more on prostate cancer, visit the Prostate Cancer Foundation Web site, *www.prostatecancerfoundation.org.*

Urine Test May Predict Prostate Cancer

Arul Chinnaiyan, MD, PhD, director, Michigan Center for Translational Pathology, professor of pathology and urology, University of Michigan Medical School, Ann Arbor.

Michael M. Shen, PhD, professor, medicine and genetics and development, Columbia University College of Physicians and Surgeons, New York City.

Margaret K. Offermann, MD, PhD, deputy national vice president for research, American Cancer Society.

Nature.

A simple urine test that identifies small molecules that are associated with prostate cancer might some day be able to identify men who have a fast-moving, aggressive form of the disease, University of Michigan researchers report.

Called metabolites, compounds such as these are produced by the body's metabolic process. Researchers say such a test could help identify those who need aggressive treatment and might one day lead to the development of important new therapies.

"There are metabolites that might be useful in predicting the aggressiveness of prostate cancer," said lead researcher Arul Chinnaiyan, MD, PhD, director of the Michigan Center for Translational Pathology and a professor of pathology and urology.

"Metabolites, similar to genes and proteins, should also be measured in understanding cancer," he said. "They have been underappreciated relative to genes being profiled in cancer. This approach could be extended to other cancers."

However, before such a urine test could become standard medical practice, it would have to be tested in animals and then in people through clinical trials, Dr. Chinnaiyan said.

THE STUDY

For the study, Dr. Chinnaiyan's group analyzed 1,126 metabolites from 262 tissue, blood and urine samples taken from men with early, advanced and metastatic prostate cancer. From these samples, the researchers identified 10 metabolites that frequently appeared with prostate cancer, especially with advanced prostate cancer.

One of the 10 metabolites, called *sarcosine*, was the most indicative of advanced prostate cancer, the researchers found. Sarcosine levels were elevated in 79% of the samples from men with metastatic cancer (cancer that has spread) and in 42% of the samples from men with early-stage disease, the researchers found.

No trace of sarcosine was found in samples from men who did not have prostate cancer, the researchers noted.

According to the report, sarcosine was a better indicator of advanced prostate cancer than prostate-specific antigen (PSA), the current marker for the disease.

And, sarcosine's involvement in the invasiveness of the cancer suggests that blocking it might be a target for future drug development, Dr. Chinnaiyan said.

The findings are preliminary, though, Dr. Chinnaiyan noted, and it would be years before a test or treatment based on the metabolite could be available. Ideally, he said, researchers would like to find other metabolites associated with prostate cancer that would help predict the course of the disease with even more precision.

The findings were published in *Nature*.

More than 190,000 people in the United States will be diagnosed this year with prostate cancer, and almost 28,000 will die from the disease, according to the American Cancer Society.

EXPERT REACTION

Michael M. Shen, PhD, a professor of medicine, genetics and development at Columbia University College of Physicians and Surgeons in New York City, and coauthor of an accompanying article, said that the report advances the use of metabolites in understanding cancer.

"The hope is that this approach will ultimately yield a clinical application," Dr. Shen said. "For example, one could screen urine from men and not only diagnose prostate cancer, but have information that would be useful for cancer prognosis."

However, that goal is a long way off, he said. "The importance of the paper is that there is a new methodology that has not been pursued extensively before, which in combination with existing approaches may yield advances in cancer diagnosis and prognosis," he said.

Margaret K. Offermann, MD, PhD, the deputy national vice president for research at the American Cancer Society, stressed that studies are needed to see if the approach could be used in patients.

"This is not a perfect test," Dr. Offermann said. "It is not perfectively predictive of when someone is going to have prostate cancer and when that cancer is going to misbehave, but it may help in combination with PSA," she said.

And it could be a new target for treatment, she said. "Potentially, by blocking the formation of sarcosine or related compounds, it may actually help in the treatment," she explained.

info For more information on prostate cancer, visit the Web site of the American Cancer Society, *www.cancer.org,* and search "Learn about prostate cancer."

■ ■ ■ ■

New Guidelines on Prostate Cancer Screenings

Men age 75 and older no longer need to undergo annual prostate-specific antigen (PSA) testing to screen for prostate cancer, according to guidelines issued by the US Preventive Services Task Force. These guidelines are intended to reduce the number of older men who are diagnosed with prostate cancer and receive treatment (such as surgery or radiation therapy) that may lead to impotence and/or incontinence, even though such treatment does not necessarily increase the life span of an older man. Men should discuss their prostate cancer screening schedules with their doctors.

Kenneth W. Lin, MD, medical officer, US Preventive Services Task Force Program, Agency for Health Care Research and Quality, Rockville, Maryland.

■ ■ ■ ■

Silent Cancer Risk in Men

Researchers recently interviewed 24 men with immediate family members—mother, sister or daughter—who had tested positive for a BRCA1 or BRCA2 breast cancer gene.

Result: Nearly half did not realize that their relative's test results meant their own cancer risk was increased. Men with a defect in one of the genes have a 30% to 40% lifetime risk for prostate cancer versus 14% in the general population.

If a female family member tests positive for the genetic mutation: Ask your doctor if you should be tested.

Mary B. Daly, MD, PhD, senior vice president for population science, Fox Chase Cancer Center, Philadelphia.

■ ■ ■ ■

Coming Soon—Handheld Health "Cures"

A graduate student has developed prototypes for palm-sized, battery-operated, lightweight ultrasound devices that are powerful enough to treat conditions such as prostate tumors and kidney stones. Currently available therapeutic ultrasound machines weigh about 30 pounds. Tests of the new devices are currently under way.

Cornell University, Ithaca, New York.

■ ■ ■ ■

Walking Offsets Bone Loss Due to Prostate Cancer Treatment

Androgen *deprivation therapy* (ADT), commonly used for prostate cancer, can cause bone loss.

New study: In an eight-week study of 70 sedentary men who received radiation and ADT for prostate cancer, half of the men walked at a brisk pace for 20 to 30 minutes five days weekly, while the others did not exercise.

Result: The exercisers gained 0.49% in bone mass, on average, while those who did not exercise lost 2.2%, on average.

If ADT is prescribed for you: Talk to your doctor about a walking program.

Paula Chiplis, PhD, RN, clinical instructor, department of nursing, Johns Hopkins Hospital, Baltimore.

■ ■ ■ ■

Combination Therapy Slows Growth of Deadly Tumors

Researchers recently studied 875 men who had either locally advanced prostate cancer (spread to the border of, or just beyond, the prostate gland) or aggressive prostate tumors.

Result: Twelve percent of the men who received both hormone and radiation therapy died of the disease within 10 years, compared with 24% of the patients who received hormone therapy alone.

Theory: Combination therapy may slow the growth of potentially fatal tumors that are too small to detect at the time of diagnosis.

Anders Widmark, MD, professor, department of radiation sciences, Umea University Hospital, Sweden.

Marijuana Use Raises Risk for Testicular Cancer 70%

Janet Daling, PhD, epidemiologist, public health sciences division, Fred Hutchinson Cancer Research Center, Seattle.

Gary G. Schwartz, PhD, associate professor, departments of cancer biology and epidemiology and prevention, Wake Forest University, Winston-Salem, North Carolina.

Cancer online.

Smoking marijuana over an extended period of time appears to greatly boost a young man's risk for developing a particularly aggressive form of testicular cancer, a new study reveals.

In fact, researchers found that men who smoked marijuana once a week or began to use the substance on a long-term basis while adolescents incurred double the risk for developing the fastest-spreading version of testicular cancer—*nonseminoma*, which accounts for about 40% of all cases.

The findings were published in the medical journal *Cancer*.

BACKGROUND

"Since we know that the incidence of testicular cancer has been rising in our country and in Europe over the last 40 years and that marijuana use has also risen over the same time, it seemed logical that there might be an association between the two," said study coauthor Janet Daling, PhD, an epidemiologist and member of the Fred Hutchinson Cancer Research Center's public health sciences division in Seattle.

The researchers also noted that the testes could be particularly vulnerable to the effects of marijuana, given that the organ—along with the brain, heart, uterus and spleen—carries specific receptors for *tetrahydrocannabinol* (THC), the principal psychoactive ingredient in marijuana.

According to the National Cancer Institute, testicular cancer is relatively uncommon, accounting for just 1% of cancers among American men. Nevertheless, the disease is the most common type of cancer for American men between the ages of 15 and 34, the study noted.

THE STUDY

Dr. Daling and her team explored the notion of a marijuana–testicular cancer connection by analyzing data on 369 testicular cancer patients that had been collected by the Adult Testicular Cancer Lifestyle and Blood Specimen Study.

Participants were between the ages of 18 and 44, most were white or Hispanic, and all were residents of the Seattle–Puget Sound region. All had been diagnosed with the disease between 1999 and 2006. The men reported any history of marijuana use, as well as alcohol and smoking habits, and the same information was collected from about 1,000 healthy men.

RESULTS

The researchers found that current marijuana use was linked to a 70% increased risk for the disease.

Independent of known risk factors, nonseminoma risk was particularly high among men who used the drug at least once a week and among those who had started using it before age 18.

No link was found between the drug and a less aggressive and more prevalent form of the disease, known as *seminoma*, which strikes 60% of testicular cancer patients.

IMPLICATIONS

Though Dr. Daling emphasized that the findings are preliminary, she suggested that attention should be paid.

"We know very little about the long-term health consequences of marijuana smoking," she cautioned. "So, although this is the first time this association has been studied and found—and the finding does need to be replicated before we are really sure what's going on—this does give some evidence that testicular cancer may be one result from the frequent use of marijuana. And that is something that young people should keep in mind."

EXPERT COMMENTARY

The prospect of a causal relationship between marijuana use and testicular cancer raised unanswered questions for Gary G. Schwartz, PhD, an associate professor in both the department of cancer biology and the department of epidemiology and prevention at Wake Forest University in Winston-Salem, North Carolina.

"The consensus is that most testicular cancer is thought to originate with lesions in utero, and that the peak age for testicular cancer to actually occur begins, really, right after adolescence," he noted. "That's when hormones released during puberty appear to promote [full-blown] cancer by essentially throwing fuel on the lesion fire, following a relatively long latency. So it's a little hard to understand how exposure to marijuana beginning at that point could somehow play an immediate causal role.

"But certainly, the idea that cannabis may cause cancer cells to proliferate is interesting," Dr. Schwartz acknowledged. "It could, however, also be that recreational drug use is simply a marker for affluence, since we know that testicular cancer is traditionally a disease that is more common among the affluent."

info For more information on marijuana and its effects on cancer, visit the Web site of the National Cancer Institute, *www.cancer.gov,* and search "marijuana."

■ ■ ■ ■

Cancer Linked to Hand Changes

Palmar fasciitis and polyarthritis syndrome (PFPAS), a thickening or curling of the palm and swelling of the fingers that gives the palms a wooden appearance, has been linked to cancers of the prostate, blood, lung, breast, pancreas and ovaries. This rare condition primarily affects older people.

Theory: Connective tissue growth factor, a chemical signal in the body, may trigger both the growth of malignancies and overgrowth of connective tissues in the palm.

If your palms suddenly become thickened: Consult a physician who specializes in internal medicine.

Richard Stratton, MD, consultant physician, Royal Free Hospital, London.

■ ■ ■ ■

Better Ovarian Cancer Testing

In a study of 496 pre- and postmenopausal women who had undergone surgery for diagnosis and treatment of pelvic masses, researchers measured preoperative levels of the proteins HE4 and CA-125 in the women's blood. The presence of the two proteins accurately identified 94% of postmenopausal women and 75% of premenopausal women with ovarian cancer as high risk for malignancy.

Important: The CA-125 test is currently available, but it is not as sensitive as the combination of blood tests in predicting ovarian cancer. A blood test for HE4 is under FDA review. If approved, it should be widely available soon.

Robert C. Bast, Jr., MD, professor, department of experimental therapeutics, M.D. Anderson Cancer Center, Houston.

Yes, You Can Detect Ovarian Cancer Before It's Too Late

Robert P. Edwards, MD, professor of obstetrics, gynecology and reproductive sciences at University of Pittsburgh School of Medicine, director of gynecologic oncology research and vice chairman of clinical affairs at Magee-Womens Hospital, and senior investigator at Magee-Womens Research Institute, all in Pittsburgh.

Some cancers of the female reproductive tract have obvious early warning signs. For uterine cancer, it's bleeding after menopause. For cervical cancer, it's a Pap smear that shows abnormal cells. But ovarian cancer—cancer of the glands that produce eggs and manufacture the hormones estrogen and progesterone—often has no obvious symptoms.

Reasons: In the spacious abdominal cavity, a tumor can grow undetected for years...and cancer cells can silently spread via the peritoneal fluid in the abdominal cavity.

Result: Among women whose ovarian cancer is caught and treated early—while it is still confined to the ovary—the five-year survival rate is 93%. Unfortunately, of the estimated 22,000 women in the US who are newly diagnosed with ovarian cancer each year, 80% already have cancer that has spread to other parts of the body. For them, the five-year survival rate could be just 20% to 30%.

Self-defense: Determine your level of risk, then follow the protective guidelines below.

Important: Watch for these subtle, easy-to-miss warning signs of ovarian cancer...

- **Abdominal swelling or bloating**
- **Pelvic pressure or abdominal pain**
- **Feeling full quickly when eating**
- **Urgent and/or frequent urination.**

These same symptoms can be caused by irritable bowel syndrome or urinary incontinence. *However, they are more likely to indicate ovarian cancer when symptoms...*

- **Appeared within the last year**
- **Are severe**
- **Occur almost every day**
- **Last for more than a few weeks.**

AT HIGH RISK

The average woman's risk for ovarian cancer is relatively small—for every 100 women, fewer than two get the disease. However, certain factors significantly worsen these odds. For instance, for every 100 women who inherit a mutated form of the genes linked to breast cancer (BRCA1, BRCA2), 16 to 60 of them—depending on the specific mutation—are likely to develop ovarian cancer.

You are at high risk if any of these apply...

- **Two or more first-degree relatives** (mother, sister, daughter) have had ovarian or breast cancer.
- **Three or more second-degree relatives** (grandmother, aunt) have had ovarian or breast cancer.
- **You have a personal history of breast cancer** diagnosed before menopause.

You are at intermediate-high risk if...

- **You have one first-degree relative** who has had ovarian cancer.

Self-defense: If your risk is high or intermediate-high, maximize your chances for early detection...

- **Get genetic counseling.** The counselor maps your family history to determine if genetic testing (for instance, for the BRCA1 and BRCA2 genes) is appropriate. Genetic counseling is available at many university-based cancer centers.

Referrals: National Cancer Institute, 800-422-6237, *www.cancer.gov.*

- **Have frequent screening tests.** *At least once per year, see your gynecologist for a...*
    - Pelvic exam, during which the doctor manually examines the ovaries and uterus.
    - Transvaginal ultrasound, in which a probe is placed in the vagina to check for ovarian tumors.
    - Blood test for CA-125, a protein produced by ovarian cancer cells. *New study:* This test detected about half of early-stage ovarian cancers... and about 80% when used with a symptom questionnaire among high-risk women.

If any of these test results are suspicious, your doctor may order a magnetic resonance imaging (MRI) or computed tomography (CT) scan.

- **Consider a laparoscopic exam.** A thin, lighted tube inserted via a small incision in the navel region allows the doctor to visually examine the ovaries.
- **Ask your doctor about preventive surgery.** Surgical removal of the ovaries (*oophorectomy*) reduces the odds of ovarian cancer by about 95%. (It does not provide 100% protection because microscopic cancer cells already may have existed prior to the surgery.) Insurance generally covers the cost.

Downside: If you are premenopausal, oophorectomy leads to abrupt menopause, which may cause severe hot flashes, mood swings and vaginal dryness. Hormone therapy can ease these symptoms—but may increase risk for breast cancer and heart disease.

AT SLIGHTLY INCREASED RISK

Even if you are not at high or intermediate-high risk, your chances of getting ovarian cancer may be above average. *Studies have linked increased risk with the following factors...*

- **Age.** Two-thirds of ovarian cancer patients are 55 or older.
- **Ethnicity.** The disease is most common among Caucasians.
- **Menstrual history.** Ovulation increases ovarian cancer risk. If you began to menstruate

before age 12 and/or reached menopause after age 55, your risk is greater.

•**No history of oral contraceptive use.** The Pill prevents ovulation, so women who have taken it for at least two years are at lower risk.

•**History of infertility.** This link may be due to increased ovulation and/or decreased progesterone.

•**History of endometriosis** (overgrowth of the tissue lining the uterus). The link is unclear but may be due to increased inflammation.

The more of these risk factors you have, the more vital it is to get annual pelvic exams. Also, ask your doctor if a CA-125 blood test and ultrasound are warranted for you.

AT AVERAGE RISK

Unfortunately, there is no reliable screening test for ovarian cancer that is appropriate for women who have no risk factors. Studies show that on average, periodic ultrasounds and/or CA-125 testing provide no benefit for women at average risk—no increased level of detection, no lower death rate from the disease—but do lead to unnecessary tests and even surgeries when small cysts are mistaken for cancer.

Several new blood and urine screening tests have received much publicity lately. Called *proteomics*, this emerging field of research seeks to identify biomarkers for ovarian cancer. But although the early news about these tests was promising, subsequent larger studies showed that none were effective in increasing cancer detection or survival.

Bottom line: If you're at average risk, the only recommended screening tool for ovarian cancer is the all-important annual pelvic exam.

■ ■ ■ ■

Powder Raises Risk for Ovarian Cancer

Researchers had theorized that inflammation of the ovaries could lead to ovarian tumors—but a recent study found no link.

What does raise risk: Family history...using talcum powder in the pelvic region...and endometriosis (in which the uterine lining migrates outside the uterus).

Penelope M. Webb, DPhil, researcher, Queensland Institute of Medical Research, Brisbane, Australia, and investigator on a study of more than 3,000 women, published in *International Journal of Cancer.*

■ ■ ■ ■

Robot Surgery—Better for Bladder Cancer

Robotic surgery is now being used to perform bladder removal procedures (*cystectomies*) that result in similar outcomes and fewer complications for bladder cancer patients compared with traditional open cystectomies. During the robotic procedure, the doctor makes several small incisions in the abdomen, inserts surgical instruments and a tiny camera and removes the bladder. A new channel is created for urine to pass from the body. The robotic procedure also spares the nerves, enabling men to return to normal sexual function after surgery.

If you have bladder cancer: Ask your doctor if robotic cystectomy is an option for you.

Douglas Scherr, MD, associate professor of urology, Weill Cornell Medical College of Cornell University, New York City.

■ ■ ■ ■

Less Invasive Surgery Effective for Colon Cancer

Surgeons usually perform open surgery—making large incisions in the abdominal wall—to view and remove cancerous colon tissue.

Recent finding: An analysis of 12 studies found no differences in rates of surgical complications, cancer recurrence or survival between open surgery and laparoscopic surgery, which involves much smaller incisions and the use of tiny cameras.

Bottom line: Consider a surgeon trained in laparoscopic surgery—it involves less pain and quicker recovery.

Esther Kuhry, MD, PhD, Namsos Hospital, Namsos, Norway, and leader of a review involving 3,346 patients, published in *The Cochrane Library.*

Best Ways to Prevent Colon Cancer

JoAnn E. Manson, MD, DrPH, is a professor of medicine and women's health at Harvard Medical School and chair of the division of preventive medicine at Brigham and Women's Hospital, both in Boston. She is one of the lead investigators for two highly influential studies on women's health—the Harvard Nurses' Health Study and the Women's Health Initiative. Dr. Manson is author, with Shari Bassuk, ScD, of *Hot Flashes, Hormones and Your Health* (McGraw-Hill).

As many as seven out of 10 cases of colorectal cancer could be prevented. While a few risk factors can't be helped—risk rises with age, a personal history of inflammatory bowel disease and/or colorectal *adenomas* (precancerous polyps), or a family history of adenomas or colorectal cancer—simple steps provide significant protection. *What the studies are suggesting...*

- **Get screened.** A doctor inserts a thin flexible tube with a tiny camera into the colon via the rectum to detect and remove adenomas and cancerous growths.

Problem: Only 43% of US women get the recommended screening.

Best: Get screened every five to 10 years starting at age 50. If you're at elevated risk, ask your doctor about starting earlier.

- **Boost vitamin D.** This may inhibit the growth of tumors and the blood vessels that feed them. Many doctors recommend taking at least 1,000 international units (IU) daily.

- **Eat folate-rich foods**—cruciferous and dark green leafy vegetables, beans, peas and citrus fruits. Folate promotes DNA replication and repair.

- **Cut back on meat.** Increasing consumption of red meat (beef, pork) and processed meat (cold cuts, hot dogs) by four ounces per day boosts colorectal cancer risk by about 28% and 36%, respectively.

Possible culprits: Iron, a pro-oxidant that damages DNA...growth-promoting hormones fed to the animals...carcinogenic compounds created during cooking or processing. Limit red and processed meat to two servings weekly.

- **Limit alcohol.** Colorectal cancer is 41% more common among women who consume three or more drinks daily than among nondrinkers. Alcohol may reduce the body's stores of folate.

Best: Have no more than one drink per day.

- **Don't smoke.** In a study of 469,019 women, colorectal cancer deaths were about 33% to 51% more common among current smokers who had smoked for 20 years or more than among women who never smoked. The sooner you quit, the sooner your risk will fall. For help, visit *www.smokefree.gov.*

- **Watch your weight.** More than 20% of colorectal cancers in US women are due to excess pounds, which contribute to insulin resistance (inability of cells to properly use the hormone insulin), inflammation and overgrowth of cells lining the gut.

- **Move your body.** Exercise helps balance levels of insulin and other hormones. It also speeds passage of food and bile salts through the gut, possibly shortening the exposure of intestinal walls to potential carcinogens.

Wise: Exercise 30 minutes or more daily.

- **Consider a daily aspirin.** This may reduce colorectal cancer risk when taken at 325 milligrams (mg) daily for 10 years or more. However, aspirin also increases risk for gastrointestinal bleeding —so talk to your doctor about weighing the benefits and risks.

When Heartburn Is Deadly

Anil Minocha, MD, professor of medicine at Louisiana State University and staff gastroenterologist and director of nutrition support at Overton Brooks VA Medical Center, both in Shreveport, Louisiana. He is author of *How to Stop Heartburn* (Wiley).

Nearly everyone suffers from heartburn from time to time, but frequent episodes (two or more times weekly) can signal a condition that must be taken seriously. Chronic heartburn, also known as gastroesophageal reflux disease (GERD), can lead to internal bleeding and scarring—even a deadly form of cancer. More than 20 million Americans have GERD.

Alarming finding: The number of people hospitalized for conditions related to GERD doubled between 1998 and 2005, according to the US government's Agency for Healthcare Research and Quality.

WHAT GOES WRONG

When you eat or drink, food and liquid move from your mouth to the esophagus, where a valve, called the lower esophageal sphincter, relaxes to allow the food and liquid to pass into your stomach. The lower esophageal sphincter then squeezes shut to keep stomach contents from backing up (a process known as reflux) into the esophagus.

Some degree of reflux occurs normally—including after meals. But when reflux becomes excessive, causes complications or affects quality of life, it is called GERD.

Symptoms that may be misdiagnosed: GERD—with or without heartburn—also can be characterized by chronic hoarseness or cough, sore throat or asthma, conditions that occur when gastric contents come in contact with the upper respiratory tract.

A LIFE-THREATENING DANGER

No one knows exactly why some people suffer from frequent reflux. But regardless of the cause, chronic reflux can lead to injury and bleeding in the esophagus, which sometimes affects swallowing. With time (sometimes just a few years), cells lining the esophagus can become precancerous as a result of chronic inflammation. This condition, known as Barrett's esophagus, can lead to esophageal cancer, which is often fatal and is the most rapidly increasing cancer in the US.

Important: Because GERD can lead to serious, even life-threatening complications, see a doctor if you have heartburn two or more times weekly—or if you have symptoms (difficulty swallowing, unexplained chronic cough or hoarseness) that don't respond to standard treatment, such as medication and lifestyle changes.

GETTING THE RIGHT DIAGNOSIS

A primary care doctor or gastroenterologist usually diagnoses GERD on the basis of the symptoms described earlier. In some cases, the doctor will perform endoscopy, in which a thin, flexible, fiber-optic tube is passed through the throat to examine the esophagus and upper part of the stomach.

Ask your doctor about: An esophageal acidity test. With this procedure, a tiny device is placed in the esophagus to monitor levels of acidity for 24 hours (very high levels usually indicate GERD). This test typically is used when a patient has not responded to treatment or has atypical symptoms (such as chronic cough or hoarseness).

BEST MEDICATION CHOICES

Over-the-counter (OTC) antacids, such as TUMS, Rolaids and Maalox, neutralize stomach acid and may help relieve heartburn, but they do not heal the injury to the esophagus caused by reflux.

People who have frequent heartburn usually get better results from acid-reducing prescription medication, such as H2 blockers, including *ranitidine* (Zantac) and *famotidine* (Pepcid), or proton pump inhibitors (PPIs), including *omeprazole* (Prilosec) and *esomeprazole* (Nexium). Some of these medications are available OTC.

Ask your doctor about: Potential side effects of long-term use of PPIs, which include reduced absorption of vitamin B-12, calcium and magnesium, higher risk for bone fractures and increased risk for respiratory infections.

SMALL CHANGES THAT HELP

If followed conscientiously, lifestyle changes can eliminate the need for medication in up to 20% of GERD sufferers. *My advice...*

- **Check your medications.** Calcium channel blockers and beta-blockers taken for high blood pressure or heart disease, as well as some antidepressants and anti-anxiety medication, can reduce lower esophageal sphincter (LES) pressure and may worsen GERD. If you have heartburn symptoms, ask the doctor who prescribed your medication about alternatives.
- **Modify your eating habits.** Small, frequent meals leave the stomach quickly, thus providing less opportunity for reflux.

Avoid foods that may worsen GERD: Onions, chocolate and fatty foods reduce LES pressure, allowing reflux to occur.

• **Sleep right.** If you're troubled by reflux when you sleep, place a foam wedge under the mattress or wooden blocks under the bedposts to elevate the head of your bed by four to six inches.

Important: Extra pillows under your head will not do the job. They will raise your head, but won't change the angle between your stomach contents and your LES.

ALTERNATIVE APPROACHES

Stress causes the LES to relax more often. This will increase the occurrence of reflux episodes. Practicing a regular stress-reduction technique, such as deep-breathing exercises, has been shown to reduce the amount of acid in the esophagus. *Also helpful...*

• **Acupuncture.** This ancient Chinese practice is most likely to help people diagnosed with "slow stomach"—that is, their GERD is worsened by food taking longer to leave the stomach. Acupuncture can improve the movement and emptying of stomach contents.

• **Probiotics,** such as *Lactobacillus acidophilus* and *Lactobacillus bifidus,* are "friendly" bacteria that reduce the harmful effects of acid in the esophagus.

My advice: Eat yogurt or kefir containing "live, active" cultures twice daily.

THE SURGICAL OPTION

Surgery usually is an option if drug treatment and alternative approaches have failed.

In the standard procedure, called *fundoplication*, part of the upper stomach is wrapped around the LES to strengthen it. This operation can be performed with tiny incisions (laparoscopically), rather than by opening the chest.

In one study of 100 individuals, 90% expressed overall satisfaction with the surgery. Although 80% continued to take anti-reflux medications, most took lower doses than before the surgery. Some new procedures, which involve injections or sutures to tighten the LES, are promising but as yet unproven.

Important Alcohol–Esophageal Cancer Link Will Save Lives

PLoS Medicine news release.

People who experience facial flushing when they drink alcohol are much more likely to develop alcohol-related esophageal cancer, say American and Japanese experts.

ENZYME DEFICIENCY LINKED TO CANCER

Facial flushing, nausea and increased heart rate when drinking alcohol occurs in about a third of East Asians (Chinese, Japanese and Koreans), mainly due to an inherited deficiency in an enzyme called *aldehyde dehydrogenase 2* (ALDH2). There is increasing evidence that people with this deficiency are at much higher risk for alcohol-related esophageal cancer (specifically squamous cell carcinoma) than people with fully active ALDH2, the experts wrote in an article in *PLoS Medicine.*

ESOPHAGEAL CANCER ONE OF DEADLIEST

However, many doctors and people with alcohol-flushing response aren't aware of this increased risk. This lack of awareness is "unfortunate as esophageal cancer is one of the deadliest cancers worldwide, with five-year survival rates of 15.6% in the United States, 12.3% in Europe and 31.6% in Japan," noted Phillip Brooks, PhD, and colleagues at the US National Institute on Alcohol Abuse and Alcoholism, and Akira Yokoyama, MD, of the Kurihama Alcohol Center in Japan.

BE AWARE OF FLUSHING FROM ALCOHOL

"Our goal in writing this article is to inform doctors firstly that their ALDH2-deficient patients have an increased risk for esophageal cancer if they drink moderate amounts of alcohol, and secondly, that the alcohol flushing response is a biomarker for the ALDH2 deficiency," according to the researchers.

ALDH2 deficiency can be determined by asking patients about previous episodes of alcohol-induced flushing, the experts said.

"As a result, ALDH2-deficient patients can then be counseled to reduce alcohol consumption, and high-risk patients can be assessed for endoscopic cancer screening," Dr. Brooks and colleagues said.

REDUCING RATES OF ESOPHAGEAL CANCER

There are about 540 million people worldwide with ALDH2 deficiency, which means even a minor reduction in the rate of alcohol-related esophageal cancers would save a large number of lives.

info For more information about esophageal cancer, visit the Web site of the Mayo Clinic, *www.mayoclinic.com,* and search "esophageal cancer."

Pamper Your Pancreas

R. Matthew Walsh, MD, vice chairman of surgery in the department of hepato-pancreatic-biliary surgery at the Cleveland Clinic in Cleveland, Ohio. He has published numerous scientific papers on pancreatic disease, gastrointestinal surgery and related topics.

Acute pancreatitis (inflammation of the pancreas) causes telltale symptoms that are usually unforgettable for the sufferer. The pancreas is a gland that produces hormones (insulin and glucagon) that are needed to store and mobilize glucose, the body's primary energy source. The pancreas also pumps out digestive juices that break down proteins, fats and carbohydrates.

An attack typically comes on suddenly and triggers searing pain in the upper abdomen, often spreading to the back. Eating makes the pain worse. Nausea and vomiting are common.

Acute pancreatitis is a medical emergency. Most people get better after a few days in the hospital, but in about 5% of cases, the condition is fatal due to such complications as infection, breathing problems and kidney failure. *Common causes...*

- **Gallstones** can block the duct that carries bile (fluid secreted by the liver and stored in the gallbladder) and pancreatic secretions into the digestive system. These secretions back up into the pancreas, activating its enzymes. Surgery may be necessary to remove gallstones blocking the pancreatic duct.

Self-defense: If you have gallstones that have caused symptoms, such as pain in the upper middle or right part of the abdomen and nausea and/or vomiting, consider having your gallbladder removed.

- **Alcohol** can damage the liver and, in some people, it can harm the pancreas. Binge drinking (beer, wine or whiskey) often triggers the attack.

Self-defense: If you drink excessively (more than two drinks daily for men and more than one drink daily for women), abstain from alcoholic beverages.

- **Medications,** such as antibiotics, corticosteroids and diuretics, can, in rare cases, lead to acute pancreatitis.

Self-defense: If you experience an attack shortly after you started taking a drug, ask your doctor whether there is another medication that you can take instead. *Other conditions affecting the pancreas...*

CHRONIC PANCREATITIS

Chronic pancreatitis may follow repeated episodes of acute pancreatitis, or result from an inherited abnormality in the anatomy of the gland, but 70% of cases are caused by prolonged alcohol abuse.

Most of the time, chronic pancreatitis results in pain that flares up periodically over months or even years. Weight loss is common, because the pancreas cannot produce enough enzymes to break down food. Chronic pancreatitis is often difficult to diagnose—abdominal pain is common to any number of disorders, and blood tests may not detect abnormalities.

Latest development: A test known as *endoscopic retrograde cholangiopancreatography* helps doctors diagnose chronic pancreatitis. With this test, the doctor passes a thin tube through the stomach and into the small intestine. Dye is injected to make the bile and pancreatic ducts visible on an X-ray.

Tests that assess pancreatic function, which is measured by determining if the pancreas is producing the appropriate levels of digestive enzymes, also help make the diagnosis.

New thinking: Only recently have doctors begun to appreciate that in some people chronic pancreatitis is an autoimmune disorder—the body's tissues attack the gland for unknown reasons (as occurs with rheumatoid arthritis or lupus). This type of chronic pancreatitis can be diagnosed with a blood test and treated with drugs, such as steroids, that help reduce inflammation.

For most cases of chronic pancreatitis, there is no medical cure. A low-fat diet and pain medication may reduce symptoms. Also, pancreatic enzyme pills can be taken with meals to aid the absorption of nutrients. When symptoms do not improve with these approaches, a surgical procedure to drain secretions from the pancreas or remove diseased parts of the gland is performed.

Treatment advances: Patients who do not respond to other treatments may be candidates for removal of the pancreas. This can be followed by transplantation of insulin-producing cells (islet cells) from the patient's own cells or from another person into the patient's liver—a minor outpatient procedure that can be performed with a local anesthetic. Another option is a pancreas transplant—this is major surgery that requires a one- to three-week hospital stay.

CANCER OF THE PANCREAS

Each year, about 30,000 Americans are diagnosed with pancreatic cancer. The risk for pancreatic cancer is two to three times higher for smokers. Chronic pancreatitis also increases the risk.

Early-stage pancreatic cancer rarely produces symptoms, and when they do appear, they are usually vague—mid- or upper-abdominal pain, weight loss and fatigue. Only 5% of patients survive five years after diagnosis, primarily because the malignancy is difficult to detect before it spreads.

Caution: If you develop diabetes later in life (after age 60), ask your doctor to evaluate you for pancreatic cancer. Pancreatic cancer is diagnosed twice as often in people who have developed diabetes than it is in those without diabetes—particularly in the two years after diabetes appears.

If pancreatic cancer runs in your family: You should consider screening if you have two first-degree relatives (such as a parent or sibling) who have had pancreatic cancer. Screening strategies include annual endoscopic ultrasound and biopsies of the pancreas.

Recent finding: A study in the journal *Annals of Surgery* found that fewer than one-third of people diagnosed with early-stage pancreatic cancer—a time when treatment may be most effective—actually have surgery to remove the pancreas. Patients were less likely to be offered surgery if they were treated at community hospitals, rather than major cancer centers. They also were less likely to be offered surgery if they were older than age 65.

info To find a medical center with expertise in treating pancreatic cancer, consult the list of Comprehensive Cancer Centers designated by the National Cancer Institute (800-422-6237, *http://cancercenters.cancer.gov*).

■ ■ ■ ■

A Big Belly Raises Pancreatic Cancer Risk Among Women

Obese women who carry weight in their midsections are 70% more likely to develop pancreatic cancer. Obesity also has been linked to breast, colon and other cancers.

Juhua Luo, PhD, department of medical epidemiology and biostatistics, Karolinska Institute, Stockholm, Sweden, and leader of a study of 251 women, published in *British Journal of Cancer.*

■ ■ ■ ■

Antibiotics that Prevent Stomach Cancer

The *Helicobacter pylori* bacterium causes chronic stomach inflammation and peptic ulcers, which can progress to gastric cancer.

Recent finding: The sooner antibiotics are given, the more effectively they reverse cell damage that leads to cancer, animal studies show.

Best: See your doctor without delay if you have *H. pylori* symptoms—persistent abdominal pain, bloating, tarry stool—especially if you have a family history of peptic ulcers or gastric cancer.

James G. Fox, DVM, director, division of comparative medicine, Massachusetts Institute of Technology, Boston, and coauthor of a study published in *Cancer Research*.

The Anticancer Diet From a Doctor Who Survived Cancer

David Servan-Schreiber, MD, PhD, a neuroscientist and clinical professor of psychiatry at University of Pittsburgh School of Medicine. He is cofounder of the university's Center for Integrative Medicine and author of *Anticancer: A New Way of Life* (Viking). *www.anticancerbook.com.*

At any given time, the average person might have thousands of cancer cells in his/her body. Individually, these abnormal cells are harmless, but any one of them could potentially proliferate and form a mass of cells (in other words, a tumor) that damages normal tissues and can spread to other parts of the body. About one-third of us will eventually get full-fledged cancer.

Often people who get cancer have created impairments in their natural defenses, allowing cancer cells to survive and proliferate. About 85% of all cancers are caused by environmental and lifestyle factors. We can't always control our environments, but we can control what we eat. Diet is one key factor that determines who gets cancer and who doesn't.

Example: Asian men have just as many precancerous microtumors in the prostate gland as American men, yet they are as much as 60 times less likely to develop prostate cancer. It's not a coincidence that their diets are far healthier, on average, than those consumed by men in the US. Asian men eat far more fruits and vegetables than Americans and relatively little red meat. They also tend to eat more fish and soy foods, and they drink more tea, especially green tea. These and other dietary factors allow their immune systems and other natural defenses to prevent cancer cells from proliferating.

My story: I was a physician in Pittsburgh when I was first diagnosed with a brain tumor in 1992. With the benefit of hindsight—and years of research into the origins and development of cancer—I have come to understand that my previous lifestyle, particularly my poor diet, fostered a procancer environment. For example, a typical lunch for me was chili con carne, a plain bagel and a can of Coke.

CAUSES OF CANCER

It can take years for cancer cells to turn into tumors—assuming that they ever do. This lag time means that we have many opportunities to create an anticancer environment in our bodies.

There are three main factors that promote the development of cancer...

- **Weakened immunity.** The immune system normally patrols the body for bacteria and viruses, as well as for cancer cells. When it spots something foreign, it dispatches a variety of cells, including natural killer cells, to destroy the foreign substance. In people who eat an unhealthy diet—not enough produce, too much alcohol, very little fish and so on—the immune system works less efficiently. This means that cancer cells can potentially slip under the radar and eventually proliferate.
- **Inflammation.** Millions of Americans have subclinical chronic inflammation. It doesn't cause symptoms, but it can lead to heart disease and cancer. Chronic inflammation can be caused by infection, a diet low in antioxidant nutrients and even emotional stress. It's accompanied by the release of *cytokines* and other inflammatory chemicals. Inflammation also prevents the immune system from working efficiently.
- **Angiogenesis.** Cancer cells, like other cells in the body, need blood and nourishment to survive. They send out chemical signals that stimulate the growth of blood vessels that carry blood to and from the cancer.

This process is called *angiogenesis*—and it can be strongly influenced by what we eat.

Example: People who eat no more than 12 ounces of red meat weekly can reduce their overall risk for cancer by 30%. Red meat stimulates the release of inflammatory chemicals that inhibit *apoptosis,* the genetically programmed cell death that prevents uncontrolled growth.

CANCER FIGHTERS

The best cancer-fighting foods...

•**Fatty fish.** The omega-3 fatty acids in fish reduce inflammation. Oncologists in Scotland have measured inflammatory markers in the blood of cancer patients since the 1990s. They have found that patients with the lowest levels of inflammation are twice as likely to live through the next several years as patients who have more inflammation.

Laboratory studies indicate that a high-fish diet can reduce the growth of lung, breast, colon, prostate and kidney cancers. Naturally, people who eat more fish tend to eat less red meat.

Important: The larger fatty fish, such as tuna, are more likely to be contaminated with mercury and other toxins. The best sources of omega-3s are smaller fatty fish, such as sardines, anchovies and small mackerel.

•**Low-glycemic carbohydrates.** The glycemic index measures the effects of the carbohydrates in foods on blood glucose levels. Foods with a high glycemic index, such as white bread and table sugar, cause a rapid rise in insulin as well as a rise in insulin-like growth factor (IGF). IGF stimulates cell growth, including the growth of cancer cells. Both insulin and IGF also promote inflammation.

Data from the Harvard Nurses' Health Study indicate that people who eat the most high-glycemic foods (these same people tend to be sedentary and overweight) are 260% more likely to get pancreatic cancer and 80% more likely to get colorectal cancer.

Recommended: Unprocessed carbohydrates that are low on the glycemic scale, such as whole-grain breakfast cereals and breads (with whole wheat, barley, oats, flaxseeds, etc.)... cooked whole grains, such as millet, quinoa and barley...and vegetables, such as broccoli, cauliflower and peppers.

Also important: Reduce or eliminate refined sugar as well as honey.

Better: Agave nectar, available at most health food stores. Extracted from cactus sap, it's sweeter than sugar or honey, yet it has a glycemic index four to five times lower. You can use agave nectar just as you would sugar or honey—by adding it to cereals, tea and so on. Because of the liquid content of the syrup, you'll generally want to reduce the amount of other liquids in baked goods. Substitute three-quarter cup of agave nectar per one cup of any other sweetener.

•**Green tea.** Between three and five cups daily can significantly reduce your cancer risk. A chemical in green tea, *epigallocatechin gallate* (EGCG), inhibits angiogenesis. Green tea also contains *polyphenols* and other chemical compounds that reduce inflammation and activate liver enzymes that break down and eliminate potential carcinogens.

In men who already have prostate cancer, consuming five cups or more of green tea daily has been associated with reduced risk of progressing to advanced cancer by 50%. In women with certain types of breast cancer, three cups daily reduced relapses by 30%. Because black tea is fermented, it has a lower concentration of polyphenols and is less protective than green tea.

•**Soy foods.** The *isoflavones* in tofu, soy milk, edamame (green soybeans) and other soy foods help prevent breast cancer, particularly in women who started eating soy early in life. These compounds, known as *phytoestrogens*, have estrogen-like effects. They occupy the same cellular receptors as the body's estrogen yet are only about one-hundredth as active. This means that they may slow the development of estrogen-dependent tumors.

Recommended: Three servings of soy per week—but only for women who are cancer-free. Avoid soy if you have or had cancer—there's some concern that the estrogen-like compounds in soy might promote tumor growth in women who have a type of breast cancer that is sensitive to estrogen's effects.

•**Turmeric.** No other food ingredient has more powerful anti-inflammatory effects. In laboratory studies, the active ingredient curcumin in the spice turmeric inhibits the growth of many different cancers. It helps prevent angiogenesis and promotes the death of cancer cells.

In India, people consume an average of one-quarter to one-half teaspoon of turmeric daily. They experience one-eighth as many lung cancers as Westerners of the same age...one-ninth as many colon cancers...and one-fifth as many breast cancers.

•**Asian mushrooms,** such as shiitake, maitake and enokitake. They're available in most supermarkets and gourmet stores and are one of the most potent immune system stimulants. Among people who eat a lot of these mushrooms, the rate of stomach cancer is 50% lower than it is among those who don't eat them. One to two half-cup servings weekly probably is enough to have measureable effects.

•**Berries.** Berries contain *ellagic acid,* which strongly inhibits angiogenesis. Aim for one-half cup per day.

•**Dark chocolate.** One ounce contains twice as many polyphenols as a glass of red wine and almost as much as a cup of green tea. Laboratory studies indicate that these compounds slow the growth of cancer cells.

Look for a chocolate with more than 70% cocoa. The "lighter" milk chocolates don't contain adequate amounts of polyphenols—and the dairy component of milk chocolate blocks the absorption of polyphenols.

Breakthrough Cancer Fighter—Wheat Germ Extract

Mark A. Stengler, ND, naturopathic physician in private practice, La Jolla, California...adjunct associate clinical professor at the National College of Natural Medicine, Portland, Oregon...author of many books, including *The Natural Physician's Healing Therapies* and coauthor of *Prescription for Natural Cures* (both from Bottom Line Books)...and author of the *Bottom Line/Natural Healing* newsletter.

Wheat germ was one of the original health foods. The "germ" is the most nutritious part of the wheat seed. Today fermented wheat germ extract (FWGE) is showing promise as a potential breakthrough for treating cancer patients.

The evidence: A number of cell, animal and human studies support the use and benefits of FWGE as an adjunct therapy, meaning one that is used as part of a broader treatment program.

•**Colorectal cancer.** A study of 170 patients who had received conventional treatments for colorectal cancer found that those who also took 9 grams (g) of FWGE daily for six months had less risk of developing new cancers. The cancer spread among only 8% of the patients receiving FWGE, compared with 23% of those getting only conventional treatment.

•**Oral cancer.** Researchers compared 22 patients with oral cancer who took FWGE with 21 patients not receiving the supplement. FWGE reduced the risk for cancer progression by 85%.

•**Melanoma.** For one year, FWGE was given to 22 patients with advanced (stage 3) melanoma, and their progress was compared with 24 similar patients not receiving FWGE. Patients taking FWGE were half as likely to die from melanoma during this time.

•**Chemotherapy-induced infections.** Researchers studied 22 children and teenagers with different types of cancer. The 11 children who received FWGE had significantly fewer infections and fevers while receiving chemotherapy.

•**Animal studies.** Many studies suggest benefits from FWGE for leukemia as well as breast, ovarian, gastric and thyroid cancers. In one study, laboratory rats received both FWGE and vitamin C in the treatment of lung, skin and colon cancers. The combination prevented the cancer from spreading, but vitamin C alone did not. In another study, FWGE worked better alone than it did with vitamin C to treat kidney cancer.

HOW IT WORKS

FWGE appears to work by starving cancer cells of glucose, prompting their death...and by enhancing immune cell activity. Wheat germ contains chemicals that seem to have anticancer properties, and fermentation increases their concentration.

Note: FWGE is very different from the regular wheat germ you can buy at health food stores. It comes in a powder and is sold in health food stores and on-line.

Good brands: Avemar (*www.avemar-alternativetherapy.com*) and OncoMar (800-647-6100, *www.xymogen.com*).

MY ADVICE

If you would like to begin taking FWGE, check with your physician about incorporating it into your treatment program. I recommend one packet a day, which equals 9 g. You can mix it into a glass of cold water and then drink it —or substitute a non-citrus juice, such as apple or cranberry (citrus can deactivate FWGE's active ingredient).

FWGE is not cheap—it costs about $160/month—but I think the expense is worth it, given the early indications that it may improve cancer survival rates.

Good news: FWGE is generally safe, and any side effects, such as diarrhea and flatulence, occur only occasionally.

Natural Ways to Ease Chemo Side Effects

Jamison Starbuck, ND, a naturopathic physician in family practice in Missoula, Montana. She is past president of the American Association of Naturopathic Physicians and a contributing editor to *The Alternative Advisor: The Complete Guide to Natural Therapies and Alternative Treatments* (Time-Life).

Chemotherapy can be lifesaving for cancer patients, but because it is very strong medication, it is rife with troubling—sometimes debilitating—side effects. Among the most common are nausea, mouth sores, diarrhea or constipation, and neuropathy (nerve pain). Pain medications, antinausea drugs and stool softeners are among the treatments that conventional doctors prescribe most often to manage these side effects. However, there are other options. In my patients undergoing chemotherapy, I've used several natural medicines that have proven to be highly effective while also being safe and relatively free of side effects.

It's crucial to remember that natural therapies should never be used during chemotherapy without the consent of an oncologist (medical doctor who specializes in cancer treatment). In a recent study, researchers found in a laboratory trial that vitamin C rendered chemotherapy less effective—perhaps due to the vitamin's antioxidant properties, which can counteract the drug's ability to kill cancer cells. This subject is hotly debated among cancer researchers, and more studies are needed for us to understand the action of vitamin C in cancer treatment.

Meanwhile, if you are suffering from chemotherapy side effects, ask your oncologist about the following natural therapies (supplements and homeopathic preparations are available at health food stores), which have been well studied and have been shown to be effective...

Acidophilus and ***bifidus*** are probiotics—"friendly" bacteria in the intestinal tract. Chemo typically reduces these bacteria, making patients more susceptible to gastrointestinal problems such as yeast infections (candidiasis).

My advice: Begin a regimen of acidophilus and bifidus supplements five days before the first chemo treatment and continue for at least one month after chemotherapy ends. A typical dose is four billion units of acidophilus and two billion units of bifidobacteria twice daily, taken with food.

Acupuncture has been shown in studies to reduce the nausea so often caused by chemotherapy. Some cancer centers now have acupuncturists on staff.

My advice: If you suffer from chemo-induced nausea, ask your oncologist to refer you to a licensed acupuncturist.

Glutamine is a naturally occurring amino acid that helps to repair and regenerate the lining of the gastrointestinal tract. It has been shown to reduce mouth sores and gastrointestinal irritation caused by chemotherapy.

My advice: For one minute, swish a mixture of 4 grams (g) of glutamine powder, dissolved in room-temperature water, in the mouth, then swallow it. Do this twice daily while undergoing chemotherapy. People with kidney or liver disease should not use glutamine.

Traumeel is a homeopathic therapy that helps ease chemo-induced neuropathy.

My advice: Take two drops of the liquid form in one ounce of water three times daily or one tablet under the tongue three times daily during chemotherapy. Traumeel is manufactured by Heel (800-621-7644, *www.heelusa.com*).

The Amazing Cancer Recovery Diet

Mitchell Gaynor, MD, clinical professor of medicine at Weill Cornell Medical College of Cornell University and founder and president of Gaynor Integrative Oncology, both in New York City. He is author of several books, including *Nurture Nature/Nurture Health* (Nurture Nature), and *Sounds of Healing: A Physician Reveals the Therapeutic Power of Sound, Voice and Music* (Broadway). *www.gaynoroncology.com.*

When you are facing cancer, it is more important than ever to follow a nutritious diet that strengthens your immune system and helps your body detoxify. This often is challenging, however, because some cancer treatments interfere with the body's ability to take in or use nutrients. *Cancer patients undergoing chemotherapy and/or radiation often experience...*

- **Damage to salivary glands resulting in a dry mouth,** difficulty swallowing and unpleasant changes in taste.
- **Nausea and vomiting.**
- **Impaired absorption of nutrients and calories** due to changes in the normal intestinal bacteria.

These factors and the resulting loss of appetite deplete the body's stores of nutrients and can lead to excessive weight loss that impedes your recovery, strains your immune system and adds to fatigue.

The following nutrition plan is designed for cancer patients undergoing treatment—as well as for those who finished treatment within the past year—to help rebuild nutrient reserves. All supplements below are sold at health-food stores and/or online.

Important: Discuss your diet and supplement use with your oncologist—this helps the doctor determine the best treatment and follow-up regimen for you. *What to do...*

- **Eat plenty of protein.** Protein helps repair body tissues and prevent unwanted weight loss. It also helps minimize the memory and concentration problems ("chemo brain") common among patients on chemotherapy. The recommended dietary allowance (RDA) for women is 38 grams (g) of protein per day and for men it is 46 g—but for cancer patients, I recommend at least 70 g per day.

Example: With breakfast, include one egg (7 g) and eight ounces of unsweetened soy milk (8 g)...with lunch, a cup of lentil soup (10 g) and eight ounces of low-fat yogurt (12 g)...as a snack, two ounces of almonds (12 g)...with dinner, three ounces of chicken or fish (21 g) or one cup of soybeans (29 g).

Helpful: Consider a protein supplement—such as Biochem Sports Greens & Whey, which provides 20 g of protein per one-ounce serving.

Have eight ounces of low-fat yogurt or kefir daily. Check labels and choose unsweetened brands with live, active cultures of lactobacillus acidophilus and bifidobacterium. Chemotherapy and radiation destroy beneficial bacteria in the gut. Restoring them with probiotics helps alleviate nausea, optimizes immune system function and reduces production of cancer-promoting chemicals.

Alternative: Try a probiotic supplement that contains at least one billion colony-forming units (CFUs) per gram. Choose coated capsules to protect the probiotics from stomach acids. Take on an empty stomach upon awakening and also one hour before lunch and dinner.

Good brand: Natren Healthy Trinity (866-462-8736, *www.natren.com*).

- **Boost fiber.** This combats constipation, a common side effect of chemotherapy. Aim for six to 10 servings of whole grains daily.

Examples: One slice of whole-grain bread ...one-half cup of cooked brown rice, rolled barley, millet or buckwheat...one-half cup of old-fashioned oatmeal.

Also eat seven to 10 servings of fruits and vegetables daily, which provide fiber and cancer-fighting *phytonutrients* (plant chemicals). If you have lost your taste for vegetables, have juice instead—it is easier to swallow. Carrots, celery, watercress and beets make delicious juices. Juicers are sold at kitchenware stores ($50 to $150).

- **Focus on anti-inflammatory foods.** The same enzyme that causes inflammation also may increase levels of compounds that allow cancer cells to grow. Lowering the body's inflammatory response may be protective.

Best: Eat cold-water fish (salmon, sardines, herring, mackerel, cod) at least three times per week—these are rich in anti-inflammatory omega-3 fatty acids. I recommend avoiding tuna, swordfish and shark, which may contain mercury and other contaminants.

Alternative: Take 2.5 g of a fish oil daily with food.

Also helpful: Use curry powder liberally to spice up vegetables, meats and poultry—it is a natural anti-inflammatory.

- **Eat foods rich in calcium, magnesium and vitamin D.** These bone-building nutrients are especially important for cancer patients who take steroid medication to control nausea, because steroids can weaken bones. Increase your intake of foods that provide calcium (low-fat dairy, fortified cereals, leafy green vegetables)...magnesium (nuts, beans, quinoa)...and vitamin D (fish, fortified dairy). Also supplement daily with 1,500 mg of calcium citrate...400 mg of magnesium...and 1,000 international units (IU) of vitamin D-3.
- **Minimize intake of sugar and white flour.** Eating these foods temporarily increases your levels of insulin-like growth factor (IGF), which has hormonelike effects. Although the long-term consequences are unclear, some research suggests a link between high IGF levels and cancer, especially of the breast and colon.
- **Drink plenty of fluids.** Dehydration contributes to decreased salivation...promotes inflammation...and stresses the kidneys and liver, making it harder for these organs to detoxify the body. Drink at least six eight-ounce glasses of water, broth or tea per day.

Beneficial: Green tea contains compounds that may inhibit angiogenesis (creation of blood vessels that feed cancer cells).

- **Opt for organic.** Conventionally grown produce often has pesticide and herbicide residues that stress the liver. Choose organic free-range chicken and beef from grass-fed cows to minimize exposure to antibiotics and hormones in the feed of nonorganic animals. Remove the skin from poultry and fish before cooking, even if organic—skin tends to store a high concentration of toxins.

Helpful: A dietitian who specializes in oncology nutrition can help monitor your nutrient intake and recommend alternatives if certain foods are difficult to eat.

Referrals: American Dietetic Association, 800-877-1600, *www.eatright.org.*

New Studies Show Cell-Phone Users at Greater Risk for Cancer

David O. Carpenter, MD, director of the Institute for Health and the Environment and a professor in the department of environmental health sciences at the University at Albany, both in Rensselaer, New York. He coauthored the scientific paper "Setting Prudent Public Health Policy for Electromagnetic Field Exposures," which appeared in *Reviews on Environmental Health.*

Until recently, there was no long-term scientific evidence that cell phones posed any health threats.

Now: Research that raises questions about cell-phone safety has begun to emerge. As a precaution, Germany, France and India, among other countries, have recommended limiting exposure to radiation from cell phones.

The wireless communication industry and other commercial groups have argued that the recent scientific findings about possible dangers from cell phones are inconclusive. Some doctors agree.

So, what is the truth?

David O. Carpenter, MD, a renowned expert on the health risks associated with exposure to electromagnetic radiation, shared his thoughts on the subject...

What is radiation, and what are the most common sources? Radiation refers to energy that occurs in the form of electromagnetic waves (produced by man-made sources, such as X-rays) or particles (found in natural radioactive substances, such as uranium). All radiation is part of an electromagnetic spectrum that has various frequencies and wavelengths, ranging from high to low.

Scientists agree that high-frequency (ionizing) radiation, such as that found in X-rays, can break chemical bonds in the body and damage DNA, potentially causing cancer and birth defects. Ultraviolet (UV) rays from the sun, another form of ionizing radiation, are known to increase skin cancer risk.

But there is controversy about the health effects from lower-frequency (nonionizing) radiation. This includes radio-frequency radiation from cell phones and extremely low frequency radiation from power lines and electrical appliances.

Why don't scientists agree about the health effects of exposure to nonionizing radiation? In my view, there are many reasons, from the economic and political clout of the communications and electrical power industries to our society's heavy reliance on technologies that emit these types of radiation.

But one primary reason for the controversy is the assertion by many physicists that nonionizing radiation cannot have a biological effect because it does not have enough energy to heat tissue—what they call a "thermal" effect. Cell phones, for example, must use radio-frequency radiation levels that do not cause measurable heating.

However, there is scientific evidence suggesting that nonionizing radiation can have biological effects—even if radiation levels do not produce a thermal effect. These include breakage of DNA structure, which can lead to cell mutations and, in turn, to cancer. In addition, studies have linked cell-phone radiation to poor sperm quality and/or reduced sperm count.

What is the scientific evidence linking cell-phone use to cancer? The *American Journal of Epidemiology* published findings from researchers in Israel who compared the lifetime cell-phone use of 1,300 healthy adults with 500 adults who were newly diagnosed with benign or malignant tumors of the salivary gland. The researchers found a 50% greater risk for such a tumor in heavy cell-phone users who usually held the phone on the side of the head where the tumor developed. Also recently, Swedish researchers who analyzed several studies found a doubling of risk for acoustic neuroma (a tumor of the auditory nerve) and glioma (a potentially deadly brain tumor) after 10 years of heavy cell-phone use.

Why do you believe this research is more credible than that cited by the wireless industry and some doctors who say there is no proof that cell phones are harmful? It's true that there are no definitive studies showing that cell phones cause cancer or other health problems, but there also is no proof that cell phones are absolutely safe. The existing evidence is based on observational studies that look for health effects associated with certain behaviors, including cell-phone use.

The research results have been mixed—that is, some studies have found no health risks associated with cell-phone use, while some other studies (especially the more recent and longer-term ones) have. A definitive study—though admittedly impractical—would have to measure all aspects of electromagnetic field exposure (including that from power lines, appliances, cell phones and radio and television transmission) over a decade or more.

Based on the current evidence, do you believe that people should take steps to limit their exposure to nonionizing electromagnetic radiation? Yes. There is no reason to wait until scientists have dotted every "i" and crossed every "t" before you take action to minimize your exposure. Young children—whose brains and bodies are still developing and therefore are more vulnerable to electromagnetic exposure—are particularly at risk.

What are your recommendations for cell phones? The key principle to remember is that exposure to electromagnetic radiation declines as you increase your distance from the source.

For cell phones, I recommend using these devices only when absolutely necessary and when a corded landline phone is not available.

Seven Ways to Keep Your Cell Phone from Harming Your Health

Ronald B. Herberman, MD, is the director of the University of Pittsburgh Cancer Institute, a National Cancer Institute–designated Comprehensive Cancer Center. He is also associate vice chancellor for cancer research, Health Sciences, Hillman professor of oncology and professor of medicine at the University of Pittsburgh School of Medicine.

The director of the University of Pittsburgh Cancer Institute (UPCI) recently issued a memo warning faculty members and staff about possible dangers associated with long-term cell-phone use. The memo is based on the UPCI's analysis of the existing data. *Key points...**

• **Use the speaker-phone mode, whenever possible, or a wireless Bluetooth headset, which produces significantly less electromagnetic emission than a normal cell phone.** Use of an earpiece attachment (with a wire) also may reduce radiation exposure. (More research is needed on such earpieces.)

• **Avoid carrying your cell phone on your body.** If you must do so, make sure that the cell phone's keypad is positioned toward your body so that the transmitted electromagnetic fields move away from you. (Even when not in use, cell phones continue to connect to relay antennas. This will expose the user to electromagnetic radiation.)

• **Use text messaging rather than making a call, whenever possible.** This limits the duration of exposure and the proximity to the body.

• **Do not keep your cell phone near your body at night**—for example, under the pillow or on a bedside table—particularly if you're pregnant. Keep the phone at least three feet away.

• **Avoid using your cell phone when the signal is weak or when moving at high speed,** such as in a car or train—this automatically increases the phone's power as it repeatedly attempts to establish a connection to a new relay antenna.

• **Choose a cell phone with the lowest possible Specific Absorption Rate (SAR),** which is a measure of the strength of the magnetic field absorbed by the body. (Check the phone manual or Web sites, such as *http://reviews.cnet.com*, that review technology products. In the US, the SAR value limit is 1.6 watts per kilogram.)

*To read the complete list of recommendations, go to the UPCI Web site, *www.upci.upmc.edu*.

5

Diabetes Update

Low Blood Sugar May Raise Dementia Risk

Older individuals with type 2 diabetes who have been hospitalized with severe low blood sugar levels seem to have a greater risk of developing dementia, new research suggests.

It's not yet clear whether less severe episodes of low blood sugar, which are more common, are also linked with an increased dementia risk, according to a study in *The Journal of the American Medical Association* (JAMA).

The issue is an important one, with an ever-growing population of people suffering from type 2 diabetes. In the United States alone, some 24 million people have the condition, with lots more to come as the population ages.

Hypoglycemic episodes are marked by dizziness, fainting and even seizures.

THE STUDY

Researchers followed 16,667 patients with type 2 diabetes, average age 65, from 1980 to 2007. Twenty-two years of the follow-up were devoted to chronicling hypoglycemic episodes, and more than four years were spent following dementia diagnoses.

THE RESULTS

"Hypoglycemic episodes that were severe enough to require hospitalization or an emergency-room visit were associated with a greater risk of dementia, particularly for patients who had multiple episodes. And these findings, a little bit to our surprise, were independent of glycemic control," said study author Rachel A. Whitmer, PhD, a research scientist at Kaiser

---

Teleconference with Rachel A. Whitmer, PhD, research scientist, division of research, Kaiser Permanente, Oakland, California.

Nir Barzilai, MD, director, Institute for Aging Research, Albert Einstein College of Medicine and the Montefiore Hospital Diabetes Clinic, New York City.

Michael Horseman, PharmD, associate professor, pharmacy practice, Texas A&M Health Science Center, Irma Lerma Rangel College of Pharmacy, College Station.

The Journal of the American Medical Association.

Permanente in Oakland, California. "Episodes of hypoglycemia may be associated with neurological consequences in patients already at risk for dementia. This study seems to suggest that hypoglycemia is one of the reasons people with type 2 diabetes are at a higher risk for dementia. It also adds to the evidence base that balance of glycemic control is a critical issue, and particularly for the elderly."

People with type 2 diabetes are at a 32% greater risk for dementia, although the reasons for that are not clear. People with prediabetes are also at greater risk, Dr. Whitmer noted.

POSSIBLE EXPLANATIONS

The association that was found could be attributable to any of a number of possible mechanisms, including accelerated death of nerve cells in the brain or reduced blood supply to the brain, the authors stated. Such a link could also be a result of too much insulin over time, again possibly contributing to neuronal damage or other brain changes.

However, the study looks at association only, and doesn't actually prove any cause-and-effect link between the two conditions, cautioned Nir Barzilai, MD, director of the Institute for Aging Research at Albert Einstein College of Medicine and the Montefiore Hospital Diabetes Clinic in New York City.

"It could be fluctuation of glucose. We know that hyperglycemia [high blood sugar] is also very toxic to the cells. All those things cannot be dissected on a study like this," he said.

Dr. Whitmer also noted that hypoglycemia is likely only one reason for the heightened risk of dementia in individuals with type 2 diabetes.

But the whole picture is likely to be much more complicated, Dr. Barzilai said. "The glucose concentrations in the brain are much, much lower than in the [rest of the body], and it takes it a long time to actually adjust if you change the peripheral glucose for the brain to have lower glucose," he explained. "Not only that, but the neurons in the brain are really not fed by glucose but by other metabolites. The rest of the body, when glucose goes down, will feel it. The brain is a totally different story."

BALANCING BLOOD SUGAR

Although balanced blood-sugar control is a good strategy in theory, it's difficult to attain and difficult to monitor.

"The trouble is, when you try to keep blood sugar within the normal range, there's a higher risk of hypoglycemia," said Michael Horseman, PharmD, an associate professor of pharmacy practice at the Texas A&M Health Science Center Irma Lerma Rangel College of Pharmacy. "There hasn't been a study that I'm aware of where they made a serious attempt to keep blood sugar in the normal range that didn't have episodes of hypoglycemia."

Dr. Barzilai agreed. "You give them a little bit of insulin, and they get hypoglycemia. You give them a little less and the glucose goes very high. It's individual. It's not that you know what to do with every patient.

"It does underline the fact that if we had drugs that didn't produce hypoglycemia, we certainly would be better off," he added.

info Visit the American Diabetes Association Web site, *www.diabetes.org/type-2-diabetes.jsp,* for more on type 2 diabetes.

When Blood Sugar Control Is Bad for Your Health

Simon Finfer, MB, senior staff specialist in intensive care, Royal North Shore Hospital of Sydney, Australia.
Silvio E. Inzucchi, MD, professor, medicine, Yale University School of Medicine, New Haven, Connecticut.
The New England Journal of Medicine.
Canadian Medical Association Journal news release.
American Diabetes Association/American Association of Clinical Endocrinologists, joint statement.

People hospitalized in intensive care units, or ICUs, often experience spikes in blood sugar, and current practice is to try to lower these levels.

But a recent study found that this strategy might actually boost the person's risk of death by 10%.

"Intensively lowering blood glucose in critically ill patients is not beneficial and may be harmful," said Simon Finfer, MB, a senior staff specialist in intensive care at Royal North Shore Hospital in Sydney, Australia, and lead author of the study. "Based on our findings, we do not recommend pursuing a normal blood glucose level in critically ill patients."

Expert groups remain cautious about the study's findings, however. In a joint statement the American Diabetic Association (ADA) and the American Association of Clinical Endocrinologists (AACE) warned against "letting this study swing the pendulum of glucose control too far in the other direction, where providers in hospitals are complacent about uncontrolled hyperglycemia."

The study was published in *The New England Journal of Medicine.*

BACKGROUND

Intensive glucose lowering has been recommended to control high blood sugar, which is common in people who are acutely ill and has been associated with organ failure and death.

THE STUDY

For the study, Dr. Finfer's team randomly assigned more than 6,100 ICU patients to either intensive or conventional blood sugar control. The researchers used infusions of insulin to achieve specific blood sugar levels. The participants were then followed for 90 days.

"We found that intensively lowering blood glucose levels increased a patient's risk of dying by 10%," Dr. Finfer said. Overall, 24.9% of those whose blood sugar was controlled by conventional means died within 90 days compared with 27.5% of those who were given intensive infusions—about a one-tenth rise. The percentage of people who experienced hypoglycemia, or low blood sugar, was also higher in the intensely treated group compared with the conventional care group.

The findings reveal that the current practice of intensively lowering blood glucose increases the risk of death among patients in the ICU, Dr. Finfer said.

NEW GUIDELINES NEEDED

"International guidelines should be revised to reflect this new evidence," he said. "Many professional organizations recommend very tight glucose control for ICU patients. They will now need to take this new evidence into consideration and adjust their recommendations accordingly."

EXPERT REACTION

Silvio E. Inzucchi, MD, a professor of medicine at Yale University School of Medicine and author of an accompanying journal editorial, believes the findings might change clinical practice in the ICU.

The study "raises a big question mark about intensive blood sugar control in intensive care patients," Dr. Inzucchi said. "We used to think that keeping the sugar levels in the normal range was a good thing. This study says the opposite. The truth is probably somewhere in the middle.

"Get the sugars down, but keeping them in the slightly elevated range, is probably not a bad thing, at least during the short course of most hospitalizations," he said. "Medicine is always changing as new evidence emerges. We need to incorporate new findings into our practice patterns."

EXPERT GROUP REACTION

For their part, the ADA and AACE stress that doctors must still closely monitor and manage the blood sugar levels of very ill patients.

The findings "should not lead to an abandonment of the concept of good glucose management in the hospital setting," the groups said in their joint statement. They also pointed out that the study compared patients receiving either very strict glucose control or, in the conventional treatment arm, less strict but still well-controlled blood sugar management.

ADA and AACE have also convened a special inpatient task force to examine the issue. "Until more information is available, it seems reasonable for clinicians to treat critical care patients with the less intensive—yet good—glucose-control strategies used in the conventional arm [of the study]."

info For more information on controlling blood sugar, read the articles available at the Diabetes In Control Web site, *www.diabetesincontrol.com.*

Stay-Well Secrets for People with Diabetes or Prediabetes

Theresa Garnero, advanced practice registered nurse (APRN), certified diabetes educator (CDE) and clinical nurse manager of the Center for Diabetes Services at the California Pacific Medical Center in San Francisco. She is the author of *Your First Year with Diabetes: What to Do, Month by Month* (American Diabetes Association).

We've all heard that diabetes is on the rise in the US, but few people realize the degree to which older adults are disproportionately affected.

Frightening statistic: Nearly one out of every three Americans over age 65 has diabetes, the highest rate among all age groups. Another one out of three older adults has a precursor to diabetes known as "prediabetes"—defined as a fasting blood sugar (glucose) level of 100 milligrams per deciliter (mg/dL) to 125 mg/dL.

Many people downplay the seriousness of diabetes. That's a mistake. Because elevated glucose can damage blood vessels, nerves, the kidneys and eyes, people with diabetes are much more likely to die from heart disease and/or kidney disease than people without diabetes—and they are at increased risk for infections, including gum disease, as well as blindness and amputation. (Nerve damage and poor circulation can allow dangerous infections to go undetected.)

And diabetes can be sneaky—increased thirst, urination and/or hunger are the most common symptoms, but many people have no symptoms and are unaware that they are sick.

Despite these sobering facts, doctors rarely have time to give their patients all the information they need to cope with the complexities of diabetes. Fortunately, diabetes educators—health-care professionals, such as registered nurses, registered dietitians and medical social workers—can give patients practical advice on the best ways to control their condition.*

*To find a diabetes educator near you, consult the American Association of Diabetes Educators, 800-832-6874, *www.diabeteseducator.org*.

Good news: Most health insurers, including Medicare, cover the cost of diabetes patients' visits with a diabetes educator.

What you've probably never been told about diabetes...

SAVVY EATING HABITS

Most doctors advise people with diabetes or prediabetes to cut back on refined carbohydrates, such as cakes and cookies, and eat more fruits, vegetables and whole grains. This maximizes nutrition and promotes a healthy body weight (being overweight greatly increases diabetes risk). *Other steps to take...*

•**Drink one extra glass of water each day.** The extra fluid will help prevent dehydration, which can raise glucose levels.

Never skip meals—especially breakfast. Don't assume that bypassing a meal and fasting for more than five to six hours will help lower glucose levels. It actually triggers the liver to release glucose into the bloodstream.

Better strategy: Eat three small meals daily and have snacks in between. Start with breakfast, such as a cup of low-fat yogurt and whole-wheat toast with peanut butter or a small bowl of whole-grain cereal and a handful of nuts.

Good snack options: A small apple or three graham crackers. Each of these snacks contains about 15 g of carbohydrates.

•**Practice the "plate method."** Divide a nine-inch plate in half. Fill half with vegetables, then split the other half into quarters—one for protein, such as salmon, lean meat, beans or tofu...and the other for starches, such as one-third cup of pasta or one-half cup of peas or corn. Then have a small piece of fruit. This is an easy way to practice portion control—and get the nutrients you need.

•**Ask yourself if you are satisfied after you take each bite.** If the answer is "yes," stop eating. This simple strategy helped one of my clients lose 50 pounds.

•**Be wary of "sugar-free" foods.** These products, including sugar-free cookies and diabetic candy, often are high in carbohydrates, which are the body's primary source of glucose. You may be better off eating the regular product, which is more satisfying. Compare the carbohydrate contents on product labels.

GET CREATIVE WITH EXERCISE

If you have diabetes or prediabetes, you've probably been told to get more exercise. Walking is especially helpful. For those with diabetes, walking for at least two hours a week has been shown to reduce the risk for death by 30% over an eight-year period. For those with prediabetes, walking for 30 minutes five days a week reduces by about 60% the risk that your condition will progress to diabetes. *But if you'd like some other options,*** *consider...*

• **"Armchair workouts."** These exercises, which are performed while seated and are intended for people with physical limitations to standing, increase stamina, muscle tone, flexibility and coordination. For videos or DVDs, go to *www.armchairfitness.com* or call 800-453-6280.

Cost: $39.95 per video or DVD.

• **Strength training.** This type of exercise builds muscle, which burns more calories than fat even when you are not exercising.*** Use hand weights, exercise machines or the weight of your own body—for example, leg squats or bicep curls with no weights. Aim for two to three sessions of strength training weekly, on alternate days.

• **Stretching—even while watching TV or talking on the phone.** By building a stretching routine into your daily activities, you won't need to set aside a separate time to do it. If your body is flexible, it's easier to perform other kinds of physical activity. Stretching also promotes better circulation. Before stretching, do a brief warm-up, such as walking for five minutes and doing several "arm windmills." Aim to do stretching exercises at least three times weekly, including before your other workouts.

CONTROL YOUR BLOOD GLUCOSE

If you are diagnosed with diabetes, blood glucose control is the immediate goal. Newer devices that test blood glucose levels can be used for self-monitoring.

Good choices: OneTouch Ultra from LifeScan...Bayer's Contour...or Freestyle from Abbott Laboratories.

The hemoglobin A1C test, which is ordered by your doctor and typically is done two to four times a year, determines how well glucose levels have been controlled over the previous two to three months.

If you have prediabetes: Don't settle for a fasting glucose test, which measures blood glucose after you have fasted overnight. It misses two-thirds of all cases of diabetes. The oral glucose tolerance test (OGTT), which involves testing glucose immediately before drinking a premixed glass of glucose and repeating the test two hours later, is more reliable. If you can't get an OGTT, ask for an A1C test and fasting glucose test.

If you have diabetes or prediabetes, you should have your blood pressure and cholesterol checked at every doctor visit and schedule regular eye exams and dental appointments. *In addition, don't overlook...*

• **Proper kidney testing.** Doctors most commonly recommend annual microalbumin and creatinine urine tests to check for kidney disease. You also may want to ask for a *glomerular filtration rate* test, which measures kidney function.

• **Meticulous foot care.** High glucose levels can reduce sensation in your feet, making it hard to know when you have a cut, blister or injury. In addition to seeing a podiatrist at least once a year and inspecting your own feet daily, be wary of everyday activities that can be dangerous for people with diabetes.

Stepping into hot bath water, for example, can cause a blister or skin damage that can become infected. To protect yourself, check the water temperature on your wrist or elbow before you step in. The temperature should be warm to the touch—not hot.

STAY UP TO DATE ON MEDICATIONS

Once diabetes medication has been prescribed, people with diabetes should review

**Consult your doctor before starting a new exercise program.

***If you have high blood pressure, be sure to check with your doctor before starting a strength-training program—this type of exercise can raise blood pressure.

their drug regimen with their doctors at every visit. *Insulin is the most commonly used diabetes drug, but you may want to also ask your doctor about these relatively new medications...*

•**DPP-4 inhibitors.** These drugs include *sitagliptin* (Januvia), which lowers glucose levels by increasing the amount of insulin secreted by the pancreas. DPP-4 inhibitors are used alone or with another type of diabetes medication.

•**Symlin.** Administered with an injectable pen, *pramlintide* (Symlin) helps control blood glucose and reduces appetite, which may help with weight loss. It is used in addition to insulin.

If you have prediabetes or diabetes: Always consult a pharmacist or doctor before taking any over-the-counter products. Cold medicines with a high sugar content may raise your blood glucose, for example, and wart removal products may cause skin ulcers. Pay close attention to drug label warnings.

■ ■ ■ ■

Take This Prediabetes Quiz

If you are age 65 or older, you are at increased risk for prediabetes regardless of the characteristics described below. For this reason, you should ask your doctor about receiving a fasting glucose test.

If you are under age 65, answer the following questions and speak to your doctor about receiving a fasting glucose test if you score a total of 5 or higher.

Age	**Points**
20–27	0
28–35	1
36–44	2
45–64	4
Sex	
Male	3
Female	0
Family History of Diabetes	
No	0
Yes	1
Heart Rate (beats per minute)*	
Less than 60	0
60–69	0
70–79	1
80–89	2
90–99	2
Greater than 100	4
High Blood Pressure	
No	0
Yes	1
Body Mass Index (BMI)**	
Less than 25	0
25–29.9	2
30 or greater	3

*To determine your heart rate, place the tips of the first two fingers lightly over one of the blood vessels in your neck or the pulse spot inside your wrist just below the base of your thumb. Count your pulse for 10 seconds and multiply that number by 6.

**To determine your BMI, consult the National Heart, Lung and Blood Institute Web site, *www.nhlbisupport.com/bmi.*

Annals of Family Medicine

Two-Drug Combo Drops Kidney Problems by 20%

American Society of Nephrology news release.

A combination of two blood pressure–lowering drugs reduced the risk of kidney disease by about 20% in people with type 2 diabetes, according to a recent study.

THE STUDY

Researchers analyzed data from a study that included more than 11,000 patients with diabetes. The patients were randomly selected to receive either a placebo or a combination of the angiotensin-converting enzyme (ACE) inhibitor *perindopril* and the diuretic *indapamide.* Most of the patients had high blood pressure, but 20% had blood pressure less than 130/80.

THE RESULTS

After an average follow-up of four years, patients taking the blood pressure–lowering drugs were 21% less likely to have kidney disease than those in the placebo group. The researchers also found that kidney function returned to normal among some patients who had early signs of diabetes-related kidney disease before they started taking the drugs.

Even in patients who didn't have high blood pressure, the drug combination reduced the risk for kidney disease.

IMPLICATIONS

More research is needed, but these results suggest that patients with type 2 diabetes might be considered for antihypertensive treatment even if they have normal blood pressure, said the authors of the study, which appeared in the *Journal of the American Society of Nephrology*.

info For more information about diabetes and kidney disease, visit the Web site of the National Kidney Foundation, *www.kidney.org,* and search "diabetes and kidney disease."

■ ■ ■ ■

Drug Helps Block Diabetes in People with Early Symptoms

About 21 million people in the US have impaired glucose tolerance, a prediabetic condition that is diagnosed through blood tests. According to recent research, impaired glucose tolerance is 81% less likely to turn into full-blown diabetes if patients take the prescription drug *pioglitazone* (Actos).

Possible side effects: Weight gain...edema (swelling)...increased fracture risk in postmenopausal women.

Ralph A. DeFronzo, MD, professor of medicine and diabetes chief, University of Texas Health Science Center, San Antonio, and leader of a study of 602 people with impaired glucose tolerance, presented at the 68th Scientific Sessions of the American Diabetes Association.

Warning! Diabetes Drug that Doubles Risk for Fractures

Mark A. Stengler, ND, naturopathic physician in private practice, La Jolla, California...adjunct associate clinical professor at the National College of Natural Medicine, Portland, Oregon...author of many books and the *Bottom Line/Natural Healing* newsletter.

Researchers at Wake Forest University have found that Avandia and Actos, two drugs that control type 2 diabetes, can almost double the risk for hip fractures in women.

Both medications—*rosiglitazone* (Avandia) and *pioglitazone* (Actos)—belong to a class of drugs known as *thiazolidinediones*. This is not the first time that these drugs have made headlines. In 2007, it was found that those who took rosiglitazone were at increased risk for heart attack. The FDA required warnings about heart attack and congestive heart failure to be added to rosiglitazone's label.

In the pharmaceutical industry, drugs are monitored through a practice known as postmarketing surveillance. Health-care professionals and the public voluntarily let the FDA know about any adverse effects experienced while using a drug. Manufacturers also are required to report any adverse events involving their drugs. Neither system is reliable. The disturbing new findings about Avandia and Actos emphasize the need for more rigorous monitoring and reporting of side effects.

Many patients with diabetes can reduce or eliminate the need for medication with proper diet and exercise, along with certain natural supplements—including chromium...ginseng...and PolyGlycoplex (also known as PGX), a blend of fiber including glucomannan and Pycnogenol (extract from pine bark). If you must take medication to control your diabetes, talk to your physician about drugs other than Avandia and Actos. *Metformin* (Glucophage) has a long history as a reliable diabetes medication.

■ ■ ■ ■

Are You Taking Byetta?

A few people with diabetes taking the drug Byetta have died after developing pancreatitis. There have been about six reported deaths involving pancreatitis among the one million people who have used Byetta since the Food and Drug Administration approved the drug in 2005.

But: The pancreatitis may not have caused the deaths—one patient weighed more than 400 pounds and had extensive gallstones...another had a relapse of leukemia.

Bottom line: No drug is completely safe. In this particular drug's case, the benefits may far outweigh the risks.

Stanley Mirsky, MD, associate clinical professor of metabolic diseases, Mount Sinai School of Medicine, and an internist in private practice, both in New York City. His most recent book is *Diabetes Survival Guide* (Ballantine), coauthored by Joan Rattner Heilman.

Coming Soon—Pain-Free Glucose Monitoring!

Paturi V. Rao, MD, departments of endocrinology and metabolism and medicine, Nizam's Institute of Medical Sciences University, Hyderabad, India.

Charles F. Burant, MD, PhD, professor, internal medicine, University of Michigan, Ann Arbor.

Umesh Masharani, MD, associate clinical professor, medicine, University of California, San Francisco.

Journal of Proteome Research.

Scientists say they are on the verge of developing a saliva test for monitoring type 2 diabetes, a test which might someday replace invasive blood tests.

For the first time, researchers from Oregon and India have identified proteins in saliva that appear more frequently in people with diabetes than in nondiabetics. Using these proteins, they are working to develop a test to monitor and perhaps diagnose the condition.

The report was published in the *Journal of Proteome Research.*

THE STUDY

For the study, Paturi V. Rao, MD, from the departments of endocrinology and metabolism and medicine at Nizam's Institute of Medical Sciences University in Hyderabad, India, and colleagues analyzed saliva samples from people with and without type 2 diabetes. Their goal was to find proteins associated with the blood sugar disease.

The researchers found 65 proteins that occurred twice as frequently in the people with diabetes than in those without the condition.

LESS PAINFUL GLUCOSE TESTING

Using these proteins, Dr. Rao's team hopes to develop a noninvasive test for diabetes screening, detection and monitoring.

Dr. Rao's group thinks the pain involved with current diabetes monitoring causes many people with diabetes to be lax in monitoring their condition. A noninvasive test could make it easier and less painful for patients to keep track of their blood sugar levels.

"As recent studies have shown that early, multifactorial intervention in diabetes prevents cardiovascular complications and mortality, advances in understanding molecular aspects of preclinical diabetes will further facilitate accurate diagnosis and early intervention," said the authors.

EXPERT COMMENTARY

Diabetes expert Charles F. Burant, MD, PhD, a professor of internal medicine at the University of Michigan, isn't convinced that a test using proteins in saliva is needed.

Dr. Burant noted that diabetes and prediabetes already have an accurate marker—glucose. "Thus, this is interesting biochemistry and raises questions why these changes occur, but the clinical utility is unclear," he said.

Umesh Masharani, MD, an associate clinical professor of medicine at the University of California, San Francisco, doesn't think this approach is going to replace current blood tests any time soon.

"This is an interesting and novel approach," Dr. Masharani said. "I do not think this approach will be used in the diagnosis or treatment of diabetes any time in the near future. It is interesting, I think, for research studies in diabetes."

info To follow more news updates about diabetes, visit the DiabetesMonitor Web site, *www.diabetesmonitor.com.*

■ ■ ■ ■

Better Blood Sugar Control

One group of type 1 diabetes patients did conventional blood tests several times daily. Another group used tiny sensors (which patients place under the skin every few days using an insertion device) to continuously monitor blood sugar. With constant feedback on when to eat or take insulin, sensor users had better blood sugar control—reducing risk for diabetes complications. Prescription sensor systems can cost about $10 per day. Some insurance plans cover them.

Roy W. Beck, MD, PhD, executive director, Jaeb Center for Health Research, Tampa, and head of a study of 322 diabetes patients, published in *The New England Journal of Medicine*.

■ ■ ■ ■

OJ Raises Diabetes Risk by 24%

It only takes one cup of orange juice per day to raise diabetes risk by about 24%, according to new research.

Reason: The juice's high sugar content causes a spike in blood glucose levels.

Diabetes Care.

■ ■ ■ ■

Measure Sugar *Before* Meals

Individuals with diabetes should measure blood sugar before meals to best establish their long-term blood sugar levels, says Stanley Mirsky, MD. Premeal sugar level is more closely aligned with long-term levels than standard blood sugar measurements taken two hours after a meal. Postmeal levels are still important to measure the effects of the meal on blood sugar.

Important: Those with diabetes should maintain a low-sugar and low-carbohydrate diet.

Stanley Mirsky, MD, associate clinical professor of metabolic diseases, Mount Sinai School of Medicine, and an internist in private practice, both in New York City. His most recent book is *Diabetes Survival Guide* (Ballantine), coauthored by Joan Rattner Heilman.

■ ■ ■ ■

Web Site for Diabetes Management

Log on to *www.sugarstats.com* to keep track of your blood glucose levels...medication usage...food intake...and exercise. People with diabetes can use the free site to help manage their disease and share information with their health-care providers.

■ ■ ■ ■

Exercise Helps Arthritis And Diabetes

When researchers recently analyzed physical activity among adults with both arthritis and diabetes, nearly 30% of them were sedentary, compared with 21% of those with diabetes alone, 17% of those with arthritis alone and 11% of those with neither condition.

Theory: People with both arthritis and diabetes remain inactive because they are concerned about worsening pain and joint damage, both of which can be exacerbated by excess body weight.

If you have arthritis and diabetes: Try arthritis-friendly workouts, such as walking, cycling and swimming, to help control your arthritis and diabetes.

Charles Helmick, MD, lead scientist, arthritis program, Centers for Disease Control and Prevention, Atlanta.

When Wounds Won't Go Away...

Steven J. Kavros, DPM, a podiatrist, assistant professor of orthopedic surgery and certified wound specialist at Mayo Clinic in Rochester, Minnesota. He has published several papers on diabetic and vascular wound care in peer-reviewed medical journals.

If you get a scrape or other superficial wound, it usually heals in a week or two. But some wounds don't go away so quickly—especially if you're an older adult, are confined to a bed or wheelchair, or have diabetes or some other condition that interferes with your blood circulation.

Latest development: New, highly effective therapies and the proliferation of wound-care centers staffed by doctors and other health-care professionals (often located at large medical centers or university hospitals) are helping to prevent amputations, life-threatening infections and other serious complications.*

WHY WOUNDS BECOME CHRONIC

If a wound doesn't heal within six weeks, it is considered chronic and requires special care. Poor blood flow, which cuts off the supply of oxygen and nutrients that are needed for healing, is a common cause of chronic wounds.

Basic care for all chronic wounds usually involves cleansing (to remove foreign matter and bacteria-laden debris)...debridement (to remove dead and damaged tissue)...and dressing (often treated with a medicinal preparation, such as an antimicrobial solution, to prevent the growth of bacteria).

COMMON CHRONIC WOUNDS

•**Diabetic foot ulcers.** Among Americans with diabetes, 15% will develop a foot ulcer, and many of them will ultimately require amputation of the foot—usually because the patient has developed a life-threatening condition, such as gangrene (decay and death of tissue due to insufficient blood supply).

Why are people with diabetes at such high risk for foot ulcers?

The disease not only impairs healthy blood flow, but also inhibits the body's ability to fight infection. In addition, neuropathy (a type of nerve damage that often occurs in people with diabetes) can cause nerve pain and decrease sensation, so pressure and injury may go unnoticed.

Diabetic ulcers typically occur at points of prolonged or repeated pressure on the skin and underlying tissue—for example, the big toe or front part of the foot.

Self-defense: People with diabetic foot ulcers should wear properly fitting shoes. They also may need a podiatrist to check for abnormalities in their gaits, perhaps with the aid of a computerized scan of pressure points on their feet. Special shoe inserts (orthotics) can help adjust the position of the foot to relieve pressure points.

•**Venous ulcers.** When veins, which carry blood back to the heart, don't function properly, blood can pool in the legs, causing swelling and discoloration and disrupting the supply of fresh blood with its oxygen and bacteria-fighting immune cells. This sets the stage for venous ulcers to develop.

Self-defense: The main treatment for a venous ulcer is compression (wrapping the leg, under a doctor's supervision, with an elastic bandage or special stocking to reduce swelling and improve blood flow). Venous ulcerations that don't respond to standard therapy may require surgery to close off the failing veins, which improves blood flow back to the heart and reduces venous pressure in the leg.

•**Arterial ulcers.** Atherosclerosis, the buildup of fatty deposits (plaque) that narrows the coronary arteries, also may impair circulation to the limbs. If circulation is further inhibited by a tiny blood clot, tissue may die, causing an arterial ulcer, typically on the toes or an ankle.

Self-defense: The most effective treatments for arterial ulcers are much like those used for coronary artery disease—the doctor may thread a catheter into the affected artery and inflate a balloon to open it up, possibly inserting a stent (tiny wire mesh tube) to keep it open.

A severe blockage may require bypass surgery—as with a coronary bypass, a blood vessel (taken from elsewhere in the body) is implanted to "bypass" the blockage.

•**Pressure ulcers.** Also known as bedsores, these afflict people who are confined to a bed or wheelchair. Immobility causes constant pressure, which cuts off circulation (for example, in the tailbone). About 9% of hospitalized patients develop pressure ulcers, usually during the first two weeks of their stay.

Self-defense: Pressure ulcers require the same care as other chronic wounds. Bedsores often can be prevented by regularly changing an immobile person's position (every two hours), which distributes pressure more evenly.

*To find a wound-care specialist in your area, consult the American Academy of Wound Management (202-457-8408, *www.aawm.org*).

BREAKTHROUGH THERAPIES

A chronic wound is a magnet for bacteria—the dead tissue and moisture provide a hospitable environment for germs to thrive.

Recent development: A treatment available at many wound-care centers uses low-frequency ultrasound to break up biofilm (a microscopically thin layer of film containing bacteria) on the wound. This stimulates the production of cells that fill in the wound with new tissue and help keep the area clean.

Caution: Notify your physician promptly if your wound shows signs of infection, such as pain, odor, redness, pus or streaks along the affected limb, or if you have a fever (above 99°F). Infections require antibiotic treatment.

Wounds that refuse to heal despite treatment may require one of the other latest therapies typically available at wound-care centers...

- **Cell therapy involves placing a bioengineered skin substitute over the wound.** This film-like material secretes substances that stimulate your own cells to grow tissue that will close the wound. Cell therapy is often used for resistant diabetic or venous ulcers.
- **Hyperbaric oxygen therapy,** which is mainly used for diabetic ulcers, involves sitting or lying for about 90 minutes in a room or chamber that contains 100% oxygen at two to three times normal air pressure. Breathing this supercharged air promotes wound healing by raising oxygen levels in the blood.
- **Negative pressure wound therapy,** used for diabetic and arterial ulcers, involves placing a sponge or foam dressing over the wound and attaching a device that suctions off waste fluids and infectious material, thus stimulating the growth of new tissue.

■ ■ ■ ■

New Technique Reduces Risk For Diabetic Foot Ulcers by 30%

For patients with diabetes, open sores on the feet heal slowly, due to impaired sensation and circulation. In a recent study, 225 patients with type 2 diabetes did a daily foot inspection for 18 months and received education and therapeutic footwear. Half the patients also used an infrared skin thermometer (a probe that is placed on the skin) to measure foot temperature twice daily. Whenever a difference of more than 4°F was detected between the right and left foot, patients curtailed physical activity until temperatures normalized.

Result: Temperature-taking patients were 30% less likely to develop ulcers.

My view: Measuring skin temperature is a noninvasive way for diabetes patients to identify inflammation—a warning sign of an impending ulcer—so they can allow time to heal. The thermometer the study used, Diabetica Solutions' TempTouch Thermometer, is available without a prescription (800-246-3395, *www.temptouch.com*) for $99 and is covered by some insurance plans.

Mark A. Stengler, ND, naturopathic physician in private practice, La Jolla, California...adjunct associate clinical professor at the National College of Natural Medicine, Portland, Oregon...author of many books and the *Bottom Line/Natural Healing* newsletter.

■ ■ ■ ■

Older Treatment Better at Saving Eyesight

Several years ago, early reports of success suggested that injection of steroids into the eye was a promising new treatment for diabetic macular edema (retinal swelling).

Surprising study: After two years of treatment, vision had worsened substantially in 28% of patients treated with steroids...but in only 19% of patients given the traditional laser therapy. Steroid users also had more side effects, including cataracts and increased eye pressure.

David Brown, MD, ophthalmologist and retina specialist, Methodist Hospital, Houston, and local principal investigator of a study of 693 people, published in *Ophthalmology*.

■ ■ ■ ■

Easy Eye Scan Detects Diabetes

An experimental test uses specialized photographs of the eye to detect tissue damage caused by diabetes. The test is noninvasive and faster than blood-glucose testing—and could allow an earlier diagnosis.

University of Michigan Kellogg Eye Center.

■ ■ ■ ■

Does Diabetes Cause Hearing Loss?

When researchers recently analyzed hearing test results and related questionnaires for about 5,000 Americans, they found that hearing loss was about twice as common in people who had diabetes than in those without diabetes.

Theory: Diabetes may cause hearing loss by damaging nerves and blood vessels in the inner ear.

If you have been diagnosed with diabetes: Ask your doctor to refer you to a hearing specialist (audiologist), so you can receive a hearing test.

Catherine Cowie, PhD, director, diabetes epidemiology program, National Institute of Diabetes and Digestive and Kidney Diseases, Bethesda, Maryland.

■ ■ ■ ■

Get a Fatty Liver in Shape With Exercise

Excess fat in the liver can lead to cirrhosis and liver failure, especially in diabetes patients, necessitating dialysis or a transplant. Liver fat was reduced by an average of 34% among type 2 diabetes patients who did 45 minutes of moderate aerobic exercise (walking, cycling) plus 20 minutes of weight lifting three times weekly for six months. Waistlines shrank an average of two inches.

Kerry Stewart, EdD, professor of medicine, Johns Hopkins University School of Medicine, Baltimore, and leader of a study of 77 diabetes patients, reported at the annual meeting of the American Association of Cardiovascular and Pulmonary Rehabilitation.

■ ■ ■ ■

Diabetes Linked to Colon Cancer

In a recent analysis of data for 45,000 women, those with diabetes were 1.5 times more likely to develop colorectal cancer during an eight-and-a-half-year period than women without diabetes.

Theory: Elevated levels of insulin (a hormone that helps regulate blood sugar) may stimulate cancer-cell growth. These findings are believed to apply to men as well.

If you have diabetes: Control your blood sugar levels, and ask your doctor how often you should have a colonoscopy.

Andrew Flood, PhD, assistant professor, division of epidemiology and community health, University of Minnesota, Minneapolis.

You Can Reverse Diabetes with Food!

Neal D. Barnard, MD, an adjunct associate professor of medicine at the George Washington University School of Medicine and Health Sciences and president of the nonprofit Physicians Committee for Responsible Medicine. He is author of numerous books, including *Dr. Neal Barnard's Program for Reversing Diabetes* (Rodale). *www.nealbarnard.org.*

Cut calories and keep careful track of the fat, protein and carbohydrates (including sugar) you eat—those are the usual dietary recommendations for adults with type 2 diabetes (commonly referred to as adult-onset or non-insulin-dependent diabetes).

Trap: In my experience, many people who follow these recommendations still don't reap the promised benefits—weight loss, reduced need for medication and fewer complications.

My approach is dramatically different—and it works. My research team and I conducted a series of studies with hundreds of patients, and we discovered that it is possible to improve blood-sugar levels through diet alone.

Big payoff: People can now control—and even reverse—their type 2 diabetes. While the diet won't reverse type 1 (or juvenile) diabetes, it will reduce risk for diabetic complications and help to minimize use of insulin.

WHERE IT STARTS

If you have type 2 diabetes, your body has become resistant to insulin, the hormone that carries glucose (sugar) into your cells, where it is used for energy.

The cause: Tiny droplets of fat have accumulated inside your muscle cells and are interfering with their ability to use insulin. Glucose can't get into your cells properly, which means that it builds up in your blood instead.

What if you could remove that accumulated fat from inside your cells? You would improve your body's ability to use insulin, get your blood sugar under control—and possibly even reverse your type 2 diabetes.

The best way to do this is by changing the way you eat. *With my three-step program, you can eat as much as you want of certain foods, because this approach focuses solely on what you eat, not how much...*

THE THREE-STEP PROGRAM

1. Avoid all animal products, including red meat, poultry, fish, dairy and eggs, as well as dishes and baked goods containing these ingredients. Animal protein is harmful to the kidneys. And the principal ingredient of dairy products, even low-fat or nonfat, is sugar in the form of lactose.

2. Minimize fats, and food made with fats, including cooking oils, salad dressings, mayonnaise, margarine and peanut butter, plus fried foods and naturally fatty foods, such as avocados and olives.

3. Consume lots of fruits, vegetables and whole grains. These foods are low on the glycemic index—meaning that they act slowly on your blood sugar.

Best choices: Whole-grain breads (wheat, pumpernickel, rye), other whole grains (barley, oats, bulgur, brown rice and corn), plus beans, lentils, sweet potatoes (which contain natural sugar but do not raise blood sugar rapidly), green vegetables, most fruits (except watermelon and pineapple, which are naturally sugary) and tofu. Nuts and seeds are also good in small amounts—unless you need to lose weight. In that case, it's best to avoid them.

Also: Herbal or regular tea and coffee are fine. Skip the soda and fruit juice, though, as these drinks are high on the glycemic index. I recommend avoiding diet soda as well. Although the reasons are not clear, people who stop drinking diet soda often lower their blood glucose. I also advise that you take a daily multivitamin/mineral supplement and a daily vitamin D supplement of 1,000 international units.

Bonus: If you follow these guidelines, you'll get plenty of fiber, which has many health benefits including helping to control blood sugar. And don't worry—you'll get enough protein from eating beans, leafy green vegetables, seeds and nuts.

MAKING THE CHANGE

If this all sounds like a very low-fat "vegan" diet, that's because it is. *To help yourself ease into this new program...*

- **Throw out all animal products and oils and foods that contain them.**
- **Make a list of foods you like that fit into the plan.** Then go to the store and buy a week's worth so you can test-drive the diet.

Helpful: There are plenty of healthy convenience foods on the market, like frozen cheese-free veggie pizza with a whole-wheat or rice crust, low-fat vegetarian chili and frozen vegan enchiladas.

- **Follow my plan to the letter for three weeks.** Your blood sugar should start to drop within the first week and will continue to improve. Your blood pressure may drop as well. You'll have more energy, and you may lose some weight (up to a pound a week). By the end of the third week, you won't be able to imagine going back to your old way of eating.

Our cravings go away because of a simple biological fact—we crave today what we had yesterday. Once you've gotten your diabetes under control, you can treat yourself to small amounts once in a while of, say, chocolate and other favorite foods. You may even find that you're satisfied with more healthful substitutes, such as strawberries drizzled with chocolate syrup instead of a candy bar.

Best of all, after a few months, you may be able to cut back or even eliminate some of your medications.

Note: Always discuss medication changes with your doctor first.

GET MOVING

I recommend exercise as something you add to a healthy diet. It should not be considered a substitute for eating better.

Best: If you can manage a brisk walk for half an hour a day (or longer!), definitely do it.

If you are overweight or have joint or heart problems, you may not be able to do much exercise in the beginning. Before long, however, you'll feel so much better, you'll want to start moving. And once you find a form of exercise that's appropriate for you—and that you enjoy—exercise becomes a lot more fun...and your diabetes becomes even less of a health concern.

Study Proves This Herb Lowers Insulin Levels Even After High-Carb Meals

Mark A. Stengler, ND, naturopathic physician in private practice, La Jolla, California...adjunct associate clinical professor at the National College of Natural Medicine, Portland, Oregon...author of many books and the *Bottom Line/Natural Healing* newsletter.

Salacia oblonga is an herb commonly used in traditional Ayurvedic medicine to treat diabetes and obesity. Researchers fed 66 people with type 2 diabetes test meals on three separate occasions. Study participants were given a high-carbohydrate liquid meal or the liquid meal plus Salacia oblonga (*S. oblonga*) at a dosage of either 240 milligrams (mg) or 480 mg.

Result: Compared with the control meal alone, the 240-mg dose of S. oblonga lowered blood sugar by 14%...and the 480-mg dose lowered it by 22%. The amount of insulin, a hormone that regulates blood sugar, produced in response to the meal was reduced by 14% and 19%, respectively (high insulin contributes to inflammation in the body). These reductions were especially impressive given the high-carb meal (carbs raise blood sugar and insulin).

This herb prevents carbohydrates from being broken down in the digestive tract, allowing less glucose into the bloodstream—and resulting in lower blood glucose and insulin levels. Studies have shown it to be safe, and side effects are uncommon. People who have mild-to-moderate elevation in glucose levels, as well as those with diabetes, should talk to their doctors about S. oblonga.

Note: Three of the study authors are employed by Abbott Laboratories, which funded the research. However, two other studies with humans also have shown the benefits of S. oblonga.

New Technique Frees People from Insulin Injections

Richard Burt, MD, associate professor of medicine at the Feinberg School of Medicine, Northwestern University, Chicago.

Weimin He, PhD, assistant professor, Center for Environmental and Genetic Medicine, Texas A&M Health Science Center Institute of Biosciences and Technology.

Spyros Mezitis, MD, PhD, endocrinologist, Lenox Hill Hospital, New York City.

The Journal of the American Medical Association.

A particular type of stem cell transplantation using the patient's own cells led to short-term freedom from insulin injections in 20 of 23 patients newly diagnosed with type 1 diabetes participating in an experimental protocol in Brazil.

One patient even managed to go four years without needing outside sources of insulin, although the average was 31 months, said the authors of a report in *The Journal of the American Medical Association* (JAMA).

The patients also kept their blood sugar under control, which is key to preventing complications from diabetes. And, the authors stated, increased C-peptide levels indicated that the pancreas's beta cells were alive and well.

"We were trying to preserve islet beta cell mass—the cells that produce insulin—by stopping the immune system attack on these cells," said senior study author Richard Burt, MD, of Northwestern University Feinberg School of Medicine in Chicago. "Why new onset? Because we wanted to make sure there were still some islets there. We don't believe stem cells form islet cells, but if the islet cells are still there, there might be regeneration if we stop the attack soon enough."

The technique may not prove effective in patients with longstanding disease, warned Weimin He, PhD, an assistant professor at the

Center for Environmental and Genetic Medicine at Texas A&M Health Science Center Institute of Biosciences and Technology.

BACKGROUND

Beta cells secrete insulin, the hormone that is critical in moving and storing blood sugar and, thus, maintaining stable blood-sugar levels. In type 1 diabetes, an autoimmune disorder, the patient's body attacks its own beta cells.

Restoring the body's innate ability to produce insulin has been the holy grail of diabetes research. Some patients have received transplantations of insulin-producing cells from a donor, but none have remained free of exogenous (outside) insulin for longer than five years, said Spyros Mezitis, MD, PhD, an endocrinologist with Lenox Hill Hospital in New York City. This was because the body eventually started attacking those cells as well.

The current approach is more hopeful, because it involves the patient's own stem cells, not only bypassing the possibility of rejection but also allowing, theoretically, an unlimited number of future cells to be produced, he said.

PREVIOUS STEM CELL STUDY FINDINGS

A 2007 study by the same group of researchers had found that *autologous* (using the patients' own stem cells) *nonmyeloablative hematopoietic stem cell transplantation* (HSCT) allowed type 1 diabetes patients to revert to not using outside insulin, at least for a time.

"That was the first time in history we achieved normal blood sugar and A1c [the average blood sugar for the previous two to three months] levels and were drug-free after one intervention," Dr. Burt said. "But the criticism was that maybe this insulin independence was a freak prolonged honeymoon period."

"It takes time for the body to attack and break down the insulin-producing cells," explained Dr. Mezitis. "So the cells continue producing insulin, then, as the body attacks the cells, they die out."

NEW STUDY DETAILS

In this report, the authors found beta-cell improvements in 23 patients, ages 13 to 31, who were recently diagnosed with type 1 diabetes.

All participants underwent HSCT, which involved removing the patient's own blood stem cells then reinjecting them into the body.

Twenty patients were able to stop injecting insulin, 12 of them for a mean of 31 months. Eight patients had to start taking insulin again at a low dose.

Not only were blood sugar levels normalized among those individuals who no longer needed outside insulin or needed less outside insulin; C-peptide levels also rose significantly.

In other words, the beta cells seemed to be working, at least partially. There were some side effects noted, but no deaths among the participant group.

The study was funded in part by Genzyme Corp. and Johnson & Johnson-LifeScanBrazil.

info For more information on type 1 diabetes, visit the National Library of Medicine Web site, *www.nlm.nih.gov*, and search "type 1 diabetes."

Breakthrough Research Uses Viruses to Cure Diabetes

M. William Lensch, PhD, affiliate faculty, Harvard Stem Cell Institute, HHMI/Children's Hospital Boston, Harvard Medical School.

We're accustomed to thinking of viruses as "bad guys" that the world would be better without—but now that scientists have used a virus to transform a non-insulin-producing pancreatic cell into one that produced insulin, we may need to reconsider that position. Adding to the achievement is that the "programming" of the cell was done without use of sometimes controversial stem cells. This is a major breakthrough in the field of regenerative medicine, which aims to regrow or repair missing or damaged tissue.

In the study, which was published in the journal *Nature,* Douglas A. Melton, PhD, codirector of the Harvard Stem Cell Institute, and his fellow researchers used a modified virus to activate three key genes in non-insulin-producing pancreatic cells in mice. Within three days, the "infected" cells started producing insulin—far faster than the several weeks it's known to take to transform stem cells into specific organ tissues.

EXCITING RESULTS

The findings are incredibly exciting for other researchers in the field of regenerative medicine as well. "This paper really got a lot of people's attention," says M. William Lensch, PhD, affiliate faculty at the Harvard Stem Cell Institute, who wasn't himself involved with Melton's research. "It expands the possible universe of where regenerated cells can come from and how to get there—that's exciting."

WHAT IT MEANS FOR PEOPLE

Though remarkable, it's important to note that this type of cell reprogramming is still a long way from becoming a viable mainstream treatment—it has yet to be tried in humans, and long-term safety is still to be determined.

Nonetheless, it deserves attention because of the thinking behind it—the idea that you can quickly, relatively easily and with no political debate change a cell that's close to what's needed into exactly what's needed, perhaps to treat cancer, liver disease, cardiovascular disease and more.

■ ■ ■ ■

Fight Diabetes—Deliciously!

In a recent study, 24 herbs and spices were analyzed and found to contain high levels of polyphenols, antioxidant compounds that block the formation of inflammation-promoting substances that raise diabetes risk. Levels were highest in ground cloves...followed by cinnamon (shown in earlier research to help fight diabetes)...sage...marjoram...tarragon...and rosemary.

Instead of seasoning with salt: Consider trying these herbs and spices.

James L. Hargrove, PhD, associate professor, department of foods and nutrition, University of Georgia, Athens.

How to Prevent 9 in 10 Diabetes Cases

JoAnn E. Manson, MD, DrPH, a professor of medicine and women's health at Harvard Medical School and chair of preventive medicine at Brigham and Women's Hospital, both in Boston. She is one of the lead investigators for two highly influential studies on women's health—the Harvard Nurses' Health Study and the Women's Health Initiative. Dr. Manson is author, with Shari Bassuk, ScD, of *Hot Flashes, Hormones and Your Health* (McGraw-Hill).

The statistics are shocking—more than 23% of Americans age 60 and up now have diabetes, a deadly disease that can lead to heart disease, stroke, blindness, amputation, kidney failure and coma. Yet the Nurses' Health Study (NHS), which tracked 84,941 women for 16 years, suggests that about 90% of cases could be prevented.

With type 2 diabetes (the most common form), either the pancreas does not produce enough insulin (a hormone needed to convert glucose into energy) or the body's cells ignore insulin. Certain risk factors cannot be helped—a family history of diabetes...a personal history of polycystic ovary syndrome or diabetes during pregnancy...delivering a baby with a birth weight of nine pounds or more...or being non-Caucasian. However, the majority of risk factors are within your control.

- **Avoid "diabesity."** Researchers coined this term to emphasize the interconnection between obesity and diabetes. In the NHS, obese women were 10 times more likely to get diabetes than women of normal weight.

Theory: Fat cells—particularly those deep inside the belly—produce hormones and chemical messengers that trigger inflammation so that cells become resistant to insulin. Even modest weight loss can cut diabetes risk in half.

- **Stand, don't sit.** Just getting off the couch can help. NHS participants had a 14% increased risk for diabetes for every two hours per day spent watching TV—and a 12% decreased risk for every two hours per day spent standing or walking around at home.

Even better: A brisk one-hour walk daily can reduce diabetes risk by 34%.

•**Skip soda and fruit punch.** Soft drinks sweetened with sugar are the largest single source of calories in the US diet. Daily soda drinkers tend to take in more calories, gain more weight and develop diabetes more often than others.

Wise: Drink water or unsweetened beverages.

•**Choose the right fats.** Polyunsaturated fats—found in corn oil, soybean oil, nuts and fish—may affect cell membranes in a way that improves insulin use. Trans fats, found in some packaged and fast foods, and stick margarines, may have the opposite effect.

•**Limit red meat.** In the NHS, a one-serving-daily increase in red meat (beef, pork, lamb) or processed meat (cold cuts, hot dogs) increased diabetes risk by 26% and 38%, respectively.

Theory: Higher iron and preservative levels in meat products may damage the pancreas.

•**Go for whole grains.** Compared with refined grains (white flour, white rice), whole grains minimize blood sugar fluctuations, easing demands on the pancreas...and provide more magnesium, which makes insulin more effective.

•**Consider coffee.** In studies involving about 200,000 people, drinking four to six cups of coffee daily was associated with a 28% reduction in diabetes risk compared with drinking two or fewer cups daily. Chlorogenic acid, an antioxidant in regular and decaf coffee, may make cells more responsive to insulin.

■ ■ ■ ■

When Fat Hips Are Good

Abdominal fat increases a person's risk for type 2 diabetes.

But: Fat just beneath the skin on hips and thighs actually may improve insulin sensitivity (the ability of the body's cells to recognize and properly respond to insulin).

Theory: Subcutaneous fat produces *adipokines*, hormones that have beneficial effects on glucose metabolism.

C. Ronald Kahn, MD, vice-chairman, Joslin Diabetes Center, Mary K. Iacocca Professor of Medicine, Harvard Medical School, Boston, and leader of an animal study published in *Cell Metabolism.*

Hidden Dangers of Sleep Problems

Lawrence J. Epstein, MD, instructor in medicine at Harvard Medical School in Boston and medical director of Sleep HealthCenters, a Brighton, Massachusetts–based network of specialized sleep medicine centers. He is author of *The Harvard Medical School Guide to a Good Night's Sleep* (McGraw-Hill).

Most people assume that lack of sleep is more of an annoyance than a legitimate threat to their health. But that's a mistake. Lack of sleep—even if it's only occasional—is directly linked to poor health. If ignored, sleep problems can increase your risk for diabetes and heart disease.

About two out of every three Americans ages 55 to 84 have insomnia, but it is one of the most underdiagnosed health problems in the US. Even when insomnia is diagnosed, many doctors recommend a one-size-fits-all treatment approach (often including sleep medication) that does not correct the underlying problem.

Everyone should have a comfortable mattress...keep the bedroom cool (about 68°F to 72°F)...and dim or turn out the lights (production of the sleep hormone melatonin can be inhibited in the presence of light). Keep TVs and computers out of the bedroom—both can be stimulating, rather than relaxing. But these basic steps may not be enough.

To treat specific sleep problems...

IF YOU WAKE UP TOO EARLY IN THE MORNING

Early risers often have advanced sleep phase syndrome (ASPS), seen most commonly in older adults. With this condition, a person's internal body clock that regulates the sleep-wake cycle (circadian rhythm) is not functioning properly. ASPS sufferers sleep best from 8 pm to 4 am.

My solutions: Reset your circadian rhythm with a light box (a device that simulates natural light with lightbulbs). They don't require a doctor's prescription and are available for $100 to $500 online or from retailers, such as Costco. Most use a light box for 30 minutes to an hour daily at sundown. (Those with ASPS may need long-term light therapy.) If you have cataracts, glaucoma or a mood disorder (such as bipolar disorder), consult your doctor before trying light therapy. Patients with retinopathy should avoid light therapy.

Also helpful: To help regulate your internal clock so that you can go to bed (and get up) later, take a 3- to 5-milligram (mg) melatonin supplement each day. A sleep specialist can advise you on when to use light therapy and melatonin.*

IF YOU CAN'T STAY ASLEEP

Everyone wakes up several times a night, but most people fall back to sleep within seconds, so they don't remember waking up.

Trouble staying asleep is often related to sleep apnea, a breathing disorder that causes the sufferer to awaken repeatedly during the night and gasp for air. Another common problem among those who can't stay asleep is periodic limb movement disorder (PLMD), a neurological condition that causes frequent involuntary kicking or jerking movements during sleep.

My solutions: If you are unable to improve your sleep by following the strategies already described, consult a sleep specialist to determine whether you have sleep apnea or PLMD.

Sleep apnea patients usually get relief by losing weight, if necessary...elevating the head of the bed to reduce snoring...using an oral device that positions the jaw so that the tongue cannot block the throat during sleep...or wearing a face mask that delivers oxygen to keep their airways open. PLMD is usually treated with medication.

IF YOU CAN'T GET TO SLEEP

Most people take about 20 minutes to fall asleep, but this varies with the individual. If your mind is racing due to stress (from marital strife or financial worries, for example) or if you've adopted bad habits (such as drinking caffeine late in the day), you may end up tossing and turning.

My solutions: Limit yourself to one cup of caffeinated coffee or tea daily, and do not consume any caffeine-containing beverage or food (such as chocolate) after 2 pm. If you take a caffeine-containing drug, such as Excedrin or some cold remedies, ask your doctor if it can be taken earlier in the day.

*To find a sleep center near you, consult the American Academy of Sleep Medicine (708-492-0930, *www.sleepcenters.org*).

Helpful: If something is bothering you, write it down and tell yourself that you will deal with it tomorrow.

Also helpful: At night, turn the clock face away from you so you don't watch the minutes pass. If you can't sleep after 20 to 30 minutes, get up and do something relaxing, such as meditating, until you begin to feel drowsy.

IF YOU CAN'T GET UP IN THE MORNING

If you can't drag your head off the pillow, sleep apnea or a delayed sleep phase (DSP) disorder might be to blame. DSP disorder makes it hard to fall asleep early, so you stay up late and then struggle to get out of bed in the morning.

My solutions: To treat DSP disorder, progressively stay up for three hours later nightly for one week until you reach your desired bedtime. By staying up even later than is usual for you, you'll eventually shift your circadian rhythm. Once you find your ideal bedtime, stick to it. Also consider trying light-box therapy each morning upon arising. Light helps advance your body clock so that your bedtime should come earlier. Taking 3 mg to 5 mg of melatonin one hour before bedtime should also make you sleepy at an earlier hour.

IF YOU CAN'T STAY AWAKE DURING THE DAY

If you're getting ample rest—most people need seven and one-half to eight hours a night—and are still tired, you may have narcolepsy. This neurological disorder occurs when the brain sends out sleep-inducing signals at inappropriate times, causing you to fall asleep and even temporarily lose muscle function. Sleep apnea or periodic limb movements also can leave people feeling exhausted.

My solutions: Figure out how much sleep you need by sleeping as long as you can nightly (perhaps while on vacation) for one to two weeks. At the end of that period, you should be sleeping the number of hours you need. Give yourself that much sleep time nightly. If you remain sluggish, ask your doctor about tests for sleep apnea, PLMD—or narcolepsy, which is treated with stimulants, such as *modafinil* (Provigil), that promote wakefulness.

Drug News

Epilepsy Drug Saps Baby's Intelligence

When a pregnant woman with epilepsy takes the medication *valproate* (Depakote), her baby's intelligence may be lowered for at least three years, a recent study suggests.

Reporting in *The New England Journal of Medicine,* researchers found that when tested at age 3, children who were exposed to valproate in the womb had IQ scores up to nine points lower than children exposed to other epilepsy medications in utero.

The problem is, many women with epilepsy can only get good control of their seizures when using valproate.

BACKGROUND

While the majority of children born to women with epilepsy are normal, animal studies have suggested that exposure to epilepsy medications might be associated with "cognitive and behavioral difficulties," according to background information in the study.

To assess what effects these medications might have on babies, the Neurodevelopmental Effects of Antiepileptic Drugs (NEAD) study was begun. The study includes 309 children from 25 epilepsy centers in the United Kingdom and the United States. All of the mothers were taking one of four epilepsy medications during pregnancy—valproate, *carbamazepine* (Tegretol), *lamotrigine* (Lamictal) and *phenytoin* (Dilantin).

The researchers plan to assess the children periodically until they're 6 years old. The current report focuses on outcomes when the children were 3 years old.

STUDY FINDINGS

After compensating for other factors that might influence a child's intelligence—such as mater-

Kimford Meador, MD, professor of neurology, Emory University School of Medicine, Atlanta.

Inna Vaisleib, MD, pediatric neurologist and epileptologist, Children's Hospital of Pittsburgh.

The New England Journal of Medicine.

nal IQ, maternal age, the dose of antiepileptic medication, gestational age at birth and the mother's intake of folic acid—the researchers found that children exposed to valproate during pregnancy had significantly lower IQ scores than those exposed to the other medications.

The average IQ for children exposed in the womb to lamotrigine was 101, for phenytoin it was 99, and for carbamazepine it was 98. Children exposed to valproate in the womb scored an average of 92 on the IQ test, according to the study.

The researchers also found that the drug's effect on IQ was "dose-dependent," meaning that the higher the dose of medication, the more effect on the child's intelligence.

RECOMMENDATIONS

"We're not saying never use valproate, but try other drugs first," said the study's lead author, Kimford Meador, MD, a professor of neurology at Emory University School of Medicine in Atlanta. "We don't think that valproate should be used as a first choice for any woman of childbearing age. Other drugs should be used first."

Dr. Meador said the recommendation pertains to all women of childbearing age, not just pregnant women, because more than half of all pregnancies are unplanned, and any damage that may occur to the baby may occur before a woman even realizes that she's pregnant. Additionally, the drug has been shown to cause congenital birth defects in about 10% of children exposed to it in the womb, according to Dr. Meador.

For women currently taking valproate, Dr. Meador emphasized that no one should stop taking epilepsy medication abruptly, because this could result in seizures.

"Don't stop taking any medications without talking to your doctor," Dr. Meador stressed. "But, if you're on this medication, ask your doctor about it."

Dr. Meador said the researchers suspect that the medication may cause a loss of brain cells in the baby, like fetal alcohol syndrome does.

EXPERT COMMENTARY

"The take-away message is that the danger of neurocognitive impairment is real with the use of *valproic acid* (valproate)," said Inna Vaisleib, MD, a pediatric neurologist and epileptologist at Children's Hospital of Pittsburgh.

"Not using valproic acid in women of childbearing age is a good idea, as approximately half of all pregnancies are unplanned," she said, adding that "epilepsy is common, and about one in 200 pregnant women are receiving antiepileptic drugs."

Dr. Vaisleib cautioned strongly against stopping any medications without first consulting a neurologist, because seizures can also be damaging to a growing fetus, as well as to the expectant mother.

Info To learn more about epilepsy and pregnancy, visit the Epilepsy Foundation's Web site, *www.epilepsyfoundation.org,* and search "pregnancy."

Popular Osteoporosis Drugs May Cause Jaw Problems

Parish Sedghizadeh, DDS, MS, assistant professor of clinical dentistry, University of Southern California School of Dentistry, Los Angeles.

James Liu, MD, chairman, department of obstetrics and gynecology, MacDonald Women's Hospital at Case Medical Center, University Hospitals, Cleveland.

Merck & Co. statement.

Journal of the American Dental Association.

The proportion of people taking widely prescribed oral osteoporosis drugs who develop a nasty jaw condition may be much higher than previously thought, a recent study suggests.

Previous reports had indicated that the risk of developing *osteonecrosis of the jaw* (ONJ) after taking *bisphosphonates* were "negligible," although there was a noted risk in people taking the higher-dose intravenous form of the drug.

ONJ is characterized by pain, soft-tissue swelling, infection, loose teeth and exposed bone.

But Parish Sedghizadeh, DDS, MS, an assistant professor of clinical dentistry at the University of Southern California School of Dentistry in Los Angeles, said his clinic is seeing one to four new cases a week, compared to one a year in the past. This led him to investigate the phenomenon and publish the findings in the *Journal of the American Dental Association.*

"This is more frequent than everybody would like to think it is," said Dr. Sedghizadeh, lead author of the study.

BACKGROUND

Bisphosphonates are medications used to reduce the risk for bone fracture and to increase bone mass in people with osteoporosis. They're also used to slow bone "turnover" in people who have cancer that has spread to their bones, and in people who have the blood cancer multiple myeloma.

Use of bisphosphonates has been associated with other problems in the past, including an increased risk of atrial fibrillation (a type of abnormal heart rhythm), unusual fractures of the thighbone, and inflammatory eye disease.

THE STUDY

After searching the USC School of Dentistry's medical records database, the study authors found that nine of 208 patients taking the bisphosphonate *alendronate* (Fosamax) had active ONJ, a prevalence of about 4%. All were patients who had undergone some kind of dental procedure, such as having a tooth removed.

Fosamax is the most widely prescribed oral bisphosphonate and has been the 21st most prescribed drug in the United States since 2006, according to the study.

The jaw complication has been seen in patients taking Fosamax for as little as one year. It seems to occur most frequently after routine tooth extraction, the study authors said.

THEORY

Although no one is sure why bisphosphonates seem to have this effect only on jaw bones, Dr. Sedghizadeh speculated that the drugs may make it easier for bacteria to adhere to bone that is exposed after a tooth extraction.

Previously, experts had thought that ONJ in people taking intravenous bisphosphonates was related to their underlying condition (for example, cancer), not to the actual drug, explained James Liu, MD, chairman of obstetrics and gynecology at MacDonald Women's Hospital at Case Medical Center, University Hospitals in Cleveland.

IMPLICATIONS

Dr. Liu said the finding "does not mean that women should stop taking the drug if they're on it. It does mean that there may be more frequent side effects than was previously known."

The USC School of Dentistry now screens every patient for bisphosphonate use.

"As a school now, we don't have complications any more, we only have referrals," Dr. Sedghizadeh said. "We put patients on anti-microbial, anti-fungal rinse one week preoperatively or postoperatively. If they have been on bisphosphonates six months or a year or longer, then we have a prevention protocol which has been very, very effective."

MANUFACTURER MAKES STATEMENT

According to a statement released by Merck & Co., which makes Fosamax, the new study "has material methodological flaws and scientific limitations, making it unreliable as a source for valid scientific conclusions regarding the prevalence of ONJ in patients taking alendronate."

info To learn more about bisphosphonates and ONJ, visit the Web site of the American Dental Association, *www.ada.org,* and search "ONJ."

Fosamax: Bad to the Bone

Mark A. Stengler, ND, naturopathic physician in private practice, La Jolla, California...adjunct associate clinical professor at the National College of Natural Medicine, Portland, Oregon...author of many books and the *Bottom Line/Natural Healing* newsletter.

The popular drug *alendronate* (Fosamax) has been prescribed to millions of people (mostly women) suffering from osteoporosis, a weakening of the bones that often comes with aging. But two new findings indicate that the drug also can cause some significant health problems.

- **Physicians at Weill Medical College of Cornell University** found that Fosamax may increase risk for fractures of the thighbone (femur). Researchers reviewed 70 people with femur fractures and identified a type of break specific to patients who had been taking Fosamax for more than four years. (Incidentally, the breaks happened despite the subjects' suffering minimal or no trauma.)

Reason: Fosamax works by inhibiting bone cells known as osteoclasts, which break down bone so it can rebuild itself, and in some patients, this inhibits bone repair.

- **The FDA reported in 2008 that Fosamax** (and similar drugs) can cause incapacitating pain in bones, joints and/or muscles for reasons unknown.
- **A study in *Archives of Internal Medicine* found that postmenopausal women who had used Fosamax**—even if they had stopped taking it—were at higher risk for atrial fibrillation, a heart rhythm problem. This may be due to inflammation or decreases in calcium and phosphate levels, affecting how blood flows through arteries.

My thoughts: I recommend patients avoid taking Fosamax and other osteoporosis drugs in the bisphosphonate family. There are ways to increase bone density and strength without drugs. I recommend a pH-balanced diet…walking or other regular weight-bearing exercise…supplementing with bone-enhancing nutrients, such as calcium, magnesium, vitamin D and the mineral strontium daily…and addressing deficiencies in hormones, such as testosterone (especially important for postmenopausal women, who are at greatest risk for osteoporosis).

■ ■ ■ ■

Monthly Osteoporosis Pill Approved

A once-a-month, 150-milligram tablet of *risedronate* (Actonel) for prevention and treatment of postmenopausal osteoporosis is now FDA-approved. A recent study showed similar increases in bone mineral density (BMD) between patients taking monthly doses and those taking the approved daily dose, which was previously shown to decrease the risk for fractures. Monthly users were more likely to experience diarrhea as a side effect.

Also recently approved: A once-yearly osteoporosis drug, *zoledronic acid* (Reclast), given intravenously.

Karen Mahoney, spokesperson, Center for Drug Evaluation and Research, FDA, Silver Spring, Maryland.

■ ■ ■ ■

Cholesterol Drugs Do Not Strengthen Bones

Some preliminary research suggested that cholesterol-lowering statin drugs, such as *atorvastatin* (Lipitor), had beneficial effects on the skeleton.

But: A recent clinical study of postmenopausal women found that Lipitor had no effect, either positive or negative, on bone mineral density.

Michael R. McClung, MD, director, Oregon Osteoporosis Center, Portland, and coauthor of a study of 626 women, published in *Journal of Clinical Endocrinology and Metabolism.*

Nausea Drug Shows Promise Against Opioid Addiction

Stanford University news release.

A drug currently used to treat nausea can prevent symptoms of withdrawal from illegal and prescription opioid drugs, such as heroin, morphine and codeine, a recent study shows.

The Stanford University scientists behind the research added that it can do so without some of the serious side effects caused by existing treatments for addiction to these drugs.

BACKGROUND

Opioid abuse is rising at a faster rate than any other type of illicit drug use, yet only about a quarter of those dependent on opioids seek treatment. "One barrier to treatment is that when you abruptly stop taking the drugs, there is a constellation of symptoms associated with withdrawal," said lead author Larry F. Chu, MD, an assistant professor of anesthesia at Stanford University School of Medicine.

Those symptoms include agitation, insomnia, diarrhea, nausea and vomiting. Current methods of treating withdrawal symptoms aren't completely effective or cause severe side effects, requiring constant patient supervision.

"What we need is a magic bullet, something that treats the symptoms of withdrawal, does not lead to addiction and can be taken at home," Dr. Chu added.

NEW STUDY

Initial tests in mice showed that the drug *ondansetron* (Zofran) blocks certain 5-HT3 receptors involved in withdrawal symptoms, the researchers said. They then tested it in eight healthy, non-opioid-dependent volunteers who were given two doses of morphine—once without ondansetron and once with it—and found withdrawal symptoms were reduced in humans.

The study appeared in the *Journal of Pharmacogenetics and Genomics.*

EFFECTIVELY TREATING OPIOID ADDICTION

The Stanford team plans to continue testing the effectiveness of ondansetron in treating opioid addiction and to conduct a clinical study to determine the effectiveness of an ondansetron-like drug in treating opioid addiction.

However, the researchers noted that ondansetron alone can't solve the problems caused by opioid addiction, which is a long-term, complex process that involves both physical and psychological factors.

"This is not a cure for addiction. Treating the withdrawal component is only one way of alleviating the suffering. With luck and determination, we can identify additional targets and put together a comprehensive treatment program," said principal investigator J. David Clark, MD, a professor of anesthesia at Stanford.

info To learn more about opiate withdrawal, go to the National Institutes of Health Medline Plus Web site, *www.nlm.nih.gov/medlineplus,* and search "opiate withdrawal."

When Antibiotics Turn Deadly

B. Joseph Guglielmo, Jr., PharmD, professor and chair of the department of clinical pharmacy at the University of California, San Francisco (UCSF), and founder of the Antimicrobial Management Program at UCSF Medical Center. He is a coauthor of *Applied Therapeutics: The Clinical Use of Drugs* (Lippincott Williams & Wilkins).

Antibiotics are among the most frequently prescribed drugs in the US. What most people don't realize is that because drug companies generally do not make much profit by developing oral antibiotics, there are few new options available. That's why it's especially important that the available drugs be used correctly. Taking the wrong antibiotic can allow infections to linger—and sometimes become life-threatening. *What you need to know...*

WHEN TO TAKE AN ANTIBIOTIC

The immune system in healthy adults is very effective at eliminating minor infections—even ones caused by bacteria. Antibiotics are needed only when an infection overwhelms the immune system's ability to stop it or when an infection is too dangerous (or too painful) to be allowed to clear up on its own.

Examples: A bacterial infection of the lungs can be fatal, so it is almost always treated with antibiotics. Bacterial ear infections generally will go away without treatment, but antibiotics may decrease the duration of symptoms.

Good rule of thumb: Most infections of the ears, sinuses and respiratory tract are viral and don't require antibiotics.

How to tell: Viral infections of the respiratory tract usually start to improve in five to seven days. If you get worse after that time, there's a good chance that the infection is bacterial and may require antibiotics.

SHOULD YOU GET A CULTURE?

Doctors usually can guess which organism is causing an infection—and choose the right antibiotic—just by reviewing a patient's description of his/her symptoms.

However, cultures (taken from a throat swab, for example) should be used when it's unclear what's causing an infection—or when previous antibiotics weren't effective. In otherwise healthy adults, antibiotics start to ease symptoms of an infection within 24 hours. Symptoms that don't improve within two days may indicate an incorrect initial diagnosis or antibiotic choice.

BEWARE OF SIDE EFFECTS

Nearly every antibiotic may cause diarrhea, intestinal cramps or yeast infections in the mouth or vagina. That's because the drugs not only kill harmful microbes, but also reduce the numbers of "good" bacteria that keep harmful bacteria and fungi in check.

Besides the general side effects, each antibiotic also has other risks. *For example...*

•***Amoxicillin* plus *clavulanate* (Augmentin),** commonly used for certain respiratory tract infections, may cause skin rashes and hives.

•***Doxycycline* (Doryx),** for chronic eye infections and Lyme disease, increases sensitivity to sunlight.

•***Ciprofloxacin* (Cipro),** for urinary tract infections, can cause headache, abdominal pain and vomiting.

WHAT TO TAKE FOR COMMON INFECTIONS

Most effective antibiotics for common medical conditions...

•**Bacterial pneumonia.** Most cases are caused by an organism called *Streptococcus pneumoniae,* but some patients are infected with multiple and/or "resistant" organisms.

Main treatment: Hospitalized patients with community-acquired pneumonia usually are given an intravenous antibiotic, such as *ceftriaxone* (Rocephin) with *azithromycin* (Zithromax), or a "respiratory" fluoroquinolone, such as *levofloxacin* (Levaquin).

•**Ear infections.** Even doctors have difficulty differentiating viral from bacterial ear infections. Antibiotics often are used "just in case." If the infection is bacterial, the symptoms will start to abate within 24 hours of starting an antibiotic.

Main treatment: Amoxicillin for seven to 10 days. Patients with a history of antibiotic use for ear infections may have resistant organisms and will probably be given a broad-spectrum cephalosporin antibiotic, such as *cefdinir* (Omnicef). Similarly, patients who are allergic to amoxicillin may be given a cephalosporin antibiotic if the allergy is mild—or a fluoroquinolone, such as levofloxacin, if the allergy is severe.

•**Sinus infections.** Recent research by the Cochrane Collaboration, which reviews health-care practices and research evidence, found that about 80% of patients with sinus infections recover within two weeks without antibiotics.

However, a viral sinus infection can sometimes progress to a more serious, secondary bacterial infection. Patients with sinus pain that lasts for more than a week to 10 days—or who have a period of recovery followed by a painful relapse—probably need antibiotics.

Main treatment: The same as that used for ear infections.

•**Skin infections are usually due to *Staphylococcus aureus* or *Streptococcus pyogenes,*** common bacteria that can enter the skin through a cut or scrape.

Recent danger: A virulent, drug-resistant form of staph, known as methicillin-resistant *Staphylococcus aureus* (MRSA), can cause cellulitis, a life-threatening infection even in healthy adults.

What to look for: Although most localized skin infections will clear up on their own, an area of skin that is red and feels warm and tender and might spread rapidly could be cellulitis. In severe cases, the center area will turn black as the tissue degenerates. Treatment of MRSA usually requires consultation with an infectious-disease specialist.

•**Urinary tract infections** (UTIs) usually occur when fecal bacteria enter the urethra. Women get UTIs more often than men because of the close proximity of the urethra to the anus.

Mild UTIs often will clear up on their own. In studies, about two-thirds of women who take a placebo will recover within seven to 10 days, compared with 80% to 85% of those taking antibiotics. However, antibiotics are usually recommended both for symptom relief and to prevent a UTI from progressing to pyelonephritis, a dangerous kidney infection.

Main treatment: *Trimethoprim* plus *sulfamethoxazole* (Septra or Bactrim), a combination treatment usually taken for three days.

Important: If you get two or more UTIs a year, you may have resistant organisms. Your doctor may perform a urine culture to identify the organism, which will determine the appropriate antibiotic.

Caution: Don't combine ciprofloxacin with antacids or iron supplements—both can interfere with the absorption of this antibiotic.

■ ■ ■ ■

Green Tea Helps Antibiotics Fight Superbugs

Researchers in Egypt examined whether drinking green tea while taking an antibiotic would affect the medicine's ability to fight bacteria. Green tea was tested in combination with antibiotics against 28 different infectious microorganisms.

Result: Drinking even a small amount of green tea while on an antibiotic increased the drug's antibacterial effect. Also, green tea made 20% of antibiotic-resistant bacteria vulnerable to one of the cephalosporin antibiotics, such as *cephalexin* (Keflex), which they usually resist.

Green tea could play an important role in an age of antibiotic-resistant superbugs. This study is an example of how a natural substance can be used synergistically—to enhance the effectiveness of a traditional medication.

Mark A. Stengler, ND, naturopathic physician in private practice, La Jolla, California...adjunct associate clinical professor at the National College of Natural Medicine, Portland, Oregon...author of many books and the *Bottom Line/Natural Healing* newsletter.

■ **Also from Dr. Mark Stengler...**

Antibiotics—Rheumatoid Arthritis Cure or Controversy?

For the two million or so Americans who suffer from rheumatoid arthritis (RA), the symptoms—joint stiffness, inflammation and soreness—can be unbearably painful. RA, an autoimmune disorder, usually strikes between the ages of 30 and 50. For reasons unknown, it occurs in two to three times more women than men. Treatment includes anti-inflammatory drugs, such as *ibuprofen* (Advil, Motrin), steroids and/or disease-modifying antirheumatic drugs (DMARDS) such as *adalimumab* (Humira) and *methotrexate.* A holistic doctor may prescribe natural anti-inflammatory foods and supplements, such as fish oil, turmeric, *methylsulfonylmethane* (MSM, a sulfur-producing compound found in meat, seafood, fruits and vegetables) and the herb boswellia. But for many people, symptoms persist...and worsen as time goes on.

For some patients, a nontraditional course of treatment—long-term antibiotic therapy—may bring relief. A small but growing group of physicians, including rheumatologists and family and holistic doctors, now treat RA with antibiotics from the tetracycline family, such as *minocycline.* Patients take the drugs at a very low dose for months and sometimes years, and many report unprecedented relief. Some recover fully and can stop taking the drugs.

This approach emerged from the work of Thomas McPherson Brown, MD, from the Rockefeller Institute, a research facility in New York City. In 1951, he and his colleagues were the first to report that RA was not an infectious disease but the body's immune system reacting to a foreign invader (an antigen). They suspected that the particular antigen was from the family of mycoplasma, bacteria from the *pneumoniae* species. The most recent study on the subject, published in 2005 in *Rheumatology Journal,* suggests that bacteria could be a contributing cause for RA but concludes that more research is necessary.

To explore this further, I contacted Harry Spiera, MD, chief of rheumatology at Mount Sinai Medical Center in New York City. Dr. Spiera told me that he believes tetracycline derivatives may benefit RA sufferers, although he does not explicitly endorse this therapy.

Antibiotic use is fairly controversial because over time, the body can build up resistance to the drugs. They also can have unpleasant side effects—even at low doses—including allergic reactions, diarrhea and yeast infections.

Is it worth a try? Although the evidence is inconclusive at this point, I believe that low-dose antibiotic therapy is likely to help some RA patients. For those who are not responding to other therapies, the course of treatment is especially worth considering. However, it is crucial to work with a doctor who is experienced in this therapy.

I also recommend that patients do everything possible to strengthen their immune systems—eat a nutritious diet...avoid processed foods...and drink plenty of water to flush out toxins. You also may consider increasing your intake of "good" bacteria (in foods such as yogurt, kefir and sauerkraut) and taking a probiotic supplement of 5 billion colony-forming units (CFUs) daily. Take the probiotic two hours before or after the antibiotic. In addition, because antibiotics tend to deplete B vitamins, take a full-spectrum multivitamin/mineral or a B-complex supplement.

■ ■ ■ ■

Help for Severe Alzheimer's

The drug *donepezil*—already prescribed for mild-to-moderate-stage Alzheimer's symptoms—preserves cognitive function in late-stage Alzheimer's patients as well.

Recent finding: 63% of patients who took donepezil exhibited stable or improved memory, language, attention and recognition of their own names. The donepezil users also showed slower declines in overall social functioning than the placebo users.

Sandra E. Black, MD, professor of neurology, Sunnybrook Health Sciences Centre, University of Toronto, Canada, and leader of a study of 343 people, published in *Neurology.*

■ ■ ■ ■

Is There an Alzheimer's Cure?

In animal studies, a new drug (PBT2) dramatically improved memory and learning within days. The drug transports metal ions across cell membranes. Alzheimer's has been linked to disorders of metal ions, particularly copper and zinc. More study is needed.

Neuron.

■ ■ ■ ■

Blood Pressure Meds Lower Alzheimer's Risk

When researchers analyzed data for 2.7 million patients (median age 75) who took drugs for high blood pressure, those using angiotensin receptor blockers (ARBs), such as *candesartan* (Atacand) and *losartan* (Cozaar), were 26% to 38% less likely to develop Alzheimer's or other forms of dementia than other patients were.

Theory: ARBs may help prevent nerve cell injury from blood vessel damage in the brain, which is believed to contribute to the development of dementia. In dementia patients, ARBs may delay progression of the disease.

Benjamin Wolozin, MD, PhD, professor of pharmacology and neurology, Boston University School of Medicine.

■ ■ ■ ■

Pain Meds Prevent Alzheimer's Disease

A recent analysis based on 13,499 people found that those who tended to use aspirin and/or related painkillers called nonsteroidal anti-inflammatory drugs (NSAIDs) had up to a 23% reduced risk for the disease.

The effective drugs include *ibuprofen* (sold as Advil, Motrin and other brands) and *naproxen* (Aleve and other brands), in addition to aspirin. All were found to produce the same result. Alzheimer's is connected with inflammation in the brain, which NSAIDs counter.

Caution: The study authors do not recommend taking NSAIDs to prevent Alzheimer's but say the findings will direct further research.

Peter P. Zandi, PhD, associate professor, Johns Hopkins Bloomberg School of Public Health, Baltimore, and Christine A. Szekely, PhD, research scientist, Cedars-Sinai Medical Center, Los Angeles.

■ ■ ■ ■

Men: Taking Aspirin Affects PSA Levels

Men who take aspirin "regularly" have significantly lower prostate-specific antigen (PSA) levels than those who do not, according to a recent study. (A PSA test is used to screen men for prostate cancer.)

Impact: Aspirin use makes PSA testing less reliable. Tell your doctor about your aspirin use when scheduling a test.

Jay H. Fowke, PhD, MPH, assistant professor, Vanderbilt-Ingram Cancer Center, Nashville.

■ ■ ■ ■

Aspirin Helps Build Bone

Low doses of aspirin—81 milligrams daily—increase production of bone-forming cells. More study is needed before aspirin can be recommended as an osteoporosis preventive.

Songtao Shi, DDS, PhD, associate professor, University of Southern California School of Dentistry, Los Angeles, and leader of an animal study reported in *PLoS ONE* 2008.

■ ■ ■ ■

Amazing Ways Aspirin Protects Your Liver

Aspirin may protect the liver against damage from acetaminophen and other drugs, according to a recent study. This potent anti-inflammatory also may protect against liver disease resulting from alcohol, obesity and other causes. Clinical trials are needed to confirm aspirin's liver-protecting benefits.

Future possibility: Medicines could be formulated containing both acetaminophen and enough aspirin to ward off liver damage.

Wajahat Z. Mehal, MD, associate professor, section of digestive diseases, Yale School of Medicine, New Haven, Connecticut, and leader of a study of aspirin's effect on liver damage, published in *Journal of Clinical Investigation.*

■ ■ ■ ■

RA Drugs Raise Risk For Serious Infections

Several drugs known as *TNF blockers,* immune-suppressing drugs that treat rheumatoid arthritis, Crohn's disease and other conditions, can increase patients' risk for severe local or systemic fungal infections. The drugs—Remicade, Humira, Cimzia and Enbrel—work by suppressing the immune system, leaving some patients open to these infections. The Food and Drug Administration has ordered stronger warning labels to alert doctors to the fungal-infection risk. Patients taking TNF blockers should be aware that they are more susceptible to serious fungal infections. If you develop a persistent fever, cough, shortness of breath, unexplained weight loss and/or fatigue, seek medical attention promptly.

Jeffrey Siegel, MD, clinical team leader, FDA Division of Anesthesia, Analgesia and Rheumatology Products, Silver Spring, Maryland.

Hidden Side Effects of 10 Common Drugs

Joe Graedon, MS, a pharmacologist, and Teresa Graedon, PhD. The Durham, North Carolina–based consumer advocates specialize in drugs and supplements. Their syndicated newspaper column, "The People's Pharmacy," appears in newspapers nationwide and abroad. The couple are coauthors of 12 books, including *Best Choices from The People's Pharmacy* (Rodale), *www.peoplespharmacy.com.*

When doctors prescribe medication, the goal is to reduce troubling symptoms—or even cure a particular medical condition. But sometimes a medication's side effects can be as bad as the condition being treated.

While some side effects, such as a headache or rash, are usually easy to spot, others can be subtle, develop slowly and go undetected by both the doctor and the person taking the medication.

In many cases, the drug's side effect may even be causing—or worsening—one of the common chronic health problems mentioned in this article.

Caution: Never stop taking prescription medication without your doctor's consent. If you're concerned about side effects, call your physician for advice.

Hidden side effects may contribute to...

HIGH BLOOD PRESSURE

- **Pain relievers.** Researchers at Brigham and Women's Hospital in Boston found that older men who used nonsteroidal anti-inflammatory drugs (NSAIDs), such as *ibuprofen* (Advil) or *naproxen* (Aleve), six to seven times weekly had a 38% higher risk of developing high blood pressure (hypertension) than men who did not use an NSAID. *Acetaminophen* (Tylenol) users had a 34% increased risk.

Theory: Pain relievers may raise blood pressure because of their effect on prostaglandins, which are hormone-like chemicals that affect the dilation and constriction of blood vessels and blood flow.

Our advice: You may be able to reduce your NSAID use—and the potential for increased hypertension risk—by trying topical pain relievers, such as over-the-counter BenGay arthritis cream or the prescription topical NSAID *diclofenac* (Voltaren). Or ask your doctor about anti-inflammatory fish oil supplements. In a recent nine-month Scottish study, 39% of rheumatoid arthritis sufferers who consumed 2.2 grams (g) of omega-3 fatty acids from fish oils daily reduced their NSAID use by 30% or more.

- **Estrogen drugs that are used as hormone replacement therapy** (HRT) in postmenopausal women may raise blood pressure and increase risk for blood clots, which elevates stroke risk.

Our advice: If you use HRT, take the lowest possible dose for the shortest possible time. If you are bothered by hot flashes, consider taking the herbal supplement pine bark extract (Pycnogenol), which may provide some relief.

- ***Pseudoephedrine,*** the decongestant in Sudafed and many other cold remedies, works by constricting blood vessels to reduce nasal stuffiness, but the drug's effect can increase blood pressure.

Our advice: If you have high blood pressure, never take pseudoephedrine unless it is recommended by your doctor. For congestion, use a saline nasal wash or spray for its soothing effects.

Important: If you're taking any of the above drugs, it's crucial to monitor your blood pressure regularly. (Ask your doctor to recommend a reliable home monitor.) When starting the medication, check your blood pressure two to three times a day, gradually tapering off to once or twice a week (unless your doctor advises otherwise).

PREDIABETES/DIABETES

- **Corticosteroids,** such as *prednisone* and *methylprednisolone* (Medrol), used to treat conditions ranging from arthritis to asthma, can raise blood sugar (glucose) levels. Long-term, high-dose use can cause or exacerbate diabetes.

Our advice: If you take a steroid, report signs of elevated blood sugar, such as increased thirst, hunger and urination, to your physician.

- **Atypical antipsychotics,** such as *aripiprazole* (Abilify), *clozapine* (Clozaril) and *risperidone* (Risperdal), primarily used for schizophrenia or bipolar disorder, may elevate blood sugar levels (indirectly as a result of weight gain).

Our advice: If you take an atypical antipsychotic, tell your doctor if you show signs of elevated blood sugar (described earlier).

- **Beta-blockers,** such as *atenolol* (Tenormin) or *sotalol* (Betapace), used for high blood pressure and heart rhythm abnormalities...and thiazide diuretics, such as *chlorothiazide* (Diuril) and *indapamide* (Lozol), also used for high blood pressure and sometimes congestive heart failure, can increase diabetes risk in some people.

Our advice: If you have diabetes (or "prediabetes" blood sugar levels) and need medication for hypertension, ask your doctor about trying an angiotensin-converting enzyme (ACE) inhibitor, such as *ramipril* (Altace) or *enalapril* (Vasotec)...or an angiotensin receptor blocker (ARB), such as *losartan* (Cozaar).

MENTAL IMPAIRMENT

- **Anticholinergics,** such as *benztropine* (Cogentin), used to treat Parkinson's disease...

and *tolterodine* (Detrol), used to treat overactive bladder, block the neurotransmitter *acetylcholine* from binding to nerve cells. An eight-year study of 870 older Catholic clergy members and nuns found that those taking anticholinergic drugs were 50% more likely to show mental decline.

Our advice: If you or a loved one has memory and concentration lapses or shows signs of dementia, ask your doctor if medication may be to blame.

•**Statins,** such as *atorvastatin* (Lipitor) and *simvastatin* (Zocor). There is preliminary evidence linking very low cholesterol levels to depression, memory loss and confusion. More research is needed to determine if there's a real connection between very low cholesterol and neurological conditions.

Our advice: If you have a family history of such conditions, talk to your doctor about the potential benefits and risks of aggressively lowering your cholesterol.

VISION PROBLEMS

•**Erectile dysfunction drugs,** such as *sildenafil* (Viagra), *vardenafil* (Levitra) and *tadalafil* (Cialis), can cause vision disturbances—most commonly a blue haze or increased brightness. In rare cases, men taking ED drugs have suffered blindness from reduced blood flow to the optic nerve. But it's unclear whether the medication was to blame, since impotence itself may be a sign of vascular problems. More recently, there also have been a small number of reports of hearing loss or tinnitus (ringing in the ears) in men taking ED drugs.

Our advice: If you experience any vision or hearing symptoms, contact your doctor as soon as possible.

•**Corticosteroids may cause pressure buildup in the eye,** increasing your risk for glaucoma. Also, research has shown that cataracts may develop in up to 75% of patients taking 15 mg or more of oral prednisone daily for over a year. People who inhale steroids are at 50% increased risk for nuclear (center-lens) cataracts and 90% greater risk for posterior (back-lens) cataracts, according to an Australian study.

Our advice: If you must take long-term steroids (generally, more than one year of continued use), have your eyes examined regularly by an ophthalmologist.

Statins Raise Post-Op Delirium Risk

Donald A. Redelmeier, MD, professor, medicine, University of Toronto, Ontario, Canada.
Edward R. Marcantonio, MD, associate professor, medicine, Harvard Medical School, Boston.
Canadian Medical Association Journal.

People who take cholesterol-lowering statin drugs—which include Crestor, Lipitor, Pravachol and Zocor—are more likely to suffer delirium after surgery, a Canadian study indicates.

BACKGROUND

Delirium is a common, and commonly neglected, experience for older people after any sort of surgery, according to study lead author Donald A. Redelmeier, MD, professor of medicine at the University of Toronto.

"It's quite striking how some people are unable to recognize family members and don't know where they are," Dr. Redelmeier said. "It is sometimes prolonged and severe."

THE STUDY

The study included more than 284,000 people, 65 years of age and older, who had surgery in Ontario hospitals. The researchers reported that the incidence of delirium was one out of every 90 patients, but it was 30% more likely to occur in those taking a statin before surgery.

These statistics are almost certainly too low, however, because "there is no question that delirium is often overlooked by the surgeon or family members or even the patient himself," Dr. Redelmeier said.

His estimate is that delirium occurs after about 10% of all surgical procedures, and that the incidence is 13% among people taking statins.

Dr. Redelmeier said he looked for a possible link between statins and post-op delirium, because "all clinical trials of statins focus on otherwise healthy outpatients under normal circumstances. Whereas, from my work in hospitals, I have found that medications that are safe under normal circumstances might not be safe at the time of surgery." Blood-thinning medications such as *warfarin* (Coumadin), as well as sleeping pills, are other examples of drugs that raise delirium risks, he said.

His team published its findings in the *Canadian Medical Association Journal.*

POSSIBLE EXPLANATION

Statins might increase the risk of delirium by shunting blood away from the brain to the heart, the report proposed.

"It is plausible, but there are no biological data to support it," said one expert, Edward R. Marcantonio, MD, associate professor of medicine at Harvard Medical School and the author of an accompanying editorial.

STOPPING STATINS BEFORE SUGERY

Dr. Marcantonio was also cautious about stopping statin therapy before surgery. "Before making a change in clinical management, I usually like to see stronger evidence in doing so," he said.

Dr. Marcantonio cited other factors that argued against stopping statins. "We certainly don't know the effect of taking patients off these drugs on outcomes other than delirium, such as cardiovascular conditions," he said. "They may have cardiovascular benefits above and beyond their lipid-lowering effects."

And, Dr. Marcantonio said, "There is always the risk of the drug never getting restarted."

Dr. Redelmeier has no such doubts. An internist, he does not do surgery himself but is often called in for consultation by surgeons. "I take the position that a brief interruption, for one or two days prior to surgery, is extremely simple, and if desired, you could restart the statin right there in the recovery room after surgery, so you get protection without any interaction with anesthetics," he reasoned.

MORE DELIRIUM STUDIES NEEDED

More study is needed to settle the issue, Dr. Marcantonio said. Delirium has been underreported in the past because of reliance on reviews of medical records, he said. "One of the real advances has been development of interview tools to enable assessment of delirium in a reliable way."

Dr. Marcantonio has done such studies himself. "It is an expanding area of research. There are ongoing studies of delirium where data may be available to do this sort of evaluation," he said. "Certainly, such a study is doable, perhaps within a couple of years."

info For more information, visit the National Heart, Lung, and Blood Institute Web site, *www.nhlbi.nih.gov,* and click on "NHLBI Health Information Center."

Are Cholesterol-Lowering Drugs Making You Sick?

Mark A. Stengler, ND, naturopathic physician in private practice, La Jolla, California...adjunct associate clinical professor at the National College of Natural Medicine, Portland, Oregon...author of many books and the *Bottom Line/Natural Healing* newsletter.

Statins are cholesterol-lowering drugs, including *atorvastatin* (Lipitor), *simvastatin* (Zocor) and *rosuvastatin* (Crestor). These medications have been shown in rare instances to cause peripheral neuropathy, a condition characterized by pain and numbness in the hands and feet. A Danish study found that people taking statins were 14 times more likely to develop peripheral neuropathy than people who were not taking the drugs. One possible cause is that statins deplete the body of coenzyme Q10 (CoQ10), an antioxidant and energy-producing nutrient. One study found that after 30 days on Lipitor, patients' blood levels of CoQ10 were reduced by half.

If this happens to you, consult a holistic doctor to find a different treatment for high cholesterol. In addition, try taking 200 milligrams (mg) of CoQ10 daily, plus 1,000 mg of *acetyl L-carnitine,* an amino acid that produces energy in cells, three times daily. You should notice an improvement in eight to 12 weeks. I gave this prescription to an MD friend of mine, and his symptoms are slowly dissipating.

■ **More from Dr. Mark Stengler...**

Ouch! Statins Cause Tendon Disorders

Researchers at Rouen University Hospital in Cedex, France, identified 96 people whose tendonitis or tendon ruptures were attributed to statin therapy. In more than half of patients, the problem began within one year of starting statin therapy to lower cholesterol. Those taking *metformin* for diabetes, *fluoroquinolone* antibiotics or steroid drugs—all of which increase statins' toxicity—were at increased risk. Tendonitis improved or went away when the statins were discontinued and recurred in those who resumed the therapy.

We are learning about certain side effects only now that statins have been on the market for several years. It is unknown how these drugs increase the risk for tendon disorders. Cholesterol is needed to form tendon cell membranes, and statins seem to interfere with this process or destroy tendon cells. I think most people taking statin drugs could achieve the same cardiovascular prevention with a healthy diet, exercise and natural supplements, such as red yeast rice, plant sterols, fish oil and niacin. Talk to your doctor about treatment options.

■ **Also from Dr. Mark Stengler...**

Vytorin May Raise Cancer Risk

Are people who take the cholesterol-lowering drug Vytorin at increased risk for cancer? The Federal Drug Administration is investigating a report from a clinical trial that indicates that there might be such a link. Vytorin contains both *simvastatin* (Zocor), a statin that reduces cholesterol production by the liver, and *ezetimibe* (Zetia), which decreases cholesterol absorption from food in the small intestine. The five-year trial was developed to determine whether lowering LDL (bad) cholesterol with Vytorin reduced the risk for cardiovascular events in people with aortic stenosis, a narrowing of the heart valve. Vytorin did not appear to reduce cardiovascular risk, but a larger percentage of people treated with Vytorin were diagnosed with, and died from, cancer than those who took a placebo.

There is much debate about the safety of Vytorin. To date, two ongoing studies, which will be completed in 2010 and 2012, have not found an increased risk for cancer. But a 2007 analysis of 16 studies involving statins, published in *Journal of the American College of Cardiology,* did find an association between low LDL levels and cancer in patients taking a statin.

Since the jury is still out, I recommend that you speak to your doctor about using a medication other than Vytorin. There also is a variety of natural options, including red yeast rice, plant sterols and niacin, that can optimize cholesterol levels without serious health risks.

■ ■ ■ ■

Breakthrough Drug Therapy for COPD

Patients with chronic obstructive pulmonary disease (COPD) lose lung function. The disease remains incurable, but for the first time, drug therapy—a combination of the inhaled cortical steroid *fluticasone propionate* and the beta-agonist *salmeterol*—can slow the rate of lung function decline.

Bartolomé R. Celli, MD, is professor of medicine, Tufts University School of Medicine, Boston, and research professor of medicine, Caritas-St. Elizabeth's Medical Center, Brighton, Massachusetts. He led a trial of drug therapy for COPD involving 6,112 patients, published in *American Journal of Respiratory and Critical Care Medicine.*

■ ■ ■ ■

COPD Drugs Raise Heart Attack Risk and More

In a recent study, researchers analyzed 17 studies involving 14,783 patients with chronic obstructive pulmonary disease (COPD)—a group of lung diseases that includes emphysema and chronic bronchitis. Patients who used inhaled drugs known as *anticholinergics*, which relax airway muscles and assist breathing, had a 58%

higher risk, on average, for heart attack, stroke or death than those who did not use these drugs.

Theory: Inhaled anticholinergics may cause heart rhythm disturbances.

If you use an inhaled anticholinergic: Discuss the risks and benefits with your doctor.

Sonal Singh, MD, MPH, assistant professor of internal medicine, Wake Forest University School of Medicine, Winston-Salem, North Carolina.

■ ■ ■ ■

Better Crohn's Disease Treatment

In a two-year study of 129 patients with Crohn's disease (chronic inflammation of the digestive tract), half the patients received conventional treatment—including steroid drugs to reduce inflammation followed by the immune-suppressing drugs *azathioprine* (Imuran) and, if needed, *infliximab* (Remicade), given via infusion. The others received the same regimen without steroids.

After 26 weeks, 60% of the steroid-free group were symptom-free versus 36% of the conventional therapy group.

Geert D'Haens, MD, PhD, director, Imelda Gastrointestinal Clinical Research Center, Imelda General Hospital, Bonheiden, Belgium.

■ ■ ■ ■

Ease Itchy Eczema Flare-Ups

Eczema (dry, itchy, swollen skin) is usually treated with topical anti-inflammatory cream twice daily during flare-ups. Patients who applied *tacrolimus* (Protopic) twice weekly to lesion-prone areas even when no lesions were visible went 142 days between flare-ups, on average...versus 15 days for placebo users. Tacrolimus can cause nausea and muscle pain and may increase skin cancer risk, so ask your doctor about the pros and cons of preventive eczema treatment.

Sakari Reitamo, MD, PhD, acting professor of dermatology, University of Helsinki, Finland, and coauthor of a clinical trial of 247 adults, published in *Allergy*.

■ ■ ■ ■

New Treatment for Irritable Bowel Syndrome (IBS)

Lubiprostone (Amitiza) is currently the only FDA-approved prescription drug therapy for constipation-predominant IBS (which can also cause cramping, abdominal pain, bloating and diarrhea). Lubiprostone increases secretions of intestinal fluid, which increases intestinal motility and reduces symptoms of chronic constipation.

Julie Beitz, MD, director, Office of Drug Evaluation III, FDA Center for Drug Evaluation and Research, Silver Spring, Maryland.

■ ■ ■ ■

Impotence Drugs May Treat Brain Tumors

In recent tests on rats, the drugs Levitra and Viagra helped a cancer-fighting medicine get to the brain more effectively. It also increased survival times.

Keith L. Black, MD, chairman, department of neurosurgery, Cedars-Sinai Medical Center, Los Angeles, and leader of a study published in *Brain Research*.

■ ■ ■ ■

Viagra Worsens Sleep Apnea

Sleep apnea sufferers who take Viagra or other erectile dysfunction drugs increase their risk for oxygen deprivation during sleep.

Theory: The drugs may promote congestion of the upper airway, making breathing difficult.

Self-defense: If you have any symptoms of sleep apnea, including snoring or excessive daytime sleepiness, get tested for sleep apnea before taking an erectile dysfunction drug. If you do have sleep apnea, ask your health-care provider about alternative treatments for erectile dysfunction.

Study by researchers in the department of psychobiology, Federal University of São Paulo, Brazil, and Stanford University Medical Center, Stanford, California, published in *Archives of Internal Medicine*.

■ ■ ■ ■

Incontinence Drugs Linked to Memory Loss

People who take *anticholinergic* drugs, such as Detrol and Ditropan, to treat incontinence had a rate of cognitive decline that was one and a half times faster than people who did not take these drugs.

Self-defense: Talk to your doctor about alternate therapies.

Jack Tsao, MD, PhD, is an assistant professor of neurology at Uniformed Services University of the Health Sciences, Bethesda, Maryland, and author of a collaborative study of 870 people, presented at the American Academy of Neurology annual meeting in 2008.

■ ■ ■ ■

Reduce Lupus Symptoms 36%

An autoimmune disease, lupus causes periodic flare-ups of joint pain, rash, fever and other symptoms. *Mycophenolate mofetil* (MMF) is an immune-suppressing drug used by transplant patients to prevent rejection of donor organs.

Recent study: Lupus patients had 36% fewer flare-ups over a two-year period while taking MMF than they had during the two years prior to MMF treatment. If you have lupus, talk to your doctor about treatment options, including MMF.

Kevin Moder, MD, rheumatologist, Mayo Clinic, Rochester, Minnesota, and leader of a study of 88 lupus patients, presented at a meeting of the American College of Rheumatology.

■ ■ ■ ■

Parkinson's Risk Cut by Blood Pressure Drug

In a recent analysis of the health data for 7,374 men and women (half of whom had Parkinson's disease), those who had been taking calcium channel blockers (CCBs), such as *nifedipine* (Procardia) or *amlodipine* (Norvasc), were 23% less likely to develop Parkinson's than those who didn't take the drugs. No such effect was found for other blood pressure drugs.

Theory: CCBs may protect nerve cells in the central nervous system.

If you take blood pressure medication: Ask your doctor if a CCB is right for you.

Christoph R. Meier, PhD, associate professor, pharmacoepidemiology unit, University Hospital Basel, Basel, Switzerland.

The Hidden Dangers of Off-Label Prescriptions

Douglas Melnick, MD, MPH, a specialist in public health and preventive medicine in North Hollywood, California. He formerly worked for the pharmaceutical industry as a physician in medical affairs in support of drug marketing. Dr. Melnick is the co-author of "Off-Label Promotion, On-Target Sales," which appeared in the October 28, 2008, issue of *PLoS Medicine,* a peer-reviewed journal published by the Public Library of Science.

Of all prescriptions written for 160 common medications, about one out of every five were prescribed off-label, according to recent research. This means that the drugs were used in ways never approved by the FDA.

To learn more about this practice, we spoke with Douglas Melnick, MD, MPH, a preventive medicine physician who worked in the pharmaceutical industry...

• **What is an "off-label" prescription?** FDA approval is granted for medications that have been shown in clinical trials to be both safe and effective for a particular medical condition. However, once a drug is approved—no matter what it's approved for—doctors can prescribe it for any medical condition.

• **Why do doctors prescribe medications off-label?** For obvious reasons, pregnant women—and, until recently, most children—have been excluded from most drug studies, so few drugs have undergone the kind of testing required by the FDA in these particular groups. Therefore, a pregnant woman with, say, migraines, has little choice but to take a migraine drug off-label.

Also, it's common to discover new uses for old medications. Rather than wait for a drug company to conduct FDA-required studies on a medication's effect on a condition for which it was not approved—a process that can take years, cost hundreds of millions of dollars and might never be done—doctors use the drugs right away.

•Is this practice responsible? In some cases, it would be irresponsible not to prescribe drugs off-label. For example, aspirin was known to reduce heart attacks long before it was given FDA approval for this use. Waiting might have resulted in thousands of unnecessary deaths.

•Are there dangers associated with using drugs off-label? Most drugs that are prescribed off-label haven't been tested for such use in large populations using double-blind, placebo-controlled studies. These studies, which are the "gold standard," can take years to complete, but they are the only way to prove that a drug is both effective and safe. Some drugs that haven't been exhaustively tested for off-label uses will invariably prove to be ineffective. Others may prove to be dangerous.

For example, in 1973 the FDA approved an appetite suppressant, *fenfluramine*, for short-term use. Doctors then began prescribing it for longer periods (an off-label use) in combination with a drug called *phentermine*. Approximately 100 cases of heart-valve disease were reported in patients taking the combination drug, commonly known as Fen-Phen, before it was removed from the market.

•What role do the drug companies play? It's illegal for pharmaceutical companies to promote—through advertising, conversations with doctors or other means—off-label drug uses. However, the industry routinely engages in practices to heighten awareness of off-label use.

In some cases, a drug's off-label uses may be more lucrative than its indicated use. If a company anticipates this, it may seek FDA approval for a so-called "decoy indication."

Here's how it works: Suppose that a company develops an ulcer drug that also shows potential for cancer prevention. The company will conduct a relatively inexpensive ulcer study—because cancer studies tend to be much lengthier and expensive. When the company gets FDA approval for this drug as an ulcer treatment, it will quietly put out the word that the drug also may work for cancer.

By law, pharmaceutical sales representatives are not allowed to discuss off-label uses with doctors. There's a loophole, however, if the doctor asks first. For example, suppose a doctor learns at a dinner conference sponsored by a drug company that a new drug is being used off-label to lower blood pressure. He can ask the drug manufacturer for a packet of information that contains abstracts or articles about the medication's effectiveness in treating high blood pressure.

In addition, medical professionals (most commonly, pharmacists) who work as medical liaisons for pharmaceutical companies are allowed to discuss off-label drug use with physicians—but, again, only if the doctor first asks about off-label uses of the drug.

•Do doctors play any other role in the promotion of off-label drugs? A pharmaceutical company may recruit an influential physician to spread the word about off-label drug uses. This often is done indirectly—by funding research, for example—or more directly by providing speaking fees. The goal isn't necessarily to conduct high-level research, but to generate buzz. When word gets out that a drug may work for an off-label use—and is being used by an expert in the field—physicians around the country will be more likely to try it.

•Should patients worry about off-label prescriptions? They should, at a minimum, be aware of the practice. Every patient treated with an off-label drug is essentially taking part in an informal study. Will the drug work? Are there serious side effects? These are questions that truly get answered only during the FDA's approval process. Off-label drug uses, by definition, are more uncertain.

I suggest that patients who take any medication ask their doctors the following questions...

•Is this drug FDA-approved for my condition? If not, why are you prescribing it? Are there other drugs that do have FDA approval?

•Do you know how many patients have been treated off-label with this drug? For how many years has it been used off-label?

14 Drugs that Need Immediate Research

Randall S. Stafford, MD, PhD, senior study author and associate professor of medicine at the Stanford Center for Research in Disease Prevention at Stanford University School of Medicine in Stanford, California.

Fourteen commonly used medications that often are prescribed "off-label"—that is, for uses for which the medications do not have FDA approval—merit immediate priority for additional study, according to researchers from Stanford University and the University of Illinois at Chicago. Questions remain regarding the safety and efficacy of these drugs when they are prescribed off-label.

The drugs in the chart are listed in the order in which researchers believe they should be studied (based, in part, on an analysis of volume of off-label drug use with inadequate evidence supporting that use).

According to researchers, this list is only a small sampling of drug uses that are not supported by sufficient scientific evidence.

Rank	Drug (brand name)	Most common on-label use	Most common off-label use*
1	*Quetiapine* (Seroquel)	Schizophrenia	Bipolar disorder maintenance
2	*Warfarin* (Coumadin)	Atrial fibrillation	Hypertensive heart disease
3	*Escitalopram* (Lexapro)	Depression	Bipolar disorder
4	*Risperidone* (Risperdal)	Schizophrenia	Bipolar disorder maintenance
5	*Montelukast* (Singulair)	Asthma	Chronic obstructive pulmonary disease
6	*Bupropion* (Wellbutrin)	Depression	Bipolar disorder
7	*Sertraline* (Zoloft)	Depression	Bipolar disorder
8	*Venlafaxine* (Effexor)	Depression	Bipolar disorder
9	*Celecoxib* (Celebrex)	Joint sprain/strain	Muscle aches
10	*Lisinopril* (Prinivil, Zestril)	Hypertension	Coronary artery disease
11	*Duloxetine* (Cymbalta)	Depression	Anxiety
12	*Trazodone* (Desyrel)	Depression	Sleep disturbance
13	*Olanzapine* (Zyprexa)	Schizophrenia	Depression
14	*Epoetin alfa* (Procrit, Epogen)	Chronic kidney failure	Anemia associated with chronic disease

*These drugs are most often prescribed off-label for psychiatric conditions, such as bipolar disorder and depression, but also are commonly used off-label for other problems, such as dementia.

■ ■ ■ ■

Better Medication Instructions

When researchers studied 2,346 older adults who took the blood thinner *warfarin* (Coumadin), those who received written instructions or written plus verbal instructions were 60% less likely to suffer a serious bleeding problem—a possible side effect—over the next two years than those who received only the instructions printed on the prescription bottle.

Self-defense: Ask for both written and verbal information on the proper use of medication.

Joshua P. Metlay, MD, PhD, associate professor, division of internal medicine, University of Pennsylvania School of Medicine, Philadelphia.

■ ■ ■ ■

Outrageous! Generic Drugs Don't Always Work Like Brand Names

The Food and Drug Administration (FDA) requires that generic drugs carry labels identical to the labels of their corresponding brand-name drugs—but this can lead to errors.

Example: There is evidence that the generic version of the antidepressant Wellbutrin XL is more quickly absorbed than the original.

Self-defense: If you switch to any generic from any brand-name drug and you notice a difference, let your doctor know immediately.

Tod Cooperman, MD, president, *ConsumerLab.com*, White Plains, New York.

Drinks that Undo Drugs' Benefits

Beverly J. McCabe-Sellers, PhD, RD, who was a professor of dietetics and nutrition at the University of Arkansas for Medical Sciences in Little Rock for more than 20 years. She continues to serve as an adjunct professor of nutrition at the university's School of Public Health and is a coeditor of the *Handbook of Food-Drug Interactions* (CRC).

If you take any kind of prescription or over-the-counter (OTC) medication, you may be unwittingly reducing its benefits and/or increasing its risks by drinking certain beverages when you swallow the drug. The potentially harmful interactions also may occur if you drink the beverage hours before or after taking the medication.

For example...

DANGERS OF GRAPEFRUIT JUICE

Grapefruit juice has long been known to alter the effects of certain medications, but not all doctors warn their patients about these potential dangers.*

Grapefruit juice contains compounds that inhibit an important enzyme called CYP3A4, which is found in the liver and intestines. CYP3A4 is one of several enzymes that help break down up to 70% of all medications.

Grapefruit juice that is made from concentrate usually contains the entire fruit, including the rind—the primary source of the compound that affects drug metabolism. Grapefruit juice that is not made from concentrate contains less of this compound. However, to be safe, it's best to avoid grapefruit juice (and grapefruit itself) altogether if you take certain medications.

Among the drugs that can interact with grapefruit juice...

*As a general guideline, it is best not to drink any juice at the same time that you take medication. Instead, use water to swallow pills.

- **Anti-arrhythmic medications,** such as *amiodarone* (Cordarone), *quinidine* (Quinidex) and *disopyramide* (Norpace), which are taken for abnormal heart rhythms.

Risks: Heart arrhythmias as well as thyroid, pulmonary or liver damage.

- **Blood pressure–lowering calcium channel blockers,** such as *felodipine* (Plendil), *nifedipine* (Procardia) and *verapamil* (Calan).

Risks: A precipitous drop in blood pressure, as well as flushing, swelling of the extremities, headaches, irregular heartbeat and, in rare cases, heart attack.

- **Cholesterol-lowering drugs,** such as *atorvastatin* (Lipitor), *lovastatin* (Mevacor) and *simvastatin* (Zocor).

Risks: Headache, stomach upset, liver inflammation and muscle pain or weakness.

- **Sedatives** such as *diazepam* (Valium) and *triazolam* (Halcion).

Risks: Dizziness, confusion and drowsiness.

DANGERS OF APPLE JUICE AND ORANGE JUICE

Recent research shows that apple juice and orange juice can decrease the absorption of some drugs if the juice is swallowed at the same time as the pill. Grapefruit juice is also believed to have this effect.

Specifically, researchers found that apple, orange and grapefruit juice decrease the absorption of...

- **Allergy medication** *fexofenadine* (Allegra).
- **Antibiotics,** such as *ciprofloxacin* (Cipro) and *levofloxacin* (Levaquin).
- **Antifungal drug** *itraconazole* (Sporanox).
- **Blood pressure–lowering beta-blockers,** such as *atenolol* (Tenormin).
- **Chemotherapy drug** *etoposide* (Toposar).

If you are taking any of these drugs, it is probably safe to drink apple or orange juice (and eat whole fruits) at least two hours before or three hours after taking the medications. Check with your doctor first. Avoid grapefruit juice (and grapefruit itself) altogether.

DANGERS OF COFFEE

Coffee can interact with certain medications in a variety of ways. Do not drink coffee at the same time that you take any medication. *Limit daily consumption of coffee to one to two cups if you take...*

•**Antacids.** Because coffee contains acid, it counteracts the effectiveness of OTC antacids such as calcium carbonate (TUMS) and Maalox.

•**Aspirin or other medications in the NSAID (nonsteroidal anti-inflammatory) group,** such as *ibuprofen* (Advil) or *naproxen* (Aleve). Because coffee increases stomach acidity, combining it with these drugs may increase risk for gastrointestinal side effects, including stomach irritation and bleeding.

•**Bronchodilator *theophylline* (Elixophyllin),** used to treat asthma or emphysema. Consuming coffee with the bronchodilator can slow the breakdown of the drug, leading to higher blood levels and an increased risk for nausea, vomiting, palpitations and seizures.

•**Monoamine oxidase inhibitor (MAOI) antidepressants,** such as *phenelzine* (Nardil) and *selegiline* (Eldepryl). The combination may increase anxiety.

•**Osteoporosis drug *alendronate* (Fosamax).** Studies show that coffee (and orange juice) can inhibit absorption of Fosamax by 60%. If you take Fosamax or any other osteoporosis medication, ask your pharmacist about foods or other beverages that may interact with the drug.

DANGERS OF CRANBERRY JUICE

In the United Kingdom, there have been at least eight recent reports of bleeding in patients (one of whom died) after they drank cranberry juice with the blood-thinning medication *warfarin* (Coumadin).

Health officials were unable to definitively link the bleeding to the combination of cranberry juice and warfarin, but it's probably safest to avoid cranberry juice altogether if you're taking this medication. Cranberry juice has been shown to inhibit a key enzyme that is responsible for warfarin metabolism, but more research on this interaction is needed.

If you take another drug with blood-thinning effects, such as aspirin, you can probably drink cranberry juice occasionally (no more than four ounces—at least two hours before or three hours after taking the medication). Consult your doctor for advice.

DANGERS OF MILK

The calcium in milk can interact with certain medications. *Drink milk at least two hours before or three hours after taking...*

•**Antacids,** such as calcium carbonate products (Rolaids) or sodium bicarbonate products (Alka-Seltzer and Brioschi). Drinking milk with these antacids can cause milk-alkali syndrome, a condition characterized by high blood calcium levels that can lead to kidney stones or even kidney failure.

•**Antibiotics,** such as tetracyclines and *ciprofloxacin* (Cipro). Calcium blocks absorption of these drugs, decreasing their effectiveness. Calcium-fortified juices are believed to have the same effect.

BETTER DRUG METABOLISM

Our bodies need nutrients to properly metabolize most medications. Chief among these nutrients is protein. Though we tend to eat less protein as we age—due to a variety of reasons, such as dental problems that make it harder to chew meat—we actually require more of this nutrient, since our bodies become less efficient at digesting and utilizing it.

Because the lining of the small and large intestines—where drugs are absorbed—regenerates every three to seven days, you need a continual supply of protein to maintain healthy levels of the enzymes that promote metabolism of medications.

To facilitate drug metabolism: Aim to eat about half a gram of protein daily for every pound of body weight.

Good sources: Fish, meats, eggs, peanut butter and soybeans.

B vitamins also play a key role in drug metabolism. Food sources rich in B vitamins include meats, fortified cereals, bananas and oatmeal.

Helpful: If you skip breakfast and aren't much of a meat eater, consider taking a multivitamin supplement containing the recommended daily intake of B vitamins.

info To learn more about drug-beverage interactions, go to the FDA Web site, *www.fda.gov* and search "drug interactions."

7

Emotional Well-Being

Coming Soon— A Pill that Erases Bad Memories

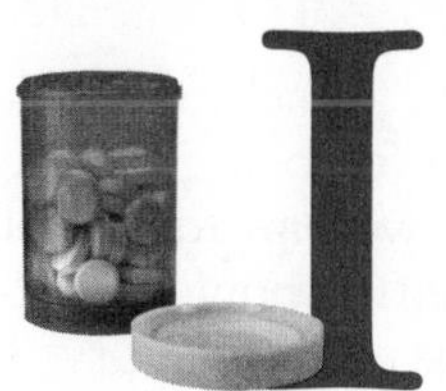

Imagine being able to decouple bad memories from the fear and anxiety they produce with just a pill. That's the promise of a recent report from Dutch researchers that was published in the journal *Nature Neuroscience.*

BACKGROUND

Human memory often is compared to computer storage. Some memories exist in a sort of neurological flash RAM, whereas others are stored for the long term, on the brain's hard disk. The analogy works to a point, but it isn't perfect, as it turns out to be quite difficult to permanently erase files in the brain's memory banks.

"Fear memories can be surprisingly resilient," explained Mark Bouton, PhD, a professor of psychology at the University of Vermont.

THE STUDY

To try to break at least the physiological hold these fears have over individuals, Merel Kindt, PhD, head of the department of clinical psychology at the University of Amsterdam, induced a fear response in 60 undergraduate students at the university.

The study lasted three days. On the first day, the subjects learned to associate images of spiders with a mild electrical shock. Fear was measured by assessing each individual's startle response—how much his or her eyes blinked in response to the stimulus. That fear memory was then consolidated—written to the hard disk, if you will.

The next day, the memory was recalled, but only after the subjects had been given a placebo or *propranolol* (Inderal), a beta-blocker typically

Mark Bouton, PhD, professor, psychology, University of Vermont, Burlington.

Merel Kindt, PhD, head, department of clinical psychology, University of Amsterdam.

Jane Taylor, PhD, professor, psychiatry, Yale University, New Haven, Connecticut.

Nature Neuroscience online.

used to treat high blood pressure and other heart conditions.

The idea, Dr. Bouton explained, is that at this point, the memory becomes "open to modification"—just as a computer file can be changed and then rewritten to the hard disk.

Propranolol had already been shown to impact memory reconsolidation in rodents. Would it have the same effect in people?

The answer came on day three, when the subjects were tested again. The physiological response to the fear-inducing cue—pictures of spiders—was eliminated in the propranolol group, but not in the placebo group, Dr. Kindt found.

IMPLICATIONS

Such findings could one day help individuals suffering from pathological anxiety disorders from the debilitating physiological effects of their fears. Yet many questions remain, experts note, such as how permanent the effect is, and whether it can affect traumatic memories that may be decades old.

EXPERT REACTION

"I think it's a very interesting study," said Jane Taylor, PhD, a professor of psychiatry at Yale University, who studies memory reconsolidation in rats. "It will be interesting to know how long-lasting this effect is, and whether it only works on recently consolidated memories."

Dr. Bouton echoed that sentiment. "This study is a solid step forward in our understanding of how to reduce fear," he said. "The big question is whether this treatment will reduce all forms of relapse, including the return of fear that can occur with the passage of time.

"In principle," said Dr. Bouton, "this is a step toward finding a clinical treatment for people with pathological fears."

info For more information, visit the National Institute of Mental Health Web site, *www.nimh.nih.gov*, click on "Mental Health Topics" and then choose "Anxiety Disorders."

Secret to Letting Go Of Toxic Memories

Thomas H. Crook III, PhD, CEO of Cognitive Research Corp. and a psychologist in private practice in St. Petersburg, Florida. He is an affiliate professor of psychiatry and behavioral medicine at University of South Florida College of Medicine in Tampa, a former research program director for the National Institute of Mental Health and author of numerous books, including *The Memory Advantage* (Select Books). *www.cogres.com.*

Good or bad, happy or sad, our memories are a huge part of who we are. They can help us repeat our successes, motivate us to learn from our mistakes and provide the framework for our sense of ourselves as individuals.

But when painful or counterproductive memories echo over and over in our heads, they drain our mental energy and lessen our joy.

Self-defense: Learn how toxic memories form —then develop skills to defuse their power.

ORIGINS OF MEMORIES

Much of the way we see ourselves is rooted in childhood experiences, and the memories of those early events can be intense. Not every unpleasant childhood experience becomes a toxic memory, however. In fact, similar situations can create similar memories—yet produce very different effects.

Example: Two women remember feeling humiliated in first grade for being unable to read. Whenever the first woman thinks of this, she also reminds herself of how she excelled at math. For her, this early memory is tied to feelings of success. But when the second woman recalls her six-year-old self, she views those first failures with reading as the start of every struggle she has ever faced and every challenge she has ever avoided. For her, this unhappy memory is toxic.

Not all toxic memories are rooted in childhood. They can form at any time, especially during emotional upheaval.

For instance: The memory of losing a job turns toxic if a man feels enraged whenever he thinks of it. The memory of a bitter divorce becomes toxic if someone is too afraid ever to date again. The memory of her father's dying is toxic if a woman sobs uncontrollably every time she pictures his face, even years after his death.

An exceptionally traumatic event, such as being a victim of a violent crime, understandably can cause extreme fear, anger and sadness. But the memory turns especially toxic if the victim turns that blame inward—believing, for instance, "I was sexually assaulted because I danced too provocatively"—rather than rightfully blaming the assailant.

HOW MEMORIES CAN HURT

If poisonous memories repeatedly invade our thoughts, reinforcing negative feelings about ourselves or others, we may have...

- **Diminished pleasure in life,** as even happy occasions are overshadowed by images from the past.

  Example: At her daughter's wedding, a woman obsesses about how aloof her own mother was. Such thoughts increase a person's risk for depression and/or anxiety disorders.

- **Low self-esteem and missed opportunities for growth.**

  Example: Having always been picked last for teams in gym class, a man habitually labels himself as clumsy—and refuses to try any new sports.

- **Inability to respond appropriately to new situations.**

  Example: Continued resentment over having been laid off may negatively affect a person's manner and the impression he or she makes on job interviews.

- **Chronically elevated levels of stress hormones.** These have damaging effects on blood pressure, blood sugar, digestion and immunity, increasing risk for heart disease, diabetes and gastric disorders.

BREAKING THE HABIT

A toxic memory turned constant companion is as much a bad habit as a bad memory—and like any bad habit, it can be broken. *Steps...*

1. Select a favorite positive memory. You can choose an event that specifically contradicts your toxic memory (for instance, the day you learned to ski despite being a "hopeless klutz") ...or choose a completely unrelated experience, such as your first date with your spouse.

2. Write down as many details as you can recall. Where did you go? What did you wear? Did you dance to a certain song or see a stunning sunset? How did that first kiss feel? Tap into all your senses.

3. Practice conjuring up this happy memory. Let this personal "movie" play inside your head during relaxed moments. Soon you'll be able to recall it vividly at will, even when stressed or depressed.

4. Mentally hit an "eject" button whenever a toxic memory pops into your head, replacing it with thoughts of the happy memory.

FULFILLING EMOTIONAL NEEDS

If the technique above isn't working, your toxic memory may be more than a bad habit —it may be fulfilling some unmet need. Ask yourself, "How am I benefiting by holding on to this painful memory?" This insight will help you explore more productive ways to meet that need, thus diminishing the power of the toxic memory. *Consider...*

- **Does thinking of yourself as unlucky let you avoid taking responsibility for your life?** On a sheet of paper, make two columns, labeled "good luck" and "bad luck," then list examples from your own life of each type of experience. You will see that your whole life hasn't been a series of misfortunes. Next, identify the role played by your own efforts—rather than good luck—in creating each positive experience...and give yourself due credit.

- **Is there a certain pleasure for you in resenting other people for past unpleasantness?** (Be honest with yourself!) Develop a habit of doing small favors that make people respond to you in a positive way. Smile at everyone you pass on the sidewalk, yield to other drivers trying to enter your lane, say a sincere "thank you" to a surly cashier. A conscious and voluntary decision to be of service to others can help you overcome old resentments, relegate toxic memories to the past and find pleasure in the here and now.

If you feel traumatized: After an extremely traumatic experience, it is normal to fixate on the event for a time. However, if you are seriously disturbed by recurrent memories of the trauma months or even years later, you may have post-traumatic stress disorder (PTSD). Symptoms include nightmares or obsessive mental reenactments of the event...frequent fear or anger ...trouble concentrating...feelings of guilt, hopelessness or emotional numbness.

Defusing traumatic memories may require the help of a mental-health professional.

Recommended: Cognitive-behavioral therapy (CBT), which focuses on changing harmful thought patterns rather than on lengthy exploration of past experiences.

Referrals: National Association of Cognitive-Behavioral Therapists, 800-853-1135, *www.nacbt.org*. With CBT, even seriously toxic memories can become more manageable—and you can move on with your life.

Empathy Might Be Genetic

Oregon Health & Science University news release.

Genes may play a role in a person's ability to empathize with others, suggests a US study involving mice.

THE STUDY FINDINGS

Researchers trained highly social mice to identify a sound played in a specific cage as negative by also having squeaks of distress come from a mouse in that cage. But a genetically different strain of mice that were less social were unable to learn the same negative connection.

The study was published in the online journal *PLoS ONE.*

IMPLICATIONS

The results indicate that the ability to identify and act on another's emotions may have a genetic basis, said the University of Wisconsin-Madison and Oregon Health & Science University researchers. They added that understanding empathy in mice might improve knowledge about social interaction problems that occur in many human psychosocial disorders, such as autism, schizophrenia, depression and addiction.

"The core of empathy is being able to have an emotional experience and share that experience with another. We are basically trying to deconstruct empathy into smaller functional units that make it more accessible to biological research," said study coleader Jules Panksepp, a University of Wisconsin-Madison graduate student.

"Deficits in empathy are frequently discussed in the context of psychiatric disorders like autism. We think that by coming up with a simplified model of it in a mouse, we're probably getting closer to modeling symptoms of human disorders," Panksepp explained.

"Mice are capable of a more complex form of empathy than we ever believed possible," said Garet Lahvis, PhD, assistant professor of behavioral neuroscience at Oregon Health & Science University. "We believe there's a genetic contribution to the ability for empathy that has broad implications for autism research and other psychosocial disorders."

Future studies will examine the genetic differences between the highly social and less-social strains of mice in an attempt to identify specific genes that may play a role in empathy.

info For information on teaching children empathy, visit the Nemours Foundation Web site, *http://kidshealth.org/classroom,* and search "empathy."

Good Relationships Make You Healthier

Mark A. Stengler, ND, naturopathic physician in private practice, La Jolla, California...adjunct associate clinical professor at the National College of Natural Medicine, Portland, Oregon...author of many books, including *The Natural Physician's Healing Therapies* and coauthor of *Prescription for Natural Cures* (both from Bottom Line Books)...and author of the *Bottom Line/Natural Healing* newsletter.

In working to ensure good health, people often overlook a subtle but extremely important factor. That is, quite simply, other people. We all need others, as Tom Hanks vividly demonstrated in the movie *Cast Away,* when his character's survival rested in part on "interactions" with a painted face on a volleyball. Fortunately, most of us have ample opportunity to connect with real people—spouses, partners, children, relatives, friends, colleagues. We know instinctively that connecting raises our spirits and fosters good feelings. From a medical standpoint, we now know without any doubt whatsoever that human connection profoundly affects our physical health.

Meaningful research concerning relationships and health started with a seminal study in Alameda County, California, in 1979. It showed that being socially integrated (married, close with family and friends, belonging to groups) was closely associated with longevity.

Meaning: Individuals who form close bonds with other people typically live longer than those without meaningful relationships.

GREATER SOCIAL CONNECTIONS RESULT IN RESISTANCE TO ILLNESS

Sheldon Cohen, PhD, from Carnegie Mellon University in Pittsburgh, has become a prominent researcher in this area. Using the common cold as a marker of wellness, Cohen discovered in numerous studies that greater social connection results in more resistance to illness.

Recently Dr. Cohen completed a study in which he used a unique method of measuring social connection. He analyzed the autobiographies of 96 psychologists and 220 literary writers for words that indicated close relationships—father, mother, brother, sister, neighbor and the like. He found that the writers who lived longest had included more of these words in their life stories than had the writers who died younger. In addition, the Australian Longitudinal Study on Aging, which included 1,500 people age 70 or older, discovered that those who had the most extensive network of friends and confidants lived an average of 22% longer than those who did not.

NEGATIVE INTERACTIONS

While good relationships can affect your health in positive ways, the opposite also is true. A 2007 study from University College in London asked 9,011 men and women about their closest relationships. Participants who described the most negative interactions in those relationships were 34% more likely to develop heart disease, on average, than those who reported more positive interactions. Another project at Rush University Medical Center in Chicago discovered that lonely people were more likely to fall prey to Alzheimer's disease.

IN MY EXPERIENCE

Not long ago, I had the opportunity to witness how powerful a good relationship can be in restoring a person to good health. My patient, a man in his early 60s, is a high-powered real estate professional. He doesn't like to admit that anything in his life isn't going well, but as his physician, I was aware of his soaring blood pressure and fatigue that was becoming so pronounced that it interfered with his work. Finally the man admitted that he had been terribly unhappy in his marriage for several years. I urged him to see a marriage counselor with his wife. Fortunately, they took my advice.

After about six months, the couple had made substantial progress. They were once again communicating with each other—and growing closer. At about that time, treatments for the husband's fatigue and blood pressure problems began to take effect. There is no question in my mind that these two developments were related.

WHEN RELATIONSHIPS GET ROCKY

Of course, we can't simply "prescribe" good relationships for ourselves. Human beings by nature have varying opinions, tastes and desires —and so some disagreement is always part of dealing with other people. That is not the issue, however, when it comes to health. The issue is how you go about disagreeing.

In a 10-year study of 4,000 residents of Framingham, Massachusetts, 32% of men and 23% of women reported that they habitually bottled up their feelings during spats with their spouses. Keeping quiet didn't seem to upset the men, but for women, the study's finding about this so-called "self-silencing" was astonishing. During the decade-long study, wives who habitually suppressed their feelings and held their tongues during arguments were four times more likely to die than were the women who spoke up.

ADVICE FOR GOOD RELATIONSHIPS AND BETTER HEALTH

To get insight about the attitudes and actions that improve close relationships, I talked to Alexa Elkington, MS, a marriage and family therapist in Las Vegas who leads workshops to help people communicate better. *Here are the key points that she says help strengthen the quality of our interactions—thus contributing to health and happiness…*

•**Accept differences.** Instead of trying to change others, recognize and accept that they are who they are—full of strong points and weak, lovable qualities and some that aren't so lovable…in other words, completely human.

•**Think positive.** You can decide to view other people's annoying small habits as big negatives …as neutral behavior…or even as charming quirks. For example, grown children visiting your home are apt to leave a dish or two in the sink, just as they did as kids. You can get fired up about it or smile at their consistency.

•**Appreciate.** Remember to say thank you even for small actions—including chores that the other person is "supposed" to do. Gratitude cheers the heart and increases warm feelings.

•**Be understanding.** Recognize and respect that your style of handling conflict may be different from the other person's. Those who easily speak up find it hard to understand someone who stays quiet, for instance. But it is important to accept the difference…and for "self-silencers" to protect their health by learning to speak up.

Loving the Spouse You Have…Secrets to A Happily-Ever-After Marriage

Mark O'Connell, PhD, clinical instructor of psychology at Harvard Medical School in Boston and at Cambridge Hospital in Cambridge, Massachusetts. He also is a marriage therapist in private practice in Chestnut Hill, Massachusetts, and author of *The Marriage Benefit: The Surprising Rewards of Staying Together* (Springboard). *www.markoconnellphd.com.*

When a marriage becomes contentious, cold or boring, too many couples point fingers or pack bags, lamenting lost dreams of marital bliss. Yet the disappointments behind today's dismal divorce rate often result not from truly unacceptable situations (serial affairs, spousal abuse)—but instead stem from couples' seriously unrealistic expectations of what a marriage can and should be.

The fix: By recognizing that relationships evolve over time and adapting to those inevitable changes, we can come to understand ourselves better…love our spouses better…and experience a deeply satisfying partnership that will last the rest of our lives.

MONEY MATTERS

One way we measure happiness is by comparing ourselves with people around us—and in that regard, the most tangible factor is wealth. When your neighbor's house is nicer or your brother's paycheck is bigger, whom are you likely to resent? Your spouse.

Be realistic: More money is not the key to permanent peace, because there always will be people who are richer. *Instead, resolve the underlying conflict by figuring out what money means to each of you…*

•**Is money a sign of self-worth**—because you were ashamed of growing up poor or for another reason? If so, remind yourself of nonmaterial achievements—the way you raised wonderful children together or serve as community leaders.

•**Is money a safeguard against insecurity**—because you were horrified when a cousin lost her home or you experienced some other financial trauma? Work with a financial planner to set up a long-term budget.

•**Is money an expression of love**—because your father lavished your mother with jewelry? Appreciate the way your husband shows his love by bringing you breakfast in bed.

Helpful: Make a list of your top five financial goals, and have your husband do the same. Together, compare the lists…agree on several goals you both share…and brainstorm ways to achieve them. When you know what truly matters, money becomes merely a means to an end, not the end goal itself.

BEDROOM BATTLES

He wants more sex…she wants more cuddling. She craves variety…he's happy on top. Toss in the influence of Hollywood—gorgeous couples who are eternally lusty and lip-locked—and unrealistic expectations about sex can run wild.

Be realistic: Take a compassionate look at the underlying reasons why lovemaking has become disappointing. Maybe she avoids sex because she thinks her body is not as beautiful as it once was. Maybe he sticks with one position not because he's indifferent to your preferences, but because he's worried about losing his erection. The key is to talk specifically about what you need or want—and encourage your spouse to do the same. When you both share honestly and listen with open minds, you can reach a satisfying compromise and find joy in your continuing mutual attraction.

Try this: Agree to share a kiss (a real kiss, not a peck) at least once a day—not necessarily with the goal of having it lead to intercourse, but simply to enhance the bond between you. Research shows that kissing sparks sexual desire and reduces levels of the stress hormone cortisol. Less stress is always a good thing—in or out of the bedroom.

AGE PREJUDICE

Have you ever caught sight of yourself in a mirror and thought, "Who is that old person?" Looking at your spouse can be like looking in that mirror. In those wrinkles, you see evidence of your own advancing age—and wish you didn't have to be reminded.

Be realistic: Growing old actually can improve a marriage—once you give up the fantasy that starting over with someone else will automatically make you feel young again.

The trick: Face up to whatever bothers you about aging. Perhaps you're disappointed that your bad shoulder has put an end to your tennis games together...or you're afraid that your spouse's couch potato habits will lead to a heart attack. If so, try new activities together that can accommodate your not-as-young body, such as bicycling...or gently suggest going for walks with you because you want your spouse to be with you for years to come.

IDEALIZATION OF LOVE

If only we could bottle that passion of the first year of a relationship, when romance made life dreamy. But it's biologically impossible to sustain that intensity of feeling day in and day out for years on end.

Reason: The early stages of romance are associated with big physiological changes—in fact, the brain pathways that govern falling in love appear to be the same as those involved in addiction. However, studies using magnetic resonance imaging (MRI) suggest that about 18 months into a relationship, brain chemistry again begins to alter—this time in ways that promote a change in focus from romance and lust to long-term attachment and contentment.

Be realistic: If love stayed at a fevered pitch, we would never get anything else done...and we would never move past the starry-eyed stage and really get to know each other. Love between two people is not stagnant or defined solely by romance—it is a combination of fascination, friendship, passion, shared purpose, trust, continuity and companionship.

What to do: Make a list of everything your spouse does that pleases you. Does she listen to your mother's endless complaints with a kind ear? Is he a thoughtful planner—for fun activities as well as important life issues? Does he keep his word? Look for the qualities you value in any long-term friendship. You both share a commitment to family and support each other in times of crisis—and that kind of partnership provides a path to lifelong marital happiness.

■ ■ ■ ■

Good Marriages Help Women Destress

After a busier-than-usual day at work, women who come home to a loving spouse have a bigger drop in the stress hormone cortisol than women whose marriages are less happy. Men's cortisol levels drop when they come home regardless of the state of their marriages.

Darby E. Saxbe, CPhil, researcher, University of California, Los Angeles, and leader of a study of 30 married couples, published in *Health Psychology*.

■ ■ ■ ■

Touch Lowers Stress by 34%

Married couples who give each other back rubs or touch each other affectionately in other ways for at least 30 minutes three times a week have 34% lower levels of stress. Researchers found that being affectionate releases the hormone oxytocin, which may protect against stress-related illnesses.

Julianne Holt-Lunstad, PhD, assistant professor, department of psychology, Brigham Young University, Provo, Utah, and leader of a study published in *Psychosomatic Medicine.*

Use Native American Know-How to Ease Pain and Stress

Lewis E. Mehl-Madrona, MD, PhD, clinical assistant professor of family medicine at the University of Hawaii School of Medicine and associate professor, department of psychology, Argosy University in Honolulu. He is the author of four books, including *Coyote Medicine: Lessons from Native American Healing* (Touchstone). *www.mehl-madrona.com.*

For centuries, Native American healing has been practiced in North America. It encompasses a number of beliefs and rituals used by the more than 500 tribes of North America to treat people with emotional or physical conditions. As a medical doctor and Native American healer, I find that people often benefit from complementary care that includes these traditional practices.

Because Native American healing is so embedded in the tribal culture, it's not something an individual can dabble in on her own. However, it does include a spiritual element from which you can gain insights that promote well-being plus healing practices you can do while honoring your own traditions.

A SPIRITUAL PRACTICE

The spirit plays an integral part in Native American healing, which is as much a philosophy as a science. Typically, conventional Western medicine aims to fix the part of the body that ails. In contrast, Native American medicine considers the spirit inseparable from the healing process and so aims to heal the whole person. There is no separation between the body parts and the person...the person and the community...and the community and the natural environment.

Whereas Western medicine looks to eliminate the particular disease, Native American medicine asks, "What can the disease teach the patient?" The answers empower the patient with awareness, confidence and tools to help her take charge of her health.

Native Americans believe that many illnesses stem from spiritual problems. A person who thinks negatively, has an unhealthful lifestyle or has an imbalance of body, mind, spirit and community is more likely to become ill. Native American healing practices aim to reestablish balance and restore the patient to a healthy and spiritually pure state.

There is no scientific proof that Native American healing can cure disease. However, many people find that the practices reduce pain and stress, encourage emotional well-being and improve quality of life.

THE RITUAL RETREAT

The retreat is an essential element of Native American healing. It is vital to wellness to take time out for a periodic respite—once a year at a minimum. A typical retreat takes place in a natural and safe environment, away from urban and residential areas. It consists of four days and nights of fasting, prayer and meditation.

Often a retreat begins and ends with a sweat lodge ceremony. This takes place in a dome-shaped structure made from tree branches. Inside, water is periodically poured over heated rocks to create a hot, steamy environment. The ceremony of the sweat lodge helps to purify the body's blood, heart, lungs, liver and kidneys... free the mind of distractions and bring mental clarity...and provide a sense of connection to the planet and the spirit world.

Though it's not possible to recreate the sweat lodge experience without being enmeshed in Native American culture, you can create your own personal retreat. *Whether for a few hours or a few days...*

•**Go to a place where you feel safe,** protected and connected to nature—to the open sky, towering trees, earth beneath you. This reduces stress and promotes relaxation.

•**Fast.** Most healthy people can safely go without eating or drinking for 24 hours. (If you have any medical problems, you may need to shorten your fast or avoid fasting—ask your doctor.) Longer fasts, such as the traditional four-day fast, should be done only under the supervision of an experienced healer.

•**Sit still and meditate for whatever amount of time feels right.** Even a short period of meditation helps you understand that you don't really need to do all the things you normally worry about...puts you in touch with your spiritual side...and helps you open up to whatever lesson may come. Use any meditation techniques you want—deep breathing, imagery, mantras, prayer.

The science: From the viewpoint of Western medicine, fasting and meditating can decrease the activity of the sympathetic nervous system (which controls the "fight-or-flight" response and production of stress hormones, among other functions)...and increase the activity of the parasympathetic nervous system (which controls the body's "rest and repose" functions). The result is deep relaxation, which gives the body an opportunity to repair itself, reduce anxiety and alleviate depression.

The tradition: Nearly every culture has methods of reflection, renewal and rejuvenation. There is benefit in engaging in rituals that have been handed down for thousands of years. Honoring such traditions can provide a healing sense of connectedness, well-being and peace.

▪ **More from Dr. Mehl-Madrona...**

Experience Native American Healing Firsthand

Want to learn more about Native American culture? *You can...*

•**Attend powwows.** Often open to the public, these include singing, dancing and perhaps opportunities to make contact with healers.

Information: *www.powwows.com* or *www.nativegatherings.com.*

•**Visit a holistic center for classes** on Native American practices...and an environment suitable for personal retreats.

Recommended: Heyokah Retreat Center, Santa Fe, New Mexico (505-989-8981, *www.heyokahcenter.org*)...Kripalu Center, Stockbridge, Massachusetts (866-200-5203, *www.kripalu.org*) ...Omega Institute, Rhinebeck, New York (877-944-2002, *www.eomega.org*).

Beware of "Native Shamanism" seminars. These lump together bits of Native American ceremonies with Wicca (a pagan religion), New Age spirituality and Eastern medicine—which can trivialize and weaken the Native American healing experience.

Healing Secrets from Bernie Siegel, MD

Bernie Siegel, MD, a pioneer in mind-body medicine and the founder of Exceptional Cancer Patients (*www.ecap-online.org*), a nonprofit organization that provides resources and programs based on mind-body-spirit medicine. He is also author of many books and audio programs, including *Love, Medicine and Miracles* (Harper), *Help Me to Heal* (Hay House) and the CD *Healing Meditations: Enhance Your Immune System and Find the Key to Good Health* (Hay House).

Words are powerful tools—especially for people who are dealing with any kind of illness. Doctors often tell cancer patients, for example, that their treatment is designed to "destroy" or "attack" cancer cells.

All of this is good and well if these words make a patient feel more powerful. But all too often, this approach has the opposite effect and makes those who are ill feel that they are at war with their own bodies—and their health suffers as a result. Why does this happen?

Even if you are "assaulting" an illness—be it cancer, heart disease, diabetes or any other serious ailment—your body is designed to shift into a self-protection mode in the midst of this assault. When threatened, our bodies release stress hormones to fuel a quick escape from whatever is endangering us, and our immune function (one of the keys to overcoming virtually all types of illness) becomes suppressed. Some people feel energized by a good fight, and they approach their health challenge with the precision of a sergeant leading his/her troops. Others, on the other hand, feel completely at odds with such an approach.

This was the case for Dave, a Quaker friend of mine who developed cancer. His oncologist told him, "I am going to kill your cancer." Dave quietly responded, "I am a Quaker. I don't kill anything," and he walked out the door.

Dave ended up consulting a different doctor for his cancer treatment and worked with me on alternative therapies that included imagery and therapeutic drawing. Because the aggressive words used by his initial doctor felt so wrong to Dave, he began a regular practice of visualization that included images of his white cells "carrying away"—rather than destroying—his cancer cells.

I also introduced Dave to drawing, which gave him an opportunity to conceptualize and reproduce images of the healing he sought for his body. You don't need any artistic skill to benefit from therapeutic drawing. It's designed to help patients grapple with questions and fears about their illnesses and their treatment options. Dave lived 12 years after his doctor had given him one to two years to live.

If you think all of this sounds unscientific, I don't blame you. When I first became involved in mind–body medicine more than 30 years ago, I was skeptical, too. I was a surgeon, and I believed that the scalpel was all-powerful. Then I began examining the evidence and could no longer deny how our minds—and mental well-being—can affect our response to illness. It's been shown that women who have lung cancer or melanoma tend to live longer than men who have the same type of malignancy. We know that this is not a result of female hormones—studies also show that married men who have prostate or bladder cancer generally live longer than single men who have the same cancers. According to my observations, it's all about having positive connections with others. In fact, I am firmly convinced that women are more likely than men to have strong emotional connections that can literally extend their lives.

This point is illustrated by a woman I once knew who was a devoted mother at the time of her cancer diagnosis. "I have nine kids, and I can't die until they are all married and out of the house," she told me. Twenty-three years later, when her last child left the house, her cancer returned and soon proved to be fatal. I have seen similar stories in the hundreds of cancer patients I have known and worked with over the years. What saddened me about the woman with nine children is that she no longer felt that her life had meaning once all of them had left the house.

So before you embark on a new medical treatment, ask yourself two important questions...

- **Does my mind feel at ease with the type of therapy I am considering—or am I simply complying with my doctor's wishes?** If the treatment doesn't feel right, is there a way that I can mentally frame it differently? Even a treatment that has potentially unpleasant side effects, such as chemotherapy, can feel "right" if it is undertaken in the spirit of extending a life that has meaning. The treatment becomes a "labor pain of self-birth"—seen in this way, the side effects are diminished when you're undergoing the therapy to give yourself a new life.
- **Is there anything I can do to live my life more fully in the midst of my health challenge?** Staying mentally healthy is an invaluable tool. When you heal your life and find peace of mind, your body is much more likely to get the message, too.

■ ■ ■ ■

Herb Slashes Stress by 62%

Researchers in the US and India gave 98 chronically stressed men and women the herb ashwagandha (at a dose of 125 milligrams, or mg, 250 mg or 500 mg) or a placebo daily.

Results: Participants taking the lowest dose reported a 40% reduction in anxiety after 30 days. After 60 days, their anxiety was reduced by 62%...their levels of cortisol, a stress hormone, decreased by 15%...*dehydroepiandrosterone* (DHEA), an antiaging and antistress hormone, increased by 13%...and C-reactive protein (CRP), a marker for inflammation and heart disease risk, decreased by 32%.

Those taking higher doses noticed even more improvement, while the placebo group showed no significant changes.

For my patients who are under chronic stress or for whom testing reveals elevated cortisol, I recommend 125 mg to 250 mg of ashwagandha daily. Look for the type used in this study, known as Sensoril, which is highly concentrated and available in health food stores from companies such as Natural Factors, Jarrow and Life Extension.

Mark A. Stengler, ND, naturopathic physician in private practice, La Jolla, California...adjunct associate clinical professor at the National College of Natural Medicine, Portland, Oregon...author of many books and the *Bottom Line/Natural Healing* newsletter.

■ ■ ■ ■

Workplace Aggression Hurts More Than Sexual Harassment

Compared with employees who were sexually harassed, those who were bullied, belittled, excluded or ignored reported more stress, anger and anxiety and less job satisfaction.

Possible reason: Organizations are prepared to help victims of sexual harassment, but bullying often is more subtle and is not illegal—so victims have to fend for themselves.

Sandy Hershcovis, Phd, assistant professor, University of Manitoba, Canada, and leader of a review of 110 studies, presented at an American Psychological Association Conference.

Surprising Disease–Depression Connection

Charles Raison, PhD, assistant professor in the mind-body program, department of psychiatry and behavioral sciences at Emory University in Atlanta...and Esther Sternberg, MD, director of the integrative neural immune program at the National Institutes of Health in Rockville, Maryland. Dr. Sternberg is a research professor at American University in Washington, DC, and author of *The Balance Within: The Science of Connecting Health and Emotions* (W. H. Freeman). Her Web site is *www.esthersternberg.com*. Drs. Raison and Sternberg collaborate on clinical research.

It is an unfortunate double jeopardy—being sick can make you depressed...and being depressed can make you sick. New research shows that many chronic illnesses, including heart disease, diabetes and osteoporosis, have this two-way connection to depression.

Consequences can be grave. In a recent study, heart attack patients who were depressed had a two- to fourfold increased risk of dying within five years, compared with heart attack patients who were not depressed. In a global study from the World Health Organization involving 245,000 people, those with a chronic illness fared far worse if they also were depressed.

One in eight women experiences depression at some point, compared with only one in 16 men—a gender discrepancy due primarily to hormonal differences. That means it is especially important for women who are depressed to get regular checkups to screen for chronic illness... and for women who have a chronic disease to be alert for signs of depression. Self-help strategies and/or professional care can protect both your mental and physical well-being.

EXPLAINING THE CONNECTION

Scientists are trying to learn more about how disease and depression interact. *What the evidence suggests...*

- **How disease can lead to depression.** Common sense tells us that a woman with a chronic illness might feel sad—but physiologically speaking, the explanation may involve an overactive immune system.

Theory: Inflammation is part of the body's normal healing process...but if the immune system fails to turn off the inflammatory mechanism at the appropriate time, inflammation becomes long-lasting and widespread. This can alter metabolism and damage blood vessels, bones and other body tissues, bringing on a variety of chronic illnesses and disrupting the balance of neurotransmitters (brain chemicals) that affect mood, triggering depression.

Recent studies show that the following conditions may be linked to depression—cancer... heart disease...diabetes...fibromyalgia (a syndrome of widespread pain)...psoriasis (patches of scaly, red skin)...rheumatoid arthritis (an autoimmune disease)...and stroke.

•**How depression can lead to disease.** It is logical that a depressed woman may not take care of herself well enough to guard against illness, but this is only a partial explanation. Physiologically, depression is linked to high levels of stress hormones—which in turn may raise blood pressure and cholesterol levels...promote accumulation of harmful abdominal fat...impair digestion...and hamper immune function. Along with depression comes increased production of proteins called cytokines, which cause widespread inflammation. This can trigger changes in the brain that reduce its resistance to dementia.

Recent studies suggest that people who suffer from depression may be at increased risk for Alzheimer's disease...asthma...breast cancer... cardiovascular disease...diabetes...gastric ulcer... high blood pressure...osteoarthritis...osteoporosis ...and thyroid disease.

DEFENSE AGAINST DEPRESSION

Getting relief from depression can help prevent chronic illness or make an existing illness easier to deal with. Yet even though up to 90% of depressed people can be treated effectively, only one in three seeks treatment. *To overcome depression...*

•**Develop realistic expectations.** You may pessimistically assume that your physical prognosis is worse than it really is...or you may be overly optimistic, then feel crushed if your progress is slow. Either attitude can negatively affect your motivation to participate actively in your own physical recovery.

What helps: Be proactive. Write down all of your questions about your condition, treatment and prognosis, and review them with your doctor. Use the Internet to find a national association that addresses your illness, or ask your doctor if he/she knows of one. Be sure to take medication as prescribed, and keep all of your doctor appointments.

•**Eat foods rich in omega-3 fatty acids.** Omega-3s reduce inflammation and aid neurotransmitter function. Research suggests that omega-3s may be better absorbed from food than from supplements.

What helps: Have at least four servings weekly of omega-3–rich foods.

Good choices: Two tablespoons of ground flaxseeds or flaxseed oil...one-quarter cup of walnuts...three ounces of herring, salmon or sturgeon...one cup of navy beans, cabbage, cauliflower, squash or leafy green vegetables.

•**Stay active.** Exercise releases endorphins, brain chemicals that lift mood and block pain.

What helps: Don't tell yourself, I feel too lousy to work out. Ask your doctor or physical therapist to recommend exercises that you can do—such as water aerobics, which is easy on joints and bones...or slow stationary cycling, which won't overtax the heart.

•**Strengthen social ties.** You may hesitate to tell loved ones how down your illness makes you feel for fear of burdening them—yet emotional support is vital to healing.

What helps: Remember that your illness affects your family and friends, too. Everyone will feel better if emotions and concerns are discussed honestly.

•**Know when to get professional help.** Many people incorrectly assume that depression is an unavoidable part of physical illness, so they don't seek treatment.

What helps: Learn the symptoms of depression —sleeping too much or too little, unintended weight gain or loss, low energy, persistent sadness, frequent crying, irritability, feelings of hopelessness, poor concentration, low libido or lack of interest in daily activities. If you have any thoughts of suicide or if you experience two or more of the symptoms above for more than two weeks, tell your doctor.

• **Consider psychotherapy.** A form called cognitive behavioral therapy helps depressed patients replace negative beliefs and behaviors with positive ones.

What helps: Talk to a therapist experienced in treating depression linked to chronic illness. Ask your primary care physician to refer you to a suitable mental-health professional.

• **Try natural nonprescription supplements.** Sold at health food stores, these may relieve mild-to-moderate depression. If you use pharmaceutical medications, get your doctor's approval before taking natural supplements to avoid possible adverse interactions.

What helps: Ask your doctor about appropriate dosages and usage guidelines for the following...

- *5-adenosylmethionine* (SAMe)
- *5-hydroxytryptophan* (5-HTP)
- St. John's wort
- Vitamin D.

• **Consider pharmaceutical antidepressants.** These medications work by slowing the removal of neurotransmitters from the brain.

What helps: Antidepressants often are very effective, though it may take trial-and-error to find one that works for you and does not cause side effects (such as nausea, weight gain, drowsiness and low libido).

Useful: Ask your doctor about the new cytochrome P450 blood test, which helps identify genetic factors that influence your response to certain antidepressants.

■ ■ ■ ■

Obesity Is Depressing!

In middle age, obese women are twice as likely to be depressed as nonobese women —and depressed women are twice as likely to be obese as nondepressed women.

Possible reason: The stigma of obesity damages self-esteem...which contributes to feelings of hopelessness and depression...which can make it harder to lose weight.

To break the cycle: Seek help from a mental health professional.

Gregory Simon, MD, psychiatrist and researcher, Group Health Cooperative, Seattle, and leader of a study of 4,641 women ages 40 to 65, published in *General Hospital Psychiatry.*

■ ■ ■ ■

Phone Therapy Can Be Effective

Researchers recently analyzed 12 studies on psychotherapy for adults that was conducted by telephone and involved at least four sessions (typically 45 to 50 minutes each).

Result: About 8% of patients discontinued treatment soon after its start compared with an average dropout rate of nearly 47% for those receiving traditional face-to-face psychotherapy. Telephone therapy also appeared to be as effective at treating depression as office visits.

Theory: Telephone psychotherapy transcends barriers to office sessions, such as transportation problems or juggling appointments with work and family obligations. Anyone who is considering discontinuing psychotherapy treatments because of time constraints or transportation problems should ask his/her therapist if phone therapy is an option.

David Mohr, PhD, professor of preventive medicine, Feinberg School of Medicine, Northwestern University, Chicago.

Get Much-Needed Counseling for Lots Less

Joseph A. Rogers, founder and executive director of the National Mental Health Consumers' Self-Help Clearinghouse, Philadelphia, which is funded by a grant from the US Department of Health & Human Services. He also is chief advocacy officer for the Mental Health Association of Southeastern Pennsylvania. He served on the Congressional Task Force on the Rights and Empowerment of Americans with Disabilities. *www.mhselfhelp.org.*

Rising unemployment rates, falling home values and battered retirement portfolios can take a toll on our mental health as well as our finances. Difficult economic times exacerbate depression, anxiety and other emotional problems.

Psychotherapy can help us cope with emotional and psychological issues. The trouble is that the same economic problems that are causing anxiety and depression also are making it difficult for people to afford the rates charged by professional therapists, which often exceed $100 per hour.

Health insurance can help pay therapists' bills, but not all policies provide extensive coverage for counseling...and employees who lose their jobs in this recession typically lose their health insurance as well.

How to find high-quality counseling that's affordable...

SLIDING SCALE FEES

Some therapists reduce their hourly fees for clients who cannot afford to pay the full amount. Call therapists recommended by your doctor or family and friends. Explain why you are seeking therapy...be upfront about your limited financial resources...and ask if they will charge on a sliding scale.

If a therapist says yes, ask for details about the sliding scale policy to make sure that your bills will be manageable—some sliding scales slide much further down than others. If the therapist doesn't have a sliding scale, ask if he knows a local therapist who does.

GROUP THERAPY

Ask local therapists if they offer group therapy appropriate for your needs. Five to 10 patients typically meet with the therapist at one time. That allows the therapist to charge each patient significantly less.

If a therapist does not offer relevant group therapy, ask if he/she can recommend someone who does.

COMMUNITY MENTAL HEALTH AGENCIES

Many regions have community mental health organizations run by either the county or city government or a nonprofit organization. These agencies often provide low-cost counseling for perhaps $5 to $50 per hour. If your local mental health agencies do not provide low-cost counseling, they might be able to refer you to area counselors who do.

To find resources in your community, check your local Yellow Pages under the heading "Mental Health." You also can search for organizations in your area at the Web site of the nonprofit group Mental Health America (*www.nmha.org,* under "Help" select "Find treatment" then "Mental Health America affiliate"). Or contact my organization, the National Mental Health Consumers' Self-Help Clearinghouse (800-553-4539, *www.mhselfhelp.org*).

EMPLOYEE ASSISTANCE PROGRAMS

Your employer might provide free or low-cost access to local therapists through an "employee assistance program." These programs sometimes are available even to members of employees' immediate families. Ask your employer's benefits coordinator if such a program exists at your company.

Therapy provided through an employee assistance program typically is covered by the employee's health insurance or paid for by the employer. At the very least, the employer likely has negotiated a below-market therapy rate.

Participation in employee assistance programs normally is confidential, so the employer does not know which employees seek therapy.

RELIGIOUS LEADERS

Some ministers, priests, rabbis and other community religious leaders have master's degrees or even doctorates in counseling and extensive counseling experience. Contact your church or other area religious organizations to see if a pastoral counselor is available.

Pastoral counselors typically charge lower rates than other therapists with comparable levels of experience. Some waive their fees entirely for patients with limited financial resources. This varies, however, so ask about fees before arranging an appointment.

If your house of worship does not have a counselor, it might be able to refer you to other local religious organizations that do or to private counselors in the region who charge on a sliding scale.

LOCAL UNIVERSITIES

Universities that have schools of psychology, counseling or social work sometimes offer inexpensive therapy to members of the public. The therapy typically is provided by graduate students who need experience to earn counseling degrees or licenses. They probably are new to the field, but their efforts will be overseen by qualified professors.

Contact the school of counseling or social work at any local university and ask if there is a program providing low-cost counseling to the public. If not, the school might be able to refer you to inexpensive therapists in the region, such as recent graduates.

HELP HOTLINES AND "WARM" LINES

The National Suicide Prevention Lifeline (800-273-8255) offers free counseling over the phone, 24 hours a day, for people in severe emotional distress and suicidal crisis.

Some local mental-health organizations offer "warm lines," which are like hotlines, only they provide nonemergency phone counseling. These call centers typically are staffed by volunteers, not by professional counselors, but they are a useful free option for those who need someone to talk to.

Ask your county's mental-health agency if there are any relevant warm lines in your region ...or type "warm line," the name of your state and the name of your condition (such as "depression" or "addiction") or symptoms into a search engine such as Google to see what comes up.

SELF-HELP SUPPORT GROUPS

Support groups let participants meet with others who are facing similar psychological or emotional issues. There usually is no professional therapist present, but the groups are free and can be helpful.

Ask local churches or the social work departments of area hospitals if there are support groups in the region for people coping with your particular issue. If this is not helpful, use Google to search for a national nonprofit organization that deals with your condition, then contact this organization to see if someone there can point you to support groups in your region.

Example: The Depression and Bipolar Support Alliance has a network of more than 1,000 peer-run support groups. It also offers online support groups. (Call 800-826-3632, or go to *www.dbsalliance.org,* select "Find Support," then "Find a support group near you.")

HELP WITH PSYCHIATRIC DRUG COSTS

Most major pharmaceutical companies have "patient assistance programs" that provide their prescription drugs—including psychiatric drugs—for free or at greatly reduced costs. Only patients who have no health insurance and very limited financial resources are likely to qualify.

The Web site of the Partnership for Prescription Assistance, an organization sponsored by the pharmaceutical industry, can help you determine whether you are eligible (888-477-2669, *www.pparx.org*).

Or contact the pharmaceutical company directly to inquire about its patience assistance programs. The Web site of the National Alliance on Mental Illness lists the applicable 800 numbers for many commonly prescribed psychiatric drugs. (Call 800-950-6264, or go to *www.nami.org,* under "Inform Yourself" select "About Medication," then "Prescription Drug Assistance Program.")

■ ■ ■ ■

Ease Anxiety with Prayer

Anxiety disorders are three times more common among women who were once religiously active but later stopped attending worship services than among women who have always been religiously active. Women's mental health may be tied closely to social networks—including ones built at a house of worship.

Joanna Maselko, ScD, assistant professor of public health, Temple University, Philadelphia, and leader of a study of 718 people, published in *Social Psychiatry and Psychiatric Epidemiology.*

Choosing the Best Psychotherapy for You

Jonathan Jackson, PhD, clinical professor of psychology at Adelphi University and director of Adelphi's Center for Psychological Services at the Derner Institute of Advanced Psychological Studies, both in Garden City, New York.

Research has shown that emotional problems can be just as disabling—and deadly—as physical illnesses. Depression, for example, can worsen a variety of serious health ailments such as heart disease, diabetes, arthritis and asthma.

Latest development: A US law has recently been passed that requires health insurers to provide equal coverage for the treatment of physical and emotional problems beginning in 2010. This change will allow more people to afford psychotherapy.

HOW PSYCHOTHERAPY WORKS

Psychotherapy involves communication between a therapist and the person seeking help, usually in a series of weekly individual sessions ($75 to $200 each, depending on the part of the country where you live) that typically last 45 to 50 minutes each.

Important: You are most likely to get good results from psychotherapy if you work with a competent therapist who makes you feel understood and accepted. A recommendation from a physician, trusted friend, relative or member of the clergy is often helpful.

In many states, anyone can call himself/herself a therapist, but only licensed practitioners are sure to have appropriate training and qualifications. Clinical psychologists (who hold an advanced degree, such as a doctor of philosophy, PhD, in psychology or a doctor of psychology, PsyD)...social workers (who hold a master's degree in social work with an emphasis in clinical approaches)...and psychiatrists (medical doctors who can prescribe medication)—among many other practitioners—all can be licensed to practice psychotherapy.

To verify that a therapist is licensed by the professional body that governs his specialty, contact your state's health department.

Most therapists specialize in a particular type of therapy or a combination of therapies.

Best types of therapy include...

COGNITIVE BEHAVIORAL THERAPY (CBT)

Main premise: Psychological problems are tied to irrational beliefs and thoughts—for example, a depressed person thinking that everything in his life is bad. When the irrational beliefs are replaced with more realistic ones, symptoms typically improve.

What it's good for: Depression, anxiety, obsessive-compulsive disorder, eating disorders and post-traumatic stress disorder.

Typical duration: Six to 20 sessions.

PSYCHODYNAMIC THERAPY

Main premise: Difficulties in the present are rooted in feelings and actions from your earlier life.

What it's good for: Difficulty forming or maintaining relationships and interpersonal conflict at work or with friends or family members.

Typical duration: Because patterns that are identified in psychodynamic therapy can be subtle and elusive, it may last for six months to two years or more.

INTERPERSONAL THERAPY (IPT)

Main premise: Psychological problems result from difficulties in connecting and communicating with other people.

What it's good for: A person who lacks satisfying relationships or is adjusting to life changes (divorce or job loss, for example).

Typical duration: IPT generally adheres to a timetable, such as 12 to 16 weekly sessions, established at the onset of therapy.

THERAPY SETTINGS

Even though most psychotherapy occurs in individual sessions with the patient and a therapist, there are other settings in which the therapies described earlier may be used alone or in combination.

Among the most common...

- **Group therapy.** A group of five to 10 people meet and give one another feedback—most often, in the presence of a therapist.

What it's good for: A specific problem that participants share—such as anger, a phobia, panic attacks, social anxiety or grief.

Typical duration: Groups that focus on problems that are shared by its members (such as those described above) are likely to be limited to 12 to 20 sessions. Other groups, which tackle long-standing issues, such as emotional isolation or excessive dependency, can go on indefinitely. Members may stay for several months or years and then be replaced by new members. Sessions generally last 60 to 90 minutes for both types of groups.

Important: Insurance often does not cover group therapy, which typically costs 50% to 75% of the cost of individual therapy.

• **Family therapy.** This approach is based on the belief that a person's emotional difficulties are related to the way his entire family interacts. Usually, all available family members—the more the better—gather to clarify the roles each plays and the relationships among them.

What it's good for: Any issue in which the resources of an entire family can be tapped to address the problems of a member, including an adult child, a grandparent or a divorced spouse. Family therapy also can help families deal with the serious illness or death of a member.

Typical duration: Twelve to 20 weekly sessions. The cost of family therapy, which is covered by some insurance plans, is determined by the length of the session (typically 90 to 120 minutes each).

• **Couples therapy.** By meeting with both partners at the same time, the therapist can hear each partner's complaints and watch them interact. This allows the therapist to help the couple identify problematic patterns—such as repeated criticism or refusal to change—and make suggestions.

What it's good for: Marital crises (such as infidelity) or frequent fighting, particularly when the same issues come up repeatedly.

Typical duration: Weekly sessions for 20 weeks to a year.

Important: Insurance often does not cover couples therapy. Sessions typically run 60 to 90 minutes with fees set accordingly.

DO YOU NEED MEDICATION?

Medication should be considered when symptoms, such as depression or anxiety, are severe enough to interfere with your ability to function—particularly if therapy alone hasn't resolved your difficulties. In some cases, medication enhances the effectiveness of psychotherapy—and vice versa. Medication can be prescribed by a psychiatrist, psychiatric nurse or primary care physician.

■ ■ ■ ■

New Mood-Boosting Therapy

In a study of 32 people who were dissatisfied with their lives (some had been diagnosed with depression), those who attended weekly two-hour group "hope therapy" sessions (focused on identifying and reaching goals) for eight weeks had better self-esteem and fewer depression symptoms than those who did not attend the sessions.

Theory: When people learn to be more hopeful, their lives improve.

Jennifer Cheavens, PhD, assistant professor of psychology, Ohio State University, Columbus.

Free Yourself from Negative Feelings!

Judith Orloff, MD, assistant clinical professor of psychiatry, University of California, Los Angeles, and a psychiatrist in private practice in Los Angeles. She is creator of YouTube's Intuition and Emotional Freedom channel (*www.youtube.com/judithorloffmd*) and author of *Emotional Freedom: Liberate Yourself from Negative Emotions and Transform Your Life* (Harmony). *www.drjudithorloff.com.*

Everyone has moments of fear, flashes of anger and twinges of envy. But if your life is dominated by a painful or damaging emotion—paralyzing dread, uncontrollable fury or incessant envy—you are imprisoned by your feelings. Stress rises, self-image suffers, relationships falter...and you lose the ability to simply celebrate life.

You can become free. The key is to master specific techniques that help transform negative feelings into positive ones.

What to do: Consider the three common emotional traps below. Which descriptions trigger a wince, a sigh or some other sign of self-recognition? Those are areas where you can benefit most by working toward emotional freedom. *Here's how to...*

TRANSFORM FEAR INTO COURAGE

An emotional response to real or imagined danger, fear can make you abandon good sense and hold you in a chronic state of stress.

Examples: Fear of being alone may keep you trapped in a demeaning relationship even though you know that you should get out...fear of economic insecurity may keep you awake with worry night after night.

What to do...

- **Identify the source.** Make a list of the things you are afraid of. Then ask yourself where those fears came from. Did a hypercritical parent make you fear that you were unworthy of love? Did growing up poor make you chronically anxious about money? By recognizing such origins, you can predict which situations set off your fear, such as arguing with your husband or incurring an unexpected expense. This helps you feel less panicked when your body's automatic fight-or-flight response to fear causes your heart to race and your muscles to tense.

- **Shift your internal response.** Be on the lookout for the fearful inner voice that catastrophizes every situation—I can't afford a new roof. The water damage will ruin the house, and I'll wind up on the street. When fear speaks, talk back to yourself with the voice of reason—I have options. I can negotiate with the roofer or sell Aunt Jane's old silver to pay for the repairs.

- **Take courageous action.** Identify an easy first step toward changing your situation, then do it.

Example: If you fear leaving a bad relationship, first confide in a trusted friend or therapist. After you accomplish that, take another small step—such as setting a limit on how much time you spend each week with the person you are trying to distance yourself from. Slowly but surely, you will get unstuck from fear as your confidence and courage grow.

CHANGE ANGER INTO TRANQUILITY

Occasional irritation is normal, but if you often are on the verge of a blowup, you must address the true sources of your anger. Emotional freedom comes from improving situations when possible...and accepting situations over which you have no control. *What to do...*

- **Acknowledge the underlying emotions.** Anger often masks feelings of being vulnerable, unappreciated, excluded or powerless. A furious outburst ("You're a terrible friend!") makes others feel defensive or angry in return—but admitting to the deeper emotion ("I felt hurt when you invited the rest of the book club to your party but didn't include me") is likely to elicit compassion and a desire to make amends.

- **Ask specifically for what you want.** Instead of demanding, "Stop being a slob!" say to your spouse, "I'd appreciate it if you would put your dirty dishes in the dishwasher." Limit your comments to the present rather than dredging up past grievances.

- **Recognize your own role.** How are you contributing to the situations that make you angry? Perhaps you are left off of guest lists because you always argue about politics during parties. Perhaps your spouse leaves the housework to you because you are too critical. Changing your own behavior can prevent future fury.

- **Soothe yourself.** When a situation is beyond your control (the long line at the post office, the heavy traffic), giving way to anger leads only to behavior that you'll regret—such as speaking rudely to the postal clerk or endangering yourself and others by tailgating.

Better: Use a relaxation technique, such as deep breathing or listening to calming music, to safely dissipate frustration.

TURN ENVY INTO SELF-ESTEEM

Envy is the desire to have for yourself the advantages or accomplishments of another person. At the root of envy is a sense of your own inferiority.

- **Look for a pattern of putting yourself down.** Ask yourself if you habitually point out your own shortcomings ("I'm an idiot with numbers")...compare yourself negatively ("They are more outgoing than I am")...or deny your own needs ("It's okay if you smoke in the car. Don't worry about my asthma"). Like envy, these signal low self-esteem. Catch yourself when you make such remarks, and replace them with thoughts of self-affirmation—I am well-read...I exercise and keep fit...I deserve to breathe clean air.

• **Become the best you can be.** Look objectively at the person you envy and identify the attributes that you admire. Which of those traits can you work toward? Maybe you can't aspire to your rich cousin's designer wardrobe, but you can emulate her cheerful disposition. Rather than focusing on the ways in which you and she are different, list ways in which you are similar—you both volunteer, you both have new grandsons—and foster a positive connection by talking with the other person about the things that you have in common. Once you feel more positive about yourself, you'll be able to sincerely celebrate the successes of others.

• **Lend a hand.** Look around for people who are struggling, and use your talents to provide assistance—for instance, tutoring at a local school or organizing a charity fund-raiser. When you start to see yourself as competent and compassionate, you'll admire yourself more...be more confident of others' affections...and feel little cause for envy of anyone else.

Right Way to Give Advice

Judy Kuriansky, PhD, is a clinical psychologist and sex therapist on the faculty of Columbia University Teacher's College in New York City. She is author of five books, including *The Complete Idiot's Guide to a Healthy Relationship* (Alpha). *www.sexualtherapy.com/therapists/jkuriansky.htm*.

Unless it is carefully worded, advice can offend despite your good intentions. *What's hurtful, what's helpful...*

Hurtful: "You should." If you tell your friend he should get out of that marriage, he may get angry if this isn't what he wants to hear...or feel pressured if he's not ready to follow through.

Helpful: Ask questions that encourage clarification of facts and feelings, such as, "If you left, where would you go?" and "How would the kids react?" This helps elicit your friend's choice—at which point your suggestions for implementing that decision will be appreciated.

Hurtful: "I had that problem." If you interrupt a friend's story ("I felt a lump in my breast once, too..."), she feels alone because you're not focusing on her.

Helpful: Ask for details and offer practical assistance—"When is your biopsy? May I drive you?" Only after discussing your friend's situation completely should you share your experience and counsel.

Hurtful: "You'll get over it." To move past a problem, a person must face up to it, not avoid it. If a friend loses his job, and your automatic response is, "Stop fretting...you will find something better," ask yourself why. Are you too worried about your own job security to think about another's situation?

Helpful: Allow your friend to fully voice the hurt—afterward you'll both feel more ready to explore opportunities that lie ahead.

How to Keep Your Cool No Matter What

Jeffrey Brantley, MD, director of the Mindfulness-based Stress-Reduction program at Duke University Center for Integrative Medicine, Durham, North Carolina, and author of *Calming Your Anxious Mind* (New Harbinger).

Ever feel like blowing up—or melting down? Whether it's due to cramped living quarters or cranky coworkers, almost everyone feels stressed occasionally.

Women are especially vulnerable: They typically feel tremendous pressure to remain calm—to serve as family peacemaker or to project professionalism at work—but physiological responses to stress make this tough.

Example: Your ex-husband threatens to boycott your son's graduation, or your department is given an impossible deadline. Your body reacts by producing the stress hormones cortisol and adrenaline, which elevate your blood pressure and flood your bloodstream with glucose (sugar). Heart racing, palms sweating and stomach churning, you feel like your body has been hijacked by your emotions. The more you worry about losing control, the more your stress hormones rise.

Solution: Practice mindfulness, a technique rooted in Buddhist tradition. It can calm and focus the mind, slow the heart rate, reduce the need for oxygen and quickly ease muscle tension. *The basics...*

1. Assess what's happening—not in the situation, but within yourself. Are your hands shaking? Head pounding? Recognizing these signs for what they are—normal responses to stress—reduces their power to upset you further.

2. Be compassionate toward yourself. Instead of a judgmental rebuke ("Crying again? Big baby!"), silently say, "My body is giving me a message. I will listen and learn from it."

3. Shift your focus. Rather than fretting about a physiological response that you can't control, such as a flushed face or choked voice, concentrate on one you can control—your breathing. Slow, deep, rhythmic inhalations and exhalations help you to regain a sense of mastery over your physical reactions.

4. Reconnect with your body—and disconnect from the crisis around you. Take a quick walk, do some yoga poses in the restroom, or simply close your eyes and gently massage your temples for a few moments.

5. Take action. Consciously free your mind from resentful or hopeless thoughts ("My ex is a jerk!" or "I'm just no good at this job"). Reflect calmly on specific solutions, such as family counseling or assistance from coworkers, that will allow you to regain control over the situation —and yourself.

Can Reading Make You Happier?

University of Alabama at Birmingham news release.

Among older adults, the better they're able to read, understand and use health and medical information, the happier they are, suggests a US study.

THE STUDY

Researchers asked 383 people age 50 and older if they could read and answer questions on medical forms without assistance. They also asked them to rate their level of happiness.

Participants who had the most difficulty reading and understanding medical forms were more than twice as likely to report being unhappy as those with higher literacy levels, the study found.

The study was published online in the journal *Social Indicators Research.*

POSSIBLE EXPLANATION

This finding might have to do with a sense of control, explained lead author Erik Angner, PhD, an assistant professor of philosophy and economics at the University of Alabama at Birmingham. Feeling in control—which could be undermined by poor health literacy—has been linked to higher happiness scores.

The researchers suggested that improving health literacy should be a critical part of programs designed to boost health among older adults.

About 90 million Americans have problems understanding and using health information, according to a 2004 Institute of Medicine report.

info To learn more, visit the Web site of the US Department of Health and Human Services, *www.hhs.gov,* and search "health literacy."

■ ■ ■ ■

Senior Years Are the Happiest

A recent study has found that "with age comes happiness" and "life gets better in one's perception as one ages."

Key: Older people gain perspective on their achievements, placing greater value on what they have accomplished and becoming more accepting of what they haven't. The study was based on interviews of about 28,000 people ages 18 to 88, conducted from 1972 to 2004. Its findings are consistent across time. It found that at age 88, one-third of Americans reported being "very happy," compared with only about 24% of people in their 20s.

American Sociological Review, 1430 K St. NW, Washington, DC 20005.

Getting Back to Life After the Death of a Spouse

Phyllis Kosminsky, PhD, a clinical social worker specializing in grief, loss and trauma at the Darien, Connecticut–based Center for Hope/Family Centers, a nonprofit organization. She also is in private practice in Pleasantville, New York, and Norwalk, Connecticut. She is author of *Getting Back to Life When Grief Won't Heal* (McGraw-Hill).

The death of a spouse is among the greatest sources of grief. We not only lose the person who may be closest to us, we lose the person who most likely helped us function in the world and whom we depended on to help us through life's traumas. The loss of a spouse might leave us feeling more alone and helpless than we ever have felt before.

MIXED EMOTIONS

Naturally there are feelings of sadness, but surviving spouses have other feelings as well...

• **A sense of unreality.** In the weeks after a spouse's death, it is hard to accept the fact that the person with whom we have shared our life is gone. Many surviving spouses catch themselves momentarily forgetting that their partner has died. It might cross their minds to call the spouse to say they are going to be late...or to buy his/her favorite food at the market.

• **Difficulty concentrating.** It is common for surviving spouses to experience a sense of disorganization and difficulty concentrating in the weeks or months after the death. They might feel lethargic and uninterested in going out or doing anything at all.

• **Anger.** Surviving spouses sometimes are surprised to discover they feel angry, even at the departed spouse for dying.

• **Relief.** In some cases, a spouse's death brings feelings of relief, particularly if the spouse who passed away had been suffering or had come to require huge amounts of care.

• **Guilt.** When surviving spouses feel anger or relief, they often feel guilty about these feelings. Some surviving spouses also feel guilty because they imagine that they could have treated their partner better during the marriage.

GRIEVING

Some books about loss discuss the grieving process as if one stage of grief leads predictably to the next. In reality, grief does not always progress according to a preset pattern. Some surviving spouses find that life begins to return to normal within a few months, while for others, it takes years. *The grieving process tends to take a long time when...*

• **Each spouse had a clearly defined role in the marriage,** and the surviving spouse must develop new skills to perform the tasks that the departed partner once handled.

• **The spouse's death involved extended or significant suffering.** Seeing a spouse in agony can cause post-traumatic stress. Professional counseling can help surviving spouses cope with this.

• **The death is sudden or unexpected.** In this situation, the surviving spouse must come to terms with the loss of a partner as well as the shattering of illusions that the world is safe.

There is no "correct" amount of time to grieve the death of a spouse. Grief usually eases as time passes. You feel more hopeful and more like yourself six months after the death than you did three months after...and even better three months after that. (Of course, there will be good days and bad days throughout.) If this is not the case, it might be time to seek counseling.

COPING

There is no way to avoid the grief you will feel following the loss of your spouse—it would not even be healthy to try to avoid it. *There are, however, some ways to keep the grieving process moving in the right direction...*

•**Acknowledge the range of your feelings.** Some widows and widowers try to ignore any emotions they feel after their spouses' deaths, aside from grief and sadness. They think it isn't reasonable to feel anger, relief or guilt. If you deny yourself the right to experience these emotions, you will find it difficult to deal with your grief as well.

Example: A woman was mired in grief five years after the death of her husband. She was unwilling to admit to herself that she was angry with him for being financially irresponsible. Only when she came to terms with this anger was she able to move beyond her grief.

•**Put your feelings into words.** Talking about loss can help you cope. Speak with a friend or a counselor—or join a bereavement support group. A hospital, hospice or religious organization often can help you find a group in your area.

If you prefer not to share your feelings verbally, write them in a journal or in an unsent letter to the departed spouse.

•**Remain connected with friends.** It is normal to want privacy following the death of a spouse—but don't remain isolated longer than you must. As soon as you feel you could manage to go out and spend time with friends, do so—do not wait until you actually want to go out. Spending time with other people gives you an opportunity to focus on something other than your loss, reducing the odds that you will be pulled into the downward spiral of depression.

•**If you do not feel ready to resume close relationships,** pick activities that let you interact with other people but that keep the chitchat to a minimum, such as playing tennis or going to a movie.

•**Balance activity and free time.** Exercise, join clubs, do volunteer work or engage in other activities that get you out of the house and get your mind off your loss as soon as you feel able to do so. Do not become so busy that you have no free time to reflect, however. Try to find at least a few minutes of unscheduled time each day when you can relax, either at home or outside taking a walk.

•**Get enough sleep.** Schedule enough sleep time that you wake feeling rested. That might mean more than eight hours a night at first. If you're having trouble sleeping, talk with your doctor. Sleep deprivation makes any kind of emotional healing that much more difficult.

•**Give yourself what your spouse would have given you.** Surviving spouses sometimes feel cheated out of long-planned vacations and promised gifts when their partners pass away. Giving these gifts to yourself can help you overcome these emotions.

Example: Take that long-planned trip to Europe with a close friend.

Caregiver's Guide to Emotional Well-Being

Barry J. Jacobs, PsyD, a clinical psychologist and family therapist, and director of behavioral sciences for the Crozer-Keystone Family Medicine residency program in Springfield, Pennsylvania. He is a clinical assistant professor at Temple University and an adjunct faculty member at the University of Pennsylvania School of Nursing, both in Philadelphia. He is author of *The Emotional Survival Guide for Caregivers* (Guilford).

When a loved one is seriously ill or disabled and you take on the task of providing his/her care, it's natural to focus your energies on meeting that person's needs. The financial and physical demands you face may quickly become evident, yet the emotional impact often goes unrecognized—even though it may be the most challenging element of all. *Evidence...*

•**In a study in *Archives of Internal Medicine*, 14% of end-of-life caregivers reported significant financial strain**...18% reported significant physical strain...and 30% reported significant emotional strain.

•**Emotional stress leaves caregivers vulnerable to depression**—sometimes even more vulnerable than the person to whom they tend.

• **In another study, caregiving spouses who reported emotional strain** were 63% more likely to die within four years of the studied period than caregivers who did not feel such strain.

If you're a caregiver, you need to protect yourself as well as your loved one.

Helpful: Knowing what to expect as you move through the various emotional stages of becoming a caregiver...and developing specific strategies for coping.

GETTING OVER THE SHOCK

When a loved one suffers a sudden medical crisis, such as a serious injury, a woman can be thrust into the role of caregiver with no preparation. She may assume optimistically—and often unrealistically—that things will soon return to normal as the patient recovers.

In other cases, caregiving duties grow gradually as a parent or spouse ages or develops a progressive illness, such as Parkinson's disease or Alzheimer's disease. The caregiver may not be able to admit to herself how much the loved one's condition is deteriorating.

Either way, the caregiver's instinctive reaction to the shock is denial. Initially, this tendency to minimize the impact of the illness can help give the caregiver the strength to do what needs to be done. But persistent denial can compromise a caregiver's ability to make sound decisions.

Example: If your mother can no longer walk without risking a fall, but you cannot recognize the need to insist that she use a walker or wheelchair, it jeopardizes her safety.

Support strategies: It is best to face reality. To see your loved one as she is now rather than as she used to be, keep a log of her symptoms and abilities—recording other family members' observations as well as your own. Learn enough about her medical condition so that you can understand the treatment options and prognosis. This way, you and her doctors can agree on a medical objective, such as prolonging life or, later, simply making the patient as comfortable as possible.

LIVING WITH NEGATIVE FEELINGS

Many caregivers are heartened to experience positive emotions, such as pride in their ability to help and a deepened sense of devotion. But there are bound to be negative emotions, too, such as resentment and dread. You may feel resentful about being burdened...then guilty over the resentment...then angry for having been made to feel guilty.

You also may experience conflicting emotions toward the loved one himself as you struggle with the changes in the nature of your relationship.

Example: Suppose that, after your husband's stroke, you need to feed and bathe him as you would a child—and this clashes with your longtime image of him as a partner, peer and lover.

Support strategies: Remember that negative feelings about caregiving are normal and predictable—they do not invalidate your love. To overcome resentment and restore mutual respect, it helps to promote a patient's capabilities as much as his comfort—perhaps by being as dedicated to his physical therapy exercises as you are to his personal needs.

Strongly negative feelings also can be a helpful signal, alerting you to a need to adjust your plans. For example, taking care of an ill brother does not necessarily mean that he must live in your home forever, so stay open to all the options.

ACHIEVING BALANCE

Some caregivers worry that they're not doing enough, so they disproportionately expend time and energy on the loved one. This can be detrimental to their other relationships.

Example: If you devote yourself to taking care of an adult child with a progressive illness, you may neglect your spouse, other children, extended family and friends.

Losing ties with other people deprives you of support. The more isolated you become, the more susceptible you may be to depression and other health problems. This risk increases if you come to define yourself solely as a caregiver, losing your sense of personal identity.

Support strategies: Chronic medical conditions unfold over years, so they need to be handled much like a marathon—by pacing yourself. Talk to your doctor or a mental health professional if you show signs of burnout, such as constant fatigue, insomnia, irritability, cynicism or feelings of helplessness. Be committed to staying connected to others. Carving out time to go to dinner with your husband, play bridge with friends or attend a function at your house of worship will help replenish your spirit.

■ **More From Dr. Barry Jacobs...**

Help for Caregivers

Family caregivers can get information, support and/or referrals to professional counselors through these organizations...

•**Family Caregiver Alliance,** 800-445-8106, *www.caregiver.org.*

•**National Alliance for Caregiving,** 301-718-8444, *www.caregiving.org.*

•**National Family Caregivers Association,** 800-896-3650, *www.thefamilycaregiver.org.*

•**Strength for Caring,** 866-466-3458, *www.strengthforcaring.com.*

•**Well Spouse Association,** 800-838-0879, *www.wellspouse.org.*

What to Buy to Make You Happier!

Ryan Howell, PhD, assistant professor, psychology, San Francisco State University.

Katherine L. Muller, PsyD, director, psychology training and cognitive behavior therapy program, Montefiore Medical Center, and assistant professor, psychiatry and behavioral sciences, Albert Einstein College of Medicine, New York City.

Society for Personality and Social Psychology annual meeting, Tampa, Florida.

Although everyone knows that money can't buy happiness, purchasing life experiences instead of material possessions may increase your well-being, recent research suggests.

In a study that asked more than 150 college students to rate a recent purchase intended to make them happy, researchers found that people were more satisfied with purchases of life experiences, such as a trip to the beach or for a meal.

The findings were presented at the annual meeting of the Society for Personality and Social Psychology in Tampa, Florida.

THE STUDY

The study included 154 students from San Francisco State University, average age 25. About one-third of the group was white, nearly one-quarter were Asian-American, 11% were multi-racial, 15% were Hispanic, and about 4% were black.

The researchers asked each student to rate a recent purchase they made specifically with the intent of increasing their happiness. Half were told to write about a life experience purchase, while the other half was asked to write about a material purchase.

According to study coauthor Ryan Howell, PhD, an assistant professor of psychology at San Francisco State University, they asked for purchases made with the intent of increasing happiness so they didn't end up comparing a trip to the beach purchase to a box of pencils.

The students reported feeling more alive and invigorated with the purchase of a life experience, said Dr. Howell.

POSSIBLE EXPLANATIONS

There are likely a few reasons this is true, according to Dr. Howell. One may be that purchasing life experiences often brings someone closer to another person and satisfies a natural human need to be connected to others.

Another reason is that experiences provide "memory capital" that you can draw on in less happy times.

"Once you buy something, there's no reason to hold that memory," explained Dr. Howell. "But with a life experience, you can't take anything home. The only thing you can take with you is a memory, and we tend to focus our memories on the intense emotion we felt during the experience or on how it ended. Memories have an inherent bias, and you remember the best parts of life experiences."

IMPLICATIONS

The really good news from his study, given today's economic climate, is that life experience purchases don't have to be expensive to bring happiness, said Dr. Howell.

"A lot of the experiences were physical activities, like paying for park or beach admission," Dr. Howell noted.

However, Dr. Howell said that the findings probably don't apply to everyone. If you can't pay your mortgage, material things might increase your happiness more.

"As people drop closer to the poverty line, they tend to get more satisfaction with material things. The effect of purchasing life experiences probably becomes strong as you become more wealthy," he said.

EXPERT REACTION

"In this economy, being able to buy an item or an experience just for happiness is a luxury. I wonder for those who haven't had their basic needs met, if this would help as well?" said Katherine L. Muller, PsyD, director of the cognitive behavior therapy program at Montefiore Medical Center and an assistant professor of psychiatry and behavioral sciences at Albert Einstein College of Medicine in New York City.

"But if you do have disposable income, this could be something to consider, and you might want to make a conscious choice to try an experiential purchase," Dr. Muller said.

"I think there's real value in the idea that memory is really the only thing you can take with you," Dr. Muller continued. "And, social connectedness definitely creates more of an imprint, perhaps making the purchase more salient, because you shared it."

info To learn more about positive psychology, visit the Web site of the American Psychological Association, *www.apa.org/monitor,* and search "where happiness lies."

Meditation for Folks Who Don't Like to Meditate

Roger Walsh, MD, PhD, professor of psychiatry and human behavior in the School of Medicine, and of anthropology and philosophy in the School of Humanities, both at University of California, Irvine. He has done extensive research on Asian philosophies, religion and the effects of meditation and has received more than 20 national and international awards. He is author of *Essential Spirituality: The 7 Central Practices to Awaken Heart and Mind* (Wiley), which contains a foreword by the Dalai Lama.

We have heard all about the benefits of meditating. For decades, studies have shown that meditation helps with depression, anxiety, stress, insomnia, pain, high blood pressure, self-esteem, self-control, concentration and creativity. Yet for many people, meditation seems daunting. Maybe you find it hard to sit still...to clear your mind...to make the time...or to stick with it long enough to experience the effects.

Key to success: Choose a technique that suits your personality, schedule and level of experience, then do it consistently. Twenty minutes or more daily is a good goal, but even five minutes is helpful if you do it every day—and some techniques take almost no time at all.

IF YOU ARE A BEGINNER...

The methods below are effective yet simple enough for a novice. Start with just a few minutes, and work your way up.

- **Single-tasking.** A time-crunched society encourages multitasking—so you sort mail while on the phone and listen to audiobooks while driving.

What you may not know: The simple act of focusing fully on a single task is a meditative exercise. It improves your powers of concentration, alleviates stress and boosts mood by enhancing your appreciation of the here and now.

Try: Once or twice each day, give your complete attention to just one activity.

Example: When you fold the laundry, don't turn on the TV—just enjoy the softness of the fabrics and the soothing rhythm of your hand motions.

• **Focused breathing.** Sit in a quiet place, on the floor or in a chair, keeping your back straight so your lungs can expand. Pay attention to your breathing. Feel the air moving through your nostrils as you slowly inhale and exhale...feel your abdomen rise and fall. Then choose either of these sites (nostrils or abdomen) and focus fully on the sensations there. Soon you may notice that your mind has wandered. Don't berate yourself—this happens even to experienced meditators. Simply return your attention to the breath.

• **Centering prayer.** Choose a phrase or a word that is spiritually meaningful for you, such as God is love or shalom. With each breath, repeat it silently to yourself. Again, if your thoughts start to stray, just calmly return to your prayer.

IF YOU HATE TO SIT STILL...

Some people can't stop squirming when they try to meditate.

Solution: Moving meditation.

• **Qigong, tai chi or yoga.** These practices combine specific movements with a contemplative focus on the body, so you exercise while you meditate. Many health clubs, adult-education centers and hospitals offer classes in these kinds of techniques.

Referrals: National Qigong Association (888-815-1893, *www.nqa.org*)...American Tai Chi Association (703-477-8878, *www.americantaichi.net*)...Yoga Alliance (888-921-9642, *www.yogaalliance.org*).

• **Mindful eating.** Eat a meal alone, in silence, savoring the experience. When you first sit down, spend a moment enjoying the colors and aromas of the food. Take a bite and chew slowly. How do the taste and texture change as you chew? What sensations do you perceive as you swallow?

Surprise: You are meditating. Continue to eat as consciously as you can, never rushing.

IF YOU CAN'T FIND THE TIME...

Some days you may not have even five minutes to meditate—but you can take a moment.

• **Three breaths.** Whenever you feel tense, take three long, deep breaths. Even a few conscious inhalations and exhalations will calm you. Also use cues in your environment as regular reminders to focus and breathe deeply.

Example: Take three slow breaths every time you hang up the phone...walk through a doorway...or get into your car.

• **Beauty in the moment.** Three times a day, look around you and notice something lovely —the scent of someone's perfume, the happy sound of children playing. Explore the experience with your full attention.

Example: A light breeze is blowing. Watch the graceful way it makes the grass sway...listen to it whisper as it moves through the trees...feel its gentle touch on your cheeks. Notice your emotions of pleasure and appreciation—and carry them with you as you continue through your day.

■ **More from Dr. Roger Walsh...**

Secrets to Better Meditation...

If you are an accomplished meditator and want to enrich your experience, try these more advanced techniques...

• **Contemplative reading.** Select a brief passage—two or three sentences—from a philosophy book, religious text or other writing that is meaningful to you. Read it slowly and reflectively, over and over. If your reading brings up insights, ponder them. If your mind drifts to unrelated thoughts, return to reading.

• **Inquiry.** Sit and focus on your breathing. When a thought, feeling, sound or other sensation enters your awareness, instead of turning your attention back to the breath, explore the experience. Does it seem to have a shape or image associated with it? Does it change or fade away as you examine it? *Examples...*

• You notice a tickle in your shoulder. As you study it, you note that it feels diffuse...then localizes in one spot...then moves to a different area and prickles...then disappears.

• You are feeling anxious. Rather than trying to figure out what is causing this, note where the anxiety manifests in your body (a fluttery stomach, a tight muscle)...any images and thoughts associated with it...and how those images and thoughts change as you observe them. When a particular sensation passes, return your attention to your breath until the next sensation enters your awareness...then explore this new one. Over time, this enhances awareness and acceptance.

8

Family Health

Flu Rates Go Up When Humidity Goes Down

Flu viruses survive longer and are more easily transmitted when humidity levels are low, Oregon researchers say. Humidity is at its lowest in the middle of winter—January and February—and this also happens to be peak time for flu.

BACKGROUND

A link between humidity and flu prevalence and transmission has long been suspected, but the focus has been on relative humidity, not absolute humidity, according to the Oregon State University (OSU) study. Relative humidity is the ratio of air water vapor content to the saturating level, which varies with temperature. Absolute humidity refers to the actual amount of water in the air, irrespective of temperature.

THE STUDY

In this recent study, the Oregon team reanalyzed data from a 2007 Mount Sinai School of Medicine study that identified a weak relationship between flu transmission and relative humidity. The reanalysis revealed a strong link between absolute humidity and flu virus survival and transmission.

"The correlations were surprisingly strong. When absolute humidity is low, influenza virus survival is prolonged, and transmission rates go up," said study author Jeffrey Shaman, PhD, an atmospheric scientist at OSU who specializes in ties between climate and disease transmission.

CONCLUSIONS

Dr. Shaman and colleague Melvin Kohn, MD, MPH, an epidemiologist with the Oregon Department of Health Services, concluded that relative humidity explains only about 36% of flu virus survival and 12% of transmission, while absolute humidity explains 90% of flu virus survival and 50% of transmission.

Oregon State University news release.

Their findings were published in the *Proceedings of the National Academy of Sciences.*

"In some areas of the country, a typical summer day can have four times as much water vapor as a typical winter day—a difference that exists both indoors and outdoors," Dr. Shaman said. "Consequently, outbreaks of influenza typically occur in winter when low absolute humidity conditions strongly favor influenza survival and transmission."

info For tips on preventing the flu, visit the Web site of the American Academy of Family Physicians, *http://familydoctor.org,* and search "flu prevention."

Swine Flu: Your Questions Answered

William Schaffner, MD, president-elect of the National Foundation for Infectious Diseases in Bethesda, Maryland. Dr. Schaffner is professor and chairman of preventive medicine at Vanderbilt University School of Medicine in Nashville.

On June 11, 2009, the World Health Organization declared the global outbreak of swine flu (also known as H1N1) to be a pandemic.

To learn more about the swine flu, we spoke with infectious disease expert William Schaffner, MD. *Here, he answers your questions...*

•How common is swine flu? The Centers for Disease Control and Prevention (CDC) released its estimate of H1N1 cases in the United States on December 14, 2009. From April through mid-November, 2009, the estimate is between 34 million and 67 million, with between 7,000 to 14,000 deaths.

To put this in perspective, up to 50 million Americans get normal, seasonal flu in an average year and about 36,000 die from it.

•Isn't swine flu more dangerous than regular flu? Not necessarily. In the 1990s, the average number of yearly hospitalizations due to seasonal flu was more than 200,000. Contrast this number with the mid-range estimate of the number of hospitalizations due to H1N1: 213,000, according to the CDC. The difference is that the bulk of cases, hospitalizations and deaths due to the H1N1 are occurring in people younger than 65, rather than in those 65 or older.

•Why are young people more at risk? About 64% of swine flu patients are between the ages of five and 24. Only about 1% of confirmed cases occurred in people 65 years old or older. Possible reason: In general, children are the main flu reservoirs. They haven't been exposed to as many viruses as older adults and thus are less likely to have protective antibodies.

In addition, millions of older adults have been exposed to related flu strains in the past. They developed antibodies that appear to offer at least partial protection against swine flu.

•Who is at risk for getting seriously ill? People with diabetes, heart disease, cancer and other diseases that weaken the immune system. Pregnant women also are at greater risk. These groups of people are at greater risk for getting seriously ill with seasonal flu, too.

New finding: Researchers noted that obese patients with swine flu were more likely to get seriously ill than thinner patients. This probably is because very large individuals have more difficulty expanding their lungs, which increases the risk for fluid buildup and pneumonia.

•How is the disease transmitted? Flu mainly is spread by droplet transmission. Someone sneezes, coughs or merely exhales, and virus-filled droplets are expelled. If you inhale the virus or get it in your nose or eyes, there's a good chance that you'll develop the flu. The virus also can survive in eye and nose secretions on the hands.

Wash your hands often. It won't eliminate the risk of getting swine flu, but it reduces the odds.

•Do face masks help? The surgeons masks that many people wore when the virus first emerged might have limited the spread somewhat. However, the CDC doesn't recommend them, because it is difficult to assess their potential effectiveness in community settings.

Exception: The N95 respirator, designed to be worn by workers in hazardous environments, can be tightly sealed around the face and probably is effective in protecting you from getting the infection. The problem is that these masks are hot and uncomfortable, and they make it difficult to breathe. They aren't practical for daily life.

• **Should I see a doctor if I think I have swine flu?** If you're sick, call your doctor. Don't risk infecting other people in the doctor's office or emergency room. Many doctors will give flu-related advice and sometimes a prescription for an antiviral drug over the phone. In general, the only people who really need to worry are those who feel extremely ill and those with a high risk of getting the flu (such as those with impaired immunity or lung disease). If you fall into this category, have a prearranged plan with your doctor.

■ ■ ■ ■

Mom's Diet May Affect Baby's Sex

Women who ate high-calorie diets with a wide range of nutrients around the time of conception were more likely to deliver boys. Women who ate breakfast cereal daily had more boys...those who seldom ate cereal had more girls.

Caution: Even if you hope for a girl, do not restrict calories—your baby needs nutrients. Do not avoid cereal—it often has folic acid, which combats birth defects.

Fiona Mathews, PhD, lecturer, University of Exeter, England, and head of a study of 740 women, published in *Proceedings of the Royal Society B: Biological Sciences.*

■ ■ ■ ■

Brainy Babies Come from Moms with Big Hips

Researchers analyzed data from the National Center for Health Statistics. On average, children born to mothers with relatively more fat in the hip area and narrower waists performed better on tests of cognitive function than other children did.

Theory: Women with hourglass figures store more fat on their thighs and buttocks...and this fat contains polyunsaturated fatty acids that aid fetal brain development.

William Lassek, MD, adjunct assistant professor of epidemiology, University of Pittsburgh, and coauthor of a study of 16,325 women, published in *Evolution and Human Behavior.*

■ ■ ■ ■

New Procedure Boosts Fertility in Men

As many as 15% of adult men in the US have varicoceles, varicose veins impeding blood flow through the testicles, which sometimes affect fertility.

Now doctors can do a minimally invasive venous embolization—a procedure that blocks blood flow to the varicocele—by passing a catheter through the groin. This improves the motility of sperm.

Recent finding: Within six months of having the procedure, more than 25% of patients reported that their partners were pregnant. Rare side effects include minor bleeding and inflammation in the scrotum.

Sebastian Flacke, MD, PhD, associate professor of radiology, Tufts University School of Medicine, Boston, and vice chair for research and development, department of radiology, Lahey Clinic, Burlington, Massachusetts, and author of a study of 223 patients, published in *Radiology.*

■ ■ ■ ■

Fans Help Babies Survive SIDS

Sudden Infant Death Syndrome (SIDS) may occur when babies' access to fresh air is blocked.

Study: Infants who slept in a room with a fan were 72% less likely to die of SIDS...those who slept in a room with an open window were 36% less likely.

Theory: Airflow reduces the chance of rebreathing trapped carbon dioxide.

De-Kun Li, MD, PhD, MPH, senior research scientist, Kaiser Permanente, Oakland, California, and head of a study of 497 babies, published in *Archives of Pediatric & Adolescent Medicine.*

■ ■ ■ ■

Warning: Bumper Pad Danger

All 22 bumper pads examined in a recent study were found to carry a risk of causing suffocation or strangulation.

Reasons: An infant's head can get wedged between the pad and mattress...and some pads have ties longer than the industry standard of nine inches.

Bradley Thach, MD, professor of pediatrics and staff physician, St. Louis Children's Hospital, and head of a study of crib bumper deaths, published in *The Journal of Pediatrics*.

■ ■ ■ ■

Autism Twice as Likely in Tiny Babies

Autism risk is more than double among infants who are born prematurely or at low birth weight. Risk is higher for premature and low-birth-weight girls than for similar boys, even though autism itself is more common in boys. About one in 150 children in the US is autistic.

Diana Schendel, PhD, lead health scientist, National Center on Birth Defects and Developmental Disabilities, Centers for Disease Control and Prevention, Atlanta, and researcher on a study of 565 children, published in *Pediatrics*.

■ ■ ■ ■

Quit Smoking for a Happier Baby

Researchers rated nine-month-old babies on mood, receptivity to new things, and eating and sleeping regularity. Compared with babies whose mothers smoked throughout pregnancy, babies whose mothers gave up cigarettes while pregnant were significantly more easygoing.

Upshot: Here's yet another reason to quit smoking.

Kate E. Pickett, PhD, Department of Health Sciences, University of York, England, and leader of a study of about 18,000 babies, published in *Journal of Epidemiology and Community Health*.

■ ■ ■ ■

Breast-Feeding Boosts IQ

Mothers were urged to feed newborns only breast milk for at least three months. At age six, these children did better academically and scored six points higher on IQ tests, on average, than their peers who in infancy had received other foods in addition to breast milk. Breast milk contains high levels of nutrients that promote brain growth.

Recommended: Nurse exclusively for at least three months and preferably six months.

Michael S. Kramer, MD, professor of pediatrics, epidemiology and biostatistics, McGill University and Montreal Children's Hospital, both in Montreal, and leader of a study of 13,889 children, published in *Archives of General Psychiatry*.

Anesthesia in Toddlers Raises Learning Disability Risk Over 50%

Robert T. Wilder, MD, PhD, consultant, anesthesiology, Mayo Clinic, and associate professor of anesthesiology, Mayo Medical School, Rochester, Minnesota.

Randall Clark, MD, chairman, American Society of Anesthesiologists committee on pediatric anesthesia, and chairman, anesthesiology, Children's Hospital Denver.

Anesthesiology.

Children who have had anesthesia two or more times by the age of three may be at a higher risk of developing learning disabilities later, recent research suggests.

Although this is the first human study to indicate such an association, it's still unclear if the anesthesia is the culprit, or if some other factor is at play.

BACKGROUND

Prior animal studies have suggested that anesthesia drugs might affect the developing brain.

One study in 2008 found that youngsters who had hernia surgery under the age of three showed almost twice the risk of behavioral or developmental problems later compared with kids who hadn't had surgery. Researchers suspect that exposure to general anesthesia during these operations might have played a role in the jump in risk. Other studies have demonstrated a similar link.

THE STUDY

The authors of this latest study scoured the educational and medical records of all 5,357 children born in five towns in Olmsted County, Minnesota, between 1976 and 1982, and who had lived in the same county at least until the age of five.

Generally, the children who had been under anesthesia had received *halothane* and nitrous oxide (laughing gas). Halothane is no longer available in the United States, according to the study, but newer drugs that work by similar mechanisms have replaced it. Nitrous oxide is used widely in this country.

Children's brains are still rapidly developing during these early years of life and are therefore vulnerable to insults, the researchers noted.

THE RESULTS

The team said that just one exposure to anesthesia did not up the risk of developing a learning disability before the age of 19. Two exposures, however, increased the risk by 59%, while three or more exposures increased the risk by a factor of 2.6. Children who stayed under anesthesia for longer periods of time also faced a greater degree of risk.

But the association could also be due to the stress from the surgery itself or to the fact that children who undergo multiple surgeries at such a young age are sicker and therefore more likely to develop learning disabilities in general, the study suggested.

IMPLICATIONS

"We don't want to alarm parents," said Robert T. Wilder, MD, lead author of the study appearing in *Anesthesiology.* "We have an association here between kids who received two or more anesthetics in surgery and an increase in learning disabilities, but we don't have clear causality that it was the anesthetics that caused the learning disabilities."

"Even if I knew for a fact that anesthesia might be increasing the risk for learning disabilities, my advice would still be, if your kid needs to have surgery done, they're better off having the anesthetic," added Dr. Wilder, who is a consultant in anesthesiology at the Mayo Clinic in Rochester, Minnesota, and an associate professor of anesthesiology at the Mayo Medical School. "Of course, you don't want to submit your kid to any unnecessary surgical or medical procedure, but that would have been my advice before studying this."

EXPERT REACTION

One expert noted that the issue is of utmost concern to anesthesiologists.

"This is more information on an area that has been of intense interest to anesthesiologists," said Randall Clark, MD, chairman of the American Society of Anesthesiologists committee on pediatric anesthesia and chairman of anesthesiology at Children's Hospital Denver. "We're all very concerned about this and are working hard to see if it has implications for human infants, but we don't have any clear evidence that that's the case yet."

"Research in this area is ramping up dramatically, and we are working with the FDA [US Food and Drug Administration] to get answers to these questions," he added.

And, Dr. Clark noted, "very little of total elective surgery is done in the age ranges where we think children might be of risk. These are needed procedures and, to the best of our knowledge, the need for the procedure would outweigh what we now know are potential risks."

DISCOVERING NEW ANESTHETICS

If future research does point to the anesthesia as the guilty party, new anesthesia agents may mitigate the effect.

But, Dr. Wilder pointed out, "even though finding new drugs might be the holy grail, that won't be easy."

info For more information about children and anesthesia, visit the Web site of the Society for Pediatric Anesthesia, *www.pedsanesthesia.org*, and click on "Parent & Families."

■ ■ ■ ■

Safer Scans for Kids

Children are more susceptible to the effects of X-rays or CT scans, so the less exposure they get to the radiation used for these tests, the better.

Best: Talk to the doctor and radiologist about using the lowest levels possible. Ask if alternative tests that do not use ionizing radiation, such as magnetic resonance imaging (MRI) or ultrasound, may be substituted. Ask about the facility's average repeat rate—the number of times an image typically must be redone in order to obtain the necessary diagnostic quality. The national average repeat rate is 5%. If the facility's rate is higher than that, consider having your child's imaging done at another facility.

Helene Pavlov, MD, FACR, radiologist-in-chief, Hospital for Special Surgery, New York City.

Are Sneaky Sources of Aluminum Harming Your Family's Health?

Mark A. Stengler, ND, naturopathic physician in private practice, La Jolla, California...adjunct associate clinical professor at the National College of Natural Medicine, Portland, Oregon...author of many books, including *The Natural Physician's Healing Therapies* and coauthor of *Prescription for Natural Cures* (both from Bottom Line Books)...and author of the *Bottom Line/Natural Healing* newsletter.

You may think of aluminum mostly as a handy foil for wrapping leftovers, but in fact, aluminum is just about everywhere...in our air, water, soil and food. It also is in many drugs...as well as in household and personal products, such as kitchen pans and antiperspirants.

I am concerned about the aluminum humans have added to our surroundings. Although conventional medicine has long maintained that aluminum is not a problem for most people, the holistic view is that any metal is unsafe when present in excess.

Unfortunately, there is limited research on the risks of aluminum buildup in the body. *What we know for certain...*

- **Aluminum can accumulate in the bones,** liver, kidneys and brain.
- **It is toxic to the nervous system.**
- **It can cause brain cells to degenerate.**

Symptoms of aluminum toxicity include headache...fatigue...bone pain...anemia (low red blood cell count)...and dementia. Because these symptoms can mimic those of other medical conditions, doctors often do not recognize aluminum as the root cause of the problem. That is why, whenever I see such symptoms in my patients, I order a urine test to check aluminum levels.

RISKY VACCINES?

I am especially concerned about aluminum in vaccines, for children in particular. Shots that are supposed to help keep us healthy may, in this way, do us harm.

A decade ago, the biggest concern around childhood vaccines had to do with *thimerosal,* a preservative that contains mercury. As clear evidence of mercury's toxicity mounted, demands were made that thimerosal be removed from vaccines. Manufacturers finally complied, eliminating or reducing it to trace levels in all vaccines. This was possible because thimerosal was not crucial to the effectiveness of the vaccine.

But aluminum is a different story. It makes vaccines work better. It allows the body's immune system to more easily recognize the vaccine and get busy creating antibodies against the disease being targeted. Eliminating the aluminum would necessitate a complete reformulation of current vaccines—plus many years of clinical trials to determine whether new alternatives were effective.

In healthy adults, the current guideline for a safe amount of aluminum delivered via a vaccine is considered to be up to 850 micrograms (mcg). Many of the vaccines typically given to adults—for tetanus, diptheria, pertussis (whooping cough), HPV and Hepatitis A and B—contain aluminum. I would argue that no amount of aluminum is healthy.

However, adults have, on average, five liters of blood, and they generally do not receive multiple vaccinations at the same time. These factors make the consequences of receiving an aluminum-laced vaccine less worrisome for them than it is for children. In newborns, as pediatrician Robert W. Sears, MD, points out in *The Vaccine Book* (Little, Brown), an acceptable aluminum dose ranges from just 10 mcg to 20 mcg. Yet this number is far exceeded by some of the new vaccines.

Example: The Hepatitis B shot with 250 mcg, which was added by the American Academy of Pediatrics to the childhood vaccination schedule in the early 1990s. Furthermore, throughout the first year of life, several vaccines are administered at each checkup. Add up the amount of aluminum in all the vaccines recommended in a single round—given at two months of age, four months and six months—and you will see that babies are getting as much as 1,225 mcg in a single vaccination day. For a one-year old, the known safe amount is only about 50 mcg daily.

Much of what is known about aluminum's effects in human infants comes from research in premature babies. Years ago, it was discovered that preemies who received more than 10 mcg to 20 mcg of aluminum in their intravenous feeding solutions each day suffered aluminum toxicity in their bones and brain tissue, resulting in impaired neurologic and mental development. Aluminum is now filtered out of such solutions. Yet preemies are still allowed to receive a Hep B vaccine with 250 mcg of aluminum!

Safer steps you can take...

- **Ask your doctor for aluminum-free vaccines for the family.** Certain vaccine brands contain little or no aluminum.

Examples: Fluzone and FluMist for influenza...Pneumovax for pneumonia...RotaTeq for rotavirus. The Centers for Disease Control and Prevention has a complete list on its Web site, *www.cdc.gov/vaccines.*

- **Do not receive more than one vaccine per month.** Ideally, adults and children should space out getting any shots that have aluminum by three or more months. *The Vaccine Book* offers a safer vaccination schedule for children.

SNEAKY SOURCES

Each person in the US ingests, on average, about 30 milligrams (mg) to 50 mg of aluminum daily, according to the National Library of Medicine.

Reason: Aluminum can be present in a number of common substances, including...

- **Air**—via dust from mining and agricultural processes.
- **Baking aids,** such as cake mixes, baking powder and self-rising flour. Try aluminum-free varieties, available from Bob's Red Mill (800-349-2173, *www.bobsredmill.com,* and in natural food stores).
- **Beverages**—from the cans that hold juice, soda, beer, infant formula.
- **Cheeses (processed).**
- **Cookware, utensils (some brands) and aluminum foil**—it is especially important to avoid using these items when preparing acidic substances, such as tomato sauce, which make them more likely to leach aluminum.
- **Health and beauty products,** including antiperspirants, shampoos and sunscreens.
- **Jet fuel.**
- **Medications,** including some antacids and anti-diarrheals, and buffered aspirin.
- **Nondairy creamers.**
- **Tap water,** especially fluoridated.

Watch for "alum-" on labels. Once you are aware of these sneaky sources, you can take care to avoid them as much as possible. More research is needed to understand how aluminum affects our health and to formulate guidelines about its use. When it comes to aluminum—or any toxic metal—it's better to be safe than sorry.

While we all should watch our exposure to aluminum, certain people are at especially high risk for aluminum toxicity. *I recommend all adults be tested at some point, but it is especially important for...*

- **People with severe memory problems or dementia,** including Alzheimer's disease.
- **People with neurological problems,** such as tremors and neuropathy (nerve pain).
- **Children with learning or developmental disorders** (autism, ADHD).

• **Anyone with impaired kidney function.**

• **Those with known aluminum exposure,** such as workers in factories where it is used.

Your doctor can perform the test, or you can purchase a hair analysis kit to use at home (Mineral Check test, $79.95, 888-891-3061, *www.bodybalance.com*). If your aluminum levels appear to be elevated, see a holistic doctor for urine or stool testing to confirm that excess aluminum is present.

If so, your doctor should prescribe a chelating agent—a drug that binds to metal, pulling it out of the body's tissues and sending it into the blood. It can then be filtered through the liver and kidneys and excreted via urine and stool. After three months or more, your doctor will want to retest you to see if your aluminum level has dropped. I have had great success using this therapy and detoxifying supplements for my patients.

■ ■ ■ ■

Is Flavored Yogurt Making Your Child Hyper?

Some FDA-approved additives—including allura red, known as Red No. 40...and tartrazine, known as Yellow No. 5—can cause significant increases in hyperactivity in some children under age 10. These colors are added to many foods, including yogurt, so check labels carefully.

William Sears, MD, pediatrician, Sears Family Pediatrics, Capistrano Beach, California, and coauthor of *The Healthiest Kid in the Neighborhood* (Little, Brown).

Grandparents Great at Helping Kids Through Tough Times

American Psychological Association news release.

Grandparents might be known for spoiling grandchildren, but a recent study says they might also be helping the kids improve their social skills and behavior.

Spending time with Grandma and Grandpa especially appears to help children from single-parent, divorced/separated or stepfamily households, according to the report, published in the *Journal of Family Psychology.*

STUDY FINDINGS

Shalhevet Attar-Schwartz, PhD, of the Hebrew University of Jerusalem, and her team interviewed 11- to 16-year olds from England and Wales. They found that the more conversations the youths had with a grandparent, including asking for advice or even money, the better they got along with their peers and the fewer problems they had, such as hyperactivity and disruptive behavior.

"This was found across all three family structures," Dr. Attar-Schwartz said. "But adolescents in single-parent households and stepfamilies benefited the most. The effect of their grandparents' involvement was stronger compared to children from two-biological-parent families."

The study did not look at children who lived solely with their grandparents, though.

IMPLICATIONS

"Grandparents are a positive force for all families but play a significant role in families undergoing difficulties," said Dr. Attar-Schwartz, the study's lead author.

"They can reduce the negative influence of parents separating and be a resource for children who are going through these family changes," she said.

The findings have great implications for people in the United States, the authors said, because American grandparents are increasingly sharing living space with their grandchildren. A 2004 US Census Bureau survey found that more than five million households include a grandparent and a grandchild under 18, up 30% since 1990.

info For more on raising safe and healthy children, visit the Web site of the Centers for Disease Control and Prevention, *www.cdc.gov/family.*

Surprising Childhood Sign of Depression Later On

University of Washington news release.

Antisocial behavior among young elementary school girls, and increased anxiety in either boys or girls that age, tend to predict whether they develop depression in adolescence, a recent study shows.

However, showing signs of depression in first or second grade did not mean adolescent depression was imminent, said the report published in *The Journal of Early Adolescence.*

THE STUDY

University of Washington researchers followed more than 800 predominantly white children for seven years, starting when they were in first or second grade. Children, parents and teachers provided information that measured the students' levels of depression, anxiety, antisocial behavior and social competency. Parents were also asked about family and marital conflict, family stress and parental depression.

THE FINDINGS

"When all the risk factors were analyzed, antisocial behavior and anxiety were the most predictive of later depression. It just may be that they are more prevalent in the early elementary school years than depression," said study lead author James Mazza, PhD, associate professor of educational psychology at the University of Washington.

"One finding from this study that is a mind-grabber is that young children can identify themselves as being anxious and depressed," Dr. Mazza said. "When they had scores that were elevated, we were a bit surprised, because we thought they would say, 'My life is fun, and I play a lot.' Nevertheless, they are able to understand and report feeling depressed or anxious, and tell us so. This suggests giving health surveys in early elementary school is a good idea, and we should talk to kids in the first and second grades because they can give us valuable information."

While doctors may start assessing children as young as six for depression, middle-school age is usually when the condition is first recognized or diagnosed in children. That is the time when the genders split, with more girls showing signs of depression than boys.

"Boys with early antisocial behavior typically go on to show more antisocial behavior, while girls may turn inward with symptoms, morphing into other mental health problems such as depression, eating disorders, anxiety and suicidal behavior during adolescence," he said.

info To learn more, visit the Web site of the National Institute of Mental Health, *www.nimh.nih.gov,* and search "Depression in children and adolescents."

Dads Put Children at Risk for Bipolar Disorder

American Medical Association news release.

Children of older fathers are at an increased risk for bipolar disorder. That's the conclusion of a recent study by Swedish researchers who compared 13,428 people with bipolar disorder to more than 67,000 people without the condition.

Bipolar disorder is a common, severe mood disorder involving an alternating pattern of emotional highs (mania) and lows (depression). Other than a family history of psychotic disorders, few risk factors for the condition have been identified.

STUDY FINDINGS

"After controlling for parity (number of children), maternal age, socioeconomic status and family history of psychotic disorders, the offspring of men 55 years and older were 1.37 times more likely to be diagnosed as having bipolar disorder than the offspring of men aged 20 to 24 years," said Emma M. Frans, of the Karolinska Institute in Stockholm.

Children of older mothers also had an increased risk, but the risk was less pronounced than that associated with older fathers. In cases of early-onset bipolar disorder (diagnosed before age 20), the effect of the father's age was much stronger, while the mother's age had no effect, the study found.

EXPLANATION

"Personality of older fathers has been suggested to explain the association between mental disorders and advancing paternal age. However, the mental disorders associated with increasing paternal age are under considerable genetic influence," according to the study authors.

This suggests a genetic link between the advancing age of the father and bipolar and other disorders among children, the researchers said.

"As men age, successive germ cell replications occur, and de novo (new, not passed from parent to offspring) mutations accumulate monotonously as a result of DNA copy errors," the researchers noted.

"Women are born with their full supply of eggs that have gone through only 23 replications, a number that does not change as they age. Therefore, DNA copy errors should not increase in number with maternal age. Consistent with this notion, we found smaller effects of increased maternal age on the risk of bipolar disorder in the offspring."

The study was published in the journal *Archives of General Psychiatry.*

info To learn more about bipolar disorder, visit the Web site of the Depression and Bipolar Support Alliance, *www.dbsalliance.org.*

■ ■ ■ ■

Shampoos and More that Are Bad for Boys

Personal-care products, such as lotions, hair gel, shampoo and soap, that contain tea tree oils can cause *gynecomastia* (enlarged breasts) in rare cases. Gynecomastia dissipates when these products are no longer used.

Kenneth Korach, PhD, chief of the laboratory of reproductive and developmental toxicology, National Institute of Environmental Health Sciences, Research Triangle Park, North Carolina, and coauthor of a study published in *The New England Journal of Medicine.*

9

Heart Disease

Pneumonia Vaccine Lowers Risk of Heart Attack

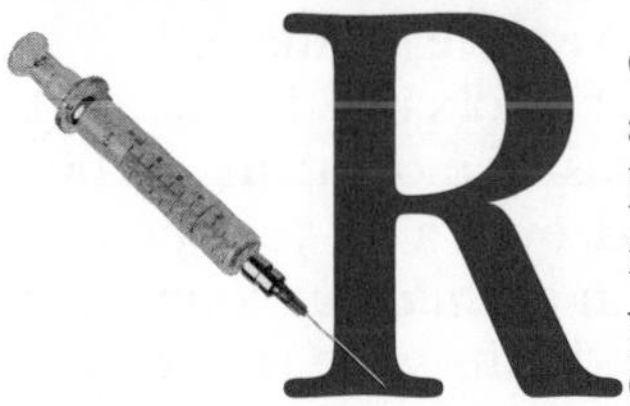

Receiving a vaccination against pneumonia can halve the risk of having a heart attack two years later, a recent Canadian study finds.

THE STUDY

The study compared 999 people admitted to Canadian hospitals for heart attacks, with 3,996 admitted for other reasons. It found no difference in heart attack rates between those who did or did not have the pneumococcal vaccine in the previous year. However, there was a 50% lower heart attack rate for those who received the vaccine two years earlier.

THEORIES

There are plenty of theories and many statistics linking pneumonia with heart attacks, said Mohammad Madjid, MD, a senior research scientist at the Texas Heart Institute.

Indeed, "many years ago, at the start of the 20th century, scientists believed that heart attacks had an infectious origin," Dr. Madjid said. That belief has been pushed aside as studies showed the importance of risk factors, such as high blood pressure, high cholesterol, obesity and diabetes.

"But in every epidemic of influenza, there is a sharp rise in the number of heart attacks," Dr. Madjid continued. "You have more people dying of heart attacks than of pneumonia."

One reason is that pneumonia increases the inflammation of coronary arteries, which is associated with the risk of a heart attack, he said. "When you have this infection, inflammation doubles and triples," Dr. Madjid added.

Mohammad Madjid, MD, senior research scientist, Texas Heart Institute, Houston.

David Fisman, MD, medical epidemiologist, Ontario Public Health Laboratories, Canada.

Canadian Medical Association Journal.

PREVIOUS STUDY CORROBORATES EVIDENCE

The new report parallels that of a study reported two years ago, said David Fisman, MD, a medical epidemiologist at the Ontario Public Health Laboratories. That study of 63,000 people hospitalized between 1999 and 2003 found that the 12% of patients who had gotten the pneumococcal vaccine were 40% to 70% less likely to die than the 23% who had not been vaccinated.

Lower rates of heart attack, kidney failure and other problems were also seen in the vaccinated group, Dr. Fisman added.

WHO SHOULD GET THE VACCINE?

Pneumococcal vaccine is recommended by the US Centers for Disease Control and Prevention for everybody aged 65 and older and for persons with chronic ailments, such as heart disease. The government goal is to have 90% of the over-65 population get the vaccine. The actual rate, however, "is much less than it should be," Dr. Madjid said.

Pneumococcal vaccine is controversial, because "it is difficult to show that it actually decreases the risk of pneumonia," Dr. Fisman said. But there have been studies indicating not only that the vaccine decreases the risk for pneumonia, but also that when pneumonia does occur, it is less severe in those who have been vaccinated, he said.

"If they did get pneumonia, they were less likely to get bacteremia, bacteria in the blood," Dr. Fisman said. "Heart disease may be an inflammatory process, and infection is a physiological challenge that generates an inflammatory response.

"This study is consistent with a number of studies showing that having the vaccine makes it less likely that people will die of pneumonia or heart disease," Dr. Fisman said. "The important take-home message is that pneumococcal vaccine gets a bad rap. It saves lives. It is a lot safer to vaccinate people than to pull them back from the brink when they have a heart attack."

info To learn more about vaccines and immunizations, go to the Web site of the Centers for Disease Control and Prevention, *http://www.cdc.gov/vaccines/default.htm.*

■ ■ ■ ■

Respiratory Infection Linked to Heart Attack and Stroke

In the week following a severe respiratory infection, such as influenza, patients have at least twice the risk for heart attack or stroke as people who did not have respiratory infections.

Self-defense: Wash hands often...get a flu shot yearly.

Tom Meade, DM, professor of epidemiology, London School of Hygiene and Tropical Medicine. Dr. Meade was coresearcher of a study of 20,363 people, published in *European Heart Journal.*

Holiday Heart Problems

Keith B. Churchwell, MD, assistant professor of medicine and radiology at Vanderbilt University School of Medicine in Nashville. He is executive director at the Vanderbilt Heart and Vascular Institute.

The holidays bring more than gifts and good cheer. They also bring an increase in deaths from heart disease, with spikes both on Christmas Day and New Year's Day. The trend is so predictable that cardiologists now refer to the "Merry Christmas Coronary" and the "Happy New Year Heart Attack."

A research team led by Robert A. Kloner, MD, looked at death records of more than 220,000 people who had died over a 12-year period. The study, published in *Circulation*, found that about one-third more deaths were recorded in December and January than from June through September.

The holidays also bring a rise in hospital admissions for nonfatal cardiac events, including angina (chest pain).

IS COLD WEATHER TO BLAME?

It was once thought that cold weather was the primary reason for holiday-related heart attacks. However, the *Circulation* study looked only at patients in Los Angeles County, where temperatures generally are mild all year.

Cold weather can play a small role in the incidence of cardiovascular events, especially for people with existing heart disease. It can increase the body's response to stressful conditions, which can put people at heightened risk, particularly when they engage in more vigorous activities (such as shoveling snow) than they're accustomed to.

The holidays themselves, however, present other risks...

INCREASED ALCOHOL

People socialize more—and drink more—during the holidays. Excessive alcohol can be toxic to the cardiovascular system, particularly in people with heart disease. Alcohol both depresses heart function and irritates the top heart chambers (the atria). The irritation can lead to atrial fibrillation, a dangerous change in the heart's normal rhythm.

One of my patients, a young woman who usually didn't drink, had shared a bottle of champagne with a friend. That's not a lot of alcohol, but within 24 hours, she went into atrial fibrillation. Fortunately, her heart rate was back to normal after 24 hours.

What to do: Don't use the holidays as an excuse to drink more than usual. Stick to the guidelines recommended by the American Heart Association—no more than one drink daily for women...two drinks daily for men.

LARGE MEALS

People eat more often during the holidays, and they tend to eat more, on average, at each meal. After a meal, blood is directed to the intestines to aid in digestion. In patients with atherosclerosis—blockages in the coronary arteries that can restrict blood flow to the heart—the reduction in cardiovascular circulation can result in angina, chest pain caused by decreased blood.

Also, people tend to eat richer foods during the holidays. High-fat meals make the coronary endothelium—the inner lining of blood vessels—more reactive. This can cause an increase in coronary spasms, constrictions that further impede coronary circulation.

What to do: Eat normal serving sizes, particularly if you've been diagnosed with atherosclerosis, angina or other heart condition. Don't "save" calories so that you can eat more at a special meal.

Don't add salt. Excessive sodium can cause fluid retention, resulting in spikes in blood pressure in some people. In patients with existing high blood pressure or impaired heart function, an increase in salt can lead to increased risk for heart failure or pulmonary edema, a buildup of fluid in lung tissue.

INCREASED STRESS

The holidays are one of the most stressful times of year. People are interacting more with relatives (with whom they may or may not be on good terms)...fighting crowds at the malls...traveling...attending parties...and/or worrying about finances. There's a direct correlation between stress and cardiovascular events. During stressful situations, people with cardiovascular disease are more likely to experience coronary spasms—and sometimes chest pain that can indicate angina or a heart attack.

There's also a condition called stress-induced cardiomyopathy, which can cause heart attack–like symptoms in response to intense stress. It is seen predominantly in women and is thought to occur when a stress-related surge of adrenaline stuns the heart. Most people recover without long-term harm, but in rare cases, it can be fatal.

What to do: Take steps to minimize holiday stress—by not overbooking your social calendar...walking away from (instead of confronting) unpleasant social situations...and keeping up with regular exercise and relaxing activities.

WINTER INFLUENZA

The flu season peaks between the months of December and March. Flu is potentially dangerous for everyone, but heart patients are especially vulnerable. There's evidence that the inflammation that accompanies flu may destabilize arterial plaque and increase the risk for clots, the cause of most heart attacks.

What to do: An annual flu vaccination is the best protection. The Centers for Disease Control and Prevention recommends the vaccine for adults age 50 and older...any adult with a heart, lung, kidney or metabolic disease (such as diabetes)...and those patients with compromised immune systems.

Get vaccinated in October or November. This gives your body time to create the necessary antibodies prior to the peak influenza season.

MEDICAL DELAYS

People who are caught up in holiday excitement—or who don't want to spoil the holiday fun of others—may delay seeking medical care even if they're having chest pain or other heart symptoms. They also are more likely to forget to take medications, such as anticoagulants and blood pressure drugs.

What to do: Stay on top of your health throughout the holiday season. Put medications in a place where you'll see them—and if you have worrisome symptoms (see "Even Heart Attack Survivors Don't Recognize Heart Attack Symptoms" on page 162), don't wait until the end of the holidays or even the end of the day to get medical attention. Don't delay—immediately call 911.

■ ■ ■ ■

Car Exhaust May Harm The Heart

Living near heavily traveled roads is related to arteriosclerosis (hardening of the arteries), which can lead to heart attack.

Self-defense: Avoid being outside on days when air quality is very poor. Check air quality at *www.weather.com* (click on "Health").

Barbara Hoffman, MD, MPH, head of environmental epidemiology, Institute for Medical Informatics, Biometry and Epidemiology, University of Duisburg-Essen, Germany, and leader of a study of 4,494 people, published in *Circulation*.

Heart Patients Need Cleaner Air

Mark A. Stengler, ND, naturopathic physician in private practice, La Jolla, California...adjunct associate clinical professor at the National College of Natural Medicine, Portland, Oregon...author of many books and the *Bottom Line/Natural Healing* newsletter.

Harvard Medical School researchers followed 48 patients, ages 43 to 75, who had been hospitalized for a heart attack, unstable angina (severe chest pain) or worsening coronary artery disease. Participants wore Holter monitors, which record heart activity as patients go about their normal routines. Researchers compared the results with pollution ratings.

Findings: Increased levels of pollutants caused by traffic were associated with a change in the heart's ability to conduct electrical signals. This may be a sign of inadequate blood flow to the heart. Effects were greatest within the first month after hospitalization.

Pollution particles from traffic seem to reduce blood flow through the heart arteries, increase inflammation and blood thickness and interfere with the electrical activity of the heart. Using a high-efficiency particulate air (HEPA) purifier to filter out air pollutants, especially in the bedroom, is particularly important for those recovering from heart disease. It is also a good idea to stay away from exposure to pollution by avoiding driving in heavy traffic for a few weeks after discharge from the hospital.

Living Well with Atrial Fibrillation from A Woman Who Has It

Mellanie True Hills, founder of *StopAfib.org*, an advocacy group dedicated to educating the public about the signs, risks and treatment options for atrial fibrillation. Based in Decatur, Texas, she is author of *A Woman's Guide to Saving Her Own Life: The HEART Program for Health and Longevity* (Healthy Ideas).

Mellanie True Hills was leading a hectic life as a technology consultant when, at age 51, one of her coronary arteries became blocked and she experienced heart attack–like symptoms. The emergency surgery that followed saved—and changed—her life. She quit her job to start the American Foundation for Women's Health, a nonprofit women's health advocacy group, but then developed atrial fibrillation, a heart rhythm disruption. She struggled with the disorder for two years—and then underwent surgery, which cured her. She then created *StopAfib.org* (part of the American

Foundation for Women's Health), a clearinghouse for information on atrial fibrillation.

Atrial fibrillation, or A-fib, as it is commonly called, is the most common type of irregular heartbeat. Several million Americans currently have A-fib—and it's likely that many more have it without knowing it. According to the Mayo Clinic, the risk of A-fib increases with age, affecting about 5.1 million Americans—and the numbers are rapidly increasing.

A-fib occurs when the electrical signals that trigger each heartbeat are disrupted, causing the atria (the heart's two upper chambers) to beat faster or quiver instead of contracting as in a normal heartbeat. As a result, blood pools in these chambers instead of being pumped onward. *While this may sound benign, A-fib can lead to serious health problems, including...*

• **Stroke.** A-fib causes a fivefold increase in stroke risk. Pooled blood in the atria can form blood clots—like debris on the edges of a stagnant lake. Stroke occurs when a clot breaks off and blocks an artery leading to the brain.

• **Congestive heart failure.** Atrial fibrillation can cause the heart to work less efficiently. If left untreated, this can lead to congestive heart failure.

Bottom line: If you think that A-fib can't kill you, you're wrong.

SYMPTOMS

A-fib symptoms vary from person to person. *Some of the most common include...*

• **Heart "skips" a few beats, then races.**

• **Erratic heartbeat.**

• **Dizziness and feeling light-headed.**

• **A feeling of having butterflies,** a bag of wiggly worms or a fish flopping in the chest.

• **Pressure in the chest or throat similar to a heart attack.**

• **A feeling of constriction around the left bicep.**

Symptoms can last for a few minutes or days at a time (a condition known as paroxysmal, or intermittent, atrial fibrillation) but terminate on their own. In others, symptoms may continue for days, months or even years (a condition called persistent A-fib).

A-fib episodes can be scary. I was always worried about passing out and having a stroke. Since I had blood clots during my first episode, I carried a cell phone everywhere and was afraid to be alone or far from a hospital.

Helpful: Be alert to what might trigger an episode, for example, smoking, caffeine, alcohol, exercise and especially stress. Some believe even white flour, white sugar and food additives are triggers.

DIAGNOSIS

The usual way to diagnose A-fib is with an electrocardiogram (ECG). For this test, electrodes are placed on the chest to record the heart's electrical activity. However, a regular EKG won't pick up intermittent A-fib unless you're having an episode at the time you're examined. In these cases, your doctor may recommend that you wear a Holter monitor—a portable EKG device that records all heart activity for up to 48 hours—or an event monitor that's worn for a few weeks, which you activate when you feel an A-fib episode occurring.

MEDICATIONS

For A-fib patients, there are two treatment goals—to reduce blood clot risk and to control the heart rate or rhythm. *Types of medication used to accomplish this...*

• **Blood-thinning (anticoagulant) medication—typically *warfarin* (Coumadin)—** can lower the risk for a stroke-causing blood clot. These medications are considered critical for many with A-fib. Coumadin can be problematic for many people, as it was for me. For genetic reasons, I was never able to keep my blood viscosity in the normal range. Many people have a gene that makes it difficult to stabilize their blood on Coumadin.

• **Rhythm control medication.** These drugs, which include sodium channel blockers and potassium channel blockers, are used to restore the heart's normal rhythm. While the drugs help to control A-fib, they don't cure the underlying rhythm problem, and they lose effectiveness after a few years. Some are even toxic to various organs.

•**Rate control medication.** These drugs slow the heart rate by blocking some of the electrical signals in the atria. They also relax blood vessels. I took the beta-blocker *metoprolol* (Toprol XL) daily. It proved effective at stopping episodes once they started, so I carried pills with me wherever I went.

Talk to your doctor about finding the right combination of medications that work for you.

A procedure known as electrical cardioversion, in which the heart is given a jolt of electricity to "reset" its electrical signals, may also be used when a patient is having an event.

SELF-CARE

Identifying and avoiding your personal triggers may be effective in minimizing episodes. Supplements, such as magnesium, potassium and omega-3 fatty acids, have been found by some people to be helpful, although there is little scientific proof that they work.

Maintaining adequate hydration is also important. Dehydration can trigger A-fib and raise the risk for blood clots (it makes the blood more viscous).

A-fib is also correlated with sleep apnea. People with A-fib who have untreated sleep apnea are more likely to revert to A-fib after cardioversion. If you suspect that you have sleep apnea, get it diagnosed and treated.

OTHER OPTIONS

Many patients respond well to medication and/or electrical cardioversion. For some patients, however, A-fib comes back again because medications lose their effectiveness or never worked in the first place. *For this group—and for those who prefer not to take medication for the rest of their lives—two highly effective options may provide a permanent cure...*

•**Catheter ablation.** A catheter is threaded into the heart through a vein in the leg or neck, and the energy in its tip is used to kill a small area of heart tissue. The dead tissue, known as a conduction block, stops the erratic electrical signals from reaching the heart. Although there is some risk of complication, this procedure has become safer at centers where it is performed often.

•**Surgical ablation.** An energy source is applied to the surface of the heart to create a conduction block. Called maze surgery, this was previously conducted only as open-heart surgery, but there is now also a minimally invasive version. I underwent the latter and it cured my A-fib completely—and gave me back my life.

Omega-3s May Heal Atrial Fibrillation

Mark A. Stengler, ND, naturopathic physician in private practice, La Jolla, California...adjunct associate clinical professor at the National College of Natural Medicine, Portland, Oregon...author of many books and the *Bottom Line/Natural Healing* newsletter.

If you have atrial fibrillation (abnormal heart rhythm), you are probably taking a prescription blood thinner, such as *warfarin* (Coumadin), to help prevent blood clots. Atrial fibrillation tends to occur with age, as electrical conductance of the heart goes awry. People with atrial fibrillation are at increased risk of blood clots, stroke and heart failure, so it is important to regulate your heart rhythm as best you can. Many natural therapies can help. Studies demonstrate that consuming oily fish containing omega-3 fatty acids five or more times weekly can lower your risk by almost one-third or, in some cases, resolve abnormal rhythm in those who already have it. I recommend that my patients consume cold-water fish, such as sardines and wild salmon (broiled or baked), three times a week and also take fish oil supplements containing 1,500 milligrams (mg) of combined *eicosapentaenoic acid* (EPA) and *docosahexaenoic acid* (DHA). I also suggest taking the antioxidant *coenzyme Q10* (100 mg two to three times daily), the amino acid *L-carnitine* (1,500 mg twice daily) and magnesium (200 mg twice daily). Talk to your doctor before taking these supplements, especially if you take blood thinners.

■ ■ ■ ■

Statins May Help Your Heartbeat

With atrial fibrillation, the heart quivers instead of beating normally. Blood pools and clots may form, increasing stroke risk.

New research: Postmenopausal women with heart disease who took cholesterol-lowering statin drugs were 55% less likely to develop atrial fibrillation than women who did not.

Wise: Ask your doctor about the pros and cons of statins.

Cara Pellegrini, MD, electrophysiology fellow, University of California, San Francisco, and author of a study of 2,673 women, presented at a meeting of the Heart Rhythm Society.

How to Protect Yourself from Deadly Cardiac Arrest

Prediman K. Shah, MD, director of the division of cardiology and the Atherosclerosis Research Center at Cedars-Sinai Heart Institute in Los Angeles. He is a professor of medicine at the David Geffen School of Medicine at the University of California, Los Angeles, and was the chief of the editorial committee of the Screening for Heart Attack Prevention and Education (SHAPE) Task Force, which developed screening guidelines to help prevent heart attacks.

When Tim Russert, the NBC correspondent and moderator of *Meet the Press*, died suddenly at the network's Washington, DC, bureau, it was widely reported that a heart attack had caused his death.

Russert did have a heart attack, but the actual cause of death was sudden cardiac arrest (SCA), a usually fatal disruption of the heart's normal rhythm. Each year, more than 325,000 Americans die from SCA.

A heart attack can lead to SCA, but not all SCA cases result from a heart attack. The difference is significant because the conditions don't require all the same treatments—or the same emergency care.

More than half of heart attack victims survive, and they often have symptoms—the classic ones include chest pain, shortness of breath and sweating, while the less well-known ones include dizziness, fatigue and even jaw pain.

In contrast, the survival rate for SCA is 10% or less, and the condition usually causes no symptoms. Patients typically collapse and die without warning.

What you need to know to protect yourself—or a loved one...

AN ELECTRICAL PROBLEM

Most heart attacks are caused by a plumbing problem. Typically, a blood clot forms on top of a ruptured plaque (fatty buildup) in a coronary artery. The clot (or clots) prevent blood from reaching the heart, sometimes leading to death.

SCA is usually due to an electrical problem. The electrical impulses that regulate the heartbeat become too rapid (ventricular tachycardia), chaotic (ventricular fibrillation) or both.

Result: The heart can't pump blood. Without proper emergency care, SCA victims die within minutes of the event.

THE RIGHT EMERGENCY CARE

Immediate emergency care is crucial for a person who suffers SCA. For every minute of ventricular fibrillation, the chance of survival decreases by about 10%.

Best approaches...

- **Jumpstart the heart.** An automated external defibrillator (AED), which is about the size of a laptop computer and costs about $1,500 when purchased online, can increase the odds of survival by twofold to fourfold—and even more if it's located and used within the first minute or two after an attack.

AEDs are easy to use. Once the device is turned on, a computerized voice tells bystanders exactly what to do, such as when (and where) to attach the electrodes to the victim's chest and when to push buttons. The machine analyzes the heart's rhythm. If a patient is experiencing SCA, the machine will instruct the operator to press a "shock" button to restart the heart. The heart rhythm will again be analyzed to determine if more shocks are needed.

Because about 80% of SCAs occur in the home, many adults—and particularly those with SCA risk factors (such as a previous heart attack or a family history of heart disease)—should consider buying an AED. In some cases, insurance will cover the cost of the device.

•**Chest compressions.** Bystanders without access to an automated defibrillator can at least double an SCA victim's odds of survival by giving continuous chest compressions as soon as he/she collapses.

What to do: Put the heel of one hand in the center of the chest, place your other hand on top of the first hand for strength, and push the breastbone down one to one-and-a-half inches. Try to give about 100 compressions a minute—and keep giving them until emergency help arrives or the patient revives. If the victim is not breathing and SCA is suspected, don't waste time checking for a pulse or giving mouth-to-mouth resuscitation. These steps slow down the administration of heart compressions.

Important: Most states have "Good Samaritan" laws that protect bystanders who administer emergency care from personal liability.

•**Hospital care.** SCA patients who survive long enough to reach an emergency room undergo a series of treatments that can increase the odds of survival by a factor of four. After being given shocks and/or chest compressions to restart the heart and restore circulation to the heart and brain, SCA patients also may receive induced hypothermia (available in about 25% of US hospitals). With this procedure, the body temperature is rapidly lowered (with a cooling blanket or with cooled intravenous fluids) to about 89.6°F. This improves the chances for neurological recovery.

TREATING SURVIVORS

Patients who survive SCA require ongoing treatment to prevent subsequent attacks.

Two main approaches...

•**Restore the heart's rhythm.** An implantable cardioverter defibrillator (ICD) is a surgically implanted device that continuously analyzes heart rhythms and administers electrical shocks, as needed, to prevent ventricular fibrillation. The device is about 98% effective in interrupting ventricular arrhythmias.

•**Radio-frequency ablation.** With this nonsurgical procedure, the doctor uses a catheter to deliver a burst of radio-frequency energy (similar to microwave heat) to destroy clusters of damaged heart-muscle cells.

Success rate: Up to 90%.

UNDERLYING CAUSES

SCA has several underlying causes. *Among the most common...*

•**Coronary artery disease.** Most victims of SCA are later found to have significant atherosclerosis (accumulations of plaque) in two or more coronary arteries. Impaired circulation can damage the heart and disrupt its electrical activity.

•**Muscle abnormalities.** Patients who have suffered a previous heart attack may have scarring or other types of damage that alter normal heart rhythms.

•**Too-rapid heartbeat.** In some genetically predisposed patients, the release of the hormone adrenaline during exercise or from stress can speed up the heartbeat to the levels associated with ventricular tachycardia, leading to SCA.

LIFESAVING TESTS

If you have been diagnosed with heart disease or have had a prior heart attack, ask your doctor to refer you to an electrophysiologist, a cardiologist who specializes in heart-rhythm disturbances.

You probably will be advised to undergo a test that uses an ultrasound of the heart to measure your ejection fraction (a percentage measurement of blood that's pumped out of a filled ventricle with each heartbeat). Patients with readings below 30% to 35% have a significant risk for SCA and may be candidates for an ICD.

Also important: The presence of calcium within the coronary arteries means that a patient has atherosclerosis and needs to be vigilant about managing coronary risk factors. Coronary artery calcium screening is recommended for all men age 45 and older and women age 55 and older. The only exceptions are adults with no coronary risk factors and patients who already have been diagnosed with atherosclerosis.

The Hidden Heart Condition Doctors Miss

C. Noel Bairey Merz, MD, director of the Women's Heart Center and the Preventive and Rehabilitative Cardiac Center at Cedars-Sinai Heart Institute in Los Angeles and professor of medicine at the David Geffen School of Medicine at University of California, Los Angeles. She is chair of the National Institutes of Health–sponsored Women's Ischemic Syndrome Evaluation (WISE) study, which investigates methods for diagnosis and evaluation of heart disease in women.

You're awake (again!) in the middle of the night, worrying about finances, when suddenly you feel a stab of pain in your chest. It's not the first time such chest discomfort has accompanied stress. What's happening?

Answer: You may have small vessel heart disease, or coronary microvascular disease (MVD). By impairing blood flow in the heart's tiniest arteries—the twigs of the arterial tree—MVD can lead to a heart attack or heart failure.

When the Women's Ischemic Syndrome Evaluation (WISE) study began more than a decade ago, MVD was found to play a major role in heart disease in women. You may never have heard of MVD—and your primary care physician may know next to nothing about it—even though it affects up to three million American women, most of them over age 45. *What women must know about this potentially deadly disease...*

WOMEN'S ARTERIES ARE DIFFERENT

Scientists don't yet know the exact cause of MVD, but they are focusing on several likely factors. Because men are far less prone to MVD, a key to understanding the disease seems to lie in the ways in which arteries differ between the sexes. *Women's arteries are...*

- **More likely to spasm.** Women have much larger variations in hormone levels, day to day and over a lifetime, than men do. Such variations may affect arteries, which have hormone receptors, and lead to vascular reactivity—arteries that are likely to spasm, limiting or halting blood flow.
- **Smaller.** It is not only that women, on average, are smaller than men. Even after adjusting for average body area, women have relatively smaller arteries—perhaps because they have less testosterone, a hormone that powers tissue growth. The tinier the blood vessel, the more vulnerable it is to spasm.
- **Prone to smoother plaque.** Plaque is a fatty material that builds up on inner walls of arteries, impairing blood flow. In men, plaque typically forms big lumps. Although women may have as much plaque as men, in women it often spreads out smoothly and evenly—which makes it harder to detect.

DIFFICULT TO DIAGNOSE

Many women with MVD have the classic signs of heart disease—angina (chest pain) and/or shortness of breath upon minor exertion, such as when walking up stairs. To check for heart disease, doctors typically begin with a stress test, which measures heart function and blood pressure while the patient walks on a treadmill. If results suggest a problem, the patient is given an angiogram—an injection of dye into the arteries which is followed by an X-ray to detect blockages.

Problems: With MVD, the angiogram may not find threatening obstructions in large blood vessels because smooth plaque is not easily detected...and the test may not be sensitive enough to find abnormalities in small blood vessels.

Result: The woman is assured that she does not have heart disease—though in fact she does. Because she goes untreated, she continues to be at high risk for heart attack or heart failure.

What many doctors don't know: Persistent chest pain and an abnormal stress test are indications of MVD—and sufficient reason for treatment—even when the angiogram is normal.

Many doctors also are not aware that about 50% of women with MVD do not have the typical "exertional" symptoms. Instead, these women have angina when they're upset or stressed—even if they are sitting or lying down.

Reason: Anxiety or stress can trigger the release of stress hormones, such as adrenaline, that can affect the small blood vessels and bring on angina. Yet doctors may not recognize the link between this type of "nonexertional" chest pain and heart disease.

Self-defense: If you have persistent chest pain but your doctor says that you don't have heart disease, get a second opinion. This is especially important if your doctor attributes your symptoms to heartburn, hiatal hernia or gallbladder disease even though tests do not confirm any of those diagnoses and treating those conditions does not stop the pain. To find a cardiologist who is knowledgeable about MVD, contact a top medical center for a referral.*

Best: A coronary reactivity test is the gold standard for determining the extent and severity of—and the most appropriate treatment for—MVD. First, a wire is inserted into a coronary artery and blood flow is measured...then a substance that dilates small blood vessels is injected, and blood flow is measured again. Currently, the test is available at only a limited number of medical centers. As knowledge of MVD increases, the test should become more widely available. Ask your cardiologist if this test is appropriate for you. Insurance may cover the test.

MVD TREATMENTS

Treatment of MVD aims to ease symptoms and reduce risk factors for heart attack and heart failure. *Treatment may include...*

- **Lifestyle changes.** As with any form of heart disease, follow your doctor's guidelines for eating a heart-healthy diet with no more than 30% of calories from fat...doing aerobic exercise, such as brisk walking, for 30 minutes a day...maintaining a healthy weight...managing stress...and not smoking.

- **Medication.** Your doctor may prescribe one or more drugs...

  - A beta-blocker to block the action of adrenaline, thereby slowing heartbeat, lowering blood pressure and easing angina.

  - An ACE inhibitor to reduce heart attack risk by blocking production of *angiotensin,* a compound that narrows arteries.

  - Baby aspirin, taken at 81 milligrams (mg) daily, to reduce the risk for artery-clogging blood clots.

  - Statin medication to lower LDL or "bad," cholesterol.

  - *Ranolazine,* nitroglycerine and/or a calcium channel blocker to improve blood flow.

- **Enhanced external counterpulsation therapy (EECP).** Inflatable pressure cuffs are wrapped around the legs from the calves up to the hips. The cuffs inflate and deflate in time with the heartbeat, improving circulation and blood vessel health.

Drawback: EECP treatment requires a one-hour session, five days a week, for seven weeks. While EECP has not been clinically tested specifically for MVD, it has been proven to be effective for easing angina in cases of heart failure—and many experts say that EECP has helped their MVD patients whose angina was not sufficiently relieved by lifestyle changes and medication.

*Among the top medical centers that treat MVD are Cedars-Sinai Medical Center in Los Angeles...Emory University Hospital in Atlanta...Harvard Medical School's Brigham and Women's Hospital in Boston...Mayo Clinic in Rochester, Minnesota...Stanford University School of Medicine in Stanford, California...and University of Florida at Gainesville.

Risky Prescriptions for Heart Attack Patients

P. Michael Ho, MD, PhD, cardiologist, Denver VA Medical Center.

Gregg C. Fonarow, MD, professor, cardiology, University of California, Los Angeles.

Byron Lee, MD, associate professor, cardiology, University of California, San Francisco.

The Journal of the American Medical Association.

Heart attack patients given the blood thinner Plavix, plus a *proton pump inhibitor* (PPI), a class of drug used to treat acid reflux, may be at increased risk for death or another heart attack, a recent study finds.

Many patients are given *clopidogrel* (Plavix) to help reduce the risk of another heart attack after treatment for a first heart attack. Plavix makes blood platelets less sticky, helping to prevent clots from forming.

Many doctors also prescribe PPIs, such as *omeprazole* (Prilosec) and *esomeprazole* (Nexium), which are drugs used to help prevent gastroesophageal reflux, but they help prevent gastrointestinal (GI) bleeding while taking Plavix.

"A lot of patients are on Plavix and also a lot of patients are being prescribed PPI medication just prophylactically to prevent a stomach bleed," said lead researcher P. Michael Ho, MD, a cardiologist at the Denver VA Medical Center.

THE STUDY

For the study, Dr. Ho's team collected data on 8,205 patients discharged from 127 Veterans Affairs hospitals after suffering a heart attack or an episode of unstable angina. Among these patients, 63.9% were prescribed a PPI drug.

The researchers found that 29.8% of patients given a PPI and Plavix died or were rehospitalized, compared with 20.8% of the patients given Plavix alone. The combination of Plavix plus a PPI was associated with a 25% increase in the risk of dying or being rehospitalized, compared to the use of Plavix alone.

The findings were published in *The Journal of the American Medical Association*.

CORROBORATING STUDY

Researchers reported in the *Canadian Medical Association Journal* that people taking Plavix and a proton pump inhibitor after a heart attack had a dramatically higher risk of a second heart attack than those taking Plavix alone.

PREVENTING DANGEROUS DRUG INTERACTIONS

The study doesn't change the reasons for prescribing Plavix, Dr. Ho said. "But both clinicians and patients should look at why the PPI is being prescribed. It shouldn't be prescribed prophylactically just to prevent a GI bleed, because there might be an interaction between the PPI and Plavix," he said.

A proton pump inhibitor should only be prescribed to patients who have had a stomach bleed, since they are at higher risk of another bleed, Dr. Ho said.

Patients taking Plavix should discuss the use of PPIs with their doctor, Dr. Ho said. "This should be an individualized decision between the patient and the physician about whether patients should be on a PPI or whether there are alternative medications for reflux or stomach problems," he said.

EXPERT REACTION

Gregg C. Fonarow, MD, a professor of cardiology at the University of California, Los Angeles, thinks this study shows that PPIs used with Plavix should be limited to patients at risk for gastrointestinal bleeding.

"While further studies in different patient populations are needed, use of clopidogrel without a proton pump inhibitor may be preferred," Dr. Fonarow said.

"The FDA [Food and Drug Administration] has recently communicated that it is conducting a safety review regarding potential interactions of these two commonly prescribed medications," he added.

Byron Lee, MD, an associate professor of cardiology at the University of California, San Francisco, thinks this study may suggest using medications other than PPIs to prevent gastrointestinal bleeding.

"This study is very worrisome because so many of our patients are on both Plavix and a proton pump inhibitor," Dr. Lee said. "To lower the risk of recurrent heart attacks, we should probably think about switching some of these patients from proton pump inhibitors to H2 blockers [such as Zantac or Tagamet], at least temporarily."

info For more information on heart attack, visit the Web site of the American Heart Association, *http://americanheart.org*, and search "what is a heart attack?"

■ ■ ■ ■

Taking a Statin Can Save Your Life

In a recent study, patients who stopped taking statin drugs after their heart attacks were 88% more likely to die within the next year than those who never took statins. Those who started taking statins after a heart attack were 28% less likely to die. Statins are cholesterol-lowering drugs, such as *rosuvastatin* (Crestor), *atorvastatin* (Lipitor), *pravastatin* (Pravachol) and *simvastatin* (Zocor).

Stella Daskalopoulou, MD, PhD, is assistant professor of medicine, McGill University, Montreal, Quebec, and lead author of a study of 9,939 heart attack patients, published in *European Heart Journal*.

When a Cardiologist Can't Help Your Heart

Jeptha P. Curtis, MD, assistant professor of internal medicine, Yale University School of Medicine, New Haven, Connecticut.

Stephen C. Hammill, MD, professor of medicine, Mayo Clinic, Rochester, Minnesota.

Journal of the American Medical Association.

Chances are you've never heard of electrophysiology, but it's a medical subspecialty you should know about if you are one of the 100,000 or so Americans who will have a heart defibrillator implanted this year.

BACKGROUND

An implantable cardioverter defibrillator monitors the heart's rhythm and delivers a shock if needed to keep an aberrant heart beating regularly. And the incidence of in-hospital complications is significantly lower when the implant is done by an electrophysiologist rather than an ordinary cardiologist, a thoracic surgeon or another specialist, according to a study published in *The Journal of the American Medical Association.*

"Electrophysiology is a subspecialty within cardiology," explained study author Jeptha P. Curtis, MD, an assistant professor of internal medicine at the Yale University School of Medicine's section of cardiovascular medicine. "You have to undergo two years of advanced training on the electrical activity of the heart to be eligible for board certification."

THE STUDY

The study of a registry of 111,293 defibrillator implants, done between January 2006 and June 2007, found that 70.9% of them were performed by electrophysiologists, 21.9% were performed by other cardiologists, 1.7% by thoracic surgeons and 5.5% by other specialists.

When an electrophysiologist did the procedure, complications occurred in 3.5% of cases. The incidence was 4% for other cardiologists, and 5.8% for thoracic surgeons, according to the study.

IMPLICATION

"Our study suggests that, in general, people are better served by having them [defibrillators] implanted by electrophysiologists," Dr. Curtis said.

SPECIALIZED DEFIBRILLATOR

Another marked difference found in the study concerned people who require an implanted defibrillator that provides cardiac resynchronization therapy (CRT-D). "These are patients with heart failure, in which the heart is not only weak and inefficient but also beats in a disorganized way," Dr. Curtis explained.

While a standard implanted defibrillator has one or two "leads"—electrical wires attached to deliver impulses to the heart muscle—a CRT-D device uses three leads to keep the heart beating properly. Nearly one-third of the people in the study met criteria for a CRT-D implant, and the likelihood that they would get one was significantly higher when the procedure was done by an electrophysiologist, the study said.

CRT-D devices were implanted by electrophysiologists in 83.1% of such cases, compared with 75.8% when the implants were done by other cardiologists, 57.8% by thoracic surgeons and 74.8% by other specialists.

RECOMMENDATIONS

So a physician's training in electrophysiology can rightly be a matter of concern for someone getting a defibrillator, Dr. Curtis said. "I think it is reasonable for a patient to ask a doctor what his qualifications are," he said. "It would be very reasonable for patients to ask implanting physicians what are their results, what are the numbers."

Such information should be available at most large medical centers, and "having that information available should be part of normal quality assurance," Dr. Curtis said.

Stephen C. Hammill, MD, is a member of the study group, a professor of medicine at the Mayo Clinic, a past president of the Heart Rhythm Society, and a qualified electrophysiologist. He said the study shows that "across the board as a group, electrophysiologists have a better outcome than cardiologists or thoracic surgeons.

"But it does not show what individual physicians' outcomes are," Dr. Hammill added. His recommendation is that anyone considering a defibrillator implant "needs to speak with his or her physician and be sure that the physician is comfortable with the level of expertise and training of the individual who will do the implant."

FOLLOW-UP STUDY NEEDED

Further study is needed to see whether the benefits of having an implant done by an electrophysiologist continue after hospital discharge, Drs. Curtis and Hammill said. "We need a follow-up study to see what happens over time," said Dr. Curtis.

info For more information on defibrillators, visit the Mayo Clinic Web site, *www.mayoclinic.com*, and search "implantable cardioverter defibrillator."

Best Health Tips For Anyone with Heart Disease

Wayne M. Sotile, PhD, director of psychological services for the Wake Forest University healthy exercise and lifestyle programs in Winston-Salem, North Carolina, and a special consultant in behavioral health at the Center for Cardiovascular Health, Carolinas Medical Center in Charlotte, North Carolina. Dr. Sotile is author of *Thriving with Heart Disease* (Free Press).

A diagnosis of heart disease is much more than a medical problem. It also requires sufferers to cope with changes in their day-to-day living and to come to grips with the realities of a chronic life-threatening illness.

Among the heart problems that can present the greatest challenges are heart failure (inadequate pumping action of the heart) and heart rhythm problems, such as ventricular tachycardia and ventricular fibrillation, which are typically treated with an implantable cardioverter defibrillator (ICD).

If people with heart failure and ICD wearers adopt the right habits, they can have a dramatic influence on how they feel—and perhaps even extend their lives.

HEART FAILURE

About five million Americans have heart failure. The older you are, the more likely you are to have the condition (it affects 10% of people age 70 and older). Symptoms include fatigue... shortness of breath...and swelling, especially in the ankles, or weight gain (both can be due to water retention).

How people with heart failure can stay as healthy as possible...

- **Cut down on salt to counter your body's tendency to retain water.** The goal is generally no more than 2,000 mg of sodium per day—about half what the average American consumes. Most salt comes from processed foods—not the shaker. Read labels. Avoid processed foods and never add salt to your food. Your taste buds will adjust to a salt-free diet much more quickly than you might expect.

- **Limit fluids.** Follow your doctor's advice about fluid intake. Consuming even a little extra fluid can lead to undue heart strain. Be aware that foods with a high liquid content, such as Jell-O and ice cream, count as fluids.

- **Weigh yourself daily.** If you gain more than three pounds in a day or five in a week, call the doctor. You're probably retaining water.

- **Avoid caffeine and alcohol.** Caffeine in coffee, tea and cola makes your already overworked heart beat more rapidly, increases the amount of oxygen it needs and may disrupt your heart rhythm. Alcohol can weaken the heart muscle. Ask your doctor if you need to cut back or eliminate beverages and/or foods that contain alcohol and caffeine.

- **Take your medications.** Many people with heart failure will need to take medications such as diuretics (to help the body excrete excess fluid)...beta-blockers (to reduce the force of the heart's contractions)...and anticoagulants (to help prevent blood clots from forming in the heart chambers) for the rest of their lives. Failure to take medicines as prescribed is a leading cause of hospitalization.

- **Balance rest and activity.** Heart failure limits how much your body can do. To reduce fatigue, get sufficient sleep (including an afternoon nap if you need one)...and spread your tasks throughout the day.

At the same time, regular exercise has been shown to increase energy in people with heart failure—and sometimes even help them live longer. The challenge is to find an exercise level that will strengthen—not overtax—your heart.

Most important: Start slowly...to reduce strain on your heart, use leg rather than arm muscles (walking generally is the best exercise for heart failure patients)...and stop immediately if you become dizzy or short of breath or have chest pain.

Best option: Enlist your doctor's help in designing an exercise plan and/or enroll in a cardiac rehabilitation program. To find one near you, consult the American Association of Cardiovascular and Pulmonary Rehabilitation, 312-321-5146, *www.aacvpr.org.*

• **Tend to your relationships.** In a recent study, University of Pennsylvania researchers found that heart failure patients who got along well with their spouses were significantly more likely to be alive at a four-year follow-up point than those who had less harmonious relationships.

LIVING WITH AN ICD

An ICD is an electronic device about the size of a deck of cards that automatically delivers a shock when the heart rate accelerates to the point where life-threatening fibrillation (dangerously fast heart rate) may be imminent. (Similar electronic devices, known as pacemakers, signal the heart to beat when the heartbeat is too slow.)

Even though ICDs can be lifesavers, most people who wear one of the devices worry about getting a shock at the wrong time or not receiving a shock when one is needed. *What you can do to adjust to wearing an ICD...*

• **Don't limit your activities unnecessarily.** Normal activity—including sex, exercise, job stress, arguments or excitement at a movie or ball game—will not accelerate your heart rate enough to trigger the ICD. The best way to reduce the number of shocks you receive is to take your heart medication regularly.

• **Take sensible precautions.** Electromagnetic interference (EMI) can disrupt ICD operation or trigger an inappropriate shock. For that reason, ICD patients cannot have a magnetic resonance imaging (MRI) scan, which creates a large, powerful magnetic field.

ICD wearers can talk on cell phones but should keep them more than six inches from the implant site (use a belt holster instead of your shirt pocket).

Although the ICD may set off metal-detecting devices used at public places, such as airports, walking through one is generally safe if you don't linger. The handheld wand used by security personnel can disrupt ICD operation, so ask to be "patted down" instead. (When you receive an ICD, you should be given a card that identifies you as an ICD wearer.)

Electric shavers, remotes, televisions and microwave ovens typically present no risk for those who wear ICDs.

• **Remain calm if you have an ICD "storm."** If you receive more than one shock in 24 hours, go to a hospital emergency room. The ICD device could need an adjustment or your heart medications may need to be modified.

An estimated 16% of people with ICDs have such "storms," which can cause wearers to fear that they are suffering a potentially fatal heart rhythm disturbance or that the device is running amok. To put the trauma behind you, talk about it with supportive people, such as loved ones and your health-care providers.

■ ■ ■ ■

Even Heart Attack Survivors Don't Recognize Heart Attack Symptoms

When quizzed about the signs of heart attack, 46% of those questioned answered less than 70% of questions correctly.

Surprising: All the participants had either survived a heart attack or been treated for blocked arteries. Women, people younger than 60 and those who were seeing a cardiologist rather than an internist or a general practitioner tended to answer more of the questions correctly.

Problem: Quickly recognizing the signs of a heart attack significantly improves the likelihood of survival. Common symptoms include discomfort in the chest and/or upper body, shortness of breath, cold sweat, nausea and light-headedness.

Kathleen Dracup, RN, FNP, DNSc, dean and professor, University of California, San Francisco, School of Nursing, and lead researcher of a study of 3,522 heart attack patients, published in *Archives of Internal Medicine*.

■ ■ ■ ■

Never Ignore Chest Pain

When health information for 1,957 patients was reviewed one year after the patients had suffered a heart attack, nearly 20% of them reported suffering chest pain (*angina*), a treatable condition that indicates significant heart disease. These patients were more likely to be depressed or smoke than those in the study who did not have angina.

If you have had a heart attack: See your doctor if you suffer any chest pain or depression symptoms—or need help quitting smoking.

Thomas M. Maddox, MD, staff cardiologist, Denver VA Medical Center.

■ ■ ■ ■

Mild Thyroid Problems Linked to Serious Heart Failure

In a 12-year study of 3,065 adults, those with untreated subclinical hypothyroidism (a mildly underactive thyroid) were twice as likely to develop congestive heart failure (inadequate pumping action of the heart) as those with normal thyroid function.

Theory: Subclinical hypothyroidism results in less-efficient heart contractions.

If you have an underactive thyroid: Ask your doctor if you should take thyroid medication and/or be monitored for heart problems.

Douglas C. Bauer, MD, professor of medicine, epidemiology and biostatistics, University of California, San Francisco.

Nutrition Plan to Pump Up Your Heart

JoAnn E. Manson, MD, DrPH, a professor of medicine and women's health at Harvard Medical School and chair of the division of preventive medicine at Brigham and Women's Hospital, both in Boston. She is one of the lead investigators for two highly influential studies on women's health—the Harvard Nurses' Health Study and the Women's Health Initiative. Dr. Manson is author, with Shari Bassuk, ScD, of *Hot Flashes, Hormones and Your Health* (McGraw-Hill).

Despite its scary name, heart failure doesn't mean that the heart has failed completely—it means that the heart's pumping ability is reduced and cannot meet 100% of the body's need for blood flow. Blood backs up in veins...fluid builds up in lungs...and kidneys retain fluid. Symptoms include shortness of breath, persistent coughing, increased heart rate, fatigue and leg swelling.

Heart failure is the leading cause of hospitalization in the US among women and men age 65 and older, though female patients are more likely to be disabled by it. About 40% to 50% of patients die within five years.

Diabetes quintuples the risk for heart failure ...obesity doubles it. High blood pressure or a history of heart attack increases risk two- to threefold—but half of all women who develop heart failure have no previous diagnosis of heart disease. *Nutritional strategies that may reduce your risk...*

- **Boost vitamin D.** In a German study, heart disease patients with vitamin D deficiency were nearly three times more likely to develop heart failure than those with normal levels.

Theory: Vitamin D may counteract genetic and hormonal effects that raise blood pressure and cause abnormal heart muscle overgrowth. Get at least 1,000 international units (IU) daily from diet (fish, fortified dairy foods) and/or supplements.

- **Consume more marine omega-3 fatty acids.** In an Italian study, heart failure patients who took 1,000 milligrams (mg) daily of fish oil were significantly less likely than those given placebos to be hospitalized or die.

Goal: Eat fatty fish (herring, mackerel, salmon) at least twice weekly.

But: Even daily fish may not supply the 1,000 mg of omega-3s that heart disease patients need—so these people should consider fish oil supplements.

•**Eat more whole grains.** A US study of more than 14,000 people found that for each one-serving-daily increase in whole grains, heart failure risk fell by 7%. Aim for two to three servings daily. Try unfamiliar ones—farro, bulgur, barley, quinoa.

•**Limit eggs and high-fat dairy foods.** The US study found that heart failure risk rose by 23% for each one-serving-per-day increase in eggs...and by 8% for each one-serving-per-day increase in high-fat dairy.

Prudent: Have eggs only a few times per week...stick with low- or nonfat dairy foods.

•**Avoid high-dose vitamin E supplements.** Contrary to previous beliefs, vitamin E does not protect against heart disease and stroke. In fact, it is linked to increased heart failure risk. The amount of vitamin E in a multivitamin is fine, but there is no basis for taking separate high-dose supplements of vitamin E.

■ ■ ■ ■

Hawthorn Relieves Heart Failure Symptoms

With heart failure, the heart's pumping action fails to effectively circulate blood. Fluid builds up in the lungs and elsewhere, causing fatigue and shortness of breath.

Recent finding: Patients with mild-to-moderate heart failure who took herbal hawthorn extract had significant improvement in symptoms.

Theory: Hawthorn may boost the heart's contraction strength, improving blood flow.

Possible side effects: Nausea, dizziness, digestive complaints.

Recommended: Ask your doctor about usage and dosage.

Max Pittler, MD, deputy director of complementary medicine, Peninsula Medical School, Exeter, England, and coauthor of a study of 855 patients, published in *The Cochrane Library.*

■ ■ ■ ■

Calcium Puts Healthy Women at Risk for Heart Disease

Based on current guidelines, women are considered to be at low risk for heart disease if they do not smoke, do not have diabetes, and have normal blood pressure and cholesterol levels.

New finding: Among these supposedly low-risk women, about 5% actually may be at increased risk for heart attack or stroke due to a significant buildup of calcium in coronary arteries.

Best: Discuss this risk with your doctor.

Phillip Greenland, MD, director, Northwestern University Clinical and Translational Sciences Institute, Chicago, and coauthor of a study of 3,601 women, reported in *Archives of Internal Medicine.*

■ ■ ■ ■

Better Heart Disease Screening

In a recent study, 3,601 women received computed tomography (CT) chest scans to detect calcium deposits in the coronary arteries, a heart disease risk factor not included in the Framingham score, a well-known heart disease risk assessment that relies on such factors as cholesterol and blood pressure levels.

Result: 30% of the women rated as "low risk" by the Framingham risk score had detectable coronary calcification.

If you are at risk for cardiovascular disease: Ask your doctor if you should have a CT scan to screen for coronary calcification.

Susan G. Lakoski, MD, MS, assistant professor of cardiology, University of Texas Southwestern Medical Center at Dallas.

■ ■ ■ ■

The Statin Drug That Doesn't Work for Women

Clinical trials of cholesterol-lowering *atorvastatin* (Lipitor) found evidence that the drug reduced heart attack risk for men—but not women. Ads for Lipitor fail to disclose this. Statins can have serious side effects—review pros and cons with your doctor.

Theodore Eisenberg, JD, professor of law, adjunct professor of statistical sciences, Cornell Law School, Ithaca, New York, and coauthor of a meta-analysis of drugs' effects on cardiovascular risk, published in *Journal of Empirical Legal Studies*.

■ ■ ■ ■

Giving Birth Prematurely Predicts Heart Risk

Women who had delivered before 37 weeks of pregnancy were more than twice as likely to have heart disease decades later as women who had delivered at full term (after 37 weeks).

Theory: Inflammation and blood fats may affect both pregnancy and heart health.

Best: Women with a history of preterm delivery may benefit from early cardiac interventions, such as exercise and weight control.

Janet M. Catov, PhD, assistant professor of obstetrics, gynecology and reproductive sciences, University of Pittsburgh, and leader of a study of 446 women, published in *American Journal of Epidemiology*.

■ ■ ■ ■

Psoriasis Tied to Heart Disease

Patients with severe psoriasis at age 30 had more than three times the risk for a heart attack compared with those of the same age without psoriasis.

Theory: Inflammation plays a role in the development of both psoriasis and cardiovascular disease.

If you have psoriasis: Ask your doctor to screen you at least every two years for high blood pressure and obesity...and at least every two to five years for elevated cholesterol and triglyceride (blood fat) levels and diabetes—all are cardiovascular disease risk factors.

Lyn C. Guenther, MD, professor and chair, division of dermatology, University of Western Ontario, London, Ontario, Canada.

■ ■ ■ ■

Surprising Heart Attack Risk Factor

In a recent study of nearly 15,000 people, researchers found that kidney stone disease (buildup of crystals in the kidneys from substances in urine) was up to three times more likely to occur in those with metabolic syndrome—heart attack and stroke risk factors, such as diabetes and high blood pressure.

Theory: People with metabolic syndrome have a propensity to develop highly acidic urine, which raises kidney stone risk.

If you have kidney stones: Ask your doctor whether you need testing for metabolic syndrome.

Bradford West, MD, fellow, department of nephrology, University of Chicago.

■ ■ ■ ■

Getting Drunk Raises Heart Attack Risk

Women who drank alcohol to the point of intoxication at least once a month were six times as likely to suffer a heart attack (not necessarily while drinking) as women who drank at least monthly but not enough to be intoxicated.

Best: Never drink to the point of intoxication.

Joan M. Dorn, PhD, adjunct associate professor, department of social and preventive medicine, University of Buffalo, and leader of a study of 1,885 women, published in *Addiction*.

Can This Patient Be Cured? Heart Palpitations

Mark A. Stengler, ND, naturopathic physician in private practice, La Jolla, California...adjunct associate clinical professor at the National College of Natural Medicine, Portland, Oregon...author of many books, including *The Natural Physician's Healing Therapies* and coauthor of *Prescription for Natural Cures* (both from Bottom Line Books)...and author of the *Bottom Line/Natural Healing* newsletter.

Mandy, a 49-year-old cosmetics salesperson, had been experiencing a strange fluttering sensation in her chest once or twice a day for two months. Understandably concerned, she scheduled a visit with a cardiologist. An electrocardiogram showed that the electrical activity of her heart was normal. Results of blood work and other tests came out normal, too. But Mandy was still experiencing heart fluttering, so she came to see me.

After reviewing her symptoms, health history and heart function, I asked about her lifestyle. First, her dietary habits—Mandy said she didn't consume much caffeine or sugar, both of which can trigger heart palpitations (the medical term for "fluttering") in some people. She did tell me that she had noticed the sensation became more pronounced whenever she drank alcohol, so she tried to avoid it. Her stress level? Like many people, Mandy described it as "up and down"—yet she said that the fluttering was no more intense during high-stress periods than during times of relative calm.

Next, I asked about her menstrual cycle. Mandy said her periods were starting to become irregular and that she experienced occasional hot flashes. She said that she had noticed an increase in the fluttering sensation about four to five days before her menses began. I told her that due to hormonal fluctuations, heart palpitations are fairly common in women during menopause and just before, during the stage called perimenopause.

I performed a comprehensive hormone test, which showed that Mandy's progesterone level was quite low. Progesterone affects circulation, specifically in the coronary arteries, and blood flow to the heart. Supplementing with natural progesterone has helped many of my patients with exactly the sort of palpitations Mandy was experiencing. For her, I prescribed a natural progesterone cream and recommended that she apply it to her forearms each evening, except during her menstrual flow.

In addition, I suggested that she take supplements of calcium and magnesium, both twice daily, morning and evening. These minerals help relax the nervous system and regulate heart rate and rhythm. Within two weeks, Mandy's daily heart palpitations had vanished. Now, three years later, Mandy feels that fluttering sensation only very occasionally. She no longer uses the progesterone cream, but she does find that if she stops taking the calcium and magnesium supplements for more than a week or so, mild palpitations return.

I have found that progesterone deficiency is a greatly underdiagnosed cause of heart palpitations in women of menopausal age. Many end up on cardiovascular medications, such as beta-blockers (*atenolol,* for example), which can cause fatigue. Addressing the root issue—which often is, as in Mandy's case, progesterone deficiency—is a better bet for safely and effectively correcting the problem.

Could Food Sensitivities Be Causing Your Heart Problems?

Leo Galland, MD, director, Foundation for Integrated Medicine, New York City. His latest book is *The Fat Resistance Diet* (Broadway). *www.fatresistancediet.com*. Dr. Galland is a recipient of the Linus Pauling award.

When James, a 62-year-old accountant, first came to see me, he was suffering from troubling heart palpitations and unpleasant side effects from the very drugs that had been prescribed to calm his irregular heartbeat.

"I don't know which is worse—the palpitations or the drugs that were supposed to prevent them," he said at our first meeting.

James's problem had started a few years earlier with an occasional flutter in his chest. More recently, the sensation had occurred every day and was so severe and persistent that he felt dizzy and was unable to concentrate at work. James's doctor had told him that the problem was most likely a *cardiac arrhythmia* (irregular heartbeat) caused by *premature ventricular contractions* (PVCs).

This is a common irregularity in which the normal rhythm of the heart is disrupted by a beat that comes too early followed by a compensatory pause as the heart attempts to resume its usual rhythm. The beat that follows the pause tends to be very strong, frequently causing the sensation of fluttering or palpitations. Some people have PVCs and don't know it, while others feel every single irregular heartbeat. There are many causes of PVCs, including caffeine, alcohol, stress or stimulant drugs as well as thyroid problems, nutritional deficiency (such as a magnesium deficiency)—and even heart disease.

Important: Any irregularity in heartbeat should be evaluated by a physician, as it can be a sign of heart disease.

James's doctor did not specialize in heart conditions, so he referred James to a cardiologist, who performed an exercise stress test and an ultrasound of the heart. James "passed" these tests with flying colors, and his blood tests revealed no obvious cause of PVCs. In the absence of a known underlying condition to treat, James was prescribed a drug called a beta-blocker (commonly used to treat high blood pressure, glaucoma and migraines) to suppress the extra heartbeats. The medication completely prevented the PVCs, but it made James feel sluggish and caused erectile dysfunction.

James was concerned about the side effects of the beta-blocker when he consulted me. But we both really wanted to get to the root of his palpitations. To do so, I took a very detailed history, which ultimately led to the solution.

Since childhood, James had experienced mild eczema and occasional migraine headaches. These were easily controlled with medications, including a steroid cream (*hydrocortisone*) for the eczema and an antimigraine drug called a *triptan*. Because both eczema and migraine are strongly associated with food allergy—especially when they first develop during childhood—I decided to investigate the possibility that James's palpitations were being triggered by food.

Food sensitivity is not unusual in adults. Estimates show that it affects about nine million adults in the US. Over the past 30 years, I have seen a wide variety of symptoms caused by food sensitivity, including headaches, skin rashes, palpitations, asthma, joint pain, gastrointestinal disturbances (such as heartburn and diarrhea), muscle tics and spasms, profound mood swings and difficulty falling asleep or staying asleep. Once food sensitivity is suspected, the next step is to identify the food triggers. The most reliable way to do this is by using an "exclusion diet"—avoiding common foods that the person regularly eats or drinks. For most people with chronic symptoms, the troublesome food is milk (or milk products), wheat, corn, yeast, eggs and/or soy. I asked James to follow an exclusion diet for a week while tapering down his use of the beta-blocker. By the end of the week, James was free of palpitations—and as a bonus, his eczema had begun to clear up, probably because he was sensitive to one or more of the foods he had eliminated.

The next step was for him to systematically reintroduce the foods he'd avoided—one at a time every three days to see if any of them triggered palpitations. In James's case, the culprit proved to be wheat. Avoiding wheat-containing foods (such as wheat cereals, pasta, bread and baked goods) completely eliminated his palpitations and cleared most of his eczema. The frequency of his migraine headaches was cut by two-thirds.

CORRECT DIAGNOSIS: FOOD SENSITIVITY

Lesson for all: If you have symptoms such as those described in this article (with no known cause) and have a personal or family history of allergies, eczema, asthma and/or migraines, consider food sensitivity as a possible trigger. Ask your primary care physician to refer you to a health professional who specializes in food sensitivities for an evaluation.

Low Levels Are Best For Your Heart

Stephen J. Nicholls, MBBS, assistant professor, molecular medicine, Cleveland Clinic.

Jonathan Tobis, MD, director, interventional cardiology research, David Geffen School of Medicine, University of California, Los Angeles.

Journal of the American College of Cardiology.

The tightest control of the major risk factors for heart disease seems to provide the greatest protection against cardiovascular trouble, a recent study shows.

And so the current guidelines for risk factors, such as blood pressure and low-density lipoprotein (LDL) cholesterol, might need to be tightened even further, said Stephen J. Nicholls, MD, an assistant professor of molecular medicine at the Cleveland Clinic, and author of the report, which appeared in the *Journal of the American College of Cardiology.*

"It is clear that each benefit we have in terms of lowering LDL cholesterol and blood pressure is going to be important. The lower you get those measurements, the better," Dr. Nicholls said.

THE STUDY

Dr. Nicholls and his colleagues looked at data on the arteries of 3,437 men enrolled in seven different trials at the Cleveland Clinic. Ultrasound of the arteries provided information on the volume of the fatty deposits in the linings of the blood vessels—deposits that can grow until they block blood flow, causing a heart attack or stroke.

The least amount of growth was seen in those men who had the lowest levels of LDL cholesterol, the "bad" kind of cholesterol that contributes to the fatty deposits, and the lowest levels of blood pressure.

"The rationale for the current analysis was the belief that you should get lower LDL cholesterol and lower blood pressure, and that the benefit is greatest in getting both low," Dr. Nicholls said. "In fact, patients who had the best results in terms of growth of the deposits were those with the lowest LDL and lowest blood pressure."

CHOLESTEROL AND BLOOD PRESSURE GUIDELINES

Specifically, the least growth was seen in men with LDL blood cholesterol readings under 70 milligrams per deciliter and systolic blood pressure (the top number) under 120, he said.

The guideline for blood pressure says that men at risk can have systolic readings as high as 140 (having consistent systolic readings from 120 to 139 is called "prehypertension"). With blood cholesterol, the current recommendation is for an LDL level of 100 for men at high risk of heart disease, with "consideration" being given to lowering it to 70.

"If you are at high risk, LDL should be below 70," he said. "For blood pressure, you get the greatest benefit if it is below 120."

EXPERT COMMENTARY

An accompanying editorial coauthored by Jonathan Tobis, MD, of the University of California, Los Angeles, said the results did not necessarily indicate that tighter control of cholesterol and blood pressure would be beneficial.

"You need clinical endpoints to know," said Dr. Tobis, director of interventional cardiology research at the UCLA's David Geffen School of Medicine. "They have positive effects on total plaque volume, but the question is whether that corresponds to clinical events such as myocardial infarction [heart attack] and stroke. I suspect that they do, but we haven't proven that yet, and these trials don't prove it."

The composition of a fatty deposit might be as important as its size, Dr. Tobis said. Some plaques might be less stable than others, thus prone to rupture and block a blood vessel, he said. "One of the studies included in the report showed that aggressive lowering of LDL reduced the size of the deposits, but we don't know clinically if that makes a difference or not," Dr. Tobis said. "Lowering LDL enough might stabilize a plaque so that you get an adequate result."

MORE CLINICAL STUDIES NEEDED

Dr. Nicholls said he agreed with that assessment. While the study indicates that lowering existing guideline levels for LDL cholesterol and high blood pressure could reduce risk considerably, he noted that "we need a lot more clinical studies showing that putting the guidelines below those levels would be beneficial."

info For more information, visit the Web site of the National Heart, Lung and Blood Institute, *www.nhlbi.nih.gov*, and search "high cholesterol."

High Blood Pressure Traps that Could Kill You

Samuel J. Mann, MD, a hypertension specialist at NewYork-Presbyterian Hospital and professor of clinical medicine at Weill-Cornell Medical College, both in New York City. He is author of *Healing Hypertension: A Revolutionary New Approach* (Wiley).

Getting your blood pressure checked is a routine part of most physical exams. But how the measurement is taken and the treatment your doctor recommends if you have high blood pressure (hypertension) can have a profound effect on your health.

High blood pressure occurs when the force with which blood travels through the arteries is higher than it needs to be. Blood pressure readings consist of two measurements—systolic pressure (top number) measures the force as the heart contracts...diastolic (bottom number) represents the pressure between beats. Hypertension typically is defined as 140/90 mmHg or above, although readings above 120/80 mmHg are considered higher than optimal.

It's well-known that hypertension is often "silent" (causing no symptoms) and that it can lead to death or disability due to heart attack... stroke...and kidney damage.

What you may not know: One-third to one-half of all patients who take medication for hypertension lower their blood pressure insufficiently ...take the wrong drugs...or suffer unnecessary side effects.

Samuel J. Mann, MD, a renowned hypertension specialist at New York-Presbyterian Hospital in New York City, shares his insights about these and other dangers...

Trap: Getting inaccurate blood pressure readings. The equipment in doctors' offices and home arm-cuff blood pressure monitors are usually accurate, but how they're used can greatly affect readings. *Three common mistakes...*

Mistake 1: **Rushing the test.** It takes five to 10 minutes of sitting quietly for blood pressure to stabilize. Testing too quickly can produce a reading that's considerably higher than your usual resting blood pressure.

Mistake 2: **Using a cuff that's too small.** Doctors often use the same blood pressure cuff on all patients—but if you have a large arm, the reading can be artificially high. Ask your doctor whether the blood pressure cuff size is right for you.

Mistake 3: **Talking while blood pressure is being measured.** It can add 10 millimeters or more to the systolic (top number) reading.

Trap: Ignoring "white-coat hypertension." Up to 20% of people exhibit elevations in blood pressure in the doctor's office even though their pressure at home is normal. This phenomenon, known as white-coat hypertension, sometimes is due to the anxiety many people experience when they go to the doctor.

We used to think that white-coat hypertension was insignificant. Now, a study published in the *Journal of Human Hypertension* shows that people who exhibit this trait do face higher risks—for both heart attack and true hypertension at some point in their lives—than those whose office blood pressure is normal.

It's not yet clear why these patients have higher risks. Studies of patients who perform home monitoring suggest that their pressure tends to be slightly higher than what's considered optimal even if it's not high enough to be classified as hypertension.

Warning: Some people with white-coat hypertension are undertreated because their doctors tend to ignore elevated office readings while not paying attention to a gradual rise in home readings. Others are overtreated based on the elevated office readings, even though home readings are normal.

Helpful: Patients with hypertension—or those at risk of getting it (due to such factors as family history and being overweight)—should use a home monitor to check their blood pressure two or three times a week. Take three readings each time, waiting about one to two minutes between each measurement.

Trap: Overtreating hypertension because of high readings obtained at times of stress. It's clear that blood pressure rises sharply at moments when people are angry, anxious or stressed. Many people have their blood pressure checked—or check it themselves—at such times, and their doctors increase medication based on these readings.

Helpful: Blood pressure elevation during emotional moments is normal. If your blood pressure is otherwise normal, an increase in medication usually is not necessary.

Trap: Taking the wrong drug. Up to 25% of patients with hypertension take a beta-blocker to lower blood pressure. This type of drug inhibits the kidneys' secretion of the enzyme renin, which results in lower levels of *angiotensin II,* a peptide that constricts blood vessels.

Beta-blockers also reduce the rate and force of heart contractions. However, most beta-blockers, including the widely prescribed *metoprolol* (Lopressor) and *atenolol* (Tenormin), have the undesirable effect of reducing blood flow.

These effects often result in fatigue. Many patients don't even realize how fatigued they are until they stop taking the beta-blocker and experience a sudden boost in energy.

Fact: The majority of patients with hypertension who suffer from fatigue due to a beta-blocker don't even need to take this drug.

For most patients, it's best to start with other drugs or drug combinations, such as a diuretic (sodium-excreting pill) and/or an angiotensin-converting enzyme (ACE) inhibitor or an angiotensin receptor blocker (ARB).

Exception: Beta-blockers are usually a good choice for patients with hypertension who also have underlying coronary artery disease or who have had a heart attack.

If you need a beta-blocker: Ask your doctor about newer versions, such as *nebivolol* (Bystolic), that dilate arteries. Nebivolol is less likely to cause fatigue.

Trap: Switching to a newer drug—without good reason. Even if people are getting good results with the blood pressure medication they are taking, there's often a temptation to switch to a newer drug. Some newer drugs may have features that are an improvement over older medications, but others may offer little advantage and are not worth the extra cost.

Example: *Aliskiren* (Tekturna) is the first FDA-approved medication in a new class of blood pressure drugs known as renin inhibitors. Aliskiren inhibits the blood pressure–raising effects of the renin-angiotensin system. However, it is no more effective at lowering blood pressure than older treatments, such as ACE inhibitors or ARBs.

Switching drugs does make sense if you're not achieving optimal control—or if your current treatment is causing side effects. But for most patients, the older drugs are both effective and well-tolerated—and much less expensive.

Trap: Taking medication unnecessarily. It's estimated that only about 40% of patients with hypertension achieve optimal control by taking a single drug (monotherapy). Most patients will eventually need multiple drugs—but monotherapy is effective for some patients, particularly those with mild hypertension (defined as systolic pressure of 140 mmHg to 159 mmHg and/or diastolic pressure of 90 mmHg to 99 mmHg).

Adding drugs invariably increases both the cost of treatment and the risk for side effects. If a drug doesn't work within a few weeks, then switching drugs is an alternative to simply adding drugs. Or if a second drug is added and it normalizes your blood pressure, your doctor may consider reducing the dose of—or stopping—the first drug.

■ ■ ■ ■

Hot Weather Heats Up Your Blood Pressure

When researchers reviewed the records of 6,400 people, in those age 66 or older who were being treated for high blood pressure, nighttime systolic blood pressure (top number) averaged five points higher when the temperature ranged from 77.9°F to 90.5°F than when it was 30.7°F to 43.2°F.

If you have hypertension and are 66 or older: Ask your doctor to review your blood pressure treatment during the summer.

Pietro Amedeo Modesti, MD, PhD, associate professor of internal medicine, University of Florence, Italy.

The All-New Blood Pressure Control Diet

C. Tissa Kappagoda, MD, PhD, professor of medicine, preventive cardiology program, University of California, Davis. Dr. Kappagoda has published more than 150 medical journal articles on heart health.

For the first time, high blood pressure that is uncontrolled is more common in women than in men—yet women are less likely to be prescribed treatment, such as blood pressure–lowering medication. High blood pressure, or hypertension, doesn't hurt or cause other obvious warning signs, but it damages arteries in ways that can lead to stroke, heart attack, kidney problems and cognitive impairment. *More concerns for women...*

- **Hypertension now affects nearly one in four American women.** Rates in women are rising even as rates in men are falling.

About 35% of women who have hypertension go untreated.

- **Blood pressure is the force that blood exerts against the arterial walls.** It is reported as two numbers. The top number, or systolic pressure, is the pressure as the heart pumps. The bottom number, or diastolic pressure, is the pressure as the heart rests between beats. Normal, healthy blood pressure is below 120/80 millimeters of mercury (mmHg)...hypertension is diagnosed at 140/90 mmHg or higher.

Problem: Up to 70% of people who are told that they are fine because their blood pressure is in the "high normal" range actually are at serious risk. Systolic pressure of 120 to 139 and/or diastolic pressure of 80 to 89 indicates prehypertension —which often progresses to hypertension.

Good news: You can significantly reduce blood pressure by changing what you eat. You must do more than just cut back on salt—although following this common advice helps—but the simple strategies below are worth the effort.

If you already have hypertension or have "high normal" blood pressure...are at risk due to being overweight or having a family history of blood pressure problems...or simply want to be as healthy as possible, this diet is for you.

Bonus: These habits often lead to weight loss—which also lowers blood pressure.

HAVE MORE...

- **Berries.** Berries are high in *polyphenols,* micronutrients that relax blood vessels.

Study: Hypertension patients who ate berries daily for two months lowered their systolic blood pressure by up to seven points—which could reduce risk for heart-related death by up to 15%.

Action: Eat one cup of fresh or frozen berries daily.

- **Fat-free milk.** A study found that people who ingested the greatest amounts of low-fat dairy were 56% less likely to develop hypertension than those who ate the least.

Theory: The active components may be the milk proteins whey and/or casein, which help blood vessels dilate.

Action: Have eight to 16 ounces of fat-free milk per day. Evidence suggests that fat-free milk is best—higher fat milk and other dairy products may not work as well.

- **Potassium-rich fruits and vegetables.** Potassium counteracts the blood pressure–raising effects of sodium.

New study: Prehypertension patients with the highest sodium-to-potassium intake were up to 50% more likely to develop cardiovascular disease within 10 to 15 years, compared with those who had the lowest ratio.

Action: Among the generally recommended five or so daily servings of fruits and vegetables, include some potassium-rich choices, such as bananas, citrus fruits, lima beans, potatoes and sweet potatoes (with skin), tomatoes and yams. Talk to your doctor before increasing potassium if you take blood pressure or heart medication (diuretic, ACE inhibitor or ARB blocker) or if you have kidney problems.

- **Fiber.** Studies suggest that fiber lowers blood pressure, though the mechanism is unknown. The fiber must come from food—fiber supplements do not offer the same benefit.

Action: Check food labels, and aim for at least 25 grams of fiber daily.

Good sources: Whole fruits (juice has less fiber)...raw or lightly cooked vegetables (overcooking reduces fiber)...beans and lentils...high-fiber breakfast cereals...and whole grains, such as barley, brown rice, oats, quinoa and whole wheat.

EAT LESS...

•**Meat.** Often high in cholesterol and saturated fat, meat contributes to the buildup of plaque inside arteries—a condition called atherosclerosis. Hypertension significantly increases the risk that atherosclerosis will lead to a heart attack or stroke.

Action: If you have been diagnosed with both atherosclerosis and hypertension, a good way to reduce your cardiovascular risk is to adopt a vegetarian or near-vegetarian diet.

Also: Avoid other sources of saturated fats, such as high-fat dairy, and palm oil.

If you are concerned about getting enough protein, increase your intake of plant proteins.

Good sources: Soy foods (edamame, soy milk, tofu)...beans, lentils, peas...nuts and seeds.

If you have hypertension or prehypertension but no atherosclerosis, limit yourself to three weekly four-ounce servings of animal protein. Stick with low-fat meat, fish or poultry.

•**Salt.** Sodium raises blood pressure by increasing blood volume and constricting blood vessels. Some people are more sensitive to salt than others—but limiting dietary salt is a good idea for everyone.

Recommended: Healthy people up to age 50 should limit sodium to 2,300 mg per day (about one teaspoon of salt)...older people and anyone with prehypertension or hypertension should stay under 1,500 mg daily (about two-thirds of a teaspoon of salt).

Action: Instead of salt, add flavor with pepper, garlic and other seasonings. Do not use seasoning blends that contain salt. Avoid processed and canned foods unless labeled "low sodium."

PROS AND CONS OF...

•**Red wine.** Like berries, red wine contains heart-healthy polyphenols.

But: Polyphenols relax blood vessels only when exposure time is short, as with light-to-moderate alcohol consumption. Heavy drinking actually reduces the blood vessels' ability to relax, negating polyphenols' benefits.

Advised: If you choose to drink alcohol, opt for red wine and have no more than one glass per day.

Alcohol-free option: Polyphenol-rich unsweetened dark grape juice.

•**Coffee, tea and soda.** Some evidence links caffeine to increased blood pressure.

Advised: Opt for caffeine-free beverages.

Good choice: Herbal tea. A recent study suggests that drinking three cups daily of a blend that includes the herb hibiscus can lower systolic blood pressure by about seven points.

•**Chocolate.** Small studies suggest that dark chocolate helps lower blood pressure.

Theory: Cocoa contains antioxidant *procyanidins,* which boost the body's production of nitric oxide, a chemical that relaxes blood vessels.

But: Chocolate is high in sugar and fat, both of which contribute to weight gain.

Advised: If you want an occasional dessert, a small piece (one-half ounce) of dark chocolate is a good choice.

■ ■ ■ ■

"Grow" a Healthier Heart!

Stem cells injected into the hearts of heart failure patients might stimulate the growth of blood vessels and repair damaged tissues—and could reduce the numbers of transplant procedures.

Methodist DeBakey Heart & Vascular Center.

Amazing Stem Cell Breakthroughs for Heart, Arteries and More

Jan Nolta, PhD, director of the University of California at Davis Stem Cell Center and Research Program. Dr. Nolta has authored or coauthored more than 75 scientific papers as well as 15 book chapters related to stem cells. She is editor of the textbook *Genetic Engineering of Mesenchymal Stem Cells* (Springer).

Until recently, most of the news about stem cells focused on those derived from human embryos. These so-called "undifferentiated" cells have been heralded for their potential to treat—or even cure—diseases ranging from Alzheimer's and Parkinson's to diabetes and spinal cord injuries.

Embryonic stem cells are capable of producing heart cells, blood cells, brain cells—or any one of the more than 200 other types of specialized cells in the body. Although research related to embryonic cells is promising, it still is preliminary and has been performed only on laboratory animals. Human embryonic stem cell clinical trials will not begin for at least one year—and embryonic stem cells remain controversial, because some people believe that it is unethical to use the cells for medical purposes.

Now: Researchers are discovering new uses for adult stem cells, which have long been used in transplants (from the patient's own bone marrow or blood...or from the bone marrow of someone who is a genetic match) to treat leukemia, lymphoma and, more recently, as an adjunct therapy for advanced malignancies of the prostate, kidney and bladder.

LATEST BREAKTHROUGH

Researchers at the University of California at Davis have for the first time identified adult bladder stem cells—which might be used in the future to regenerate replacement bladder tissue in people whose bladders are too small or don't function properly, such as adults with spinal cord injuries or bladder cancer. These findings were reported in the May 2008 online issue of the *American Journal of Physiology-Renal.*

Other exciting research: Elsewhere, hundreds of recent clinical trials in the US and around the world show that adult stem cells found in specific tissues and organs, such as the heart, muscles and bones—or "harvested" from the patient's blood or bone marrow—can treat a variety of medical conditions, including congestive heart failure, rheumatoid arthritis and multiple sclerosis.

At the UC Davis Stem Cell Center, we often refer to adult stem cells as the "paramedics of the body" because they move very quickly to areas of tissue damage and secrete substances that repair tissue and improve blood flow.

Future research at our center will study the use of adult stem cells for, among other problems, repairing heart tissue after a heart attack...and restoring restricted blood flow in peripheral artery disease (PAD), a blockage in the arteries, occurring mainly in the legs.

Some current research in these areas...

HEART DISEASE

A review article in an issue of the *Journal of the American Medical Association* cited more than 30 studies that have been conducted using adult stem cells in people who have had heart attacks or who suffer from cardiovascular disorders.

How they work: Adult stem cells from the bone marrow or blood may generate compounds, including proteins, that stop cell death and promote the body's own capacity to regenerate blood vessels.

Results have included fewer deaths from heart disease...an 18% improvement in the strength of the heartbeat, on average...less severe angina (chest pain)...fewer arrhythmias (abnormal heart rhythms)...slower rates of new arterial blockage...and better daily functioning.

PERIPHERAL ARTERY DISEASE

About 10 million Americans suffer from peripheral artery disease. When the disease advances to the point where pain in the lower legs is nearly constant, and leg wounds and ulcers won't heal, the condition is called *critical limb ischemia* (CLI). CLI affects 1.4 million Americans. Every year, 100,000 people with CLI lose a toe, foot or an entire leg to amputation.

Latest development: In January 2008, researchers at Northwestern University Feinberg School of Medicine began studying 75 people with CLI for whom all standard therapies, including the use of a balloon-tipped catheter to open blocked arteries, had been unsuccessful.

Half the CLI patients were given a drug that stimulated the release of CD34+ cells (a type of adult stem cell) from their bone marrow. The cells were then collected via an intravenous line, and a sophisticated machine "purified" that mixture to increase the concentration of CD34+ cells. The patients were injected intravenously with the cells. Researchers hope the cells will accumulate in—and help repair—the damaged arteries as well as attract other adult stem cells to the area.

Other promising research...

AUTOIMMUNE DISEASES

In the 1990s, doctors began to use stem cell transplants to treat autoimmune diseases, in which the white blood cells of the body's immune system attack a particular organ or type of tissue—for example, the joints in rheumatoid arthritis...the coverings (sheaths) of nerves in multiple sclerosis...and the pancreas in type 1 diabetes. The transplants were performed to generate new white blood cells that would not attack the body.

Recent clinical studies have used adult stem cells to repair tissue damaged by...

- **Crohn's disease.** Two-thirds of the 21 patients treated had complete remission of this form of inflammatory bowel disease.
- **Lupus.** Nearly two-thirds of the 26 patients treated were "event-free" for five years from the symptoms of this autoimmune disease. Lupus can attack the skin, joints, heart, lungs, blood, kidneys and brain.
- **Multiple sclerosis.** Of 21 patients, none had progression of this neurological disease over two years, and 62% were improved.

info To learn more about participating in a clinical trial using adult stem cells, consult the National Institutes of Health's Web site, *www.clinicaltrials.gov.*

10

Natural Remedies

Coconut Oil May Help Fight Childhood Pneumonia

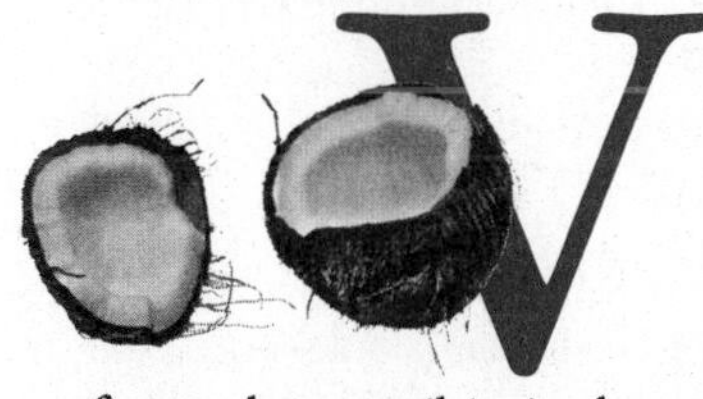

Virgin coconut oil, added to antibiotic therapy, may help relieve the symptoms of community-acquired pneumonia in children faster than antibiotic therapy alone, according to a recent study.

Children who received coconut oil therapy along with antibiotics had fewer crackles (a wheezing sound in the lungs), a shorter time with an elevated breathing (respiratory) rate and fever, better oxygen saturation in the blood and shorter hospital stays, the study finds.

"Earlier normalization of respiratory rate and resolution of crackles could also mean possible earlier discharge," said the study's lead author, Gilda Sapphire Erguiza, MD, a pediatric pulmonologist at the Philippine Children's Medical Center in Quezon City.

The study's findings were presented at a meeting of the American College of Chest Physicians.

BACKGROUND

Community-acquired pneumonia is an infection of the lungs that is contracted outside a hospital setting. It is a serious infection in children and affects as many as 34 to 40 per 1,000 children in Europe and North America, according to the American Academy of Family Physicians (AAFP). Infections of the lower respiratory tract are one of the leading causes of childhood mortality in developing countries, according to the AAFP.

THE STUDY

The current study included 40 children between the ages of three months and five years.

Gilda Sapphire Erguiza, MD, pediatric pulmonologist, Philippine Children's Medical Center, Quezon City, Philippines.

Daniel Rauch, MD, director, pediatric hospitalist program, New York University Langone Medical Center, and assistant professor of pediatrics, New York University School of Medicine, New York City.

American College of Chest Physicians' annual meeting.

Morbidity and Mortality Weekly Report.

All had community-acquired pneumonia and were being treated intravenously with the antibiotic *ampicillin*.

Half of the group was randomized to also receive oral virgin coconut oil in a daily dose of 2 milliliters per every kilogram of weight. The oil was given for three days in a row.

The researchers found that the respiratory rate returned to normal in 32.6 hours for the virgin coconut oil group versus 48.2 hours for the control group who did not receive the coconut oil, according to the study. After three days, patients in the control group were more likely to still have crackles than those in the coconut oil group—60% of the controls still had crackles compared with 25% of the coconut oil group.

Those in the coconut oil group also had fevers for a shorter time, had normal oxygen saturation faster and had shorter hospital stays. However, Dr. Erguiza explained that these differences were not enough to be statistically significant.

POSSIBLE EXPLANATION

How might the coconut oil work to ease pneumonia? Dr. Erguiza hypothesized that the lauric acid in coconut, which is known to have antimicrobial properties, boosts the effectiveness of ampicillin.

EXPERT COMMENTARY

"This is a very interesting but small study. The jury's still out as to whether there's a real benefit here," said Daniel Rauch, MD, director of the pediatric hospitalist program at New York University Langone Medical Center.

Dr. Rauch said he wouldn't discourage a parent from trying this treatment, as long as they were still using antibiotics, but he said it's important that children aren't forced to take virgin coconut oil. The concern, he said, is that if a child is forced to ingest something that he or she doesn't really want to, they may end up choking on it and aspirating the oil into the lungs, which is very dangerous.

info To learn more about pneumonia, visit the National Library of Medicine Web site at *http://medlineplus.gov* and search "pneumonia."

The Real Secret to Fixing All Your Health Problems

Henri Roca, MD, medical director, Greenwich Hospital Center for Integrative Medicine, Greenwich, Connecticut. He is a diplomate of both the American Academy of Family Practice and the American Board of Integrative Holistic Medicine and serves on the Louisiana State Board of Medical Examiners Complementary and Alternative Medicine Advisory Board.

Think of your health as a pot on the stove that's about to come to a boil. Conventional medicine would try to slam a lid on the pot and hold it down tight. That may work at first, but unless the heat is also turned down, the pressure under the lid will build up and the pot will boil over anyway. What alternative therapies try to do is reduce the intensity of the flame under the pot. In both cases, we're trying to keep the pot from boiling over.

The difference is that with integrative medicine, we're trying to keep that flame turned way down and keep it from bringing the pot to a boil at all.

This combination of conventional medicine and alternative treatments works so well that today many hospitals (including the one where I work) offer integrative medicine centers. When we incorporate alternative treatments, we're looking at ways to help people with certain lifestyle issues that are out of balance and will eventually cause illness. We're looking at the whole person—mind, body and spirit.

CREATING BALANCE

Our goal is to bring balance back—instead of allowing an imbalance to continue until it develops into serious symptoms. Through poor eating habits, lack of exercise and exposure to chemicals (pesticides and added hormones) in the air we breathe, water we drink and food we eat, we put a huge burden on the body. By using integrative medicine, we can reduce that burden and help the body detoxify.

How it works: By supporting the liver, the kidneys and the intestines. If any of these organs don't function correctly, we will develop serious disease sooner or later.

Do you suffer from such common disorders as acid reflux, stomach ulcers, obesity, diabetes, menstrual irregularities, skin rashes, allergies, asthma or digestive problems? Many of my patients do. All those diagnoses are related, because the human system is a web of interactions and no single diagnosis can stand alone. Instead of giving someone three or four or 10 diagnoses with three or four or 10 pills to treat them, we work to bring that entire system back into balance. *Treatments I use include...*

- **Herbal products.**
- **Biofeedback or other types of mind-body techniques,** such as visualization.
- **Meditation or techniques that utilize deep, mindful breathing.**
- **Traditional Chinese medicine,** such as acupuncture.
- **Homeopathy.**

There's no single best treatment that works for everyone. We look closely at the patient as an individual and choose treatments based on what is most likely to be effective for him/her. *But there are some important general guidelines that may apply to you...*

CHRONIC DISEASES

When we have situations in life that impact our bodies significantly, such as chronic disease or stress, our nutrients are used up very quickly. We need to replenish them—if we don't, then chronic diseases can worsen or we may develop new disease.

Examples...

- **Depression often occurs after a person has been under significant stress that continues over a long period.** Under these circumstances, by replenishing basic nutrients necessary to create natural mood-regulating chemicals in the brain, we can potentially diminish depression symptoms. We don't automatically put any depressed person on an antidepressant medication. Sometimes we do so in conjunction with vitamin therapy, but the goal is to eventually lower the medication dosage or stop it altogether.
- **High blood pressure (hypertension) can be caused by a magnesium deficiency.** In that case, we might prescribe medication to lower blood pressure but also recommend a diet with more magnesium (or use magnesium supplements).

WHEN TO CHOOSE ALTERNATIVE THERAPIES

Conventional practitioners worry that by using alternative methods, some patients will end up delaying treatment until the condition has worsened...or even until it's "too late" in the case of life-threatening conditions. That's a valid concern, but rarely do I ever tell anyone that it's appropriate to use only conventional medicine or only an alternative approach.

Emergencies: When there's a truly dangerous medical condition—for example, blood pressure that's so high that the patient is in serious danger of having a heart attack or stroke...or a serious bacterial infection needing antibiotics... or cancer that might respond to chemotherapy, radiation and/or surgery—then conventional medicine, through the emergency room if necessary, is definitely the way to go.

But what if your blood pressure has just begun to increase? Then you could choose standard blood pressure medication to protect yourself from complications and worsening disease... and use an integrative approach to rebalance the system and turn off the fire. The ultimate goal is to reduce the medication dose or to stop the drugs completely.

In the case of a life-threatening illness, such as cancer, alternative therapies are not cures. Instead, integrative medicine focuses on supporting the person through the conventional treatment process and can be very effective in helping with the pain, fatigue and nausea associated with chemotherapy and radiation treatments.

Similarly, integrative medicine can be very helpful for treating chronic diseases, such as multiple sclerosis, where fatigue is a big problem. Integrative medical doctors are board-certified by the American Board of Integrative Holistic Medicine. You can find a doctor near you by checking its Web site, *www.holisticboard.org.*

■ ■ ■ ■

Drug-Free Ways to Reduce Blood Pressure

Mind–body therapies reduce high blood pressure as effectively as medication does. They can be used alone or as an adjunct to traditional drug therapy.

Helpful: Do yoga, meditate and/or visualize a relaxing scene. As with drugs, sustained results require regular use.

Ather Ali, ND, MPH, assistant director of Integrative Medicine Research at the Yale-Griffin Prevention Research Center, Derby, Connecticut, and leader of a review of 12 studies, presented at a meeting of the American Public Health Association.

The Mozart Prescription For Lower Blood Pressure

Jean Tang, PhD, assistant professor, College of Nursing at Seattle University, Seattle, Washington.

Robert Ostfeld, MD, cardiologist, associate professor of clinical medicine, Montefiore Medical Center, New York City.

American Heart Association's conference of the Council for High Blood Pressure Research, Atlanta.

Listening to relaxation tapes or classical music by Mozart reduces your blood pressure if you listen at least three times a week.

In a study of 41 seniors living in retirement communities, researchers found that regularly listening to relaxation tapes reduced average systolic (the top number) blood pressure readings by nine points, while those who regularly listened to Mozart saw a seven-point reduction in their blood pressure.

"This is a simple program that's very easy to do, and blood pressure did decrease," said the study's lead author, Jean Tang, PhD, an assistant professor at the College of Nursing at Seattle University in Washington. But, she added, "It won't replace medicine. It can only reduce blood pressure to a certain point—it's like making lifestyle changes."

Tang presented the findings at the American Heart Association's conference of the Council for High Blood Pressure Research in Atlanta.

THE STUDY

Two groups of seniors were randomly assigned to listen to a 12-minute relaxation tape with the sound of ocean waves, instructions for breathing and relaxation exercises or to a 12-minute Mozart sonata. Each group was asked to participate three times a week for four months.

Researchers took blood pressure readings before and after the intervention. At the end of the study, researchers asked participants to continue listening to the relaxation tape or to Mozart three times a week, if possible. Follow-up blood pressure readings were taken at one month and three months after the end of the study.

The average blood pressure for the relaxation tape group fell from 141/73 before the beginning of the study to 132/70 four months later. For the Mozart group, the average blood pressure fell from 141/71 before the study to 134/69 after the study.

After the three-month post-study period, the researchers found that only about half of the seniors had continued listening to the relaxation tapes or to Mozart three times a week. Tang said the reduction in blood pressure only persisted for those who continued with the program.

IMPLICATION

"High blood pressure is clearly a very significant and common problem. Approximately one in four people have hypertension, and about two-thirds of people with hypertension aren't adequately controlled," said cardiologist Robert Ostfeld, MD, of Montefiore Medical Center in New York City.

"This is a small, but very interesting study on a very safe and doable intervention," he added, but noted, "It's not clear if the reduction is sustained over time."

Dr. Tang said using a relaxation tape with instruction is likely a good supplementary treatment for lowering blood pressure. Eating right and exercising are also important, said both Dr. Tang and Dr. Ostfeld. "Exercise is the fountain of youth," added Dr. Ostfeld.

IMPORTANT

Both experts cautioned that relaxation exercises or listening to classical music are additional ways to help lower blood pressure, but they could not replace blood pressure medication.

info For more information on controlling blood pressure, visit the American Academy of Family Physicians' Family Doctor Web site, *http://familydoctor.org*, and search "blood pressure."

■ ■ ■ ■

A Tea that Lowers BP

Reduce blood pressure (BP) with hibiscus, commonly found in blended herbal teas, says Diane L. McKay, PhD.

Recent finding: After drinking eight ounces of hibiscus tea three times a day for six weeks, participants' systolic (top number) blood pressure dropped by an average of seven points—about as much as with standard hypertension drugs. People with higher blood pressure had an even larger drop. Pure (unblended) hibiscus tea can be found on the Internet.

Diane L. McKay, PhD, a scientist in the Antioxidants Research Laboratory at the Jean Mayer USDA Human Nutrition Research Center on Aging at Tufts University, Boston. She led a study presented at a meeting of the American Heart Association.

Turn Placebos Into Power Medicine

Richard L. Kradin, MD, a pulmonologist, internist, anatomic pathologist and researcher at Massachusetts General Hospital and associate professor of pathology at Harvard Medical School, both in Boston. He has written more than 150 medical articles and serves as codirector of Harvard Medical School's postgraduate study on Mind/Body Science. Dr. Kradin is author of *The Placebo Response and the Power of Unconscious Healing* (Routledge).

Researchers at several American institutions recently reported that half of 679 American doctors who had been surveyed said they regularly prescribed placebos to their patients. This news came as a shock to many people—and raised serious ethical questions.

Everyone knows what placebos are—"sugar pills" or "dummy pills" that masquerade as medication. But is it that simple?

There's a lot more to the question than meets the eye, according to Richard L. Kradin, MD, one of the country's foremost experts on the use of placebo treatments. *He answers questions below...*

What exactly is a placebo?

It's any type of therapeutic intervention—for example, a fake or unproven medication, or a simple talk with the doctor—that, in and of itself, is judged to have no therapeutic capacity. When it works, the success is attributed to an activation of what's called the "placebo response."

How is the placebo response believed to work?

Before there were any scientific medical treatments, people got sick and got well. In species such as ours, some of these responses involve the body's ability to restore states of physical and mental well-being. This self-soothing process is key to the placebo response.

Certain memories are probably involved. For example, children are usually soothed by their parents. Their mothers kiss minor hurts to make them better. They are given pills and told the medicine will make them well. When adults are sick and receive care from someone who's supposed to help them, the situation can reawaken this capacity to be soothed. After a visit to the doctor, some people report that they feel better right away.

Can a person who has a serious illness be healed by the placebo response?

There are people who appear to have been cured of cancer by what might be termed the placebo response. In one case, an experimental chemotherapy drug—later shown to be inactive—was highly effective in a patient as long as he believed it was capable of curing his cancer. But that scenario is quite rare.

Placebos seem best able to restore well-being when problems are minor, such as a headache or stomachache. It's important to remember that the placebo response isn't necessarily separate from real therapeutic responses brought about by effective treatment, but part of them. If you take a drug that works, the placebo response may make it work better. Many of the factors involved in the placebo response have been scientifically confirmed in a number of studies on the topic.

Do placebos do more for some people than for others?

In most clinical trials, one-third of patients who receive a sugar pill feel better. But it's hard to predict which people will respond positively to placebo treatment.

Trust and expectation increase the chance of a positive response. If you believe that a drug or treatment is likely to help you, the odds are that it will work as a placebo.

If the doctor or other caregiver conveys a sense of competence and authority, and the visit to the doctor's office promotes relaxation and trust, these factors also seem to elicit the placebo response. The doctor's ability to listen and make patients feel that they're understood is important. If the doctor doesn't convey his/her own belief that the intervention will work, the chances are good that it won't work.

Can a placebo have harmful effects?

Negative, or so-called nocebo, responses are quite common. For example, about 25% of participants in clinical trials report side effects after receiving a harmless pill. Similarly, a certain proportion of adverse reactions to prescribed medications are no doubt due to the nocebo response.

Here, too, expectation plays a role. Nocebo effects commonly occur after a patient reads the drug package insert that lists, often in alarming detail, a medication's potential side effects. The health-care provider can elicit the nocebo response, too. People sometimes leave the office of a brusque, uncaring doctor feeling much worse, and getting little benefit from the medication the doctor prescribed. If a caregiver expresses too many doubts about the treatment, patients detect that as well.

Is it ethical for a doctor to prescribe a drug as a placebo without the patient's consent?

In many situations, with many types of people, conveying the entire truth, including doubts surrounding the treatment, may not be in the patient's best interest in terms of therapeutic outcome. On the other hand, if a doctor is caught prescribing a placebo, he risks losing his credibility. Most placebos are prescribed unwittingly by doctors who prescribe a medication "off-label"—for an unapproved use—in the belief that it will help.

By the same token, when I talk in detail with a patient about a particular drug's potential side effects, as mandated by law, I can see fear well up in his face. Is that the role of a healer? I'm not so sure.

Can medical consumers harness the power of their own placebo responses?

Yes. In choosing a health professional, you should try to find someone you can trust and have confidence in. Don't go to anyone who doesn't evoke this trust. It's possible for a doctor to be brusque and still convey the confidence that a patient needs. Some people respond well to that kind of personality.

Know yourself. If you leave a treatment situation feeling doubtful and not reassured, you're probably in the wrong place.

How can you minimize nocebo effects?

I suggest to my patients that they read the medication package insert only if they experience a side effect, to check whether it is a common one. I believe it's better to stay modestly informed—and to respect the expertise of the doctor or other health professional.

Important: Any side effect that is not short-lived should be reported to your physician so that potentially serious adverse reactions are not missed.

You should be a working partner in your treatment and have some idea of what's going on. But when people start involving themselves in the fine details, it tends to have a disturbing effect on mind-body processes—either resulting in a nocebo response or limiting the advantages of the placebo response.

Wristbands Ease Nausea After Radiation

University of Rochester Medical Center news release.

Acupressure wristbands might help cancer patients experience nearly 25% less nausea during radiation treatments, a recent study says.

The finding, published in the *Journal of Pain and Symptom Management*, also discounted the common belief that such non-Western medical treatments act more as a placebo than an effective treatment.

"We know the placebo effect exists—the problem is that we don't know how to measure it very well," said study author Joseph A. Roscoe, PhD, a research associate professor at the James P. Wilmot Cancer Center at the University of Rochester Medical Center. "In this study, we attempted to manipulate the information we gave to patients to see if their expectations about nausea could be changed. As it turned out, our information to change people's expectations had no effect, but we still found that the wristbands reduce nausea symptoms."

The wristbands put pressure on a "nausea point" identified by traditional Chinese acupuncture. The pressure acts to change the flow of chi (energy), according to the Eastern belief.

THE STUDY

The study involved 88 people who experienced nausea after radiation treatments for cancer. Some were given wristbands to wear, and the others were not. And about half of those in the wristband group were also given information that explicitly said the wristbands cut down on nausea, whereas handouts given to the others with wristbands contained more neutral information.

THE RESULTS

Those with wristbands experienced a 24% decrease in nausea, regardless of which set of information they were given before the experiment. The group without wristbands reported just a 5% lessening of nausea.

info For more information about alternative therapies that stimulate the flow of energy, visit the Web site of the Alternative Medicine Foundation, *www.amfoundation.org/energywork.htm.*

Acupuncture Cuts Dry Mouth in Cancer Patients

University of Texas M.D. Anderson Cancer Center news release.

Acupuncture reduces severe dry mouth (*xerostomia*) among patients receiving radiation for head and neck cancer, a small pilot study suggests.

BACKGROUND

"The quality of life in patients with radiation-induced xerostomia is profoundly impaired," said study senior author Mark S. Chambers, DMD, a professor in the dental oncology department at the University of Texas M.D. Anderson Cancer Center in Houston. "Symptoms can include altered taste, dental decay, infections of the tissues of the mouth, and difficulty with speaking, eating and swallowing. Conventional treatments have been less than optimal, providing short-term response at best."

THE STUDY

This study included 19 patients with xerostomia who'd completed radiation therapy at least four weeks earlier. They were given two acupuncture treatments a week for four weeks. Acupuncture points used in the treatment were located on the ears, chin, index finger, forearm and lateral surface of the leg.

The acupuncture treatments resulted in improvements in physical well-being and xerostomia symptoms, the researchers said.

The study was published online in the journal *Head & Neck*.

LARGER CLINICAL TRIAL PLANNED

The researchers are planning a phase 3, placebo-controlled clinical trial.

"Although the patient population was small, the positive results are encouraging and warrant a larger trial to assess patients over a longer period of time," Dr. Chambers said.

info To learn more about dry mouth, go to the Web site of the National Institute of Dental and Craniofacial Research, *www.nidcr.nih.gov*, and search "dry mouth."

Ease Pain and Boost Your Mood with Reiki

Aurora Ocampo, RN, CNS, clinical nurse specialist at The Continuum Center for Health and Healing, Beth Israel Medical Center, New York City. *www.healthandhealingny.org*.

Reiki (pronounced RAY-key) is a healing art traced to spiritual teachings from Japan in the early 20th century. The name combines two Japanese words, *rei* (universal) and *ki* (life energy). Reiki practitioners use the technique to help ease clients' anxiety and stress...chronic or postsurgical pain...menopausal hot flashes...menstrual cramps...migraines...and nausea and fatigue from chemotherapy.

How it works: The principle is that the practitioner taps into a universal life energy that exists within and around us...then channels this energy to the client, enhancing the body's innate healing abilities. The modern scientific theory is that reiki promotes profound relaxation, increasing levels of pain-relieving, mood-boosting brain chemicals called endorphins.

What to expect: During a typical 60-minute reiki session, the client (fully dressed) sits in a chair or lies on a massage table. The practitioner places his/her hands, palms down, on or just above a dozen or so different spots on the client's body, holding each position for several minutes. Clients become deeply relaxed, and some perceive sensations of warmth or tingling at the spot being treated.

Cost of treatment: About $75 to $100 per session.

How to find a practitioner: Reiki has no formal licensing process, so locating an experienced practitioner is largely a matter of word-of-mouth.

Helpful: Get a referral from a local hospital that has an integrative medicine center.

Bottom line: While no large-scale clinical trials on reiki have yet been done, studies show benefits from various touch therapies. There are no negative effects from reiki. If you have a serious health problem, try reiki as an adjunct to standard medical treatment. Some people say that reiki works only due to a placebo effect—and that may be so. However, practitioners often encounter clients who are skeptical at first...but who, after experiencing reiki firsthand, report that the therapy has helped them.

Drug-Free Ways to Fight Colds

Effie Poy Yew Chow, PhD, RN, founder and president of East West Academy of Healing Arts in San Francisco, *www.eastwestqi.com*. A licensed acupuncturist, qigong grandmaster and registered psychiatric and public health nurse, she was appointed by President Clinton to the original 15-member White House Commission on Complementary and Alternative Medicine Policy. Dr. Chow is coauthor of *Miracle Healing from China: Qigong* (Medipress) and a member of the *Bottom Line/Women's Health* advisory board.

When a cold makes you miserable, you want relief fast. But drugs designed to ease cold symptoms can have side effects—increased blood pressure and heart rate, gastric upset, blurred vision, trouble concentrating, insomnia.

Instead, I recommend the practices of traditional Chinese medicine, which have been used for thousands of years. These practices may ease inflammation...fight infection...boost the immune system...and promote the healthful flow of qi (energy) through the body.

YIN OR YANG?

According to traditional Chinese medicine, two seemingly opposing yet interdependent natural forces called yin and yang must be in balance for a person to maintain good health. When one force predominates, illness results.

Colds can be characterized as either yin or yang. With a yin cold, you have chills...feel exhausted...and want to crawl into bed. With a yang cold, you have a fever...perspire...and feel agitated. *To reestablish the body's natural balance...*

•**Feed a yin cold**—primarily with yang foods. Yang foods are warming. Generally, they include meat, chicken and fish...and vegetables that grow in the earth, such as carrots, beets, jicama, turnips and yams. Eat as much as you comfortably can. Drink three six-ounce cups of ginger tea daily—ginger has anti-inflammatory and antiseptic effects.

Also soothing: Submerge yourself up to your earlobes in a bathtub of comfortably hot water mixed with Epsom salts.

•**For a yang cold, eat lightly.** Avoid yang foods, and focus on cooling yin foods—especially green vegetables, sprouts, fruits and other foods that grow in the open air. Drink eight to 10 cups of water daily. Also drink two or three cups of garlic tea daily—garlic is an antibacterial, antiviral and anti-inflammatory agent.

To make garlic tea: Boil a cup of water...add a clove of garlic cut in half...steep five to 10 minutes...remove garlic...add honey and lemon juice to taste.

Also helpful: Use garlic liberally in cooking.

TIME-HONORED REMEDIES

Many traditional treatments may be helpful no matter what type of cold you have. Products mentioned below are sold at health-food stores, Asian markets and/or online. Check with your health-care provider before taking supplements, especially if you have a chronic health condition or take any medication. *Consider...*

•**Loquat syrup.** Made from the yellow pear-shaped loquat fruit, this syrup quiets coughs and soothes sore throats. Try a brand called Nin Jiom Pei Pa Koa cough syrup or a natural loquat extract. See product labels for dosage guidelines.

•**White Flower Analgesic Balm.** This brand-name product combines essential oils of wintergreen, menthol, camphor, eucalyptus, peppermint and lavender.

To relieve nasal congestion: Put a drop of White Flower on your palm, rub palms together, then bring your hands up to your nose (avoiding the eyes) and inhale for four to eight breaths. Repeat up to four times daily as needed.

To ease headache or body aches: Massage a few drops into achy areas. May be used up to four times daily.

•**Acupressure.** This practice stimulates certain points along the body's meridians (energy channels) to eliminate qi blockages. To open sinuses, squeeze the acupressure point on the fleshy area between your thumb and index finger, near the thumb joint. The more blocked your qi is, the more tender this spot may feel. Apply enough pressure to cause mild discomfort. Hold for several minutes, then switch sides. Repeat as needed.

•**Acupuncture.** This can clear even serious sinus congestion, sometimes in a single session. The acupuncturist inserts one or more very fine needles at specific points on the body, depending on the individual's needs, to restore qi flow.

Referrals: American Association of Acupuncture and Oriental Medicine (866-455-7999, *www.aaaomonline.org*).

•**Cupping.** Some acupuncturists and massage therapists provide this treatment. A small glass or bamboo cup is heated and then placed on the person's back for about five minutes. The heat creates a vacuum that pulls on the skin and underlying muscle, improving qi flow and blood circulation to bring healing nutrients to the body's tissues. Cupping sometimes leaves a red mark on the skin—not a burn, just a result of the suction—which fades within a few days. If the practitioner opts to leave the cup on the back for a longer period of time, slight bruising may result—but again, this soon fades.

•**Diaphragmatic breath work.** This technique uses the diaphragm as a piston to improve oxygen flow and blood circulation and relieve congestion. Sit or stand up straight to allow lungs to fill...gently draw in air through your nose (if you're not too congested), letting your abdomen expand outward...then pull your abdomen in so that it pushes the air out through your mouth. Continue for one minute. Consciously repeat several times daily, aiming for this to become the way you automatically breathe throughout the day.

• **Tui na massage.** This Chinese system of massage vigorously stimulates acupressure points and manipulates muscles and joints to promote qi flow. To find a practitioner, contact the National Certification Commission for Acupuncture and Oriental Medicine (904-598-1005, *www.nccaom.org*), and check for practitioners certified in "Asian bodywork." Other types of massage also can be helpful.

■ **More from Dr. Chow...**

Nutrients that Keep You Cold-Free

The best defense against colds is to avoid getting them in the first place. That requires a strong immune system—and certain nutrients can help.

Advised: In addition to a daily multivitamin, take any or all of the following supplements. For maximum effect, use year-round.

• **Coenzyme Q10 (CoQ10).** This vitamin-like substance boosts cellular energy. *Recommended dosage:* 100 milligrams (mg) to 200 mg twice daily.

• **Fish oil.** This is rich in the omega-3 fatty acids eicosapentaenoic acid (EPA) and docosahexaenoic acid (DHA), which reduce disease-promoting inflammation. Take fish oil liquid or capsules at a dosage that provides 3,000 mg daily of combined EPA and DHA.

• **Vitamin D.** This is a fat-soluble vitamin that benefits the body in many ways, including by strengthening the immune system. I recommend taking 2,000 international units (IU) daily of vitamin D-3 (cholecalciferol).

Alternative: Take one teaspoon of cod-liver oil daily for each 50 pounds of body weight.

Natural Ways to Prevent Pneumonia

Jamison Starbuck, ND, a naturopathic physician in family practice in Missoula, Montana. She is past president of the American Association of Naturopathic Physicians and a contributing editor to *The Alternative Advisor: The Complete Guide to Natural Therapies and Alternative Treatments* (Time-Life).

Even though many people think of pneumonia as a wintertime illness, it can strike during any season of the year. It can be caused by one of many different types of bacteria, viruses, fungi—or even an injury, such as exposure to chemical fumes (from a chlorine spill, for example). People who are at greatest risk for pneumonia are older adults and newborns, smokers, heavy drinkers, people with preexisting lung disease or compromised immune systems, or anyone who is bedridden or has limited mobility (which increases risk for buildup of mucus in the lungs). Fortunately, you can take steps to protect yourself. *My secrets to avoiding pneumonia...*

• **Consider getting a pneumonia vaccination.** Discuss the vaccine with your doctor if you are age 65 or older—or at any age if you have congestive heart failure, a compromised immune system, liver or lung disease or diabetes, or if you are a smoker or heavy drinker. The vaccine can help prevent a common type of pneumonia caused by the *Streptococcus pneumoniae* bacterium.

• **Take vitamin A daily.** Vitamin A deficiency can cause drying of the respiratory-tract lining and a reduction in cilia, the hairlike tissues that move mucus and debris out of the lungs. Both changes make the lungs vulnerable to infection and inflammation. A total daily dose of 10,000 international units (IU) of vitamin A can help keep your lungs healthy.

Caution: Vitamin A is toxic when consumed in high doses over long periods of time. Consult your doctor before taking more than 10,000 IU of vitamin A daily. If you have liver disease or are pregnant, do not take supplemental vitamin A. In addition, some research suggests that smokers should not take vitamin A supplements.

•**Get more vitamin C daily.** The results of studies on the immune-enhancing effects of vitamin C have been mixed. However, I'm convinced—based on my clinical experience—that a daily dose of vitamin C does, in fact, help the immune system resist disease and is essential to combating the immune-draining effects of stress, a chief cause of illness.

I recommend a daily total of 1,000 milligrams (mg) of vitamin C.

•**Treat upper respiratory infections (URIs) promptly and effectively.** Quite often, pneumonia develops from the spread of inflammation caused by a viral infection, such as bronchitis. My advice: Rest (forgo your usual activities, including going to work)...and hydrate (drink 68 ounces of water daily). For a cold or bronchitis, I recommend drinking a tincture made from extracts of the powerful antiviral botanical medicines elder, echinacea, eyebright and licorice—15 drops of each in one ounce of water, 15 minutes before or after meals, every four waking hours for several days.

Caution: Omit licorice if you have high blood pressure or heart disease—the herb may affect blood pressure or cause heart problems.

•**Don't delay a doctor visit if you suspect pneumonia.** Typical symptoms include a cough, fever, shortness of breath and fatigue. An early diagnosis increases your chance of a good outcome.

■ ■ ■ ■

Osteoarthritis Eased by Topical Remedies

In a study of 204 people with osteoarthritis of the hands, those who rubbed *arnica* gel (an herbal remedy) over their affected joints three times a day for 21 days had similar improvements in pain, grip strength and hand-function measures as those who used 5% *ibuprofen* gel. Unlike oral ibuprofen and other nonsteroidal anti-inflammatory medications, topical arnica and ibuprofen gel generally do not cause stomach upset.

Theory: Both of these therapies have anti-inflammatory effects. If you have osteoarthritis of the hands ask your doctor if arnica gel or ibuprofen gel is appropriate for you.

Jörg Melzer, MD, researcher, Institute of Complementary Medicine, University of Zurich, Switzerland.

Nine Ways to Keep Joints Young

Joanne M. Jordan, MD, MPH, professor and chief of the division of rheumatology, allergy and immunology, University of North Carolina, and director of the Thurston Arthritis Research Center, both in Chapel Hill. She is the principal investigator on numerous large clinical studies.

Exciting developments are occurring in the field of arthritis research. In many cases, even among people who are genetically predisposed to arthritis, unless there also is an environmental or lifestyle trigger (being a smoker, for instance) to spur the onset of the disease, chances are good that arthritis will never develop.

What this means: Far from being an inevitable result of aging or an inescapable fate for those with a family history of the disease, arthritis is quite possibly preventable...and many of the same strategies that guard against the development of arthritis also help slow its progress, making the condition more manageable if you do get it.

What it is: Arthritis is an umbrella term for more than 100 conditions that affect the joints. Osteoarthritis, which is by far the most common type, involves the deterioration of the cartilage that covers the ends of bones, leading to pain and loss of movement as bone rubs against bone. Among young adults, osteoarthritis most often is seen in men—but after age 45, women sufferers outnumber men. Second-most common is rheumatoid arthritis, an autoimmune disease in which the immune system attacks and inflames the *synovium* (membrane lining the joints). One of the most severe types of arthritis, it affects women twice as often as it does men.

What to do: Follow the steps below to help prevent various types of arthritis...

• **Reduce the weight load on your knees.** The more you weigh, the more likely you are to get arthritis in the knees.

Helpful: Even if genes place you at increased risk, dropping your excess weight—or perhaps even as little as 10 to 12 pounds—makes your arthritis risk drop, too.

• **Guard against joint injury.** People who have had any type of knee or shoulder injury are more likely to eventually develop arthritis in that joint than people with no such history of injury.

Prudent: To help prevent neuromuscular injuries that can place added stress on joints, warm up for five minutes before you exercise or perform any strenuous activity (shoveling snow, moving furniture)...and stretch afterward. Watch out for hazards that could lead to falls and bone fractures, such as icy sidewalks and cluttered floors.

• **Avoid repetitive motions.** Some evidence suggests a link between osteoarthritis and activities that require repetitive use of specific joints, such as continuous typing or cashiering.

Self-defense: Vary your motions as much as possible...and take frequent breaks.

• **Minimize exposure to infection.** Arthritis can develop after a person contracts certain infections, such as salmonella, erythema infectiosum ("fifth disease") or hepatitis B.

Theory: These infections trigger cellular damage, especially in people genetically predisposed to arthritis.

Precautions: Wash hands often...avoid contact with people who have infections.

• **Stay away from cigarettes.** Toxic chemicals in smoke appear to damage joint fibers—so refrain from smoking and minimize your exposure to secondhand smoke.

To quit smoking: Visit *www.smokefree.gov* for referrals to quit lines and advice on how to stop smoking.

• **Exercise for 75 minutes or more each week.** In a recent study, women in their 70s who exercised for at least an hour and 15 minutes weekly for three years reported significantly fewer joint problems than women who exercised less. Doubling that workout time was even more beneficial.

Good options: Walking, tai chi, yoga, swimming, weight lifting.

• **Eat the "Big Three" anti-arthritis antioxidants.** Antioxidants neutralize molecules called free radicals that cause tissue damage. Some observational studies suggest that three in particular may guard against arthritis.

Findings: In a study of more than 25,000 people, researchers found that those who developed arthritis ate, on average, 20% less *zeaxanthin* and 40% less *beta-cryptoxanthine* than those who did not get arthritis. Both of these antioxidants are found in yellow-orange fruits and vegetables (apricots, pineapple, peppers, winter squash)...zeaxanthin also is found in leafy green vegetables (arugula, chicory, kale, spinach). Another study of 400 people showed that those with the highest blood levels of *lutein*—also found in leafy greens—were 70% less likely to have knee arthritis than those with the lowest levels.

Sensible: Boost your intake of foods rich in these three important antioxidants.

• **Get the "Top Two" vitamins.** In one study of 556 people, those with the lowest blood levels of vitamin D were three times more likely to have knee osteoarthritis than participants with the highest levels. A larger clinical study is in progress, so it is too early to make specific recommendations—but it probably is wise to include plenty of vitamin D–rich foods (such as fish and low- or nonfat dairy) in your diet.

Observational studies also suggest that vitamin C helps keep arthritis from progressing—perhaps by stimulating the production of collagen, cartilage and other connective tissues in the joints.

Healthful: Foods high in vitamin C include citrus fruits, peppers and sweet potatoes.

• **Do not neglect omega-3 fatty acids.** These natural anti-inflammatories appear to reduce the risk of developing arthritis (especially rheumatoid) and to ease symptom severity in people who already have the disease.

Best: Ask your doctor about taking fish oil supplements that provide the omega-3s *eicosapentaenoic acid* (EPA) and *docosahexaenoic acid* (DHA).

Interesting: You have an advantage if you were born, raised and currently live in the western part of the US.

Recent finding: Compared with women in the West, those in other areas of the country have a 37% to 45% higher risk for rheumatoid arthritis.

Possible influences: Regional differences in lifestyle, diet, environmental exposures and/or genetic factors.

What to do: You can't necessarily change where you live, of course—but if your location suggests an increased risk for arthritis, you can be extra conscientious about following the self-defense strategies above.

■ ■ ■ ■

Omega-3 Eases Some Alzheimer's Symptoms

Supplementing with 2.3 grams daily of omega-3 fatty acids reduced agitation in Alzheimer's disease patients who carried the APOE gene (revealed by genetic testing)...and eased depression in patients without the gene.

Maria Eriksdotter Jönhagen, MD, PhD, associate professor, department of neurobiology, Karolinska Institutet, Sweden, and researcher of a study of 200 Alzheimer's patients, published in *International Journal of Geriatric Psychiatry*.

■ ■ ■ ■

Fight Hot Flashes with Supplements

In a study of 120 menopausal women, one group took omega-3 fatty acid supplements three times daily for eight weeks, while another group took placebos.

Result: Among women who had hot flashes before the study began, those who took omega-3 supplements had an average of 1.6 fewer hot flashes daily, compared with a decrease of 0.50 in the placebo group.

Theory: Omega-3s may play a role in regulating the interaction of brain chemicals that have been linked to hot flashes.

If you have hot flashes: Ask your doctor about trying an omega-3 supplement.

Michel Lucas, PhD, epidemiologist and nutritionist, Laval University, Quebec City, Canada.

■ ■ ■ ■

Ease Symptoms of Lupus

This chronic inflammatory disease can affect many body systems and organs.

Recent study: Lupus patients who took 3 grams of omega-3 fish oil supplements daily for 24 weeks showed significant improvement in lupus symptoms, such as fatigue, joint pain, skin rashes and mouth ulcers. Cardiovascular benefits: There also was an improvement in blood vessel function and a reduction in cell-damaging molecules.

Best: Patients with lupus should ask their doctors about daily supplementation with omega-3 fish oils.

Stephen Wright, MD, specialist registrar in rheumatology, Queen's University of Belfast, Northern Ireland, and lead investigator of a study on fish oils and lupus, presented at a meeting of the American College of Rheumatology.

Soothe MS Symptoms—Naturally

Mark A. Stengler, ND, naturopathic physician in private practice, La Jolla, California...adjunct associate clinical professor at the National College of Natural Medicine, Portland, Oregon...author of many books and the *Bottom Line/Natural Healing* newsletter.

Regular B vitamin injections, especially B-12 (weekly during flare-ups or monthly for prevention) can help alleviate some of the troubling symptoms of multiple sclerosis (MS), such as fatigue, blurred vision, loss of balance and tremors. Extra doses of B vitamin supplements taken daily to prevent flare-ups also work well. In addition, taking vitamin D at high levels—3,000 international units (IU) daily—may be a worthwhile consideration. This may help reduce inflammation, which can bring about or worsen symptoms, and balance the immune system, which is thrown off kilter in patients with MS. Supplements of calcium (500 milligrams/mg) and magnesium (250 mg), both taken twice daily, can help with muscle spasms.

Other recommendations: Patients should avoid eating foods that can trigger symptoms—margarine...cooking oils, such as safflower and corn oil...packaged foods that list hydrogenated oils...and saturated fats (found in red meat and whole milk), and opt for more polyunsaturated fats, such as flaxseeds, flax oil and hempseed oil, and fish, such as sardines and salmon. MS patients also may benefit from a daily dose of supplemental fish oil. I recommend taking 1,500 mg of *eicosapentaenoic acid* (EPA) and *docosahexaenoic acid* (DHA) and 500 mg of *gamma-linoleic acid* (check labels).

Weight Loss Supplements—What Works...What Won't

Jane Guiltinan, ND, a clinical professor at Bastyr Center for Natural Health, Seattle. She is also a past president of the American Association of Naturopathic Physicians.

Unscrupulous marketers claim that three supplements suppress appetite. Should you try them? No. *What doesn't work—and what does...*

• **Never take ephedra (*ma huang*).** This stimulant does suppress appetite—but at the price of increased heart rate, nervousness and agitation. In moderate-to-large doses, ephedra has killed people. The FDA banned ephedra from dietary supplements in the US in 2004—yet it still is marketed illegally.

• **Skip *garcinia cambogia*.** This fruit from India contains a compound called *hydroxycitrate*. In animal studies, rats given hydroxycitrate ate less and lost weight—but there is no evidence that garcinia has the same effect on humans. Short-term studies (12 weeks) have not revealed safety problems, but no long-term studies have been done.

• **Don't waste money on hoodia.** A plant found in Africa, hoodia is said to fool your brain into thinking that you're full. It is not a stimulant, so it's probably safe—but no published long-term studies on humans show that it's effective.

• **Do drink plenty of water.** People often mistake thirst for hunger and eat when they should be hydrating.

• **Opt for hot tea or coffee.** In my experience, hot beverages curb hunger better than cold drinks do. Also, caffeine is a stimulant with a mild appetite-suppressing effect. To avoid insomnia, limit caffeinated beverages to a few per day.

• **Eat "volume" foods that fill you up—** such as high-fiber, low-calorie carrots, broccoli, salad greens, apples and brown rice.

• **Eat more often.** Go no more than three hours without a regular meal or a healthful snack, such as nut butter on whole-grain crackers. Otherwise, you end up so ravenous that when you do eat, you're more likely to consume too many calories and make poor food choices.

• **Curb sugar cravings.** Supplement with 100 micrograms twice daily of the mineral chromium—it may lessen sugar cravings by stabilizing blood sugar levels. Or consider the herb gymnema sylvestre, which may temporarily block sweet taste receptors on the tongue and also help stabilize blood sugar. Speak to a health-care professional who is knowledgeable about botanical medicine to determine the proper dosage. If you take medication to control blood sugar, do not use either supplement without your doctor's approval.

Eight Ways to Great Digestion

Jamison Starbuck, ND, a naturopathic physician in family practice in Missoula, Montana. She is past president of the American Association of Naturopathic Physicians and a contributing editor to *The Alternative Advisor: The Complete Guide to Natural Therapies and Alternative Treatments* (Time-Life).

Though sometimes overlooked by doctors, gastrointestinal (GI) health is fundamental to overall wellness. The GI tract, also known as the "gut," allows us to draw nourishment from our food and eliminate toxins. A variety of medications claim to promote intestinal health, but I prefer my own eight-step natural approach, which is both inexpensive and easy to follow. Add one new step each day. If you're like most people, your GI tract will be healthier within two weeks. *My advice...*

•**Avoid foods that cause indigestion.** Indigestion is your body's way of telling you that a certain food is not readily digestible. Instead of trying to make a food digestible by taking drugs, choose foods that you can easily digest, such as fish, brown rice and steamed vegetables.

•**Shortly after awakening in the morning, drink an eight-ounce glass of room-temperature water.** This "wakes up" the GI tract, preparing you for both digestion and elimination. Repeat this step five to 10 minutes before each meal. Avoid iced beverages, including water, with meals and 15 minutes before and afterward. Some research suggests that cold beverages decrease the secretion of digestive enzymes.

•**Squeeze fresh lemon or sprinkle vinegar on your food.** For most people, one-half teaspoon of lemon or vinegar per meal fights indigestion by increasing stomach acidity and improving the digestion of fats.

•**Take a 15-minute walk after meals.** Doing so will improve your digestion and elimination. If you can't do this after every meal, do so following the largest meal of the day.

•**Practice simple home hydrotherapy.** This practice increases blood flow to your intestines, which helps them function properly.

What to do: Finish your daily shower or bath with a 30-second spray of cool or cold water to your entire abdomen. Towel dry with brisk strokes immediately after the cool water spray.

Caution: If you have a history of stroke, check with your doctor before trying hydrotherapy.

•**Drink chamomile or peppermint tea after dinner.** These herbs soothe the lining of the stomach and intestines. Add one tea bag or two teaspoons of loose herb to eight ounces of water.

•**Use foot reflexology to relieve intestinal pain.** Massaging reflexology points on the feet is thought to help increase blood flow to and improve the function of corresponding organs or body parts.

What to do: Whenever you have GI discomfort, firmly massage (for five to seven minutes) with your thumb and forefinger the outside portion of the middle one-third of the soles of the feet. According to reflexologists, this area corresponds to the colon. Your strokes should move toward the heel.

•**Never eat when you are stressed.** Our bodies are not designed to simultaneously manage both stress and digestion. Studies show that just a few moments of relaxation, such as deep breathing or prayer, before a meal will improve the digestive process.

■ ■ ■ ■

Try Probiotics for Hay Fever

In a five-month study of 20 hay fever sufferers, one group drank about two ounces daily of yogurt containing 6.5 billion *Lactobacillus casei Shirota* (LcS), a strain of beneficial bacteria (probiotic), while the other drank yogurt without LcS.

Result: Participants who drank the probiotic drink had significantly lower blood levels of immunoglobulin E, an antibody associated with hay fever symptoms, than those who drank yogurt without LcS.

Kamal Ivory, PhD, cellular immunologist, Institute of Food Research, Norwich, UK.

IBS Expert Reveals How To Halt Symptoms Now

Nicholas J. Talley, MD, professor of medicine at the Mayo Clinic College of Medicine and chair of the department of internal medicine at Mayo Clinic Florida, both in Jacksonville. An internationally known expert on IBS, Dr. Talley has had more than 500 articles published in medical journals and is author of *Conquering Irritable Bowel Syndrome* (BC Decker).

Are you nervous about venturing too far from your bathroom for fear of a sudden attack of diarrhea? Or do you live in dread of your next spell of days-on-end constipation? Either way, the culprit could be *irritable bowel syndrome* (IBS).

This condition afflicts up to 20% of Americans—and two to three times as many women as men. Patients may experience constipation, diarrhea or both...plus abdominal pain, bloating and/or nausea. Symptoms may be constant...or flare up in response to specific triggers...or pop up at random. No medical tests can confirm IBS—nothing shows up in blood or stool samples, X-rays or even exploratory surgery to examine the digestive tract.

No one knows exactly what causes IBS, but research suggests four main components...

- **Genetics.** IBS tends to cluster in families.
- **Inflammation.** Many people have their first IBS bout after an intestinal infection... which causes inflammation in the gut (digestive tract)...which provokes physiological changes that render the gut vulnerable to certain triggers long after the infection is gone.
- **Intestinal organisms.** Billions of beneficial bacteria grow in the gut. With IBS, this "garden" may be altered through a change in the type or balance of bacteria present.
- **Brain–gut link.** The brain and gut "cross-talk." That's why anxiety can affect the digestive system—for instance, causing butterflies in your stomach when you're nervous.

New finding: Gut changes from IBS can cause depression. The gut has receptors for serotonin, a nerve communication chemical that promotes feelings of well-being. If the gut is unhappy, the brain often becomes unhappy.

If you have persistent symptoms, see a gastroenterologist. IBS is diagnosed by ruling out other possible causes of symptoms, such as a parasitic infection, celiac disease or colon cancer.

FLARE-UP PREVENTION

Once a bout of IBS gets started, it is hard to quell—so it is best to keep symptoms from flaring up.

- **Take a probiotic supplement to add "good" bacteria to the gut.** Best is *Bifidobacterium infantis,* which may dampen the inflammatory response, improving regularity and reducing bloating.

Recommended: Nonprescription Align (800-208-0112, *www.aligngi.com*), one capsule daily. Try it for a month. If it doesn't help, stop. If it does help, continue indefinitely.

- **Identify your food sensitivities.** Certain foods trigger gut inflammation in certain people.

Common culprits: Chocolate, coffee, corn, dairy, eggs, nuts, onions, wheat. Pick one food, and eliminate it from your diet for five days to see if you feel better...then reinstate it, and see if you feel worse. Test foods one by one, swearing off those that bring on symptoms. If you have trouble identifying problem foods, consult a nutritionist.

- **Move your body to get your bowels moving properly, too.** Bloating and pain can make walking, even at a moderate pace, feel awkward—so experiment with various workouts to find one that's comfortable.
- **Reduce stress.** Get enough rest. Relaxing: Have a weekly massage, practice yoga, go to the movies with friends, try a new hobby.
- **Consider hypnosis.** Studies suggest that hypnosis may help IBS patients.

Referrals: National Board for Certified Clinical Hypnotherapists (301-608-0123, *www.natboard.com*).

HELP FOR ACUTE SYMPTOMS

When IBS flares up, various treatments aim to relieve individual symptoms.

For constipation...

•**First, try a fiber supplement.** Best for IBS-related constipation is *psyllium* (in nonprescription Metamucil, Fiberall and Konsyl). Because fiber may worsen bloating, start with a low daily dose, even less than the product label calls for—for instance, one-half to one teaspoon of powdered Metamucil mixed with water. Work up over one month to three to six teaspoons per day in two divided doses. Continue indefinitely.

•**Switch to a nonprescription laxative if fiber doesn't help.** Most effective is *polyethylene glycol* (PEG) 3350, found in MiraLax and GlycoLax, which pulls water into the bowel, adding moisture to stool so it passes more easily. Take one heaping teaspoon daily, dissolved in water, for as long as symptoms persist.

•**Consider prescription medication if nonprescription laxatives don't help.** The drug *lubiprostone* (Amitiza) increases secretion of fluid in the intestines, making it easier to pass stool. Side effects may include nausea, diarrhea and headache.

Caution: This drug has not been studied in women who are pregnant.

For diarrhea...

•**Take a nonprescription diarrhea drug.** I recommend Imodium Advanced, which combines *loperamide* (the active ingredient in regular Imodium) with *simethicone*, a gas reducer. The label says to take two tablets at the first sign of diarrhea plus one tablet after each loose stool. If that does not help, ask your doctor if you should try a higher dosage.

•**Try fiber.** Take one teaspoon of psyllium. If diarrhea improves within 24 hours, continue taking psyllium daily. If symptoms worsen after you take the one-teaspoon dose, try taking half a teaspoon the next day. If diarrhea again worsens or gets no better, discontinue use.

For additional symptoms...

•**Ease pain.** Take over-the-counter or prescription pain medication...or one or two enteric-coated peppermint oil capsules three times a day.

•**Minimize bloating.** Take one or two activated charcoal pills 30 minutes after meals. Do not use within two hours of taking other medications, as charcoal can interfere with other drugs.

•**Reduce nausea.** Take 1 gram (g) to 1.5 g of ginger in capsule form daily, in two divided doses. Also use acupressure—with a fingertip, firmly press for several minutes on the inside of either forearm, one inch above the wrist crease, in the center between the two tendons.

Surprising Ways a Chiropractor Can Help You

Karen Erickson, DC, a chiropractor in private practice in New York City and a spokesperson for the American Chiropractic Association. She is author of several academic texts on the role of chiropractic in integrative health care and is on the board of trustees at New York Chiropractic College, New York City.

Well-designed studies have shown that chiropractic care (often just called "chiropractic") is at least as effective—and sometimes more effective—than conventional medicine for treating certain types of physical complaints.

Emerging research indicates that chiropractic affects more than just the spine and surrounding muscles. It has been used to successfully treat a variety of conditions, including digestive complaints and ear infections.

Ways chiropractic can help...

DIGESTIVE DISORDERS

A survey of 1,494 patients found that 22% reported digestive relief following chiropractic treatments, even though the majority had never mentioned any digestive issues to their chiropractors.

Many of the spinal nerves that are affected by chiropractic manipulation control digestive functions. Patients who undergo routine manipulations may experience changes in their levels of digestive fluids, the speed at which food moves through the intestinal tract or the strength and/or frequency of intestinal contractions.

We're often told by patients that manipulations for, say, neck or low-back pain not only helped their musculoskeletal complaints but also resulted in improvement in constipation, irritable bowel syndrome and other digestive issues.

Digestive problems need to be medically diagnosed first, but the most effective treatments involve an integrative approach, which can include chiropractic. I often get referrals from medical doctors of patients with constipation, colitis or irritable bowel syndrome.

Help for colic: A study published in *Journal of Manipulative and Physiological Therapeutics* found that colicky babies treated with chiropractic cried about three hours less daily than they did before, compared with a one-hour reduction in those given the drug *dimethicone*, a standard treatment. The manipulations given to children are very gentle. Many have a reduction in colic after just one or two treatments. Look for a chiropractor who specializes in the problems of children.

TENSION HEADACHE

The headaches that we all get from time to time often are related to the cervical spine in the neck. Known as *cervicogenic* headaches, these occur when vertebral misalignments cause muscle tightness or spasms. The tension begins in the neck but can radiate through the occipital nerves that rise upward from the base of the skull.

A study that compared patients receiving chiropractic care for tension headaches with those who were treated with the antidepressant *amitriptyline* showed reduction in both the frequency and pain intensity of these types of headaches. Most important, the chiropractic patients sustained these improvements after the treatment period, unlike patients who were treated with medication.

In a typical treatment, the chiropractor attempts to realign the cervical joints by manipulating the neck and head. The main goals of the treatment, apart from adjusting the vertebrae, are to increase the patient's range of motion, relax the surrounding muscles and decrease pain and inflammation.

People who have only recently started getting headaches often will improve after one or two sessions with a chiropractor. Those who have suffered from headaches for years probably will require multiple treatments before they start to notice a significant improvement.

Also important: The chiropractor will take a detailed history to learn why there is excess misalignment in the neck. This usually is due to lifestyle issues. For example, many of us look down at our computer monitors, which puts excessive tension on the neck. Raising the monitor to eye level can correct this. Women may be advised to carry a handbag rather than a heavy shoulder bag. Cradling your phone between your neck and shoulder also can cause problems. If you often find yourself doing this, get a headset.

It's not clear if chiropractic is as effective for migraines, but preliminary research suggests that chiropractic manipulations may affect nerves that control vascular expansion and contraction, a key component of migraines.

EAR INFECTIONS

Some adults and virtually all children accumulate fluids in the eustachian tube, the passage between the throat and middle ear. The fluid is a perfect medium for viruses and bacteria, which can cause otitis media, an infection or inflammation of the middle ear.

Many studies have shown that chiropractic can relieve and prevent ear infections without antibiotics. The treatments, which include chiropractic adjustment and massage of the lymph nodes along the neck and around the ear, help drain excess fluid. The adjustment helps regulate the nervous system, which in turn helps drain the eustachian tube and promotes long-term drainage.

SINUSITIS

People with chronic sinusitis (inflammation of the mucous membranes in the sinuses) rarely get long-term relief from antibiotics or other types of conventional medicine, such as antihistamines and decongestants. Chiropractic can sometimes relieve all or most of the typical symptoms, such as facial pain and nasal congestion.

People with chronic sinusitis often have a misalignment in the cervical vertebrae. Chiropractic adjustments may help sinuses drain more efficiently. The treatment for sinusitis also includes applying pressure to the sinuses near the eyebrows and on either side of the nose.

REPETITIVE STRESS DISORDERS

Most repetitive stress injuries, including tennis elbow, are caused by tendonitis, an inflammation of the fibrous tissue that connects muscles to bones. Carpal tunnel syndrome, another type of repetitive stress injury, is caused by nerve inflammation in the wrist.

Doctors usually treat these conditions with anti-inflammatory drugs, including steroid injections in severe cases. For carpal tunnel syndrome, surgery to "release" pressure on the nerve is sometimes recommended.

Chiropractic, a more conservative approach, is effective for virtually all types of repetitive stress disorders. Manipulations to realign joints and improve range of motion can reduce pressure on tendons and nerves. The movements also improve lymphatic drainage, which reduces inflammation, improves circulation and accelerates healing.

info To find a chiropractor, go to the American Chiropractic Association Web site, *www.amerchiro.org*, and click on the "Find a Doc" icon.

Sneeze, Laugh, Jump For Joy—Incontinence Cures That Work!

Mark A. Stengler, ND, naturopathic physician in private practice, La Jolla, California...adjunct associate clinical professor at the National College of Natural Medicine, Portland, Oregon...author of many books, including *The Natural Physician's Healing Therapies* and coauthor of *Prescription for Natural Cures* (both from Bottom Line Books)...and author of the *Bottom Line/Natural Healing* newsletter.

It's one of those topics that no one likes to talk about. Urinary incontinence, involuntary leaking of urine, can cause embarrassment, interfere with daily life and intimacy, and diminish quality of life and self-esteem.

More than 13 million Americans—most of them women—cope with the disorder. Many people turn to prescription drugs and surgery to help, but there are many natural approaches that work—without the side effects or dangers of drugs and surgery.

Incontinence occurs for many reasons. In women, it can result from thinning urethral tissue after menopause. Some studies show an increased rate of incontinence due to vaginal childbirth, which can damage or stretch the pelvic floor muscles. Other studies show that the rate of incontinence is no different in women who have not given birth vaginally.

Additional risk factors: Pelvic surgeries... prolonged straining due to chronic constipation...repetitive heavy lifting...obesity...urinary tract infections...smoking and lung disease (with chronic cough)...some diseases, including multiple sclerosis, diabetes and Parkinson's disease...stroke...spinal cord injury ...and a number of medications, including muscle relaxants.

Men, too, are affected by all types of incontinence. In addition to many of the factors above, prostate problems and nerve damage also can cause incontinence in men.

NATURAL APPROACHES

I spoke with one of my colleagues, Tori Hudson, ND, from Portland, Oregon, about the most effective approaches to treating incontinence in women and men. Dr. Hudson is author of *Women's Encyclopedia of Natural Medicine* (McGraw-Hill). These natural approaches and supplements treat all types of incontinence. Patients should experiment to find the approach that works best for them.

• **Lifestyle changes.** Lifestyle changes may resolve your incontinence.

Example: Losing weight—excess weight can press on the bladder, creating the urge to urinate. Other changes: Resolve constipation problems, and avoid medications that contribute to incontinence, such as diuretics, as well as caffeine (even decaffeinated drinks affect some people). Carbonated drinks, tea, citrus juices and artificial sweeteners also can aggravate the condition.

• **Exercise your muscles.** Even patients who don't have incontinence should regularly do Kegel exercises to strengthen the muscles of the pelvic floor. While mainly associated with women, Kegel exercises also can help men strengthen their pubococcygeus muscle. Studies show that in women with stress incontinence caused by bladder pressure from laughing or coughing, the faithful practice of Kegel exercises achieves a 40% to 60% reduction of the problem.

How to do Kegel exercises: Both men and women can locate their muscles the same way—by stopping the flow when urinating. To do Kegels, contract the muscles for a count of 10, release for 10, and then contract for 10. Repeat five to 10 times in a row, three times a day any time—while waiting for a red light to change...lying in bed...sitting at your desk.

A more advanced technique: For men and women who have difficulty isolating the right pelvic muscles, biofeedback, involving electrical stimulation of the pelvic muscles, can help. Sensors are placed near the pelvis. When a patient contracts the correct muscles, he/she can see the result on a computer screen and thus be trained to recognize and exercise those muscles.

An alternative for women: Cone-shaped weights are inserted into the vagina. This is for women with mild-to-moderate incontinence who have some pelvic floor strength (they must be able to hold the cones in place). Cones come in 20- to 100-gram weights. Insert the lightest for 15 to 30 minutes while going about daily activities. Weights are gradually increased as holding them becomes easier.

•**Bladder training.** Usually performed along with Kegel exercises, bladder training helps patients learn to hold urine longer. When they need to urinate, they hold their urine for five minutes before using the bathroom. When that gets easier, they hold it for 10 minutes, eventually building up to using the bathroom every three to four hours. Another technique: Scheduled bathroom trips. Patients first use the bathroom every hour and then gradually extend the time between visits.

•**Eliminate certain foods.** Food sensitivities can cause or worsen urinary incontinence, possibly by irritating the nervous system and bladder. One of my patients eliminated dairy from her diet, and it greatly improved her incontinence. Another eliminated orange juice with success. Other common sensitivities include wheat...other glutenous grains, such as barley...corn...peanuts...soy...sulfites (common food preservatives)...and sugar substitutes.

What to do: For about a month, investigate your potential food sensitivities by recording what you eat and drink. Make note of days when urine leakage is worst. If you notice a pattern, eliminate a possible problem food for several days. If you are sensitive to that food, you should see improvement within two to three days.

CONSIDER SUPPLEMENTS

Several supplements have proven successful for treating incontinence in men and women. Begin by trying one supplement at a time for two months before deciding whether it helps.

•**BetterWOMAN or BetterMAN.** These high-quality blends of more than a dozen Chinese herbs reduce all types of incontinence. In one study, women with incontinence took 400-milligram capsules twice a day for 60 days. They reported a 70% decrease in urinary urgency and a 73% decrease in urinary frequency. Follow instructions on the label (888-686-2698, *www.betterwomannow.com* for both products).

•**Uriplex.** Made of pumpkin seed extract, this herbal formula is believed to strengthen the pelvic muscles and help maintain bladder function. At least one study showed it to be about 60% successful in decreasing all types of incontinence. Available only through physicians (natural or otherwise), Uriplex is made by Integrative Therapeutics (800-931-1709, *www.integrativeinc.com*). Follow the instructions on the label.

•**Vaginal estrogen suppositories or creams.** These more conventional treatments also work—and I often recommend them to female patients. Available by prescription, these suppositories and creams can improve vaginal muscle tone and help support the bladder.

Quiet the Ringing in Your Ears

Aaron G. Benson, MD, clinical adjunct professor, division of otology/neurotology (ear health), department of otolaryngology–head and neck surgery, at the University of Michigan Health System in Ann Arbor. Also in private practice in Maumee, Ohio, he specializes in hearing disorders, *www.toledoent.com.*

Perhaps you hear a high-pitched ringing... perhaps a buzzing, chirping, whistling or whirring. Nobody else can hear it—but the quieter it gets around you, the worse the noise in your head. This bothersome condition, tinnitus, afflicts an estimated 10% to 16% of Americans.

Tinnitus most often develops when a person has hearing loss caused by nerve damage from prolonged or extreme exposure to loud noise. It also can be a side effect of antibiotics, aspirin, diuretics and some cancer drugs. Tinnitus usually appears after age 50 but is increasingly common in younger people due to high-volume use of personal music players (iPod, Walkman). It can occur during pregnancy due to increased blood volume—and may or may not go away after delivery.

Tinnitus usually is not a serious health problem, but it should be evaluated—so consult an otolaryngologist.

Referrals: American Tinnitus Association, (800-634-8978, *www.ata.org). There is no cure, but various strategies can ease symptoms and help you cope...*

- **Cut caffeine and salt.** Caffeine (in coffee, tea, cola and chocolate) constricts blood flow to the ear...and salt can raise blood pressure, aggravating tinnitus.
- **Keep ears clean.** Excessive earwax can muffle outside noises and amplify internal ringing.

Home remedy: Mix hydrogen peroxide with an equal amount of water, and place two drops in each ear weekly. Or see your doctor to have your ears irrigated.

- **Reduce stress.** Muscle relaxation, meditation, biofeedback, exercise and other techniques that reduce stress may alleviate symptoms.
- **Fill the room with white noise.** A constant low-level background sound masks the inner ringing. In a quiet room and at bedtime, turn on a fan or tabletop fountain, or use a white-noise machine (about $30 to $60 at home-products stores).
- **Wear a tinnitus masker.** This miniature white-noise device resembles a hearing aid and fits behind or in the ear.

Cost: About $2,000. To obtain one, ask your doctor for a referral to an audiologist.

- **Try a hearing aid.** This eases tinnitus for about half of people with significant hearing loss. It amplifies outside sounds, which obscures inner sounds.
- **Retrain your brain.** A new treatment provided by trained audiologists, tinnitus retraining therapy (TRT) may help up to 80% of patients. Sometimes improvement is noticed after just a few sessions. Typically, you attend weekly or monthly hour-long sessions during which you wear a special hearing aid programmed with a facsimile of your particular tinnitus sound. You are shown how to train your brain to be less sensitive to the ringing.

Rarely, tinnitus may be caused by a tumor. Call your doctor without delay if your tinnitus sounds like a pulsing or whooshing...is heard on only one side of your head...or is accompanied by dizziness or a sudden decrease in ability to discriminate between similar words, such as cat and hat.

■ ■ ■ ■

Sound Sleep Secret

Certain aromas have a calming effect that can help bring on sleep.

Helpful: Make a sachet to place under your pillow. You'll find most of the items you need at natural food stores.

In a bowl, toss together two tablespoons of corncob chips (sold as bedding at pet shops) and four drops each of lavender essential oil and lemon essential oil...cover and let stand overnight. Uncover and stir in one-half cup of dried hops...and one-quarter cup each of dried lavender buds and lemon verbena leaves. Place mixture inside a small fabric drawstring sack (about six inches square). Refill the sack with a fresh batch of herbal stuffing every two to three weeks or when the aromas start to fade.

Dorie Byers, RN, intensive care nurse and herbalist, Bargersville, Indiana, and author of *Natural Beauty Basics: Create Your Own Cosmetics and Body Care Products* (Vital Health).

Kitchen Cabinet Cures That Lower Cholesterol... Ease Pain and More

Ann Kulze, MD, a primary care physician and founder and CEO of Just Wellness, LLC, which specializes in corporate and group wellness seminars, Mt. Pleasant, South Carolina. She lectures widely on the topic of nutrition and disease prevention and routinely recommends the everyday use of disease-fighting herbs and spices. She is author of *Dr. Ann's 10-Step Diet: A Simple Plan for Permanent Weight Loss and Lifelong Vitality* (Top Ten Wellness and Fitness, *www.dranns10steps.com*).

Spices and herbs not only boost the flavor of your food, they also boost your health. Powerful plant compounds known as phytochemicals are found in high concentrations in many spices and herbs. Phytochemicals help fight heart disease, cancer, Alzheimer's, type 2 diabetes, arthritis and other diseases.

Here are the seasonings to add liberally to your food as often as possible. Unless otherwise noted, fresh herbs and spices offer a higher concentration of phytochemicals, but dried still are powerful.

SUPER SPICES

The following spices have been shown to be particularly beneficial to our health...

•**Cinnamon.** Cinnamon has an almost medicinal power. Studies have shown that cinnamon enhances the metabolism of glucose and cholesterol and thus may provide protection from type 2 diabetes and cardiovascular disease.

A study reported in *Diabetes Care* highlighted cinnamon's favorable impact on the blood fat levels of people with type 2 diabetes. After eating one to six grams (about one-quarter to one-and-one-quarter teaspoons) of cinnamon daily for 40 days, overall levels of unhealthy blood fats dropped significantly—up to 26% for total cholesterol and 30% for triglycerides (a type of blood fat).

Even healthy people can benefit from cinnamon's impact on blood sugar, according to a study in *The American Journal of Clinical Nutrition.* Adding cinnamon to rice pudding significantly decreased the test subjects' normal, post-dessert elevations of blood sugar.

Interestingly, at least some of this effect was related to the spice's ability to delay how quickly food leaves the stomach and enters the intestines. In this regard, cinnamon also may be helpful in reducing appetite and hastening weight loss by enhancing satiety (feeling full).

Suggested uses: Cinnamon can be added to oatmeal, cereal and yogurt...coffee and tea... pumpkin and apple dishes...and rice and beans for an Indian touch.

•**Turmeric.** Curcumin (turmeric's active ingredient) is a potent, naturally occurring anti-inflammatory agent. It may even be one of the best all-round spices for disease protection and antiaging. Inflammation plays a central role in most chronic diseases.

Turmeric can also be considered "brain health food." Research studies on mice demonstrate turmeric's ability to reduce the buildup of plaque in the brain that is associated with Alzheimer's and cognitive decline. Laboratory research has shown that turmeric also has potent anticancer properties.

Suggested uses: Add turmeric to your favorite bean, poultry, seafood, tofu and rice dishes, as well as to soups and stews. Turmeric often is used in classic Indian dishes, such as curries.

MORE HEALTH HELPERS

•**Cilantro.** Cilantro is high in the vitamins A and K and beta-carotene, and like any dark, leafy green, it is full of beneficial phytochemicals, including a natural antibiotic called *dodecenal.* In a University of California, Berkeley, laboratory study, dodecenal killed the bacteria *Salmonella* more effectively than a powerful prescription antibiotic.

Suggested uses: Add fresh, chopped cilantro to salsa, guacamole, omelets, salads, soups and stews.

•**Ginger.** Ginger is an anti-inflammatory superstar. It suppresses the action of inflammatory cytokines and chemokines. For people plagued with motion sickness or morning sickness or experiencing postoperative nausea and vomiting, ginger—fresh or dried—has proved to be an effective, safe option. The phytochemicals in ginger also are valuable for boosting immunity, especially to combat viral infections.

Suggested uses: Dried powdered ginger is even more potent than fresh. Add it to sauces and salad dressings, or sprinkle it on salad, poultry or seafood. You also can add a thumbnail-sized piece of raw ginger to hot tea. Ginger is delicious in its candied form, and pickled ginger is perfect with sushi.

•**Parsley.** One tablespoon of fresh parsley provides more than half of the daily recommended value of vitamin K. It's also rich in vitamin A, lutein and zeaxanthin (which promote eye health) and provides nature's most concentrated source of flavonoids, plant pigments that provide health benefits. Parsley is among those plants that may be particularly useful for combatting cancer, allergies and heart disease.

Suggested uses: Add fresh chopped parsley to salads, pasta and rice dishes, soups and stews. Parsley is a main ingredient in the Mediterranean cracked-wheat dish tabouli.

•**Rosemary.** This savory herb contains phytochemicals that can reduce the formation of cancer-causing compounds known as *heterocyclic amines* (HCAs). HCAs can form when meat is cooked at high temperatures.

Preliminary research also indicates that rosemary may enhance insulin sensitivity, improving the action and efficiency of insulin in the body, aiding in a healthy metabolism and slowing the aging process. And it turns out that Shakespeare's Ophelia wasn't all that far off when she said that rosemary is for remembrance. According to a study in *Journal of Neurochemistry*, rosemary contains the compound *carnosic acid* (CA), which helps protect the brain.

Suggested uses: I always add one teaspoon of dried rosemary or a tablespoon or two of fresh to a pound of ground meat before grilling burgers. Rosemary also is good in lamb and potato dishes, soups and stews.

Five Popular Herbs With Surprising Healing Powers

Holly Phaneuf, PhD, an expert in medicinal chemistry and the author of *Herbs Demystified* (Da Capo). She is a member of the American Chemical Society.

You may know that the tiny, fiber-rich seeds of the flax plant can be used as a laxative and that ginger helps ease nausea. But can you name any of the other health benefits provided by these plant-derived remedies?

Few people can. Yet, credible scientific evidence shows that many herbs that are well-known for treating a particular ailment have other important (but little-known) uses.* *For example...*

ARTICHOKE LEAF

Artichoke leaf extract is used by some people with mildly elevated cholesterol levels as an alternative to prescription statin drugs. Exactly how the herb works is unknown, but animal studies suggest that it inhibits *HMG CoA-reductase*, an enzyme that plays a key role in the liver's production of cholesterol.

In a placebo-controlled, randomized study conducted at the University of Reading in England, adults who took 1,280 milligrams (mg) of artichoke leaf extract daily for three months reduced their cholesterol levels by 4.2%, on average, while levels increased by 1.9%, on average, in those taking a placebo.

What else artichoke leaf can do: Calm indigestion. In a placebo-controlled, randomized study, patients rated their chronic indigestion as significantly improved after taking artichoke leaf extract twice daily for six weeks. Tests on rats suggest that the herb stimulates the gallbladder's production of bile, which helps facilitate the digestion of dietary fat.

*If you use prescription drugs and/or have a chronic medical condition, such as diabetes, cancer or heart disease, speak to your doctor before trying herbal remedies. In some cases, herbs may interfere with medication or cause an undesired effect on a chronic medical problem. Women who are pregnant or breast-feeding also should consult a doctor before taking herbs.

Typical dose: About 320 mg daily of artichoke leaf soothes digestive complaints. This dosage can be taken until the indigestion is no longer a problem.

Caution: Avoid artichoke if you are allergic to plants in the daisy family or if you have gallstones (artichoke appears to make the gallbladder contract).

FLAX

Often used as a gentle laxative, the seed of the flax plant (flaxseed) contains fiber and phytonutrients known as *lignans*—a combination that helps draw water into the gut to speed digestion. For laxative effects, eat one tablespoon of whole or ground seeds (sprinkled on cereal, for example) daily. Be sure to drink at least eight ounces of water when eating flaxseeds to prevent them from forming a temporary blockage in the intestines.

What else flaxseed can do: Help prevent cancers of the breast and prostate. Lignans form estrogen-like compounds that inhibit the body's production of the hormone in women and men. This effect is believed to reduce risk for estrogen-dependent malignancies, including some breast and prostate cancers.

Typical initial dose: One to two tablespoons of ground flaxseed daily, which can be increased gradually to as many as five tablespoons daily.

Grinding flaxseed (in a coffee grinder, for example) rather than eating it whole releases more of its cancer-fighting compounds. Also, ground flaxseed is better than flaxseed oil, which lacks the plant's beneficial lignans unless they are replaced during the manufacturing process.

Helpful: Be sure to refrigerate flaxseed to prolong freshness and preserve potency.

Caution: Do not consume flaxseed within two hours of taking an oral medication—flaxseed may interfere with absorption of the drug.

GARLIC

With its powerful blood-thinning effects, garlic is widely used to help prevent artery-blocking blood clots that can lead to a heart attack or stroke. The typical recommendation for this purpose is one clove of fresh garlic or one-half to three-quarters of a teaspoon of garlic powder per day.

What else garlic can do: Help prevent stomach and colorectal cancers. The National Cancer Institute funded an analysis of 23 clinical studies that linked garlic consumption (raw, cooked or from garlic supplements) to a 10% to 50% decrease in risk for these types of cancers. This cancer-fighting effect is believed to result from the antioxidant activity of garlic's sulfur-containing molecules. Garlic also is a popular remedy to stave off the common cold, but research on its virus-fighting properties has shown mixed results.

Recommended: A fresh crushed garlic clove four to seven times a week.

GINGER

Ginger is widely used to treat nausea, including that due to motion sickness (one-quarter to one-half teaspoon of ginger powder)...and chemotherapy (one to two teaspoons daily of ginger powder). Ginger is believed to quell queasiness by stopping intense stomach motions that can interfere with digestion.

What else ginger can do: Relieve arthritis pain. With its aspirin-like effects, ginger inhibits both COX-1 and COX-2 enzymes, two substances that are involved in the production of inflammatory hormones known as *prostaglandins.*

Typical dose: One-quarter to one-half teaspoon daily of ginger powder.

TURMERIC

In India, turmeric is a popular remedy for indigestion. It contains curcumin, an oily, yellow pigment that appears to prevent gut muscles from contracting and cramping.

What else turmeric can do: Relieve arthritis, morning stiffness and minor sprains. Turmeric reduces levels of an inflammatory, hormone-like substance known as *PGE2.* In lab studies, researchers also are finding that turmeric helps prevent colorectal and skin cancers, but its cancer-fighting mechanism has not yet been identified.

In addition, turmeric is being studied for its possible role in decreasing risk for Alzheimer's disease. Test-tube and animal studies suggest that turmeric interferes with the formation of amyloid plaque, a hallmark of this neurodegenerative disease.

Recommended: Consume turmeric powder regularly by adding it to food, such as dishes with Indian flavors.

Caution: Because turmeric can cause gallbladder contractions, people with gallbladder problems should avoid the herb.

Controversial Herb Is a Powerful Disease Fighter

Mark A. Stengler, ND, naturopathic physician in private practice, La Jolla, California...adjunct associate clinical professor at the National College of Natural Medicine, Portland, Oregon...author of many books, including *The Natural Physician's Healing Therapies* and coauthor of *Prescription for Natural Cures* (both from Bottom Line Books)...and author of the *Bottom Line/Natural Healing* newsletter.

The herb wormwood (*Artemisia absinthium*) has a long history of use in Europe and China as a remedy for digestive disorders. But wormwood has been dogged by controversy. That's because it is a flavoring and color agent in absinthe, an alcoholic beverage that was banned in the US and Europe in the early 1900s because it was thought to cause hallucinations and even insanity. A component of wormwood—the chemical thujone—was believed to have these mind-altering properties. But some experts have since questioned the science behind this belief, and in the 1990s, Europe lifted the ban on the manufacture and consumption of absinthe...without any related increase in mental illness. In 2007, the US government began allowing thujone-free absinthe to be imported into the country, and herbal wormwood is widely available in health-food stores. *Recent research shows that this controversial herb may be helpful in fighting some insidious health conditions...*

•**Crohn's disease.** A study published in 2007 by doctors at Yale University School of Medicine found that wormwood significantly reduced symptoms of Crohn's disease, a form of inflammatory bowel disease that is difficult to treat. Forty patients were given either 750 milligrams (mg) of wormwood extract (brand name: SedaCrohn) or placebos twice daily for 10 weeks. After eight weeks, 13 of the 20 patients (65%) taking wormwood had almost a full remission of symptoms. As a result, they were able to reduce their use of corticosteroid drugs. For most of the patients taking placebos, symptoms worsened.

•**Malaria.** A very close relative of wormwood called sweet wormwood (*Artemisia annua*) has been found beneficial in treating malaria, which is caused by a mosquito-borne parasite. Although most Americans are not likely to contract malaria, the disease is still a major problem in Africa and throughout the developing world. The World Health Organization has approved the use of wormwood-based compounds in the treatment of malaria—a sign of the herb's efficacy and safety.

•**Parasitic infections.** Wormwood has a long history of use in traditional Chinese medicine and in Western naturopathic medicine for treating a variety of parasitic infections. I have found that a wormwood tincture (10 drops three times daily) or capsule (200 mg) helps rid the body of parasites in the digestive tract.

•**Cancer.** Some research suggests that extracts of wormwood might have anticancer benefits. However, the research has been limited to small-scale cell and mouse studies. Some companies are hyping wormwood as a potential cancer fighter, but at this point, I do not believe there is enough evidence to justify its use in treating cancer.

What about the risk? The amount of thujone in herbal preparations is extremely small—I have never found a problem with its use. In fact, thujone also is found in the culinary herb sage, commonly used as a rub for Thanksgiving turkeys.

Important: Work with a physician if you suspect that you have any of the conditions mentioned here, and ask about wormwood as a possible treatment. My patients have not experienced any hallucinations or other side effects as a result of the doses I prescribe.

■ ■ ■ ■

Black Tea Protects Against Parkinson's

When researchers analyzed health data for 63,257 adults, they found that those who drank at least 23 cups of black tea monthly (caffeinated or decaffeinated) had a 71% lower risk for Parkinson's disease over a 12-year period than those who drank less black tea. Intake of green tea had no effect on Parkinson's risk.

Theory: Black tea contains complex antioxidants that may help protect against Parkinson's disease.

Louis C. Tan, MD, senior consultant, department of neurology, National Neuroscience Institute, Singapore.

■ ■ ■ ■

Parkinson's Patients Dance Their Way to Better Balance

People with Parkinson's disease who took tango lessons improved their mobility compared with study subjects who attended traditional exercise classes instead. The dancers also had better balance and were at lower risk for falling.

Gammon M. Earhart, PhD, assistant professor of physical therapy, anatomy and neurobiology and neurology, Washington University School of Medicine, St. Louis, and coauthor of a study reported in *Scientific American*.

11

Nutrition, Diet and Fitness

The Health Beef with Red Meat

Diets high in red meat and in processed meats shorten life span, not just due to cancer and heart disease, but due to Alzheimer's, stomach ulcers and an array of other conditions as well, a US National Cancer Institute study has found.

In fact, reducing meat consumption to the amount eaten by those who ate the least (the bottom 20%) could save 11% of men's lives and 16% of women's, according to the study.

"The consumption of red meat was associated with a modest increase in total mortality," said Rashmi Sinha, PhD, lead author of the study published in the *Archives of Internal Medicine.*

"This fits together with the findings of the American Institute for Cancer Research and the World Cancer Research Fund and the American Cancer Society, which recommend limiting the consumption of red meat," added Dr. Sinha, who is a senior investigator with the nutrition epidemiological branch in the cancer epidemiology and genetics division at the Cancer Institute. Dr. Sinha noted that this is the first time that meat consumption has been linked to overall mortality.

BACKGROUND

Previous studies of red meat had mostly found an association with cancer incidence. Last year, US National Cancer Institute researchers reported that a quarter-pound hamburger or a small pork chop eaten daily could put you at increased risk for a variety of cancers.

The message from the latest study echoes that finding: The more red meat and processed

Rashmi Sinha, PhD, senior investigator, nutrition epidemiological branch, division of cancer epidemiology and genetics, US National Cancer Institute, Bethesda, Maryland.

Jay Brooks, MD, chairman, hematology/oncology, Ochsner Health System, Baton Rouge, Louisiana.

Michael Thun, MD, vice president emeritus, epidemiology and surveillance research, American Cancer Society, Atlanta.

American Meat Institute, Washington, DC.

Archives of Internal Medicine.

meats you consume, the greater your risk for dying of cancer.

THE STUDY

For the study, the researchers looked at what more than a half-million people, ages 50 to 71, were eating over the span of a decade. Participants tended to be white and educated with fewer smokers and more vegetable-and-fruit eaters than in the general population. During that time, more than 71,000 people died.

THE RESULTS

Men and women eating the highest amount of red meat were found to have a 31% and 36%, respectively, higher risk for dying from any cause, than those eating the least amount.

Women eating the most processed meat were 25% more likely to die early than those eating the least of this type of meat, while men had a 16% increased risk, the study found.

Causes of death for those in the study included diabetes, Alzheimer's disease, ulcers, pneumonia, influenza, liver disease, HIV, tuberculosis and chronic obstructive pulmonary disease.

Dying from cancer also was more likely among those eating the most red meat: 22% higher for men, 20% for women. The risk for death from cancer increased 12% for men and 11% for women who ate the greatest amount of processed meat.

Similarly, the risk of dying from cardiovascular disease among those eating the most red meat was higher by 27% for men and 50% for women. For processed red meat, the risk was 9% higher for men and 38% higher for women.

Meat contains many carcinogens as well as saturated fat, which might explain the increased mortality risk, the authors stated.

MEAT INDUSTRY RESPONDS TO STUDY

But the American Meat Institute objected to the conclusion, saying in a statement that the study relied on "notoriously unreliable self-reporting about what was eaten in the preceding five years. This imprecise approach is like relying on consumers' personal characterization of their driving habits in prior years in determining their likelihood of having an accident in the future.

"Meat is an excellent source of zinc, iron, B-12 and other essential vitamins and minerals," the statement continued. "The US Dietary Guidelines say to eat a balanced diet that includes lean meat. In this way, you derive a wide array of nutrients from many different sources. It's the best return on a nutritional investment you can get."

EXPERT REACTION

Jay Brooks, MD, chairman of hematology/oncology at Ochsner Health System in Baton Rouge, Louisiana, described the study's findings as "provocative."

"The question is, how much of it is the meat and how much is the extra calories," Dr. Brooks said. "Calories *per se* are a strong determinant for death from cancer and heart disease. This should make us think about our calorie intake.

GUIDELINES FOR MEAT CONSUMPTION

Michael Thun, MD, vice president emeritus of epidemiology and surveillance research at the American Cancer Society, said the study's findings "support previous studies as well as supporting the American Cancer Society nutrition guidelines."

Those guidelines include choosing fish, poultry or beans instead of beef, pork and lamb; choosing leaner cuts of meat; and baking, broiling or poaching meat rather than frying or charbroiling it.

info For more information on healthy eating, visit the Web site of the American Dietetic Association, *www.eatright.org*, and click on "Food and Nutrition Information."

■ ■ ■ ■

Bottoms Up! Wine Blocks the Harmful Effects of Meat

Digestion of the fat in meats, such as beef and poultry, leads to the release of toxic chemicals in the body. These chemicals have been linked to cancer and heart disease.

But: The toxins are neutralized by antioxidants called *polyphenols* in red wine.

Self-defense: Eat meat only occasionally—and have a glass of red wine with your meal when you do.

Shlomit Gorelik, MSc, department of pharmaceutics, Hebrew University of Jerusalem, and leader of a study reported in *Journal of Agricultural and Food Chemistry.*

■ ■ ■ ■

Red Meat Raises Blood Pressure

When researchers followed more than 28,000 women over 10 years, those who ate more than one-and-a-half servings daily of red meat (for example, six to nine ounces of beef) were 35% more likely to develop high blood pressure than those who ate no red meat. Researchers believe similar results would apply to men.

Theory: Saturated fats, cholesterol, animal protein and heme iron (the type in red meat) may play a role in raising blood pressure.

To lower your risk for high blood pressure: Limit your intake of red meat, and substitute other protein sources, such as fish, legumes, soy and low-fat dairy foods.

Lu Wang, MD, PhD, instructor in medicine, Brigham and Women's Hospital, Boston.

Age-Proof Your Muscles For Better Health

Mark A. Stengler, ND, naturopathic physician in private practice, La Jolla, California...adjunct associate clinical professor at the National College of Natural Medicine, Portland, Oregon...author of many books, including *The Natural Physician's Healing Therapies* and coauthor of *Prescription for Natural Cures* (both from Bottom Line Books)...and author of the *Bottom Line/Natural Healing* newsletter.

As we age, we steadily lose muscle mass. It's a fact that many falls and bone fractures result not from weak bones, but from insufficient muscle to support ourselves as we go about our lives.

It's easy to preserve muscle or reverse age-related muscle loss, which doctors call sarcopenia. You can do this through diet, exercise and supplements or any combination of these. The more you do, the more you will ensure that you lead an active, independent and productive life long into your 60s...70s...80s...and beyond.

THE POWER OF PROTEIN

The word protein comes from the Greek *proteios,* which essentially means first and foremost. This hints at just how important protein is for life and health. In addition to forming our muscles, protein constitutes much of the tissue of the internal organs. And bone is a matrix of proteins and minerals. Proteins also are the building blocks of hormones, immune cells, neurotransmitters and other biochemicals.

For too many years now, doctors and dietitians have warned patients about the dangers of eating too much protein. That view now is changing, but too slowly in my opinion. It turns out that many people, particularly seniors, do not consume enough high-quality protein. High-quality protein foods contain all the essential amino acids, the compounds that are the building blocks of protein. Poultry is one example. Fish is another, and it has an added benefit since many cold-water types, such as salmon and sardines, are high in the healthful type of omega-3 fatty acids. Eggs, in moderation, are another option, especially those enriched with omega-3s.

Best: Eat a variety of proteins, including fish, poultry and legumes, such as kidney beans and lentils. A legume might be low in one particular amino acid, but chances are you'll eat another food rich in that amino acid that will make up for it.

Over the course of one year, one of my older patients, a 90-year-old man, lost a great deal of weight and strength. (If a person is overweight, losing weight is healthy. In his case, it wasn't.) He was able to gain weight—increasing muscle, not fat—and enhance his strength simply by consuming more protein.

Important: Protein is both essential and safe. However, people with kidney disease should consume relatively small amounts of protein daily because high amounts can stress the kidneys. If you have reduced kidney function or any type of kidney disease, speak to your physician first before changing the amount of protein you consume.

EAT MORE PROTEIN EVERY DAY

There are lots of ways to get more protein into your diet. Here are the protein amounts for some common foods. Do the math—you'll see that it's not hard to boost intake.

- **Chicken (white meat),** 3.5 oz = 31 g protein
- **Turkey,** 3 oz = 28 g protein
- **Beef round roast (preferably grass fed),** 3 oz = 25 g protein
- **Tuna,** 3 oz = 24 g protein
- **Salmon,** Chinook, 3 oz = 21 g protein
- **Pumpkin seeds,** ¼ cup = 19 g protein
- **Pork roast,** 3 oz = 21 g protein
- **Black beans (boiled),** 1 cup = 15 g protein
- **Chickpeas (boiled),** 1 cup = 15 g protein
- **Shrimp,** 6 large = 8.5 g protein
- **Skim milk,** 1 cup = 8 g protein
- **Walnuts,** ¼ cup = 4 g protein
- **Brown rice (cooked),** 1 cup = 4 g protein
- **Peanut butter,** 1 tbsp = 4 g protein
- **Broccoli,** 1 cup = 3 g protein

THE ROLE OF VEGETABLES

Most plant foods have less protein than fish, poultry, beef and other meats, but they are good protein sources because they are low in fat and high in fiber.

What you might not know: Vegetables and fruits help build muscle, but not because of their protein content. Plant foods are rich in potassium and bicarbonate, which result in a more alkaline pH (pH is the body's alkaline-to-acid ratio). Most other foods make your body more acidic, and acidosis triggers muscle wasting. A recent Tufts University study found that higher intake of foods rich in potassium, such as fruits and vegetables, can help preserve muscle mass in older men and women.

THE BENEFITS OF EXERCISE

I can't overstate the benefits of regular exercise, particularly resistance activities (weight lifting) for preserving and increasing muscle. As I have explained, muscle is mostly made of protein. Exercise stimulates the conversion of dietary protein to muscle. The more exercise you do, the better. Going for a daily brisk walk is a good way to start. Consider advancing to hand weights, larger weights, cycling or swimming. Alternate activities to avoid boredom. Resistance exercise, such as weight lifting, will reverse sarcopenia even if you consume relatively little protein, according to an article in *Journal of Physiology,* because the physical activity stimulates the conversion of protein to muscle.

TAKE VITAMIN D DAILY

Vitamin D is needed to make muscle. It ensures that calcium, which is essential for transporting proteins to muscle tissue, is absorbed. If you don't already do so, take 1,000 international units (IU) of vitamin D daily.

GETTING PROTEIN FROM SUPPLEMENTS

As I have mentioned, protein consists of compounds called amino acids, so think of taking amino acid supplements as a way of getting more protein.

Some exciting recent research has focused on using amino acid supplements to increase muscle mass and strength while reducing body fat and fatigue. These supplements won't give you a bodybuilder's physique, but they can help reverse age-related muscle loss.

Beware: Not all amino acid supplements are alike. Many of the protein powder supplements that come in huge containers in health food stores or pharmacies have poor-quality proteins (such as soy) and lots of sugar. These are not worth using.

I recommend these protein supplements...

- **Multi amino acids.** These supplements, available at most health food stores, provide between eight and 11 different amino acids. Recent studies have shown impressive benefits in seniors after they took these supplements. One of the studies, reported in *The American Journal of Cardiology,* found that people who took daily amino acid supplements had significant increases in muscle after six months—and experienced even more of an increase after 16 months, reaching the normal levels found in peers without sarcopenia. I often recommend multi amino acids because they come closest to being a complete protein (one that contains all of the amino acids). One good example is Country Life's Max Amino Caps (800-645-5768, *www.country-life.com*). Follow instructions on the label.

Alternatives: Use supplements that contain individual amino acids. *Beta-alanine, l-ornithine* (which seems to help women especially) and *l-leucine,* known to help convert protein to muscle, are what I recommend. For each, follow instructions on the label.

Prevent Alzheimer's And Boost Your Brainpower with the Mediterranean Diet

Nikolaos Scarmeas, MD, assistant professor, neurology, Columbia University Medical Center, New York City.
Gary Kennedy, MD, director, geriatric psychiatry, Montefiore Medical Center, New York City.
Alice H. Lichtenstein, DSc, Gershoff Professor of Nutrition Science and Policy, Tufts University, Boston.
Archives of Neurology.

Chalk up another endorsement for the so-called Mediterranean diet: The eating regimen, which is rich in fruits, vegetables, fish and olive oil, may help the brain stay sharp into old age, a recent study suggests.

Following the healthful diet reduced the risk of getting mild cognitive impairment—marked by forgetfulness and difficulty concentrating. And it also cut the risk of developing Alzheimer's disease if cognitive impairment was already present, said study lead author Nikolaos Scarmeas, MD, an assistant professor of neurology at Columbia University Medical Center in New York City.

The study was published in the *Archives of Neurology.*

Previous research has found that people who follow the Mediterranean diet are at less risk of developing a variety of diseases, including heart disease, cancer and Parkinson's disease.

THE STUDY

The Columbia researchers evaluated nearly 1,400 people without cognitive impairment and 482 people with mild cognitive impairment, and then followed them for an average of 4.5 years. The participants—average age 77—also completed a food frequency questionnaire, detailing what they had eaten during the past year.

The researchers divided the participants into three groups—those who adhered regularly to the Mediterranean diet, those who adhered moderately to it, and those who adhered somewhat or not at all. Then they evaluated the participants' cognitive functioning.

STUDY RESULTS

The researchers found that the diet helped prevent both mild cognitive impairment and also the risk of further decline, even if people weren't entirely strict in their adherence to the diet.

"As compared to the group that ate very little or not at all of the Mediterranean diet, those who ate it to a moderate degree had 17% less risk of developing mild cognitive impairment," Dr. Scarmeas said. "Those who adhered a lot had a 28% less risk of developing mild cognitive impairment."

The diet also helped those who already had mild impairment. "Compared to those who adhered not at all or very little, those who ate the Mediterranean diet to a moderate degree had a 45% reduction in risk of going from mild cognitive impairment to Alzheimer's disease. Those who adhered a lot had a 48% reduction in risk of going from mild cognitive impairment to Alzheimer's," he said.

Dr. Scarmeas said previous research he conducted found that a greater adherence to the Mediterranean diet was associated with a lower risk of Alzheimer's disease.

THEORY

It's not known exactly how the diet may help keep the brain healthy, Dr. Scarmeas said. One possibility is that it might reduce inflammation, which plays a role in brain disease. Or it might work by improving cardiovascular risk factors, such as high cholesterol, he said.

EXPERT PERSPECTIVES

"You see what is called a dose response. The more stringently you follow the Mediterranean diet, the better the outcome," noted Gary Kennedy, MD, director of geriatric psychiatry at Montefiore Medical Center in New York City.

Alice Lichtenstein, DSc, Gershoff Professor of Nutrition Science and Policy at Tufts University in Boston, said, "It's encouraging to see the results—those reporting the healthier dietary pattern seem to do better." What remains to be seen, she added, is whether it was the specific diet that helped people avoid cognitive decline or if those people who ate properly had other healthy habits that decreased their risk.

All three experts agreed: Until more evidence is in that the Mediterranean diet keeps brains sharp, there are plenty of other reasons to follow it, including heart health.

info To learn more about the Mediterranean diet, visit the Women's Heart Foundation Web site, *www.womensheart.org*. Under the "Exercise & Nutrition" pull-down menu, choose "Mediterranean Diet."

Superfoods for Your Brain

Mark Hyman, MD, founder of The UltraWellness Center in Lenox, Massachusetts. He is on the board of advisers and faculty of Food As Medicine, a professional nutrition training program at The Center for Mind-Body Medicine, Washington, DC. He is author of many books on wellness, including *The UltraMind Solution* (Scribner). *www.ultrawellness.com.*

The aging American population is facing a sharp increase in diagnosed cases of dementia. Alzheimer's disease and other forms of dementia affect about 10% of people 65 and older. Among those in their mid-80s and older, up to half have a significant degree of cognitive impairment.

Millions of younger Americans suffer from less obvious mental impairments, including mild memory loss and diminished alertness, as well as brain-related disorders, such as depression and chronic anxiety.

Research clearly shows that some foods can improve mental performance and help prevent long-term damage. *Best choices...*

• **Sardines.** They have two to three times more omega-3 fatty acids than most other fatty fish. Our bodies use omega-3s for the efficient transmission of brain signals. People who don't get enough omega-3s in their diets are more likely to experience learning disabilities, dementia and depression.

Bonus: Omega-3s reduce inflammation and inhibit blood clots, the underlying cause of most strokes.

Fatty fish also are high in choline, a substance used to manufacture one of the main neurotransmitters (*acetylcholine*) involved in memory.

Recommended: Three cans of sardines a week. Sardines are less likely to accumulate mercury or other toxins than larger fish.

Caution: Many people believe that flaxseed is an adequate substitute for fish. Although it contains alpha-linolenic acid (ALA), a type of omega-3, only about 10% of ALA is converted to *docosahexaenoic acid* (DHA) or *eicosapentaenoic acid* (EPA), the most beneficial forms of omega-3s and the ones that are plentiful in fish oil.

If you don't like sardines, you can take fish oil supplements (1,000 milligrams twice a day).

• **Omega-3 eggs.** They're among the best foods for the brain because they contain folate along with omega-3s and choline. Folate is a B vitamin that's strongly linked to mood and mental performance. A Finnish study of 2,682 men found that those with the lowest dietary intakes of folate were 67% more likely to experience depression than those with adequate amounts.

Recommended: Up to eight eggs a week. Only buy eggs that say "Omega-3" on the label. It means that the chickens were given a fish meal diet. Eggs without this label contain little or no omega-3s.

• **Low-glycemic carbohydrates.** The glycemic index ranks foods according to how quickly they elevate glucose in the blood. Foods with low glycemic ratings include legumes (beans, lentils) and whole-grain breads. They slow the release of sugars into the bloodstream and prevent sharp rises in insulin.

Why it matters: Elevated insulin is associated with dementia. For example, diabetics with elevated insulin in the blood have four times the rate of dementia as people without diabetes. Elevated insulin damages blood vessels as well as neurons. The damage is so pronounced that some researchers call Alzheimer's disease "type 3 diabetes."

Recommended: Always eat natural, minimally processed foods. They're almost always low on the glycemic index. For example, eat apples instead of applesauce...whole-grain bread instead of white bread...or any of the legumes, such as chickpeas, lentils or soybeans.

•**Nuts.** They're among the few plant foods that contain appreciable amounts of omega-3 fatty acids. They also contain antioxidants, which reduce brain and arterial inflammation that can lead to cognitive decline.

Most of the fat in nuts is monounsaturated—it lowers harmful LDL cholesterol without depressing beneficial HDL cholesterol—important for preventing stroke.

Recommended: One to two handfuls daily. Walnuts and macadamia nuts are among the highest in omega-3s, but all nuts are beneficial. Avoid highly salted and roasted nuts (the roasting changes the composition of the oils). Lightly toasted is okay.

•**Cruciferous vegetables, such as broccoli, Brussels sprouts, cauliflower and kale.** They contain detoxifying compounds that help the liver eliminate toxins that can damage the hippocampus and other areas of the brain involved in cognition.

Recommended: One cup daily is optimal, but at least four cups a week. Cooked usually is easier to digest than raw.

•**B-12 foods.** Meat, dairy products and seafood are our only source (apart from supplements) of vitamin B-12 in the diet. This nutrient is critical for brain health. A study published in *American Journal of Clinical Nutrition* found that older adults with low levels of vitamin B-12 were more likely to experience rapid cognitive declines. Older adults have the highest risk for B-12 deficiency because the age-related decline in stomach acid impairs its absorption.

Recommended: Two to three daily servings of organic lean meat, low-fat dairy (including yogurt) or seafood.

Also important: I advise everyone to take a multinutrient supplement that includes all of the B vitamins.

•**Green tea.** It's a powerful antioxidant and anti-inflammatory that also stimulates the liver's ability to break down toxins. Recent research indicates that green tea improves insulin sensitivity—important for preventing diabetes and neuro-damaging increases in insulin.

Recommended: One to two cups daily.

•**Berries, including blueberries, raspberries and strawberries.** The darker the berry, the higher the concentration of antioxidant compounds. In studies at Tufts University, animals fed blueberries showed virtually no oxidative brain damage. They also performed better on cognitive tests than animals given a standard diet.

Recommended: One-half cup daily. Frozen berries contain roughly the same level of protective compounds as fresh berries.

Eight Easy Ways to Eat Better—and Feel Great

Jamison Starbuck, ND, a naturopathic physician in family practice in Missoula, Montana. She is past president of the American Association of Naturopathic Physicians and a contributing editor to *The Alternative Advisor: The Complete Guide to Natural Therapies and Alternative Treatments* (Time-Life).

If improving your diet has ever been a personal goal for you—or perhaps a New Year's resolution—I have good news. There are some very practical and simple steps you can take to reach this goal—and you don't have to make radical changes that are next to impossible to sustain.

Several years ago, a patient named Eugene asked me how he could improve his eating habits. As I told Eugene, the key is substituting a few healthful foods for some of the less nutritious items that most people eat. *My advice...*

•**Use plain, low-fat yogurt instead of milk, ice cream or sour cream.** Yogurt offers all of the nutrition of milk plus the addition of beneficial bacteria that help improve digestion and nutrient absorption and fight overgrowth of yeast. Yogurt is an excellent choice for breakfast or a snack. It can be used on vegetables, in soup or as a healthful dessert. If you don't like the taste of plain yogurt, add your own honey, maple syrup, fresh fruit and/or nuts.

•**Replace iceberg lettuce with chopped red chard leaves.** Iceberg lettuce provides few nutrients. By replacing it with red chard, you can add vitamin A, iron and fiber to your salads.

•**Try romaine lettuce leaves in place of bread.** Romaine lettuce is firm enough to be filled with spreads or something more substantial, such as tuna or turkey. Simply roll up the leaf as you would a sandwich wrap. Romaine "sandwiches" will help you reduce calories, contribute to your daily fiber intake and improve your digestion.

•**Use sesame butter instead of peanut butter.** Sesame butter is a richer source of calcium and healthful omega-3 fatty acids.

•**Substitute ground flaxseed for flour.** Ground flaxseed is more nutritious than wheat flour and is a great source of fiber and a form of heart- and brain-healthy omega-3s. Add ground flaxseed to oatmeal or cereal or substitute ground flaxseed for one-third of the flour in recipes for muffins and breads.

•**Add a few bok choy leaves to soup.** Like chard, bok choy is high in folic acid (needed for red blood cell formation) and iron—and the compounds that give the leafy, green vegetable its bitter quality aid digestion. To improve the nutritional value of even canned soup, sprinkle several coarsely chopped bok choy leaves on top when it's steaming hot and almost ready to eat. Cover and let simmer for four minutes.

•**Eat parsley regularly.** It's rich in vitamin C, helps freshen your breath and reduces intestinal gas. Chop it up raw and add it to green salads or tuna. Or make a batch of parsley pesto (substitute parsley for some or all of the basil in a pesto recipe).

•**Go vegetarian one day a week.** Use crumbled tempeh (fermented soy) instead of ground beef in chili or soups. Also, scramble tofu, instead of eggs, with onions and veggies for breakfast. Avoiding meat for just one day a week will help reduce your cholesterol levels.

Surprising Facts About Cow's Milk

Dennis A. Savaiano, PhD, dean of the College of Consumer and Family Sciences and professor in the department of foods and nutrition at Purdue University in Lafayette, Indiana. He has authored or coauthored numerous studies on lactose intolerance, published in peer-reviewed biomedical journals.

If you grew up in the US, you were probably admonished to drink cow's milk for its bone-building calcium. But do you still follow that advice?

As adults, many people give up cow's milk because they don't like its taste...don't like the way cows are raised (on "factory farms")...or have difficulty digesting lactose (the primary sugar in cow's milk and other dairy products).

Good news: There are more good-tasting milk options available than most people realize.

MILK FROM ANIMAL SOURCES

Milk is a good source of calcium—one eight-ounce cup contains about 300 milligrams (mg) of the mineral (nearly one-third of the daily recommended intake for adults age 50 and under and about one-quarter of the daily recommended intake for adults over age 50). Milk also contains vitamin D (needed to absorb calcium) and protein, an important nutrient that helps us maintain strength and muscle tone as we age.

However, about 5% of infants are allergic to cow's milk. Symptoms include diarrhea, runny nose and hives. Most children outgrow the allergy by age two or three.

Because whole cow's milk contains saturated fat, which can contribute to obesity and heart disease, it's usually best to drink nonfat or 1% milk. *Milk options...*

•**Lactose-free cow's milk.** About one out of every four American adults has lactose intolerance. This condition, which is different from a milk allergy, causes stomach pain, diarrhea, bloating and/or gas after milk or other dairy products that contain lactose are consumed. But lactose can be removed from milk.

Examples: Lactaid and Land O Lakes Dairy Ease.

• **Cow's milk (with meals).** Studies show that many people who believe they are lactose intolerant can drink milk without suffering any symptoms as long as it's consumed with a meal, which helps slow the digestion of lactose.

If you've stopped drinking cow's milk due to lactose intolerance and would like to try reintroducing it: Drink one-quarter to one-half cup of milk with a meal twice daily. Within a few days, try drinking a full cup of milk with a meal. Most people who have identified themselves as being lactose intolerant can adapt to this level of milk consumption within two weeks—the length of time that it usually takes intestinal bacteria to activate the body's lactases (enzymes that break down lactose).

If you have gas or loose stools, reduce your milk intake to one-quarter cup daily until the symptoms subside. If this does not work, see a doctor. You may have another condition, such as irritable bowel syndrome, which causes cramping, abdominal pain, constipation and diarrhea.

• **Kefir.** Kefir is a slightly sour fermented milk drink produced by "friendly" probiotic bacteria and yeasts found in kefir grains. Kefir, which has a milkshake-like consistency, is an option for some people who are lactose intolerant.

Example: Lifeway Lowfat Kefir.

• **Goat's milk.** Like cow's milk, goat's milk contains lactose and is a good source of calcium, vitamin D and protein. Goat's milk has a refreshingly tart, almost sour taste.

Example: Meyenberg Goat Milk.

Kefir and goat's milk are available at health food stores and some supermarkets.

PLANT-BASED MILKS

Plant-based milks are lactose-free and offer health benefits of their own. Most of these milks contain only small amounts of calcium and vitamin D, so they are usually fortified with these nutrients. Some plant-based milks are flavored (vanilla and chocolate, for example), but these varieties can contain up to 20 grams (g) of sugar per cup. Check the label for the sugar content to avoid unnecessary calories. Choose a lowfat plant-based milk whenever possible. Plant-based milks, which can be used in baking and cooking, are available at health-food stores and most supermarkets. *Choices include...*

• **Soymilk.** This milk has a mild, bean-like flavor and contains heart-healthy soy protein. In addition, some studies, though inconclusive, suggest that the phytoestrogens (naturally occurring compounds with estrogen-like effects) in soy may help reduce the risk for breast and prostate cancer.

Example: Silk Organic Soymilk.

Caution: Anyone who has had breast or prostate cancer or who is at high risk (due to family history, for example) should consult a doctor before consuming soy—in some cases, phytoestrogens are believed to stimulate the growth of certain hormone-dependent malignancies.

• **Nut milks.** People who don't like the taste of soy milk often prefer almond or hazelnut milk.

Examples: Blue Diamond Almond Breeze and Pacific Foods Hazelnut Milk.

• **Oat milk.** The fiber in this milk, which has a mild, sweet taste, may help lower cholesterol levels.

Example: Pacific Foods Oat Milk.

• **Hemp milk.** Derived from shelled hempseeds, this creamy, nutty milk contains a balance of fatty acids that are believed to fight heart disease and arthritis.

Example: Living Harvest Hempmilk.

• **Rice milk.** For many people, rice milk, among all the plant-based milks, tastes the most like cow's milk. Rice milk has less protein than cow's milk and soymilk, but it can be consumed by some people who are allergic to cow's milk.

Example: Rice Dream.

Berries May Help Prevent Wrinkles

Federation of American Societies for Experimental Biology news release.

You probably already knew that berries are nutritious. But recent research shows that a compound found in nuts, berries and other fruits might help prevent wrinkles and repair skin damage caused by the sun.

THE STUDY

Researchers in Korea applied *ellagic acid,* an antioxidant found in raspberries, strawberries, cranberries and pomegranates, to human skin cells in the lab as well as to the skin of hairless mice that had been exposed to strong, ultraviolet rays.

In the human cells, ellagic acid reduced the inflammatory response and the destruction of collagen, both major causes of wrinkles.

Researchers had a similar result in 4-week-old mice. Baby mice are often used in dermatology studies because their skin is similar to that of humans.

For eight weeks, 12 hairless mice were exposed three times a week to increasing ultraviolet radiation. The exposure would have been strong enough to cause sunburn and skin damage in humans, according to the researchers, from Hallym University in South Korea.

Half of the exposed mice were given daily topical applications of ellagic acid, even on the days in which they did not receive UV exposure. Ellagic acid was not applied to the other mice.

The mice that did not receive ellagic acid developed wrinkles and thickening of the skin that indicates sun damage.

The mice that received the ellagic acid showed less wrinkle formation. The study was presented at the Experimental Biology meeting in New Orleans.

HOW IT WORKS

In human skin cells, ellagic acid protects against ultraviolet damage by blocking production of *matrix metalloproteinase enzymes* that break down collagen and reduce the expression of ICAM, a molecule involved with inflammation.

info For more on preventing sun damage, visit the Web site of the American Academy of Family Physicians, *http://familydoctor.org,* and search "prevent sun damage."

The Wonder Vitamin That Helps Your Heart, Eyes, Bones and Even Fights Cancer

Reinhold Vieth, PhD, a professor in the department of nutritional sciences and the department of laboratory medicine and pathobiology at Mount Sinai Hospital, University of Toronto, Canada. He is also director of the bone and mineral laboratory at Mount Sinai Hospital in Toronto. Dr. Vieth has studied vitamin D for more than 30 years and has written more than 70 related professional articles.

Until recently, physicians rarely diagnosed deficiencies of vitamin D except in occasional cases of childhood rickets (a disease in which the bones do not harden).

Now: One in three Americans is considered to be deficient in vitamin D—and most of them don't know it, according to the US National Center for Health Statistics.

How did vitamin D deficiency become such a widespread problem so quickly—and what should be done about it? Reinhold Vieth, PhD, a leading expert on vitamin D, provides the answers below.

NEW DISCOVERIES

To produce adequate levels of vitamin D naturally, you must expose your skin (without sunscreen) to ultraviolet B (UVB) rays from the sun for about 15 minutes, as a general guideline, twice a week. If you use sunscreen, your body makes little or no vitamin D. Generations ago, when large numbers of Americans began working indoors—thus reducing their exposure to sunlight—their average vitamin D blood levels declined. Some food sources, such as egg yolks and sardines, provide small amounts of the vitamin.

More recently, average blood levels of vitamin D in the US have remained fairly constant. What has changed is the amount of scientific research pointing to the importance of the vitamin.

An overwhelming body of evidence shows that vitamin D not only affects the bones (by facilitating the absorption of calcium), but also may play a key role in fighting a wide variety of ailments, including cardiovascular disease... autoimmune diseases (such as rheumatoid arthritis, lupus and multiple sclerosis)...chronic bone or muscle pain (including back pain)... macular degeneration...and increased susceptibility to colds and flu.

A number of studies also have shown a link between adequate blood levels of vitamin D and lower risk for some types of cancer, including colon, lung, breast and prostate cancers as well as Hodgkin's lymphoma (cancer of the lymphatic system).

Important new finding: In a study of 13,000 initially healthy men and women, researchers at Johns Hopkins found that vitamin D deficiency was associated with a 26% increase in death from any cause during a median period of nine years.

HOW VITAMIN D HELPS

Recent scientific discoveries have demonstrated that vitamin D is critical for the health of every organ in the body. By acting as a signaling molecule, vitamin D helps cells "talk" to each other, which in turn helps control how they behave. Cellular communication is essential for healthy biology.

To understand the function of vitamin D, think of paper in an office—you need paper to send memos and create reports. With enough paper, communication occurs easily. Without adequate paper supplies, the office may continue to function, but some important messages will not be communicated and mistakes will be made. Similarly, without enough vitamin D, your body is more likely to experience a breakdown of cellular communication that can lead to the conditions described above.

ARE YOU AT RISK?

Vitamin D deficiency is considered a "silent disease" because it can occur without any obvious signs. When symptoms do occur, muscle weakness and musculoskeletal pain are common.

Recent study: People with a severe vitamin D deficiency were more than twice as likely to die of heart disease and other causes than people with normal levels of vitamin D.

Among those at greatest risk for a vitamin D deficiency...

- **People over age 50.** Beginning at about age 50, our skin progressively loses some of its ability to convert sunlight to the active form of vitamin D.

- **People with dark skin (anyone who is of non-European ancestry).** Dark skin pigmentation offers some protection from skin cancer because it naturally filters the sun's cancer-causing ultraviolet B (UVB) rays. However, these are the same rays that we need to produce vitamin D.

- **People with limited sun exposure.** Those who live in most parts of the US, except the extreme South, do not produce enough vitamin D from sun exposure in the winter months. Elderly people who may spend less time outdoors also are at increased risk for vitamin D deficiency.

AVOIDING A DEFICIENCY

Many doctors now advise their patients to receive a blood test that measures levels of 25-hydroxy vitamin D—a form of the vitamin that acts as a marker for vitamin D deficiency. If you are concerned about your vitamin D levels, ask your primary care physician for the test—it typically costs $75 or more and is covered by some health insurers.

My recommendation: Get the test in the winter. If done in the summer, when you are likely to get more sun exposure, the test may reflect higher vitamin D levels than is typical for you at other times of the year.

As research confirming vitamin D's health benefits continues to mount, medical experts have raised the recommended blood levels for the vitamin—currently, levels of 30 nanograms per milliliter (ng/mL) are considered adequate—but a more desirable range for most people is 31 ng/mL to 90 ng/mL.

The US adequate intake level for vitamin D (from food and/or supplements) is 400 international units (IU) per day for adults under age 70 and 600 IU for adults age 70 and older.

However, the consensus among vitamin D researchers is that most adults should be taking vitamin D supplements totaling 1,000 IU daily...and 2,000 IU daily might be even better for meeting the body's needs. Ask your doctor what the right dosage is for you. Either dosage can be taken along with a multivitamin.

It is nearly impossible to get enough vitamin D from diet alone. In the US, milk and other dairy products and some breakfast cereals are fortified with vitamin D. Other food sources such as salmon, sardines, egg yolks and beef liver also provide small amounts.

How difficult is it to get 1,000 IU of vitamin D per day from food? You would need to drink about 10 cups of vitamin D–fortified milk or orange juice...eat 30 sardines...or eat 55 egg yolks.

Helpful: When choosing a vitamin D supplement, look for vitamin D-3 (cholecalciferol). It is twice as potent as vitamin D-2 (ergocalciferol).

Caution: Because vitamin D is fat-soluble (stored in the body), consuming more than 10,000 IU daily (or 70,000 IU weekly) can lead to toxic reactions, such as weakness, nausea and vomiting.

▪ More from Reinhold Vieth, PhD...

Sunny Rooms Don't Help with Vitamin D

Ultraviolet B (UVB) rays, which stimulate the production of vitamin D in the body, do not pass through glass. In general, to produce adequate levels of vitamin D naturally, you must expose your skin—without sunscreen—to sunlight for about 15 minutes twice a week. It also is important to get vitamin D from food such as salmon, sardines, egg yolks, fortified milk and cereals, as well as from daily supplements. Vitamin D aids in the absorption of calcium, which helps form and maintain strong bones, and provides protection against osteoporosis. The vitamin also may protect against other disorders, including cardiovascular disease and autoimmune diseases, such as multiple sclerosis and rheumatoid arthritis.

▪ ▪ ▪ ▪

C Is for Strong Bones

In a four-year study of 606 men and women, researchers found that men with the highest intake of vitamin C (314 milligrams daily) from food and supplements had the lowest levels of bone loss in the hip. Vitamin C is required for the formation of collagen, the main protein in bone. There was no similar finding in women, possibly because they already had adequate vitamin C levels.

For strong bones: Strive to eat five to nine servings daily of vitamin C–rich fruits and vegetables (such as strawberries and red peppers).

Katherine L. Tucker, PhD, director, dietary assessment and epidemiology research program, Human Nutrition Research Center on Aging, Tufts University, Boston.

▪ ▪ ▪ ▪

Save Your Sight

In a recent study of 4,400 adults, those with the highest levels of sun exposure and the lowest blood levels of the antioxidants zeaxanthin, vitamin C and vitamin E were four times more likely to have advanced age-related macular degeneration (AMD) than were those with less sun exposure and high antioxidant levels. AMD occurs when the *macula* (an area of the retina) deteriorates.

Self-defense: Eat at least five servings daily of antioxidant-rich produce, such as apples, oranges and leafy greens—and when outdoors, wear sunglasses and a wide-brimmed hat.

Ian S. Young, MD, PhD, professor of medicine, Queens University, Belfast, Ireland.

Calcium Lowers Risk of Hip Fractures and More

JoAnn E. Manson, MD, DrPH, a professor of medicine and women's health at Harvard Medical School and chair of the division of preventive medicine at Brigham and Women's Hospital, both in Boston. She is one of the lead investigators for two highly influential studies on women's health—the Harvard Nurses' Health Study and the Women's Health Initiative. Dr. Manson is author, with Shari Bassuk, ScD, of *Hot Flashes, Hormones and Your Health* (McGraw-Hill).

The typical midlife woman in the US consumes about 700 milligrams (mg) of calcium daily—far less than the recommended 1,200 mg for women age 50 and older. Perhaps this would improve if more women were aware of recent research showing how directly calcium's ability to prevent bone loss translates into better health.

Until recently, there was scant evidence that calcium cut the risk for hip fracture, a common and disabling complication of thinning bones. As part of a large study called the Women's Health Initiative (WHI), my colleagues and I conducted a seven-year clinical trial of calcium and vitamin D supplementation. More than 36,000 postmenopausal women were assigned to take either placebos or daily supplements of calcium at 1,000 mg plus vitamin D at 400 international units (IU), in two divided doses. Compared with placebo users, women who consistently took their pills as prescribed decreased their hip fracture risk by 30%...while in the 60-and-up age group, risk was reduced by 21% whether or not the pills were taken consistently. The benefit might have been even greater if higher doses of vitamin D had been tested—many experts now recommend 800 IU to 1,000 IU daily. *Calcium also may protect against...*

- **Colorectal polyps.** Small trials of calcium supplementation report reductions in risk for precancerous polyps called colorectal adenomas. In the WHI, however, calcium supplementation did not lower colorectal cancer risk. Research is ongoing.
- **Weight gain.** Although the effect was modest, WHI participants assigned to calcium supplementation were less likely to gain weight.

Theory: Calcium may positively affect fat metabolism.

The news about heart health: Although a recent small trial suggested that calcium supplements may contribute to cardiovascular problems, the much larger WHI study found that calcium plus vitamin D supplements did not increase heart attack or stroke risk.

Good dietary sources of calcium are low-fat dairy foods...canned oily fish with bones (sardines, salmon)...calcium-fortified orange juice and cereals...broccoli, collard greens and kale.

Few women are able to get enough calcium from food alone.

Best: Take a daily calcium supplement, preferably along with vitamin D to maximize absorption.

Options: Calcium carbonate (Caltrate, Viactiv) requires stomach acid for proper absorption, so you must take it with a meal or snack...calcium citrate (Citracal) is more convenient because it can be taken without food, but you need a higher dose to get the same amount of actual (elemental) calcium.

Excess calcium can increase kidney stone risk, impair kidney function and interfere with magnesium absorption.

National guidelines: Do not exceed 2,500 mg of calcium daily from all sources. If you supplement with more than 500 mg, take it in divided doses at least two hours apart.

Can This Patient Be Cured? Supplement Sensitivity

Mark A. Stengler, ND, naturopathic physician in private practice, La Jolla, California...adjunct associate clinical professor at the National College of Natural Medicine, Portland, Oregon...author of many books, including *The Natural Physician's Healing Therapies* and coauthor of *Prescription for Natural Cures* (both from Bottom Line Books)...and author of the *Bottom Line/Natural Healing* newsletter.

When Carrie, a 55-year-old homemaker, first came to see me five years ago, she was experiencing a multitude of symptoms, including migraines, fatigue, mood problems with depression and irritability, hair loss and irritable bowel symptoms, including extreme bloating. I took a medical history, performed a physical exam and ordered lab tests. I took a close look at her thyroid (which regulates metabolism) and adrenal glands (which produce the hormones needed to deal with physical and mental stress). The dysfunction of either can cause fatigue and some of the other symptoms Carrie described. As it turned out, her thyroid and adrenal gland function were both deficient—so I prescribed natural hormone replacement for thyroid support and supplements to bolster the adrenal glands.

At times, Carrie thought that the hormone replacement improved her energy, but her fatigue and bloating persisted. Over the next year, we adjusted the dose of her thyroid supplement, but this did not seem to help her feel better consistently. Sometimes she felt better...sometimes, worse.

NEXT STEP: DIGESTION PROBLEMS

To help with her digestive problems and fatigue, I tested Carrie for sensitivity to gluten, a protein found in wheat and some other grains. It came back positive, so it seemed likely that avoiding gluten would resolve Carrie's digestion problems, but after two months, we both were disappointed in the result. I then prescribed digestive enzymes and probiotics (helpful bacteria for the gut) to help with Carrie's digestion and lack of energy, but this too resulted in only a mild benefit.

I was puzzled. Something was going on with Carrie that wasn't on my radar. The best strategy in a situation like this is to assess everything a patient is doing and taking to determine where the bottleneck might be.

THE REAL CULPRIT

In addition to the supplements I had prescribed, Carrie also was taking a multivitamin. I had her stop taking it to see what would happen. To our surprise, her energy and digestive function improved within five days. To confirm that the multivitamin had been the culprit, Carrie started taking it again—and sure enough, within three days, her fatigue and bloating returned with a vengeance.

I took a close look at her multivitamin. There was nothing out of the ordinary in its composition, but it was clear that either Carrie was having a reaction to one of the ingredients or that there was a contaminant in it. I put her on a different multivitamin and had her continue with the thyroid supplement and natural hormone replacement, and she felt much better.

Every once in a while, I have a patient who is sensitive to a supplement or a medication, and it causes unexpected symptoms (such as fatigue or depression) or mimics those of other medical conditions (such as chronic fatigue or irritable bowel syndrome). The human body can be sensitive in surprising ways.

The Fat that May Keep You Thin

Aaron Cypess, MD, PhD, research associate, Joslin Diabetes Center, and instructor, Harvard Medical School, Boston.

Spyros Mezitis, MD, endocrinologist, Lenox Hill Hospital, New York City.

Ian Murray, PhD, assistant professor of neuroscience and experimental therapeutics, Texas A&M Health Science Center College of Medicine, College Station.

The New England Journal of Medicine.

Take note of the brown revolution—the brown fat revolution, that is. Three separate groups of scientists on two continents have independently verified that adult humans do possess this "good," slimming form of fat, previously thought only to be present in children and rodents.

The tissue is metabolically active and the more of this fat you have, the leaner you tend to be, experts say. That's because brown fat helps regulate body temperature by generating heat.

And according to experts, insights on how to tweak brown fat's magic qualities could lead to anti-obesity treatments.

"The general public and most scientists didn't know this existed," said Aaron Cypess, MD, PhD, a research associate at Joslin Diabetes Center and instructor at Harvard Medical School in Boston. "We say it's there and could be used as a treatment for obesity and diabetes."

Dr. Cypess is lead author of one of the studies, all three of which were published in *The New England Journal of Medicine.*

THE DISCOVERY OF BROWN FAT

While too much everyday "white" fat causes obesity, brown fat actually helps burn calories and may help us lose weight. Babies have some, but most scientists studying metabolism and obesity had abandoned the idea that adults (other than rodents) might harbor this potentially useful tissue.

That is, until imaging specialists mentioned that they had been seeing this type of tissue for years while studying cancer patients, basically considering it a nuisance factor.

"It was in a corner of the scientific literature the rest of us were not necessarily aware of," Dr. Cypess said. "Nuclear medicine experts didn't like it, because it gets in the way of seeing tumors."

So scientists interested in metabolism harnessed the latest imaging technologies to investigate this lost piece of the obesity puzzle.

STUDY #1

Using combined positron-emission tomographic and computed tomographic (PET-CT) scans, Dr. Cypess and his team found a wide prevalence of brown fat tissue in human adults. It was twice as common in women as in men (7.5% versus 3.1%).

The fat was indicative of overall leanness, the researchers noted, since heavier people, especially older, heavier people, had less brown fat than skinnier people. People taking beta-blockers—drugs used to treat high blood pressure and other conditions—also tended to have less brown fat. Beta-blockers have been linked with weight gain.

Younger adults had more brown fat, and this type of fat was more active in colder weather, stated the authors, who were supported by funds from various sources, including drug makers Pfizer Inc. and Merck & Co.

STUDY #2

In a second study, Dutch researchers found that all but one of 24 young men studied had brown fat. Yet in keeping with the previous study's findings, brown fat was less active in males who were carrying extra pounds.

The tissue was also active in cold temperatures only, which makes sense, given our need to keep warm in colder climes and seasons.

STUDY #3

The final study, from researchers in Finland and Sweden, showed that lower temperatures activated brown fat tissue in adults. This could shed light on how humans expend energy.

IMPLICATIONS

"This is the first time we're finding out that there is active brown fat in adult humans, but the question is if this can be applied—if we can use medication to make this brown fat more active and help people lose weight," said Spyros Mezitis, MD, an endocrinologist with Lenox Hill Hospital in New York City.

"With obesity treatments, we now can't lose more than 10 percent," Dr. Mezitis said. This finding opens the possibility of new drugs that will treat obesity in a more effective manner, he added.

EXPERT REACTION

One expert believes the findings from the three studies have several drawbacks. Ian Murray, PhD, assistant professor of neuroscience and experimental therapeutics at Texas A&M Health Science Center College of Medicine, noted that only a small percentage of people overall had brown fat, and very few heavy people had it.

Also, the tissue's activity seemed to be concentrated around the adrenal gland, which is known to play a role in the regulation of stress and body temperature, Dr. Murray added.

"It might be that lean people have better energy regulation than fat people," he reasoned. "You can modulate this early on before people get obese...so that a larger percentage of people can develop or maintain this fat. That is another [potential] therapy, more preventive than curative."

Dr. Cypess agreed that more study is needed. "As much as scientists want to be first, we really all want to be right," he said. "With three of us showing these things, we feel that this is all probably true, and we are very optimistic now for potential treatments for obesity."

info For more on obesity and weight control, visit the Web site of the Centers for Disease Control and Prevention, *www.cdc.gov.* Click on "Healthy Living" and then "Overweight and Obesity."

Why a Big Belly Is Worse than Just Being Overweight

JoAnn E. Manson, MD, DrPH, a professor of medicine and women's health at Harvard Medical School and chief of the division of preventive medicine at Brigham and Women's Hospital, both in Boston. She is one of the lead investigators for two highly influential studies on women's health—the Harvard Nurses Health Study and the Women's Health Initiative. Dr. Manson is author, with Shari Bassuk, ScD, of *Hot Flashes, Hormones and Your Health* (McGraw-Hill).

To gauge whether they are a healthy size, many people rely on a scale, height-and-weight chart or mathematical formula that calculates body mass index (BMI). Yet new research reveals that a tape measure more accurately predicts a person's risk for many major health problems. That's because waist measurement indicates the amount of belly fat—the fat that accumulates deep in the abdomen, around the intestines, liver and other internal organs. Belly fat is linked to a strongly elevated risk for diabetes, heart disease, stroke, high blood pressure and abnormal cholesterol levels...some types of cancer, including breast and colorectal cancers...and dementia.

Surprising: Having a big belly is more dangerous than simply being overweight or even obese. In a 16-year study of 45,000 female nurses, women whose waists measured 35 inches or more were much more likely to die prematurely than women with waists of less than 28 inches—even when their weight was within the normal range for their height. Women in the middle range had a small-to-moderate increase in risk. *Reasons...*

- **Belly fat may be more metabolically active than other fat,** releasing free fatty acids (fat cell products that circulate in the bloodstream) directly to the liver. This can lead to insulin resistance (inability of the body's cells to use insulin properly) and widespread inflammation, both of which significantly increase diabetes and heart disease risk.
- **Belly fat may be a sign of fat deposits in the liver and around the heart,** which can impair organ function.
- **After menopause,** the tendency to accumulate belly fat increases as women produce less estrogen relative to androgens (male hormones). Androgens promote abdominal fat.

To measure: Wrap a tape measure around your torso at the level of your navel—usually slightly below the narrowest part of the abdomen. The tape should be snug but not cut into your flesh. For women of any height, a waist size of less than 30 inches is optimal...30 inches to 35 inches indicates moderately elevated health risk...and more than 35 inches indicates high risk. *To reduce belly fat...*

- **Lose weight.** Often the first fat to go is abdominal fat. Even a modest loss of 10% of your starting weight confers great health benefits.
- **Reduce stress.** Stress causes adrenal glands to release the hormone cortisol, which promotes belly fat.
- **Get the right kinds of exercise.** You cannot melt away belly fat with targeted abdominal exercises, such as sit-ups. Instead, engage in aerobic activity, such as brisk walking and racket sports. Doing three hours of aerobic exercise weekly can eliminate about 50% of the excess risk for heart disease associated with belly fat and up to 25% of the excess risk for diabetes.

Also healthful: Resistance exercises (such as using arm and leg weights).

Supercharge Your Metabolism.... Supercharge Your Energy

Mark A. Stengler, ND, naturopathic physician in private practice, La Jolla, California...adjunct associate clinical professor at the National College of Natural Medicine, Portland, Oregon...author of many books, including *The Natural Physician's Healing Therapies* and coauthor of *Prescription for Natural Cures* (both from Bottom Line Books)...and author of the *Bottom Line/Natural Healing* newsletter.

Imagine a simple nutritional protocol that not only boosts your metabolism but also your energy levels! It is one I prescribe in my clinic daily—and I want to share it with you.

Even if you are in good shape and in relatively good health, you probably don't have the vitality that came so naturally when you were younger. Many of my patients also complain about putting on weight even when they still eat and exercise much as they did when they were younger. You already know that carrying excess weight contributes to or complicates a multitude of serious conditions—among them diabetes, arthritis, heart disease, and even several types of cancer. Carrying even a few extra pounds makes us feel slower...less ready to live with energy and zest...older.

Many people are resigned to these changes, assuming that slowing down and fattening up are inevitable parts of aging. Not so! You can't turn back the clock, but you can rev up your metabolism so it is closer to where it was when you were younger. In recent years, I have had great success prescribing "metabolism superchargers"—critical nutrients that revitalize the body's energy production. My patients tell me that these substances give them more energy, and I have seen many patients of all ages lose excess pounds.

THE ENERGY THIEVES

Your basal metabolic rate is the speed at which your body burns calories while at rest. When it slows, as it usually does with age, you burn fewer calories.

Result: Your energy level begins to flag...you gain weight.

But what is "energy" to our bodies? Here's a brief (I promise!) biology refresher to help you understand. Our physical strength, stamina and vigor originate within cell structures called mitochondria. Mitochondria generate *adenosine triphosphate* (ATP), a chemical that affects our metabolism and produces energy—both the fuel that cells need to do their work and the vitality we feel in our bodies. As we age, mitochondrial function gradually declines...as does the actual number of mitochondria.

One reason: The numerous toxins to which the body is exposed over the years, including environmental metals and other pollutants, radiation, alcohol, infections...hormone imbalances, such as hypothyroidism...inherited mitochondria mutations...some medications... and, in elite athletes, the stress caused by chronically overexercising—ultimately damage some mitochondria and interfere with replication of new mitochondria cells.

Decreased mitochondrial function also contributes to diseases. The mitochondria's slowed ability to make ATP is often a common denominator of two conditions that involve extreme fatigue—chronic fatigue syndrome and some cases of fibromyalgia.

Chronic heart disease often follows decreased ATP production, and it appears that heart failure is caused by a lack of ATP production in the heart muscle cells. Other age-related conditions seem to cause decreased ATP production as well—these include ischemic heart disease (due to blocked arteries)...angina...arrhythmia... Alzheimer's disease...Parkinson's disease...and Huntington's disease.

THE NATURAL WAY TO BOOST YOUR ENERGY

Considerable research demonstrates that certain natural nutrients, taken as supplements, can increase energy by directly increasing mitochondrial functioning and ATP production. In other words, they can supercharge your metabolism. Healthful foods do boost metabolism, but not enough to make a real difference in energy or weight to people who need help in those areas.

My suggestion: For three months, take all of the following nutrients daily (all are available at many drugstores and most health food stores). Then assess whether your energy has increased and whether it feels as if your weight has become easier to control with appropriate food choices and exercise. I find that most people experience an energy boost (if you don't experience this, stop taking the supplements), and about 75% of patients find that this regimen helps with weight control. If you are pleased with your increased energy, you can continue to take these supplements indefinitely—as I do.

- **Coenzyme Q10 (CoQ10).** This nutrient is found in every cell in the body and is required for ATP production. It is a potent antioxidant, helping to protect mitochondria from damage. The generally recommended dosage is 100 milligrams (mg) once daily with a meal. For people with severe fatigue—those who have trouble carrying out daily activities—I advise taking 100 mg two or three times each day with meals. Continue the higher dosage for a few months. When your energy level improves, try to cut back to 100 mg daily. CoQ10 is a mild blood thinner so if you are on blood-thinning medication it is particularly important to consult your doctor before taking this supplement.

•**L-carnitine.** This chemical derived from the amino acids lysine and methionine exists in most cells and serves a dual purpose—it transports long-chain fatty acids into the mitochondria to be used as fuel...and removes waste products such as lactic acid and ammonia. Researchers have concluded that L-carnitine helps to reduce body fat...increase muscle mass...increase the capacity for physical activity...minimize fatigue...and improve cognitive functions, such as arithmetic, memory and orientation (an awareness of one's environment with reference to time, place, and people). My recommended dosage is 1,500 mg (that's 1.5 grams) twice daily. Side effects are uncommon, but can include digestive upset—in which case, take it with food or reduce your dosage slightly.

•**Resveratrol.** Recently publicized as the "healthful" component of red wine in animal studies, this potent antioxidant has been shown to help increase the number of mitochondria in muscles and other tissues and to reduce fat deposits in the body. Resveratrol activates the SIRT1 gene, which promotes longevity, and also contributes to better glucose and insulin control in men with type 2 diabetes (which leads to better energy and weight control). In my practice, I am also finding that resveratrol helps with metabolism in general. My colleague, Carrie Louise Daenell, ND, in Denver, works extensively with fatigue and weight issues. She has her patients take all the nutrients discussed here and says that 75% of her patients improve in energy and weight—but, she adds, it is resveratrol that seems to give the greatest benefits for weight control.

My recommended resveratrol dosage for adults to improve metabolism and weight control: 125 mg daily. It is generally well tolerated, though occasionally people experience nausea or loose stool—in which case take with food or start with a lower dose and build up over time.

•**D-ribose.** This is a type of sugar found in all the body's cells. It helps to restore energy by prompting the mitochondria to recycle ATP that has broken down...and it acts as another fuel source besides glucose, especially in the muscles and in particular the heart. In a study at The Fibromyalgia and Fatigue Centers in Dallas, patients with either fibromyalgia or chronic fatigue syndrome were given 5 g of d-ribose three times daily for between 15 and 35 days. Patients had few side effects, and 66% showed significant improvement in energy, sleep, mental clarity, pain intensity and overall well-being. My recommended dosage of d-ribose for the average person is 5 g twice daily. If you feel light-headed after taking d-ribose, take it with meals. Although d-ribose is a type of sugar, it is safe for people with type 2 diabetes.

You aren't likely to hear much talk about mitochondrial dysfunction from practicing physicians in the conventional Western medical community. That's because researchers are just beginning to demonstrate that it is very common and plays an important role in our metabolism, energy levels and weight. Furthermore, as I mentioned earlier, new research is on the horizon. The recommendations you read here are well ahead of the curve, but you can adapt them into your life now. These plus a healthful diet and regular exercise should enable you to enjoy vibrant energy, a greater zest for life—more happiness!

Yummy Foods that Help You Burn More Fat

Emma Stevenson, PhD, senior lecturer, Northumbria University, Newcastle Upon Tyne, England.
Barry Braun, PhD, associate professor, kinesiology and director, Energy Metabolism Laboratory, University of Massachusetts, Amherst.
The Journal of Nutrition.

The type of carbohydrates you eat before a workout may influence how much fat you burn during your exercise session, recent research suggests.

Women who ate a breakfast rich in carbohydrates that do not cause a spike in blood sugar

—think muesli, yogurt, skim milk—burned 50% more fat during a post-breakfast workout than did those who ate a breakfast rich in the kind of carbohydrates known to make blood sugar rise sharply, such as cornflakes and white bread.

BACKGROUND

Carbs that cause a sharp blood sugar rise are known as high-glycemic index (GI) carbs. Those that don't are called low-GI index carbs.

While other researchers have also found that a low-glycemic menu is beneficial to fat-burning, the recent study has some unique points, noted lead author Emma Stevenson, PhD, a senior lecturer at Northumbria University in Newcastle Upon Tyne, England. She conducted the study while at the University of Nottingham.

"Most of the research in the effects of the glycemic load of pre-exercise feeding has been carried out in male subjects," Dr. Stevenson said. Most of it also has focused on endurance athletes, not the bulk of the population.

NEW STUDY

Instead, the new study included eight women of a typical healthy weight who averaged 24 years of age. On two different occasions, the women ate either a high- or low-GI breakfast, and then walked on a treadmill for 60 minutes three hours later. Dr. Stevenson's group drew blood samples before the breakfast, and also during and after the exercise, to measure parameters such as free fatty acids, which are a marker for fat burning.

Each breakfast totaled about 265 calories, but the low-GI meal had more fiber, the team noted.

The average amount of fat oxidized during the exercise was 7.4 grams after eating the low-glycemic meal but just 3.7 grams after the higher GI meal, a nearly 50% difference.

POSSIBLE EXPLANATION

Why the disparity? High-glycemic index carbs are known to spur a big spike in blood sugar, and the researchers believe that a meal rich in low-GI carbs, which elicit a lower blood sugar response, may boost the body's use of body fat, rather than blood sugar, for burning.

Mars UK, the candy company, funded the study. It is published in *The Journal of Nutrition.*

RECOMMENDATION

The take-home message, according to Dr. Stevenson: To burn more fat, focus on the low-GI foods. Low-GI foods tend to be whole grains, porridge, some whole grain cereals, soy and linseed bread, she said.

EXPERT COMMENTARY

The new study makes sense and builds on previous research, said Barry Braun, PhD, director of the Energy Metabolism Laboratory at the University of Massachusetts, Amherst, who has done his own research on post-workout eating.

While Dr. Stevenson's study findings are limited to healthy-weight women, Dr. Braun said he suspects it will also hold true for those hoping to shed excess pounds. "Eating large amounts of high-GI carbs right before exercise is probably as detrimental for overweight people as it is for normal-weight," he said.

Like Dr. Stevenson, he said he is talking about pre-exercise meals for those who work out at less than triathlon intensity. "There may be a place for these high-GI carbs" when an athlete needs high energy immediately, such as before running a marathon, Dr. Braun said.

POST-WORKOUT MEAL

Last year, Dr. Braun's own research found that the type of food eaten after exercise can make a difference in weight control—even for everyday exercisers.

Based on his studies, Dr. Braun suggests that eating a meal low in carbohydrates after working out at moderate intensity is potentially better for weight control than eating a meal high in carbs.

info For more on choosing healthy carbohydrates, visit the Harvard School of Public Health Web site, *www.hsph.harvard.edu/nutritionsource,* and click on "carbohydrates."

■ ■ ■ ■

Women Can't Control Hunger As Well as Men

After a night of fasting, women and men were asked to suppress their hunger when presented with favorite foods. Brain scans showed that food-related brain activity decreased in men but not in women.

Theory: Female hormones play a role in the brain's reaction to food.

Gene-Jack Wang, MD, professor of psychiatry, Mount Sinai School of Medicine, New York City, and lead author of a study of 23 people, published in *Proceedings of the National Academy of Sciences.*

■ ■ ■ ■

Are "TV Dinners" Making You Fat?

People eat nearly 300 more calories when watching TV during a meal.

Recent study: Compared with their normal eating habits, participants consumed 36% more pizza and 71% more macaroni and cheese when eating in front of the TV.

Theory: TV distracts you from realizing you are full.

Best: Turn off the TV during meals...or carry only a single serving into the TV room and leave the rest in the kitchen.

Heather L. Kirkorian, PhD, postdoctoral research associate, department of psychology, University of Massachusetts, Amherst, and leader of a study published in *Physiological Behavior.*

Drop Pounds with Pine Nuts...and Other Great Tricks to Lose Weight

Jodi Citrin Greebel, RD, CDN, a registered dietitian and president of Citrition, LLC, a nutrition consulting company in New York City. She is coauthor, with Melissa Gibson and Katie Nuanes, of *The Little Black Apron: A Single Girl's Guide to Cooking with Style & Grace* (Polka Dot).

Most weight-loss diets are hard to stick to. That's because you have to eliminate 3,500 calories to lose just one pound a week and that comes to 500 calories a day. This degree of calorie restriction can make people feel hungry all the time—and reluctant to stick with any diet for very long. That's also why it is hard for people to maintain the weight that they do lose. Roughly 95% of those who lose weight are unable to maintain the weight loss longer than a year or two.

Better: Eat foods that curtail appetite and increase feelings of fullness. People who do this naturally take in fewer calories overall and are more likely to maintain their weight loss.

What to eat...

- **Protein at every meal.** Protein is a natural appetite suppressant. People who often feel hungry probably aren't getting enough protein.

Self-test: Eat a regular meal or snack. If you're hungry again within two hours, the meal probably didn't include enough protein.

Protein should make up about 25% of every meal—three ounces to six ounces of protein is ideal. Good protein sources include chicken, seafood, lean red meats, egg whites, beans and low- or nonfat dairy.

Trap: Many traditional breakfast foods, such as a bagel or a Danish, are high in calories but low in protein. People who start the day with these foods invariably want to eat more within a few hours, adding unnecessary calories.

Always include protein with your morning meal—by spreading peanut butter on whole-wheat toast, for example.

Also helpful: High-protein snacks, such as string cheese or yogurt. They're more satisfying than carbohydrate snacks, such as pretzels or chips.

- **More fat.** Until recently, weight-loss experts advised people to eat less fat. This made intuitive sense because fat has about twice the calories as an equal amount of protein or carbohydrate. But today, after about 15 years of low-fat dieting, Americans are heavier than ever.

Reason: People who don't feel satisfied on a low-fat diet often eat excessive carbohydrates to make up the difference.

Fat is a satisfying nutrient. You may feel full after eating a lot of carbohydrates, such as pasta or bread, but you'll still want more. Fat, on the other hand, makes you crave less food, so you'll be less likely to fill up on additional calories.

Have a little fat with every meal. If you're having a salad, for example, use full-fat dressing in moderation rather than fat-free. Add a tablespoon of olive oil when making pasta sauce. A slice of cheese or a serving of cottage cheese also provides satisfying amounts of fat.

Easy does it: Use fats only in small amounts to avoid excess calories. One tablespoon of olive oil, for example, has about 120 calories. Small amounts curtail your appetite without adding too many calories.

• **A handful of pine nuts.** A hormone called *cholecystokinin* (CCK) has been found to increase feelings of fullness. About one ounce or a small handful of pine nuts (which actually are seeds, not nuts) stimulates the body to release CCK. This reduces appetite and helps you feel fuller even when you take in fewer calories overall.

• **Fiber, especially early in the day.** High-fiber diets increase feelings of fullness and aid in weight loss. High-fiber foods also may stimulate the release of appetite-suppressing hormones.

Virtually all foods that are high in fiber, such as fruits, vegetables, legumes and whole grains, are relatively low in calories. People who eat a lot of these foods tend to feel full even when they take in fewer calories during the day.

Try to get 25 to 30 grams of fiber daily. Beans are high in fiber, with about six grams in one-half cup. Blackberries are another excellent source, with about eight grams of fiber per cup.

• **Spicy foods as often as possible.** Cayenne, jalapeños, curries and other spicy foods contain *capsaicin* and other compounds that may increase metabolism and cause the body to burn slightly more calories. More important, these foods appear to affect the "satiety center" in the brain, causing people to feel more satisfied and consume fewer calories.

• **Water before a meal.** Drink a full glass of water before you start eating, and keep sipping water throughout the meal. Water takes up space in the stomach. Or you can start your meal with a broth-based soup (not a cream soup, which is higher in calories). People who consume liquids before and during meals consume fewer calories than those who go straight to the main course.

Caution: Avoid high-calorie liquids. Americans consume about 20% more calories now than they did 20 years ago. Many of these calories come from soft drinks, sports drinks and coffee beverages that include sugar and cream. Some of these drinks contain 400 calories or more, which could result in almost one extra pound of weight a week if consumed daily.

Good Mood Foods That Help You Lose Weight, Too

Susan Kleiner, PhD, RD, a Mercer Island, Washington–based nutritionist who has worked with Olympic athletes, professional sports teams and Fortune 500 company executives. She is author of *The Good Mood Diet: Feel Great While You Lose Weight* (Springboard), *www.good mood-diet.com,* and *Power Eating* (Human Kinetics).

It's long been known that our eating habits can have a dramatic effect on our overall health. Now a growing body of scientific evidence shows that the foods we eat can either improve—or harm—our mood.

Bonus: Mood-boosting foods will help you lose weight if you have some extra pounds to shed. They can give you the mental and physical energy to be active as well as the nutrition that best supports physical activity, muscle growth and fat burning. People of normal weight can adapt these food recommendations to their daily calorie needs.

FEEL-GREAT BUILDING BLOCKS

The basic nutrients in our food each play a role in optimizing our mood and energy levels...

• **Carbohydrates** are viewed negatively by most people who are trying to eat healthfully. But, in fact, these nutrients—when eaten in the proper form—are crucial to maintaining mood.

Here's why: Your mood is largely determined by a proper balance of brain chemicals (neurotransmitters). One key neurotransmitter, serotonin, is strongly linked to positive feelings.

Surprising fact: The brain uses the amino acid tryptophan, which is contained in most dietary proteins, to manufacture serotonin. But to cross from the bloodstream to the brain, tryptophan must compete against other amino acids. Carbohydrates help displace the other amino acids, thus increasing the amount of tryptophan that gets through—and the amount of serotonin that is produced.

A steady stream of carbohydrates will help your brain reach ample levels of tryptophan.

Best carbohydrate sources: Fruits (such as bananas, blueberries, mangoes, oranges, pomegranates and strawberries) and vegetables (such as broccoli, spinach, yams and carrots). These foods not only supply carbohydrates, but also contain water and fiber that slow the rate at which the carbohydrates are digested and absorbed into the bloodstream.

Helpful: When your favorite fruits and vegetables are out of season, frozen versions (without added sauces) are economical and convenient.

- **Fats,** like carbohydrates, have been pegged as "no-nos." But dietary fats should not be eliminated altogether—they make foods satisfying.

Surprising fact: Fats are essential in keeping brain-cell membranes supple and well-functioning. For example, the omega-3 fatty acids found in certain fish (such as salmon, mackerel and sardines) have been shown to improve mood in people who are depressed.

Best fat sources: In addition to fish, try olives (any type), nuts, seeds, avocados, extra-virgin olive oil and cold-pressed canola oil.

- **Proteins** can be converted into blood sugar (glucose)—but slowly, to keep glucose on an even keel. These nutrients also help keep metabolism (how fast you burn calories) high.

Surprising fact: Proteins are the raw materials from which neurotransmitters, including serotonin, are manufactured.

Best protein sources: Lean organic meat (beef, pork or lamb) or poultry...fish...low-fat or fat-free dairy products...eggs...and legumes (such as pinto beans or lentils).

GOOD MOOD MEALS

After three hours of not eating, glucose levels fall and so do your spirits and energy levels. To avoid "panic eating," have a meal or substantial snack every two to three hours. *For example...*

Breakfast: ½ cup of shredded wheat cereal...2 tablespoons of raisins...1 cup of fat-free milk...1 egg (cooked without butter or margarine).

Mid-morning snack: 1 cup of fat-free milk ...omelet from 4 egg whites or 2 ounces of sliced turkey.

Lunch: 1 cup of bean soup (low-sodium canned soup is okay)...tuna salad (without mayonnaise, but with reduced-fat salad dressing made with olive oil and vinegar)...and mixed greens.

Afternoon snack: Orange...mini-carrots with 1 tablespoon of natural-style peanut butter.

Dinner: 1 cup of whole-wheat pasta tossed with 1¼ tablespoons of pesto (homemade or store-bought)...4 ounces of chicken (grilled, broiled, baked or roasted)...2 cups of sliced cucumber...at least 1 cup total of carrots and cherry tomatoes...and 1¼ cups of fresh strawberries with 1 tablespoon of full-fat dairy whipped topping (it has only a few more calories than a "lite" version).

Evening snack: 1 cup of hot cocoa made with fat-free milk, 1 to 2 rounded teaspoons of unsweetened cocoa powder and Splenda (one packet or to taste) or another sweetener, such as agave nectar (a syrup derived from a desert plant). It is sold in health food stores.

EXERCISE–MOOD CONNECTION

Exercise not only helps control your body weight, but also has been shown to improve mood and reduce depression (as effectively as medication, in some studies). At a minimum, get 30 minutes of activity (at the level of brisk walking) five to six days a week.

■ ■ ■ ■

Sniff Mint to Lose Weight

In a recent finding, people who sniffed peppermint oil every two hours ate almost 350 fewer calories a day than those who did not.

Possible reason: Peppermint boosts alertness, so people who smell it may be less likely to snack because of fatigue or boredom.

Bryan Raudenbush, PhD/L pharm, associate professor of psychology and director of undergraduate research, Wheeling Jesuit University, Wheeling, West Virginia, and coauthor of a study of 27 adults, published in *Appetite.*

■ ■ ■ ■

Skip MSG to Stay Slim

People who used the flavor enhancer monosodium glutamate (MSG) the most were nearly three times as likely to be overweight or obese as people who did not use MSG, a recent study found—even though calorie consumption and physical activity levels were the same in both groups. MSG may affect the part of the brain that helps regulate appetite and fat metabolism. Check food labels—many processed and Asian foods contain MSG…as do the flavor-enhancing ingredients yeast extract, hydrolyzed protein and calcium caseinate.

Ka He, MD, assistant professor of nutrition and epidemiology, University of North Carolina at Chapel Hill School of Public Health, and author of a study of 752 people, published in *Obesity.*

Lose a Pound a Day and Keep It Off—Secrets From Dr. Rob Huizenga Of *The Biggest Loser*

Rob Huizenga, MD, associate professor of clinical medicine at University of California, Los Angeles. He specializes in sports and weight-loss medicine and is the medical adviser for *The Biggest Loser,* the NBC-TV reality series whose contestants compete to lose the most weight. He is author of *Where Did All the Fat Go: The WOW! Prescription to Reach Your Ideal Weight—and Stay There* (Tallfellow).

One of the most effective weight-loss strategies was developed for *The Biggest Loser,* the popular NBC reality show. The first 64 contestants—all of whom were obese —lost an average of about 60 pounds each over five months, three times more than most people lose on standard diets.

Admittedly, the participants were in a highly artificial environment. People in real life don't have full-time trainers, around-the-clock peer pressure and cameras recording every move.

As an experiment, the producers arranged for 36 people who weren't on the show to follow a similar program.

Result: The participants lost nearly as much as those who were on the show.

The secret: Less emphasis on calories and more on hard exercise.

Important: To be safe, get a medical checkup before starting any intense exercise program and tell your doctor what you intend to do.

EXERCISE LONG

The Surgeon General advises overweight individuals to lose weight by walking for 10 minutes three times a week, gradually increasing the amount to 150 minutes a week. Unless you're a racewalker, this level of exercise burns only about 525 calories. It takes nearly a week to lose just one pound.

Better: Prolonged, vigorous exercise. Working out intensely for one hour, twice a day, burns up to 2,500 calories in obese women and 3,000 to 4,000 in obese men. That adds up, on average, to about one pound a day.

Important: The assumption has always been that obese men and women are incapable of long exercise. Not true. Many of our participants were morbidly obese and had been completely sedentary. They struggled at first, but nearly all were able to complete the program.

EXERCISE HARD

It's the only way to lose appreciable amounts of weight. Suppose that your only exercise is walking. You would have to do it for 5.5 hours a day in order to lose 1% of your body weight in a week. Those who exercise more intensely can get the same results in a day.

The average woman who goes from sedentary to very fit with vigorous exercise gains six to seven pounds of muscle. Each pound of muscle burns at least an extra 30 calories a day.

STAY ON SCHEDULE

People who work out at the same times every day—once in the morning and again in the afternoon or evening—tend to stick with it more reliably than those who "get around to it."

Also important: Do not quit exercising if you get hurt. Doctors used to tell people to curtail their workouts after injuries. Now we know that injuries heal faster when people keep moving—although you might need to switch to a different exercise. If you hurt your ankle, for example, you might need to swim for a few weeks instead of jog. However, if the pain is worse the next day, even after you changed the exercise, see your doctor.

FUEL UP AFTER WORKOUTS

Muscle cells are more responsive to insulin in the 30 minutes following a workout. People who have a high-protein, high-carbohydrate drink during this period absorb more nutrients and have accelerated muscle growth.

You can use a commercially made muscle-recovery drink, such as Endurox (available online and at health-food stores). Or make your own by blending about a cup of skim milk with fresh or frozen fruit and a high-protein powder, such as whey (follow directions on the label).

YOU STILL CAN EAT

The good thing about this plan is that you don't have to avoid anything. Healthy foods, such as fresh produce, fish and whole grains, are important, but you don't need to be fanatical.

Even the quantities aren't that important. The participants in our program lost dramatic amounts of weight, even though they practiced only modest calorie restriction—the women consumed an average of about 1,400 calories a day and the men had about 1,800.

The program works because people who slightly curtail calories and exercise vigorously gain the necessary muscle to burn even more fat. Just as important, eating an almost-normal diet prevents the body from shifting into "starvation mode," in which it tries to conserve calories—the point at which weight loss slows or stops altogether.

Foods that Make Exercise "Easier"

Heidi Skolnik, MS, CDN, a certified dietitian nutritionist and director of sports nutrition for the Women's Sports Medical Center at the Hospital for Special Surgery in New York City. A regular contributor to NBC's *Today* show, she also is a sports nutrition consultant to the New York Giants football team and the School of American Ballet.

You already know that a regular exercise routine—ideally, at least 30 minutes of vigorous activity daily—is among the smartest steps you can take to protect your health.

What you may not know: Consuming the right foods and fluids is one of the best ways to improve your exercise performance.

If your body is not properly fueled—regardless of the type, frequency or intensity of physical activity—your energy levels are more likely to wane, your muscles will be more susceptible to fatigue and soreness, and you'll find it harder to maintain your desired weight. *My secrets...*

•Remember to drink enough fluids before exercise. Research shows that about half of people who work out in the morning are dehydrated when they begin to exercise.

Why is fluid consumption so important? When you're dehydrated, your heart must pump harder to get blood to your muscles. Being dehydrated also impairs your ability to perspire and cool yourself.

Advice: Drink one cup of water or a sports drink, such as Gatorade, before your workout and another during your workout. If your workout is vigorous or lasts more than 60 minutes, you may need to consume more fluids.

Also remember to drink fluids throughout the day. You don't have to limit yourself to water. Milk, tea, coffee, fruit juice and carbonated beverages also count toward your daily fluid intake.

Caution: Your risk for dehydration is increased if you take a diuretic drug, have diabetes or are an older adult—the body's thirst center functions less efficiently with age.

•Don't exercise on an empty stomach. When you don't eat for several hours—including the time when you're sleeping—your blood sugar levels decline. This can leave you with less energy for physical activity and at risk for injury.

The quickest solution is to consume carbohydrates, which are your body's primary energy source. Carbohydrates are found mainly in starchy foods, such as grains, breads and vegetables, as well as in fruit, milk and yogurt.

Advice: If you're exercising before breakfast, first have half a banana or a slice of toast. If you're exercising just before lunch, eat a healthful midmorning snack—and a mid- to late-afternoon snack if your workout is before dinner. It's okay to eat the snack right before your workout.

• **Eat a balanced breakfast.** Eating a good breakfast helps get your metabolism going—and may help you consume fewer calories during the rest of the day.

Advice: Choose whole-grain foods (such as oatmeal or whole-grain cereal or toast) to fuel your muscles...a serving of dairy (yogurt, low-fat milk or cheese) or another protein (such as eggs or Canadian bacon) to promote muscle repair... and fruit (such as a mango, berries or melon) for vitamins and disease-fighting phytonutrients.

• **Fill in your nutritional "gaps" with lunch.** Like breakfast, your midday meal should include healthful carbohydrates and protein.

Advice: At lunch, get some of the nutrients you may not have included in your breakfast. For example, if you ate fruit in the morning, eat vegetables at lunch. If your breakfast included a dairy product as your protein source, eat lean meat or fish at lunch.

Example of a healthful lunch: A salad with grilled chicken, legumes, peppers, broccoli and an olive oil–based dressing.

• **Eat an evening meal.** If you exercise late in the afternoon or after work, don't skip your evening meal. You may wake up the next morning with a "deficit" that can lead you to overeat.

Advice: Strive for a balance of unprocessed carbohydrates (such as brown rice or vegetables), lean protein (such as fish or poultry) and a little healthful fat (such as nuts or olive oil).

Example: A shrimp and vegetable stir-fry served over one-quarter cup of brown rice.

■ ■ ■ ■

"Alarming" Exercise Routine

Adults received handheld personal digital assistants (PDAs) that beeped morning and evening to prompt them to answer questions about where, how and how much they were exercising. They engaged in physical activity for five hours per week, on average—compared with just two hours per week for study participants given only informational handouts.

Motivating: Program your PDA, cell phone or computer calendar to cue you to exercise.

Abby King, PhD, professor, departments of medicine and health research and policy, Stanford Prevention Research Center, Stanford University School of Medicine, California, and leader of a study of 37 people, published in *American Journal of Preventive Medicine.*

The Affordable, In-Home Strength Workout that Beats the Machines

Doris St-Arnaud, a Trois-Rivières, Quebec–based 25-year veteran of the fitness industry and author of several books about using stability balls, including *Stability Ball Exercises with Weights* (available at Balls 'N' Bands, 864-346-0945, *www.ballsnbands.com*). She also serves as a stability ball training master trainer in Canada and Europe.

As you age, one of the simplest—yet most effective—actions you can take to maintain your ability to perform everyday activities, such as carrying shopping bags and climbing stairs, is to build muscle strength.

What you may not know: The expensive, freestanding weight machines that are found in gyms around the country are not always the best way to build strength.

Important new finding: When 30 people exercised twice weekly for 16 weeks, researchers found that those who used "free-form" equipment, such as hand weights, improved their strength by 115% versus 57% when freestanding exercise equipment, such as a leg-press machine, was used.

Why the big difference? According to exercise physiologists, weight machines primarily strengthen the muscles that are needed to move the weights in the designated range of motion, while free-form equipment works the primary muscles that lift the weight and, to a greater degree, the nearby muscles that support and stabilize the primary muscles.

For even greater benefits: While performing free-form strength-building exercises, sit or lie on an inflatable "stability ball." This helps strengthen another set of muscles, called stabilizers. These include the postural muscles in the lower back, abdomen and thighs.

The following exercises, which work all the major muscles in the body, can be performed in about 20 minutes in your home.*

To get started: Everything you need to perform these exercises is available at sporting-goods or discount stores—three pairs of hand weights (starting at about $8 a pair)...three pairs of strap-on ankle weights (starting at about $10 a pair)...and an inflatable stability ball (starting at about $20).

The hand and ankle weights you choose should be light enough so that you can do at least eight repetitions of each exercise but heavy enough so that you can't do more than 15 repetitions.

Example: A woman who is just beginning to strength-train may start with two-pound hand or ankle weights, while a male beginner may start with five-pound weights. Once you can easily perform 15 repetitions, switch to a heavier weight. Increase the weight by one to three pounds at a time depending on the strength of the muscles worked.

To choose the proper size stability ball: Follow the instructions on the package, using your height as a general guideline. Inflate the ball so that your knees and hips are at the same level when you sit on it.

For each of the following exercises, perform one set of eight to 15 repetitions unless otherwise noted...**

*Rest at least 48 hours between workouts to allow for adequate muscle recovery, and always check with your doctor before beginning any exercise program.

**If you prefer not to use a stability ball, you can perform the arm curl, triceps press and leg lift while sitting in a chair...the fly while lying on your back...and the reverse leg lift and back rise while lying on your stomach (on a mat or bed).

•Arm curl.

Primary muscles used: Biceps (fronts of the upper arms).

Among the secondary muscles used: Fronts of the shoulders, the upper back and sides of neck.

What to do: While holding a weight in each hand, sit on the stability ball with your feet on the floor, your elbows next to your waist. Keeping your elbows in this position, lift the weights toward your shoulders. Return slowly to starting position.

•Triceps press.

Primary muscles used: Triceps (backs of the upper arms).

Among the secondary muscles used: Fronts of the shoulders and pectorals (front of the chest).

What to do: While holding a weight in each hand, sit on the ball with your abdominal muscles tightened and your back straight. Extend both arms overhead, palms facing each other and elbows slightly flexed. Keeping your elbows stationary, bend them to lower the weights to the backs of your shoulders. Return slowly to starting position with arms overhead.

•Leg lift.

Primary muscles used: Quadriceps (fronts of the thighs).

Among the secondary muscles used: Iliopsoas (muscles connecting the pelvis to the front of the hip).

What to do: Place a weight on your right ankle and sit on the ball with your palms holding the sides of the ball for added stability. Straighten your weighted leg with your heel resting on the floor, then flex your ankle so your toes point upward. Lift your weighted leg as high as you comfortably can. Return slowly to the starting position. Perform a second set of eight to 15 repetitions with your left leg.

•Fly.

Primary muscles used: Pectorals.

Among the secondary muscles used: Fronts of the shoulders, triceps and biceps.

What to do: While holding a weight in each hand, sit on the stability ball and carefully "walk" forward until your lower back rests on the ball. Keep your feet and knees shoulder-width apart with your knees directly above your heels. Extend your arms above your chest, elbows slightly bent and palms facing each other. Lower your left arm to the side until it's in line with your shoulders. Return slowly to the starting position. Perform a second set of eight to 15 repetitions with your right arm.

- **Reverse leg lift.**

Primary muscles used: Buttocks.

Among the secondary muscles used: Hamstrings (backs of the thighs).

What to do: Place a weight on your left ankle, then face the ball with your knees slightly bent and lean forward to rest your trunk on the ball. Keep your feet shoulder-width apart with both hands flat on the floor for extra stability. While holding your weighted leg straight, lift it off the ground as high as you comfortably can, then slowly lower it again without touching it to the floor. Perform a second set of eight to 15 repetitions with the right leg.

- **Back rise.**

Primary muscles used: Lower back.

Among the secondary muscles used: Backs of the shoulders, and middle and upper back.

What to do: Rest your trunk on the stability ball and lower your head so your chin also rests on the ball. Hold a weight in each hand and place your hands in front of your forehead with your palms facing down. Keeping your head in line with your trunk, lift your head, shoulders and chest off the ball and pull your elbows back toward your hips.

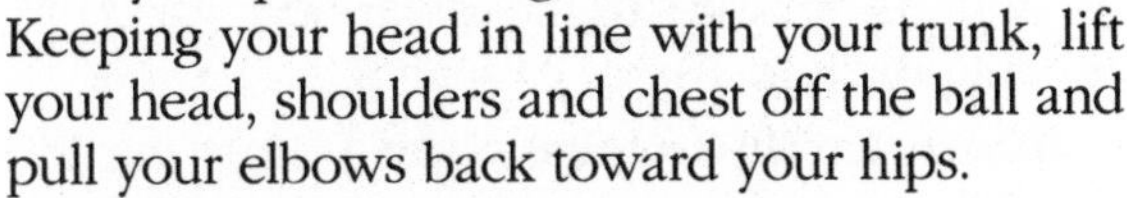

Exercise illustrations by Shawn Banner.

Exercise for Your Body Type

Edward J. Jackowski, PhD, founder and CEO of Exude, Inc., a New York City–based fitness company (*www.exude.com*) that specializes in one-on-one fitness training. He is author of *Escape Your Shape: How to Work Out Smarter, Not Harder* and *Hold It! You're Exercising Wrong* (both from Fireside). He is also the New York City fitness representative for the American Diabetes Association.

Little-known fact: The shape of a person's body—Hourglass, Spoon, Cone or Ruler*—dictates the type of exercise he/she should be performing to get health and fitness benefits.

Solution: A six-year medical study shows that by selecting exercises according to your body type, you can begin to address the built-in imbalances of your body.**

WHAT'S YOUR BODY TYPE?

Your body type has nothing to do with how tall, short, slim or chunky you are. It has to do with where your weight—both fat and muscle—accumulates on your body. *Your body is most likely...*

- **Hourglass**—if you carry most of your weight in your upper and lower body...and there's a significant difference (six inches or more) between the circumference of your chest and waist or between your hips and waist.
- **Spoon**—if you carry most of your weight in your hips, thighs and buttocks.
- **Cone**—if you carry most of your weight in your back, chest, arms and stomach.
- **Ruler**—if there's not much difference in the circumference of your chest, waist and hips... and you tend to put on weight around your midsection.

If you're not sure of your body type: You're probably overweight. Follow the recommendations below for the Hourglass body type until you've lost some of your weight. As you slim down, your natural shape will emerge.

*These body types are registered trademarks of Exude, Inc., and the fitness prescriptions for them are patented.

**Check with your doctor before beginning a new exercise program.

HOURGLASS

About 40% of women and 20% of men have an Hourglass body type. People with this type require exercises that burn fat without adding muscle mass in the upper and lower body areas.

Recommended exercises...

Main aerobic exercises: Jump rope...stationary bicycling with low resistance (level 1 to 3)...jumping jacks...fast walking (a pace of 3 to 4.5 mph) on a flat surface...elliptical machines with no resistance.

Main resistance exercises: Weight machines with light weights (10 pounds or less for the upper body and less than 25 pounds for the lower body) and a high number of repetitions (25 to 50 per exercise)...upper-body exercises with a four-pound aerobic (weighted) bar (for women) or 12- to 15-pound aerobic bar (for men)...leg extensions with light weight and high repetitions (25 to 50 per exercise).

Exercises to avoid...

Aerobic: Step classes...spinning classes...high-impact aerobics.

Resistance: Any upper- or lower-body exercises using high resistance or weights...any exercise using ankle weights.

SPOON

About 30% of women and 10% of men have a Spoon body type. Spoons require exercises that quickly burn fat in the lower region of the body and build muscle in the upper region.

Recommended exercises...

Main aerobic exercises: Jump rope...stationary bicycling with low resistance (level 1 to 3) and high revolutions per minute (90 to 120)...fast walking (3 to 4.5 mph) on a flat surface.

Main resistance exercises: Upper-body exercises with moderate to heavy weights (10 pounds or more) and low repetitions (8 to 10 per exercise)...lower-body exercises with low resistance (less than 25 pounds) and high repetitions (25 to 50 per exercise).

Exercises to avoid...

Aerobic: Elliptical machines and stair climbers...Rollerblading...swimming...long-distance running...spinning...step classes...high-impact aerobic classes.

Resistance: Squats...lunges...leg presses...any lower-body exercises with moderate to high resistance or weights.

CONE

About 30% of men and 10% of women have a Cone body type. Cones need to concentrate on building bulk in the lower body and endurance in the abdomen and upper body.

Recommended exercises...

Main aerobic exercises: Spinning...stair climbers...stationary bicycling with moderate to high resistance (level 4 or higher)...slow walking (3 mph or less) on an incline or hills...step classes.

Main resistance exercises: Leg presses, leg extensions and leg curls (done on weight machines) using moderate to heavy resistance (50 pounds or more) and low repetitions (8 to 10 per exercise)...upper-body exercises with low resistance (10 pounds or less) and high repetitions (25 to 50 per exercise)—especially push-ups, pull-ups and dips.

Main flexibility exercises: Hamstring and upper-body stretches.

Exercises to avoid...

Aerobic: Rowing...aerobic or step classes using hand weights.

Resistance: Any upper-body exercises with moderate to high resistance or weights.

RULER

Approximately 40% of men and 20% of women have a Ruler body type. Rulers need to focus on building muscle and overall strength.

Recommended exercises...

Main aerobic exercises: Step classes...spinning...stationary bicycling or elliptical machines with moderate to high resistance (level 7 to 15)...walking on an incline or hills (3.7 to 4.3 mph)...swimming.

Main resistance exercises: Squats, lunges and leg presses...all upper- and lower-body exercises using moderate to heavy resistance or weights (10 pounds or more for the upper body, 50 pounds or more for the lower body) and low repetitions (8 to 10 per exercise).

Main flexibility exercises: Hamstring and quadriceps stretches.

Exercises to avoid...None.

■ ■ ■ ■

Inactivity Raises Disease Risk—Quickly

Researchers asked 18 healthy men to reduce the number of steps they took daily from either 6,000 or 10,000 steps to about 1,400 steps by using a car or elevators.

Result: After two weeks, the men had higher levels of blood sugars and fats that raise risk for diabetes, heart disease and other diseases.

Theory: When excess blood fats and sugars don't clear the bloodstream quickly—a process promoted by exercise—they can adversely affect metabolic functions.

Self-defense: Aim to exercise for at least 30 minutes (in at least five-minute segments) most days of the week.

Frank Booth, PhD, professor, department of physiology, University of Missouri College of Medicine, Columbia.

Feel-Good Exercises You Can Do in Bed

Genie Tartell, DC, RN, a New York City–based chiropractor and registered nurse who focuses on physical rehabilitation. She is coauthor of *Get Fit in Bed* (New Harbinger).

Think about the last time you really stretched your body. Didn't you feel great afterward?

Unfortunately, most people—including many who are physically active—don't do enough to improve their muscle tone, flexibility and strength. To help people incorporate a simple workout regimen into their daily routines, I have devised a program that can be performed in a comfortable setting you are bound to visit each day—your bed.

These bed exercises not only increase your strength, flexibility and endurance, but also stimulate production of the mood-enhancing brain chemical serotonin, leaving you feeling calm and relaxed. As a result, most people find that they sleep better when they do these exercises at night, and feel invigorated if they do the routine in the morning.

The following exercises are designed for anyone but are particularly helpful for people who are confined to bed (while recovering from an illness or injury) and for those unable to find time during the day to exercise. They can be completed in just 10 minutes a day.

Important: When performing each movement, breathe in slowly for a count of four... hold for a count of one...then exhale through pursed lips for a count of four.

ALTERNATE LEG LENGTHENER

Purpose: Tones and stretches the spine and pelvis, which bears much of the upper body's weight.

What to do: While lying on your back with your body centered on the bed and your hips and legs flat on the bed, stretch your right leg forward by pushing with the heel of your right foot. Return your leg to the starting position. Do the same stretch with your left leg. Repeat five times with each leg.

HIP SIDE TO SIDE

Purpose: Tones and stretches the hips and low back.

What to do: While lying on your back with your hips flat on the bed, rock your hips gently—as far as comfortable—to the right and then to the left. Keep your upper body stable. Repeat five times in each direction.

ARMS-SHOULDER SEESAW

Purpose: Tones and stretches the shoulders and upper back.

What to do: While lying on your back, place your arms at your sides. Slide your right arm and shoulder toward your right foot. Next, raise your right shoulder toward your head, while at the same time sliding your left arm and shoulder toward your left foot. Then raise your left shoulder toward your head, while lowering your right arm and shoulder toward your right foot. Repeat five times on each side, moving your shoulders up and down like a seesaw.

ARMS TOWARD THE HEADBOARD

Purpose: Stretches the shoulders and rib cage, allowing for deeper, more relaxed breathing.

What to do: While lying on your back, extend your arms behind your head. Stretch your right arm toward the headboard of your bed or the wall behind you. Return your right arm to your side and then extend your left arm behind you. Repeat five times on each side.

ELBOW–KNEE PISTON

Purpose: Strengthens your abdominal muscles while increasing your heart rate (improves heart muscle strength and endurance).

What to do: While lying on your back, raise your knees and, using your stomach muscles, lift your upper body toward them. Bend your arms so that your elbows are pointing at your knees. Bring your left elbow toward your right knee, then return to the starting position. Then bring your right elbow toward your left knee, maintaining a continuous pumping motion. Repeat six times.

COBRA

Purpose: Builds upper body strength (important for daily activities such as bathing and cooking).

What to do: Lie on your stomach with your elbows bent and palms flat on the bed next to your shoulders. Fully straighten your arms to lift your upper body so that it curves into a cobra-like position. Hold for a few seconds, then return to the starting position. Repeat three times.

MODIFIED BOW

Purpose: Tones and strengthens the back and improves muscular coordination.

What to do: Lie on your stomach with your arms at your sides. Raise your legs and upper body simultaneously (only to a level that is comfortable), then reach back with your arms as if you are trying to touch your raised feet. Hold for a few seconds, then return to the starting position. Repeat three times.

SWIMMING IN BED

Purpose: Strengthens the arms and legs, while increasing heart rate and stimulating blood flow throughout the body.

What to do: While lying on your stomach, move one arm forward, then move it back while moving the other arm forward, simultaneously kicking your legs. Repeat 20 times, counting each arm movement as one repetition.

BRIDGE

Purpose: Cools down the body and directs blood flow away from the legs to the heart, reducing risk for blood clots in the legs.

What to do: Lie on your back with your knees bent, feet flat on the bed and your arms at your sides. Tighten your buttock muscles as you lift your pelvis toward the ceiling—until your pelvis is in line with your thighs. Then gently lower your body back to the bed. Repeat five times.

Important: If you think any of these exercises may be too strenuous for you, check with your doctor before trying them.

Exercise illustrations by Shawn Banner.

■ ■ ■ ■

Easiest Exercises Boost Energy the Most

A recent study followed people who had unexplained constant fatigue. For six weeks, one group did no exercise...another group did 20 minutes of moderately intense stationary cycling three times weekly...a third group cycled for the same amount of time at a much slower pace. In both exercise groups, energy increased by 20% over the sedentary group—but the lowest-intensity exercisers reported the least fatigue.

Patrick O'Connor, PhD, codirector, Exercise Psychology Laboratory, University of Georgia, Athens, and leader of a study of 36 people, published in *Psychotherapy and Psychosomatics.*

20-Minute Cellulite Solution

Wayne Westcott, PhD, fitness research director at South Shore YMCA and adjunct professor of exercise science at Quincy College, both in Quincy, Massachusetts. He is author or coauthor of more than 20 books, including *No More Cellulite* (Perigee) and *Get Stronger, Feel Younger* (Rodale).

When scientists say there's "no such thing" as cellulite, they mean that cellulite is not a distinct type of body tissue, but it is ordinary fat. Yet for nearly nine out of 10 women, that unwanted dimpling on the hips and thighs is undeniably real.

How it got there: Fibrous cords connect the skin to the underlying muscle. When the fat layer that lies between the skin and the muscle is too thick, the cords are pulled tight and fat cells bulge out between them, causing that "cottage cheese" look. *And cellulite gets worse with age...*

- **The typical woman loses muscle mass** at an average rate of about five pounds per decade from ages 20 to 50...and perhaps more rapidly after menopause.
- **As muscle mass decreases,** metabolism slows, the body burns fewer calories and the ratio of fat to muscle rises.
- **Supporting connective tissues** (such as collagen) break down and lose elasticity, making cellulite more pronounced.

What doesn't help: A swarm of creams, wraps, massage techniques and mechanical devices purport to eliminate cellulite, typically by "melting away fat." None addresses the underlying physiological causes. Even dieting can backfire if you overdo it, because your body may break down muscle as well as fat to get the energy that it needs, raising your fat-to-muscle ratio.

What does help: Strength training, which rebuilds muscle and burns calories. It also boosts metabolism.

Best: Three times a week, do the following exercises. The routine takes about 20 minutes.*

You need only three simple kinds of equipment. Go to a gym or buy your own equipment at a sporting-goods store or online (try *www.spriproducts.com*). Within four to six weeks, you should see a noticeable reduction in cellulite.

*Check with your doctor before beginning any exercise program.

MEDICINE BALL

A medicine ball is a weighted ball about six to eight inches in diameter. Holding one while doing the following two moves adds extra weight that makes your lower body work harder—and as a bonus, tones the upper body, too. To start, choose a ball with which you can do eight to 12 repetitions per side. Once you work your way up to 15 reps, switch to a ball about one to two pounds heavier. Typically, a woman starts with a two- to four-pound ball and works up to six, eight or 10 pounds.

Cost: About $20 to $40 per ball.

Target zones: Front and back of thighs... buttocks.

- **Lunge.** Stand with feet shoulder-width apart, holding ball between hands at waist level, about six to eight inches in front of you. Bend elbows to bring ball up to chest level...at the same time, with right foot, lunge forward about two to three feet, bending right knee to a 90-degree angle so that it is directly above foot. Step out far enough so that your knee does not move past your ankle (left leg will be slightly bent, heel up). Hold lunge position for three seconds, keeping back straight...then push off with right foot and return to standing, bringing ball back down. Do 10 to 15 reps, then repeat on left. (Avoid this exercise if you have knee problems.)
- **Knee lift.** Stand with feet shoulder-width apart, holding ball between hands at waist level. Step right foot back about two to two-and-a-half feet, keeping right leg straight and bending left knee slightly. Elbows straight, raise ball in front of you to head height.

Bring right knee forward and up as high as you can... bend elbows and bring ball down to touch knee...then step back again with right foot as you straighten arms and raise ball to head height. Do 10 to 15 reps, then repeat on left.

RESISTANCE TUBES

Resistance tubes are elastic tubes about four feet long with handles on each end. They vary in thickness—start with a tube with which you can do eight to 12 reps per side. When you can do 15 reps, switch to a thicker tube.

Cost: About $5 to $15 per tube.

Target zones: Inner and outer thighs.

•**Hip adduction.** Attach one handle to a secure anchor (such as around a bed leg). Loop other handle securely around your right foot (push past toes as far as possible so it doesn't fly off).

Sit on floor, with knees straight and legs spread, so tube is straight out to the right of your right foot. With hands on floor behind you, use inner thigh muscles to slide right leg in to meet left leg. Hold three seconds, then slowly slide right leg back out to spread-leg position. Do 10 to 15 reps, then repeat with left leg.

•**Hip abduction.** Attach one handle to a secure anchor, and loop other handle around right foot (as in the previous exercise).

Sit on floor, with knees straight and legs together, so tube is straight out to the left of your right foot, crossing over left ankle. With your hands on the floor behind you, use outer thigh muscles to slide right leg out to the right until legs are spread as much as possible. Hold three seconds, then slowly slide right leg back to meet left leg. Do 10 to 15 reps, then repeat with left leg.

DUMBBELLS

To start, use a pair of dumbbells (hand weights) with which you can do eight to 12 reps. When you are able to do 15 reps, switch to weights two to three pounds heavier. Typically a woman starts with five-pound weights, building up to as much as 15 pounds.

Cost: About $10 to $30 per pair.

Target zones: Front and back of thighs... buttocks.

•**Squat.** Stand with feet shoulder-width apart, one weight in each hand, arms down at sides. Keeping torso erect and head in line with spine, bend knees (as if sitting on a chair) until thighs are nearly parallel to floor. Do not allow knees to move forward past toes. Hold for three seconds, then return to standing. Do 10 to 15 reps.

•**Step-Up.** Stand at bottom of a stairway, facing steps, one weight in each hand, arms down at sides. (If you have balance problems, hold a weight in one hand and hold on to banister with the other hand.)

Place entire left foot flat on first step, then rise until you are standing on the stair. Step back down, again moving left foot first. Do 10 to 15 reps, then repeat on the right side.

Exercise illustrations by Shawn Banner.

Bone-Building Exercises

Raymond E. Cole, DO, clinical assistant professor, department of internal medicine, Michigan State University College of Osteopathic Medicine, East Lansing. He is director of the Osteoporosis Testing Center of Michigan in Brooklyn, Michigan, and author of several books, including *Best Body, Best Bones: Your Doctor's Exercise Rx for Lifelong Fitness* (Wellpower). *www.drraymondcole.com.*

Women whose bones are fragile and porous—due to the severe loss of bone density that characterizes osteoporosis—often avoid exercise for fear that jarring or twisting motions could cause fractures.

Done properly, however, exercise is not only safe for people with osteoporosis or its milder form, osteopenia, it actually can reduce or even reverse bone loss. For people whose bones are still healthy, exercise helps ensure that osteoporosis never develops.

Reason: When a muscle exerts tension on a bone, it stimulates specialized cells that increase new bone formation. Also, when muscles that contribute to balance are strengthened, falls (and resulting fractures) are less likely.

Keys: Doing the types of workouts that build bone most effectively...and modifying techniques as necessary to avoid overstressing already weakened bones.

What to do: Start by exercising for 10 to 20 minutes several times a week, gradually building up to 30 minutes a day six days per week. Alternate between a strength-training workout one day and an aerobic activity the next.

Important: Before beginning the exercise program below, ask your doctor which instructions you should follow—the ones labeled "If you have healthy bones" or the ones labeled "If you already have bone loss."

STRENGTH TRAINING FOR BONES

The only equipment you need are hand weights (dumbbells) and ankle weights (pads that strap around the ankles), $20 and up per pair at sports equipment stores.

For each exercise, begin with one set of eight repetitions (reps). If you cannot do eight reps using the suggested starting weights, use lighter weights. Over several weeks, gradually increase to 10, then 12, then 15 reps. Then try two sets of eight reps, resting for one minute between sets...and again gradually increase the reps. When you can do two sets of 15 reps, increase the weight by one to two pounds and start again with one set of eight reps.

Keep your shoulders back and abdominal muscles pulled in. With each rep, exhale during the initial move...hold the position for two seconds...inhale as you return to the starting position. Move slowly, using muscles rather than momentum. Do not lock elbow or knee joints.

UPPER BODY

These exercises build bone density in the shoulders, arms and spine.

If you have healthy bones: Stand during the exercises. Start by holding a five-pound weight in each hand...over time, try to work up to eight, then 10, then 12 pounds.

If you already have bone loss: To guard against falls, sit in a straight-backed chair while exercising. At first, use no weights or use one- or two-pound weights...gradually work up to three-, then five-, then a maximum of eight-pound weights if you can. Avoid heavier weights —they could increase the risk for vertebral compression fractures.

•Arms forward.

To start: Bend elbows, arms close to your body, hands at chest-height, palms facing each other.

One rep: Straighten elbows until both arms are extended in front of you, parallel to the floor...hold... return to starting position.

•Arm overhead.

To start: Raise right arm straight overhead, palm facing forward.

One rep: Bend right elbow, bringing right hand down behind your head...hold...return to starting position. Do a set with the right arm, then with the left.

•Arms up-and-down.

To start: Have arms down at your sides, palms forward.

One rep: Keeping elbows close to your sides, bend arms to raise hands toward shoulders until palms face you...hold...lower to starting position.

MIDBODY

This strengthens and stabilizes "core" muscles (abdomen, back, pelvic area). By improving body alignment, it helps prevent falls and reduces pressure on the vertebrae, protecting against compression fractures of the spine. No weights are used.

If you have healthy bones: Do this exercise while standing...or try while lying on your back, with knees bent and feet flat on the floor.

If you already have bone loss: Done while standing, this is a good option for osteoporosis patients who are uncomfortable exercising on the floor. If you have balance problems, hold on to a counter...or sit in a chair.

•Tummy tuck/pelvic tilt.

To start: Arms at sides, feet hip-width apart.

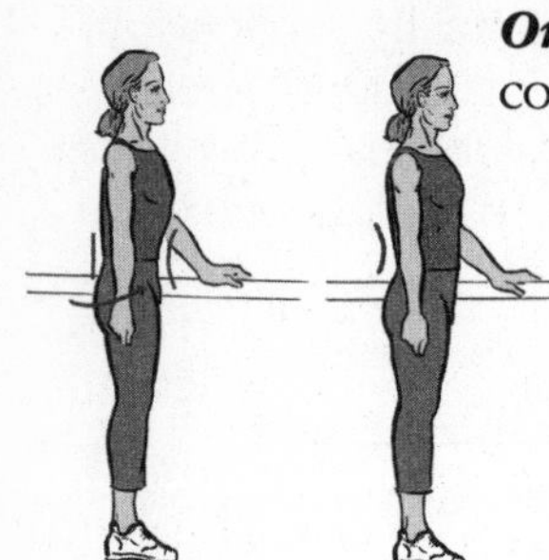

One rep: Simultaneously contract abdominal muscles to draw your tummy toward your spine, tighten buttocks muscles, and tilt the bottom of your pelvis forward to flatten the arch of your back...hold...return to starting position.

LOWER BODY

These moves increase bone density in the legs and feet. For each rep, raise the leg as high as possible without leaning...hold for two seconds...return to starting position.

Advanced option: Try not to touch your foot to the ground between reps.

If you have healthy bones: Start by wearing a two-pound ankle weight on each leg... gradually increase to 10 pounds per ankle.

If you already have bone loss: Hold on to a counter for balance. To begin, use no weights...build up, one pound at a time, to five pounds per ankle.

•Leg forward-and-back.

To start: Stand on your right foot.

One rep: Keeping both legs straight, slowly swing left leg forward and up...hold...swing leg down through the starting position and up behind you...hold...return to starting position. After one set, repeat with the other leg.

•Leg out.

To start: Stand on your right foot.

One rep: Keep both legs straight. Slowly lift left leg out to the side...hold...return to starting position. After one set, repeat with the other leg.

BONE-BENEFITING AEROBICS

•Biking, stationary cycling, swimming and rowing are good for heart health—but they do not protect against osteoporosis.

Better: Weight-bearing aerobic activities in which you're on your feet, bones working against gravity, build bone mass in the hips and legs.

If you have healthy bones: Good choices include jogging, dancing, stair climbing, step aerobics, jumping rope, racket sports and interactive video games, such as Wii Fit and Dance Dance Revolution. If you enjoy walking, boost intensity by wearing a two- to 20-pound weighted vest ($50 and up at sports equipment stores).

Warning: Do not wear ankle weights during aerobic workouts—this could stress your joints.

If you already have bone loss: Refrain from high-impact activities (running, jumping) and those that require twisting or bending (racket sports, golf). Do not wear a weighted vest.

Safe low-impact options: Walking, using an elliptical machine (available at most gyms), qigong and tai chi.

Exercise illustrations by Shawn Banner.

Better Breathing for Those with COPD

Ronald G. Crystal, MD, professor and chairman of the department of genetic medicine of the Weill Cornell Medical College, where he is also the Bruce Webster Professor of Internal Medicine, director of the Belfer Gene Therapy Core Facility and chief of the division of pulmonary and critical care medicine at the NewYork-Presbyterian Hospital/Weill Cornell Medical Center in New York City. He has published more than 700 scientific articles.

The lung disorder chronic obstructive pulmonary disease (COPD) kills about 125,000 Americans every year—more than accidents, diabetes, Alzheimer's disease or influenza. But treatment can be a challenge because half of the 24 million Americans with

COPD don't know they have the disease, often assuming that their symptoms are due to smoking, poor physical fitness and/or aging.

Good news: With proper testing, COPD can be diagnosed early—when treatment is most effective. And even though COPD cannot be cured, you still can lead an active, healthier life and slow the progress of the disease.

HOW THE LUNGS WORK

To visualize the airways, think of an upside-down tree—the trunk is the windpipe...the large branches are tubes called bronchi...and the twigs, bronchioles. At the tip of the bronchioles are about 300 million tiny air sacs called alveoli, where microscopic blood vessels (capillaries) help remove carbon dioxide from the bloodstream and replace it with oxygen.

Most people with COPD have chronic bronchitis and emphysema. In emphysema, the airways and air sacs lose their elasticity, like old hoses and balloons...in chronic bronchitis, inflamed airway walls thicken, while their cells pump out airway-clogging mucus (sputum)... and the walls of air sacs collapse. Chronic bronchitis (marked by a chronic cough that may produce sputum) involves the bronchi...emphysema (characterized by severe breathlessness) involves the bronchioles and alveoli.

The earliest symptom of COPD might be a chronic cough with or without sputum. Later, you may find yourself unexpectedly short of breath while carrying groceries or climbing stairs. As the disease advances, you may wheeze, have difficulty taking a deep breath or sometimes feel like you can't breathe at all.

DIAGNOSE THE PROBLEM EARLY

Because the lungs have so much capacity and strength, the early stages of COPD are often symptom-free—but a medical test known as spirometry can detect the disease.

Spirometry uses a breathing device to measure lung capacity (the amount of air lungs can hold) and strength (exhalation speed after taking a deep breath). During the test, the patient blows into a large tube connected to a spirometer (a recording device). The test, which takes about five minutes, can be done in a doctor's office—usually by a pulmonologist (lung specialist)—or at a hospital.

Problem: Many primary care physicians don't use spirometry.

Solution: If you are a current or former smoker...have early symptoms of COPD (as previously described)...have asthma...or were exposed for years to secondhand smoke or occupational dust and fumes (other common causes of COPD), ask your doctor for spirometry and a chest X-ray, which can detect signs of lung cancer and emphysema. Both tests should be done annually—more often if you have COPD symptoms.

THE RIGHT EXERCISE

Exercise and lung rehabilitation help reduce and control breathing difficulties, improve quality of life, and decrease the use of medical care and the length of hospital stays. *Best choices...**

- **Lower-body training.** Walking or riding a stationary bicycle.

Benefit: Strengthens leg muscles to help you move about more easily and for longer periods of time.

- **Upper-body training.** Strength-training exercises (using hand weights or exercise machines) for the arm and shoulder muscles.

Benefit: Stronger muscles support the rib cage and improve breathing. Ask your doctor how often and how long you should perform such exercises.

STRENGTHEN YOUR BREATHING

Strengthening the muscles used for breathing is also important.

Recent study: When researchers studied 40 people with COPD, those who learned "pursed-lip breathing" (designed primarily for patients with severe COPD) had sustained improvement in overall physical functioning. *To perform pursed-lip breathing...*

Step 1: **Relax your neck and shoulder muscles.** Inhale slowly through your nose and count to two in your head.

*These exercises should be performed as part of a pulmonary rehabilitation program. To find a program near you, contact the American Association of Cardiovascular and Pulmonary Rehabilitation (*www.aacvpr.org*).

Step 2: **Pucker your lips as if you are whistling.** Exhale slowly and gently through your lips while you count to four or more in your head.

Use this breathing technique often throughout the day—not only during exercise (including walking) but also while engaged in daily activities, such as climbing stairs.

COPD PREVENTION

Quitting smoking is the most important step to prevent COPD as well as to slow and reduce its severity.

Smoking causes about nine out of 10 cases of COPD—with the remaining cases probably due to long-term exposure to secondhand smoke, fumes and/or dust.

If you are a smoker, talk to your doctor about a smoking-cessation plan. Don't give up—you may have to try two to three times before quitting for good.

Diet also may play a role in COPD prevention, according to studies.

Recent finding: When researchers analyzed diet and health data from more than 70,000 women, those who ate a diet rich in fruit, vegetables, fish and whole grains had a 25% lower risk of developing COPD, while those eating refined grains, cured and red meats, desserts and french fries had a 31% higher risk. Similar results were found in men.

CHOOSING MEDICATION

The newest, most effective drug treatment for COPD combines two medication stalwarts in one inhaler—a bronchodilator that opens the airways and a corticosteroid that decreases inflammation.

Two of these combination-drug inhalers are now available—Advair combines the bronchodilator *salmeterol* and the corticosteroid *fluticasone*...Symbicort combines the bronchodilator *formoterol* and the corticosteroid *budesonide.* Studies have shown that people with COPD who use either of these inhalers have improved lung function, better overall health and less breathlessness compared with those who use either a corticosteroid or a bronchodilator alone.

Choosing the Best Type Of Yoga for You

Timothy McCall, MD, a board-certified internist in Oakland, California, medical editor of *Yoga Journal* and author of *Yoga as Medicine: The Yogic Prescription for Health and Healing* (Bantam). Dr. McCall leads workshops and retreats on yoga and yoga therapy around the country and worldwide. *www.drmccall.com.*

Yoga is powerful medicine. It can improve balance, flexibility and posture... strengthen muscles and bones...lower blood pressure, ease pain and boost immune function...heighten sexual functioning...alleviate stress and depression...and bolster spiritual well-being.

Key: Finding a style that fits your abilities, temperament and goals. *With your doctor's okay, consider...*

•**Anusara.** This playful, warm-hearted and physically challenging style emphasizes body alignment (often with hands-on adjustments from the teacher) and a positive mindset that looks for the good in all people.

Best for: Physically fit people who want to be part of a like-minded community.

•**Ashtanga ("power" yoga).** A vigorous practice, it includes a fixed series of postures that flow rapidly and continuously, accompanied by energizing breathing techniques.

Best for: People who can handle an intense workout, want to build stamina and strength, and enjoy a set routine.

•**Bikram ("hot" yoga).** An invariable sequence of 26 poses is performed in a studio heated to at least 100°F to loosen muscles, tendons and ligaments.

Best for: People in good health who don't mind heat and want improved flexibility. Bikram, like other vigorous styles, may not be appropriate for frail or older students or those with serious illnesses.

•**Integral.** Beginning classes include gentle poses, breathing techniques, meditation and discussions of ancient yoga texts. The principle of selfless service (such as volunteer work) is emphasized. Some centers offer special classes for students with physical limitations or health problems (such as heart disease or cancer).

Best for: People interested in traditional Indian yoga that includes more than just poses.

•**Iyengar.** Emphasizing meticulous body alignment, this style makes use of blocks, straps and other props so students with limited flexibility can safely and comfortably assume poses. Teacher training requirements are among the strictest.

Best for: Anyone new to yoga or especially in need of better body alignment, such as people with arthritis or back pain.

•**Kripalu.** A blend of Western psychology and Eastern philosophy, this practice provides a safe place to explore emotional issues. Meditation and chanting accompany moderately vigorous and sometimes improvised movement.

Best for: People looking for stress relief and emotional release.

•**Kundalini.** This style includes a wide variety of breathing techniques, intense physical movements, chanting and meditation. The focus is on raising energy rather than on precise body alignment.

Best for: People who are seeking to build prana (life force) and who are open to yoga's spiritual dimensions.

•**Viniyoga.** Gentle flowing poses are held only briefly. Safety and breath work are emphasized. Teachers often focus on private one-on-one sessions rather than group classes.

Best for: People who are new to yoga or out of shape or who are looking to use yoga to help alleviate any of a variety of chronic ailments.

To find a class: Yoga Alliance (888-921-9642, *www.yogaalliance.org*) registers teachers who complete a certain number of hours of training in specific styles. If you have a medical condition, contact the teacher to see if a particular class is appropriate for you or to ask about private lessons. Yoga therapy has been shown in studies to be effective for a wide range of conditions, from diabetes and arthritis to cancer and chronic lung disease.

12

Pain Treatments

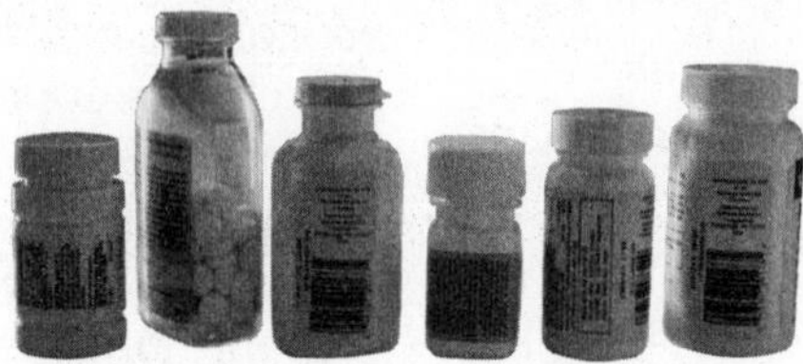

Higher Temperatures Trigger Migraines

If you think that changes in the weather bring on migraines, it might not be all in your head. Harvard researchers report in a recent study that people are more likely to visit emergency rooms with severe pain from migraines if the outside temperature is above normal.

Barometric pressure has an effect, too, although it is not as significant, say the researchers.

KEEP TEMPERATURE IN MIND

The findings do not definitively prove that the weather causes migraines. Nor are they "a reason to stay indoors or move to a different part of the country," said study author Kenneth J. Mukamal, MD, an internist at Beth Israel Deaconess Medical Center in Boston.

"But this does tell us that when we identify migraine triggers, we need to keep temperature in mind," he said.

BACKGROUND

An estimated 28 million Americans suffer from migraine headaches, perhaps as many as 17% of women and 6% of men. The headaches can disable sufferers, forcing some to flee to quiet, darkened rooms for relief.

Treatments include painkillers, biofeedback and a newer class of drugs called *triptans.*

Many people report "triggers" that cause their migraines, including red wine, chocolate, menstrual cycles and lack of sleep. Others blame changes in the weather. Previous studies on possible environmental causes of migraine have suggested they're on to something.

THE STUDY

In the study, researchers examined the records of 7,054 emergency room patients who were treated for migraines at Beth Israel Deaconess Medical Center between 2000 and 2007.

Kenneth J. Mukamal, MD, internist, Beth Israel Deaconess Medical Center, Boston.

Richard Lipton, MD, director, Montefiore Headache Center, Montefiore Medical Center, New York City.

Neurology.

The researchers tried to find links between the number of headache cases and levels of temperature, barometric pressure and humidity. They also looked at air pollution levels.

The study was published in *Neurology*.

THE RESULTS

The researchers found that the number of emergency visits for headaches would rise by an average of 7.5% within 24 hours if the temperature rose by 9 degrees Fahrenheit above the expected temperature.

In a hypothetical example, the hospital would expect to see 7.5% more headache patients 24 hours after the temperature was 90 degrees instead of a typical 81 degrees.

High temperatures alone, such as those in the summer, were not as much of a trigger. The most influential factor was whether a particular day was hotter than expected.

"Warmer days were associated with higher risk, even in the winter," Dr. Mukamal said.

The researchers also found that drops in barometric pressure made headache visits more likely 48 to 72 hours later. Pollution did not seem to have an effect on headaches.

POSSIBLE EXPLANATION

Why might the weather affect migraines? Barometric pressure could affect the layer of fluid that protects the brain inside the skull, said Richard Lipton, MD, director of the Montefiore Headache Center at Montefiore Medical Center in New York City. But the effect of temperature, he said, is mystifying.

WHAT TO DO

"If someone knows that they're vulnerable to changes in temperature, what they might do is be cautious about the things they can control," he said. "If you know the temperature is changing, that might be a good day to make sure you get your regular amount of sleep, avoid red wine, chocolate and the other triggers."

info The National Institute of Neurological Disorders and Stroke Web site, *www.ninds.nih.gov,* has more information on migraine. Under "Health Information," click on "M" and then choose "Migraine."

Breakthroughs in Migraine Relief

Robert Kunkel, MD, an internist and consultant at the Center for Headache and Pain at the Cleveland Clinic Neurological Institute in Cleveland. He is a past president of the National Headache Foundation and the American Headache Society and author of *Headaches: A Cleveland Clinic Handbook* (Cleveland Clinic).

For many of the nearly 30 million Americans who suffer from migraines, the standard treatments, such as over-the-counter and prescription medication, do not always provide relief.

Latest development: A variety of new and highly effective therapies are now available for treatment of migraines.

DRUG COMBINATION EASES MIGRAINE

Migraines cause moderate-to-severe pain that usually occurs on one side of the head. The exact cause of these headaches is unknown, but many experts believe that the attack starts in the brain, where pain receptors become activated when arteries widen and become inflamed.

Sumatriptan (Imitrex) and similar drugs, known as triptans, affect pain receptors and constrict dilated arteries in the brain. These drugs are among the most effective treatments for migraine pain. However, triptans have little effect on inflammation of arteries in the brain, another component of migraines.

New approach: Combining sumatriptan with *naproxen sodium* (Aleve), an over-the-counter nonsteroidal anti-inflammatory drug (NSAID). The combination works better than either drug alone because it reduces arterial dilation and inflammation.

Scientific evidence: When Philadelphia researchers recently looked at 1,111 patients who experienced two to six migraines per month in the period preceding the study, about half of those given sumatriptan plus naproxen were pain-free within two hours, compared with about 16% of those given a placebo. This approach can be tried by combining any triptan with any NSAID, including ibuprofen (Motrin) or aspirin.

Caution: If you have a history of ulcers or stomach upset when taking NSAIDs, talk to your doctor before trying this approach.

HEART REPAIR REDUCES MIGRAINE RISK

Between the left and right atrial chambers of the heart, there is an opening known as the *foramen ovale* that is present in all newborns. The foramen ovale, which aids in fetal circulation, normally seals shut in the first years of life.

In up to 18% of Americans, the opening doesn't completely seal. This defect may increase risk for migraines—perhaps because small blood clots that normally would be dissolved in the lungs instead bypass the lungs and are pumped out of the heart, then into small blood vessels in the brain.

New approach: Surgical repair of the heart defect.

Scientific evidence: For several years, doctors have noticed that some patients who undergo surgery or catheterization (threading a small tube from the groin to the heart) to repair the heart defect reported fewer migraines. A study is currently under way to determine if this approach is an effective treatment for migraine in people who have the heart defect.

BETTER SLEEP PREVENTS HEADACHES

People who sleep poorly tend to get more headaches than those who sleep well. That's because poor sleep alters the body's natural biorhythms. Disturbed sleep is especially problematic for people with "transformed migraine" —a condition in which periodic migraines begin to occur on a daily or near-daily basis.

New approach: Counseling (from a primary care doctor or sleep specialist) to learn better sleep habits.

Scientific evidence: When researchers at the University of North Carolina studied 147 patients with transformed migraine, most had poor sleep habits, including watching TV in bed. Patients who received counseling on good sleep habits, such as adhering to a specific schedule for going to bed and rising, had a 29% decrease in headache frequency and a 40% decrease in headache intensity. Patients who did not receive such counseling did not improve.

MAGNETIC DEVICES QUELL PAIN

About 20% of migraine patients experience an aura, which may include visual symptoms, such as seeing zigzagging lines, along with other sensory changes (tingling sensations in an arm or leg). In those patients, auras typically precede migraine pain by 20 to 30 minutes.

New approach: *Transcranial magnetic stimulation* (TMS), a technique involving the use of a handheld device that is placed against a person's head and sends a magnetic pulse to interrupt the brain's erratic electrical signals. TMS, which has been available only in hospitals, now is being investigated for home use. If approved by the FDA, the TMS device will be sold at pharmacies with a doctor's prescription.

Scientific evidence: A recent study of 201 migraine patients found that 39% of those who used TMS were pain-free after two hours, compared with 22% in a control group that used a sham device.

NEW TRIPTANS ON THE WAY

Triptan drugs are available in tablets, injections and a liquid nasal spray. An injection of sumatriptan can stop a migraine in five to 10 minutes...oral and nasal forms work within 30 to 60 minutes.

The drugs aren't perfect, however. Injections are inconvenient and uncomfortable, and the oral forms require relatively high doses, which can cause adverse effects, including high blood pressure. Nasal sumatriptan sprays work quickly, but are not widely used because they have an unpleasant taste and can cause gagging when spray residue drips into the back of the throat.

New approach: A spray powder that is administered to the nasal membranes. The powder is more easily absorbed than liquid spray and reduces drips into the throat.

Scientific evidence: A recent study found that patients using the powder form achieved maximum blood concentrations of sumatriptan in 20 minutes—a rate that is comparable to that of injections. The powder is being studied by pharmaceutical companies and could be available within a few years.

■ ■ ■ ■

Better Headache Care

When 108 people with cluster headaches (severe headaches that occur in cyclical patterns) took the calcium channel blocker *verapamil* (Calan) for headache prevention, about 19% of the patients developed irregular heartbeat and 37% had slower-than-normal heart rates.

If you take verapamil for cluster headaches: Ask your doctor for an electrocardiogram (ECG) each time the dosage is increased. If the dose remains the same, get one every six months.

Peter Goadsby, MD, PhD, professor of clinical neurology, National Hospital for Neurology and Neurosurgery, London.

How to Break the Headache–Insomnia Cycle

Jason C. Ong, PhD, assistant professor, behavioral sciences, Rush University Medical Center, Chicago.

Frederick de la Vega, MD, neurologist, Scripps Memorial Hospital, La Jolla, California.

Journal of Clinical Sleep Medicine.

Headache sufferers often treat their pain by taking naps to sleep it off, but they run the risk of developing insomnia by disrupting their normal sleep patterns and perpetuating the cycle of headaches, a recent study shows.

"Going to sleep was one of the main things people tried to treat their headaches, and they rated it a very effective treatment," said study author Jason C. Ong, PhD, an assistant professor of behavioral sciences at Rush University Medical Center in Chicago. "It could be that people are taking naps or using sleep as a way to try to cope with pain, but that could actually lead to more sleep disturbance at night."

THE STUDY

The researchers recruited 65 women from undergraduate psychology courses at a university in the southeastern United States, 32 of whom suffered from tension-type headaches (TTH), while the other 33 women experienced minimal pain and were placed in the control group.

Fifty-eight percent of the headache sufferers said that sleep problems triggered their headaches, while only 18% of the control group said that was the case. Eighty-one percent of the headache sufferers also reported using sleep to manage their pain, a coping mechanism they rated as the most effective self-treatment.

IMPLICATIONS

"The most important aspect of the study suggests that a very common coping strategy for TTH—going to sleep or taking naps—may interfere with the normal physiological drive to sleep, thus causing insomnia which is a trigger for TTH," said Frederick de la Vega, MD, a neurologist at Scripps Memorial Hospital in La Jolla, California.

"It's a catch-22," said Dr. Ong. "Going to bed might help relieve your pain, but when you try to go to sleep at night, what happens then?"

Further studies are needed to determine if insomnia actually causes headaches (or vice versa) or whether the two are simply related, Dr. Ong said.

The study was published in the *Journal of Clinical Sleep Medicine.*

MOST EFFECTIVE HEADACHE TREATMENTS

Developing more effective pain-management strategies may be the best way to disrupt this headache–insomnia cycle, the researchers said. Unfortunately, different types of headaches may call for different treatments, and it's often difficult to determine the best approach.

"The treatment for migraines is somewhat different than TTH," said Dr. de la Vega. "The question is whether better management during wake-hours, so as to avoid just taking a nap, could prevent the disruption of the physiology of sleep at night. That answer is uncertain but makes intuitive sense."

According to Dr. Ong, "Doing some kind of relaxation technique is one way to cope with pain, so that might be one thing to attempt. Are there existing interventions that might be helpful for people who have both insomnia and headaches or do we have to come up with something else?"

The experts agreed that people who suffer from headaches or insomnia should see a doctor to discuss the best individual treatment.

"The main thing is that if people have headaches and also sleep difficulties, they should communicate that information to their health-care provider," said Dr. Ong.

"Migraine sufferers should see their primary doctor or preferably a neurologist," added Dr. de la Vega. Appropriate medications should be tried, food/activity triggers should be avoided, and if insomnia is a trigger, an assessment of sleep habits may be helpful, he said.

info For more information on headaches, visit the Web site of the National Institutes of Health, *http://health.nih.gov/topic/HeadacheandMigraine.*

Seven Common Myths That May Give You A "Pain in the Neck"

Scott Haldeman, DC, MD, PhD, a clinical professor of neurology at the University of California, Irvine, an adjunct professor of epidemiology and public health at the University of California at Los Angeles, and an adjunct professor of research at Southern California University of Health Sciences in Whittier, California. He presided over the Bone and Joint Decade 2000 to 2010 Task Force on Neck Pain and Its Associated Disorders.

Neck pain is one of the most common of all ailments—affecting 30% to 50% of Americans each year—but it's also one of the least understood by medical professionals. As a result, anyone who suffers from neck pain is likely to be offered an array of different treatments—most of them unproven.

Latest development: Recently, an international task force published in the peer-reviewed medical journal *Spine* one of the most extensive reports ever created on the diagnosis and treatment of neck pain. The task force, which I led, was comprised of 50 researchers from nine countries whose specialties ranged from neurology and chiropractic to orthopedic surgery and physical therapy.

We analyzed more than 1,000 studies to create the most up-to-date recommendations about which neck pain treatments are truly effective—and which are not. In the process, the task force uncovered some surprising facts that dispel many popular myths about neck pain. *For example...*

Myth 1: To successfully treat neck pain, you must know its exact cause.

Reality: The evidence shows that it's virtually impossible to identify a specific cause for most neck pain. Instead, it appears to be a very complex phenomenon that is affected by the neck pain sufferer's overall physical and mental health and daily physical and emotional stresses.

If your doctor or health-care provider says he/she doesn't know the exact cause of your neck pain, don't think less of him—he's just being honest.

Myth 2: Seeing more than one doctor will increase your odds of getting relief for your neck pain.

Reality: The evidence shows just the opposite—the more doctors you see, the longer your neck pain is likely to last. How could this be true? The most likely explanation is that patients who see multiple doctors end up focusing excessively on their pain, which creates psychological stress that makes the pain worse.

Also, by relying on others to "cure" them, these neck pain sufferers often take less responsibility for doing things that will actually make them feel better. The same is true for people who get neck X-rays or magnetic resonance imaging (MRI) scans. Research shows that these scans usually have no value in determining the cause of neck pain and even can be misleading, since they often detect changes, such as small disk bulges or misalignments, that are also seen in patients who do not have neck pain. However, imaging tests (such as X-rays) may be necessary to check for fractures if the patient has suffered serious trauma, such as in a car accident.

Important: Even though trips to multiple doctors are not helpful when you have neck pain, you should at least get screened by a physician who is experienced in treating neck pain (ask your primary care doctor for a referral) to rule out infection, a tumor or serious trauma such as a fracture (these conditions collectively account for 1% of neck pain cases). Initial screening also should include tests for cervical *radiculopathy*, a condition in which pressure on a nerve in the neck (due to a herniated disk) causes pain, numbness or weakness down the arm. About 5% of neck pain is due to cervical radiculopathy.

For the 94% of patients with ordinary neck pain, the best next step is to begin treating the pain with therapies that are proven to have some effectiveness (such as those described below), rather than seeing more doctors.

Myth 3: Surgery is often effective for ordinary neck pain.

Reality: There's no research showing that surgery has any positive impact on ordinary cases of neck pain. The only time that surgery is useful is in treating cervical radiculopathy. This operation involves removing the herniated disk to take pressure off the compressed nerve. Surgery also may be needed if a tumor or infection is present.

Myth 4: Rest is one of the best treatments for neck pain.

Reality: Our review found that any treatment that reduces activity and mobility in the neck actually delays recovery. This includes bed rest (even a day or two), neck collars and stopping work and other ordinary activities. If you exercise regularly or have a physically demanding job, you may need to reduce your activity level somewhat—but you should remain active.

Myth 5: Heating pads, cold packs and other such treatments speed neck pain recovery.

Reality: The medical evidence shows that "passive" treatments, such as heating pads, cold packs, ultrasound, electrical stimulation and injecting medication, including steroids or anesthetics, into "trigger points" have no effect on the duration of neck pain. In some patients, however, such therapies may offer temporary relief from neck pain. If so, they should use these therapies as necessary to improve their ability to function.

Myth 6: Some treatments for neck pain should be used indefinitely.

Reality: Just as there is no single cause of neck pain, there is no single "magic bullet" for treating it either. Our review found that certain therapies designed to increase mobility of the neck appeared to help in many cases, but that patients often had to try several treatments before finding one that worked for them.

Treatments found to be effective were chiropractic manipulation...active physical therapy (in which the patient is given movement exercises rather than simply being treated with ultrasound and/or heat)...and exercise such as walking, swimming or low-impact aerobics.

Patients also improved when they combined these therapies with other treatments that reduce inflammation and stiffness. Among the most effective were acupuncture...massage... and over-the-counter anti-inflammatory medication, such as *ibuprofen* (Advil) or *naproxen* (Aleve). There's very little research on whether preventive steps, such as ergonomic adjustments to chairs, improving posture or using a cervical foam pillow, have any effect, but these approaches may be helpful for some people.

Whichever approach you choose, try it for two weeks. If your condition hasn't improved by then, stop it and try another approach. If the treatment is helping, four weeks of the therapy should be enough—research shows that treating neck pain any longer than this won't offer additional improvement.

Myth 7: Stress does not play a significant role in neck pain.

Reality: Studies clearly show that stress and anxiety make neck pain worse. Our review also found that people who take charge of their own treatment—by trying different therapies and/or activities that provide pain relief—tend to recover faster. This is your best hope for relieving neck pain.

Safer, Easier Way to Heal a Herniated Disk

Society of Interventional Radiology news release.

A shot of ozone and oxygen may prove to be a safe, effective and less invasive way to relieve the pain of a herniated disk, US researchers say.

BACKGROUND

Small spongy disks normally act as shock absorbers between the vertebrae, but when one is damaged, it may bulge or break, putting pressure on spinal nerves. The standard treatments for severe pain caused by herniated disks are either open discectomy or microdiscectomy, surgeries that require the removal of disk material through an incision.

STUDY FINDINGS

But one study of more than 8,000 patients found that injecting a gas mixture of oxygen and ozone into a herniated disk significantly relieves the pressure put on the nerves, easing patients' pain. A second study showed that the oxygen/ozone treatment works by reducing disk volume through ozone oxidation; the reduced volume eases disk pressure on the nerves.

The findings were presented at the Society of Interventional Radiology's annual meeting in San Diego.

STUDY DETAILS

In the study of more than 8,000 patients, those who had the oxygen/ozone treatment reported their pain lessening by an average of nearly 4 points, based on a 10-point scale (with 0 being no pain and 10 representing the worst pain experienced). The patients' ability to conduct everyday tasks—such as washing and dressing themselves or even just standing up—also improved by more than 25% based on the rating scale used.

"Oxygen/ozone treatment of herniated disks is an effective and extremely safe procedure. The estimated improvement in pain and function is impressive when we looked at patients who ranged in age from 13 to 94 years with all types of disk herniations," said Kieran J. Murphy, MD, an interventional neuroradiologist and vice chair and chief of medical imaging at the University of Toronto in Canada.

COMPARISON TO SURGICAL TREATMENT

"Equally important, pain and function outcomes are similar to the outcomes for lumbar disks treated with surgical discectomy, but the complication rate is much less (less than 0.1 percent)," Dr. Murphy said. "In addition, the recovery time is significantly shorter for the oxygen/ozone injection than for the diskectomy."

Much of the research into oxygen/ozone therapy has been done in Italy, where it is believed as many as 14,000 individuals have been treated in the past five years.

"There are millions of people with back pain who suffer and who can't work because of their pain. Undergoing invasive surgical diskectomy puts you on a path where you may be left with too little disk. Taking out a protruding disk may lose the shock absorption that naturally resides between them in the spine," said Dr. Murphy. He predicts that this procedure will become standard in the United States within the next five years.

info The US Department of Health & Human Services has more information on how to prevent back pain at *www.healthfinder.gov.* Search "prevent back pain."

Best Ways to Relieve Back Pain Today

David G. Borenstein, MD, who has a private practice at Arthritis and Rheumatism Associates and is a clinical professor of medicine at George Washington University Medical Center, both in Washington, DC. He is author of *Back In Control* (M. Evans and Company) and coauthor of the physician textbook *Low Back Pain* (W.B. Saunders).

With back pain, treatment advances occur so rapidly that often it is difficult for patients to keep up with the latest developments. *What you need to know to find the right back-pain therapy...*

COMMON CAUSES OF BACK PAIN

Back pain can result from a variety of underlying conditions. If you experience back pain for more than two to four weeks, it's important to see an internist or family physician to identify the problem.* The cause of back pain can be pinpointed by a careful examination.

Herniated disk, which is among the most common causes of back pain, occurs when the soft material inside one or more of the "cushions" (disks) between spinal vertebrae oozes through a split in the disk's tough outer shell (herniation) or causes the shell to bulge outward.

Sciatica occurs when a herniated or bulging disk presses against the sciatic nerve, which exits from the lower (lumbar) spine, usually causing severe pain on one side of the body in the buttock and down the back of the leg.

Compression fractures, the breakdown of one or more spinal vertebrae, are usually caused by osteoporosis, while muscle strain and muscle spasm typically result from physical activity.

CHOOSING THE RIGHT MEDICATION

Best choices...

•Anti-inflammatory medication.

Typically used for: Back pain due to muscle spasms or strain. Mild-to-moderate back pain usually improves within a few weeks with the use of over-the-counter anti-inflammatory medication, such as *ibuprofen* (Advil), and home treatments, such as ice packs.

What you may not know: To minimize swelling and inflammation, ice or a cold pack should be applied to the painful area—10 minutes several times daily—for only two days after the pain starts. Thereafter, it's better to use heat—for 10 minutes several times daily. Heat (from a heating pad, a towel soaked in hot water or a hot bath or shower) relaxes your muscles and increases blood flow to the painful area, which speeds healing.

•Steroids.

Typically used for: Severe back pain due to a herniated disk. An injection of cortisone or another steroid in the epidural space, which surrounds the sciatic nerve, reduces inflammation within hours. The injection can be administered in a doctor's office and doesn't require an anesthetic. The treatment, which may be repeated two or more times for any episode of sciatica, generally is safe, with only a low risk for infection. Between 50% and 60% of patients injected with an epidural steroid report less pain and disability.

What you may not know: Patients who don't get steroid injections tend to have the same level of relief over a one-year period, according to recent research.

OTHER OPTIONS

•Alexander Technique.

Typically used for: Back pain due to spasms or muscle strain. This technique involves analyzing musculoskeletal patterns—such as a patient's posture—and creating movements that are designed to improve posture and "release" muscular tension.**

New finding: When 579 patients with chronic (more than three months) or recurrent (three or more weeks) low-back pain were followed for one year, those treated with the Alexander Technique had less pain than those who received massage or conventional treatments, such as physical therapy.

What you may not know: Patients who receive as few as six lessons in the Alexander Technique have been shown to do as well as those who took 24 lessons.

Caveat: The study lasted for only one year, so the long-lasting benefits are unknown.

•McKenzie Method.

Typically used for: Patients with pain caused by one or more herniated disks. The McKenzie Method, also known as Mechanical Diagnosis and Therapy (MDT), involves an extensive assessment to identify the patient's pain response to repeated test movements, positions and activities. Precise pain-eliminating exercises and posture modifications are then recommended. MDT educates patients in lifestyle practices that not only decrease pain, but also help restore function and independence.***

*Sudden onset of back pain accompanied by fever, numbness or weakness in the legs or groin area and/or loss of bladder or bowel control may indicate an infection or other serious condition. Seek immediate medical attention.

**To find a trained Alexander Technique practitioner, consult the American Society for the Alexander Technique, 800-473-0620, *www.alexandertech.org.*

***To find a certified McKenzie provider in your area, consult the McKenzie Institute, 800-635-8380, *www.mckenziemdt.org.*

There's no long-term (more than one year) data on outcomes from MDT, but it does seem to be effective for some patients with sciatica from a herniated disk.

What you may not know: Research has shown that the initial McKenzie assessment procedures can be as reliable as diagnostic imaging, such as X-rays, in determining the source of pain.

SURGICAL APPROACHES

If back pain is not relieved by medication and/or other therapies, surgery is an option. *For example...*

•**Diskectomy (removal of the herniated portion of a disk,** which relieves pressure on a nerve).

Typically used for: Excruciating back pain due to a herniated disk. This surgery used to be routinely recommended for a herniated disk with sciatica because doctors thought that unrelieved nerve irritation could lead to permanent disability, such as muscle weakness or persistent pain. In fact, this rarely happens, but surgery can help patients recover more quickly and may lead to better outcomes in some cases.

An influential study published in *The Journal of the American Medical Association* found that back patients who had surgery had virtually the same recovery rates as those who were treated with oral anti-inflammatory medication and physical therapy. The only difference was that patients in the surgery group recovered within a few months, while those who didn't have surgery took longer to recover—up to two years, in some cases. (Over time, the herniated portion of a disk can be spontaneously reabsorbed by the body.)

What you may not know: Researchers who tracked 1,244 patients with herniated disks—and associated back and leg pain—for four years found that those who had surgery improved more in physical functioning and had less pain than those in the nonsurgical group.

Bottom line: Most patients with sciatica will recover without surgery. But those who have surgery will usually recover more quickly—and, in some cases, regain more mobility.

•***Kyphoplasty.***

Typically used for: Compression fractures. With this relatively new approach, the doctor threads a balloon guided by a catheter into the open space inside a vertebra. The balloon is then inflated, which pushes the surrounding bone back to its normal shape. A cement-like substance is then injected to reinforce the vertebra.

What you may not know: Kyphoplasty can repair compression fractures and eliminate related symptoms in 75% of cases.

■ ■ ■ ■

Best Treatment for Spinal Stenosis

Researchers studied 654 men and women with *spinal stenosis* (narrowing of the spinal canal).

Result: Patients who had surgery (in most cases, removal of excess bone, ligament and soft tissue to make more room for nerves) reported significantly greater function and less disability than those who had nonsurgical care that included physical therapy and nonsteroidal anti-inflammatory drugs. Few postsurgical complications were reported.

If you have spinal stenosis: Ask your doctor if surgery is right for you.

James N. Weinstein, DO, chairman, department of orthopedics, Dartmouth Medical School, Hanover, New Hampshire.

Can This Patient Be Cured? Sciatica

Mark A. Stengler, ND, naturopathic physician in private practice, La Jolla, California...adjunct associate clinical professor at the National College of Natural Medicine, Portland, Oregon...author of many books, including *The Natural Physician's Healing Therapies* and coauthor of *Prescription for Natural Cures* (both from Bottom Line Books)...and author of the *Bottom Line/Natural Healing* newsletter.

I have had many patients tell me that they experience a combination of lower back pain and an unpleasant radiating tingle down one leg and sometimes into the foot or toes. These symptoms are called sciatica, and they typically stem from a disk problem in the lower back.

Debbie, a 57-year-old writer and mother of two, experienced constant lower back pain, a sharp pain down her right leg, plus numbness in her right foot and toes. Also, her left hip felt as if it were constantly about to "go out." The pain caused her to limp, and she used a cane to help her walk.

A doctor prescribed painkillers, which helped to alleviate Debbie's discomfort. A chiropractor provided some relief, but the pain and numbness remained. Debbie's back pain had accelerated after she spent two days in a hospital bed, being treated for diabetes-related complications.

After examining Debbie, I told her I was concerned that she had a compression of one or more of the disks (collagen and gel pads that cushion the bones of the spine) in her lower back. I referred her to a neurologist, who ordered a magnetic resonance imaging (MRI) scan to view the spine. Sure enough, she had two bulging disks that were squashing the nerve roots as they exit the spine. The pressure was causing her back pain and sciatica. Additional nerve tests showed that there was decreased nerve sensation to the right foot.

I suggested Debbie try spinal decompression, a procedure that is gaining popularity among chiropractors and some osteopathic doctors. The treatment works by creating negative pressure —essentially, a vacuum—inside the disk to pull in the bulge or herniation (when a disk has actually broken open), relieving pressure on the affected nerves. Spinal decompression also increases the flow of blood and nutrients back into the disk, allowing the body to heal the injury.

How it works: The patient lies down fully clothed on his/her back or stomach, with pads comfortably securing the upper body and pelvis. Computer-controlled tension stretches the lower back, separating the vertebrae by miniscule increments and creating the vacuum effect.

The treatments are painless. Each lasts 15 to 30 minutes, and patients usually require a series of 15 to 30 visits, one to three per week.

Cost: $80 to $100 per visit. You can find a practitioner through the American Spinal Decompression Association (888-577-4625, *www.americanspinal.com*).

Note: Spinal decompression is not advised for people with severe osteoporosis or nerve damage, pregnant women or those who are very obese.

Debbie noticed great relief after just five treatments. After her 20th treatment, she reported a substantial improvement in her back pain and sciatica. She also began to feel sensation in her right toes and foot again. She is 80% improved and continuing the treatments.

■ ■ ■ ■

Acupuncture Eases Back Pain

In a study of 1,162 people with chronic low back pain, one group received acupuncture and another group received conventional therapy using painkillers, physical therapy and exercise. Those who had 10 half-hour acupuncture sessions over six weeks were nearly twice as likely to report improvements in pain and functional ability as patients given conventional therapy.

Theory: Acupuncture triggers a pain-dulling response by the central nervous system.

If you have chronic low-back pain: Ask your doctor if you should try acupuncture.

Heinz G. Endres, MD, clinical epidemiology specialist, Ruhr-University Bochum, Germany.

■ ■ ■ ■

Back Pain Relief from A Vitamin!

After taking vitamin D supplements for three months, 95% of patients with chronic back pain reported improvement. Low levels of vitamin D may soften bone surfaces, leading to pain. Increasing vitamin D improves calcium absorption and bone health.

Best: Ask your doctor about taking 1,000 international units (IU) of vitamin D-3 daily...or 2,000 IU daily if you have back pain.

Stewart B. Leavitt, PhD, editor of the Web site Pain Treatment Topics (*www.pain-topics.org*) and leader of an analysis of 22 studies on back pain.

■ ■ ■ ■

Omega-3s Relieve Pain As Well as Drugs

Omega-3s, found in fish and fish oil supplements, block inflammation and accompanying pain.

Study: 60% of participants with neck or back pain who were given 1,200 milligrams (mg) of fish oil per day reported relief after two to four weeks, and almost all of that group were able to discontinue their use of nonsteroidal anti-inflammatory drugs (NSAIDs), such as Vioxx and Motrin. The study also found that most patients taking fish oil had no significant side effects.

Joseph C. Maroon, MD, professor, and vice-chair, department of neurological surgery, University of Pittsburgh School of Medicine, and lead author of a study of 250 people, published in *Surgical Neurology.*

You Don't Need Drugs To Fight Arthritis

Harris H. McIlwain, MD, founder of the Tampa Medical Group and an adjunct professor of medicine at the University of South Florida College of Public Health in Tampa. A board-certified rheumatologist and former chair of the Florida Osteoporosis Board, Dr. McIlwain is coauthor of *Diet for a Pain-Free Life* (Da Capo).

Scientists have long known that inflammation is largely responsible for the pain associated with osteoarthritis (age-related wear-and-tear arthritis) and rheumatoid arthritis (an autoimmune disease that causes joint swelling and pain).

That's why people with arthritis have relied heavily on nonsteroidal anti-inflammatory drugs (NSAIDs), including aspirin and *ibuprofen* (Advil) —even though only an estimated half of arthritis sufferers get adequate relief by taking such medication.

NSAIDs also can cause side effects, such as gastrointestinal bleeding. Prescription NSAIDs, such as *celecoxib* (Celebrex), may increase the risk for heart attack in high-risk individuals, especially if taken at maximum doses.

New thinking: Whether you have osteoarthritis or rheumatoid arthritis, you can dramatically reduce pain and/or stiffness by adopting an "anti-inflammatory lifestyle." This approach focuses not only on weight control and exercise, but also on strategies such as using certain spices and reducing stress, which are just now being recognized for their effects on arthritis.

Even if you must take prescription medication for rheumatoid arthritis or occasionally use NSAIDs for acute flare-ups of osteoarthritis or rheumatoid arthritis, the following inflammation-fighting strategies may allow you to reduce—or even eliminate—your reliance on medication.

ELIMINATE "HIGH-TEMPERATURE" FOODS

Anything that's usually cooked at very high temperatures—mainly meats and fried foods—is likely to contain large amounts of compounds called advanced glycation end (AGE) products, which trigger inflammation in the body.

Scientific evidence: Several studies, including research conducted at Mount Sinai School of Medicine in New York City, have shown that consumption of AGE-containing foods is linked to increased risk for arthritis and other chronic diseases associated with inflammation.

What to do: I advise most of my patients to eliminate all red meat (poultry is acceptable) as well as processed foods and snacks, which are typically high in saturated fat and/or trans-fatty acids. Most people who eliminate these foods notice a significant reduction in arthritis pain within three weeks.

EAT MORE PLANT FOODS

Even though obesity is skyrocketing in the US, it affects no more than 6% of vegetarians—a fact that appears to have important implications for people with arthritis.

Scientific evidence: A study recently published in *Nutrition and Metabolism* found that arthritis sufferers who adopted a plant-based diet—particularly one rich in the so-called "super-antioxidants" (described below)—had significant reductions in pain.

The explanation? A plant-based diet is low in inflammatory chemicals and high in plant compounds that fight inflammation in the body. It also promotes weight loss.

What to do: Everyone with arthritis should eat little or no red meat...consume high-fiber foods, including legumes (such as black beans and lentils) and whole grains...and consume two to three daily servings of foods with the highest levels of anti-inflammatory compounds. *These include...*

- **Dark berries,** such as elderberries, black currants, blueberries, cranberries, cherries and blackberries (fresh or frozen). They are up to 50% higher in antioxidants than most fruits and vegetables. Consume one serving (for example, three-quarters of a cup of blueberries or 10 large cherries) daily.
- **Red grapes.** These contain resveratrol, a compound that inhibits the pain-causing COX-2 enzyme—the same mechanism that is used by the drug celecoxib. Red wine also contains resveratrol. Eat about 18 red grapes—and/or drink five ounces of red wine daily (purple grape juice can be substituted for red wine).
- **Citrus and other vitamin C–rich foods.** These greatly reduce inflammation and help the body repair damaged cartilage. A study in the *American Journal of Clinical Nutrition* found that people with high blood levels of vitamin C had a 45% reduced risk for inflammation. Eat one to two servings daily of vitamin C–rich foods, such as oranges and strawberries. Most daily multivitamins also provide sufficient vitamin C (60 milligrams, or mg, daily).
- **Cold-water fish** (such as salmon, mackerel and sardines) and omega-3-containing nuts (such as walnuts, almonds and pecans). The omega-3 fatty acids found in these foods reduce levels of inflammatory chemicals in the body. Eat four ounces of cold-water fish daily and about one-half ounce (a small handful) of nuts daily. As alternatives, natural peanut butter without added fat or sugar (one tablespoon daily) and ground flaxseed (about three tablespoons daily) are good sources of omega-3s.
- **Green or black tea.** Both contain polyphenols, compounds that inhibit joint inflammation. Drink two to three cups daily.

USE ANTI-INFLAMMATORY SPICES

A number of kitchen spices and herbs, including turmeric and garlic, are powerful antioxidants that can relieve joint pain even when consumed in quantities used for cooking. Ginger is among the most potent and the best studied.

Scientific evidence: A study of 247 arthritis patients published in *Arthritis & Rheumatism* found that 63% who took an extract of ginger twice daily had less knee pain.

What to do: Use one teaspoon of fresh or dried ginger daily—the amount needed for noticeable anti-inflammatory effects. Also, add turmeric and garlic to dishes whenever possible.

TRY GLUCOSAMINE

Most studies indicate that glucosamine sulfate supplements don't help with acute pain, particularly when compared with anti-inflammatory drugs. However, glucosamine sulfate does appear to slow the breakdown of joint cartilage and can help prevent arthritis from worsening.

What to do: Ask your doctor about taking 1,500 mg of glucosamine sulfate daily. The addition of chondroitin, a compound often combined with glucosamine, doesn't seem to make a difference.

Caution: Because glucosamine is derived from the shells of shellfish, people with shellfish allergies should avoid it.

Also helpful: *S-adenosylmethionine* (SAM-e), a supplement that seems to lessen arthritis pain.

Recommended dose: 1,200 mg daily, taken with glucosamine sulfate or alone. Be sure to check with your doctor before taking SAM-e. It may interact with some drugs, including certain antidepressants.

MANAGE NEGATIVE EMOTIONS

Chronic stress increases levels of cortisol, a hormone that triggers the release of inflammatory compounds known as cytokines, and contributes to weight gain.

Scientific evidence: A recent Duke University study found that volunteers who were prone to anger and suffered from depression had levels of *C-reactive protein* (CRP), a protein associated with pain and inflammation, that were two to three times higher than levels in calmer volunteers.

What to do: Anything that relaxes you—meditation, yoga, walking in nature or visiting with friends. People who learn to set their stress aside, even for brief periods, have lower levels of pain-inducing chemicals.

Choosing the Best Cane for You

American Geriatrics Society news release.

When it comes time to use a cane to walk or support you after an injury, don't grab any old stick, advises the American Geriatrics Society.

Getting a cane tailored to your body and needs, and using it properly, is vital to its success and your health, according to the society's president, John Murphy, MD.

"A common use of canes is for arthritis in the hip," said Dr. Murphy. "For patients using a cane for pain in one hip, the cane should be held in the hand opposite the affected leg. The cane should then move forward with the affected leg."

Dr. Murphy offered several tips for selecting a cane...

- **Check the tip: A rubber tip is a must for traction.** Check the tip often, and replace it when the tread is worn.

Get a grip: Find one that feels comfortable when held. A person who has arthritis or an injury that affects the fingers and hands might need a specialized grip.

Adjust for your body: When standing, the elbow should be at a 30-degree angle when the cane is held next to the leg. When your arm is at your side, the cane's top should be parallel with your wrist.

Natural Ways to Fight Fibromyalgia

Alan C. Logan, ND, lecturer at Harvard School of Continuing Medical Education in Boston and nutrition editor of the *International Journal of Naturopathic Medicine*. He is coauthor of *Hope and Help for Chronic Fatigue Syndrome and Fibromyalgia* (Cumberland House). *www.drlogan.com.*

Muscle aches targeting your tenderest spots...fatigue so severe that you can scarcely stand up...sleep disturbances that keep you from ever feeling rested. If these symptoms sound familiar, the problem may be fibromyalgia.

Some doctors claim that fibromyalgia is "all in the head." Yet this potentially debilitating condition is very real to the estimated five million Americans who have it—with women outnumbering men nine-to-one. As yet, it has no known cause or cure. Conventional medical care often fails to bring relief—but many alternative therapies may ease fibromyalgia symptoms. *What you need to know to feel better...*

FIGURING IT OUT

No lab test can detect fibromyalgia, and patients' blood work often appears normal. Diagnosis is based on symptoms—widespread pain that persists for at least three months plus abnormal tenderness at 11 or more of 18 specific spots on the neck, shoulders, chest, back, hips, thighs, knees and elbows. Many patients also experience headache...stiff joints...constipation or diarrhea...depression...sleep problems...and/or sensitivity to lights, sounds or smells.

Theories as to the cause of fibromyalgia include an excess of, or oversensitivity to, the neurotransmitters (brain chemicals) that signal pain...or changes in muscle metabolism and/or hormones that affect nerve activity.

Anti-inflammatory drugs, painkillers and antidepressants are only moderately effective for fibromyalgia symptoms. What's more, because patients with fibromyalgia often are very sensitive to medication, they're more likely than other people to experience side effects.

Bottom line: If drugs help you and do not cause side effects, consider complementing your medication with the therapies below. If medication is not effective or appropriate, alternative therapies offer the best chance for relief.

SOOTHING SUPPLEMENTS

The supplements below are listed in the order in which I believe they are likely to be effective for fibromyalgia. All are available at health food stores and online. Try the first one for six to eight weeks. If it helps, continue indefinitely. If it doesn't help, discontinue use. For greater relief, try the others one at a time for six to eight weeks, continuing with any or all that work for you. They generally are safe and, unless otherwise noted, can be taken indefinitely—but get your doctor's approval before using them. As a general precaution, do not use while pregnant or breast-feeding.

•**Omega-3 fatty acids,** such as *eicosapentaenoic acid* (EPA) and *docosahexaenoic acid* (DHA), may ease pain by reducing inflammation.

Source: Fish oil liquid or capsules.

Dosage: 3 grams (g) daily of combined EPA and DHA.

•**S-adenosylmethionine (SAM-e),** a naturally occurring compound in the body, may reduce fatigue and depression by increasing levels of the neurotransmitter serotonin.

Dosage: 800 milligrams (mg) to 1,200 mg daily. Do not use SAM-e if you take antidepressants or have diabetes.

•**Coenzyme Q10 (CoQ10) and *ginkgo biloba*,** taken together, may have a synergistic effect. CoQ10, a vitamin-like substance, boosts cellular energy. Ginkgo biloba, an herb, improves blood flow.

Dosage: 200 mg daily of each.

•***Chlorella*,** a type of green algae, reduced fibromyalgia pain by 22% in one study.

Possible reasons: It may boost the immune system and/or increase absorption of essential nutrients.

Dosage: 5 g to 10 g daily.

•***Nicotinamide adenine dehydrogenase* (NADH),** a vitamin-like substance, may increase energy within cells and facilitate production of the neurotransmitter dopamine, which affects mood.

Dosage: 10 mg daily.

•**Melatonin,** a hormone that regulates the "body clock," can improve sleep.

Dosage: 3 mg daily. Melatonin can affect other hormones, so using it for more than one month requires close medical supervision.

•**Probiotics,** beneficial intestinal bacteria, combat harmful bacteria that cause digestive distress...and may influence inflammatory chemicals that trigger pain and depression.

Dosage: One billion colony-forming units (CFU) of *lactobacillus* and/or *bifidobacterium* per day.

MORE ALTERNATIVE THERAPIES

Ask your doctor about...

•**Acupuncture.** This involves inserting thin needles into points along the body's meridians (energy pathways) to enhance flow of qi (life force). This may release endorphins that relieve pain.

Referrals: American Association of Acupuncture and Oriental Medicine, 866-455-7999, *www.aaaomonline.org.*

•**Aromatherapy.** This uses essential oils to lift mood, making pain less bothersome.

To use: Place two or three drops of jasmine or lavender oil in an aromatherapy diffuser.

•**Mind–body techniques.** These reduce stress.

Try: Meditation, deep breathing, biofeedback. For DVDs and CDs on techniques, contact the Benson-Henry Institute for Mind–Body Medicine (617-643-6090, *www.mbmi.org*).

•**Mud packs.** In one study, mud packs were heated to between 104°F and 113°F and applied to patients' sore areas for 15 minutes during 12 separate sessions. Pain, fatigue and physical function all improved.

Theory: Mud draws heat to muscles, reducing pain and stiffness.

Best: Ask a holistic doctor for a referral to a medical spa.

•**Myofascial trigger-point therapy.** This focuses on tender muscle areas that are anatomically similar to acupuncture points. Practitioners inject these "trigger points" with an anesthetic, then stretch muscles to relieve pain.

Referrals: National Association of Myofascial Trigger Point Therapists, *www.myofascialtherapy.org.*

•**Pool therapy.** Exercises done in a heated swimming pool for one hour three times weekly for several months can reduce fibromyalgia pain and increase stamina.

Referrals: Ask a physical therapist.

For a referral to a doctor who specializes in fibromyalgia, contact the National Fibromyalgia Association (714-921-0150, *www.fmaware.org*).

How to Heal Aches And Pains—Without Surgery or Drugs

Ming Chew, PT, a physical therapist with a private practice in New York City, *www.mingmethod.net*. He is author of *The Permanent Pain Cure* (McGraw-Hill). A former bodybuilder, Chew has worked as a physical therapist for more than 20 years. His clients include professional baseball and basketball players and golfers.

Most conventional doctors' approach to orthopedic pain and injuries is "medicate or cut." But there are alternatives.

Before resorting to powerful drugs or surgery, people who suffer from aching knees, backs, shoulders, hips or necks owe it to themselves to first try physical therapy.

Secret to permanent pain relief: A specialized form of physical therapy that focuses on fascia (the tough sheet of connective tissue found in all parts of your body) is one of the most effective —yet underused—cures for joint pain.

WHY DOES IT WORK?

Over time, the fascia (pronounced fash-ee-uh) throughout your body can become less flexible from lack of exercise. Repetitive movements, such as typing, knitting, golfing or tennis playing...bad posture...or trauma, including bruising or surgery, also affect the fascia. When the fascia tightens, your muscles no longer contract properly. This results in muscle weakness that can lead to aches and pains in other parts of the body.

Important: If the fascia is injured, it won't show up on a magnetic resonance imaging (MRI) scan, which doctors routinely use to diagnose orthopedic problems. But unhealthy fascia often is the underlying cause of joint and muscle pain.

THE KEY TO HEALTHY FASCIA

To check the resilience of your fascia, place your palm flat on a table and spread your fingers as wide as possible. Using the thumb and index finger of your other hand, pinch a fold of skin on the back of your flattened hand. Pull it up and hold it for five seconds. Then let go. If the skin snaps back and becomes completely flat instantaneously, your fascia is highly elastic and healthy. If it takes longer than two seconds, your fascia has lost some elasticity.

For the health of your fascia...

- **Stay hydrated.** The fascia in your body is 70% water. For proper hydration, drink at least 64 ounces of filtered water or purified bottled water per day if you're male or 48 ounces daily if you're female.

Eat an anti-inflammatory diet by limiting sugar consumption (including fruit juices and sweets), trans fats ("partially hydrogenated oils" found in many packaged and fast foods) and fried foods.

Take supplements to further reduce inflammation. For example, ask your doctor about taking 1.5 grams (g) to 2.5 g of fish oil per day (taken with meals)...and a daily joint-support supplement that combines glucosamine and chondroitin (components of joint tissue and cartilage, respectively)—consult a naturopathic or integrative medicine physician for advice on specific dosages and any precautions that should be taken when using these supplements.

STRETCHING TIGHT FASCIA

The following three fascial stretches address some especially common problem areas.

Important: Always warm up with two minutes of continuous movement, such as jogging in place or performing arm circles, before stretching.*

- **Hip flexor stretch.** This stretch affects the *psoas*, a muscle that connects the base of the spine to the hip bones. Tight psoas muscles are a major—and under-recognized—cause of low-back pain as well as hip and knee pain.

What to do: Place a chair on each side of your body. Kneel on your right knee and place your left leg in front of you with your left foot flat on the ground and your left knee bent 90 degrees. Place the palm of each hand on the seat of each chair.

Next, tilt your torso to the left. While maintaining this tilt, rotate your torso to the right.

*These stretches should not be performed by pregnant women or people with bone cancer, acute pain or recent muscle tears or strains.

Lift your chest and tuck your chin to your chest. Clench your buttocks to press your right hip forward. To avoid arching your back, contract your abdominal muscles.

Finally, while pressing your right foot downward, imagine that you're dragging your right knee forward and contract the muscles you would use to do this. You should feel a deep stretch in the front of your right hip. Hold for 20 seconds, keeping your buttocks firmly contracted. Relax for 10 seconds, then hold for 30 seconds more. Switch legs and repeat on the other side.

• **Shrug muscle stretch.** This stretch affects the trapezius muscle, which runs from the lower back to the outer shoulder and base of the skull. The stretch can help relieve neck stiffness, which is often due to a tight trapezius.

What to do: While seated or standing, hold your right arm five inches out from your hip, elbow straight. Bend your wrist slightly behind your body and drop your chin to your chest. Rotate your chin to the right about 30 degrees, and hold it there while you tilt the upper part of your head to the left. Press your right shoulder down hard, away from your ear and hold for 20 seconds. You should feel a stretch from the back of your head to the outer edge of your right shoulder. Rest for 10 seconds, then hold for 30 seconds more. Repeat on the left side.

• **Biceps stretch.** This stretch helps with a range of problems, including shoulder pain, tennis elbow and golfer's elbow. It also strengthens muscles in the mid-back, which helps improve posture. For this stretch, you'll need a chair and a low table.

What to do: Place the chair back against the table and sit with your feet flat on the floor. Put both arms on the table behind you with the backs of your hands facing down. Pull both shoulders backward and lift your chest. Next, walk both feet slightly leftward so your torso is rotated to the left. Straighten your right elbow and bend your right wrist up, touching the fingers and thumb of your right hand together in a point (your left hand should remain flat on the table).

Next, tilt your head to the left, and rotate it to the left so that the right side of your neck feels a stretch. Then drop your chin to your left collarbone. It should feel like a strap is being pulled from the top front of your shoulder to your elbow. Hold for 20 seconds. Rest for 10 seconds, then hold for 30 seconds more. Switch sides and repeat.

Illustrations by Shawn Banner.

A Surprising Cure for Joint and Muscle Aches

Mitchell T. Yass, PT, a licensed physical therapist who has practiced for more than 15 years. He is the founder and director of PT2 Physical Therapy and Personal Training in Farmingdale, New York, and author of *Overpower Pain: The Strength-Training Program that Stops Pain Without Drugs or Surgery* (Sentient).

When you hear the term "weight lifting," you may think of bodybuilders with bulging muscles. Only in the past few years has it become more widely known that weight lifting—often called strength training—also helps control body weight and increase bone mass.

What most people still don't know: Weight lifting can play a significant role in relieving muscle and joint pain. Even though doctors often overlook muscle weakness as a cause of pain, it is the culprit in an estimated 80% to 90% of my patients, many of whom are ages 60 to 90 and suffer from aching joints and muscles.

Surprisingly, muscle weakness contributes to pain even in people who have been told by a physician that a structural problem, such as a torn ligament or arthritis, is responsible.

WHY DO STRONG MUSCLES FIGHT PAIN?

Exercises designed to strengthen muscles improve joint function and overall body mechanics in two important ways. When the muscles of a joint are weak, the bones can move out of position, causing bone surfaces to rub together and leading to irritation and pain at the joint. Also, because muscles work together to produce movement, if one is underdeveloped, other muscles can easily become strained.

The following exercises target areas that are especially prone to pain-causing muscle weakness that often goes undetected.

The exercises require hand or ankle weights. Both are available at sporting-goods stores.

Typical cost: Hand weights—$10 a pair... ankle weights—$20 a pair.

Helpful: When choosing weights, select ones that you can lift about 10 times without straining. If your muscles are not tired by the time of the last repetition, choose a heavier weight.

For each exercise, perform three sets of 10 repetitions two to three times a week.* As you lift the weight, breathe out and count to two... as you lower it, breathe in and count to three.

Important: See a doctor if your pain was caused by a traumatic injury, such as a fall...if your discomfort is constant and/or severe...or if you have limited range of motion (less than 50% of your normal range). In these cases, the pain may be due to a problem that cannot be improved with exercise.

Best exercises to relieve...

SHOULDER AND ELBOW PAIN

What's targeted: The *rotator-cuff* muscles, which hold the humerus (upper arm) bone in place when you lift your arm. Building the rotator-cuff muscles also alleviates the strain on forearm muscles that leads to elbow pain. Rotator-cuff muscles can be strained during such activities as driving or using a computer for long periods without supporting the arms.

What to do: Sit in a chair placed at the front edge of a table with your left side a few inches from the corner of the table. Hold a weight in your left hand and rest your left elbow on the front edge of the table. Your hand should be about three inches below the tabletop with your palm facing down.

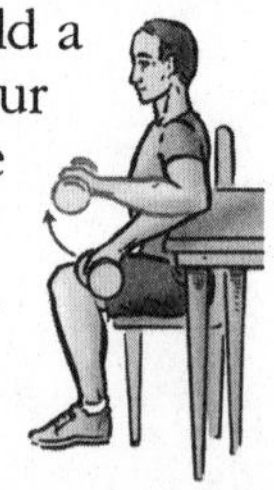

Raise your forearm, keeping your wrist straight, until your hand is about three inches above the table. Lower the weight to the starting position. Reposition the chair so that your right side is next to the table, and repeat the exercise with the weight in your right hand.

SHOULDER PAIN

What's targeted: The *posterior-deltoid* muscles located at the back of the shoulders. These muscles tend to be weaker than the front shoulder muscles due to our natural tendency to hold and carry objects in front of our bodies, which makes the chest, front shoulder and bicep muscles work harder. This imbalance can throw off bone alignment in the shoulder joints, causing pain.

What to do: Stand with your feet a little more than shoulder-width apart. Position yourself so that your knees and elbows are slightly bent and your back slightly arched. Hold a weight in each hand in front of your thighs, palms facing each other. Using your shoulders, extend your arms out to the side until the weights are about six inches from your thighs, stopping the motion before your shoulder blades begin to come together. Return the weights to the starting position.

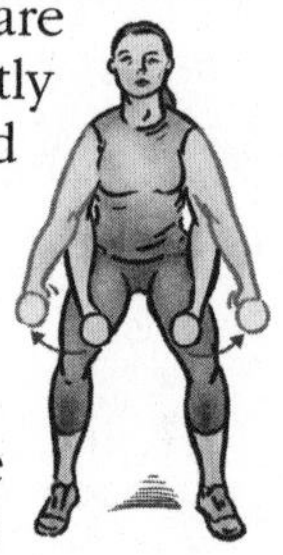

ELBOW PAIN

What's targeted: The *wrist-extensor* muscles, which run along the top of the forearm. Building these muscles relieves strains caused by gardening, playing tennis or other activities involving repetitive wrist movement, gripping or squeezing.

What to do: Sit with your feet flat on the floor directly under your knees. While holding a weight in your right hand, rest your right forearm on the top of your right thigh with your wrist about three inches directly in front of your knee and your palm facing down. Place your left hand on your right forearm to keep it steady. Using your wrist muscles, lift the weight until your wrist is fully flexed. Return to the starting position. Repeat the exercise on your left thigh, using your left hand.

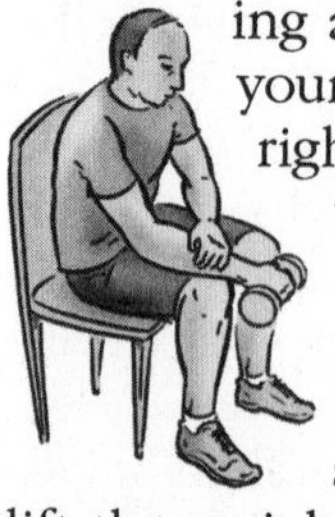

*Consult your doctor before starting any new exercise program.

HIP, KNEE AND HEEL PAIN

What's targeted: The *hip-abductor* muscles, which support your legs when you walk and climb stairs. Strengthening these muscles can relieve muscle strain at the hip joint and prevent the knee and foot from rotating toward the midline of your body when you walk (causing knee pain and heel pain)—instead of staying in line with your hip.

What to do: Lie on your right side on a carpeted floor or a mat with an ankle weight strapped to your left leg. Fold your right arm under your head and bend your right leg. Place your left hand on the floor in front of you for support. Flex your left foot (as if standing on it) and raise your straightened left leg to hip height, keeping it in line with your torso. Lower your leg to the starting position. Lie on your left side and repeat the exercise raising your right leg.

Illustrations by Shawn Banner.

Drug-Free Chronic Pain Relief

Ingrid Bacci, PhD, *www.ingridbacci.com*, a certified craniosacral therapist (a manual therapy that treats chronic pain and other conditions) and a licensed teacher of the Alexander Technique (a movement therapy). She develops and teaches seminars on chronic pain management, is a guest lecturer at the Columbia College of Physicians and Surgeons in New York City, and is author of *Effortless Pain Relief* (Free Press).

Contrary to popular belief, an injury or accident is hardly ever the only cause of chronic pain—be it a backache, throbbing knee or stiff neck or shoulder.

Surprising: Chronic pain generally results from lifestyle habits, such as the way we breathe, stand, move or hold tension in our bodies. These habits involve patterns of physical stress—expressed as muscle tension—that either can be the cause of pain or can turn injuries into long-standing problems.

For example, someone with a back injury may find that it's more comfortable to stoop forward slightly or lean to one side. Even when the original injury is healed, the body position can become a habit—and cause excessive muscle stress and pain.

KNOW YOUR BODY

If you suffer any type of chronic pain, it's essential for you to develop a heightened awareness of how your body feels...recognize physical habits that cause muscle tension...and move in ways that enhance flexibility and comfort. Even if you have severe chronic pain that requires other treatment, such as medication, the strategies described in this article also may be used to promote healing.

My advice...

***Step 1:* "Scan" your body.** Yoga, meditation and many other relaxation techniques recognize that simply observing your body's sensations without judgment can often encourage your body to spontaneously relax. When we worry about pain, we unconsciously tighten our muscles. The key is to accept whatever you feel.

Solution: When you are in bed at night, or relaxing on a sofa during the day, start by observing the sensations in your feet, then gradually travel up your entire body. Just observe your sensations. While you may feel momentary discomfort as you become aware of areas of tension, this tension will gradually dissipate, leaving you feeling more relaxed both physically and emotionally.

***Step 2:* Practice breathing deeply.** The diaphragm, located just below the lungs and heart, is a large muscle responsible for about 75% of the work involved in breathing.

Interesting fact: Because the diaphragm is attached via connective tissue and muscles to the low back and hips, tension in the diaphragm can contribute to low-back pain. When the diaphragm does not work optimally—contracting and releasing fully—secondary respiratory muscles in the upper torso must kick in to improve breathing. This contributes to upper torso fatigue and pain. People whose diaphragms are contracted and rigid tend to breathe shallowly. They are known as "chest breathers."

Solution: To relieve muscle tension, practice diaphragmatic breathing. As you breathe in this way, you will notice your breath becoming softer, deeper and slower. *What to do...*

• **While sitting or lying on your back,** put one hand on your chest and the other on your stomach.

• **Slowly inhale through your nose**—or keep your lips slightly parted and breathe slowly through your mouth.

• **If you notice that your chest is expanding,** focus more on breathing "into the belly." Your stomach should rise more than your chest with each breath.

Practice diaphragmatic breathing as often and for as long as you like. The more you practice, the more it will become your preferred way of breathing.

Helpful: If you're not sure that you are breathing in a relaxed, fully diaphragmatic way, count the number of breaths you take in one minute. If you're breathing more shallowly than you're capable of doing, you may take as many as 11 to 20 breaths a minute. If you're breathing deeply and diaphragmatically, you will take as few as four to 10 breaths a minute.

Step 3: **Work on body alignment.** As a result of years of sedentary living, most adults have poor body alignment. Since we stand and sit a great deal of the time, it is particularly important to improve alignment in these postures.

Interesting fact: Improving alignment isn't about squaring back your shoulders and being stiff. It's about using your body in more comfortable ways.

Solution: A few simple steps can help improve the way that you stand and sit, reducing pain and fatigue. *Examples...*

• **Bend your knees slightly when standing.** It reduces stress on the low back.

• **Keep your weight distributed evenly over both legs when standing**—and keep both feet pointed in the same direction, instead of turning them in or out.

• **When walking,** roll from heel to toe, pushing off through the ball of the foot and keeping the weight evenly distributed between the inside and outside of the foot.

• **When you get in and out of a chair,** bend fully at the knees and hips, keeping your torso relaxed and straight.

Step 4: **Stretch your body.** Few move enough of their muscles regularly to stay limber.

Interesting fact: Certain animals, such as cats, stretch their whole bodies each time they get up, which helps keep them limber.

Solution: Spend 15 to 30 minutes daily fully stretching your body. You can do this through a formal discipline, such as yoga, or through an activity such as free-form dancing. Put on some music you enjoy, close your eyes and move to the beat, freeing up every stiff muscle. Or simply lie on the floor and stretch in any way that feels good.

Step 5: **Release body tension.** To reduce chronic pain, it is important not only to pay close attention to your body and recognize muscle tension as it occurs, but also to let it go whenever you can.

Interesting fact: Once people learn how their bodies should feel, they're better able to make other physical changes that reduce muscle tension.

Solution: Don't ignore muscle tension. Learn how to move more "intelligently"—using minimum effort to achieve maximum results.

Examples: Grip your car steering wheel less tightly...notice whether you tense your muscles when having a stressful conversation or work long hours at a desk. Then try to relax a little bit. The more you relax, the less pain you will have.

Be Pain Free... Without Drugs

Jill Stansbury, ND, assistant professor and chair of the department of botanical medicine at the National College of Natural Medicine in Portland, Oregon, and medical director of Battle Ground Healing Arts, a naturopathic medical clinic in Battle Ground, Washington. She is coauthor of *Herbs for Health & Healing* (Consumer Guide). *http://jillstansbury.net.*

With muscle and joint pain, the cure can often be even worse than the condition.

Reason: Common pain relievers called nonsteroidal anti-inflammatory drugs (NSAIDs)—such as over-the-counter *ibuprofen* (Motrin), *naproxen* (Aleve) and aspirin, as well as prescription *oxaprozin* (Daypro) and controversial *celecoxib* (Celebrex)—have many potentially serious side effects. *NSAIDs may...*

• **Cause nausea,** vomiting, heartburn and gastrointestinal ulcers.

• **Compromise immunity** by interfering with the body's natural anti-inflammatory chemicals.

• **Thin the blood,** increasing the risk for excessive bleeding.

• **Raise blood pressure.**

• **Lead to kidney or liver failure.**

Much safer: Natural nutritional supplements and topical treatments can reduce chronic or acute pain in muscles and joints. The remedies below are available without a prescription at health food stores and/or online. (As a general precaution, do not use while pregnant or breastfeeding.) The suggested brands are examples from among many good options.

CHRONIC PAIN: SUPPLEMENTS

Nutritional supplements won't provide a quick fix—but when taken daily, they may help relieve persistent pain caused by osteoarthritis (gradual erosion of the cartilage that cushions joints), rheumatoid arthritis (an autoimmune disorder that causes chronic joint inflammation) or an old injury.

You can use any one, two, three or more of the following supplements. Often several are sold together in a combination formula. You may need to use trial and error to determine which are most effective for you.

Best: Before starting supplement therapy, it is wise to consult a naturopathic or holistic doctor for usage and dosage guidelines based on your individual sensitivities and symptoms.

If pain is mild, start with the low end of the suggested dosage ranges below to see if you get sufficient relief. For more severe symptoms, start low and work up to the higher end of the ranges if necessary. Dosages may vary by manufacturer, so follow instructions on labels.

Some supplements may cause mild stomach upset and/or gassiness. To minimize this, take with meals and/or cut back the dosage.

Important: Consult your doctor before using supplements if you have any medical problems, such as diabetes or digestive disorders...or if you are taking an antibiotic, a blood thinner, or medication to control blood sugar or blood pressure.

Supplements to try...

• **Boswellia,** a resinous plant related to frankincense, blocks production of chemicals that cause pain and swelling.

Recommended brand: Nature's Way Boswellia (801-489-1500, *www.naturesway.com*), $13.99 for 60 307-milligram (mg) tablets.

Dosage: One tablet three times daily.

• **Bromelain,** from pineapple, has enzymes that improve circulation and reduce inflammation.

Recommended brand: Thorne Research M.F. Bromelain (800-228-1966, *www.thorne.com)*, $25.55 for 60 500-mg capsules.

Dosage: 500 mg to 1,000 mg three times per day.

• **Glucosamine sulfate is derived mainly from crustacean shells.** Molecularly, it is similar to a natural compound in the human body called *glycosamine glycans*, which is a building block for bones, ligaments and tendons.

Recommended brand: Tyler's Glucosamine Sulfate (800-277-9861, *www.houseofnutrition.com*), $40.30 for 120 500-mg capsules.

Dosage: One capsule three times daily.

• ***Harpagophytum* (devil's claw),** from the sesame family, is an anti-inflammatory and a pain reliever.

Recommended brand: Nature's Way Devil's Claw (801-489-1500, *www.naturesway.com*), $17.99 for 90 960-mg capsules.

Dosage: One capsule twice daily.

• **Turmeric (curcuma),** the main spice used in curry, limits activity of inflammatory enzymes. Do not supplement with turmeric if you have an ulcer or a problem with your gallbladder or bile duct—it can exacerbate these conditions.

Recommended brand: Gaia Herbs Turmeric Supreme (800-831-7780, *www.gaiaherbs.com*), $27.99 for 60 capsules, each equivalent to 2,500 mg of turmeric.

Dosage: One capsule once or twice daily.

•**Vitamin D,** which the body synthesizes from sunlight, also is found in fish, eggs and fortified milk. Correcting a deficiency can alleviate musculoskeletal pain. Good brands are available at drugstores and health food stores.

Dosage: 1,000 international units (IU) to 2,000 IU per day of vitamin D-3 (cholecalciferol), the most active form.

ACUTE PAIN: TOPICALS

Oils, ointments and soaks provide quick relief from the pain of muscle strains and arthritis flare-ups. For mild discomfort, try any one of the remedies below...for severe pain, use two or more. Do not use on broken skin or take internally. If skin irritation develops, discontinue use.

•**Arnica,** from a daisylike plant, improves blood flow and reduces inflammation.

To use: For stiff, aching pain, rub a palmful onto the sore area two to three times daily.

Recommended brand: Gaia Herbs Arnica Oil (800-831-7780, *www.gaiaherbs.com*), $10.99 for one ounce.

•**Castor oil comes from the castor bean plant.** Used topically, it helps blood cells function properly...combats autoimmune diseases ...and relieves pain and inflammation.

To use: Just rub a palmful onto skin of the affected area (it can be messy, so you might want to do it at bedtime).

Recommended brand: Frontier Natural Products Co-op Castor Oil (800-669-3275, *www.frontiercoop.com*), $16.09 for 32 ounces.

•**Epsom salts contain magnesium sulfate,** which fights infection and inflammation and relaxes muscles.

To use: Fill a basin or bathtub with comfortably hot water, and mix in the desired amount of Epsom salts. The stronger you make the mixture, the more effective it is—try two to three cups of salts per tub of water. Soak the affected area for 15 to 20 minutes once or twice daily, then rinse if desired.

Recommended brand: TheraSoak from Saltworks (800-353-7258, *www.saltworks.us*), $8.39 for a five-pound bag.

•**Heat rub.** Topical pain relievers (Bengay, Icy Hot) contain organic compounds, such as camphor, menthol and/or *methyl salicylate.* They work by creating a feeling of heat that overrides the nerves' transmission of pain.

To use: Products are available as ointments, creams or skin patches. Follow the manufacturer's instructions for the amount and frequency of use.

Warning: Methyl salicylate is toxic if used in excess. Do not exceed recommended dosages. Never use multiple heat rubs at once. Do not use with a heating pad or while taking medication from the salicylate family, such as aspirin or antacids.

Recommended brand: Tiger Balm Red, about $7 for four ounces, available at select drugstores and health food stores.

■ ■ ■ ■

Painkillers May Reduce Parkinson's Risk

A study of 579 men and women found that patients who regularly took two or more pills of non-aspirin nonsteroidal anti-inflammatory drugs (NSAIDs), such as *ibuprofen* (Advil), weekly for at least one month during their lifetimes had up to a 60% lower risk for Parkinson's than those who took NSAIDs less often or never.

Theory: NSAIDs' anti-inflammatory effect may halt or slow brain-cell death, a process that often occurs in the brains of Parkinson's patients. More research is needed before NSAIDs can be recommended to prevent Parkinson's.

Angelika D. Wahner, PhD, assistant research faculty, department of epidemiology, University of California, Los Angeles.

Aspirin, Tylenol or Advil? What to Reach for First

Russell K. Portenoy, MD, chairman of the department of pain medicine and palliative care at Beth Israel Medical Center and professor of neurology and anesthesiology at the Albert Einstein College of Medicine, both in New York City. Dr. Portenoy is editor in chief of *Journal of Pain and Symptom Management* and has written, coauthored or edited 17 books and more than 450 scientific papers and book chapters on aspects of pain management.

Every day, 36 million Americans take an over-the-counter (OTC) painkiller, usually *acetaminophen* (Tylenol), *ibuprofen* (Advil, Motrin) or aspirin.

We take those medications to stop a headache ...ease an arthritis flare-up...soothe a sore shoulder after a weekend of yard work...or relieve any one of the everyday aches and pains that inevitably disrupt our lives.

But do you know which painkiller to take first for maximum effectiveness and safety?

Here are the latest guidelines...

HOW PAINKILLERS WORK

All three of the most common pain relievers —acetaminophen, ibuprofen and aspirin—reduce the production of cyclooxygenase (COX) enzymes. These enzymes play a key role in the formation of *prostanoids*, biochemicals that sensitize the nerve fibers that produce pain and trigger inflammation.

What you may not know: There is no "best" OTC painkiller for every pain problem. That's because not everyone responds to pain relievers in the same way—none of these drugs works consistently for everyone or for every type of pain.

You may find that ibuprofen relieves your headaches, but it may do nothing for your spouse, who swears by aspirin when his/her temples start to throb.

Even if ibuprofen works for both your and your spouse's headaches, the amount you each need for pain relief may be different—and the amount that one person needs may cause a distressing side effect that never troubles the other.

How can you determine the right drug and dose for you, and you alone? Follow the three-step plan below.

Important: This self-care plan is best for relief of mild-to-moderate acute pain, such as a toothache or headache. It is not appropriate for chronic pain. Long-term use of any painkiller should be monitored by a doctor because of the risk for side effects. All dosages listed are for adults. Also, don't use products that combine two or more of these ingredients, such as Extra-Strength Excedrin, which includes acetaminophen and aspirin. Combination products have not been proven to work any better and may have an increased risk for side effects.

START WITH ACETAMINOPHEN

Because there's no way to tell which OTC painkiller will work best for you, it's sensible for most people (though not all) to start with the safest—the one that decades of clinical use has shown poses the lowest risk for side effects. That drug is acetaminophen.

Starting dosage: 500 milligrams (mg) to 1,000 mg.

Maximum dosage: Two extra-strength 500-mg capsules, four times daily. If you take acetaminophen repeatedly over many days, don't exceed 4,000 mg a day.

Warning: The biggest risk from acetaminophen is liver damage, which can occur when more than the maximum dosage is taken. Don't use acetaminophen at any dosage without a physician's supervision if you have a liver disease, such as hepatitis C, or a history of heavy drinking (three or more drinks a day). Although ibuprofen generally would be preferred over the other painkillers in these cases, all painkillers have added risks for people who have liver disease or are heavy drinkers.

Unless you've been drinking heavily for several months, it's probably safe to use acetaminophen as long as you have no history of liver damage.

NEXT, TRY IBUPROFEN

If acetaminophen doesn't relieve your acute pain, switch to ibuprofen or one of the other nonsteroidal anti-inflammatory drugs (NSAIDs), such as *naproxen* (Aleve) or *ketoprofen* (Actron).

Starting dosage: 200 mg to 400 mg.

Maximum dosage: Use of more than 2,400 mg daily requires monitoring by a physician because high dosages can cause serious side effects.

Precautions: Like all NSAIDs, regular use of ibuprofen can damage the gastrointestinal tract, causing problems ranging from heartburn to bleeding ulcers. *Other possible side effects...*

• **Kidney damage,** with swelling of the legs, worsening of high blood pressure and/or kidney failure.

• **Risk for blood clots,** which increase the likelihood of angina, heart attack and/or stroke. If you have unstable angina (not effectively controlled with medical care), PAD (narrowing of the arteries in the legs) or have had a heart attack, a transient ischemic attack or a stroke, or have otherwise been diagnosed with cardiovascular disease, do not take ibuprofen regularly. The more severe the circulatory disease, the greater the need for caution with ibuprofen. Acetaminophen is probably the better choice, but talk to your doctor.

ASPIRIN IS THE LAST CHOICE

If acetaminophen and ibuprofen don't work, you can try switching to aspirin, with the understanding that aspirin is the most likely of these drugs to cause side effects in most people.

Starting dosage: Two 325-mg tablets.

Maximum dosage: Do not exceed 4,000 mg daily.

Precautions: The greatest risk with aspirin is bleeding ulcers.

EXTRA BENEFITS

Many studies show a link between regularly taking some OTC pain relievers and reduced risk for chronic disease.

Example: Aspirin for cardiovascular disease. Researchers at Duke University Medical Center analyzed data from six studies involving nearly 10,000 patients with heart disease. Those who took low-dose aspirin (81 mg per day) had a 21% reduction, on average, in the risk for a "major cardiovascular event," including heart attack and stroke.

However, studies showing other benefits of pain relievers are inconclusive—some show a benefit, and others don't. *The following findings from recent scientific studies are intriguing, but they are not yet the basis for practical recommendations...*

• **Alzheimer's disease.** Researchers at Johns Hopkins Bloomberg School of Public Health analyzed results from six studies and found that people who regularly used painkillers, such as ibuprofen and aspirin, had a 23% lower risk of developing Alzheimer's.

• **Cancer.** Researchers at the American Cancer Society analyzed data from nearly 70,000 men and 76,000 women and found that long-term daily use of aspirin (at least 325 mg per day) was associated with reduced cancer risk by 15% compared with people not taking aspirin, including a 30% lower risk for colorectal cancer and a 20% reduced risk for prostate cancer. Other researchers have found a 15% reduction in breast cancer risk among those who regularly use aspirin.

• **Parkinson's disease.** In a study of nearly 600 people, researchers at UCLA School of Public Health found that regular users of aspirin or ibuprofen (two or more pills a week for at least one month) had up to a 60% lower risk for Parkinson's than people who were infrequent users or nonusers.

Injection Helps Cancer Patients Live Pain Free

Giovanni Carlo Anselmetti, MD, Institute for Cancer Research and Treatment, Turin, Italy.

Mark Montgomery, MD, associate professor, radiology, Texas A&M Health Science Center College of Medicine, Temple, Texas, and director, interventional radiology, and vice chair, education in radiology, Scott & White Healthcare, Temple, Texas.

Susan Bukata, MD, associate professor, orthopaedics, University of Rochester Medical Center, New York.

Society for Interventional Radiology annual meeting, San Diego.

Injecting "bone cement" into areas of weakened bone in patients whose cancer has spread to their bones can literally allow these individuals to rise from their deathbeds and live the remainder of their lives relatively pain-free.

Italian researchers, who presented the findings at the Society of Interventional Radiology annual meeting in San Diego, called it the "Lazarus Effect," referring to when Jesus miraculously raised Lazarus from the dead.

"The majority of treated patients experienced significant or complete and long-lasting pain relief after osteoplasty with immediate improvement of clinical conditions and quality of life," said study author Giovanni Carlo Anselmetti, MD, of the Institute for Cancer Research and Treatment in Turin.

Indeed, a 79-year-old nun who was confined to her bed because of thyroid cancer that had spread to her pelvis stood and walked just two hours after the minimally invasive procedure.

BACKGROUND

Orthopedists who do osteoplasty generally partner with an interventional radiologist who first performs *radiofrequency ablation* (extreme heat) or *cryoablation* (freezing) to kill nerve cells near the tumor.

Osteoplasty involves injecting bone cement (they used *polymethyl-methacrylate*, or PMMA, in the study) into bony areas weakened by cancer with the help of a computed tomography (CT) scan or other image guidance.

"The procedure is analogous to vertebroplasty, which has been around for a few years, where you put little needles into the spine and inject a cement mixture," said Mark Montgomery, MD, an associate professor of radiology at Texas A&M Health Science Center College of Medicine and director of interventional radiology and vice chair of education in radiology at Scott & White Healthcare. "It uses the same kind of cement as for total hip replacement. This is the same thing, except they're just taking it into other areas," he added.

THE STUDY

The study involved 81 patients, ages 36 to 94 and mostly female, who underwent osteoplasty at least once. Seventy-four of the participants had cancer, while a handful had "benign" diseases, such as rheumatoid arthritis.

The overall patient population was larger than those seen in other studies, said Susan Bukata, MD, an orthopedic oncologist at the University of Rochester Medical Center.

Pelvic, femur, sacrum, ribs, knee and other bones were treated.

THE RESULTS

The mean pain score dropped significantly within 24 hours of the procedure. Sixty-four of the patients (79%) were able to discontinue use of narcotics and 43 (53%) also stopped using any other pain medications. Only five of the patients showed no improvement in pain. There were no deaths or major complications.

PAIN CONTROL OPTION

"It is palliative. It's not going to be a curative procedure, but we've seen dramatic improvements in pain control," said Dr. Montgomery. "There's a lack of an awareness of some of the options for patients that have painful bone metastases," he added. "It's physician education as much as it is patient education."

info To learn more about bone metastasis, visit the Web site of the American Cancer Society, *www.cancer.org*, and search "bone metastasis."

When to Consider Palliative Care

Diane E. Meier, MD, director of the Center to Advance Palliative Care (CAPC), a national organization devoted to increasing the number and quality of palliative-care programs in the US. She is also director of the Lilian and Benjamin Hertzberg Palliative Care Institute, and professor of geriatrics and internal medicine at Mount Sinai School of Medicine in New York City. Dr. Meier is a recipient of the prestigious MacArthur Fellowship.

Until recently, palliative care—a type of medical care that focuses on making a person who is seriously ill as comfortable and pain free as possible—was used only when death was imminent.

Now: Palliative care is being extended to people suffering from any stage of serious illness.

This approach has many benefits. The patient has a better quality of life...families and caregivers get more support...and medical costs are reduced. In fact, a recent study published in *Archives of Internal Medicine* found that palliative care saved hospitals up to $374 per patient per day (in pharmacy, laboratory and intensive-care costs).

To learn more about this new vision of palliative care—and how more people can take advantage of it—we spoke with Diane E. Meier, MD, one of the world's leading experts on this type of medical care and a recent winner of the prestigious MacArthur "Genius" Fellowship.

How does palliative care differ from other types of medical care?

Palliative care, which primarily is offered in hospitals (usually on an inpatient basis, but sometimes to outpatients), focuses on easing suffering by putting an emphasis on relief of a patient's pain and other symptoms, as well as overall improvement in his/her quality of life. For example, it complements ongoing care by helping patients control pain, reduce nausea, improve appetite, relieve fatigue and/or depression—and live a meaningful life despite the limitations of illness.

Palliative care can help a Parkinson's disease patient, for example, carry on with daily life by relieving such symptoms as joint pain and shortness of breath.

Are there any other advantages of palliative care?

There are several. For one, most physicians cannot always spend a great deal of time discussing treatment goals and options. A palliative care team, however, is able to give patients as much time as they need to get the information and guidance that is necessary to make the best medical decisions.

With palliative care, patients also get a team of specialists. Depending on an individual's needs, the palliative care team may include doctors, nurses, social workers, psychologists, massage therapists, chaplains and pharmacists as well as nutritionists.

Who is eligible for palliative care?

Doctors can administer palliative care to anyone who has been diagnosed with a serious, life-threatening or progressive illness that causes debilitating symptoms.

Diseases treated with palliative care include cancer, chronic obstructive pulmonary disease (COPD), congestive heart failure, kidney or liver failure, Parkinson's disease, dementia and autoimmune disorders, including multiple sclerosis and *lupus erythematosus.*

Palliative care may be particularly helpful for people with a serious or chronic illness who have been admitted to the hospital three or more times in the past year...if they visit an emergency room once a month or more...if their illness stops responding to ongoing treatment ...and/or if basic life functions—such as breathing or eating—are affected. But people can take advantage of palliative care at any time—even immediately after diagnosis or during the early stages of disease. Palliative care generally is covered by insurance.

Is palliative care the same as hospice?

Definitely not. If a doctor suggests palliative care, it does not necessarily mean that you are close to dying. It simply means that you could benefit from more extensive care to give you a better quality of life.

How does palliative care help support the patient's family?

Palliative care provides emotional support for family members, helps them navigate the health-care system and provides guidance to assist them and their loved ones in making difficult treatment choices.

What's the best way to seek out palliative care?

The first step is to approach your doctor. Sadly, most practicing physicians were not trained in palliative care, and your doctor may not know much about it. If you feel you need help describing palliative care, give your doctor a copy of this article.

Take this opportunity to clarify your understanding of your diagnosis, disease progression or treatment. And tell your doctor whether—and how much—your disease is limiting your life due to pain, depression or other factors.

What if the hospital my doctor is affiliated with doesn't offer palliative care?

At some point, all hospitals will offer palliative care. However, if your doctor is not affiliated with a hospital that provides this type of care, you may have to be proactive and seek out a hospital that does.

You can check the Web site of the Center to Advance Palliative Care, *www.getpalliativecare.org,* to see which hospitals in your area offer palliative care. Click on "Provider Directory," and search your hometown as well as surrounding cities.

About 1,300 US hospitals now offer palliative care. Once you find a nearby hospital on the list, ask your doctor for a referral to the hospital's palliative-care team.

Self-Hypnosis Really Works to Ease Pain

Bruce N. Eimer, PhD, psychologist and owner/director of Alternative Behavior Associates in Huntingdon Valley, Pennsylvania. He is a fellow and approved consultant of the American Society of Clinical Hypnosis and author of *Hypnotize Yourself Out of Pain Now!* (Crown House). *www.bestwaytostop.com.*

Following a serious car accident in 1993, I had herniated disks in my neck and lower back, which resulted in constant radiating pain. Back surgery caused tissue scarring, which led to my developing fibromyalgia (chronic widespread pain).

Chronic pain is the leading cause of disability in the US, affecting more than 90 million Americans. Painkillers, including morphine and related drugs, invariably cause side effects (ranging from constipation to confusion), can be addictive and are only marginally effective for many patients.

Better: Self-hypnosis. It doesn't eliminate pain, but it improves your ability to cope with it. It also lowers levels of pain-causing stress hormones and increases the body's production of *endogenous opioids*, substances with morphinelike effects. With self-hypnosis, I learned to alter my own relationship with pain. The pain is still there, but the suffering is controlled.

The practice of hypnotism has been distorted in movies and stage shows. You can't be hypnotized against your will, and you can't be made to do things that you don't want to do.

A hypnotic trance is merely an altered state of consciousness. It involves entering a physical and mental state of relaxation from which you redirect your attention to achieve certain goals—including the reduction of pain.

SIMPLE METHOD

Once you've learned to induce hypnosis, you can do it on your own once or twice a day—preferably for 10 minutes in the morning and 10 minutes at night (if you have trouble judging the time, set a timer with a quiet alarm). You might need more frequent hypnosis sessions if you are in severe pain. Most people notice a significant reduction in pain within two months—some improve after a single session.

One common technique to induce hypnosis is the Zarren Marble Method, developed by the noted hypnotist Jordan Zarren...

- **Sit in a comfortable chair, and hold a marble between your thumb and other fingers.** Roll it around and notice the texture, colors, patterns and tiny imperfections.
- **Notice how relaxed you are.** You're probably blinking more...your eyelids are getting heavy.
- **At this point, close your eyes and close your hand around the marble so that it doesn't drop.** Now you are in a state of deep relaxation. If you find that you're thinking of something else, just bring your mind back to the marble.

Once you've entered this hypnotic trance, you can use a number of mental techniques to reduce pain. *Try the techniques below and see which ones work best for you...*

DEEP RELAXATION

No one can consciously experience multiple sensations simultaneously. When the sensation of relaxation is dominant, you'll feel less pain.

How to do it: First, before you enter a hypnotic state, choose two or three positive thoughts that you want to implant in your mind. These might include things such as *My body is relaxed* or *With each breath that I take, I relax more and more.*

Then go into a hypnotic state, and mentally focus on the thoughts that you've chosen. If your mind drifts, bring it back to the thoughts.

Dwelling on the positive produces physical changes in the body, including a reduction in muscle tension and lower levels of cortisol and other stress hormones. Even when the pain isn't gone, you'll react to it less strongly.

DECATASTROPHIZING

Nearly everyone with chronic pain feels, at one time or another, that there's little hope for the future. Negative thinking increases pain sensations and intensifies suffering.

Decatastrophizing means to stop blowing things out of proportion. This helps separate pain from suffering.

Example: Someone might feel that life is worthless because of the pain. You can decatastrophize by limiting these negative thoughts or feelings. This can stop the transmission of pain signals.

How to do it: While under hypnosis, reframe how you think about pain. Rather than dwelling on hopelessness, for example, consider the possibility that pain has a purpose—that it can alert you that you need to do something to heal. Dwelling on pain's purpose can make you feel stronger and more in control.

You also can practice disputation—interrupting negative thoughts about pain by redirecting your attention to a thought that reduces stress. Say to yourself, *My pain is bad today, but I'm still going to get a lot done.*

DIRECTION

During self-hypnosis, dwell on thoughts that emphasize your sense of control. *Examples...*

- **When you notice an increase in pain,** tell yourself, *I know I can handle this. I've dealt with worse before.*
- **If the pain gets stronger,** repeat positive thoughts, such as, *I will not let the pain get the best of me. I know I can do things to make it more tolerable.*
- **Handle the worst moments with thoughts such as,** *This is only temporary. I will get through it.*

When the pain subsides, remind yourself that you coped well—and that you now have a plan to help make it easier the next time.

Important: Minimize physical "pain behaviors," such as grimacing, groaning and complaining. These reinforce the pain and increase disability.

DISTRACTION

The mind can process only a limited amount of information at one time. This means you can introduce sensations that compete with pain sensations.

How to do it: Create physical sensations (such as rubbing the place where it hurts) that are more pleasant than the pain sensations. Or distract yourself with mental exercises, such as listening to the sound of your breathing.

Try this: Go into a hypnotic trance, and pay attention only to your breathing. Listen to the sounds. Note the rhythm and the ways in which your breathing naturally changes.

The mental activity will reach your brain ahead of the pain sensations. This can close the "pain gate" so that you experience less pain.

DISSOCIATION

Again, focus your mind on something other than the pain. The idea is to take advantage of the divide between the conscious and unconscious minds. Your unconscious mind will be aware of the pain, but the pain will be unable to dominate your consciousness.

How to do it: Imagine that your consciousness is floating out of your body—that it is hovering overhead looking down. Think, *When my conscious mind floats away to a pleasant place, I leave the discomfort behind.*

MORE HELP

If you want to consult with a professional hypnotist, you can find one in your area by contacting the American Society of Clinical Hypnosis (ASCH), 630-980-4740, *www.asch.net.*

13

Savvy Consumer

Traveling for Treatment

David Boucher celebrated his 50th birthday by jetting to Bangkok for his first colonoscopy. He was seen by a California-educated physician and no shortage of nurses, all of whom verified his identity 15 times before the procedure.

To be sure, Boucher had a secondary motive: He is founder and president of Companion Global Healthcare, a subsidiary of Blue Cross Blue Shield of South Carolina that includes in its network 13 hospitals around the world that have been accredited by the Joint Commission International (JCI).

The JCI, which calls itself the "Good Housekeeping Seal of Approval," has accredited more than 170 hospitals outside of the United States.

An estimated six million Americans are traveling each year to such countries as India, Costa Rica, Mexico and Thailand in search of less-expensive treatments for simple and complex procedures. Even France and Belgium tend to be cheaper than the United States.

"People are going abroad for necessary medical treatments such as knee and hip replacements and cardiac procedures," said Devon Herrick, PhD, senior fellow with the National Center for Policy Analysis, in Dallas. "And in many countries, especially places like India, the quality is very high and the price can be up to 80% less expensive."

And that often includes the airline ticket.

Major US health-care players are jumping on the train, including Blue Shield of California. Its "Access Baja" health plan caters to Americans and Mexicans wanting to get medical care in northern Mexico. BridgeHealth International, based in Denver, also has an overseas network.

David Boucher, president, Companion Global Healthcare, Columbia, South Carolina.

Devon Herrick, PhD, senior fellow, National Center for Policy Analysis, Dallas.

National Center for Policy Analysis.

Medical Tourism: Health Care Free Trade.

WHAT'S DRIVING THE TREND?

"The cost of health care in the US, combined with the fact that we have a shortage in this country of physicians and, probably more acutely, nurses," responded Boucher. "At the same time, 2008 was the first year of the 'silver tsunami,' with Americans turning 62 at [a rapid] rate," he noted.

"Over half of folks turning 62 opted for early Social Security, and most do not have an employer-sponsored medical program," Boucher added. "There's going to be a sharply increasing number of people that need bypass surgery and hip and knee replacements."

LOWER COSTS FOR TREATMENTS IN FOREIGN COUNTRIES

According to the National Center for Policy Analysis, costs for treatment abroad can be as little as one-half to one-fifth the going rate in the United States. As an example, it cited New Delhi's Apollo Hospital, which charges $4,000 for heart surgery, compared with an average of $30,000 in the United States.

A "nose job" might cost $850 in India and $4,500 in the United States. An MRI in Brazil, Costa Rica, India, Mexico, Singapore or Thailand ranges from $200 to $300, but it can be three or four times that much stateside.

THE DOWNSIDE OF OVERSEAS TREATMENT

To be sure, the trend can have a downside. According to one study from researchers at the David Geffen School of Medicine at the University of California, Los Angeles, people getting kidney transplants overseas tend to experience more complications, including rejection of the organ and severe infections, than do people opting to undergo the procedure in the United States.

And what happens with follow-up care once a so-called medical tourist returns to the United States? And which country's laws prevail if there's a problem?

For the most part, those questions have no standard answers, leaving each person to resolve the issues, and any similar ones, that might come up.

DO YOUR HOMEWORK

But Dr. Herrick says that a little planning and taking some common-sense precautions can minimize the risks. *He advises anyone contemplating medical treatment abroad to...*

- **Make sure the facility is accredited by JCI or an equivalent** standard-setting organization in the destination country.
- **Check the credentials of the physicians.** Many doctors in other countries have been trained in the United States, Europe, Japan, Australia and New Zealand.
- **Find a good intermediary to help choose the right facility in the right country.** Some hospitals in developing nations have lower mortality rates than those in so-called developed nations.
- **Compare outcomes with other institutions,** regardless of where you go.

Dr. Herrick said that cost and quality of care tend to be higher in Singapore than in Thailand or India, but all three offer extremely good quality and could be considered for more complex procedures.

But he suggested that people go somewhere closer to home—such as Costa Rica or Mexico—or stay in the United States for procedures that are generally less exorbitant. Airfare and hotel costs can be prohibitive. Also, Dr. Herrick said, "most people would prefer to find a place not quite so far away as a 16-hour plane ride."

SLOWLY GROWING TREND

Overseas travel for the purpose of medical care "is in its infancy," Dr. Herrick said. "I don't think any insurer is doing it in a major, major way. People are testing the waters slowly. Most of the interest really seems to lie with self-insured plans" [in which the employer is responsible for paying the medical claims].

According to a small survey conducted by the International Foundation of Employee Benefit Plans, about 11% of employers offer overseas benefit options, although it was unclear how extensive the benefits were or if employees were using them.

The goal, proponents of the concept say, is for everyone—patients, employers, insurance companies—to end up paying less.

info To learn more about traveling for medical care, visit the Web site of the Medical Tourism Association, *www.medicaltourismassociation.com.*

The Pros and Cons of "Off-Shore" Medicine

Charles B. Inlander, a consumer advocate and health-care consultant located in Fogelsville, Pennsylvania. He was the founding president of People's Medical Society, a consumer health advocacy group active in the 1980s and 1990s, and is author of more than 20 books, including *Take This Book to the Hospital with You: A Consumer Guide to Surviving Your Hospital Stay* (St. Martin's).

In years past, "medical tourism" referred mainly to the practice of bringing people from foreign countries to the US for high-quality medical care. In recent years, the term has assumed a new definition, as US citizens leave the country for more affordable surgery and other treatments. Hundreds of thousands of Americans are seeking foreign medical care each year, and this trend is expected to grow as US insurance companies consider covering "off-shore" medicine. *But before you jump on a plane, here are some important points to consider...*

•**Is it safe?** Americans have long assumed that foreign medical care is more dangerous than that offered here at home. But high-quality medical care can be found in many places throughout the world. The Joint Commission on the Accreditation of Healthcare Organizations, the private group that accredits hospitals in the US, has an international branch (*www.jointcommissioninternational.org*) that accredits foreign hospitals. If you are thinking about going abroad for medical care, make sure that the facility you are considering has been accredited by the Joint Commission. Also, check on the training of the doctors who would be caring for you. Look for physicians who were educated at US medical schools and completed a residency in their area of specialty at a US hospital. This is not a guarantee that you will receive high-quality care, but it does give you some reassurance because it is easier to check the reputation of medical schools and residency programs in the US.

•**Will I really save money?** MedSolution, a Canadian medical-tourism firm, recently released these comparisons of costs...

•Hip replacement—$40,000 in North America, $15,000 in France and $5,800 in India...

•Coronary angioplasty—$35,000 in North America, $18,400 in France and $3,700 in India.

Many people going abroad for face-lifts and other cosmetic procedures are paying 30% to 50% of US prices.

•**Do I have all the facts?** It's usually best to use a medical-tourism firm. To find one, search the term "medical tourism" on the Internet and/or consult the informational Web site *www.medicaltourismguide.org.* The firm you select will ask for your medical records to review, and you will then be matched with a doctor and hospital. These firms handle all the details, including travel and hotel arrangements. But make sure you get references for the firm (check for complaints with the Better Business Bureau or the attorney general's office in the firm's home state) as well as the hospital and doctors they recommend to you (ask the firm for contact information for patients treated at these medical facilities).

Buyer beware: If something goes wrong with your overseas medical care, emergency treatment will be provided (your insurance probably won't cover the cost, though). Also, you have no legal recourse in the US against the overseas provider. Each country has its own malpractice laws. Most are not as protective as those in the US. Very few foreign hospitals or doctors will be of much help to you once you return to the US. Make sure that you have a doctor here who is ready to provide follow-up care.

■ **More from Charles B. Inlander...**

Six Ways to Survive Your Hospital Stay

I recently had to put all my years of experience as a medical-consumer advocate to the test when I found myself in the hospital recuperating from surgery for an enlarged prostate gland. My surgery was a success—in part because I chose a surgeon who had done the procedure, a transurethral resection of the prostate (TURP), more than 1,000 times. But my hospital stay went without major incident also because I knew what to do to avoid problems. *Here's what you—or a loved one—can do to have an equally successful hospital stay...*

• **Bring a list of your medications.** I always advise people to bring a list of all their medications—and the dosages—when they go to the doctor, but the same applies if you're headed to the hospital. Coming prepared with your medication list is one of the best steps you can take to protect yourself against medication errors. I brought my medication list and kept it on the adjustable table by my bedside. One nurse thanked me and used it to be sure that her records were correct.

• **Hang signs.** The 84-year-old man in the bed next to mine was nearly deaf and couldn't understand the questions that the doctors and nurses asked him. He would just nod and say "yes" to everything. When I realized this was happening, I made a sign with bold print that read, "You have to speak directly into my ear!" and hung it on the wall above his head. It worked. Once my roommate was able to hear the staff, they got real answers. You can make a sign for a variety of messages, such as "Contact my son/daughter (and give phone number) for any medical permissions."

• **Use the phone.** One night, I needed the nurse but was getting no response when I pushed the call button. I waited 20 minutes and finally picked up the phone, dialed "0" and asked for the nurses' station on my unit. A nurse answered on the first ring. I asked her to come to my room, and she showed up about 10 seconds later. I never had a problem again when I pushed the call button.

• **Bring earplugs.** Hospitals are noisy places. Knowing this, I brought earplugs with me and slept peacefully. A portable music player with earphones or noise-canceling headphones can provide the same escape.

• **Call home.** Twice during my three-day hospitalization, my doctor visited when no one from my family was around. So when my doctor entered the room, I got on the phone, called my wife and had the doctor talk to her at the same time he was talking to me. This is the best way to keep your family informed, and it is especially helpful if you are not feeling well or need someone to ask questions for you.

• **Check the bill.** I received a bill from the hospital that said I owed $2,600. I knew this was wrong. By going over the itemized bill (which I had requested at my discharge), I discovered that I had been inadvertently charged for services received by another patient. Because I was diligent and made a lot of calls, the insurer found the error. Since an estimated 85% of all hospital bills have errors in them, it's buyer beware!

Is Your Doctor's Cell Phone Making You Sick?

BioMed Central news release.

A new culprit has emerged in the spread of the tough-to-kill "superbug" bacteria and other infections in hospitals—mobile phones.

RECENT STUDY

Turkish researchers testing the phones of doctors and nurses working in hospitals found that 95% of them were contaminated with bacteria, including *methicillin-resistant Staphylococcus aureus* (MRSA). This particular strain can cause serious staph infections and is resistant to certain common antibiotics.

The team from the Faculty of Medicine at the Ondokuz Mayis University also found that only a small percentage of the staff—about 10%—regularly cleaned their phones.

IMPLICATION

"Our results suggest cross-contamination of bacteria between the hands of health-care workers and their mobile phones. These mobile phones could act as a reservoir of infection which may facilitate patient-to-patient transmission of bacteria in a hospital setting," said the authors of the study, published online in *Annals of Clinical Microbiology and Antimicrobials.*

PREVENTING THE SPREAD OF INFECTION

To combat the spread of disease and infections through contaminated handheld electronic devices, the authors recommended proactive strategies to disinfect and decontaminate the devices and the practice of improved hand hygiene.

info For more information about MRSA, visit the Web site of the Centers for Disease Control and Prevention, *www.cdc.gov.* Under "Diseases & Conditions" choose "MRSA."

How to Give Your Hospital a Check-Up

Michael T. Rapp, MD, JD, director of the Quality Measurement and Health Assessment Group in the Office of Clinical Standards and Quality at the US Department of Health and Human Services Centers for Medicare and Medicaid Services in Baltimore. The group evaluates measurement systems to assess health-care quality in a range of settings. Dr. Rapp, an emergency physician, served on the board of directors and as president of the American College of Emergency Physicians.

If you or a family member is hospitalized for a serious medical condition, you are likely to count on your doctor and/or other medical personnel to know the best way to treat the problem.

Latest resource: By consulting a Web site known as Hospital Compare (*www.hospital compare.hhs.gov*), you can learn how conditions that often land people in the hospital should be treated—and how more than 4,000 US hospitals (about 95% of the nation's total) measure up in administering this care.*

Created by the US Department of Health and Human Services in partnership with the Hospital Quality Alliance (a public-private collaboration to improve hospital care), the Web site details the performance of US hospitals in handling four key areas of hospital care—heart attack, heart failure, pneumonia and prevention of surgical infections.

Important: In some cases, there may be valid reasons for an exception to the recommended treatment (for example, an allergy to a particular drug).

HEART ATTACK

Until recently, there was a considerable gap in the care that hospitals across the US provided for heart patients. Now there is much more consistency in the treatment standards and the hospitals' performance. *Among the recommended measures...*

- **Aspirin on arrival.** Most heart attacks occur when a blood clot blocks a coronary artery. Patients who are given an aspirin to chew (not swallow) upon arrival at a hospital at the onset of heart attack symptoms are more likely to survive.

National average performance: 93%.

- **Clot-removing treatment within 90 minutes.** A *percutaneous coronary intervention* (PCI), in which a catheter is inserted in a coronary artery and used to remove blockages, is the fastest way to restore circulation to the heart. If the procedure is performed within 90 minutes of a patient's arrival, it can significantly improve patient outcomes.

National average performance: 60%.

Other heart-attack measures: Aspirin given at discharge, 90%...the use of angiotensin-converting enzyme (ACE) inhibitors or angiotensin receptor blockers for heart attack prevention, 85%.

HEART FAILURE

Also known as congestive heart failure, this condition occurs when the heart's pumping action is inadequate. It's often caused by high blood pressure, coronary artery disease or *cardiomyopathy* (a condition in which the heart muscle is severely damaged by infection, drug and/or alcohol use or other causes). *Among the recommended measures...*

- **Evaluation of left ventricular systolic (LVS) function.** This is an important test that tells whether the left side of the heart is pumping properly.

National average performance: 85%.

- **Discharge instructions.** Heart failure is a chronic condition that requires lifelong management. Patients should be given instructions on diet, exercise, medication use and monitoring their weight (even a small gain can signal potentially dangerous fluid retention) along with instructions to make follow-up appointments.

National average performance: 66%.

*Click the "Find and Compare Hospitals" button on the home page. By following the prompts, you can look up specific hospitals in your area or across the nation and review up to three hospitals' ratings side-by-side.

Other heart-failure measures: Use of ACE inhibitors or angiotensin receptor blockers for treatment of heart-failure symptoms, 84%.

PNEUMONIA

Pneumonia is one of the most common and potentially serious lung diseases, killing about 60,000 Americans annually. *Among the recommended measures...*

•Identify bacteria prior to giving antibiotics. Patients who come to the emergency room with symptoms of pneumonia (such as shortness of breath, chills, fever and chest pain) always should be given a blood-culture test to identify the type of bacterium causing the infection. This will help doctors to ascertain the most effective antibiotic.

National average performance: 90%.

•Antibiotics within six hours. Research has shown that pneumonia patients who are given antibiotics within six hours of arrival at the hospital have better outcomes than those who are given antibiotics later.

National average performance: 93%.

•Pneumococcal vaccine. Even when a patient already has bacterial pneumonia, giving a pneumococcal vaccine can help prevent future bacterial pneumonia infections. Every hospital patient with pneumonia should be given the vaccine.

National average performance: 75%.

Other pneumonia measures: The use of oxygenation assessment (to gauge the amount of oxygen in the patient's bloodstream and to determine if he/she needs oxygen therapy), 99%...smoking-cessation advice, 84%...the use of the most appropriate antibiotic, 86%.

SURGICAL CARE

Surgery is a routine hospital procedure but is associated with some of the highest risks. *Among the recommended measures...*

•Stopping antibiotics within 24 hours. Taking antibiotics prior to surgery can greatly reduce the risk for infection—but continuing the drugs longer than 24 hours after the operation increases the risk for stomach pain, serious diarrhea and other side effects.

National average performance: 78%.

•Steps to prevent blood clots. Certain types of surgery, particularly orthopedic procedures such as hip-replacement surgery, can result in venous thrombosis (a condition in which a blood clot forms, usually in a leg, and can travel to the lungs, causing pulmonary embolism—an often-fatal condition). Venous thrombosis is most likely to occur after procedures that make it difficult for patients to move for extended periods.

Clots can be prevented with the use of blood-thinning medications, elastic stockings or mechanical air stockings that promote blood circulation in the legs.

National average performance: 79%.

Other surgical measures: Administering preventive antibiotics one hour before incision, 82%...the use of the appropriate preventive antibiotic, 90%.

Anesthesia Alert—How to Make Sure Your Surgery Goes Smoothly

David Sherer, MD, a staff anesthesiologist at the Mid-Atlantic Permanente Medical Group in Rockville, Maryland, and a board-certified anesthesiologist in clinical practice at Falls Church Ambulatory Surgery Center in Falls Church, Virginia. He is author of *Dr. David Sherer's Hospital Survival Guide* (Claren).

What do heart disease, diabetes, heartburn and high (or low) blood pressure have in common? These are among the many conditions that can affect your response to anesthesia during surgery.

Each year, about 21 million Americans who undergo elective or emergency surgeries receive general anesthesia (a method of preventing pain by rendering a patient temporarily unconscious with drugs that are inhaled through a mask or given intravenously).

Possible complications...

•Anesthesia awareness. According to research published in *The New England Journal of Medicine,* one or two in every 1,000 people who undergo general anesthesia "wake up" to some degree during the operation.

This so-called "awareness" may allow patients to hear conversations in the operating room while they remain immobilized and unable to speak. In rare cases—about 30,000 surgeries in the US each year—patients also feel pain while they are unable to move or speak.

To avoid this problem, a patient's heart rate, blood pressure, breathing and other vital signs are closely monitored during general anesthesia. About 60% of operating rooms in the US also have bispectral index systems. These monitors record certain types of brain activity that can signal anesthesia awareness.

Among those at greatest risk: People who have low blood pressure. Because most anesthesia lowers blood pressure, people who have low blood pressure (chronic or acute, such as that due to injury-related blood loss) usually are given less anesthetic.

Also at risk: Heavy drinkers, who tend to metabolize anesthesia more quickly than people who do not drink heavily.

Self-defense: Tell your anesthesiologist if you have low blood pressure, and be completely honest about the amount of alcohol you drink.

•Coma, neurological damage or death. These devastating complications occur in about one in every 250,000 surgeries in which general anesthesia is used each year in the US. The most common cause is failure of the medical team to "ventilate"—that is, provide a means for the patient to breathe.

Among those at greatest risk: People who are obese—being overweight can cause obstruction of the airway, including the throat and larynx...those who have had prior surgery or radiation of the neck, mouth or airway—surgery or radiation to these areas can stiffen the tissues in the neck and mouth, making it more difficult to ventilate the patient...anyone with sleep apnea (temporary cessation of breathing during sleep)...or a history of difficulty when being intubated (insertion of a tube to keep the airway open) during past surgeries.

Self-defense: Tell your anesthesiologist if any of these risk factors apply to you. Even if you've never been diagnosed with sleep apnea, let him/her know if you snore at night or feel unusually tired during the day. These can be signs of sleep apnea, which obstructs the airway.

•Pneumonia. Thousands of Americans develop anesthesia-related pneumonia each year. One of the most common causes is the backup (reflux) of stomach acid, which can be inhaled (aspirated) into the lungs while a patient is under anesthesia, leading to pneumonia.

Among those at greatest risk: People who have chronic heartburn (known as *gastroesophageal reflux disease*, or GERD) or a *hiatal hernia* (in which the stomach passes partly or completely into the chest cavity)—both conditions make patients prone to aspiration...and those who are obese, have diabetes or diseases of the nervous system, such as Parkinson's disease. Obesity, diabetes and nervous system disorders increase risk for aspiration because they can delay emptying of stomach contents.

Self-defense: Your anesthesiologist may not ask about heartburn or hiatal hernia, but it's important to tell him if you are affected by these conditions. If you do have GERD, drugs that reduce stomach acid, such as *lansoprazole* (Prevacid) or *ranitidine* (Zantac), may be prescribed.

Important: Follow your hospital's guidelines on food and liquid intake before surgery.

•Heart attack or stroke. Each year, about one in 10,000 patients suffer heart attack or stroke while under anesthesia.

Among those at greatest risk: People with high blood pressure (140/90 or above) and/or heart disease. A history of high blood pressure can increase a patient's risk for stroke because of accompanying blood vessel changes, such as stiffening of the arteries. Heart disease often causes a thickening of the arteries to the heart that can lead to cardiovascular complications during anesthesia, resulting in heart attack.

Self-defense: Inform your anesthesiologist if you have high blood pressure or heart disease.

GETTING THE BEST CARE

Most surgical patients do not meet the anesthesiologist until moments before surgery. Ask your surgeon beforehand who will be administering the anesthetic and whether you can meet with him a day or two before the surgery so that he has more time to review your medical history and address any of your concerns.

Tell your anesthesiologist if...

•**You take any medications or supplements.** Blood pressure, diabetes and blood-thinning drugs are among those that may need to be discontinued prior to surgery. Speak to your surgeon for specific instructions. Herbal remedies, including St. John's wort and garlic, may need to be discontinued before the operation because they may interact with the anesthetic.

•**Anyone in your family has ever had a bad reaction to general anesthesia,** such as delayed awakening. In some cases, bad reactions to anesthesia may be genetic.

The High Risk of Using Snowblowers

Daniel Master, MD, orthopedic surgery resident, University Hospitals Case Medical Center, Cleveland, Ohio.

James G. Adams, MD, professor and chairman, Department of Emergency Medicine, Feinberg School of Medicine, Northwestern University, Chicago.

American Academy of Orthopaedic Surgeons annual meeting, Las Vegas.

Snowblowers might make clearing the sidewalk quicker and easier, but those who use them continue to show up in emergency rooms with hand injuries and accidental amputations, say medical experts.

"The injuries need to be prevented, because they're not the type of injuries that can be reconstructed," said Daniel Master, MD, an orthopedic surgery resident at University Hospitals Case Medical Center in Cleveland and the study's lead author. The nature of the tissue damage caused by snowblowers makes a full recovery extremely difficult and often leads to amputation, he said, and "even if you have the amputated part, it's essentially useless."

THE STUDY

Dr. Master and his colleagues researched snowblower-related hand injuries sustained by 22 patients he treated from 2002 to 2005 at Hartford Hospital in Connecticut. He presented their findings at the American Academy of Orthopaedic Surgeons' annual meeting in Las Vegas.

"The weather is a major factor that causes the cluster of these injuries," Dr. Master said. "When the snow is dense, the machines get clogged, and people put their hands down the chute" to clear it.

SNOWBLOWER DANGERS

Part of the problem, he found, is that people sometimes ignore the safety warnings that come with the snowblowers. "A large majority were aware of the warnings but stuck their hand down the shoot when it was running anyway," Dr. Master said.

In addition, he explained, snowblowers usually have two blades, including one that's not visible. That's the one that causes most injuries, he said. Also, there's a lag time between when you release the dead-man's switch (a lever that prevents the mechanism from rotating when it is released or the operator is not at the controls) and when the blade stops moving," Dr. Master said.

Danger apparently exists even when the machines do not seem to be running, though. Dr. Master said that when a clog is removed, the blades can spin again using stored energy.

James G. Adams, MD, professor and chairman of emergency medicine at the Feinberg School of Medicine at Northwestern University in Chicago, said that he, too, had encountered patients with snowblower-related injuries during his time at Brigham and Women's Hospital in Boston from 1995 to 2000.

"In the winter, every day, people would come in with their fingers cut off," Dr. Adams said. "I remember taking care of a doctor on the medical staff who was shoveling his driveway and cut his fingers off. When the chute got clogged, there was still tension and torque, so as soon as you got snow out, the snowblower would turn really quickly and cut your fingers off."

SAFETY CHANGES MADE, BUT INJURIES STILL OCCUR

However, he said, manufacturers "changed it so there wasn't any residual torque, and that seemed to decrease the incidence of snowblower injuries."

But it didn't eliminate them.

"It's a good general public health message," Dr. Adams said. "Any reminder to the public that snowblower injuries are still occurring and have not been completely eliminated is still a good message."

info For more information on how to prevent a snowblower or lawnmower injury, visit the Web site of the American Society for Surgery of the Hand, *www.assh.org,* and search "snowblower and lawnmower injuries."

Free Health Service—Online Medical Records

Charles B. Inlander, a consumer advocate and health-care consultant located in Fogelsville, Pennsylvania. He was the founding president of People's Medical Society, a consumer health advocacy group active in the 1980s and 1990s, and is author of more than 20 books, including *Take This Book to the Hospital with You: A Consumer Guide to Surviving Your Hospital Stay* (St. Martin's).

I know that I had an allergic reaction to a medication when I was in college, but I don't remember the name of the drug. Most people, like me, have very little documentation of their full medical history. Since state laws require hospitals and doctors to keep inactive medical records for only seven to 10 years (depending on the state), it is almost impossible to retrieve what might be helpful, personal medical information from long ago.

But all that is changing. Recently, several major Internet companies have begun offering services that allow you to securely store your personal medical information online at no charge. With online medical records, you can easily keep track of your medical history (including such information as past illnesses and treatments, tests, surgeries, allergies and adverse reactions to drugs), the medications you take and the appointments you have. If your doctor or hospital participates, you can even transfer (download) your medical records directly from their computers to your own. By centralizing your medical history, you won't have to repeat this information every time you see a new doctor. *If you want to consider putting your medical records online, here's my advice...*

• **Try out the different sites.** The four big players in online personal medical records—WebMD (*www.webmd.com/phr*)...Google (*www.google.com/health*)...Microsoft (*www.healthvault.com*)...and Revolution Health (*www.revolutionhealth.com*)—allow you to create your own medical record. Revolution Health (started by AOL founder Steve Case) and WebMD, both of which have a longer history of creating online personal medical records, are easier to use, in my opinion, and offer more options than the Google or Microsoft sites. But Google and Microsoft are moving quickly to expand their services.

Smart idea: Since all these services are free, create a short personal medical record on each site, entering data such as medications or past surgeries. I have. As the sites continue to grow, I'll choose the one I like best.

• **Take advantage of the special features.** These Web sites each offer extra. For example, when you list a medication in your medical record on Revolution Health's site, it allows you to easily link to an information sheet on that drug posted by the FDA. The WebMD site lets you complete an easy-to-use personal health assessment to learn your risks for heart disease, stroke and other conditions.

• **Talk to your doctor about online medical records.** If your doctor sends you to a specialist, you may be responsible for making sure that your medical records are forwarded to the new doctor. If you have an online medical record, it can be sent most anywhere on a moment's notice. Talk to your doctor about placing your medical records online. Not all physicians are sold on the idea—some like to maintain control over all of their patients' medical information. But having direct access to your own medical records can be lifesaving and reassuring.

■ ■ ■ ■

Is Your Doctor Blogging About You?

In a recent study, 42% of blogs (online journals) written by medical professionals contained descriptions of individual patients—17% included enough information for patients to identify themselves or their doctors.

Patients were portrayed negatively more often than positively...some blogs even included patients' photos.

Wise: Ask your doctors if they have blogs and how they protect patients' privacy.

Tara Lagu, MD, MPH, clinical scholar, University of Pennsylvania, Philadelphia, and lead author of a study of 271 blogs, published in *Journal of General Internal Medicine.*

■ ■ ■ ■

Hidden Dangers of Medical Identity Theft

A thief uses your Social Security number or insurance data to get free medical treatment—or to collect insurance money for services that were never performed.

Problem: This can cause incorrect or fictitious information about you to appear in medical databases—leading to incorrect treatment or future refusal of insurance benefits.

Thieves change the address to which claims and statements are sent, so you may not know of their actions for years.

In addition, patient privacy laws can make it harder to find out about phony information—and make doctors reluctant to change errors, for fear of liability.

Self-defense: Every year, get a copy of your medical records from all of your health-care providers and a list of benefits paid in your name by your insurer.

Question any charges or payments that you do not recognize—and contact police if you suspect fraud.

James C. Pyles, Esq., principal, Powers, Pyles, Sutter and Verville PC, a law firm specializing in health care, education and government relations, Washington, DC.

Lifesaving Medical Tests You May Need Now

David Johnson, PhD, an associate professor and chair of the department of physiology at the College of Osteopathic Medicine at the University of New England in Biddeford, Maine. He is coauthor, with David Sandmire, MD, and Daniel Klein, of *Medical Tests That Can Save Your Life* (Rodale).

Virtually everyone who seeks medical care in the US receives medical tests from time to time. But few people stop to ask whether they are getting the tests that can have the biggest impact on their long-term health.

Recent development: With increasingly sophisticated technology, diseases now can be diagnosed years—or even decades—before a patient exhibits symptoms...some drug treatments can be tailored to an individual...and serious medical conditions that go undetected can be identified. But many of these medical tests are underutilized—in part because doctors may not be aware of some of the newer tests...and they don't always have time to delve into all of a patient's potential risk factors.

Tests to ask your doctor about...

HEART DISEASE

Fatty deposits in the arteries (atherosclerosis) accumulate calcium.

- **Electron beam computed tomography (EBCT) can detect this problem.** It is perhaps the single most important advance for the early diagnosis of cardiovascular disease.

What it does: EBCT evaluates the amount of calcium in the coronary arteries. A positive EBCT may indicate cardiovascular disease—even if the patient has no symptoms. An early diagnosis allows patients to take the necessary steps—such as lowering cholesterol and exercising more—to retard the progression of the disease.

This noninvasive test takes 10 to 15 minutes and causes no discomfort. Because EBCT has been in use and studied for some time, it may be preferable to other heart imaging tests, such as multislice computed tomography, that expose the patient to more radiation than EBCT.

Who should consider this test: Men over age 35 and women over age 45—especially if they have two or more of the most common risk factors for cardiovascular disease, such as elevated cholesterol, hypertension or a family history of heart disease.

Cost: About $500.

LOW BONE DENSITY

An estimated 10 million Americans have osteoporosis, the main cause of weakened bones and fractures. The first symptom of osteoporosis is usually an unexpected fracture of the wrist, spine or hip. Low bone density (a precursor to osteoporosis) affects 34 million Americans.

• **Dual energy X-ray absorptiometry (DEXA)** can give patients an early warning.

What it does: DEXA measures bone density at the hip and spine. The test, which takes 10 to 20 minutes, is painless, noninvasive and emits one-tenth to one-quarter of the radiation emitted by a typical chest X-ray. If osteoporosis is identified before the patient suffers a fracture, steps—including exercise, increased intake of calcium and vitamin D, and sometimes medication—can be taken to increase bone density.

Who should consider this test: Women, upon entering menopause...and men age 65 and over who have risk factors for osteoporosis, such as vitamin-D deficiency, low testosterone levels or chronic use of corticosteroids.

Cost: $100 to $350.

LUNG CANCER

Lung cancer causes more deaths than any other type of malignancy. Once patients develop symptoms, such as a persistent cough, shortness of breath, coughing up bloody phlegm or weight loss, there's little chance of cure.

• **Low-dose spiral CT (LDSCT) scan** can detect lung cancer earlier than an ordinary chest X-ray. In one study, chest X-rays missed 85% of early-stage cancers that were detected by LDSCT.

What it does: While the patient is lying down, the imaging machine rotates rapidly around the body, taking more than 100 pictures of the chest. The procedure is painless and takes about 30 minutes.

Who should consider this test: Anyone with a smoking history of more than 20 "pack years" (the number of packs smoked per day multiplied by the number of years smoked). The risk for lung cancer outweighs the risks associated with radiation from the test.

Important: There's some controversy about the use of LDSCT for detecting lung cancer in asymptomatic patients. Cancers detected early are more likely to be treated successfully, but the test is so sensitive that it often will reveal harmless nodes or lesions. This may result in unnecessary follow-up tests or even surgeries.

Possible approach: If a small abnormality is revealed by the spiral CT scan, it can be repeated in several months to see if the growth changes size. A nodule that grows significantly is likely to be malignant.

Cost: $200 to $500.

DISORDERS OF THE SMALL INTESTINE

Diseases of the small intestine, such as tumors and some types of Crohn's disease (an inflammatory bowel disorder that causes severe diarrhea and abdominal pain), have traditionally been diagnosed with X-ray procedures.

However, these procedures sometimes miss small, but critical, abnormalities, such as *angiodysplasias* (small blood vessels beneath the intestinal lining that can bleed and cause anemia).

• **Capsule endoscopy** is another option.

What it does: Capsule endoscopy provides a close-up view of the inside of the small intestine (the 20-foot-long area between the stomach and large intestine) that is inaccessible with other tests, such as colonoscopy.

This new test involves swallowing a small capsule that contains a camera, which takes photographs over an eight-hour period as it moves through the intestine. Once a patient swallows the capsule, he/she can leave the doctor's office. Photographs are transmitted electronically to a receiver that the patient wears on his waist.

Later, the doctor downloads the pictures into a computer to review them. The capsule is eventually passed out of the patient's body in the stool. The procedure is generally safe, although the capsule could potentially cause a blockage in patients who have sections of intestine that are narrowed by scar tissue.

Who should consider this test: Anyone with unexplained bleeding thought to originate in the small intestine or unexplained abdominal pain or other gastrointestinal symptoms.

Cost: $1,000 to $1,200.

DEPRESSION

When prescribing an antidepressant, doctors typically rely on a person's symptoms and medical history. But some patients take a new drug for weeks or months only to discover that it doesn't work for them. Others may improve while taking a drug but then have to discontinue it because of side effects.

• **CYP450 genetic test,** a relatively new blood test, may help circumvent this process.

What it does: The CYP450 blood test identifies genes (and enzymes produced by those genes) that help predict how a specific patient is likely to react to a particular antidepressant—even before he takes the first dose. The test identifies the enzymes involved in metabolizing a small number of antidepressants, including *fluoxetine* (Prozac), *paroxetine* (Paxil), venlafaxine (Effexor), *imipramine* (Tofranil), *desipramine* (Norpramin) and *nortriptyline* (Pamelor).

Who should consider this test: Anyone who is about to start taking one of the antidepressants named above. The test can make it easier for doctors to avoid prescribing a medication that has a high probability of not working and/or causing side effects.

Cost: $500.

WHO PAYS?

Insurance usually covers the cost of the tests described in this article if the patient has symptoms of a relevant condition (such as osteoporosis) or is at high risk for the condition. The frequency of follow-up tests is based on initial test results—ask your doctor for advice.

■ ■ ■ ■

How Lab Tests Can Help

When was the last time you had blood and urine tests? Lab tests are not foolproof, but they can provide a helpful look inside the body, often identifying diseases or emerging conditions in early, possibly reversible stages. For instance, a blood test can indicate prediabetes, a precursor to diabetes that can be reversed through diet, supplements and/or lifestyle changes. It can point to anemia caused by low vitamin B-12 in seniors or an iron deficiency in premenopausal women and children. Blood tests can shed light on vitamin D deficiencies that predispose one to osteoporosis. In some patients, I have discovered elevated liver enzymes that result from sensitivities and adverse reactions to pharmaceutical medications. Urinalysis, a test that can screen for conditions with no symptoms, has helped me diagnose low-grade urinary tract infections and kidney disease.

The lesson: Even if you feel well, ask your doctor to order these tests annually—many may be covered by your insurance. As my patients have found, prevention is better than treatment.

Mark A. Stengler, ND, naturopathic physician in private practice, La Jolla, California...adjunct associate clinical professor at the National College of Natural Medicine, Portland, Oregon...author of many books and the *Bottom Line/Natural Healing* newsletter.

Five Vaccinations Your Doctor May Forget to Give

William Schaffner, MD, professor and chair of the department of preventive medicine at Vanderbilt University School of Medicine in Nashville. Dr. Schaffner has published more than 60 professional articles on the subject and is president of the National Foundation for Infectious Diseases, *www.nfid.org*.

If you're like most adults, the only time you think about getting vaccinations is during flu season or when you're planning an overseas vacation. The majority of American adults are not protecting themselves against preventable diseases.

Problem: Only a very small percentage of American adults is receiving most vaccinations recommended by the Centers for Disease Control and Prevention (CDC). That's largely because few doctors are reminding their patients when they need to receive vaccinations.

Solution: Add vaccinations to the list of things you discuss with your doctor during your regular physical exam. Most of us know how crucial the flu vaccine can be, but there are other vaccinations that also are important. Vaccines, which generally are safe and effective, are usually covered by insurance when recommended by your doctor.

Most adults should receive vaccinations for...

TETANUS-DIPHTHERIA-PERTUSSIS

Vaccinations against tetanus (an acute disease that causes "lockjaw") and diphtheria (an infectious disease that causes difficulty breathing and swallowing) have long been given every 10 years. Now, adults are being advised to get a new combination vaccine that also protects against whooping cough, a disease caused by the bacterium *Bordetella pertussis.*

Nearly all infants are vaccinated against whooping cough, but there has been a dramatic increase in whooping cough among adults. At its worst, the cough can be strong enough to crack ribs. Adults can expose unimmunized infants and children to the disease, which can be fatal, especially in babies younger than six months.

Because the adult vaccine was introduced four years ago, not all physicians think to recommend it. When it is time for your regular 10-year tetanus-diphtheria booster, ask for the "Tdap vaccine," which covers tetanus, diphtheria and whooping cough. The combination vaccine currently is approved for people up to age 65.

SHINGLES

If you've ever had chicken pox, you carry an inactive form of the *varicella-zoster* virus, which caused the infection. Years or decades later, the virus can become activated and develop into a disease known as shingles. (The reason for the reactivation is unknown, but it often occurs when immunity is weakened by another disorder or by the use of drugs that impair immunity.) Marked by a painful rash of fluid-filled blisters, shingles usually appears on one side of the body. By age 80, half of all adults have had it.

With the shingles vaccine (administered once in adults age 60 and older), the chance of shingles and post-shingles pain, which can last for months or more in the area of the shingles outbreak, is cut by more than half.

Important: The shingles vaccine is generally covered by insurance for adults ages 60 to 65. After age 65, it is covered only under supplemental Medicare Part D insurance. If you are not covered for the shingles vaccine, the cost is typically $180 to $300. This vaccine should not be given to people whose immune systems are compromised, including those who take high-dose steroid medication and those who have received an organ transplant. Even if you've already had shingles, the vaccine may help prevent a recurrence.

PNEUMONIA

Pneumococcal pneumonia is a type of bacterial pneumonia that is a common complication of the flu. Each year, this pneumonia affects about 500,000 Americans and kills about 40,000.

The incidence of pneumococcal pneumonia starts to rise when people reach age 50—and increases even more after age 65.

The reason: Older adults are more likely to have lung disease, diabetes or other illnesses that predispose them to pneumonia.

The pneumococcal pneumonia vaccine (administered at least once during a person's lifetime) is recommended for everyone age 65 and older...anyone ages 19 to 65 with a chronic illness (such as diabetes or lung disease) or a compromised immune system (due to cancer treatment, for example, or an organ transplant).

HEPATITIS B

The *hepatitis B* virus attacks the liver. The virus is transmitted primarily through sexual intimacy and by infected blood. Mild cases may cause no symptoms, but severe cases can lead to cirrhosis, liver failure and even death.

The hepatitis B vaccine (given in a series of three shots) is recommended for adults whose occupation (such as health-care workers) or behavior (sexually active people who are not in a long-term, mutually monogamous relationship with an infection-free partner) puts them at increased risk of coming into contact with blood or body secretions infected with hepatitis B.

HUMAN PAPILLOMAVIRUS

The *human papillomavirus* (HPV) is sexually transmitted and consists of several dozen different strains. Some are relatively harmless, others cause genital warts and some cause cervical cancer. The HPV vaccine, currently recommended for all girls and women ages 11 to 26, protects women against two genital wart–causing strains and two cervical cancer–causing strains.

The vaccine (administered in three doses over a period of six months) was tested and approved for younger women to help protect them before they become sexually active. The more sexual partners a woman has, the greater the risk that she has become infected with one or more HPV strains.

The HPV vaccine is currently in clinical trials for use in women ages 26 to 45. Women over age 26 who are sexually active (and possibly infected with one or more strains of the virus) could potentially benefit from the vaccine because it protects against four strains of HPV.

Insurance covers the cost of the HPV vaccine for girls and women ages 11 to 26. Women over age 26 can ask their doctors about receiving the vaccine "off-label." This use will not be covered by insurance. The cost is about $300 to $500 for the three doses.

■ **More from William Schaffner, MD...**

Vacation Vaccinations

Ask your doctor about the following vaccinations at least six weeks, if possible, before leaving the US. This will give your body time to build maximum immunity. *Currently recommended by the Centers for Disease Control and Prevention (CDC)...*

•**Hepatitis A,** transmitted through food or water. Areas with high or intermediate risk include Greenland...all of Central and South America and Africa...and most countries in Asia and Eastern Europe.

•**Hepatitis B.** Areas with high risk include Africa, much of southeast Asia and the Middle East (excluding Israel). The vaccine is recommended for health-care workers and others who stay in these countries for long periods, as well as for travelers who have intimate relationships with residents of these countries.

•**Meningitis,** transmitted from person to person, especially in crowded conditions. The high-risk "meningitis belt" runs across central Africa, from Mali to Ethiopia.

•**Polio,** transmitted via contact with the feces of an infected person, is most common in areas where sanitation is poor. Risk is highest in Africa, India and Indonesia.

Note: Even if you had a polio vaccination as a child, you should get a booster as an adult if you're traveling to these areas.

•**Rabies,** transmitted through contact with infected animals. Risk is highest in parts of Africa, Asia, and Central and South America.

•**Typhoid,** transmitted through food and water. Areas with the highest risk include all of South Asia...and developing countries elsewhere in Asia, Africa, the Caribbean, and Central and South America.

Certain countries require a certificate of vaccination for such diseases as...

•**Meningitis and polio.** Saudi Arabia requires proof of these vaccinations during the annual pilgrimage to Mecca (due to the large numbers of visitors).

•**Yellow fever,** a mosquito-borne disease found predominantly in Central and South America, and sub-Saharan Africa.

For a more detailed summary, go to the CDC Web site, *www.cdc.gov/travel.*

■ ■ ■ ■

Fall Health Alert—Free or Low-Cost Flu Shots

Free or low-cost flu shots are available at an increasing number of locations, including county health departments and pharmacies. At most of these locations, however, the shots are offered for a very limited time. The American Lung Association's online Flu Clinic Locator (*www.fluclinic locator.org*) can search for upcoming flu shot clinics in your area so you don't miss your chance.

Virtually everyone should get an annual flu shot, particularly people over age 50...between ages two and 18...suffering from a chronic lung or heart problem...or in regular contact with someone who falls into any of these increased-risk categories. The shot usually becomes available in late September. Seasonal flu and its complications kill about 36,000 Americans each year.

Norman Edelman, MD, chief medical officer, American Lung Association, and professor of medicine, State University of New York at Stony Brook.

■ ■ ■ ■

Paying Too Much for Your Meds?

A recent survey compared prices for a three-month supply of four prescription drugs at 163 pharmacies. The incontinence drug Detrol ranged from $365 to $551...blood thinner Plavix, $382 to $541...hypothyroidism drug Levoxyl, $29 to $85...generic osteoporosis drug *alendronate*, $124 to $306.

To save money: Shop around. The survey found Costco to have the lowest prices.

Tod Marks, senior editor, *Consumer Reports*, 101 Truman Avenue, Yonkers, New York 10703.

Get Your Drugs at 50% Off—or Even Free

Edward Jardini, MD, a family physician at Twin Cities Community Hospital in Templeton, California, where he has served as chair of the pharmacy and therapeutics committee. He is author of *How to Save on Prescription Drugs: 20 Cost-Saving Methods* (Celestial Arts). His Web site is *www.howtosaveondrugs.com.*

Anyone who regularly takes prescription medication knows how pricey these drugs can be.

Fortunately, there are places where you can buy your drugs for less—or even get them for free. The key is knowing where to look.

Important: Although most low-cost drug programs have income eligibility requirements, do not assume that you won't be accepted into a program just because your income is officially too high. Many programs will consider applications on a case-by-case basis.

Best resources for finding low-cost or free medications...

DRUG DISCOUNT NETWORKS

There are some organizations that connect patients to public and private assistance programs that provide discounted or free drugs to eligible patients. *These include...*

- **Partnership for Prescription Assistance** (888-477-2669, *www.pparx.org*). This collaborative network of professional medical organizations, including the American Academy of Family Physicians, and private groups links patients with more than 475 public and private patient assistance programs that offer more than 2,500 drugs at reduced cost or no charge. Income qualifications vary by state.
- **Together Rx Access** (800-444-4106, *www.togetherrxaccess.com*). Backed by a consortium of pharmaceutical companies, this program provides a 15% to 40% discount on more than 300 brand-name and generic prescription drugs. The program targets people who don't have prescription drug coverage with annual incomes of $45,000 or less for individuals...$60,000 for a family of two...and up to $105,000 for a family of five.

PHARMACEUTICAL PATIENT-ASSISTANCE PROGRAMS

Major pharmaceutical companies have their own patient-assistance programs that offer many—though not all—drugs at a discount, or even for free, to people who cannot afford them. Eligibility requirements vary—even families earning up to $70,000 a year can qualify. Some companies evaluate applications on a case-by-case basis.

To obtain a free copy of Directory of Prescription Drug Patient Assistance Programs, call the Partnership for Prescription Assistance at 800-762-4636. To determine the manufacturer of a particular drug, ask your pharmacist or go to *www.PDRhealth.com.*

Among the pharmaceutical companies with programs...

•**Abbott Patient Assistance Program** (800-222-6885, *www.abbott.com*). Click on "Global Citizenship."

•**AstraZeneca's AZ&Me Prescription Savings Program** (800-292-6363, *www.astrazeneca-us.com*).

•**GlaxoSmithKline** (888-825-5249, *www.gskforyou.com*).

•**Lilly Cares Patient Assistance Program** (Eli Lilly; 800-545-6962, *www.lillycares.com*).

•**Merck Patient Assistance Program** (800-727-5400, *www.merck.com/merckhelps/patientassistance/home.html*).

•**Novartis Patient Assistance Foundation** (800-277-2254, *www.pharma.us.novartis.com*).

•**Pfizer Helpful Answers** (866-776-3700, *www.pfizerhelpfulanswers.com*).

•**Roche Patient Assistance Foundation** (877-757-6243, *www.rocheusa.com/programs/patientassist.asp*).

Some pharmaceutical companies also offer coupons that can be printed from their Web sites, as well as discount card programs offering savings on some products. Check the drug manufacturer's Web site for details.

To learn about more programs that can help reduce your drug bills, see the article below.

■ **More from Edward Jardini, MD...**

The Best Discount Health Programs Aren't Always Publicized

There are a number of ways to dramatically reduce your medication costs. Unfortunately, most drug-discount programs don't advertise their services, so few people are aware of all the available options. Some programs even waive income eligibility requirements.

Among the best resources...

PHARMACY BENEFIT MANAGERS

Because of their size, large companies that act as third-party managers of prescription drug programs can provide discounted medications. *Ones to consider...*

•**Caremark.** RxSavings Plus (877-673-3688, *www.rxsavingsplus.com*). This program offers a card that is accepted at more than 59,000 US pharmacies and provides an average savings of 20%. You can use the card as long as you're not receiving insurance reimbursement, including Medicare. For up to a 50% discount, order a 90-day supply by mail.

•**Express-Scripts.** Rx Outreach (800-769-3880, *www.rxoutreach.com*). Designed for low-income patients, this program sets annual income limits of less than $32,490 for most individuals or less than $43,710 a year for couples. A 90-day supply of most medications costs $20, $30 or $40, depending on the drug.

GOVERNMENT PROGRAMS

Federal, state and local governments also offer eligible patients access to low-cost drugs...

•**US Department of Veterans Affairs** (877-222-8387, *www.va.gov*). For people who were honorably discharged from active duty in a branch of the military, the VA will provide prescription drugs at a cost of $8 a month. The prescription must be written by a doctor in a VA clinic. To qualify, you must fill out application form 10-10EZ (available at local VA offices and medical centers or online at *www.va.gov/healtheligibility/application*) and provide a copy of your discharge document.

•**The VA also offers a separate health-care program,** called CHAMPVA, for family members of a veteran who has a permanent disability or who died in the line of duty or due to a service-connected disability—as long as they're not eligible for TRICARE (see below).

•**TRICARE** (*www.tricare.mil*). TRICARE is a health-care benefit for active-duty service members, reserve members, retired uniformed armed services members, their families and survivors. Widows and widowers of active-duty members also may qualify unless they remarry. The plan includes prescription coverage.

If the medication is obtained at a military treatment facility, it is free. Medications obtained at retail network pharmacies or by mail cost $3 to $22 for a 90-day supply.

•**National Conference of State Legislatures** (202-624-5400, *www.ncsl.org/programs/health/drugaid. htm#discount*). By December 2009, almost all of the states had established some type of program to provide prescription drug coverage or subsidies to low-income older adults or disabled persons who do not qualify for Medicaid. The programs vary widely—and the information is available through state departments of health or social services.

PATIENT ADVOCACY GROUPS

Some groups charge a set fee to help patients find free or low-cost medications. This works well for people who don't want to deal with the application process required for most of the drug-assistance programs.

•**The Free Medicine Foundation** (573-996-3333, *www.freemedicine.com*). This group will search for programs that can provide your drugs for little or no charge. The onetime fee of $10 is reimbursed if the group fails to find your medication for free. The service is available to people with incomes up to $88,200 for a family of four...$58,280 for couples...and $43,320 for individuals.

•**Indigent Patient Services Inc.** (727-521-2646, *www.ipsc.cc*). A onetime registration fee of $25 per person/$40 per couple is required for this program, and each prescription (usually three months' worth of medication) costs $20.

MASS-MARKET RETAILERS

Some large retail stores, such as Wal-Mart, Target, Costco and Kmart, offer low-price prescriptions on generic and some brand-name medications. Wal-Mart, for instance, offers a program that covers mostly generic drugs at a cost of $4 for a 30-day supply and $10 for a 90-day supply.

For information, go to store Web sites or ask at your local store's pharmacy.

Beware of Dangerous Supplements

Tod Cooperman, MD, president and founder of ConsumerLab.com, a White Plains, New York–based company that conducts independent testing of health, wellness and nutrition products. He is the editor of ConsumerLab.com, a subscription-based Web site ($29.95 yearly), and the book *Health, Harm or Rip-off? What's REALLY in Your Vitamins & Supplements* (Bottom Line).

When you buy a vitamin or some other type of nutritional supplement, you expect it to contain exactly what the label promises.

But about one out of every four supplements sold in the US does not meet this basic standard or has other quality problems, according to tests performed by ConsumerLab.com, an independent evaluator of supplements.*

WHAT'S REALLY IN THAT BOTTLE?

The FDA requires supplement manufacturers to list exactly what's in their products on the labels, but there's little government oversight or enforcement to ensure that the products actually match the claims that are made on the labels.

As a result, supplements often contain less (or more) of the active ingredient that is listed on the label. In other cases, some supplements are contaminated with lead or other heavy metals...or they don't break down properly in the body, reducing a person's absorption of the supplement into the bloodstream.

Among the supplements that recently failed ConsumerLab.com's independent testing...

VITAMIN C

Vitamin C is one of the top-selling vitamins in the US.

Test results: Of 23 supplements tested this year, one—Dynamic Health Laboratories Liquid Vitamin C—contained only 43.5% of the amount of vitamin listed on the label. Liquid forms of vitamin C are more prone to chemical breakdown than nonliquid supplements.

Also, the label on one product had suggested a daily dose (up to 4,000 milligrams [mg]) that

*The products listed here have been evaluated by ConsumerLab.com. Other evaluators of supplements include the US Pharmacopeia (USP) and NSF International. Talk to your doctor before taking any nutritional supplements.

exceeded vitamin C's tolerable upper intake level (UL) for adults age 19 and over. The UL, set by the National Academies of Science, is the maximum daily intake of a nutrient that is likely to pose no risk for adverse effects in healthy people. Excess vitamin C can cause stomach upset and/or diarrhea.

The Recommended Dietary Allowance (RDA) of vitamin C for adult men is 90 mg...and 75 mg for women. Some doctors recommend higher doses, but it's rare for anyone to need more than 500 mg to 1,000 mg daily.

Reliable products include...

•**Longs Wellness Vitamin C** 500 mg.

•**Nature Made Timed Release Vitamin C** 500 mg.

•**Schiff Immune Support Vitamin C** 500 mg with Rose Hips (a plant source of vitamin C).

RED YEAST RICE

Red yeast rice (made by fermenting rice with red yeast) contains cholesterol-lowering compounds, including *lovastatin*, which is similar to the active ingredient in some prescription statin drugs, and a related compound known as *hydroxy acid*. People who combine red yeast rice with lifestyle changes, such as exercise and weight loss, can experience drops in LDL "bad" cholesterol of 42%—an improvement comparable to that of a prescription statin drug.

Test results: Four of the 10 products tested had a total of only 0.1 mg to 1.3 mg of lovastatin and its hydroxy acid form per dose—levels that are far too low to have cholesterol-lowering effects. Four of the supplements were contaminated with *citrinin*, a potential toxin linked to kidney damage in animal studies.

Reliable products include...

•**Cholestene Red Yeast Rice** (600 mg per capsule).

•**Chole-Sterin Red Yeast Rice** (600 mg per capsule).

•**Healthy America Red Yeast Rice** (600 mg per capsule).

TURMERIC

Sales of turmeric supplements quadrupled from 2002 to 2006 following reports of significant health benefits, including relief from indigestion and ulcerative colitis (a potentially debilitating inflammatory bowel disorder that causes abdominal pain and diarrhea), rheumatoid arthritis and other inflammatory conditions. Some studies suggest that turmeric also may help prevent Alzheimer's disease.

Test results: Two of the 13 products tested —NSI Nutraceutical Sciences Institute Superior Turmeric Curcuma Longa and Solgar Standardized Full Potency Turmeric Root Extract—showed high levels of lead.

In adults, excess lead can cause high blood pressure, decreased fertility and loss of sensation...in children and fetuses, it can severely affect mental and physical development.

Other results: Two turmeric products failed the tests because they provided only 11.5% and 49.5%, respectively, of the active ingredients (*curcuminoids*) listed on each product's label.

Reliable products include...

•**Douglas Laboratories Ayur-Curcumin** (300 mg per capsule).

•**Himalaya Pure Herbs Turmeric Antioxidant** (400 mg per capsule).

•**New Chapter Turmeric Force** (400 mg per softgel).

PROBIOTICS

Beneficial probiotic bacteria in the intestine are essential for good health. They help balance the intestinal flora (hundreds of species of bacteria in the gastrointestinal tract) and also may stimulate the immune system.

Probiotic supplements are often used to replenish intestinal organisms that are killed by antibiotics—a common cause of diarrhea. Probiotics are also used to treat *H. pylori* infection (a common cause of ulcers).

Supplements should provide at least 1 billion viable (living) organisms...daily doses of up to 10 billion are often recommended.

Test results: Four of the 13 products tested were found not to contain 1 billion organisms per daily serving. A fifth product (Flora Source) did contain 1 billion organisms daily, but not the 30 billion listed on the label.

Reliable products include...

•**Culturelle with Lactobacillus GG,** All Natural (10 billion organisms).

•**Jarrow Formulas Enhanced Probiotic System,** Jarro-Dophilus EPS (4.4 billion to 8.8 billion).

•**Nature's Way Primadophilus Optima,** 14 Probiotic Strains Plus NutraFlora (35 billion).

■ ■ ■ ■

Herbal Remedies Can Contain Toxic Metals

A study tested 193 Ayurvedic (traditional Indian) oral medicines made in the US or India—21% contained lead, mercury and/or arsenic in amounts exceeding regulatory standards. Most likely to contain toxic metals were products labeled *rasa shastra* (a preparation combining herbs, metals, minerals and gems)...least likely were remedies from members of the American Herbal Products Association (*www.ahpa.org*).

Robert B. Saper, MD, MPH, director of integrative medicine, department of family medicine, Boston University School of Medicine, and leader of a study published in *The Journal of the American Medical Association*.

■ ■ ■ ■

Do Expiration Dates on Nutritional Supplements Really Matter?

Expiration dates on nutritional supplements do matter. However, the dates do not have to be treated as absolute deadlines. Supplements, just like medications and food, have a particular shelf life. Deteriorated products do not work as well—and could even be dangerous. Fish oil, for example, can become rancid and turn into a tissue-damaging pro-oxidant.

Most manufacturers label a product with a conservative expiration date that is well before the time the product is likely to deteriorate. I believe that nutritional supplements, if stored as recommended by manufacturers, generally can be used safely for up to three months beyond the stated expiration date.

Best: Buy supplements in quantities you expect to use before the expiration date.

Jane Guiltinan, ND, clinical professor, Bastyr Center for Natural Health, Seattle, and past president of the American Association of Naturopathic Physicians.

Bottled Water That's Worse than Tap

David O. Carpenter, MD, director of the Institute for Health and the Environment and a professor in the department of environmental health sciences at the University of Albany, both in Rensselaer, New York. He is a member of the editorial board of the *International Journal of Occupational Medicine and Environmental Health,* and an editorial adviser of *Cellular and Molecular Neurobiology.*

The average American drinks nearly 28 gallons of bottled water each year. Much of this consumer demand is fueled by the belief that bottled water is safer than tap water.

But is this really true?

There's little evidence that most bottled water is purer than what comes out of the tap in the majority of American cities. In fact, about 25% of bottled water is tap water (sometimes further treated, sometimes not) that's been repackaged and branded with a wholesome-looking label. This means that these bottled waters may be just as likely as the tap water that comes from faucets to contain contaminants, including infectious organisms, pesticide residues and heavy metals.

Caution: Bottled water may be even worse than tap water in some cases. *Potential problems...*

•**Lax oversight.** The Environmental Protection Agency (EPA) sets and enforces purity standards for municipal water. Bottled water, however, is regulated by the Food and Drug Administration (FDA)—but it is subject to inspection only when it's shipped out of state. About 60% of bottled waters are sold in the same state in which they're packaged. Therefore, they're exempt from FDA oversight and may not meet EPA standards.

•**Lack of chlorine.** Most bottled water, including that labeled "spring water," doesn't contain the disinfectant chlorine. Water without chlorine is far more likely to contain bacteria and viruses.

Bottled water companies use ozone gas (an antimicrobial agent), but this process provides disinfection for a limited time, depending on storage and other factors, according to the FDA.

COMMON DANGERS

The safest water in the US typically comes from municipal systems. Yet even "clean" tap water may contain trace levels of contaminants that can be harmful to anyone—but especially to those with chronic illnesses or impaired immunity, as well as older adults, very young children and pregnant women. *For example...*

•**Infectious organisms.** The chlorine that's added to municipal water is very effective at killing bacteria and viruses, but it has little effect on parasites, such as *Cryptosporidium*, which can lead to severe diarrhea, abdominal pain and weight loss.

The vast majority of US water systems have procedures in place that prevent *Cryptosporidium* and other parasites from reaching the tap. Water utilities are required by law to test supplies frequently and provide consumers with up-to-date information on the safety of tap water in their local areas.

To read water-quality reports for many American cities, consult the EPA at *www.epa.gov/safewater*...or for general information, call the EPA's Safe Drinking Water Hotline at 800-426-4791.

Self-defense: If there's a water-quality alert in your area (based on testing that identifies the presence of microorganisms), use bottled water—preferably water that's either distilled or filtered through reverse osmosis, a process by which water is forced through membranes, separating it from potentially harmful substances. Boiling your water also will kill all infectious organisms, including parasites.

Also helpful: An activated carbon filter will trap *Cryptosporidium*, *Giardia* and other parasites. These filters are available at home-goods stores or online for about $50 for a faucet type... and up to $150 for an under-the-sink version.

•**Pharmaceuticals.** When people take drugs, certain amounts pass through the body and are then flushed down the toilet. Wastewater treatment plants, which treat water that comes from community sewer systems, remove some—but not all—of the residues from drinking water. It's not known if these residues affect human health, but there's strong evidence that they're harming wildlife—and may be dangerous for people.

Of particular concern are residues from such medications as chemotherapy agents, psychiatric drugs and antibiotics (which could contribute to the development of antibiotic resistance). Bottled water that is repackaged tap water is just as likely to contain drug residues as tap water itself.

Self-defense: Under-the-sink or whole-house reverse osmosis filtration. Available from home-goods stores and online. Under-the-sink models cost $150 to $450...whole-house systems cost up to $3,000. Systems with particularly small-pore membranes may remove pharmaceutical contaminants.

•**Lead.** Until the 1980s, water pipes—both in homes and city systems—were often made of lead or joined with lead-based solders. Even small amounts of lead can impair intellectual development and behavior in young children. Lead also can cross the placenta in pregnant women and impair fetal health. In adults, lead has been shown to reduce memory function and raise blood pressure.

Self-defense: If you live in an older home (built before 1986), let the water run for a minute in the morning before taking a drink. Standing water in lead pipes contains trace amounts of lead.

Caution I: Don't use the hot-water tap for drinking water. Older hot-water tanks often used lead solder—and there's always standing water in the tank. The solder used in newer hot-water tanks does not contain lead, but it may contain other harmful metals. Brass faucets and fittings, which may contain lead, also can leach this metal, as can copper pipes with lead solder.

Caution II: Let the water run before drinking from a public water fountain, particularly after periods when lead may accumulate due to infrequent use.

•**Plastics.** It's not yet known if people who drink from plastic water bottles have increased health risks—but research has shown that the phthalates and other chemicals in plastics have estrogen-like effects and may cause birth defects.

Self-defense: Avoid disposable plastic bottles. People who want the convenience of bottled water should use a stainless steel bottle or a reusable, firm plastic bottle—that is not polycarbonate—and fill it from the tap. Polycarbonate bottles can usually be identified by the recycling number "7" on the bottom. Firm plastics are less likely to contain phthalates than "squishy" plastic bottles.

How Global Warming Harms Your Health

Georges C. Benjamin, MD, an internist who serves as executive director of the American Public Health Association, *www.apha.org*, and professorial lecturer at George Washington University School of Public Health, both in Washington, DC. He is former secretary of the Maryland Department of Health and Mental Hygiene, with expertise in emergency preparedness.

The World Health Organization estimates that 150,000 deaths annually, mostly in Africa and Asia, are caused by climate change—primarily related to increases in the planet's surface temperature (commonly known as global warming). The death toll is expected to double in the next 20 to 30 years.

Latest development: Health implications are also starting to be felt in the US.

LUNG DISEASES

Higher temperatures cause an increase in ground-level ozone, a gas that irritates the airways and increases the risk for asthma and other lung diseases—and exacerbates symptoms in those who already have any pulmonary disorder.

What to do: If you or a family member has a pulmonary condition or you're healthy but planning to spend a good deal of time outdoors, check the daily ozone forecast. It's available online at EnviroFlash (*www.enviroflash.info*), a program sponsored by the Environmental Protection Agency.

HAY FEVER AND MOLD

The increase in the atmospheric gas carbon dioxide (CO_2) can stimulate pollen-producing plants to release more pollen, which exacerbates symptoms in people with hay fever as well as asthma. Rising temperatures and CO_2 levels also increase the growth of molds, which attach to pollutants in the atmosphere and more readily enter the lungs.

What to do: If you or a family member has allergies or asthma, check daily pollen reports. The American Academy of Allergy, Asthma & Immunology (*www.aaaai.org/nab*) provides daily pollen and mold counts for many US states. Limit your time outdoors on "high pollen" days.

HEATSTROKE

We're seeing more heat waves nationally. In areas that once had just a few hot days a year, now there might be stretches of four, five or six days of temperatures that are 10 degrees or more above average high temperatures for a region. Heat can be deadly, particularly for the elderly.

Older adults don't sweat as much, so they're less able to dissipate heat.

Result: Their body temperature can rise to dangerous levels—and stay there.

People with impaired mobility or those taking diuretics (which promote the excretion of fluids) have a very high risk for heat-related conditions, such as heatstroke (a potentially deadly condition that causes raised body temperature and loss of consciousness). People who are overheated often feel weak, making them less able to get up for a drink of water. The combination of low fluid intake and decreased sweating is extremely dangerous.

What to do: Anyone at risk for overheating (as previously described) should have access to an air conditioner or, at a minimum, a fan. If mobility is an issue, fill a pitcher of cool water and keep it nearby. If you have difficulty getting around, consider buying an alert bracelet so you can summon help in an emergency. Even if you're in good health, drink two to four glasses of cool water per hour in extreme heat or while physically active.

MOSQUITO-BORNE DISEASES

Worldwide, 350 million to 500 million people get malaria (an infectious disease that causes high fever and chills) every year, and more than 1 million die from it.

Malaria and other mosquito-borne diseases haven't been a significant threat in the US since the early 1950s, following a successful eradication program using drainage, removal of mosquito breeding sites and pesticides. But that could change with global warming. Warmer temperatures allow mosquito populations to proliferate. According to the most recent CDC data, 1,337 cases of malaria, including eight deaths, were reported in the US in 2002.

There's been an epidemic of dengue fever (a mosquito-borne infectious disease that causes severe joint pain, headache, fever and rash) in South America. If temperatures continue to rise in the US, an increase in dengue fever (cases have been reported in Hawaii) will almost certainly occur here. A similar increase in West Nile virus (a mosquito-borne illness that causes flu-like symptoms) also could occur in the US.

What to do: To reduce mosquito populations, remove breeding sites. After it rains, look for places where water accumulates—for example, in flowerpots—and dump it out as soon as possible. Cover barbecue grills and other outdoor water "traps." Maintain rain gutters so that there is no standing water. Mosquitoes are attracted to as little as one teaspoon of standing water, and their eggs typically hatch within 48 hours.

Also helpful: Keep fish in backyard ponds. Many species, including mosquitofish and bitterlings, eat mosquito larvae. If you live in a warm, damp area where mosquitoes proliferate, wear long sleeves and pants whenever possible, and/or use a repellent, such as one containing DEET or *picaridin*. Or stay indoors during the early morning and at dusk, when mosquitoes are most active.

WATERBORNE INFECTIONS

With global warming, extreme storms and floods are likely to occur more often. These pose obvious risks for those in coastal areas—but inland regions aren't necessarily safe.

Drowning and/or water damage are obvious concerns. A bigger issue is water quality. Many metropolitan areas have sewage systems that can't handle severe downpours—water from the sewers can overflow into clean water supplies, causing outbreaks of potentially fatal bacterial infections.

What to do: Following severe downpours or floods, tune in to news channels for up-to-date reports on water quality. If there are concerns about water quality, keep a stockpile of bottled water...boil (for at least one full minute) water used for cooking, cleaning and bathing...and wash your hands often with soap and disinfected water.

Discounts on Vitamins, Face-Lifts, Lasik and Other Hidden Benefits Of Health Insurance

Robert Hurley and Samuel Gibbs, senior vice presidents at eHealthInsurance Services, Inc., a Web site where consumers can compare health insurance plans and apply for and purchase health insurance online. Hurley is an insurance industry expert formerly with Health Net, Inc., a managed health-care company. Gibbs specializes in helping companies understand health care. eHealthInsurance is not affiliated with any particular health insurance provider, *http://ehealthinsurance.com.*

Your health insurance might offer unexpected savings. Some group and individual health insurers have negotiated discounts on behalf of their members on products and services. These discounts are not always well-publicized, and many plan members don't even realize they exist. Read your health insurance company's mailings, or visit its Web site to see if there are any special discounts through your plan.

These discounts typically are categorized as "perks" rather than plan benefits, which means insurance companies can alter or discontinue them without first notifying plan members. Contact your insurance provider or the company featured in the offer to confirm that a discount still is in effect. Also, ask if any special rules or limitations apply.

COMMON DISCOUNTS

Among the benefits found in many health insurance plans...

- **Fitness club memberships.** Many health plans offer a discount of 10% to 20% or more off the cost of gym membership. This discount usually is available only at select national fitness chains, and you may have to prove that you use the gym regularly. Some plans also include discounts at yoga studios...or discounts on the purchase of fitness equipment from participating retailers.

•**Naturopathic treatments.** Some insurance companies cover these treatments. Those that don't may offer discounts of 20% or more on acupuncture, chiropractic services, massage therapy and hypnotherapy.

Example: Most Anthem Blue Cross of California members can get these discounts simply by showing their membership cards at participating providers.

•**Weight-loss programs.** Savings of 20% or more off membership in national weight-loss chains, such as Jenny Craig and Weight Watchers, are common. Even the special low-calorie meals required by some weight-loss programs may be discounted.

•**Quit-smoking programs.** Insurance plans often cover quit-smoking programs in part or in whole. Discounts might be available on nicotine patches, gum and related products.

OTHER PERKS

These perks turn up only occasionally in health insurance plans, but they are worth watching for...

•**Cosmetic surgery and dentistry.** Cosmetic procedures typically are not covered by health insurance, but some plans do offer special negotiated rates on elective surgery at participating providers. Covered procedures could include Botox injections, face-lifts and tooth whitening. The savings often are 20% or more off standard rates.

Examples: Members of Blue Cross Blue Shield of South Carolina are eligible for significant discounts on cosmetic surgery through participating providers.

•**Vision correction.** Some insurance companies offer discounts on eyeglasses, contact lenses, even laser surgery.

Example: Golden Rule (owned by UnitedHealthcare) offers 10% to 60% savings on eye exams, eyeglasses, contact lenses and LASIK laser eye surgery to their members through an affiliation with the Federation of American Consumers and Travelers.

•**Prescription and nonprescription drug coverage without a drug plan.** Even if your health plan does not include drug coverage, there might be a discount of 10% or more if you purchase your drugs at a "partner" drugstore.

•**Vitamins and supplements.** Discounts of as much as 40% to 50% sometimes are available. You will need to buy your vitamins through a designated provider to receive these savings.

•**Book discounts.** Some insurance plans have partnered with online book sellers to offer discounts of 5% or 10% on "featured" books. These books typically focus on health and/or wellness topics.

•**Travel discounts.** Some major health insurers have negotiated discount rates for their members at hotel chains, car-rental chains and amusement parks. Savings can be 10% to 20%. Read the discount terms carefully—in some cases, members must provide special discount codes or reserve their discount rates in advance...in other cases, members simply show their insurance plan membership cards upon arrival.

Example: Members of Golden Rule can get 20% discounts at participating Choice Hotels International, such as Comfort Suites and Econo Lodge...10% off Magellan's Travel Supplies...and car-rental discounts.

■ ■ ■ ■

Lower-Cost Health Insurance For Early Retirees

Health insurance for early retirees is being offered by a small number of the largest US companies. Many employees are reluctant to accept early-retirement packages because of the cost of getting their own health coverage—if they can obtain it at all. So some large companies—32 of them so far—are taking part in Retiree Health Access, an Aetna plan that helps retirees buy health insurance at discounted group rates. Fifteen of the participating companies are giving benefits to early retirees for the first time. Other insurers are setting up similar plans.

More information: Talk to your human resources department.

BusinessWeek, 1221 Avenue of the Americas, New York City 10020.

■ ■ ■ ■

A Layoff Can Put Your Flexible Spending Account (FSA) in Jeopardy

When employees are let go, they typically are allowed to spend FSA money on health-care expenses incurred while still covered by the employer's benefits plan. This coverage often ends on the last day of the month in which the employee is terminated. After that, remaining FSA money is forfeited (unless you sign up for COBRA).

Self-defense: Schedule health procedures and stock up on health products before coverage ends.

Rebecca Mazin, a human resources consultant based in Larchmont, New York, is coauthor of *The HR Answer Book* (Amacom) and editor of The HR Answer Blog. *www.allbusiness.com.*

■ ■ ■ ■

Medical Credit Cards—An Unhealthy Choice

Medical debt does not usually show up on a credit report unless it goes to collection—but consumer debt shows up immediately and can have a big impact if you pay bills late. Medical cards, offered by GE Money, Citigroup and other banks, can be used only for health-care expenses and have 0% interest rates for as long as 12 months. The cards usually are offered to people who are having trouble paying their health-care costs—making it likely that they will end up carrying a balance after the zero-interest period expires.

Self-defense: Instead of getting a medical credit card, negotiate the fee and a payment plan with the provider directly.

Gerri Detweiler, credit adviser, Ultimate Credit Solutions, Inc. (*www.ultimatecredit.com*), a personal-finance education Web site.

Best New Hearing Aids

John M. Burkey, CCC/A, FAAA, a certified audiologist and director of audiology at the Lippy Group for Ear, Nose & Throat in Warren, Ohio. A fellow of the American Academy of Audiology, he is author of *Baby Boomers and Hearing Loss* and *Overcoming Hearing Aid Fears* (both published by Rutgers University).

Hearing loss typically sneaks up slowly with often imperceptible changes occurring over a period of several years.

Most people don't even realize there is a problem until about 30% of their hearing is lost. At that stage, one of the most common red flags is an inability to hear soft consonant sounds, such as "th," "f" or "s," which causes people to miss parts of conversations—especially if the speaker is soft-spoken and/or talks while facing away.

About one-third of all people over age 65 have significant hearing loss and could benefit from hearing aids, but only about 20% of them use the devices—often because of cosmetic concerns. With new technology, however, clunky, conspicuous hearing aids have largely been replaced with devices that are barely visible.

NEW HEARING AIDS

Vanity should no longer be used as an excuse to not get a hearing aid. A variety of new technologically advanced hearing aid devices that blend with a person's skin or hair color are the norm. In addition, manufacturers now offer devices that are decorative (a flower design, for example) or come in bright colors, such as orange or neon green. *Popular choices...*

•**Mini behind-the-ear devices** are usually no more than one inch long. A tiny clear wire, which runs from behind the ear into the ear, feeds sound into the ear.

Best for: People with loss of high-pitched hearing (sounds such as birds chirping and a microwave "beep"). This is the most common type of hearing loss, often associated with noise exposure and aging.

Typical cost: $1,000 to $4,000 per ear.

•**Completely-in-the-canal devices** are the least visible style but are not as popular as the mini behind-the-ear versions. The ear canal is blocked, which can interfere with low-pitched sounds, creating a less pleasing sound quality for some people.

Best for: People with mild to moderate hearing loss who are concerned about appearance.

Typical cost: $1,000 to $4,000 per ear.

CHOOSING THE BEST MODEL

Until recently, most hearing aids were analog—they contained a relatively simple amplifier to make sounds louder. In the last few years, analog devices have been widely replaced with digital hearing aids that process sounds through a tiny computer. With digital technology, audiologists can program the device to a person's specific needs. For example, you may need to have background noise muted so you can hear conversations better in a restaurant.

How do you determine which hearing aid technology is best for you? *My advice...*

- **Don't ask for a particular brand.** Some of the best are manufactured by companies most people have never seen advertised.

Examples: GN ReSound, Oticon, Phonak, Siemens and Starkey. Choose an audiologist who handles at least three different brands.

- **Be willing to try a second brand—or model.** Everyone responds differently to particular hearing aids. One brand may create a "bright" sound that some people think sounds crisp, while others think it sounds tinny. Another brand may create a mellower sound that some people think sounds rich, while others think it sounds "muddy." If you are dissatisfied with your first choice after three or four weeks of use, return it and try another brand or style of hearing aid.

- **Consider all your hearing needs.** If you spend most of your time in quiet conversation, your needs can probably be met by a basic, entry-level digital hearing aid. However, if you go from home to a business, for example, and then to the theater and later to the airport, you need a more adaptive hearing aid, such as one that uses artificial intelligence programming. These digital devices contain microprocessors that "learn" your needs so that—with time—your hearing aid will automatically adjust to give you the right sound levels in the appropriate environments.

BUYING HEARING AIDS

After you select the size, model and brand of hearing aid...

- **Buy a hearing aid for each ear unless your hearing loss is restricted to one ear.** The brain uses input from both ears to tell the direction of sound and to focus on one speaker within a group of people. If you buy a single hearing aid, sounds will probably blur together, making it more difficult to hear clearly.

- **Insist on a money-back guarantee.** Most states are required by law to offer a 30-day money-back guarantee. (There may be a nonrefundable "trial" fee that should not exceed 10% of the hearing aid's cost.) Because hearing aids are costly and typically not covered by insurance, it's important that they provide good sound and fit the ear comfortably.

- **Don't automatically buy loss-protection insurance.** Do you routinely lose your eyeglasses or car keys? If not, then skip the loss-protection insurance you will probably be offered. It typically covers the full cost of hearing aids but costs about $200 a year.

- **Purchase wax guards.** Half of all hearing aid malfunctions are caused when too much earwax gets into the device and damages the receiver. Wax guards, available from your audiologist for about $10 each, are disposable and can be changed as often as needed.

Smile! You Can Get Dental Care for Less

Jordan Braverman, MPH, former director of legislative and health policy analysis at Georgetown University's Health Policy Center, Washington, DC. He is author of several books on health-care policy and financing, including *Your Money & Your Health* (Prometheus).

Dental care is rarely covered by Medicare... few retirees have dental insurance...and those who have dental insurance often find that their coverage is very limited.

Dental bills average around $677 per year for the typical senior, and a major procedure, such as a root canal or a dental implant, can push that tab into four or even five figures.

Exception: Medicare usually will pay dental bills if they are related to a medical incident that requires a hospital stay, such as jaw reconstruction following a car accident.

Some resources that could help you dramatically reduce your dental bills or even provide dental care for free...

HEALTH INSURANCE

Insurance can help pay dental bills. *Options to consider...*

•**Dental insurance.** If you have access to subsidized group dental insurance through an employer or former employer, it likely is worth having. If not, the case for dental insurance is less compelling.

Dental insurance typically features copayments as high as 50%...annual benefit caps in the low four figures...often long waiting periods before expensive procedures are covered...and usually only 80% coverage if your dentist is out of network. Dental insurance premiums for seniors are about $430 per year for individual plans. That's a steep price for such limited coverage, but not necessarily an awful deal if you believe that you will require significant dental work within a few years, perhaps because your dentist has warned you that a major procedure cannot be put off too much longer.

If you do decide to sign up for dental insurance, consider the policies offered through AARP. Rates on AARP dental policies often are a bit lower than what comparable individual dental coverage would cost elsewhere.

More information: Visit *www3.deltadentalins.com/aarp/.*

If you do have dental insurance, confirm that your dentist will accept it before agreeing to any procedure. Work with him/her to get the most out of the insurance if he does.

Example: If the dental work you require is not an emergency and significantly exceeds your coverage's annual benefits cap, ask your dentist if the work—and the bill—could be spread out over two or more plan years.

•**Private health insurance.** If you do not have dental insurance but have private health insurance in addition to Medicare, this health insurance could include some basic dental benefits. Read the plan literature or call the insurance company's customer service department to find out.

•**Medical flexible spending accounts (FSAs).** FSAs can substantially trim the effective cost of dental care by allowing patients to pay for health-care bills—including dental bills—with pretax dollars. Unfortunately for retirees, FSAs are available only to employees whose employers offer FSAs as part of their benefits packages.

HAGGLING

Dentists' bills often are negotiable—but only if you discuss costs before having the dental work done. Ask if you can get a senior discount or a cash discount if you pay in cash. Either of these appeals could net you savings of 5% to 10%.

Call other dentists' offices to ask their prices for the procedure. If you find a better rate, tell your dentist that you are on a tight budget and ask if he can match the lower price.

Get a second opinion before agreeing to any major procedure. There's a chance that your dentist could be recommending an expensive procedure that is not necessary. Have your dental files, including the most recent test results and X-rays, forwarded to the dentist who will provide this second opinion so that you do not have to pay to have these repeated. You will have to pay for the second opinion, but the cost of a simple office visit is so much lower than the cost of an elaborate dental procedure that it can be a smart investment if there is any chance that the original dentist was wrong.

IF YOU HAVE A LIMITED INCOME

You probably can get dental care even if your financial resources are very limited...

•**Medicaid.** Medicaid is available only to those with low incomes and limited assets. Eligibility rules and program benefits vary by state. In most states, Medicaid provides at least basic dental care for those living near or below the poverty line.

To find out if you qualify, contact your state's Medicaid Office. (Visit *www.benefits.gov,* select "Medicaid/Medicare" from the "Benefits Quick Search" menu, then choose your home state. Or call 800-333-4636 for a contact phone number for your state's Medicaid office.)

Helpful: Nursing homes are legally required to arrange for dental care for residents who use Medicaid to pay for their stays. That typically means that they must either bring a dentist to the nursing home or transport the resident to a dentist's office to receive care.

• **Local and state dental associations.** Many have programs that provide dental services for free or reduced rates to those in financial need. Services are provided by dentists who volunteer their time. Eligibility requirements vary.

State and local dental associations can be found on the Web site of the American Dental Association (ADA)—at *www.ada.org,* select "Dental Organizations" off the menu, then check both the "Constituent (State) Directory" and the "Component (Local) Directory" to find relevant associations. Or call the ADA at 312-440-2500 for your state dental association's phone number.

Example: The Connecticut State Dental Association sponsors an annual "Mission of Mercy" program that provides free cleanings, extractions and fillings on a first-come, first-served basis. Unlike most programs of this sort, Connecticut's Mission of Mercy does not require proof of limited income. Check the Connecticut State Dental Association's Web site for more information (*www.csda.com/ctmom/ctmom4.html*).

• **Public or nonprofit dental clinics.** Available in many regions, these typically charge very low rates, perhaps linked to the patients' ability to pay. In some cases, treatment is free.

Your area Agency on Aging should be able to direct you to any dental clinics in your region and might know of other local low-cost dental options for seniors. (Call the US Administration on Aging's Eldercare Locator, 800-677-1116, or use the Locator on the Web at *www.eldercare.gov* to find your local Agency on Aging if you cannot locate it in your phone book.) Your local or state dental association also might know of area clinics.

MONEY-SAVING OPTIONS

If you don't qualify for low-income dental programs, consider these options...

• **Local dental colleges.** Performed for perhaps half the usual cost, the work is done by dental students under the supervision of qualified instructors. The quality of the dental care tends to be good...however, a dental school might not provide a full range of dental services.

The American Dental Education Association Web site can help you find dental schools in your region. (At *www.adea.org,* click "About ADEA," then "Who We Are," and "Predoctoral Dental Education Programs.") Typing "dental schools" and the name of your state into Google.com also can help you find any schools in your region.

• **Retail dental centers.** Usually located in shopping malls, they typically charge 10% to 20% less than traditional dentists' offices.

■ ■ ■ ■

Web Site Rates Nursing Home Quality

The system rates nursing homes as having from one to five stars overall, and also separately on (1) the results of health inspection reports, (2) the level of staffing per resident and (3) "quality or performance," based on 10 different physical and clinical measures. To learn and compare the star ratings of nursing homes by name or geographic location, go to *www.medicare.gov/NHcompare.*

14

Stroke Prevention

Where You Live Could Raise Your Risk for Stroke

Living in neighborhoods packed with fast-food joints could increase your risk for stroke by 13%, compared to residing in places where such restaurants are less plentiful, a recent study suggests.

Whether the link proves to be causal is not known, though, said study author Lewis B. Morgenstern, MD, a professor of neurology at the University of Michigan School of Public Health.

"The only thing we are certain about is, if you live in a neighborhood with a high fast-food restaurant concentration, you are at increased risk," Dr. Morgenstern said. He presented his study at the International Stroke Conference in San Diego.

THE STUDY

Dr. Morgenstern's research team gathered data on stroke cases in Nueces County, Texas, finding 1,247 cases of ischemic stroke from January 2000 through June 2003. More than 700,000 strokes occur each year in the United States, and most are ischemic, in which blood vessels become clogged.

The researchers then determined the number of fast-food restaurants in the county—262 during that time period—and zeroed in on 64 US Census Bureau tracts to determine the number of fast-food outlets in each area.

Dr. Morgenstern said that it would be difficult to break down how many fast-food restaurants per block or per mile were in the high-concentration areas. But each census tract included about 5,000 people, and the neighborhoods in the top 25% had 33 restaurants per tract, while those in the lowest 25% had 12.

Lewis B. Morgenstern, MD, professor, neurology and epidemiology, and director, stroke program, School of Public Health, University of Michigan, Ann Arbor.

Ralph Sacco, MD, professor and chairman, department of neurology, University of Miami Miller School of Medicine.

Dean Johnston, MD, clinical assistant professor, neurology, University of British Columbia, Vancouver.

International Stroke Conference, San Diego.

THE RESULTS

Their analysis determined that "there was a 13% increased risk of stroke in the top 25% compared to the lowest 25%," Dr. Morgenstern said. The study was funded by the US National Institutes of Health.

EXPERT REACTION

"It's interesting, but we don't know if it is causal," said Ralph Sacco, MD, chairman of the department of neurology at the University of Miami Miller School of Medicine and a spokesman for the American Stroke Association.

But the findings are plausible, said Dean Johnston, MD, a clinical assistant professor of neurology at the University of British Columbia. "This suggests that diet and lifestyle factors are important for stroke prevention," he said. Fast food has been linked with obesity, and obesity increases stroke risk.

ADVICE

The bottom line for consumers? Anyone moving to a new locale should pay attention to the neighborhood, Dr. Morgenstern said, including the number of stores that sell fresh produce and the number of fast-food restaurants.

info For more information about stroke, visit the Web site of the American Stroke Association, *www.strokeassociation.org.*

■ ■ ■ ■

Deadly Aneurysm Ruptures Can Be Prevented

An abdominal aortic aneurysm (AAA) is a weak area in a large abdominal artery. If it ruptures, internal bleeding usually is fatal. But if detected before rupturing, 95% of AAA cases can be treated.

Self-defense: Consult a vascular surgeon without delay if you notice a pulsing or unexplained pain in the abdomen or low back. You may need an ultrasound to screen for AAA.

Cynthia Shortell, MD, associate professor of surgery, Duke University Medical Center, Durham, North Carolina, and chair of the women's issues committee of the Society for Vascular Surgery.

Signs Someone Is Having a Stroke

American Heart Association/American Stroke Association news release.

Most people do not know the five warning signs of a stroke and what to do if they suspect one. This is especially true of those most likely to suffer one, according to recent research.

THE SURVEY

The findings stem from a telephone survey of more than 86,000 people conducted in 11 states, the District of Columbia and the Virgin Islands. Those polled were asked five questions to determine if they knew stroke symptoms and if they knew what to do if someone was having a stroke.

Fewer than two in five people surveyed knew all five warning signs and knew to call 911, the survey found. The results were presented at the International Stroke Conference in San Diego.

Older people and those who've already had a stroke were among the groups found to be least able to recognize the symptoms of a stroke and know to immediately call 911.

No demographic group did extremely well, but minorities, people with lower incomes and those with less education did particularly poorly.

IMPLICATIONS

"We have to make sure that people know the signs and symptoms of stroke because the patient would need to get to the hospital as soon as possible to have a much higher chance of survival and to avoid potential disabilities," said the survey's lead author, Jing Fang, MD, an epidemiologist in the division for heart disease and stroke prevention at the Centers for Disease Control and Prevention in Atlanta.

STROKE WARNING SIGNS

Some of the warning signs of stroke appeared to be better known than others. About 93% of the survey respondents knew that sudden weakness in the face, arm or leg was a symptom, but only 59% knew that a sudden severe headache with no known cause was also one.

Other warning signs of stroke can include sudden vision problems in one or both eyes, sudden confusion or difficulty speaking as well as sudden dizziness, loss of balance, loss of coordination or difficulty walking.

The survey revealed "a big disparity in age, gender, race, income and education" when it comes to knowledge of warning signs, Dr. Fang said. "If we want to improve awareness, we should be more focused on those populations who were less aware of the signs," he said.

Info For more information on how to recognize a stroke, go to the "Know Stroke" page of the Web site of the National Institute of Neurological Disorders and Stroke, *http://stroke.nih.gov.*

The Stroke Warning that Can Save Your Life

Larry B. Goldstein, MD, director of the Duke Center for Cerebrovascular Disease and the Duke Stroke Center and professor of medicine (neurology) at Duke University Medical Center and the Durham VA Medical Center, all in Durham, North Carolina. He has published more than 450 journal articles and two books for health professionals and serves on the editorial boards of the journals *Stroke, Neurology, Emergency Medicine* and *Cerebrovascular Diseases.*

Have you ever had a transient ischemic attack (TIA)? Before you answer, consider the facts. An estimated five million Americans have had a TIA, but only about half of them realized what was happening. That's because the symptoms of a TIA (a temporary interruption of blood flow to the brain) can be fleeting and often are ignored. And unlike a stroke, a TIA does not cause permanent brain injury. (To learn more about TIA symptoms, take the quiz on the next page.)

Frightening statistic: Anyone who has had a TIA is 10 times more likely to have a full-blown stroke.

WHEN TO CALL 911

A TIA occurs when an area of the brain doesn't get enough blood, often due to a narrowing or blockage of an artery leading to the brain. TIA symptoms, which are the same as those for a stroke, can be subtle and sometimes last just a few minutes. *They include...*

- **Sudden difficulty with walking or maintaining balance.**
- **Sudden weakness or numbness** affecting an arm or leg on one side of the body.
- **Sudden difficulty speaking or understanding speech.**
- **Sudden vision loss in one eye** or difficulty seeing to one side.

Important: If you're having any of these symptoms, call 911. There's no way for a patient to tell if the symptoms are due to a TIA or a stroke.

Many people who have a TIA—or even suspect one—do not see a doctor. Now, an additional problem has been discovered.

Important research finding: About one in three people who visited a primary care physician after having TIA symptoms did not receive a stroke-related evaluation, including such tests as a computed tomography (CT) scan during the next 30 days. This means such people may be missing a valuable opportunity to begin treatment that could prevent a major stroke.

KEY RISK FACTORS

You're more likely to suffer a TIA or stroke if you are overweight or inactive and/or have high blood pressure, elevated cholesterol or diabetes. TIA and stroke risk also are increased by age (a person's stroke risk doubles every decade after age 55)...family history (having a parent or sibling who had a stroke before age 65)...and gender (men are at greater risk for stroke than women, but most stroke deaths occur in women).

If you have TIA symptoms that last for more than a few minutes, call 911. If they quickly resolve, ask someone to drive you to the closest emergency room as soon as possible and tell the personnel that you may be having a stroke.

What most people don't know: Patients who are immediately evaluated and treated after experiencing TIA symptoms have fewer full-blown strokes than TIA sufferers who don't receive prompt care.

GET A PROPER EVALUATION

If you have what appear to be TIA symptoms, taking the right actions can dramatically impact your long-term health. The cause of your symptoms must be determined—other health problems, such as diabetes or a brain tumor, can trigger TIA-like symptoms. If you've had a TIA, the underlying problem, such as a blood clot or a tear in a blood vessel, must be determined. *Steps should include...*

•**Immediate evaluation.** At the hospital, tests typically include a complete blood count (CBC), blood glucose measurement, a urinalysis, an electrocardiogram (EKG) and a brain imaging study, such as a CT scan.

•**Specific tests.** Depending on your case, other tests, such as a magnetic resonance imaging (MRI) scan, may be used to determine if there is a blockage in one of the arteries that supply the brain.

If atrial fibrillation (a disturbance in the electrical rhythms of the heart that can generate stroke-causing blood clots) is suspected but not detected on the initial EKG, it may be necessary to wear a heart monitor for a day to rule out the presence of intermittent atrial fibrillation. An echocardiogram (an ultrasound of the heart) also may be performed.

BEST TREATMENT OPTIONS

People who have had a TIA—as well as those who have not—may be able to reduce their stroke risk by adopting these habits...

•**Eat a diet low in saturated fats** (found in red meat and full-fat dairy products) with at least three to five daily servings of fruits and vegetables...exercise at a brisk pace (such as fast walking) 20 to 30 minutes a day most days of the week...avoid excessive alcohol intake (no more than two drinks a day for men and one drink a day for women)...stop smoking (and avoid secondhand smoke). For a healthy body weight, aim for a body mass index (BMI) of 25 or lower.

Other approaches...

•**Blood thinners.** If tests show that you have atrial fibrillation, your doctor will probably prescribe a blood thinner, such as *warfarin* (Coumadin). Other medications—known as antiplatelet drugs—may help reduce stroke risk in high-risk people without atrial fibrillation. These drugs include aspirin, the antiplatelet drug *clopidogrel* (Plavix) and a combination of aspirin and *dipyridamole* (Aggrenox).

Warning: The combination of aspirin and Plavix can increase the risk for a hemorrhagic stroke (caused by bleeding in the brain) in patients who have had a stroke or a TIA, so be sure your doctors know about all the medications you take, including aspirin.

•**Cholesterol-lowering "statin" drugs.** In a study of nearly 5,000 people who have had a TIA or stroke, those with an LDL "bad" cholesterol level of 100 mg/dL to 190 mg/dL who took *atorvastatin* (Lipitor) had a 16% drop in risk for a subsequent nonfatal or fatal stroke compared with a placebo group.

•**Blood pressure–lowering medication.** Lowering blood pressure by an average of 10 points systolic (top number) and 5 points diastolic (bottom number) can reduce risk for a post-TIA stroke by nearly 40%.

•**Surgery.** If there is a narrowing of the carotid (neck) artery that could have caused your symptoms, you may need an endarterectomy, a surgical procedure that removes artery-blocking plaque. In some circumstances (such as narrowing of the carotid artery in an area that is difficult for the surgeon to reach), your doctor may recommend inserting a stent, a tube that helps keep the blood vessel open.

■ **More from Larry B. Goldstein, MD...**

Take This Quick TIA Quiz

Up to one-third of TIA sufferers will eventually have a stroke—unless their underlying conditions are aggressively treated. *The risk for a full-blown stroke in a person who has had a TIA can be estimated by a tool that uses key factors to determine an "ABCD²" score...*

•**Age.** If over age 60—1 point.

•**Blood pressure.** If your systolic blood pressure (top number) is higher than 140 mmHg and/or your diastolic blood pressure (bottom number) is higher than 90—1 point.

• **Clinical features.** If you had weakness on one side of your body—2 points. If you had a speech disturbance without weakness—1 point.

• **Duration of symptoms.** If TIA symptoms lasted for 10 to 59 minutes—1 point. If symptoms lasted for 60 minutes or longer—2 points.

• **Diabetes.** If you have diabetes—1 point.

If your score is 4 or less, your risk for stroke within two days of a TIA is 1%...and 3% within 90 days. A score of 5 or greater indicates an 8% risk for stroke within two days...and an 18% risk within 90 days.

■ ■ ■ ■

MRIs Reveal *Real* Stroke Risk

When researchers reviewed magnetic resonance imaging (MRI) scans for 2,040 adults (average age 62) who had no stroke symptoms, they found silent cerebral infarctions (SCIs)—brain lesions that occur when clots interrupt blood flow to the brain yet do not result in noticeable symptoms—in 10.7% of the adults. These participants did suffer some brain damage, such as loss of mental skills.

Self-defense: If you have risk factors for stroke, such as atrial fibrillation (irregular heartbeat), high blood pressure, diabetes or heart disease, ask your doctor about lifestyle modifications and treatment options to reduce your risk.

Sudha Seshadri, MD, associate professor of neurology, department of neurology, Boston University School of Medicine.

Rohit Das, MD, researcher and neurologist, Boston University's School of Medicine.

■ ■ ■ ■

"Silent" Stroke Danger

Researchers analyzed data for 1,423 patients hospitalized for sudden sensorineural hearing loss—sudden, unexplained hearing loss—and 5,692 patients (mostly middle-aged or older) who were hospitalized for appendix removal.

Result: The hearing loss patients were 1.5 times more likely to suffer a stroke over the next five years than the appendectomy patients.

Theory: Sudden, unexplained hearing loss and stroke may share a common cause.

If you have sudden hearing loss: Ask your doctor whether you should have a neurological exam and blood tests to evaluate your stroke risk.

Hsin-Chien Lee, MD, MPH, assistant professor and chairman, department of psychiatry, Taipei Medical University, Taiwan.

■ ■ ■ ■

High Blood Pressure Triples Risk for Vision Loss

With retinal vein occlusion (RVO), blood vessels in the eye become blocked and may rupture, damaging eyesight.

Recent finding: Having high blood pressure more than tripled a person's risk for RVO...high cholesterol more than doubled RVO risk.

Best: Get regular eye exams, and control blood pressure and cholesterol.

Joel G. Ray, assistant professor, division of endocrinology and metabolism, St. Michael's Hospital, University of Toronto, Canada, and lead author of an analysis of 21 studies, published in *Archives of Ophthalmology.*

See a Doctor If You Have These Eye Symptoms

Neil Shulman, MD, associate professor in the department of internal medicine at Emory University School of Medicine, Atlanta, and Jack Birge, MD, medical director for performance improvement at Tanner Medical Center in Carrollton, Georgia, and clinical assistant professor of community medicine at Mercer University School of Medicine in Macon, Georgia. They are authors, with Joon Ahn, MD, of *Your Body's Red Light Warning Signals* (Delta). *www.redlightwarningsignals.com.*

Many serious health problems are first diagnosed from changes in the eyes. *Never ignore these eye symptoms...*

SUDDEN EYELID DROOP

What it may mean: If you notice that one of your eyelids has abruptly drooped lower than the other (possibly accompanied by double vision), it could indicate an aneurysm—a ballooning-out of a blood vessel in the brain. This is particularly likely when a patient's pupils are unequal in size. An aneurysm can press against nerves that control both eyelid position and pupil size.

Aneurysms aren't always dangerous, but those that rupture can cause brain damage or death. It's estimated that up to 5% of Americans have a brain aneurysm.

Causes: Most brain aneurysms are due to a natural weakness in an artery wall. Less often, they're caused by head trauma.

What to do: Get to an emergency room as fast as possible.

Treatment: Aneurysms that are large and/or are causing symptoms are typically clipped—a neurosurgeon uses a metal clip to prevent blood from flowing through the aneurysm. Small aneurysms often are best left alone.

CHRONIC EYELID DROOP IN BOTH EYES/ DOUBLE VISION

Chronic eyelid droop sometimes is accompanied by blurred or double vision, jaw fatigue or general weakness that gets worse as the day progresses.

What it may mean: These are common symptoms of *myasthenia gravis*, a condition in which nerves are unable to communicate effectively with muscles.

Causes: Myasthenia gravis is an autoimmune disease. The immune system creates antibodies that damage cellular receptors for *acetylcholine*, a neurotransmitter involved in nerve/muscle communication.

It's not clear what triggers this condition, although it has been linked to disorders of the thymus gland.

What to do: Get to a doctor as soon as possible (ideally within a week). If your symptoms are accompanied by breathing problems, you should get to an emergency room immediately.

Treatment: Most patients are treated with medications, such as *pyridostigmine* (Mestinon), which improve the transmission of nerve signals. Other medications, including steroids, may be used. The thymus gland may be removed in patients with tumors if medication fails. This may not improve symptoms—it is mainly done to reduce the risk for a future cancer.

EYEBALL PAIN (OFTEN SUDDEN)

What it may mean: In the absence of trauma, eye pain can be due to glaucoma, a buildup of pressure within the eye. (Other causes are inflammation in the eye or dry eyes.)

Causes of glaucoma: The different forms of glaucoma all cause an increase in intraocular pressure. This usually is due to impairments in drainage, which increase fluid levels within the eye.

Important: Glaucoma is the second-leading cause of blindness among American adults (behind macular degeneration). Eye pain may be the only early symptom.

What to do: If you have severe pain and/or vision loss, get to an ophthalmologist within a day of symptom appearance.

Treatment: Medications that reduce pressure by improving drainage and/or reducing fluid production.

Examples: Medicated eyedrops, such as *timolol* (Timoptic) or *brimonidine* (Alphagan). Less often, surgery may be needed to improve eye drainage.

A HAZE, BLUR OR DARKNESS IN THE FIELD OF VISION

What it may mean: A clot in a blood vessel may be blocking circulation to the retina, optic nerve or brain. Patients with this type of clot may be suffering from a stroke or be at high risk for a subsequent stroke—possibly within hours or days. (Other conditions that can cause these symptoms include inflammation in the blood vessels, a retinal detachment or inflammation of the optic nerve.)

Causes of stroke: The same risk factors for cardiovascular disease, such as diabetes, high blood pressure and smoking, also increase the risk for stroke. The optic nerve and retina are very sensitive to changes in blood flow. Even a partial blockage can cause visual changes. These changes may occur long before an actual stroke.

Important: Small clots that cause visual changes often dissolve on their own. Symptoms disappear—but the stroke risk still is there. Also, if you're having a stroke, you may not be aware of any symptom—an onlooker may be the one to alert you to a shift in behavior.

What to do: Get to an emergency room, even if the symptom is fleeting.

Treatment: Patients with clots (or a history of getting them) usually are treated with clot-dissolving (or clot-preventing) therapies. These include aspirin, *heparin*, *warfarin* or *tissue plasminogen activator* (TPA).

A procedure called *carotid endarterectomy* may be recommended for patients with large amounts of plaque in the carotid arteries. Fatty buildups in these arteries, which run from the neck to the brain, increase the risk for subsequent strokes. A test called the *carotid doppler* can be used to detect and measure the plaque.

SWARMS OF FLOATERS OR FLASHING LIGHTS

What it may mean: We all see drifting specks, or "floaters," from time to time. They occur when the clear jelly inside the eyeball (the vitreous humor) releases strands of cells that are briefly visible.

Occasional floaters are harmless—but a dramatic swarm of floaters or flashing lights can indicate a developing retinal tear or detachment, which, without immediate surgery, can cause blindness.

Causes: The retina, a light-sensitive structure at the back of the eye, can separate from the blood vessels behind it. This often happens when the vitreous humor leaks through a small tear in the retina, weakening the supportive bonds. A tear in the retina may be caused by age-related changes, trauma or extreme nearsightedness. The longer the retina remains detached, the less oxygen it receives—and the greater the risk for subsequent blindness.

What to do: See your ophthalmologist promptly—the sooner, the better. Don't wait longer than 24 hours.

Treatment: Surgery to repair the tear often is effective, but it can take months for vision to improve—and some people don't ever fully regain their normal vision.

Note: A swarm of floaters also can be caused by bleeding in the eye due to other conditions, such as abnormal blood vessel growth. This usually occurs in patients with diabetes, hypertension or sickle-cell disease.

How Brain Scientist Jill Bolte Taylor Came Back from a Stroke

Jill Bolte Taylor, PhD, a neuroanatomist affiliated with the Indiana University School of Medicine in Indianapolis. She is a national spokesperson for the Harvard Brain Tissue Resource Center, which collects human brain tissue for research. The author of *My Stroke of Insight: A Brain Scientist's Personal Journey* (Plume), she was named one of *Time* magazine's 100 Most Influential People in the World for 2008.

In 1996, Jill Bolte Taylor, PhD, a 37-year-old brain scientist, had a severe hemorrhagic (bleeding) stroke in the left hemisphere of her brain.

Taylor's cognitive abilities degenerated rapidly in the hours following the stroke. Bleeding affected the motor cortex (paralyzing her right arm)...the sensory cortex (making it difficult for her to see or hear)...and the brain's language centers (making it difficult for her to speak).

After struggling to call for help, she was taken to the hospital, where she underwent surgery two-and-a-half weeks later to remove a golf ball–sized blood clot in her brain.

Today, Taylor is completely recovered—all of her physical, cognitive and emotional abilities are intact. Her eight-year recovery refutes the widely held belief that if a stroke survivor doesn't regain a particular ability within six months, it will never be regained.

We recently spoke with Taylor, a neuroanatomist (a scientist specializing in the anatomy of the brain) who lectures widely about her stroke recovery. *The strategies she shared also can be used by all those who have had a debilitating ischemic stroke (in which a blood clot stops blood supply to an area of the brain) or any severe brain injury...*

STEP 1: MOVE TO RECOVER

People who survive a stroke often experience crushing fatigue due to the damage that occurs to brain cells (neurons)—this affects their energy levels and abilities to process information. Simple tasks, such as changing the position of your body or even opening your eyes, are extraordinarily difficult. But the same activities that restore physical strength also force individual neurons to reconnect and communicate with one another—a process that is essential for post-stroke neurological recovery.

Helpful: Any physical activity is beneficial—even basic movements, such as standing up or sitting down.

Important: When you feel rested and capable of expending the necessary energy, you should push yourself to do more and more physically each day. As I gained strength, I progressed to trying more difficult activities, such as standing at the sink and doing dishes.

STEP 2: ESCAPE THE MENTAL NOISE

Neurons that are damaged by a stroke are unable to process normal stimuli, such as bright lights or the sound of a television. As a result, visual or auditory distractions may be interpreted by the brain as mental "noise." Saturating the brain with such stimuli may make it much harder for the neurons to recover and may impede the retention of new information.

Helpful: After any kind of stroke or other brain trauma, alternate periods of sleep with briefer periods (about 20 minutes) of learning and cognitive challenges (such as those described below). Periods of sleep (as much as needed until waking up naturally) allow the brain to assimilate information that is gleaned during periods of wakefulness.

STEP 3: WORK THE MIND

The brain has remarkable "plasticity" (the ability to form new connections between the surviving neurons). After a stroke, if there is damage to the brain areas that control movement, sensory perceptions and cognition, you need to challenge these areas.

Examples...

- **Multiple-choice questions.** My mother, who was my primary caregiver, understood that asking "yes" or "no" questions didn't force me to think hard enough. That's why she asked me multiple-choice questions—for example, did I want minestrone soup or a grilled cheese sandwich? Each question forced me to relearn words.
- **Simple puzzles.** If you've had a serious stroke, putting together a simple jigsaw puzzle may be a huge challenge. You might not recognize shapes or colors. You might not have the dexterity to put the pieces together. But doing such a puzzle is a superb exercise because it forces you to work different parts of the brain at the same time.
- **Reading.** It's among the hardest tasks because, for many stroke patients, the entire concept of letters and words is lost—temporarily for some stroke survivors, but permanently for others. I had to relearn everything from scratch—that the squiggles that make up letters have names...that combinations of letters make sounds...and also that combinations of sounds make words.

Helpful: I started with children's picture books, which would be appropriate for most stroke patients who are relearning to read.

STEP 4: THE SIMPLEST STEPS

Healthy people can't begin to comprehend how complicated things seem after a stroke. When I first started walking, for example, I didn't understand the concept of sidewalk cracks. Each time I saw one, I had to stop and analyze whether it was important.

Helpful: Caregivers need to break down tasks to the simplest levels. For example, a stroke patient might not understand how to sit up in bed. He/she might need to spend days just learning how to shift body weight. In my case, I had to learn to simply hold an eating utensil before I could imagine raising it to my mouth.

STEP 5: FOCUS ON ABILITIES

When you've had a stroke, the extent of your disabilities can be overwhelming. It took me eight years before I was fully recovered. Patients can easily get frustrated and quit trying. At that point, if a patient is not aware of what recovery step needs to be taken next, he may never actually take that next step. It's normal for a stroke survivor to reach a recovery plateau, to continue to learn, then hit another plateau. There are many plateaus along the way.

Helpful: Even if progress seems exceptionally slow, remind a person who has had a stroke of the smallest successes—it may be something as simple as once again being able to hold a fork securely.

If you are the stroke survivor, use small triumphs as inspiration. In my case, it was embarrassing to drool in front of strangers, but I reminded myself that I had managed to swallow.

After my stroke, I never imagined that I would regain enough of my abilities to return to a career as a scientist and teacher. I've managed to do both—in fact, at the same level and intensity. My stroke recovery gave me an opportunity to start my life again.

■ ■ ■ ■

Aggressive Blood Pressure Control Helps Stroke Patients

Hemorrhagic strokes affect about 60,000 people in the US every year—and up to 50% of these strokes are fatal. In a recent study of 404 stroke patients, half the stroke victims had systolic pressure (the top number) lowered to 180 by intravenous drugs—and half had it reduced to 140. Patients whose blood pressure was treated more aggressively had about one-third less bleeding, and the treatment caused no major side effects. Further research is needed.

Philip Gorelick, MD, is neurology chief at University of Illinois Medical Center at Chicago, and chairman of the International Stroke Conference 2008.

■ ■ ■ ■

Exercise and Diet Better Than Surgery

In a study of patients with carotid stenosis (a narrowing of one of the main arteries that supply blood to the brain) but no symptoms of the disease, 96% of the patients had only a 1% risk for stroke (as determined by ultrasound probes that detect small blood clots or plaque that may break loose).

Implication: Because carotid surgery or stenting (use of a tube to prop open an artery) carries a 5% risk for stroke or death, most patients fare better with exercise, a healthful diet and medication.

J. David Spence, MD, director, Stroke Prevention & Atherosclerosis Research Center, Robarts Research Institute, University of Western Ontario, London, Canada.

■ ■ ■ ■

Secondhand Smoke Danger

In a recent study of 1,209 women, those who had never smoked but had been exposed to secondhand smoke at least one day a week (15 minutes daily) during a 10-year period were 67% more likely to develop peripheral artery disease (PAD)—narrowing of the peripheral arteries, commonly in the legs—than those who were never exposed. Secondhand smoke is likely to have a similar effect on men.

Theory: Carbon monoxide, nicotine, as well as other harmful substances produced by cigarette smoke can cause atherosclerosis (fatty deposits in the arteries).

Frank Hu, MD, PhD, professor of nutrition and epidemiology, Harvard University School of Public Health, Boston.

Two Drugs that Prevent *And* Treat Stroke

Jonathan Friedman, MD, associate professor, surgery, neuroscience and experimental therapeutics, Texas A&M Health Science Center College of Medicine, associate dean of the College of Medicine, Bryan/College Station campus, and director, Texas Brain and Spine Institute.
Lancet Neurology.

Two recent studies find that *acetaminophen* and statins can be of great benefit in either preventing or treating stroke.

In the first study, statin use seemed to be correlated with a lower risk of having a first stroke, according to a group of French researchers.

Meanwhile, another team in the Netherlands found that patients with a body temperature ranging from normal (98.6°F) to 102.2°F who received acetaminophen soon after the onset of a stroke fared better than patients who did not receive the drug.

Both studies were published in the journal *Lancet Neurology.*

BACKGROUND

Prior studies have suggested that the use of cholesterol-lowering statins—which include the blockbusters Crestor, Lipitor and Zocor—can cut the risk for stroke for certain patients.

STATIN STUDY

In this study, French researchers reviewed 24 studies involving more than 165,000 patients. They found that for every 39 milligram per deciliter decrease in LDL ("bad") cholesterol brought about by using statins, the risk of stroke fell by about 21%, compared to people who did not take these drugs.

The data also suggests that statin use slows the formation of blockages in the carotid arteries, two large blood vessels of the neck that supply the brain with blood.

"It crystallizes the fact that there's a direct relationship between lowering LDL and lowering the risk of stroke," said Jonathan Friedman, MD, an associate professor of surgery and of neuroscience and experimental therapeutics at the Texas A&M Health Science Center College of Medicine. "It's not just a matter of putting patients at risk for stroke on a statin and considering that a success, but actually being aggressive about lowering LDL and monitoring and making sure the response is as significant as you can expect. The amount that you lower the LDL actually matters. That wasn't so obvious to a lot of us," he said.

ACETAMINOPHEN STUDY

The second study focused on the pain reliever acetaminophen—best known in the United States under the brand name Tylenol.

BACKGROUND

According to background information in the study, many patients having a stroke experience fever, and they tend to have poorer recovery.

"The theory is that certain cells in the brain are not getting enough blood flow, and if the temperature of the body is high, then the metabolic rate of the cells is high, and they need more blood and oxygen—or they will die," Dr. Friedman explained. "If the person is cool, then perhaps the metabolism will slow down and [the brain cells] could live longer."

Currently, guidelines recommend using acetaminophen or a related drug in patients whose temperature is above 99.5°F, although, according to the authors, there has been little evidence to show that this actually improves outcomes.

STUDY DETAILS

For this study, 1,400 patients were randomly assigned to receive either acetaminophen or a placebo.

The therapy was started within 12 hours of symptoms of an ischemic stroke (the most common kind, caused by a blood clot that blocks a blood vessel in the brain) or intracerebral hemorrhage (when a blood vessel in the brain breaks and bleeds within the brain tissue).

Although giving acetaminophen did not significantly benefit the bulk of patients, 40% of patients with body temperatures ranging from normal to 102.2°F did benefit significantly, versus only 31% of those receiving a placebo.

RECOMMENDATIONS

The study authors warned that acetaminophen should not be dispensed to all patients having a stroke. And even the finding that the drug benefits those with a certain body temperature needs to be confirmed, they added.

Dr. Friedman agreed, and said that many doctors are already providing fever-relieving medicines to stroke patients who need it.

"I do not believe that most clinicians are using acetaminophen in the short term with all patients who have stroke, [although] most physicians feel that avoiding fever in people with stroke is important, and we would use acetaminophen in those who have a fever greater than 37.5°Celsius [99.5°F]," Dr. Friedman said. "But, we lack much data on that issue, and we definitely don't give acetaminophen to every patient with a stroke."

info For more information on the types of stroke, visit the Web site of the Mayo Clinic, *www.mayoclinic.com,* and search "types of stroke."

■ ■ ■ ■

Amazing! Flu Shots May Protect Against Blood Clots

With deep vein thrombosis (DVT), a blood clot that forms in a vein can be fatal if it breaks loose and travels through the circulatory system to the heart and then into the lungs.

Recent study: When 727 people who had suffered DVT episodes were compared with 727 people without the condition, those who had gotten a flu shot during the previous 12 months were 26% less likely to develop DVT.

Joseph Emmerich, MD, PhD, professor of vascular medicine, University Paris Descartes, Paris, France.

URGENT: What Every Woman Must Know About Deadly Blood Clots

Suman Rathbun, MD, director of the vascular medicine fellowship program and the noninvasive vascular laboratories at University of Oklahoma Health Sciences Center in Oklahoma City. She is the principal investigator for numerous studies on blood clots, a trustee of the Society of Vascular Medicine and an editorial board member for *Vascular Medicine*.

Every year, more Americans die from preventable blood clots than from breast cancer, AIDS and traffic accidents combined. Many people are not aware of this gigantic health threat. The problem starts when a blood clot forms in a large vein deep inside the body, usually in the calf or, less commonly, in the pelvis or abdomen. This is called a deep vein thrombosis (DVT). It can cause severe pain, swelling and permanent blood vessel damage that make it difficult to walk.

The greater danger: In some cases, part of the DVT breaks off...travels through the veins to the heart...and from there moves into the lungs. This is called a pulmonary embolism (PE). It can impede blood flow to the lungs, sometimes blocking it completely. In about 10% of cases, a PE causes death within one hour.

Risk for a DVT rises with age because valves in the veins, which help keep blood flowing, become less efficient. Primarily because of hormonal factors, some women are at higher risk than men.

A DVT most often forms when two or more of these conditions exist...

• **Damage to the inner lining of the vein,** which hinders blood flow.

• **Sluggish blood flow through a deep vein,** which allows blood to pool and gives it more time to clot.

• **A genetic disorder that causes excessive clotting.**

There are various causes for each of these conditions. *The more of the following risk factors you have, the more important it is to take steps to protect yourself...*

• **Recent surgery.** The more invasive the surgical procedure, the higher the risk for vein damage and the more blood-clotting proteins the body produces in an attempt to heal. Also, the longer a person remains sedentary after surgery, the more sluggish circulation becomes.

Reason: During normal activity, such as walking, leg muscles contract and help pump blood onward. When mobility is curtailed, blood stagnates.

Procedures linked with especially elevated DVT risk include major gynecologic surgery, such as hysterectomy due to cancer...some other cancer surgeries, particularly ovarian and pancreatic...and orthopedic surgery, such as hip or knee replacement.

Self-defense: Before surgery, ask your doctor what precautions will be taken to prevent a DVT. You may be given an anticoagulant (orally or by injection) while recovering in the hospital and perhaps for up to four weeks after discharge. You may wear sequential compression devices—inflatable cuffs placed around the lower legs to improve blood flow—before, during and/or after surgery.

Important: Follow instructions on how much and what type of postsurgical physical activity to do.

• **Leg injury.** Recent research reveals that even a slight injury, such as an ankle sprain or a torn muscle, increases DVT risk. Microscopic damage to small blood vessels can cause deep veins to narrow...swollen tissues and inactivity can slow blood flow.

Self-defense: To reduce swelling and promote healing after an injury, elevate the leg and apply an ice pack for 15 minutes every two to three hours for one to three days. After a day or two, with your doctor's okay, do gentle stretches to improve blood flow.

•**Being overweight and/or having a sedentary lifestyle.** Excess body weight is linked with leptin, a clot-promoting hormone produced by fat cells. Extra weight may be even more risky for women than for men because women's fat cells contain more estrogen—and this hormone also increases clotting. Lack of physical activity compounds the risk because it contributes to obesity and sluggish blood flow.

Self-defense: Ask your doctor for weight-loss and exercise advice.

•**Cardiovascular disease (CVD).** Various types of CVD involve blood vessel blockages and/or inflammation that can impair blood flow and increase clotting. Heart failure, in which the heart's pumping is insufficient, allows blood to back up in the veins. CVD patients who have a pacemaker or an implantable cardioverter defibrillator are at greater risk for clots because these devices can irritate vein walls.

Self-defense: If necessary, take drugs as prescribed to lower blood pressure and/or cholesterol. Don't smoke—it adds to CVD risk.

•**Genetic disorder.** Inherited disorders can cause blood to clot excessively. The most common, which affects up to 5% of Americans, is *factor V Leiden* (the V stands for "five").

Clue: A history of two or more miscarriages—because clots in the placenta can block the blood flow that the fetus needs to survive.

Self-defense: Ask your doctor about blood testing if a close relative has a clotting disorder ...you have a history of DVT...or you had multiple miscarriages.

•**Pregnancy**...birth control pills or patch... hormone-replacement therapy (HRT). Blood tends to clot more during pregnancy, perhaps to minimize bleeding during childbirth. Because estrogen promotes clotting, estrogen-based contraceptives (such as the Pill or patch) or HRT (used to relieve menopausal symptoms) increase DVT risk twofold for the average woman—and tenfold or more for a woman with a clotting disorder.

Self-defense: During pregnancy, stay active and wear knee-high support hose (sold in drugstores). If you use an oral contraceptive or a patch, ask your doctor if you should switch to a low-dose pill or an estrogen-free contraceptive, such as an intrauterine device (IUD).

If you are considering HRT, first get tested for a clotting disorder if you have a family history of blood clots or meet the testing criteria above. If you're already on HRT, use the lowest effective dose.

•**Air travel or long-distance car trips.** Spending hours virtually immobilized in the seat of an airplane or a car slows blood flow.

Self-defense: Wiggle your toes and flex your feet every few minutes. Every two hours, get out of the car or stroll the airplane aisles for several minutes. If you have a history of DVT, walk every half-hour.

Information: Venous Disease Coalition, 303-989-0500, *www.venousdiseasecoalition.org.*

■ **More from Dr. Rathbun...**

How to Spot a Clot

Deep vein thrombosis (DVT)—a clot in a deep vein—may appear suddenly or over a few days. *See your doctor today if you have any of these symptoms in one leg (or less commonly, in the pelvis or abdomen)...*

•**Pain, tenderness, swelling and/or a hardened area over a vein.**

•**Red or bluish discoloration of the skin.**

•**Unusual warmth in the skin.**

Pulmonary embolism (PE)—a clot that travels to the lungs—can be fatal. *Seek emergency care if you have any of the following...*

•**Sudden severe coughing** (with or without bloody phlegm).

•**Sharp chest pain that worsens with a deep breath.**

•**Severe shortness of breath.**

•**Racing pulse.**

•**Severe light-headedness or fainting.**

■ ■ ■ ■

Better Stroke Recovery

In a recent study of 63 patients who had suffered an ischemic stroke (caused by a blood clot), one group received an intravenous (IV) treatment to dissolve blood clots, while the other received the IV treatment and additional therapy, such as angioplasty (inserting a balloon to open a blockage in a coronary artery).

Result: Only 12% of those in the combination therapy group died within 90 days of the stroke compared with 40% in the IV treatment group.

If a family member suffers an ischemic stroke: Seek immediate treatment at a specialized stroke center, where advanced therapies for acute ischemic stroke are available. To find a stroke center near you, consult the National Stroke Association, 800-787-6537, *www.stroke.org.*

Adnan I. Qureshi, MD, executive director, Zeenat Qureshi Stroke Research Center, University of Minnesota, Minneapolis.

■ ■ ■ ■

Vitamin E Lowers Blood Clot Risk by 44%

Blood thinners, such as *warfarin* (Coumadin), help reduce the formation of blood clots deep inside veins—important because besides the pain, there is the risk of a clot traveling to the lungs or other organs, which can be dangerous, even fatal. However, if you have been clear of blood clots for four to six months, there are natural substances that you can take to help prevent future clots. In a study of nearly 40,000 women conducted by Harvard researchers, those with a history of blood clots who took 600 IU of vitamin E every other day had a 44% lower risk of developing a deep vein clot. Vitamin E has a natural blood-thinning effect, as does *nattokinase*, an enzyme found in the soy food natto and available as a supplement. Talk with your doctor about managing your condition long-term with natural supplements.

Mark A. Stengler, ND, naturopathic physician in private practice, La Jolla, California...and adjunct associate clinical professor at the National College of Natural Medicine, Portland, Oregon...author of many books and the *Bottom Line/Natural Healing* newsletter.

■ ■ ■ ■

Study Helps You Recover Faster From Stroke

About 40% of stroke patients eventually develop depression.

New research: In a one-year study, 176 stroke patients received the antidepressant *escitalopram* (Lexapro), a placebo or problem-solving therapy (a form of talk therapy designed for older adults).

Result: In the placebo group, 22% developed depression versus 12% in the talk therapy group and 8.5% who received escitalopram.

If you have suffered a stroke: Ask your doctor if treatment to prevent depression would benefit you.

Robert G. Robinson, MD, professor and head of psychiatry, University of Iowa Carver College of Medicine, Iowa City.

■ ■ ■ ■

Fun Stroke Rehab Program

A virtual-reality program makes stroke rehabilitation more fun. Patients wearing goggles see bugs flying nearby. When they successfully "smack" them, the bugs move farther away, improving the patients' range of motion.

University of Central Florida.

■ ■ ■ ■

Physical Therapy Helps Stroke Patients Improve for Years

Even two to three years after their strokes, patients still can learn to use undamaged areas of the brain to perform tasks, especially if their physical therapy includes long-term, supervised walking on a treadmill. Physical therapy typically is prescribed for only 30 to 60 days following a stroke because, until recently, it was believed that patients could make significant improvements only within that time frame.

Daniel F. Hanley, MD, department of neurology, Johns Hopkins University School of Medicine, Baltimore, and leader of a study published in *Stroke.*

Tea Helps Lower Stroke Risk Up to 21%

David Liebeskind, MD, associate clinical professor of neurology, University of California, Los Angeles.

Lenore Arab, PhD, professor, medicine and biological chemistry, University of California, Los Angeles.

Ralph L. Sacco, MD, chairman, department of neurology, University of Miami Miller School of Medicine, and spokesman, American Stroke Association.

International Stroke Conference, San Diego.

Here's some good news for java junkies and tea lovers alike: Two recent studies suggest that both beverages may lower your stroke risk.

As coffee drinking increases, the prevalence of stroke decreases, said David Liebeskind, MD, author of the coffee study and an associate clinical professor of neurology at the University of California, Los Angeles.

THE COFFEE STUDY

Dr. Liebeskind evaluated the association between coffee drinking and stroke by looking at data from the Third National Health and Nutrition Examination Survey, taken 1988–1994. He zeroed in on the 9,384 adults older than 40 who were coffee drinkers. Of those, 500 (5%) had been told by their doctor that they'd had a stroke. And 2,793 (29.8%) had self-reported stroke symptoms or a mini-stroke, also known as a transient ischemic attack.

When he looked at stroke prevalence and coffee drinking, Dr. Liebeskind found that the more coffee the adults drank, the less likely they were to have a stroke or a mini-stroke. Those who drank six or more cups a day, he found, had a stroke prevalence of 2.9%, whereas those who drank just one or two cups daily had a stroke prevalence of 5%.

The finding was presented at the International Stroke Conference in San Diego.

PREVIOUS COFFEE STUDY

This latest coffee study comes on the heels of a study published in *Circulation* that found long-term coffee consumption is linked with a lower stroke risk in women who don't smoke. To come to that conclusion, researchers followed more than 83,000 women who enrolled in the study in 1980 with no history of stroke, heart disease, diabetes or cancer.

They found stroke risk was 20% lower in those drinking four or more cups a day and 12% lower in those who had coffee five to seven times a week.

TEA STUDY

Tea drinkers may have reason to enjoy their brew, too, according to another study presented at the San Diego meeting.

Those who drink more than three cups a day had a 21% lower risk of stroke than those who sipped less than a cup daily, said study author Lenore Arab, PhD, a professor of medicine and biological chemistry at the University of California, Los Angeles.

She conducted a meta-analysis, pooling the results of nine published studies involving 4,378 strokes among more than 194,000 people, many from Asia. Black tea and green tea were studied, and it was typically caffeinated.

Increased tea consumption was associated with a decreased risk for stroke. "We see it consistently in every study," Dr. Arab said. The Unilever Lipton Institute of Tea, a research and development arm of Lipton Tea, funded the research.

Exactly how tea might reduce stroke risk isn't clear, she said. Anti-inflammatory compounds, or the amino acid theanine, both found in black and green tea, may be responsible for protecting the brain.

EXPERT COMMENTARY

The tea study is stronger than the coffee study, said Ralph Sacco, MD, chairman of the department of neurology at the University of Miami Miller School of Medicine.

The coffee study research was like a snapshot in time, asking people about coffee habits at a given point, he said.

According to Dr. Sacco, it would be better to do a study in which participants are followed over time to determine if there is a link between coffee drinking and stroke. "I don't feel this study is strong enough to recommend people drink coffee to reduce the risk of stroke," he said.

info To learn more about reducing the risk for stroke, visit the National Stroke Association Web site, *www.stroke.org,* and click on "Prevention."

■ ■ ■ ■

Walking Reduces Risk for Heart Palpitations and Stroke

About 20% of people over age 65 experience episodes of the irregular heart rhythm, atrial fibrillation (AF).

Danger: This temporary arrhythmia increases risk for stroke.

Study: More than 5,400 people age 65 or older without AF were followed for 12 years. At the end of that time, those who had walked 60 blocks a week (about three miles) on average were 44% less likely to have developed AF than those who had walked less than five blocks per week. Risk reduction was proportional to exercise.

Conclusion: Even modest regular exercise reduces risk.

Circulation, 6720 Bertner Ave., Houston, TX 77030.

■ ■ ■ ■

New Test for Stroke and Heart Attack Risk

The PLAC test is the only blood test cleared by the FDA to aid in assessing risk for coronary heart disease and ischemic stroke (when a blood vessel to the brain is blocked). The test measures the level of *Lp-PLA2,* an enzyme associated with inflammation of the arteries. The PLAC test should be used in addition to traditional risk factor assessment to identify moderate or high-risk patients for a heart attack or stroke.

Robert L. Wolfert, PhD, executive vice president and chief scientific officer, diaDexus, Inc., San Francisco.

■ ■ ■ ■

Men Underestimate Stroke Risk

When 296 men with high blood pressure (a stroke risk factor) guessed their stroke risk, 78% of them significantly underestimated it.

Theory: Many men—and women—consider themselves less likely than their peers to develop health problems, especially medical conditions linked to risk factors that can be controlled, such as smoking and excess weight.

If you have high blood pressure: Ask your doctor to assess your stroke risk.

Benjamin J. Powers, MD, assistant professor of medicine, Duke University Medical Center, Durham, North Carolina.

■ ■ ■ ■

Are You Aspirin-Resistant?

When researchers tracked 653 stroke patients who took aspirin to prevent a second stroke, they found that 20% of them were "aspirin-resistant"—that is, taking daily low-dose aspirin did not help prevent the patients' blood platelets from sticking together.

Theory: In some individuals, genetic factors may reduce aspirin's anticlotting effects.

If your doctor recommends daily aspirin: Ask him/her if you should receive a blood test for aspirin resistance.

Francis M. Gengo, PharmD, associate professor of pharmacy and neurology, University at Buffalo School of Pharmacy and Pharmaceutical Sciences & DENT Neurologic Institute, Buffalo.

■ ■ ■ ■

Restless Legs Syndrome (RLS) May Lead to Stroke

In a study of 3,433 adults, those with RLS (a neurological disorder that causes leg restlessness while awake and involuntary leg movements during sleep) were twice as likely to have a stroke or heart disease as those without RLS.

Theory: The frequent leg movements in RLS patients may cause spikes in blood pressure and heart rate that, over time, may lead to cardiovascular disease.

If you have RLS: Ask your doctor whether you need iron supplements to correct an iron deficiency (a common cause of RLS) or RLS medication.

John W. Winkelman, MD, PhD, assistant professor of psychiatry, Harvard Medical School, Boston.

15

Women's Health

Women 30% Less Apt to Get Best Stroke Treatment

Gender does indeed make a difference when it comes to suffering a stroke, recent research has shown.

Not only can stroke show itself in slightly different fashion in women than it typically does in men, but women also don't get the preferred treatment for stroke as often as men do.

Those are two of several findings on women and stroke that were presented at the International Stroke Conference in San Diego.

DIFFERENCES IN STROKE TREATMENT

In one study, Michigan State University researchers reported that women admitted to hospitals with the symptoms of stroke were less likely to be given *tissue plasminogen activator* (tPA), which was approved to treat stroke by the US Food and Drug Administration in 1996.

Study author Archit Bhatt, MD, MPH, pooled the results of 18 studies published in medical journals between 1995 and 2008. "Women were 30% less likely to have tPA compared to men," he said.

He analyzed data on more than 21,000 people who were given tPA, which is administered intravenously. When he looked just at people who got to the hospital within three hours of the start of their stroke symptoms—the crucial time window within which tPA must be given—men were still more likely to be given the clot buster, he said. In this subgroup, "women were 19% less likely to get tPA than the men," Dr. Bhatt said.

Archit Bhatt, MD, MPH, researcher, department of neurology and ophthalmology, Michigan State University, East Lansing.

Louise D. McCullough, MD, PhD, director, stroke research and education, University of Connecticut Health Center and Stroke Center at Hartford Hospital, Hartford, Connecticut.

Lynda Lisabeth, PhD, MPH, assistant professor, epidemiology, University of Michigan, Ann Arbor.

Mark P. Goldberg, MD, professor, neurology, Washington University School of Medicine, and attending physician, stroke service, Barnes-Jewish Hospital, St. Louis, Missouri.

More research is needed to figure out what triggers this gender gap, he added.

TIME IT TAKES TO GET MEDICAL HELP

However, the gender gap in treatment might be narrowing in some ways, said Louise D. McCullough, MD, PhD. Dr. McCullough is director of stroke research and education at the University of Connecticut Health Center and the Stroke Center at Hartford Hospital.

Though some experts have found that women put off getting medical help when a stroke is suspected, Dr. McCullough found differently in her research. She reviewed data on 445 people, 52% of them women, who got to the hospital within six hours of the start of symptoms. And she found no difference between men and women in the time it took to get medical help.

DIFFERENCES IN STROKE SYMPTOMS

Another study provided a possible explanation as to why treatment sometimes differs between genders.

University of Michigan researchers found that women are more likely to have "nontraditional" symptoms, such as numbness, visual disturbances or dizziness. Lynda Lisabeth, PhD, MPH, an assistant professor of epidemiology at the University of Michigan, targeted 480 people who came to the University of Michigan Hospital between January 2005 and December 2007 for a stroke or a mini-stroke.

She asked all of them about their symptoms. "Among women, 52% reported at least one nontraditional symptom, compared to 44% of men," she said.

The most common nontraditional symptom they reported was an altered mental state, such as confusion or unconsciousness. The finding that women tend to have nontraditional symptoms did not reach statistical significance, she said. But Dr. Lisabeth still thinks that awareness of the possibility of nontraditional symptoms might influence people to seek help sooner.

EXPERT REACTION

Some of the news on gender differences—specifically that nontraditional symptoms might be more common in women—was surprising to Mark P. Goldberg, MD, a professor of neurology at Washington University and a physician at Barnes-Jewish Hospital, both in St. Louis.

Knowing about such research should help the public, and doctors, become more aware, he said. "The idea that mental confusion is more common in women may change the way emergency medical service personnel are educated, for instance, with doctors alerting them to the possibility," he said.

info To learn more, visit the Web site of the National Stroke Association, *www.stroke.org,* and click on "Women and Stroke."

■ ■ ■ ■

Surgery Alert for Women

Patients often receive unfractionated heparin to prevent postsurgical blood clots. Sometimes this leads to *heparin*-induced thrombocytopenia (HIT), a decrease in platelet count that paradoxically increases clotting risk.

Recent finding: HIT is more common in women than in men.

Self-defense: Studies show that HIT risk is lower with low-molecular-weight heparin or the anticoagulant *fondaparinux* (Arixtra). Discuss the issue with your doctor before surgery.

Theodore Warkentin, MD, professor of pathology and molecular medicine, McMaster University, Hamilton, Ontario, and leader of a study of 290 people, published in *Blood.*

■ ■ ■ ■

Heart Surgery Riskier for Women

Women have a greater risk than men of dying after heart surgery.

Possible explanation: Transfusions increase the likelihood of potentially fatal postsurgical infection—and because of their lower blood volume and red blood cell count, women are much more likely to receive blood transfusions.

Safer: If you need surgery, request leukoreduced blood (from which white blood cells have been removed). This type of blood carries less risk for infection.

Neil Blumberg, MD, professor of laboratory medicine, University of Rochester Medical Center, Rochester, New York, and coauthor of a study of 380 people, published in *Journal of Women's Health.*

Good News for Women With Varicose Veins

Andrew Kwak, MD, clinical assistant professor of interventional radiology and director and founder of the laser vein treatment program at University of Pennsylvania School of Medicine in Philadelphia. He also is in private practice as director of the LUMEN Laser Center in Bryn Mawr, Pennsylvania. *www.lumenlasercenter.com.*

Far more than just a cosmetic problem, varicose veins can cause pain that interferes with daily activities—and may lead to serious health problems, such as blood clots and uncontrolled bleeding.

Good news: New treatments are safe and effective...involve minimal discomfort and downtime...and often are covered by insurance.

CONTRIBUTING FACTORS

Normally, veins carry blood back to the heart quickly, helped by tiny interior one-way valves. However, when circulation through a vein is too slow, the vein becomes enlarged, twisted and engorged with blood—a varicose vein. As the vein worsens and/or more varicose veins form, the leg may become painful and swollen. (Spider veins are similar but much smaller and do not cause pain or other health problems.)

Genetics determine in large measure who gets varicose veins. Women are most susceptible because the female hormone estrogen weakens and relaxes vein walls. Up to 25% of women and 15% of men have varicose veins. *Factors that can worsen the symptoms include...*

- **Menstrual cycle**—estrogen levels are highest midway between periods.
- **Pregnancy**—estrogen rises. Also, the growing fetus presses on a big abdominal vein, slowing blood flow out of the legs.
- **Hormone therapy or birth control pills**—estrogen is the culprit.
- **Hot weather**—heat causes blood vessels to dilate.
- **Prolonged standing**—gravity encourages blood to pool in legs.
- **Inactivity**—the leg muscles don't contract enough to help pump blood onward.
- **Being overweight**—this increases gravity's effects.
- **Leg injury**—veins may be damaged by any type of accident.
- **Aging**—older vein valves are more prone to malfunction.

SELF-HELP GUIDELINES

Varicose veins that do not cause discomfort or worrisome symptoms do not need to be treated—though as a general precaution, you should bring them to your doctor's attention at your next checkup. *To improve circulation and minimize symptoms...*

- **Exercise for at least 30 minutes daily.** Include a lower-body workout, such as cycling, swimming or walking.
- **Wear compression hose** (sold at drugstores and medical-supply stores). Avoid clothes that are tight at the knees, waist or groin.
- **Elevate legs above heart level** for 15 minutes whenever they ache.
- **When standing or sitting for long periods,** tap your toes vigorously every few minutes to work calf muscles. Take frequent breaks to walk around. Avoid crossing your legs—this position does not cause varicose veins, but it can aggravate symptoms.

TREATMENT OPTIONS

If you experience pain and swelling despite following the self-help guidelines, get medical treatment to close the affected veins. Afterward, your body automatically reroutes blood into healthy veins. Insurance usually covers treatment if self-help measures have failed to relieve symptoms. See a vein specialist—an interventional radiologist, vascular surgeon or dermatologist.

Referrals: American College of Phlebology, 510-346-6800, *www.phlebology.org.*

Treatment options...

- **Endovenous ablation.** For most patients whose varicose veins are moderate to severe, I recommend this new procedure performed with a laser or radio-frequency device. The doctor inserts a tiny tube into the vein, then heat energy from the device permanently seals the vein shut.

Cost: About $2,000 per leg. Advantages can include...

• Success rate of about 95% with low risk for complications (such as a blood clot or excessive bleeding).

• Performed in the doctor's office in about 30 minutes for laser. It may take 60 minutes for radio frequency.

• Requires only local anesthesia.

• Minimal discomfort, managed with nonprescription painkillers.

• Quick recovery—patients return to normal activities immediately and wear compression hose for one to two weeks.

• Good aesthetic results—bruising is minor and temporary, and veins disappear within a few weeks.

• **Sclerotherapy.** This office procedure works on small- to medium-sized varicose veins and requires no anesthesia. The doctor injects veins with a solution that causes scar tissue to form. This closes the vein, which then fades. Some veins must be injected more than once.

Cost: About $300 to $500 per session.

On the horizon: *Microfoam sclerotherapy.* Currently undergoing FDA testing, Varisolve is a foam that is injected into varicose veins, causing them to collapse. Varisolve is a stronger sclerosant able to treat larger and more problematic veins. The procedure may be available within two years.

Recommended: If your doctor suggests an older treatment called *phlebectomy* (vein stripping)—in which a long vein is removed through a series of small incisions—I suggest getting a second opinion. This in-hospital procedure involves more pain and a longer recovery time than today's advanced treatments.

■ **More from Dr. Andrew Kwak...**

Varicose Vein Complications

Watch out for these uncommon but dangerous complications...

• **Skin sores.** The skin around a varicose vein may break down, becoming discolored and hard. Over time, an open sore (ulcer) may form and become infected. If you notice signs of skin breakdown or develop a skin ulcer, see a vein specialist without delay.

• **Blood clot.** A clot in a varicose vein (phlebitis) can make nearby skin hot and tender...create a lump...and cause sudden swelling of the leg. If an associated clot forms in a deep vein, it may break off and travel via the bloodstream to the lungs. Called a pulmonary embolism (PE), this can be fatal. If you suspect a clot in your leg, go to the emergency room. If you have symptoms of PE—chest pain, shortness of breath, light-headedness, bloody cough—call 911.

• **Bleeding.** Due to increased pressure, a varicose vein may bleed profusely from even a minor injury—for instance, if you bang your leg or cut yourself shaving. Immediately elevate the leg above heart level, cover the wound with a clean cloth and apply firm pressure. If bleeding does not stop within a few minutes, call 911—a hemorrhage can be life-threatening.

Breast-Feeding Pumps Up Mom's Heart

Eleanor Bimla Schwarz, MD, assistant professor, medicine, epidemiology, obstetrics, gynecology and reproductive sciences, University of Pittsburgh Center for Research on Health Care, Pittsburgh.

Nieca Goldberg, MD, director, women's heart program, New York University Langone Medical Center, and associate professor, New York University School of Medicine, New York City. She is author of *The Women's Healthy Heart Program* (Ballantine).

Obstetrics & Gynecology.

Breast-feeding isn't just good for baby; it may also boost mom's cardiovascular health as she ages, recent research suggests.

Women in their 60s who had breast-fed for more than 12 months over their life span were nearly 10% less likely to develop cardiovascular disease, and significantly less likely to develop heart disease risk factors, such as high blood pressure, diabetes and high cholesterol, researchers report.

"We found that the longer women breast-feed, the lower their risk of heart attacks, strokes or heart disease," said Eleanor Bimla Schwarz, MD, an assistant professor of medicine, epidemiology, obstetrics, gynecology and reproductive sciences at the University of Pittsburgh Center for Research on Health Care.

Results of the study were published in the journal *Obstetrics & Gynecology*.

BACKGROUND

It's well established that breast-feeding can benefit infant health, yet just 11% of American mothers breast-feed exclusively for the first six months of their babies' lives.

In addition to helping babies, breast-feeding can help women lose pregnancy weight, since breast-feeding helps women burn nearly 500 extra calories a day. Breast-feeding has also been shown to improve glucose tolerance and the metabolism of cholesterol, according to the study.

Although a previous study noted a 23% reduction in heart attack risk in women who had breast-fed for a total of two years or more, it wasn't clear whether breast-feeding for shorter periods would have any long-term impact on a mother's health.

THE STUDY

To assess whether or not breast-feeding could make a difference in cardiovascular health years later, Dr. Schwarz and her colleagues used data from the Women's Health Initiative that included nearly 140,000 postmenopausal women. The average age of the women in the study was 63.

The women provided information on their diets as well as their breast-feeding history. Researchers also collected information on body mass index (BMI, a measurement that takes into account weight and height to gauge total body fat) and the women's medical histories.

All participants sent in an annual medical review during the study. The average time in the study was just under eight years.

THE RESULTS

The study authors found that women who breast-fed for one or more months were less likely to have high blood pressure, diabetes, abnormal cholesterol and cardiovascular disease, but it wasn't until after six months of total breast-feeding time that the trend toward lower heart disease risk became statistically significant, according to Dr. Schwarz.

"Even one or two months is going to improve a woman's heart health, but the longer women breast-fed, the more benefit they got," she said.

After a year of breast-feeding, the odds of having high blood pressure dropped by 12%; the odds of diabetes decreased by 20%; the rates of abnormal cholesterol levels went down by 19%; and the overall risk for cardiovascular disease fell by 9%, compared to women who never breast-fed, according to the study.

IMPLICATIONS

According to Dr. Schwarz, the reason breast-feeding may benefit women even many years later is because it "resets the body after pregnancy." There are certain hormonal and physiologic changes the body expects to go through after pregnancy and when those changes don't happen, that leaves certain body systems in a precarious situation, she said.

Nieca Goldberg, MD, director of the New York University Langone Medical Center Women's Heart Program, said many factors could be at play. "Breast-feeding really mobilizes fat stores and has an impact on cholesterol. It also increases levels of [the hormone] oxytocin, which can relax blood vessels."

STUDIES NEEDED TO CONFIRM LINK

Dr. Goldberg cautioned that the study only showed an association, not a cause-and-effect relationship. It could be that women who choose to breast-feed are women who are healthier in general, she noted.

Dr. Goldberg added that the issue still warrants further study. She said it's important for researchers to look specifically at things women do when they're young and how they might affect heart health.

info To learn more about the benefits of breast-feeding, visit the National Women's Health Information Center Web site, *www.womenshealth.gov/breastfeeding/benefits/*.

Brain-Boosting Nutrients Women Need

JoAnn E. Manson, MD, DrPH, a professor of medicine and women's health at Harvard Medical School and chair of the division of preventive medicine at Brigham and Women's Hospital, both in Boston. She is one of the lead investigators for two highly influential studies on women's health—the Harvard Nurses' Health Study and the Women's Health Initiative. Dr. Manson is author, with Shari Bassuk, ScD, of *Hot Flashes, Hormones and Your Health* (McGraw-Hill).

Certain foods may help ward off subtle age-related cognitive decline or even full-blown dementia, recent research suggests. *Nutrients linked to a clear mind and sharp memory...*

•**Folate.** In studies of people age 70 and older, those with low blood levels of folate had about twice the risk for Alzheimer's disease as those with normal levels. Folate reduces homocysteine, a dietary by-product linked to inflammation, blood clots and small blood vessel damage.

Best: Each day, eat two or more servings of folate-rich dark green leafy or cruciferous vegetables, such as spinach, romaine lettuce, broccoli and Brussels sprouts. As insurance, consider taking a daily multivitamin that provides 400 micrograms of folic acid (synthetic folate).

•**Marine omega-3 fatty acids.** Fish provide the omega-3s *eicosapentaenoic acid* (EPA) and *docosahexaenoic acid* (DHA). Studies show that people who eat fish five or more times weekly are 30% less likely to suffer a stroke than those who rarely eat fish. Frequent fish consumption also is associated with fewer "silent" (symptomless) brain lesions, as seen on imaging tests... and may reduce Alzheimer's risk. Fish oil also improves function of nerve cell membranes and boosts production of brain chemicals that allow nerve cells to communicate.

Wise: Eat salmon, tuna, herring, sardines or mackerel at least twice weekly...or take daily fish oil supplements with 400 milligrams (mg) to 1,000 mg of combined EPA and DHA.

•**Flavonoids.** Oxidation, a chemical reaction that can damage blood vessels, may be a key contributor to brain aging. Antioxidant plant pigments called flavonoids may counteract this—particularly the *anthocyanins* in deep-colored fruits such as berries, cherries and Concord grapes. In animal studies, berry extracts reversed age-related declines in spatial learning and memory as measured by how quickly the animals learned to navigate a maze.

Goal: Eat berries or deep-colored fruit at least two to three times per week.

•**Coffee.** In a study of 7,017 people age 65 and older, women who drank at least three cups of caffeinated coffee or six cups of caffeinated tea per day experienced less decline in memory over four years than those who drank one cup or less. However, caffeine can trigger digestive upset, insomnia and migraine.

Advised: Have no more than four eight-ounce cups of coffee daily.

The alcohol question: Moderate alcohol intake is linked with less cognitive decline—though this may simply reflect that people who already have cognitive problems are less likely to imbibe.

Recommended: Do not start drinking alcohol specifically to prevent cognitive decline. If you already drink, limit consumption to no more than one alcoholic beverage daily.

When Women Should Leave the Multi on the Vitamin Shelf

Sylvia Wassertheil-Smoller, PhD, professor, epidemiology and population health, Albert Einstein College of Medicine, New York City.
Rajat Sethi, PhD, assistant professor, pharmaceutical sciences, Texas A&M Health Science Center, Irma Lerma Rangel College of Pharmacy, Kingsville, Texas.
Andrew Shao, PhD, vice president, scientific and regulatory affairs, Council for Responsible Nutrition, Washington, DC.
Archives of Internal Medicine.

In yet another blow to the dietary supplement industry, researchers find no evidence that multivitamin use helps older women ward off heart disease and cancer, the top two killers of women, respectively.

"Women can be encouraged by the fact that these vitamins seem to do no harm, but they also seem to confer no benefit," said study coauthor Sylvia Wassertheil-Smoller, PhD, a professor of epidemiology and population health at Albert Einstein College of Medicine in New York City. "The kind of vitamins you get from diet is quite different, because foods are very complex and have a lot of chemicals we don't know about that interact with each other. [Eating a varied diet] is not the same as distilling it into a pill. The message is to eat a well-balanced diet, exercise and maintain weight."

BACKGROUND

Other recent studies have suggested that supplement forms of vitamins B, C, D and E, along with folic acid and beta-carotene, don't seem to have cancer-fighting abilities.

And another recent study reported that many healthy children and teenagers may be popping vitamins and mineral supplements they don't need, even while children who may actually need the supplements aren't getting them.

According to background information in the study, which was published in the *Archives of Internal Medicine,* half of Americans regularly use dietary supplements, to the tune of $20 billion a year.

Many people believe multivitamins will prevent chronic conditions, such as cancer and heart disease. Yet "convincing scientific data... are lacking," the researchers stated.

Two exceptions are folic acid use in women of childbearing age to prevent neural tube defects in babies, and avoiding beta-carotene supplements if you're a smoker.

THE STUDY

The researchers looked at 161,808 postmenopausal women participating in the government-sponsored Women's Health Initiative who were followed for about eight years. Some 40% of participants reported using multivitamins.

There appeared to be no association between multivitamin use and risk of breast, colorectal, endometrial, lung or ovarian cancers. There was also no association for cardiovascular disease or overall death.

"There was some hint that stress vitamins, which are mostly high doses of B vitamins, may have been protective for some forms of cardiovascular disease," Dr. Wassertheil-Smoller said.

One factor that was not fully studied was the role of diet. "Most of the women in the study probably did eat a fairly decent diet, meaning we don't yet necessarily know how vitamins affect women eating poorly," Dr. Wassertheil-Smoller said. "The other thing is we didn't measure other things about diet, such as sense of energy and well-being."

EXPERT REACTION

According to Rajat Sethi, PhD, an assistant professor of pharmaceutical sciences at Texas A&M Health Science Center, Irma Lerma Rangel College of Pharmacy in Kingsville, there are a lot of variables associated with this study and a randomized, controlled trial is needed. "There have been a mixture of studies where vitamins indeed have indirectly shown benefit," he said.

And Andrew Shao, PhD, vice president for scientific and regulatory affairs at the Council for Responsible Nutrition in Washington, DC, stated, "Multivitamins, like all other dietary supplements, are meant to be used as part of an overall healthy lifestyle; they are not intended to be magic bullets that will assure the prevention of chronic diseases, like cancer...From a practical standpoint, this study does not change the fact that the majority of consumers could benefit from taking an affordable multivitamin, particularly as the majority of Americans fail to consume the recommended amounts of a variety of essential nutrients established by the Institute of Medicine."

info The Web site of Oregon State University's Linus Pauling Institute has more information on a variety of vitamins at *http://lpi.oregonstate.edu* under "Micronutrient Information Center."

How to Find the Best Multivitamin for You

Alan H. Pressman, DC, PhD, CCN, certified clinical nutritionist, director of Gramercy Health Associates, New York City, and former professor of nutrition research at New York Chiropractic College, Seneca Falls, New York. He hosts the radio show "Healthline" on Air America and is coauthor of *The Complete Idiot's Guide to Vitamins and Minerals* (Alpha).

A daily multivitamin/mineral supplement helps you meet your nutritional needs—but with so many brands available, it's not easy to select one. *What to do...*

- **Choose a multi made especially for women.** Women's multis typically provide extra folic acid, which protects against heart disease, colon cancer and birth defects...and extra bone-building calcium, magnesium and vitamin D.

- **Look for an age-appropriate formula.** Before menopause, it is common for monthly blood loss to deplete the iron that red blood cells need—which is why women's multis often contain iron. Excess iron supplementation can damage organs, however—so if you're post-menopausal and have no diagnosed iron deficiency, it is wise to take an iron-free multi. Some "50+" formulas also provide extra B vitamins because the body's ability to absorb these often declines with age...and/or even higher amounts of calcium and vitamin D.

Good brands: Nature Made Multi for Her and Multi for Her 50+...One A Day Women's and Women's 50+ Advantage.

- **Supplement your supplement.** The daily value (DV)—the government-recommended daily intake—for calcium is 1,000 milligrams (mg) for women ages 19 to 50 and 1,200 mg for women over 50...the DV for magnesium is 400 mg. But many multis provide just a fraction of those DVs—otherwise, the pills would be too big.

Another problem: The DV for vitamin D is 400 international units (IU), an amount that many multis provide—yet experts advise getting 1,000 IU to 2,000 IU of vitamin D to lower risk for osteoporosis, diabetes, heart disease and some cancers.

Best: In addition to a multi, take a supplement that helps make up for these shortfalls, such as Caltrate 600-D Plus Minerals or Schiff Super Calcium-Magnesium...take additional vitamin D if necessary.

■ ■ ■ ■

Chocolate May Be Bad for Your Bones

Older women who ate chocolate daily had an average bone density 3.1% lower than women who ate chocolate less than weekly.

Possible reason: Chocolate contains oxalate, a salt that can hinder calcium absorption...and sugar, which can increase calcium excretion.

Jonathan M. Hodgson, PhD, senior research fellow, Western Australian Institute for Medical Research, Perth, and lead author of a study of 1,001 women, reported in *The American Journal of Clinical Nutrition.*

■ ■ ■ ■

Foods that Fight Wrinkles!

When dietary data for 4,025 women was analyzed in a recent study, those with high intakes of vitamin C and the essential fatty acid linoleic acid had fewer wrinkles than women with lower intakes.

Theory: Vitamin C is an important component in collagen synthesis (which keeps skin supple), and linoleic acid promotes normal skin structure.

For younger-looking skin: Eat vitamin C–rich fruits and vegetables, such as oranges and broccoli, and foods high in linoleic acid, such as soybeans and sunflower oil.

Maeve C. Cosgrove, PhD, nutritional epidemiologist, Unilever Corporate Research, Sharnbrook, Bedfordshire, UK.

■ ■ ■ ■

Should Those with Low Thyroid Avoid Soy?

Not necessarily. Low thyroid hormone (hypothyroidism) should be treated with thyroid medication, as prescribed by your doctor. Soy foods, eaten in moderation, are good sources of protein. Soy does have phytoestrogenic effects—it fools the body into thinking that it has more estrogen, which in turn may slow thyroid hormone production. But that does not mean you should avoid soy altogether—your doctor can help you find the best balance for you.

Erika T. Schwartz, MD, physician in private practice in New York City, a specialist in women's health, and author of four books, including *The Hormone Solution* (Grand Central).

Why ADHD Is Worse for Women

Kathleen G. Nadeau, PhD, director of the Chesapeake ADHD Center of Maryland, Silver Spring, and cofounder of the National Center for Gender Issues in ADHD, Washington, DC. She is coeditor of *Understanding Women with ADHD* (Advantage) and author of 11 other books on adult ADHD. *www.chesapeakeadd.com*.

Largely unheard of a generation or two ago, attention deficit hyperactivity disorder (ADHD) is now a common diagnosis for schoolchildren, especially boys. Recently, however, researchers have discovered that 4% to 8% of adult women may have ADHD—yet most of them have never been diagnosed.

ADHD (also formerly known as attention deficit disorder, or ADD) is a neurological condition that interferes with a person's ability to concentrate, organize daily life and manage time. It can wreak havoc on all areas of life, including health. Unlike a man, a woman may develop worsening symptoms in midlife and beyond due to hormonal changes.

Fortunately, help is available. Once a woman with ADHD is diagnosed and treated, her life tends to improve dramatically.

SIGNS OF ADHD

While everyone feels frazzled at times, the typical woman with ADHD feels almost constantly overwhelmed. *Far more often than average, she...*

- **Feels rushed**...arrives late...inclined to miss deadlines.
- **Procrastinates**...gets distracted...feels like she works frantically all day long but accomplishes little.
- **Has difficulty concentrating** and following directions.
- **Is easily bored**...or becomes so engrossed in an activity that she tends to neglect other responsibilities.
- **Acts impulsively**...blurts out inappropriate remarks...makes hasty decisions.
- **Misplaces things**...forgets errands.
- **Overspends**...pays bills late.
- **Has short-lived friendships** and failed marriages.
- **Is moody**...feels ashamed...feels "different" from other women.

ADHD can be costly in myriad ways. A woman suffers financially if she impulsively buys things she can't afford. She suffers professionally due to her scattershot performance—a recent study found that, in terms of productivity, employees with ADHD do the equivalent of 22 fewer days of work per year than other employees. She suffers socially if friends and family get fed up...and psychologically if her inability to cope erodes her self-esteem.

Her physical health also is at risk—for instance, she may forget her medication or mammogram appointment. Constant stress elevates levels of the hormone cortisol, which can weaken the immune system and contribute to heart disease, digestive disorders, respiratory problems, infertility and fibromyalgia (widespread muscle and joint pain). ADHD even may increase her risk for depression, addiction and/or eating disorders.

WHAT'S WORSE FOR WOMEN

Because girls with ADHD generally are not as disruptive as boys, pediatricians may overlook the disorder in girls. When these girls reach adulthood, their symptoms often are wrongly attributed to depression or anxiety—misdiagnoses that are less common among men.

Gender bias plays a role, too. Women typically are expected to be the family organizers—to plan meals, put away clutter, keep track of everyone's schedule. These tasks are difficult for women with ADHD, in whom the brain's organizational functions are compromised.

Midlife's hormonal changes can worsen a woman's symptoms significantly.

Reason: As estrogen production declines, the brain's receptors for dopamine—a brain chemical associated with happy feelings—become less receptive.

Result: Women who used to manage their ADHD fairly well may have more trouble coping during and after menopause.

Treatment can help—but that requires a diagnosis. *There is no definitive test for ADHD, so diagnosis is based on three criteria...*

- **Symptoms began many years ago.**
- **You have at least several of the symptoms above.**
- **Symptoms are severe enough to significantly affect at least two of the three main areas of life**—home, work, social aspects.

What to do: If you suspect that you have ADHD, consult a mental-health professional who works with adult ADHD patients.

Referrals: Children and Adults with Attention Deficit/Hyperactivity Disorder, 301-306-7070, *www.chadd.org.*

HOW TO COPE

The following strategies make it much easier to live with ADHD...

- **Join a support group.** The Center, A Resource for Women and Girls with AD/HD (888-238-8588, *www.ncgiadd.org*) or find an online group through *www.chadd.org.*
- **Hire a professional organizer to create systems for you for filing paperwork and storing belongings.**

Referrals: National Association of Professional Organizers, 856-380-6828, *www.napo.net/referral.*

- **Set up an automatic bill-paying system for regular expenses,** such as mortgages and car loans, through your bank's Web site.
- **Avoid food additives.** Studies suggest that artificial coloring and preservatives are linked to ADHD.
- **Supplement daily with a vitamin-B complex and with omega-3 fatty acids** (found in fish oil)—these support brain function.
- **Stabilize blood sugar.** Rapid spikes and plunges in blood sugar levels impair concentration. Include protein at every meal...avoid simple carbohydrates (white bread, cookies).
- **Get enough sleep.** Many women with ADHD are sleep-deprived because they get a "second wind" after dinner or lose track of time and stay up too late.

Helpful: Set an alarm to ring each evening to remind you when it's time for bed.

- **Practice stress-reduction techniques to clear your mind.** If it is hard to sit still for meditation or deep breathing, try yoga or tai chi.
- **Try neurofeedback,** which trains you to increase the brain-wave patterns associated with improved focus and concentration.

Referrals: The Biofeedback Certification Institute of America, 866-908-8713, *www.bcia.org.*

MEDICATION OPTIONS

If the above strategies are not sufficient to make life manageable, ask your doctor about the pros and cons of medication. ADHD drugs generally work by regulating levels of the brain chemicals dopamine and/or norepinephrine, which affect parts of the brain that control attention. Medication does not cure ADHD—when the drugs are discontinued, symptoms return.

Stimulants, such as *amphetamine* (Adderall), *methylphenidate* (Ritalin, Concerta) or *lisdexamfetamine* (Vyvanse), are most often prescribed. Fluctuations in estrogen levels may influence the effectiveness of stimulants, so women taking these drugs should be closely monitored. Side effects may include dry mouth, restlessness and high blood pressure.

Another option is an antidepressant. *Atomoxetine* (Strattera) is the first nonstimulant drug approved by the FDA for the treatment of ADHD. Other antidepressants include *bupropion* (Wellbutrin), *venlafaxine* (Effexor) and *desipramine* (Norpramin). Such drugs may be appropriate when anxiety and depression accompany ADHD. Antidepressants often are used in combination with stimulants. Side effects may include nausea, sleep problems and decreased sex drive.

If you are going through menopause and your ADHD symptoms have worsened, hormone therapy may help you by balancing your estrogen levels.

Downside: Increased heart disease and breast cancer risk.

Bottom line: ADHD is a legitimate medical problem, not a character flaw. Remember, the condition does have its benefits. Women with ADHD often have tremendous energy...are very creative...and have an adventurous nature that makes them great fun to be with.

Be Part of the Next Big Medical Breakthrough

JoAnn E. Manson, MD, DrPH, a professor of medicine and women's health at Harvard Medical School and chair of the division of preventive medicine at Brigham and Women's Hospital, both in Boston. She is one of the lead investigators for two highly influential studies on women's health—the Harvard Nurses' Health Study and the Women's Health Initiative. Dr. Manson is author, with Shari Bassuk, ScD, of *Hot Flashes, Hormones and Your Health* (McGraw-Hill).

Until about 20 years ago, researchers generally excluded women from clinical trials of drugs and other therapies, fearing possible harm to women of childbearing age—and assuming that what worked for men also would work for women.

What we now know: Women often respond differently than men do to tests and treatments.

Example: Earlier studies showed that daily low-dose aspirin significantly reduced the risk for a first heart attack among men—but later research found this benefit to be much more modest in women.

It also is important that women participate in trials for conditions that affect us more than men, such as osteoporosis and arthritis—yet few women do.

Survey: 93% of women said their doctors had never mentioned the possibility of joining a medical research study.

To find a clinical trial: For a list of recruiting studies funded by the National Institutes of Health, visit *www.clinicaltrials.gov.* For cancer trials, see *www.cancer.gov/clinicaltrials.* For links to disease-specific trials, see *www.rarediseases.org.* For more information on women and research, visit *www.womancando.org* or phone 202-223-8224.

Find out before signing on...

- **Purpose of the trial.** Studies typically test new drugs for safety and effectiveness...older drugs for long-term effects or usefulness for additional conditions...natural treatments, such as diet and exercise...or prevention methods.
- **Type of study.** Observational studies track behavior and health outcomes without intervening in participants' lives. In randomized clinical trials, participants are assigned at random to receive treatment or a placebo.
- **Benefits.** If you're healthy, volunteering for a study may provide information that helps you and others stay healthy. If you are at risk for a disease, you may learn ways to lessen your risk. If you have a disease, participating may help expand treatment options for you and others—and though you may be assigned to the placebo group, you could instead receive a breakthrough therapy.
- **Potential risks**—such as harm or side effects from the drug or test procedures. Be sure you understand the potential risks and have read the informed consent form carefully. If you have a disease, make sure you will at least get the generally accepted level of treatment for that condition.

EFFECT ON YOUR LIFE AND FINANCES

Consider whether you can handle time and travel commitments. Ask if expenses are reimbursed and/or stipends paid.

Who funds the study—government, industry or another source. A potential conflict of interest does not necessarily mean the study should be avoided, but you do want assurance that the investigators work independently from a commercial sponsor and that the sponsor cannot suppress the trial's findings.

Six Dangerous Symptoms Women Should Never Ignore

Marie Savard, MD, medical contributor for ABC News, former director of the Center for Women's Health at the Medical College of Pennsylvania (now part of Drexel University), Philadelphia, and former adviser to the American Board of Internal Medicine Subcommittee on Clinical Competency in Women's Health. A board-certified internist, she is author of three books, including *How to Save Your Own Life* (Grand Central). *www.drsavard.com.*

Conditioned to be care-givers rather than care-getters, women frequently downplay their own seemingly insignificant symptoms, such as bloating and headaches. Many doctors trivialize women's complaints, too.

Example: Among patients with chest pain, men are more likely than women to be given a screening test for heart disease, while women are more likely than men to be offered tranquilizers—even though heart disease is the number-one killer of Americans of both sexes.

Self-defense: Familiarize yourself with the conditions that a new or persistent symptom could signal, then see your doctor as soon as possible and insist on being given the appropriate diagnostic tests—the first step toward successful treatment. When a worrisome symptom suggests multiple possible causes, a thorough physical examination should help your doctor prioritize the tests.

• **Swelling** could be due to fluid retention from your period, varicose veins, eating too much salt or sitting too long. *But watch out for...*

• Chronic kidney disease—especially if swelling is severe enough to leave indentations when the skin is pressed. This common condition, which often goes undiagnosed, increases the risk for heart attack, stroke and kidney failure. *Action:* Diagnosis requires a urine test for the protein albumin...a blood test for the waste product *urea nitrogen*... and a *glomerular filtration rate calculation* based on blood and urine levels of the waste product creatinine and other factors.

• Heart failure, in which the heart's pumping action is insufficient to meet all of the body's needs. Other telltale symptoms include shortness of breath and rapid pulse. *Action:* Get blood tests and imaging tests—most importantly, an echocardiogram (heart ultrasound).

• Blood clot—if swelling appears in only one leg and the area is tender. A clot that breaks off and travels to the lungs can be fatal. *Action:* Go to the emergency room. You need an ultrasound or computed tomography (CT) scan.

• **Change in bowel habits** may signal the onset of lactose intolerance (dairy food sensitivity) or irritable bowel syndrome (bouts of constipation and/or diarrhea that are uncomfortable but not dangerous). *But watch out for...*

• Celiac disease, a genetic disorder in which gluten—a protein in wheat, rye, barley and certain other grains—damages the small intestine. Celiac disease is more common in women than men, can develop at any time, may lead to malnutrition and loss of bone density and increases the risk for digestive tract cancers. *Action:* Diagnosis is made with a *tissue transglutaminase* (tTG) and/or an *endomysial antibody* (EMA) blood test.

• Inflammatory bowel disease (IBD), which involves chronic inflammation of, and ulcers in, the digestive tract. IBD increases colorectal cancer risk. *Action:* You should have X-rays of the gastrointestinal tract. If X-rays suggest IBD, blood tests for certain types of antibodies can help determine your specific type of IBD. Also get a colonoscopy (visual examination of the colon using a flexible lighted tube) to check for precancerous polyps and cancerous growths. Abnormal tissue must be biopsied.

• Colorectal cancer, the number-two cause of cancer deaths in the US after lung cancer. Other signs include blood in the stool, abdominal pain and unexplained weight loss. *Action:* You must have a colonoscopy, including removal of suspicious polyps and biopsy of tissues.

• **Abnormal vaginal bleeding** (heavy bleeding or bleeding between periods) prior to menopause suggests fibroids (benign uterine growths)...irregular ovulation...or menstrual changes typical of perimenopause. *But watch out for...*

• Gynecologic cancer, such as cancer of the endometrium (uterine lining) or cervix. Even light vaginal bleeding can signal cancer or precancer if it occurs between cycles...and after menopause, any vaginal bleeding at all is cause for concern. *Action:* Call your gynecologist right away. If a pelvic exam and transvaginal ultrasound detect suspicious tissue, a biopsy is needed.

•**Breast changes,** such as lumps and tenderness, often are signs of benign breast cysts (fluid-filled sacs). *But watch out for...*

•Breast cancer—particularly if you also have nipple discharge, puckered or pitted skin, redness or a change in breast contours. Don't dismiss symptoms just because your last mammogram was negative—mammograms miss up to 20% of breast cancers. An aggressive type called inflammatory breast cancer is especially hard to detect with mammography because it forms no lumps, but instead causes tenderness, swelling, itching and/or redness. *Action:* If you notice something abnormal or different, a biopsy is almost certainly warranted. Your doctor also may order magnetic resonance imaging (MRI). When a woman's symptoms or high-risk status indicate a medical need for a breast MRI, insurance generally pays.

•**Headache** may occur because you are prone to tension headaches or migraines. These types of headaches are more common in women. *But watch out for...*

•Brain tumor—if you recently started having headaches, especially in the mornings, or have experienced a change in headache patterns. *Action:* Call your doctor immediately. An MRI or CT scan can rule out a brain tumor.

•Meningitis—if the headache is accompanied by a fever and stiff neck. This deadly infection causes inflammation of the membranes around the brain and spinal cord. *Action:* Go to the ER immediately. You need a lumbar puncture (spinal tap) to check for white blood cells and bacteria in the cerebrospinal fluid.

•Bleeding in the brain—particularly if head pain is sudden and extremely severe. Possible causes include a *cerebral aneurysm* (a bulging, weakened area in a brain artery)...*subarachnoid hemorrhage* (bleeding beneath the tissues covering the brain)...or *hemorrhagic stroke. Action:* Call 911. You need *magnetic resonance angiography* (MRA), which produces detailed images of blood vessels...and a lumbar puncture to check for red blood cells in the cerebrospinal fluid.

•**Chest pain** frequently can be a symptom of heartburn. *But watch out for...*

•Heart disease. Although chest pain is more typical in men with heart disease, it also is a common sign of heart trouble in women. Be especially vigilant if you have high blood pressure, high cholesterol, a history of smoking or a family history of heart problems. *Action:* If you are at risk for heart disease, ask for an ultrafast heart CT scan, a noninvasive test that measures calcium buildup in coronary arteries. Chest pain with fatigue, shortness of breath, dizziness or back pain could signal a heart attack—so call 911.

Tired All the Time? It Could Be Anemia

Shersten Killip, MD, associate residency director and assistant professor of medicine in the department of family and community medicine at University of Kentucky in Lexington. She coauthored a study on iron deficiency anemia for *American Family Physician.*

There are many types of anemia, but the most common form is iron deficiency anemia. Women usually are the ones diagnosed with iron deficiency anemia. Anywhere from 9% to 12% of non-Hispanic white women have it, and nearly 20% of black and Mexican-American women have it. About 2% of adult men have iron deficiency anemia.

It occurs when the body does not get enough iron as a result of nutritional deficiencies or because you are bleeding somewhere in your body, most likely your gastrointestinal (GI) tract. Such bleeding may be due to colon cancer, infection, ulcers, liver disease, inflammatory bowel disease, hemorrhoids or regular aspirin use.

Symptoms of iron deficiency anemia include fatigue, weakness, dizziness, shortness of breath, feeling cold in your fingers and toes, headaches, chest pain and blood in the stool.

If you have any of these symptoms, see your doctor. If he/she suspects internal bleeding, usually an endoscopy or colonoscopy is required to find the origin of the bleeding. An endoscopy involves an examination of the esophagus, stomach and first part of the small intestine. A colonoscopy examines the entire large intestine.

If no disease is detected, patients are prescribed iron supplements and usually retested in several months. Patients may also be advised to eat more of iron-rich foods, which include raisins, meat (liver is the best source), fish, poultry, eggs, legumes and whole-grain bread.

Birth Control After 40

Anita L. Nelson, MD, professor of obstetrics and gynecology, David Geffen School of Medicine, University of California, Los Angeles, and coauthor of *Contraceptive Technology* (Thomson Reuters).

During perimenopause—from your early 40s until menopause—the birth control methods you used in the past may not be appropriate.

Examples: If you have high blood pressure or a history of breast cancer, smoke or are obese, your doctor may recommend against hormone-based contraception...and natural family planning is less reliable now that menstruation is irregular. Ask your doctor about the risks and benefits of the following options (all prices are approximate). *If you're looking for...*

•**Convenience**—try an intrauterine device (IUD), a small t-shaped plastic device. A doctor inserts it into the uterus...then you simply place a finger inside your vagina monthly to feel for a string indicating that the IUD is still in place. The Mirena IUD contains a progestin hormone, can be left in for five years and often makes periods lighter. A nonhormonal IUD with copper, called ParaGard, lasts 10 years but may make periods heavier.

Cost: $400 to $500.

Alternative: Implanon is a matchstick-size plastic rod with a progestin that a doctor inserts under the skin of your arm. It works for three years. Periods often become irregular.

Cost: $600 to $700.

•**No monthly periods**—try a continuous-use estrogen/progestin oral contraceptive, such as Lybrel or Seasonique.

Bonus: No menstrual migraines or cramps.

Cost: $50 to $70 a month.

•**PMS relief**—try Yaz. This oral contraceptive, which combines a very low dose of estrogen with the progestin *drospirenone,* may alleviate premenstrual depression and irritability.

Bonus: Lighter periods.

Cost: $50 to $70 a month.

•**More comfortable sex**—try NuvaRing, a low-dose estrogen/progestin vaginal ring that increases vaginal lubrication (and often decreases menstrual flow). You insert it yourself every four weeks.

Cost: $40 to $70 a month.

The Pill—What You Need to Know at 40 and Beyond

JoAnn E. Manson, MD, DrPH, a professor of medicine and women's health at Harvard Medical School and chair of the division of preventive medicine at Brigham and Women's Hospital, both in Boston. She is one of the lead investigators for two highly influential studies on women's health—the Harvard Nurses' Health Study and the Women's Health Initiative. Dr. Manson is author, with Shari Bassuk, ScD, of *Hot Flashes, Hormones and Your Health* (McGraw-Hill).

Women in their 40s often ask, "Will it hurt my health if I keep taking birth control pills?"—while women past menopause ask, "Am I at risk because I used to take the Pill?" Here's what you need to know... and what not to worry about.

•**Pregnancy.** Women in their 40s may assume that they're too old to get pregnant—yet the unintended pregnancy rate in this age group rivals that of teens.

Current users: For many midlife women, low-dose birth control pills provide safe contraception, make periods lighter and more regular, and minimize mood swings.

Caution: The Pill is not appropriate if you are at high risk for cardiovascular problems (see below)...have a history of breast cancer...or are a smoker over age 35.

•**Cardiovascular problems.** For most women, the Pill raises the risk for heart attack, stroke and blood clots only slightly—but significantly increases risk in women already at elevated risk due to smoking, high blood pressure or diabetes.

New finding: The Pill may raise stroke risk in migraine patients.

Current users: If you have cardiovascular risk factors, ask your doctor about pills that contain only progestin (synthetic progesterone hormone). These are less likely than combined estrogen-progestin pills to boost risk.

Past users: Don't worry about past use. Cardiovascular risk drops within weeks after you stop taking the Pill.

- **Benign tumors.** Oral contraceptives are linked to liver adenomas, noncancerous growths that carry a small risk for bleeding or becoming malignant.

Current users: If you develop pain or a lump in the upper abdomen, alert your doctor—you may need to stop using the Pill. Rarely, surgery is required.

Past users: Adenomas usually shrink soon after you go off the Pill.

- **Breast cancer.** Studies are contradictory. Some suggest that long-term Pill use can raise risk slightly.

Current users: Pregnancy diminishes breast cells' sensitivity to hormonal effects. If you've never been pregnant and have taken the Pill for close to a decade or longer, ask your doctor about using nonhormonal contraception.

Past users: Be extra conscientious about mammograms and breast exams if you took the Pill in the 1960s or 1970s (when doses were higher) or before your first pregnancy...were never pregnant...or stopped taking the Pill less than a decade ago.

- **Ovarian cancer.** Ovulation itself contributes to ovarian cancer risk. The Pill halts ovulation, reducing risk.

Current users: For every five years on the Pill, risk falls by 20%.

Past users: Protective effects persist for many years after you go off the Pill. Your long-term risk for uterine cancer and possibly colon cancer also is lower, perhaps because progestin decreases cell growth in these organs.

■ ■ ■ ■

What Most Doctors Don't Tell Women About Fibroids

Most women who consulted gynecologists about fibroids (noncancerous and sometimes painful uterine growths) were offered surgery to remove the fibroids or uterus. Only 18% of patients were told of minimally invasive uterine fibroid embolization—done by interventional radiologists using X-ray guidance—in which tiny beadlike particles are injected into small blood vessels to block fibroids' blood supply, shrinking growths and easing symptoms.

John Lipman, MD, director of interventional radiology, Emory-Adventist Hospital, Atlanta, and leader of a study of 105 women, presented at a meeting of the Society of Interventional Radiology.

The "Inside" Story on Ovarian Cysts

Arnold P. Advincula, MD, clinical associate professor of obstetrics and gynecology, and director of minimally invasive surgery and multidisciplinary robotics at the University of Michigan Health System in Ann Arbor. He is a pioneer in the field of robotic gynecologic surgery.

Ovarian cysts are fluid-filled sacs that develop in a woman's ovaries. They occur in about 15% of postmenopausal women and a greater percentage of premenopausal women. Although most ovarian cysts produce no symptoms, some cause abdominal aches or pressure...discomfort during intercourse...heavy or irregular periods...bloating, indigestion and frequent urination...and/or facial and body hair growth (due to hormonal imbalances).

Dangers: A cyst can rupture, hemorrhage or lead to ovarian torsion (twisting), causing extreme abdominal pain that requires emergency care. While most cysts are benign, some can be cancerous.

CYST FORMATION

Each month during a woman's reproductive years, one of her ovaries develops a saclike follicle that releases an egg. Usually, the empty follicle eventually dissolves—but sometimes it persists and fills with fluid, forming what is called a *corpus luteum cyst*. Similarly, if a follicle does not release its egg, it can continue to grow and form a functional cyst. These are common in women who have *polycystic ovary syndrome* (PCOS) or who take fertility drugs, such as *clomiphene* (Clomid). They are rare after menopause.

Other types of benign cysts include cystadenomas, which form from cells on the ovary's outer surface...dermoids, which contain many types of cells...and *endometriomas*, which can form on the ovaries of women who have endometriosis (a condition in which tissue of the uterine lining grows outside the uterus).

DETECTION

Symptomless cysts usually are detected during a pelvic exam and confirmed with ultrasound. Occasionally, they are found when an imaging test has been done for some other reason. A blood test known as the CA-125 protein may be ordered if there are concerns about potential malignancy. If a cyst is small, causes no symptoms and is not suspected of being malignant, the doctor may opt to observe it closely through a series of follow-up exams. For premenopausal women, birth control pills can help prevent more cysts from forming but do not necessarily treat existing ones.

THE RIGHT DOCTOR

Your regular gynecologist can diagnose and treat an ovarian cyst that appears to be benign. If screening tests suggest a malignancy, see a gynecologic oncologist.

Referrals: Society of Gynecologic Oncologists, 312-235-4060, *www.sgo.org*.

TREATMENT

Options for cysts that are symptomatic...

- **Surgical removal of the cyst (cystectomy).** This usually is an outpatient laparoscopic procedure performed through tiny incisions in the abdomen. It typically is used when a cyst becomes large or painful, or on an emergency basis in cases of rupture, hemorrhage or torsion. Because ovaries remain intact, this procedure preserves fertility and normal hormone production for premenopausal women.
- **Surgical removal of one or both ovaries *(oophorectomy)*.** In cases where a cystectomy is not appropriate, the entire ovary can be removed. This often is done as an outpatient laparoscopic procedure, though sometimes more invasive surgery is needed.

Do You Really Need A Hysterectomy?

Togas Tulandi, MD, professor of obstetrics and gynecology and Milton Leong Chair in reproductive medicine at McGill University and chief of the department of obstetrics and gynecology at the Sir Mortimer B. Davis Jewish General Hospital, both in Montreal. He is coauthor of *So You're Having a Hysterectomy* (Wiley).

Imagine this scenario—a woman has uterine fibroids (benign growths on the uterine wall) that cause heavy menstrual bleeding and pelvic pain. Her doctor says that she needs a hysterectomy (surgical removal of the uterus). She complies—then experiences several days of severe postoperative pain, misses several weeks of work and feels an unexpected sense of loss. Eventually she switches to a different physician—and is shocked to learn that her hysterectomy may not have been necessary at all.

This is an all-too-common occurrence. Many women are told that hysterectomy is the only appropriate treatment for their conditions—even when medical advances may provide nonsurgical treatments or less invasive surgical options.

Self-defense: If your physician insists that a hysterectomy is the only way to go, seek a second or even a third opinion.

SURGERY WORRIES

Second only to cesarean section, hysterectomy is the most common surgical procedure performed on women in the US. By age 60, one in three women has had a hysterectomy.

Gynecologic problems often can be treated without resorting to hysterectomy—yet as many as two-thirds of women who undergo hysterectomy do so without a compelling medical necessity. *Concerns...*

•Like any major surgery, hysterectomy involves risks—the possibility of blood clots, excessive bleeding, infection and adverse reactions to anesthesia. In rare cases, the urinary tract and/or rectum are damaged during surgery.

•In premenopausal women, hysterectomy brings an abrupt end to menstruation. If ovaries also are removed, it can trigger severe or persistent menopausal symptoms, such as hot flashes, lowered libido and depression.

•Some women undergo hysterectomy only to find that the surgery does not completely relieve their symptoms. This often occurs with chronic pelvic pain (which may be caused by an undiagnosed intestinal or urinary tract problem, rather than a uterine problem) ...and with endometriosis, a condition in which tissue from the uterine lining (which should stay inside the uterus) attaches itself to organs outside the uterus.

Note: Hysterectomy is warranted for...

•Uncontrolled uterine bleeding, due to complications of childbirth, or extreme fibroid-related bleeding.

•Cancer of the uterus, cervix or ovary.

•Severe uterine prolapse (in which the uterus protrudes outside the vaginal opening).

WHAT YOU NEED TO KNOW

If your physician suggests hysterectomy, ask these questions...

•What could happen if I don't have the hysterectomy? If the risks are modest, you may prefer to continue as you are. If potential consequences are serious, such as severe hemorrhaging or debilitating pain, ask how commonly they occur.

•How urgent is my situation? Unless it's an emergency, you may be able to take several months to decide about surgery.

•Will my condition improve on its own after menopause? For example, once menstruation ends, hormones that prompt endometriosis and fibroids generally no longer cause problems—so consider whether you are close enough to menopause (which typically occurs between ages 48 and 52) to wait it out. On the other hand, uterine prolapse tends to worsen with age—so waiting won't help.

•Are there less invasive surgical alternatives or nonsurgical therapies? Discuss the risks and benefits of your treatment options (as described below), including how each affects fertility, if this is relevant for you.

•How effective are these alternatives? To put an end to symptoms permanently, hysterectomy could be the best choice. If you would be satisfied with partial or temporary improvement, try other options first.

ALTERNATIVES TO HYSTERECTOMY

Here are common gynecologic problems and treatments that may allow you to avoid having a hysterectomy...

•Abnormal vaginal bleeding, due to menstrual problems, endometriosis or *endometrial hyperplasia* (overgrowth of the uterine lining).

•Intrauterine device (IUD) with progesterone is a small hormone-coated contraceptive device that can be left in the uterus for up to five years.

•Endometrial ablation, an outpatient procedure, uses a surgical device to destroy the inner layer of the lining of the uterus, stopping or severely reducing menstrual flow.

•Endometriosis, which can cause pain, heavy bleeding and infertility.

•Oral contraceptives taken continuously—without the usual week off each month—relieve mild-to-moderate symptoms.

•*GnRH agonists* (medications that block estrogen production) temporarily halt menstruation and shrink endometrial tissue, buying you time if you are close to menopause.

•*Laparoscopic excision* involves inserting a lighted fiber-optic tube (laparoscope) and surgical instruments through small abdominal incisions, then removing the errant endometrial tissue.

•Uterine fibroids, growths that can vary in size from a speck to a melon and may number from one to hundreds. With the procedures below, fibroids may or may not recur.

•GnRH agonist medications can temporarily shrink fibroids.

•High-intensity focused ultrasound combines ultrasound waves and magnetic resonance imaging to destroy fibroid cells.

• *Myomectomy* removes individual fibroids with a laser, electrical current or scalpel.

• *Uterine* fibroid embolization shrinks fibroids by blocking their blood supply with tiny plastic beads injected into small blood vessels.

• **Uterine prolapse that is mild to moderate** (the uterus drops into the vagina but does not yet bulge out of the vaginal opening).

• Oral estrogen therapy helps thicken supporting pelvic tissues.

• Pessary is a plastic cap worn in the vagina to reposition the uterus.

IF YOU OPT FOR HYSTERECTOMY

Once the decision has been made to have a hysterectomy, discuss with your doctor...

• **What will surgery remove?**

• *Supracervical hysterectomy* removes the uterus but not the cervix. It should not be used if your Pap test reveals potentially precancerous cervical cells.

• Hysterectomy with what's called *bilateral salpingo-oophorectomy* removes the uterus, fallopian tubes and ovaries. I typically recommend this procedure to patients who are close to or past menopause.

• Total hysterectomy removes the uterus and cervix, leaving ovaries intact. This often is used for women with severe uterine bleeding.

• Radical hysterectomy removes the uterus, cervix, top of the vagina and most tissue surrounding the cervix. It is generally used to treat cancer.

• **How will the surgery be done?**

• Abdominal hysterectomy requires an abdominal incision of about six inches. I use the procedure when a woman has a very large uterus or scarring from previous abdominal surgeries. *Recovery:* About six weeks.

• Laparoscopic hysterectomy is done through several small abdominal incisions. It often is used for endometriosis or persistent pelvic pain. *Recovery:* About two weeks.

• Vaginal hysterectomy involves a small incision in the vagina through which the uterus is cut and removed. Used for uterine prolapse, it leaves no visible scars. *Recovery:* About two weeks.

Important—Understanding Pap Test Results

Alan G. Waxman, MD, professor of obstetrics and gynecology at University of New Mexico School of Medicine and medical director of University Center of Women's Health at University of New Mexico Health Sciences Center, both in Albuquerque. Dr. Waxman is an authority on cervical cancer screening and prevention.

You probably have a Pap test every one to three years—as you should! The test reveals cancer of the cervix, the internal gateway between the vagina and the uterus. More importantly, the Pap detects problematic changes before cells become cancerous, when the condition is most easily treated.

Before the Pap test was developed, cervical cancer was the number-one cause of cancer deaths in women...now it ranks 15th. But the fight is not yet won. In the US, 70% of new cervical cancers are diagnosed in women who have not had regular Pap tests or whose abnormal results were not followed up with appropriate additional testing for and treatment of precancerous lesions.

If you are among the three million to four million US women per year whose Pap results are "abnormal," you probably are confused about what this means and what to do next. *The answers you need...*

CANCER CULPRIT: HPV

Cervical cancer is almost always caused by infection with human papillomavirus (HPV). Of the more than 100 strains of this sexually transmitted virus, 15 are linked to cervical cancer. Nearly 80% of sexually active women become infected at some point, but usually HPV disappears on its own, so HPV testing is not done on a routine basis.

However: Occasionally, HPV persists and, over many years, can cause cellular changes that lead to cervical cancer.

What happens: Like any virus, HPV can take over a cell and alter its DNA. The purpose of the Pap test is to detect and grade precancerous HPV-infected cells so doctors can provide the appropriate subsequent tests and treatments to prevent the cells from progressing to cancer.

During a Pap test, the doctor uses a small brush or spatula to scrape two types of cells from the cervix—squamous cells from the epithelium (skin) on the surface of the cervix...and mucus-producing glandular cells from the endocervical canal, the narrow channel that runs from the cervix into the uterus.

The cells are transferred to a glass slide...or to a vial of liquid preservative (such as the ThinPrep or SurePath brand). Slides made from the liquid are easier to analyze. If the Pap results are abnormal, the remaining liquid can be tested for HPV.

TEST INTERPRETATION

Within a few weeks of your Pap smear, your health-care provider should notify you of the test results. If you are told simply that your results are abnormal, ask for the specific term for your type of abnormality. Then check the list below for an explanation of the term. The follow-up recommendations given are appropriate for most adult women. (Guidelines for adolescents and pregnant women differ—consult your doctor for more on these.)

A Pap test result of...

•**Negative**—or negative for *intraepithelial lesion* for malignancy—means results are normal and cervical cells look fine.

About 90% of Paps are negative.

What's next: No action is needed until your next regularly scheduled Pap test. If you are under age 30, have a Pap every one to two years. If you are 30 or older and have had three consecutive negative Paps, your doctor may suggest waiting two to three years between tests because your risk is low and cervical cancer grows slowly.

•**ASC-US**—or atypical squamous cells of undetermined significance—are slightly abnormal but not obviously precancerous. Caution is warranted—about 13% of ASC-US abnormalities are associated with a more serious or "high-grade" lesion called HSIL (described later).

What's next: Your doctor will recommend one of three courses...

•**Repeat the Pap test after six months** and again after another six months. Most women return to normal by the first repeat test—but two tests are needed for confirmation. If both repeat tests are normal, you don't need to do anything until your next annual Pap.

If your second test result also is ASC-US, your doctor will do a *colposcopy* (examination of the cervix using a magnifying instrument) and perhaps a biopsy (removal and analysis of a small tissue sample) of any abnormal area.

If your second or third Pap test indicates a "low-grade" lesion called LSIL or if it indicates HSIL, see these categories below.

•**Do an HPV test.** If it is negative, your risk of developing HSIL is just 1.4%. If the HPV test is positive, your HSIL risk is 27%—so you need a colposcopy.

•**Skip additional tests and get a colposcopy.** This is best if your most recent previous Pap result also showed ASC-US, LSIL or HSIL.

•**ASC-H** is a subcategory of atypical squamous cells with specific characteristics that might indicate HSIL.

What's next: Colposcopy and biopsy of any abnormal areas.

•**LSIL**—or low-grade squamous intraepithelial lesion—may indicate a viral skin infection, but in about 27% of cases, it hides high-grade changes.

What's next: Colposcopy and biopsy. If the biopsy is negative or if it confirms LSIL, your doctor should follow you carefully over the next year—repeating the Pap test twice at six-month intervals or doing an HPV test after 12 months. Low-grade changes usually regress without treatment. Even if the LSIL persists for two years, often the best course is to do additional Pap and/or HPV testing rather than to treat the lesion.

•**HSIL**—or high-grade squamous intraepithelial lesion—indicates more advanced precancerous changes. Fewer than one-third of these lesions disappear on their own. If not removed, they are likely to become cancerous.

What's next: Colposcopy and biopsy. *Depending on the findings, your doctor may recommend one of the following surgical treatments...*

•*Loop electrosurgical excision procedure* (LEEP). With this office procedure, abnormal tissue of the cervical lining is cut out using a loop of very thin, heated wire.

• Cone excision. In the operating room, the doctor typically uses a scalpel or laser to remove a cone-shaped area from the cervical lining and underlying tissue.

• Ablation. This office procedure uses either extreme cold (cryotherapy) or extreme heat (laser) to destroy abnormal cervical tissue.

Once the surgery is over, have a Pap test after six months or an HPV test after 12 months to make sure the HSIL hasn't come back.

• **AGC**—atypical glandular cells—are slightly abnormal glandular cells, usually from the endocervical canal or squamous tissue of the cervix.

What's next: Colposcopy and biopsy, including sampling of the endocervical canal...plus an HPV test. A biopsy of the endometrium (uterine lining) also is needed if you are age 35 or older... have abnormal menstrual bleeding...or had Pap results showing abnormal endometrial cells.

• If your biopsy and HPV test are negative, have a repeat Pap and HPV test in one year.

• If the biopsy is negative but HPV is positive, repeat the Pap test and HPV test after six months. If either test is abnormal, have another colposcopy and biopsy.

• If the biopsy is positive, the abnormal area is treated surgically.

• **AIS**—or *endocervical adenocarcinoma in situ*—indicates a high risk for cancer in the endocervical canal, where it often cannot be seen with colposcopy.

What's next: Biopsy and, if necessary, cone excision.

■ ■ ■ ■

Lifesaving Tests You Need After Hysterectomy

Often hysterectomy does not include removal of the cervix—and if you have a cervix, you still need to be screened for cervical cancer with a Pap smear and, if your doctor recommends it, a test for human papillomavirus (HPV).

But that's not the end of the story. Your gynecologist is the only one of your physicians who routinely checks for vaginal cancer. Although rare, vaginal cancer often goes undetected until it has progressed, because it causes no symptoms in the initial stages. To get an early diagnosis—which increases survival rates—your doctor must visually check your vagina and do a vaginal smear to screen for abnormal cells.

Your gynecologist also needs to check your outer genitalia for cancer of the vulva, the fourth-most-common gynecologic malignancy. In addition, the doctor should do a bimanual exam—one hand on your belly and two fingers inside your vagina—to check for ovarian cancer and colon cancer.

Lauren F. Streicher, MD, clinical assistant professor, department of obstetrics and gynecology, Northwestern University Feinberg School of Medicine, Chicago, and author of *The Essential Guide to Hysterectomy* (M. Evans).

Hot Flash Remedies That Really Work

Andrea Sikon, MD, a board-certified internist and director of primary care/women's health for the Medicine Institute at the Cleveland Clinic in Cleveland. She is certified as a menopause practitioner by the North American Menopause Society.

As many as 75% of menopausal women experience the sudden waves of body heat known as hot flashes. Episodes can be mild, causing just a few moments of discomfort...or intense enough to make a woman drip with perspiration.

Hot flashes and night sweats (which come on during sleep) are triggered by fluctuating levels of the hormone estrogen, affecting a woman's inner thermostat and causing blood vessels near the skin's surface to dilate. Typically, a hot flash ends after several minutes, though it can last a half-hour or more. Episodes generally abate after a few years—but some women continue to have hot flashes for the rest of their lives.

Here's what you should know about which remedies help...which are of questionable value ...and which are downright dangerous.

Important: Before beginning any therapy, talk to your doctor about its pros and cons and how they relate to your individual risk factors.

PRESCRIPTION DRUGS

Estrogen is the only prescription medication currently FDA-approved specifically for hot flashes, but others can be prescribed "off-label."

Most effective...

- **Estrogen therapy.** This reduces hot flashes by making up for a woman's own diminishing production of the hormone. It also eases other menopausal symptoms, such as mood swings, vaginal dryness, thinning skin and bone loss... and may reduce risk for hip fracture and colon cancer.

Caution: Estrogen therapy can increase risk for heart disease, stroke, blood clots, breast cancer and possibly Alzheimer's disease. The more time that has passed since a woman reached menopause and/or the longer she takes estrogen, the greater the risks may be.

Consider estrogen if: Hot flashes reduce your quality of life...you have additional menopausal symptoms...and your doctor says that you have no increased cardiovascular or breast cancer risk. If you have not had a hysterectomy, you also must take *progestogen* (a drug similar to the hormone progesterone) to guard against uterine cancer.

Sometimes helpful...

- **Antidepressants.** Selective serotonin reuptake inhibitors (SSRIs), such as *paroxetine* (Paxil), and serotonin/norepinephrine reuptake inhibitors (SNRIs), such as *venlafaxine* (Effexor), may relieve hot flashes by stabilizing the body's temperature-control mechanism.

New: The manufacturer of the SNRI *desvenlafaxine* (Pristiq) has applied for FDA approval of the drug as a treatment for hot flashes.

SSRIs can cause weight gain, dry mouth and decreased sex drive...and may interfere with the breast cancer drug *tamoxifen* in some women. SNRIs can cause insomnia, dry mouth, constipation or diarrhea, and high blood pressure.

Consider an antidepressant if: You cannot or do not want to use estrogen therapy and/or hot flashes are accompanied by mood swings.

- ***Gabapentin*** **(Neurontin).** In one study, this antiseizure drug was as effective against hot flashes as estrogen. Side effects may include sedation and dizziness in addition to mild or widespread swelling.

Consider gabapentin if: You also have insomnia and do not have additional symptoms better treated by estrogen or antidepressants.

- ***Clonidine*** **(Catapres).** This blood pressure drug affects the central nervous system. In some small studies, it reduced hot flashes. Clonidine can cause dizziness, fatigue, dry mouth and constipation.

Consider clonidine if: Other therapies have failed to relieve hot flashes, and you also require treatment for high blood pressure.

ALTERNATIVE THERAPIES

The FDA does not test herbs or dietary supplements. Nonprescription products labeled "natural" are not necessarily effective or even safe. If you try them, choose brands that have the United States Pharmacopeia (USP) seal to ensure purity.

Perhaps helpful...

- **Supplements of soy,** black cohosh or red clover. These have *phytoestrogens*, plant compounds with estrogen-like effects. Theoretically, they could ease hot flashes via the same mechanism as estrogen—but they also may carry similar risks.

Caution: Women who ought not take prescription estrogen (for instance, due to elevated risk for heart disease or breast cancer) should use these products only with their doctors' approval.

- **Flaxseeds.** One small Mayo Clinic study found that hot flash frequency was reduced by half in women who consumed two tablespoons of ground flaxseeds twice daily for six weeks.

Possible reason: Flaxseeds contain *lignans*, antioxidants with estrogenic effects. Get your doctor's approval before using. Drink lots of water with flaxseeds to prevent gas and constipation.

- **Acupuncture.** A few studies suggest that this is somewhat effective for hot flashes.

Best: Use an acupuncturist certified by the National Certification Commission for Acupuncture and Oriental Medicine (904-598-1005, *www.nccaom.org*).

Probably not helpful...

•**Evening primrose oil...ginseng...vitamins B, C and E.** These fared no better than placebos in studies.

Ginseng should not be used with blood thinners, stimulants or antidepressant MAO inhibitors...vitamins C and E can cause bleeding in people who take blood thinners.

•**Magnets.** Supporters claim that magnetic fields have healing powers. However, in an Indiana University study, sham magnets eased hot flashes better than real magnets.

Dangerous...

•**Over-the-counter topical progestogen cream.** Absorption varies dramatically from woman to woman. Using these without a doctor's supervision can lead to hormone imbalances.

•**Dong quai.** This herb can interfere with medications and it may also contain a potential carcinogen.

•**Kava.** This herb is intoxicating and can damage the liver.

•**Licorice extract.** In large doses, it can cause leg edema (swelling), high blood pressure and dangerously low potassium levels.

■ ■ ■ ■

Hormone Therapy Is Hard on The Heart

Hormone therapy (HT) eases menopausal hot flashes but may raise heart attack and stroke risk.

Recent study: Women whose ratio of LDL (bad) to HDL (good) cholesterol was below 2.5 had no increased cardiovascular risk from HT. For women with ratios of 2.5 or higher, HT did magnify cardiovascular risk.

Recommended: Discuss your cholesterol ratio with your doctor if you are considering HT.

Paul F. Bray, MD, professor of medicine and director of hematology, Jefferson Medical College, Philadelphia, and leader of a study of 978 women, published in *The American Journal of Cardiology.*

Best Way for Women to End Heartburn

Leo Galland, MD, director, Foundation for Integrated Medicine, and author of *The Heartburn and Indigestion Solution*. Dr. Galland is in private practice in New York City. *www.mdheal.org.*

Does hormone-replacement therapy (HRT) cause heartburn? That was the implication of recent reports associating the heartburn suffered by many postmenopausal women with use of either over-the-counter (OTC) estrogen (*phytoestrogens*/botanicals) or HRT. The data was from the Nurses' Health Study, which has been gathering information from more than 121,000 registered nurses since the 1970s.

Published in the *Archives of Internal Medicine,* the study reported that women who were using OTC products that are estrogen-based or who were on hormone-replacement therapy were one-and-a-half times more likely to report having symptoms of heartburn or other gastroesophageal reflux disease (GERD) symptoms. Leo Galland, MD, director of the Foundation for Integrated Medicine, and author of *The Heartburn and Indigestion Solution,* believes the heartburn connection is more complex.

HORMONES AND GERD

The study associates the use of estrogen products with GERD (defined in the study as heartburn that occurs one or more times a week). However, as we know, a correlation isn't the same as causation. Dr. Galland said that many factors may account for the increased risk of heartburn associated with hormone therapy used during or after menopause. Hormones like estrogen and progesterone affect how well muscles are able to contract, and therefore may contribute to heartburn by relaxing the LES valve that separates the stomach from the esophagus. This relaxation of the smooth muscle tissue in the lower esophagus lets stomach acid back up —that's what causes the burning sensation, Dr. Galland explained. It's thought that the presence of extra progesterone is probably responsible for heartburn that occurs during pregnancy and it's also a component in many treatments for menopausal symptoms.

It's important to take these and all GERD symptoms seriously, as left untreated, it can lead to precancerous tissue changes. "Prevention is important," said Dr. Galland. Taking calcium supplements is among the most effective ways to prevent GERD, he noted. He recommends following meals immediately with either a chewable product (like Viactiv or a drug store brand) or powdered calcium citrate that you dissolve in water and drink (several brands are available online). "These increase the tightness of the LES valve and also improve the ability of the esophagus to expel stomach acid back into the stomach," he explained.

For more information on soothing symptoms of GERD and, even better, how to avoid them altogether, see Dr. Galland's Web site, *http://fatresistancediet.com/alternative-medicine/gerd/.*

In the meantime, if you experience heartburn, consider the possibility that hormones, drugs or dietary supplements you're taking may contribute to the symptoms and understand that these symptoms are likely not due to excess stomach acid, but to weakness of the LES valve. See a doctor for proper hormonal assessment and symptomatic management.

When It Hurts "Down There"

Elizabeth G. Stewart, MD, assistant professor of obstetrics and gynecology at Harvard Medical School, Boston, and director of the Vulvovaginal Service at Harvard Vanguard Medical Associates, Burlington, Massachusetts. She is author of *The V Book: A Doctor's Guide to Complete Vulvovaginal Health* (Bantam).

The use of euphemisms such as "nether regions" and "privates" keeps women from speaking openly and knowledgeably about their genitals. That's one reason why many patients just say "It hurts down there," with no idea what is causing their problem or what to call it. The word to learn—*vulvodynia.* Vulvodynia (VVD) means chronic pain, irritation, burning and/or stinging sensations of the vulva (external female genitalia). Typically, pain is most severe around the vaginal opening, but it can extend from the pubic bone to the anus or thigh. Women with VVD may find it uncomfortable if not excruciating to wear slacks, ride a bike or have sex. Some feel pain even when nothing is touching the vulva. Discomfort may be constant but vary in severity...or symptom-free intervals may alternate with periods of intense pain lasting hours, days or weeks.

A TRICKY DISORDER

The exact cause of VVD is not yet known.

Basic theory: Due to a central nervous system glitch, nerve endings don't work properly and neurological messages get mixed up. *There are two types of VVD...*

- **Provoked VVD.** This is the type I see most often. It occurs when inflammation in the genital area makes nerve endings super-sensitive to contact. Clinicians are not sure what type of inflammation this might be. Possible triggers include a vaginal infection...immune system problem, such as a chronic skin disorder or semen allergy...or malfunction of the nerve endings.
- **Unprovoked VVD.** Characterized by continuous pain, this develops when there is a malfunction of the pudendal nerve, which serves the entire genital/anal area and urinary tract. It may arise from childbirth, vaginal or pelvic surgery, injury or herpes infection...then for unknown reasons, the nerve may continue to send pain signals even after the original trigger has healed.

If you have symptoms of VVD, see a gynecologist who specializes in vulvovaginal disorders.

Referrals: National Vulvodynia Association, 301-949-5114, *www.nva.org.*

With VVD, a physical exam typically reveals little—at most, there may be slight redness and mild swelling. There are no lab tests to confirm VVD. Diagnosis is made by testing for and ruling out other possible causes of vulvar discomfort, including a vaginal infection...sexually transmitted disease...shingles (a rash caused by the chickenpox virus)...or a skin disorder, such as eczema, *lichen sclerosus* or *lichen planus.*

OPTIONS FOR RELIEF

Once VVD is properly diagnosed, symptoms often can be eased or eliminated within a few weeks or months. With provoked VVD, it is critical to eliminate the root cause of the inflammation—for instance, with antifungal or antibiotic medication to clear up infection.

Physical therapy is rapidly becoming a mainstay of VVD treatment. Soaking in a warm tub or applying an ice pack to the area may bring temporary relief. *In addition, symptoms may improve with one or more of the following...*

- **Analgesic cream.** A pea-size dab of prescription *lidocaine* can be used topically up to four times daily. Often, patients apply it 15 minutes before sex. Though it stings at first, it quiets the nerves' response in the painful area (such as at the vaginal opening) and it does so without interfering with sensation in nonaffected areas (such as the clitoris).
- **Antidepressants.** A daily oral tricyclic drug, such as *amitriptyline* (Elavil), may help by raising levels of brain chemicals that affect nerve messages. The dosage for VVD often is lower than that used for depression. Side effects include dry mouth, sedation and increased heart rate. This drug may not be right for patients with cardiac or liver problems or glaucoma.
- **Antiseizure medication.** Some patients are alarmed by the idea of taking these drugs. However, the newer ones—*gabapentin* (Neurontin) and *pregabalin* (Lyrica)—have fewer side effects than older anticonvulsants. They block pain by occupying conduction channels on nerve fibers and often are effective for VVD at lower doses than those used to prevent seizures. Some patients use medication until pain is under control, then taper off...others use it indefinitely. Side effects may include sleepiness, dizziness and vision problems.
- **Oral pain medication.** Because antidepressant and antiseizure drugs take a few weeks to take effect, your doctor may suggest a short course of a prescription painkiller.
- **Topical estrogen therapy.** This can ease the postmenopausal vaginal dryness that contributes to vulvar discomfort and pain during sex. Topical estrogen therapy—a cream, vaginal ring or suppository—carries fewer risks than oral estrogen.

TRIGGER ELIMINATION

Certain activities can aggravate VVD symptoms. *What to do...*

- **Avoid biking and horseback riding,** which rub against the vulva.
- **Don't wear tight pants**—they press on the pudendal nerve.

Better: Wear skirts...skip panty hose or cut out the crotch...don't wear thongs (or any underpants at all if they hurt).

- **If intercourse is painful,** stick to sexual activities that do not involve vaginal penetration until the therapies above take effect. If sex is not painful but itching and/or burning symptoms flare up upon penetration, you may be allergic to your partner's semen. In this case, have him wear a condom.

Relief for Painful Vulvodynia

Erin Hytrek, DPT, director of communications for the American Physical Therapy Association section on women's health. A physical therapist at Physical Therapy Specialists in Sioux City, Iowa, she focuses on gynecologic health.

Patients sometimes feel embarrassed at first by the hands-on physical therapy (PT) techniques used to treat *vulvodynia* (VVD) and other chronic pelvic pain conditions—but this fades quickly as the techniques bring significant relief. *How PT works...*

In response to the chronic pain of VVD, the muscles of the pelvic floor tighten uncontrollably and eventually go into spasm. This exhausts the muscles and allows the buildup of lactic acid, thereby causing additional discomfort. *To relax muscles and reduce spasms, a physical therapist may use...*

- **External manipulation.** The therapist gently rubs and kneads the patient's pelvic region, hips, thighs and abdomen...and teaches the patient to do this technique herself.
- **Internal manipulation.** With a finger, the therapist gently stretches tight vaginal muscles. The patient also learns to do this herself.
- **Electrostimulation.** A device delivers an electrical current via sensors placed on the vulva or inside the vagina, producing controlled muscle contractions that ease spasms.

•**Biofeedback.** Sensors placed on the vulva help the patient recognize when she is succeeding at relaxing specific muscles.

The majority of VVD patients are treated successfully within six to 20 sessions of 30 to 50 minutes each, spread over several weeks or months. If PT is prescribed by a doctor, insurance generally covers it.

Referrals: American Physical Therapy Association, 800-999-2782, *www.apta.org.*

Best Cardio Workout Machines for Women

Wayne Westcott, PhD, fitness research director at the South Shore YMCA and adjunct professor of exercise science at Quincy College, both in Quincy, Massachusetts. He is author or coauthor of more than 22 books, including *No More Cellulite* (Perigee) and *Get Stronger, Feel Younger* (Rodale).

Exercise machines can provide excellent workouts. But unfortunately, a woman may wind up with injuries if she uses a machine improperly—or if the machine is not suitable for a person her size.

Benefits: Cardiovascular exercise helps you control or lose weight...reduces blood pressure and cholesterol...and boosts energy and mood.*

Do a cardio workout for 30 minutes or more at least three times a week. Begin with a five-minute warm-up, working up to your target speed...and end with a five-minute cooldown, gradually slowing your pace. For the 20 minutes in between, work hard enough to give your heart a workout, but not so hard that you risk overtaxing it.

To gauge effort: If you can talk normally, work harder...if you barely have the breath to get a word out, ease up. Interval workouts—alternating every few minutes between bursts of intense activity and periods of lighter activity—burn more calories than a single sustained pace.

*Check with your doctor before beginning any exercise program, especially if you are pregnant, are new to exercise, have recently recovered from an injury or have a chronic disease.

Recommended: Treadmill.

You walk or run on a flat or inclined surface as the treadmill records your time, mileage, heart rate and/or calories burned. A preset program can automatically generate varying speeds and inclines.

Especially beneficial for: Women with or at risk for osteoporosis (brittle bone disease). Walking is a weight-bearing exercise that increases bone density...and the treadmill's shock-absorbing platform is easier on joints than pavement.

To use: Start by setting the speed at two miles per hour, then slowly increase your pace. Move naturally, keeping your head up and staying in the center of the belt.

Safety alert: Holding the handrails while walking rapidly or running forces your body into an unnatural posture, increasing the risk for muscle strain—so once you have your balance, let go. Use a safety key with a cord that clips to your clothing and connects to the emergency "off" switch so that the treadmill belt will immediately stop moving if you fall.

Recommended: Stationary bicycle.

An upright bike looks and feels like a regular road bike. With a recumbent bike, the rider sits on a wide saddle, leaning against a backrest, legs out in front. Both types give an equally good cardio workout.

Especially beneficial for: Women with balance problems, because there is no risk of falling...and overweight women, because it supports the body and allows adjustable levels of external resistance rather than working against the user's own body weight. A recumbent bike is most comfortable for people with back problems or limited mobility.

To use: Every few minutes, alternate "sprints" of fast, low-resistance pedaling..."climbs" of slow, high-resistance pedaling...and recovery intervals of moderate, medium-resistance pedaling. To work shin muscles, use pedal straps or toe clips so that you can pull up as well as push down while pedaling.

Safety alert: Improper seat height can lead to knee injuries. When one pedal is pushed all the way down, your knee should be slightly bent—never fully extended. If the seat adjusts forward and aft, position it so that knees align with your ankles rather than extending beyond your toes. If you have narrow hips and the distance between the pedals seems too wide, see if a different brand of bike feels more comfortable. To reduce back and shoulder strain on an upright bike, raise the handlebars.

Use with caution: Stair stepper.

This machine provides a challenging workout because you work against your own body weight and your center of gravity moves up and down with every step.

Problem: Users may lean heavily on the handrails to keep their balance and to take weight off the legs. This increases the risk for injury to the wrists...and misaligns the spine, which can strain the back.

Solution: To avoid falls, keep only your fingertips on the rails, using a light touch...maintain a moderate pace that does not challenge your balance. Do not set the height of the rise too high (as if taking stairs two at a time)—the stepping motion should feel natural. For good posture, keep shoulders and hips aligned and imagine trying to touch the top of your head to the ceiling.

Note: The stair stepper may not be appropriate if you are overweight or new to exercise and feel discouraged by the difficulty of the workout...have problems with your joints...or have any trouble with balance.

Use with caution: Elliptical trainer.

This low-impact machine combines the leg motions of stair climbing with cross-country skiing to work the lower body. Some styles include movable arm poles, adding an upper-body component.

Problem: For short-legged women, the elliptical can force a longer-than-normal stride that may strain the knees, hips and/or lower back.

Solution: The goal is to move smoothly with good posture. If your movement feels awkward or jerky, decrease the stride setting (try 16 inches). If this does not help, avoid the elliptical trainer.

Workout Machines that Burn Fat and Build Muscle and Bone

Wayne Westcott, PhD, fitness research director at the South Shore YMCA and adjunct professor of exercise science at Quincy College, both in Quincy, Massachusetts. He is author or coauthor of more than 22 books, including *No More Cellulite* (Perigee) and *Get Stronger, Feel Younger* (Rodale).

Strength-training machines build muscle... fortify tendons and ligaments...increase bone density...improve posture...boost mood...and raise metabolic rate so that you burn more fat.

Best: Do a strength-training workout two to three times per week, leaving at least one day between workouts so that muscles can recover. Start with a gentle warm-up of three to five minutes, doing an activity that involves the whole body, such as jumping jacks. Then use the machines for a total of 20 to 30 minutes.

Machine styles and weight increments vary depending on the manufacturer. If the machines in your gym do not have the same increments as the starting weight guidelines below, ask a trainer if it is possible to modify the options. *On each machine...*

- **Perform one to three sets of eight to 12 repetitions,** resting for one minute between each set.
- **If you can't complete eight repetitions using the starting guidelines,** reduce the weight. When it becomes easy to complete one set of 12 reps, try two sets, then three. When it becomes easy to do three sets, it's time to increase the weight.
- **Control the motion at all times.** Count slowly to two as you raise the weight...count to four as you lower the weight. This ensures that you use your muscles and not momentum to move the weights.
- **Exhale as you raise the weight...inhale as you lower the weight.** This helps keep blood pressure down.

Finish workouts with a three-minute walk to cool down. Then do three minutes of gentle stretching to maintain flexibility, holding each stretch for 15 to 30 seconds.

Recent research: Stretching promotes additional gains in strength.

Address each major muscle group to keep muscles in balance—otherwise the weaker muscles could be prone to injury. *A complete workout typically includes...*

•Lat pull-down.

Muscles worked: The *latissimus dorsi* (upper back) and *biceps*—muscles used in daily life for lifting and carrying (for example, grocery bags).

To use: Sit tall, facing the machine, with thighs tucked beneath the pads to stabilize your lower body. Reach up, palms facing you and slightly farther than shoulder-width apart, and grasp the bar hanging overhead. Squeeze shoulder blades together as you pull the bar down a few inches in front of your face...stop at chin level...then raise the bar to starting position. Start with 35 pounds if you're in your 40s...32.5 pounds in your 50s...30 pounds in your 60s...27.5 pounds in your 70s...25 pounds in your 80s and beyond.

Safety alert: Never pull the bar behind your head. This can injure the neck and shoulders. It is safe to grasp the bar with palms facing away—but muscles get a better workout when palms face you.

•Shoulder press.

Muscles worked: Shoulders, *triceps* (back of the arms) and base of the neck—used when placing items on a high shelf.

To use: Sit erect, hips and shoulder blades pressed against the backrest. With hands at shoulder height, palms facing forward and arms bent, grasp the outer set of handles and push up until arms are nearly straight...then lower to starting position. Start with 30 pounds if you're in your 40s...27.5 pounds in your 50s...25 pounds in your 60s...22.5 pounds in your 70s...20 pounds in your 80s and beyond.

Safety alert: If you have shoulder problems, such as with your rotator cuff, use the inner handles, palms facing each other—this is easier.

•Chest press.

Muscles worked: *Pectorals* (front of the chest) and triceps—used for pushing a lawn mower or wheelchair.

To use: Sit erect with arms bent, hands at chest height, palms facing forward. Grasp the handles and press forward, elbows pointing to the sides (not down), until arms are nearly straight...then bend elbows and return to starting position. Start with 35 pounds if you're in your 40s...32.5 pounds in your 50s...30 pounds in your 60s...27.5 pounds in your 70s...25 pounds in your 80s and beyond.

Safety alert: Do not lean forward—keep head up and entire back pressed against the backrest to avoid neck and low-back strain.

•Biceps curl.

Muscles worked: Biceps and forearms—needed for lifting and carrying.

To use: Sit with arms out in front, elbows resting on the padded platform. Palms facing you, grasp handles and bend elbows to bring hands toward your chest...then straighten arms to return to starting position. Start with 30 pounds if you're in your 40s...27.5 pounds in your 50s...25 pounds in your 60s...22.5 pounds in your 70s...20 pounds in your 80s and beyond.

Safety alert: Elbows are prone to hyperextension—so to prevent joint injury when lowering the bar, stop when elbows are still slightly bent. If your lower back arches, reduce the weight to prevent back strain.

•Leg press.

Muscles worked: *Quadriceps* and hamstrings (fronts and backs of thighs), inner thighs and buttocks—vital for walking and climbing stairs.

To use: Sit and recline against the backrest, legs raised in front of you, knees at a 90-degree angle, feet flat and hip-width apart on the movable platform. Slowly straighten legs until knees are almost straight, pressing with heels to push platform away...then bend knees to return to starting position. Start with 85 pounds if you're in your 40s...80 pounds in your 50s...75 pounds in your 60s...70 pounds in your 70s...65 pounds in your 80s and beyond.

Safety alert: To protect knees, do not straighten legs completely...keep thighs parallel to align knees.

•Ab crunch machine.

Muscles worked: Abdominals—which help maintain posture and combat belly bulge.

To use: Sit and place feet behind ankle pads to stabilize lower body...grip handles and place elbows on padded rests to stabilize upper body. Using abdominal muscles, curl upper body forward to bring your chest toward your knees...then uncurl as far as possible without letting weights return to the resting position. Start with 40 pounds if you're in your 40s...37.5 pounds in your 50s...35 pounds in your 60s...32.5 pounds in your 70s...30 pounds in your 80s and beyond.

Safety alert: Keep head and spine aligned to prevent neck injury.

A Younger-Looking You —Without Surgery

Nelson Lee Novick, MD, clinical professor of dermatology at Mount Sinai School of Medicine and a cosmetic dermatologist in private practice, both in New York City. He is author of *Super Skin* (iUniverse) and winner of the American Academy of Dermatology's Leadership Circle Award. *www.youngerlookingwithoutsurgery.com.*

New nonsurgical techniques improve the appearance of "necklace lines" (bands of wrinkles encircling the neck) and "turkey wattle" (saggy chin skin and ropey vertical cords at the front of the neck)—without the pain, risks, recuperation or expense of cosmetic surgery. *Fixes for...*

- **Necklace lines.** Microdroplets of muscle-relaxing Botox (a purified form of a protein produced by the *Clostridium botulinum* bacterium) are injected at half-inch intervals along, above and/or below each band (except where covered by hair at the back of the neck). Within 14 days, as the sheetlike *platysma* muscle relaxes in the treated areas, the muscle in the nontreated areas pulls the skin taut so wrinkles smooth out.

Cost: About $500 to $750 per treatment.

- **Turkey wattle.** Botox injections down the length of each ropey cord make the platysma muscle drape more smoothly...Botox under the jawline allows the muscles above to pull the neck skin upward. Then injections of Radiesse (a synthetic gel of tiny calcium-based spheres) along the jawline and under the chin give added volume where needed to make the neck skin more taut. Radiesse also helps stimulate the body's own production of skin-firming collagen.

Cost: About $1,500 per treatment.

With either procedure: There is minor discomfort as local anesthesia is injected. Only tiny amounts of Botox are given at each site, so swallowing and breathing muscles are not affected. No recovery time or activity restrictions are needed. Minor redness, swelling and bruising disappear within two days. Botox lasts about six months...Radiesse lasts nine to 18 months.

Best Ways for Women to Survive Car Crashes

David Kelly, acting administrator, National Highway Traffic Safety Administration, Washington, DC.

Perhaps due to their smaller stature, women drivers may be especially vulnerable to injury in a collision. *To protect yourself...*

- **Sit with your chest at least 10 inches from the steering wheel.** If you sit too close, the airbag may strike you with excessive force in an accident. Slightly recline the back of your seat...and to guard against whiplash, position the headrest at head height (not neck height).
- **Tilt the steering wheel downward.** This points the airbag at your breastbone, not your head. If your steering wheel telescopes, move it closer to the dash.
- **Consider pedal extenders.** Adjustable rods connect the accelerator and brake to a second set of pedals that are easier to reach.

For a referral: National Mobility Equipment Dealers Association, 800-833-0427, *www.nmeda.org.*

- **Buckle up.** If you are pregnant, put the lap strap below your belly and the shoulder strap between your breasts and off to the side of your stomach.
- **Shop smart.** When buying a new car, look for height-adjustable seats and shoulder belts...adjustable pedals...tilting and telescoping steering wheel...low dash and hood...good visibility through all windows...airbags that adjust for the driver's height and seat position.

Editor's note: Cars that rate well for shorter drivers include BMW 3 series, Chevrolet Malibu, Honda Accord, Lexus RX330, Toyota Avalon.

Index

C